305-β2- 57 ①

00

IDEOLOGICAL DIFFERENCES
AND WORLD ORDER

IDEOLOGICAL DIFFERENCES AND WORLD ORDER

Studies in the Philosophy and Science of the World's Cultures

Edited by F. S. C. NORTHROP

Yale University Press: New Haven & London

INTRODUCTORY PREFACE

THE need for world order, bringing international disputes under the rule of law rather than leaving them subject to suicidal decisions by force, is obvious. Unfortunately, the difficulties which contemporary investigations in the social sciences and the philosophy of culture reveal to be in the way—difficulties which center in considerable part in ideological differences—are not so generally recognized yet are nonetheless evident and real. In fact, the neglect of them is probably the major reason for the failure of the League of Nations and for the serious weaknesses already evident in the Court of International Justice, in the organization of the United Nations, and in proposals for world government. It becomes imperative, therefore, if the latter institutions and proposals are to become effective, that less attention be paid momentarily to the goal of world order and that greater attention be given (a) to the ideological differences which present obstacles on the way to that goal and (b) to the methods suggested by the contemporary social sciences and the philosophy of culture for the removal of these obstacles. It is with this undertaking that this book is primarily concerned.

That its authors are many rather than one is dictated by the character of its problem. This problem requires for its understanding a knowledge of the major cultures of the world and their diverse ideologies. It is very difficult for a person living in any one culture, unconsciously or consciously dedicated to its ideology, to do justice to the quite different economic, political, legal, moral, religious, and artistic doctrines and cultural values of people of other cultures. Hence the wisdom of having the many cultures of the many nations or political parties of the world and their respective philosophies presented in a single volume by many persons, each of whom is indigenous to or expertly acquainted with the culture upon which he writes.

In this connection, it must be recorded here with regret that the sudden death of Ananda Coomaraswamy prevented, at the last moment, the inclusion of a chapter on the art of the Moslem and Hindu culture of India, and that the sickness of other writers in Soviet Russia and Latin America prevented the completion of their manuscripts on important portions of their respective cultures. The omission in the latter instances is not so serious, however, since chapters on other portions of Soviet Russian and Latin American culture are included in this book.

An investigation of the world's cultural institutions by many authors has another important advantage. It lessens the danger of focusing on one aspect of the subject matter and problem to the neglect of others. Any nation or culture is a complex of diverse human and professional interests—biological, technological, psychological, religious, literary, and artistic as well as economic, political, and legal. One of the major questions is whether a wise and successful national and international policy can be achieved by emphasis upon one factor in culture alone. Are economic considerations the decisive ones, as is so frequently assumed? Or must the differences concerning the form of political organization be resolved before agreement on a policy to meet economic needs is effective? Can new legal and political forms, such as a world constitution and world government, be introduced directly or are they the later expression of underlying psychological, anthropological, and sociological factors imbedded in the emotions, beliefs, and habits of people which must be changed first? Are religion, literature, and art mere luxuries, or is any attempt at world order which neglects them doomed to failure? Do the advent of the atomic bomb and the possibility of biological warfare make the physicist and biologist rather than the social scientist and humanist the wisest guiders of policy? Have psychology, anthropology, and history demonstrated that irrational emotions, environmental stimuli, biological heredity, or inevitable historical trends determine what will happen? Or do ideas really matter? Clearly an approach to world order which would face the difficulties must not beg these questions. Hence, the advantage of an authorship expert in many different professional disciplines as well as many different cultures and nations.

The difficulties in the way of world order center not merely in the ideological differences of the different peoples and cultures of the world but also in the methods used by social scientists and humanistic scholars in their determination and analysis of any given culture. For example, certain historians, anthropologists, sociologists, and philosophers have tended to regard social and cultural phenomena as parts of an objective, unchangeable process running either in inevitable cycles or subject to deterministic laws, men and their ideas and ideals being supposedly but mere puppets or inescapable consequences of the unalterable cultural process. Recently, however, it has been noted that the facts of a culture fail to make sense until the ideas or philosophy of the people indigenous to the culture are grasped. Once it is realized that ideas are relevant to social and cultural institutions and events and that the ideas of men can be altered by men themselves, then the way is opened for placing the fate of men and their cultural institutions and values, in significant part at least, back in their own hands. For this reason the later chapters of this volume deal with the issue concerning the respective roles of ideological and nonideological factors in social phenomena, historical processes, and human behavior, as this issue exhibits itself in contemporary anthropology, sociology, economics, psychology, and the philosophy of culture. Professor Clyde Kluckhohn's chapter on the philosophy of the Navaho Indians is placed in this later section of the volume, rather than in the earlier section which its title might suggest as more appropriate, precisely because it demonstrates the presence and key role of ideological factors in even a so-called primitive culture such as that of the Navaho Indians.

Thanks to Harcourt, Brace and Company, Harvard University Press, Longmans, Green and Company, and the Macmillan Company are herewith recorded for permission to quote at considerable length from works published by them. Appreciation to Edith Burnham must also be registered for her patience and skill in preparing the manuscripts of the many authors for the publisher, a patience and skill which are as notable as they are habitual on her part. Indebtedness, also, to all in the Yale University Press who eased the transfer of the authors' thoughts from the prepared manuscripts to the printed page is also acknowledged. The index by Helen Livingston gives ample testimony to her care and competence.

This volume has the distinction of being designed in its initial layout by Carl Purington Rollins at the time when his retirement as Printer to Yale University and the designer of books for the Yale University Press reminded men again and articulately of his distinguished contribution to the quality of the culture of his own country and the world. It is indeed appropriate under such circumstances, that this volume should be concerned with the ideals and values of the world's cultures.

Appreciation must also be recorded to Dr. Paul Fejos, the Director of Research of the Viking Fund, who conceived of this project in the first instance and to Mr. Richard C. Hunt, President of the Viking Fund, and his fellow directors, whose generous grants, both for this book and for the release of its editor from other duties, made possible its consummation. It is most fitting, also, that appreciation and credit be recorded here to Dr. Axel Wenner-Gren, who created and endowed the Viking Fund, Inc., in such a way that all who direct, vote the support of, and carry through the research which it sponsors are subject to but one condition—that, namely, of absolutely free and open scientific inquiry.

F. S. C. Northrop

New Haven, Connecticut,
November, 1948.

CONTENTS

IDEOLOGICAL DIFFERENCES

AND WORLD ORDER

I

TOWARD A NEW JUS GENTIUM

ROSCOE POUND

AT the outset I assume the need, and a very great need, of a world-wide legal order. That a world-wide regime of peace is urgently needed I suppose all agree. There are those, as there have been from antiquity, who would see such a regime established without law. But the whole history of civilization seems to answer them. To begin at the bottom, the individual man, the social unit, himself needs the restraint of the inner order of a group or association of some sort in order to keep in balance on the one hand the aggressive instinct of self-assertion and on the other hand the social instinct of cooperation which are deep-seated in each of us. In the beginnings of law the inner order of the household—household discipline—is relied on. In a kin-organized society the inner order of larger kin groups is the ordinary agency of social control. As conflicts between kin groups or between kin groups and the unorganized kinless disturb the peace and order of the community, the inner order of a larger politically organized society, maintained by administration of justice in accord with a body of authoritative grounds of decision applied by an authoritative technique—i.e., law in the lawyer's sense of that term—develops as a paramount agency. Conflicts between these political organizations lead to war, as conflict between kin groups had led to the blood feud and private war in kin-organized societies, and an inner order of a society of nations develops international law. But the ultimate resource of this stage of legal development is war, and international law, as it has been, is aptly compared to the first stage of development of the law of the state, in which the end is simply to keep the peace and the means employed are regulation of private war and buying off the desire of the wronged to have vengeance. The next step forward is a world order, doing for the world as a whole what the legal order in the state has achieved for the state. Indeed, law within the state, in the sense of the inner order of a politically organized society, has been coming to be much affected by a recent theory of the state as an instrumentality of general social service, of which maintaining the general security is only one feature. The League of Nations sought to do more in the way of service than merely to keep the peace, and the United Nations likewise undertakes to do more. Thus in view of the economic unification of the world which has been going forward and of the development of transportation and communication which has brought all lands into intimate contact, it seems clear that there is call for a world order which will not only keep the peace but do service toward the general welfare of mankind. If it did not succeed in establishing a universal regime of peaceable ordering, the League of Nations did not a little as an organization for service. But a peaceable ordering of the world must come first, just as political organization for peace and order in particular peoples reached maturity before the more inclusive idea of all-round service by the state began to be realized.

Sociologists today think of law as the inner order of groups and associations. As such it has two sides: experience and reason. It is experience developed by reason and reason tested by experience. Experience is a matter of time and place, but handed down by a traditional teaching and developed by reason it gets a universal aspect. Reason, on the other hand, is universal. To think of the world as an association with an inner order is not easy. It goes beyond experience. Indeed, it is only in the present century that jurists have been thinking of the state as a group or association, one of the many which organize certain of our activities without merging our personalities, and so as having the inner order of its own which we call law. To get beyond the state we must turn to the other side of law and look to reason. Along with the idea of universal reason there has gone from antiquity an ethical idea of law as authoritatively formulated morals, giving theories of an ideal universal law, discovered or demonstrated by reason, and deriving its authority from the intrinsic force of moral precepts addressed to men as moral beings. Later this idea of law gave way to a political idea. Law was something imposed by a politically organized society. It was made, not discovered, and required a state as a necessary presupposition. Still later we get the idea of law as the most specialized and the most organized form of social control, and of social control as directed to the maintaining, furthering, and transmitting of civilization. The idea of a *jus gentium* in its origin goes with the universal and the ethical ideas.

In the Greek city-state of the classical era there was a chronic condition of clash between oligarchy and democracy and an all but constant state of war of one city with another. In reflecting on this condition the Greek philosophers sought a universal conception of right and justice to which the conduct of individuals in their relations with others and the activities of cities with respect to other city-states should conform. Thus the idea of a universal ideal of or model for social control begins with those philosophers.

At Rome, the old strict law of the city knew only the Roman citizen or the citizen of a city which had a treaty with Rome whereby he was admitted to a partial Roman citizenship. The coming in of Greek traders and bankers and commercial contacts with other peoples required a more liberal treatment of aliens. Accordingly, in the later years of the Republic the beginnings of a universal idea are to be found in the contact of Roman lawyers and Greek philosophers, taking the form of a philosophical theory of the jus gentium. In its original sense the jus gentium was a body of legal precepts introduced into the law as a result of increased intercourse with aliens which governed the relations between citizens and aliens and between aliens themselves. Philosophical speculation as to the basis of the authority of the jus gentium may be seen in Cicero. It led to a universal theory of that part of Roman law as something obtaining among all civilized peoples. As the Roman state came to embrace substantially the whole civilized world, there was no occasion to extend the idea of the jus gentium to interstate as distinguished from interindividual relations. But the universal idea in the form of theories of natural law was handed on to be further developed in the modern world.

An idea of universality pervaded every medieval institution and activity. Men held to conceptions of a universal church and a universal empire. There was a universal language for all official action. There was universal scholarship promoted by universities to which students resorted from all lands. There were the universal ethical precepts and ethical customs of chivalry. Knights came from many countries to take part in tournaments, and men passed freely from land to land, thought of as Christians rather than as subjects of some particular authority. The knight, the scholar, the merchant were, as one might put it in the secular, political speech of today, citizens of Christendom. In time the Reformation, the division of Christendom into sects, the rise of strong central governments and growth of nationalism, and the rise of individualism on the breakdown of the relationally organized medieval society, led to a decadence of universal thought and universal institutions. But the idea remained strong through the era of nationalism and individualism and is gaining new strength today in an economically unified world in which men are coming to think once more of relations and associations, to value community interests as well as individual personality interests, and to seek to achieve human purposes through cooperation instead of solely through competitive free self-assertion. The idea of universality is the antidote to extravagant nationalism.

In the sixteenth century, after the idea of Christendom as one empire and one church had ceased to govern, the boundless faith in reason which had come in with the Renaissance undertook to supply the need of a universal world order. In the seventeenth century the great work of Grotius founded what we came to call international law as the Law of Nations, using the Roman name, jus gentium. It had a theoretical basis in natural law—an ideal universal system of moral precepts demonstrated by reason. It got its actual content chiefly from Roman law, postulated as embodied reason, applied to states on the analogy of neighboring Roman landowners. For two centuries, at least, the phrase was "the law of nature and nations." Reason was taken not only to show what precepts should be, i.e., the precepts of morals, but to demonstrate the intrinsic binding force of a moral precept so that a rule of law needed no more than a moral content to give it force. The moral-legal order of Christendom thus conceived served the purposes of three centuries reasonably well. Natural law had two sides: a creative side and a systematizing, organizing side. In giving us a law of nations it was both creative and organizing. It built up a system of morals by which the relations of states were to be guided. It systematized application of an idealized positive law, chiefly the modern Roman law, to the activities of states. But the philosophical theory, on which the law of nature and nations rested, gave way at the end of the eighteenth century. The juristic theory lapsed in the nineteenth century and the moral-legal jus gentium of the seventeenth century lost its force.

In truth, the seventeenth- and eighteenth-century theory of a law of nations grew out of and was an interpretation of the relations of states, whereas the nineteenth- and twentieth-century applications of that theory to the facts of the political world since the middle of the nineteenth century do not interpret and grow out of the facts but give the facts a juristic or metaphysical cast to make them fit the theory. The facts of an international legal order that must govern peoples, not personal sovereigns, that must deal with large indeterminate groups, swayed in varying proportion by all the conflicting elements that enter into public opinion for the time being, not with individual men or with small, continuous, cohesive groups of individuals, demand a theory that shall grow out of these facts and interpret them in terms of effective effort toward perceived ends, as the seventeenth-century law of nature and nations grew out of and interpreted the facts of its time and taught jurists to deal with those facts creatively and toward ends which it pictured. The classical law of nations grew up along with the rise and establishment of centralized absolute national governments in place of the loose congeries of vassal territories or relatively feeble royal control over local feudal authority which had prevailed in the later Middle Ages. It was a law governing men. It appealed to men and took account of men. It was not founded on a figure of speech. Its obligations were the obligations of personal sovereigns as individual men and its precepts were imposed on those sovereigns in their capacity of individual men. It was a body of law for sovereigns who ruled personally; for sovereigns of which Louis XIV became the type. Its flowering time was the classical period of that type of political order, and it begins to lose something of its real hold with the rise of a new type in the nineteenth century.

In the seventeenth century there was a generally received moral order as among individuals. Throughout Christendom men were agreed not only as to its main lines but largely as to its details. Grotius saw rightly that the main lines might be applied to men as rulers no less than to men in their private capacities. The thought of the past had confused *imperium* and *dominium*. One's jurisdiction and his ownership were co-extensive. Thus with the coming of a public law along Byzantine lines all social interests and all public interests took form juristically as individual interests of the personal sovereign. In a time when juristic theory assumed the identity of the legal with the moral, the existence of a moral order among personal rulers was a solid basis for a system.

Not only did the political changes of the rise of democratic governments undermine the law of nature and nations but its philosophical basis was undermined and the universal idea on which it had originated and proceeded gave way at the same time.

Since the sixteenth century, law, as a regime of adjusting relations and ordering conduct by the systematic application of the force of a politically organized society, has become the paramount agency of social control. This idea of law as postulating a politically organized society, a state, followed the rise of independent and, as they saw it, self-sufficient nations. It superseded the idea of law as reason, which obtained in the seventeenth and eighteenth centuries in place of the idea of law as authority, which had governed in the later Middle Ages. Law as reason was applicable to adjustment of the relations and ordering the conduct of states. Law as ordering by the force of a politically organized society was not applicable. Hence the universal idea of a jus gentium was all but lost for a time and the term went out of use.

But granting that the seventeenth- and eighteenth-century law of nations will not serve us, it does not follow that a new phase of a universal legal-moral order is not possible. In the present generation there has been a well-marked revival of the universal ideal throughout the world. In spite of the era of disillusionment which followed the first World War, in spite of the ideas spread by the Russian Revolution, philosophies which call for an ideal of universal fundamental law are widely held. Revived natural law, Neo-Thomism, and Neo-Idealism at least divide the world of thought with the give-it-up philosophies and cult of force. The new emphasis on the social interest in the concrete individual life, the balancing of individual personality values and community values in terms of civilization values, the growing emphasis on cooperation and thinking of it as directed to civilization as its end, and the unification of the social sciences all point to a universal ideal of raising human powers to their highest unfolding, a maximum of control of external or physical nature and of internal or human nature in order to satisfy human wants. In the nineteenth century and in the present we have been putting the whole weight upon the side of mastery of external or physical nature. But that mastery is only possible when and where control of internal or human nature makes division of labor possible and allows undisturbed research, investigation, and experiment.

A legal order seeks to maintain and further justice, the ideal relation among men, morals, the ideal development of individual character, and security which assures effective division of labor and is at the foundation of the economic order. There are philosophers today who tell us that the three ends, justice, morals, and security, are in an irreducible antinomy. If any one is carried out to its logical consequences it negates the others. But we are under no compulsion to see only one of these and carry it out to a logical extreme at the expense of the others. We must, as we have done in practice, keep the three in balance. That none of them can be logically developed to the extreme without impairment of the others does not mean that we are compelled to a give-it-up philosophy and complacently resigning ourselves to a regime of force. There is no need of skepticism as to a world legal order. Since the time of the Romans men have learned steadily how to do better and better the practical task of adjusting relations and ordering conduct so as to keep in check the individual instinct of aggressive self-assertion and utilize the urge to cooperative self-assertion for the advancement of civilization.

Theories of law in the lawyer's sense—i.e., a body of authoritative guides to decision applied by an authoritative technique, postulating a politically organized society—have led to a feeling that a law of nations is not possible; there must be a law of a supernational political organization, a great superstate in which all states are merged. Hence the term "sovereignty" is under attack by writers on international law because it seems to negate claims of other states as to things done in the internal conduct of a particular state and to stand behind ideas of reserved or nonjusticiable claims which have impeded the development of international administration of justice. In legal history the development of the legal order was long impeded by ideas of the dignity of the individual free man who must not be coerced into an adjudication of claims asserted against him but must in some way be induced to consent to an arbitration. In time we learned that it was not necessary to merge a man's personality in the state in order to subject certain aspects of his conduct to inquiry and ordering by authority of the state. In like manner we may learn that all states need not be merged in a great world state, in which their personality is lost, in order that their conduct may be inquired into and ordered by authority of a world legal order.

Moreover, if some think a great all-embracing superstate is a prerequisite of a world legal order there are others, adherents of the Marxian theory of disappearance of law, who would see an omnicompetent world government operating without law. At the other extreme there were the philosophical anarchists in the last century who would have done away with all government as well as with law and left everything to agreement when there was a conflict or overlapping of interests. But we have to do with groups of men who have a cultural, linguistic, literary, historical, and often religious unity, of which they are very tenacious. They often have a strong feeling of their relation to the land, of an independence of control from without, and of something setting them off from other peoples and binding the individuals for the time being together. We have had to recognize the importance of these ideas in the case of some states newly created after the first World War. We can no more dispense with the nation in this sense, in such time as can be foreseen, than we can dispense with the individual man as the social and hence legal unit, as the corporative state sought to do. Recognition of the moral worth of the individual human being was the great achievement of eighteenth- and nineteenth-century juristic and political philosophy. Appreciation of the social interest in the individual man is the significant achievement of the social philosophy of the present generation. It is not likely that any economic organization which may supervene in such time as we can foresee will bring about a legal order which can succeed in ignoring him. Groups and associations organize certain of men's activities without merging their personalities. So national personality need not be merged in world legal order. We can have a world legal order without that. As there are differences among men, so there are differences among peoples. It is not the function of law to wipe out these differences and reduce all men to a uniform cultural political pattern. We can have law as the inner order of the world without that. There will be need of adjusting the relations and ordering the conduct of nations so long as there are distinct, cohesive, organized societies.

The respect in which strong feelings of national personality and independence are most likely to impede development of a world legal order is the conception of a world-wide bill of rights by virtue of which the citizen of any state may appeal to a world judiciary against his own state. But ideas of the dignity of a state as a paramount interest are losing their force. In our formative era the American people were not willing to leave to the Supreme Court of the United States controversies between a state and the citizens of another state. It is only grudgingly that the states have in very recent times been allowing their own citizens to get relief against them in the courts of the state. When political organization of society was struggling with organized kindreds, when the centralized state was contesting with local feudal rulers, when the state was competing with the church for the hegemony in social control, the dignity of the political organization was a very important consideration.

Today we have largely outgrown the conditions that identified the dignity of the sovereignty with the general security.

If a new jus gentium in the sense of a world legal order is feasible, what may the universities do toward removing the obstacles toward establishing and maintaining it?

For five centuries following the Renaissance the humanities provided some measure of background of universality for the Western world. But they have been pushed into the background by the development of the physical sciences which have been augmenting our control over external nature. Going along with the passing of political control into the hands of the mass of the people in the society of today, the result has been a significant loss of a universal ideal as compared with the era of natural law.

Men with very different conceptions of the social order, groups of men with one ideal or picture of what ought to be and other groups with wholly divergent pictures, must live together and work together in a complex social organization. Such is the situation within each state and the condition in a world society is the same magnified. Clashes must be avoided, friction must be reduced to a minimum. And a prime cause of clash, a prime occasion of friction, is disagreement where each, referring to his picture of the nature of things, in the best of faith, is conscientiously persuaded that what he demands is absolutely and inevitably right, or that what he would interdict is absolutely and obviously wrong. Without inquiry or with little inquiry as to how and whence we get these pictures, each is apt to assume that he is justified in forcing his neighbors' lives, even his neighbors' thoughts and beliefs, into conformity with the details of his picture of things as they ought to be. He is not unlikely to identify his particular picture with the divine plan, or with eternal justice, or with the wisdom of our fathers, or with the Constitution, or Americanism, or progress, or whatever is the correct solving word or solving phrase for the time being. Uncritical acceptance of a picture of things as they ought to be, by which unconsciously all things are measured, is a chief source of intolerance, social misunderstanding, class hatred, race antagonism, group hostility, and religious animosity. How easily serious misunderstanding may be fomented and may lead to mistaken suspicions of lawmakers or administrative officers or judges who act from the best of motives, is illustrated by a type of case of which there are several examples in our law reports—cases where judges of Puritan bringing up, with a picture of a congregational polity as the necessary organization of a Christian church, have sought to enforce that polity upon a church with an episcopal or hierarchical organization as the only legally permissible church organization.

In order to understand our fellow men—and we must understand them if we are to live with them—we must understand both our own picture of things as they should be and their picture. We shall not understand them, and we shall only live with them at the cost of much friction, if we assume as a fixed starting point, with no critique of our own picture, that theirs is bound to conform in all its details to ours. Dickens put the matter well in Mr. Podsnap. Mr. Podsnap had done well in the insurance business and was prosperous. His life consisted in rising at eight, shaving close at a quarter past, breakfast at nine, going to the City at ten, and a routine ending with a comfortable dinner. All things were but expressions of this life. Nothing that could not conform thereto was to be permitted. Whatever did not fit into this scheme of things was wrong and was to be eliminated. Indeed, when any such thing was suggested, Mr. Podsnap magnificently put it behind him with a wave of his hand—and it perished from the earth. His one conclusive argument to anything inconvenient or out of his experience was "Not English."

It is not easy for the machinery of social control to operate with such a background. If it is to operate effectively, men must be led to criticize the details of their pictures of things as they ought to be. They must be led to ask whence these pictures come, whence they get their outlines, whence they derive their details. They must be led to think about them and to criticize the subject, the picture as a whole, the drawing, and the details. In particular, they need to inquire whether their pictures of the nature of things are anything more than an idealization of the conditions of their childhood, projected into another time and used as a measure for a different society.

But where are men to get the materials for criticizing their ideals of the social order and of things as they should be? What shall guide them in revising, erasing, redrawing, and retouching? Where shall they find the materials for shaping, organizing, and giving content to ideals more compatible with social life in a crowded world? There is no one answer. I am not here with the one thing needful. What I would urge is, simply, that herein is the task of organized education in the whole scheme of social control.

For one thing, education has to do with these pictures directly and immediately. It seeks directly and immediately to lead us to inquire into these pictures, both in their details and as wholes; to see whence they come, how they got their form and content, how they compare with the ideals held by men in the past, how they collate with those of other peoples, and, not the least, how they compare with those of our neighbors. More far-reaching, however, it affects these pictures indirectly by leading to unconscious criticisms. It affects men's application of them indirectly by making them aware of other possibilities, by making them less absolute and dogmatically assured, by giving them pause when they would measure all that their neighbors are and all that they do by an uncritically formed, uncritically applied personal ideal. It leads them unconsciously to reflect that the neighbor also may be measuring what they do by the neighbor's ideal. Thus it leads or at least may lead them to seek to understand their neighbor's picture of things and to see how that neighbor's ideal expresses the neighbor's claims and desires. Thus it suggests or may suggest that our own picture may be but an expression of our personal claims and desires.

Why do our pictures of things as they are, and even more of things as they should be, err so that there is a different picture behind the assured conviction of each group and each nation, each class and each bloc and at times of each man; that it or he is asserting claims in title of right and truth and justice, or in title of inexorable economic laws and the inevitable nature of things?

One cause of error is that so many pictures are drawn from insufficient or defective information. Another is that too many are drawn on a limited and insufficient experience. Yet another is that for the most part these pictures have been, as one might say, copied from pictures drawn by others, who drew them for another time, another place, or another society. In times of transition, especially in times of rapid and far-reaching transition, the latter cause of error is a potent cause of friction. The last census disclosed that the balance had then but just shifted from country to city. The change from the pioneer, rural, agricultural society of the last century to the urban, industrial society of today is a profound one. The sudden rise of great cities, the springing up of huge metropolitan areas where less than a century ago there were swamps or Indian missions or frontier outposts, makes the pictures that sufficed for our grandfathers, for our fathers, and, in the case of those who change their abode from one type of community to another, even the pictures that once sufficed for ourselves, inadequate and inapplicable. We are required, almost without warning, to revise and redraw to meet changes in the social and economic order which are so involved and reach in so many directions beyond our experience that we shrink from the task. To do this revising and redrawing intelligently, we must look at the information behind our pictures and broaden it; we must look into the experience behind them and deepen it and organize it and measure it, as far as we may, by all organized experience. Broadening of information, deepening of personal experience through comparing it with experience of others and of other times, organizing and measuring of experience—these things are the work of education.

What the universities can do in our own land and time to prepare us for a world legal order they can thus at the same time be doing for the whole world and for time to come. If in this way universities can help toward establishing a regime of universal peace, which Hebrew prophets and Greek philosophers and philosophical jurists of the last three centuries and statesmen of the nineteenth century dreamed of or planned to bring about, it must be by providing a universal background for a universal social and moral and legal order. It must be by providing a background of received ideals which will enable such a legal order to maintain itself and put down forcible self-redress between peoples, as the law of the state has put down private wars between kin groups and classes and self-redress between individuals.

Economic unification of the world has gone forward far and rapidly in the present century. But it is not enough for a basis for a new jus gentium. A reasonable cultural uniformity which, nevertheless, shall not impose the culture of any one people upon all peoples is no less required. Law does not enforce itself. Its life is in the application of its precepts and this depends ultimately on received ideals of the end of law and of what its precepts should be and how they should be applied to that end. Although these received ideals are part of the law they are not made from within by the lawmaking organs of the state but come in from without. They must be shaped to the culture of the time and place; and so the precepts of a jus gentium must be shaped to a culture of the world of its time. As things are today this shaping of ideals can be done most effectively by the universities, where those are taught who will teach those who are to lead in the thought and teaching of the future.

Education toward a world order must begin at home. We should begin by educating ourselves toward a universal ideal, not by striving to educate all peoples to our model.

I have suggested elsewhere that organized education stands in relation to social control in America today where organized religion stood in the Middle Ages. Educational institutions command the devoted support of all conditions of men as religious foundations did in the Middle Ages. Accumulated wealth is set aside to set up and maintain educational institutions in twentieth-century America, as it was set aside to establish and maintain religious foundations in the Middle Ages. Political institutions have seemed the central interest of Western peoples since the Reformation. But in English-speaking lands our faith in them is not deep. Our real and abiding faith is not in government but in education.

There is good reason for this faith. Without expecting miracles from education, and conceding that the work of organized education might be done better and that those who are doing it have very much to learn, we may yet recognize that in the society of today it bears the brunt of what is to be done in the background of social control, and is believed in and supported for that reason.

I would not depreciate what is done in this background by domestic institutions—the home and family—by organized religion, and by organized effort in trade and business and professional associations. But in these, men are set off in groups or denominations or classes or businesses. On the other hand, in organized education men are brought together. They come from households and denominations and races and groups and classes and businesses, and meet simply as fellow students. So, too, in politics where they participate as fellow citizens. But that participation, as governments are conducted, involves strife and contest and factions and parties. Education is the one major social activity in which all the elements of the people may cooperate without requiring any distinctions save those which individual qualifications for study necessarily impose. However imperfectly our educational institutions do their work, however much those institutions may fall short of our picture of what they could do and should do, are they not the capital agency in our national and social life making for the furtherance of reason and the will of God?

Thus the universities may train a generation not to an easy-going acceptance of current give-it-up philosophies but to faith in the efficacy of effort to maintain, further, and transmit civilization. Faith in the mere machinery of organization was characteristic of the last century. But behind the machinery there must be enlightened faith in an attainable goal. We do no better than we try to do and what we try to do is directed by some ideal. "Idea" and "ideal" are derived from a Greek word meaning picture. To make received a universal picture of a world order is to lay the solid foundation of a new jus gentium. By "jus" the Romans meant something more than law. Development of a universal sense of right may lead to a universal law making it effective. The jus gentium was explained by the Romans as reason. Law was defined as "the highest reason seated in nature." The law of nations of the seventeenth and eighteenth centuries, or international law as we later called it, was taken to be demonstrated by reason. Without returning to the idea of a natural law derived from pure reason as something given us, thinking only of reason as an instrument, reason may be used to oppose the cult of force in the world of today and to build a jus gentium to replace force as the measure of the claims of politically organized societies. We may vouch for the Italian and French universities of the later Middle Ages to which students went from every land. There they studied the universal civil law and the universal canon law. Thus they got a universal ideal of a law of all Christendom and were able to develop, maintain, and further law and order throughout continental Europe.

What are the limitations on the competence of the university to prepare a generation for a world legal order? The most serious limitation is to be found in the exigencies of vocational training to which our institutions are pushed more and more in the economic order of today. Writing during the Napoleonic wars, Fichte called for an all-round development of the individual man which would enable him to cast off or prevent his acquiring the suspicions and misunderstandings and prejudices which stand in the way of cooperation with others toward developing human powers to their highest possibilities. As it was, he said, each man was trained or trained himself for some profession or vocation or walk of life, and as he perfected himself for the purposes of that profession or vocation or walk of life he narrowed his outlook upon the world and came to look upon it and upon his fellow men, as it were, through the spectacles of that calling. Looking at other callings through those spectacles, he became suspicious, prejudiced, and intolerant and so largely incapable of assisting in the maintaining and furthering of civilization. Hence he urged an all-round training instead of the one-sided vocational development which he saw in the educational system of his time. The purpose, he said, must be an all-round development of men as men; not merely as fellows in a calling, citizens of a state, members of a class, or adherents of a denomination, but as men fully competent and attentive to their duties as members of a profession, as citizens, as churchmen, and yet conscious also of duties as men to rise above suspicion, prejudice, and intolerance and appreciate and work sympathetically with their fellows in every walk of life, of every political allegiance and of every creed. The defect which Fichte saw in the thorough vocational training afforded by the great German universities of the nineteenth century may explain why those institutions, training excellently for vocations, yet failed to train a people prepared to fit into a world society.

Today, when exaggerated nationalism and aggressive class consciousness are threatening to disrupt civilization, we may approach Fichte's position not from metaphysics, as he did, but from the standpoint of social psychology. We are told that no man can form an objective and unbiased judgment of a situation in which he is emotionally interested. Hence he unconsciously looks at everyone and everything from the standpoint of a profession or trade or calling or class or nation or denomination and so, even with the best of motives, proceeds upon prejudices and misconceptions which impede his relations with others. Whether in business or industry or international relations we see this manifested every day. We have had illustrations in strikes, in race riots, and in wars. It gives us a major problem of social control. Every social agency, the law, administration, international relations, and all attempts at international organization, must reckon with it. Manifestly, universities whose purpose and spirit are primarily vocational, if they do not hinder, cannot help toward a world legal order. For our present purpose the universities must at least achieve a balance between the humanistic in a broad sense and the vocational, and a reasoned relation between training for one's place in his community and for his place in the world. As things are in the educational system of today, this balance is not easy to establish.

Another serious limitation is involved in the enormous increase of specialized fields of learning and no less enormous accumulation of knowledge in each field which must be mastered if one is to go far in it. Thus the inevitable specialization in higher education tends to be developed at the expense of general ideals and principles. The ideals and principles which come to be held by the best educated in the community are likely to have been reached unconsciously or shaped unconsciously from the standpoint of a specialized field, so that the training of those to whom we should look for leadership may have narrowed rather than broadened their outlook on the world. Yet I would not deprecate the extremely specialized knowledge and minute detail, thoroughly developed in every specialized branch of learning, which obtain today. There is a good side to this even for our present purpose. It may give an assured basis for general principles and a universal ideal shaped by adequate knowledge whenever a new Aristotle comes forward to put the complex mass in the order of reason. In the meantime, however, the university which is mainly devoted to research and discovery of more and more minute fragments of truth is not in a position to do great things toward promoting a fuller and better background of understanding to support a world legal order.

Democracy also has been making the task of developing and maintaining a new jus gentium, relying upon reason and intelligently formed habits of obedience rather than upon force, a much harder one. Reason must now be brought home to the mass of the people in every land. The intelligently formed habits of obedience must become those of the bulk of each people, not merely those of the leaders and of a highly educated few.

Then, too, there is patriotism, a virtue which yet may run to chauvinism or to a conceiving of universality as a making over of all peoples to our own model. The cult of patriotism, as it came down to us from antiquity and was developed with the rise of modern nations, has its roots in the struggles of political organization of society with kin organization and religious organization, in reverence for the personal ruler as the symbol of an ordered society and personal loyalty to him, in a feeling of solidarity in a people, and in respect for the state as a guarantor of law and order. In the world of today the patriotism which has grown out of these may be kept in balance with loyalty to an ideal of a world legal order and respect for a regime which maintains and furthers world peace. One may be a better citizen of the world for being a good citizen of his state and a better citizen of his state for being a good citizen of the world. "Es ist der Geist der sich den Körper baut." It is the spirit which builds for itself the body. The body built by a world organization must get its life from the spirit. In spite of the difficulties I have set forth, the developing, fostering, and spreading of a universal spirit may well be the work of the universities.

I would not pretend that education or university education, even at the best of which it is capable, is the one thing needful toward a world moral and legal order. What I urge is that the universities may lay a foundation without which organization of the nations can achieve little. If they can do this, they should be taking steps toward doing it.

No doubt there is danger of trying to do too much; of not doing well what the universities can do because of ambitious attempts to do much more. But what I am urging is not a matter of additional courses of instruction or of an additional school or faculty within the university. It is a matter of an aim and purpose which, infusing its spirit in all instruction in all fields of learning, shall make all instruction help toward an inner order of the world. When we reflect on what has happened to the great institutions of learning which took and maintained leadership in nineteenth-century Germany, we may perhaps feel that our American universities will be consulting their own best interest in looking beyond vocational training and research and furthering an ideal of a world ordered by law.

THIS essay was read on February 21, 1947, by its author in the symposium on "The University and Its World Responsibilities," as part of the Princeton University Bicentennial celebration. It appears in print here for the first time with the generous permission of the Princeton University Bicentennial Committee.

II

THE PHILOSOPHY AT THE BASIS OF TRADITIONAL CHINESE SOCIETY

FUNG YU-LAN

TRADITIONAL Chinese society originated at a time long before the Christian era, and continued to exist, without fundamental change, until the latter part of the last century, when it began to break down with what is usually called the invasion of the East by the West but which is really an invasion of medieval by modern society. The basic factor in modern society is its industrialized economy. The use of machines revolutionized the preindustrial economy which might be agrarian like that of China or commercial like that of Greece and England. The old economy had to give way to the new, as did the old social structure. It is astonishing to see how profound is man's ignorance of history and even of contemporary affairs. The social structure of European life has changed and is undergoing changes that may be called industrial, political and social revolutions. But when the same thing happens in Asia, Occidentals are prone to call it the invasion of the East by the West.

Modern industrialism is destroying the traditional Chinese family system and thereby the traditional Chinese society. People leave their land to work in the factories, together with other people who are neither their brothers nor their cousins. Formerly they were attached to the land but now they are more mobile. Formerly they cultivated their lands collectively with their fathers and brothers, so that there were no products they could claim as their own. Now they have their own income in the form of wages received in the factory. Formerly they usually lived with their parents and perhaps grandparents but now they live by themselves or with their wives and children. Ideologically, this is known in China as the "emancipation of the individual from the family."

With this change of social structure, it is natural that filial piety, which was the ideological basis of the traditional society, should receive the most severe attacks. That is exactly what has happened in China. The attacks reached a climax during the earlier period of the Republic which was established in 1912 when the abolition of *chung* or loyalty to the sovereign as a moral principle took place. As we shall see, in traditional Chinese society, chung and *hsiao,* or filial piety, were parallel moral principles. Hsiao, once considered the foundation of all moral good, is now regarded by some critics as the source of all social evil. In one popular book of the Taoist religion it is said: "Among all the evils, adultery is the first: among all the virtues, filial piety is the first." In the earlier period of the Republic one writer paraphrased this statement by saying that among all the evils filial piety is the first, although he did not go so far as to say that among all virtues adultery is the first.

During recent years there have been fewer attacks on filial piety and the traditional family system. This fact does not mean that they have recovered much of their lost influence but rather indicates that they have almost completely lost their traditional position in Chinese society. They are dead tigers, to use a Chinese expression, and attacking dead tigers is no evidence of courage. I remember quite clearly that during my youth I often heard people arguing over the advantage or disadvantage of the traditional family system. But now it ceases to be a question of argument. People realize that they simply cannot keep it, even if they want to.

The attacks on the traditional family system have been mostly polemic in character; as a consequence some of the criticisms have failed to do justice to it. For instance, among the many criticisms a major one is that, in the traditional family system, an individual completely loses his individuality. His duties and responsibilities for the family are so many that it seems he can be only the son and grandson of his parents and ancestors, but never himself.

In answer to this criticism it may be said that an individual, in so far as he is a member of a society, must assume some responsibility for the society. The assumption of responsibility is not the same as the abolition of one's personality. Moreover, it is questionable whether an individual's burden of responsibility toward his family and society in the traditional Chinese scheme is really greater than that of an individual in the modern industrial order.

A society under the industrial system is organized on a basis broader than blood relationship. In this system the individual has less responsibility for the family but more for society as a whole. In modern industrialism the individual has less obligation to obey his parents but more of a duty to obey his government. He is less bound to support his brothers and cousins but is under greater pressure to give, in the form of income tax and community chest, to support the needy in society at large.

In modern industrialized society the family is just one of many institutions. But in traditional China the family, in the wider sense, was actually a society. In traditional China the duties and responsibilities of an individual toward his greater family were really those of an individual toward his family in the modern sense, plus those toward his state or society. It is due to this combination that the duties and responsibilities of an individual toward his family looked heavy.

So far as the traditional Chinese social philosophy is concerned, the emphasis is upon the individual. It is the individual who is a father or a son, a husband or a wife. It is by becoming a father or a son, a husband or wife, that an individual enlists himself as a member of society, and it is by this enlistment that a man differentiates himself from the beasts. In serving his father and sovereign a man is not giving up his personality. On the contrary, it is only in these services that his personality has its fullest development.

Another point to be noted is that, according to traditional social theory, although a family in the wider sense may become indefinitely large, the responsibility of the individual toward it is not without a definite limit. Within the limit there are also degrees of greater and lesser responsibility. These are expressed by what is known as the "mourning system." According to it, a man, at the death of his parents, must wear mourning dress for three years (actually twenty-five months); this is called mourning of the first degree. At the death of his grandparents he is to wear mourning dress for one year; this is called mourning of the second degree. Theoretically a man would not wear mourning dress at the death of his great-great-great-grandparents even though they lived long enough to see their great-great-great-grandchildren. This indicates that a man's duty as a son of a family has a limit, which includes only his parents, his grandparents, his great-grandparents, and his great-great-grandparents.

A man, at the death of his son, is to wear mourning dress for one year, and for shorter periods at the death of his grandson, great-grandson, and great-great-grandson. He would not wear any mourning dress at the death of his great-great-great-grandson even if he lived long enough to see his death. This indicates that his responsibility as a father of a family has a limit, which includes only his son, grandson, great-grandson, and great-great-grandson.

At the death of his brother a man is to wear mourning dress for one year, and for shorter periods at the death of the son of his father's brother, the grandson of his grandfather's brother, the great-grandson of his great-grandfather's brother, and the great-great-grandson of his great-great-grandfather's brother. This indicates that his responsibility as a brother of a family has a limit, which includes not more than the descendants of his great-great-grandfather.

Thus according to traditional social theory each individual is a center from which relationships radiate in four directions: upward being his relationship with his father and ancestors, downward being that with his sons and descendants, to the right and left being that with his brothers and cousins. In James Legge's translation of the *Li Chi* [1] there are several tables illustrating this point. Within the radius there are different degrees of greater and lesser affections and responsibilities. Persons outside the limit of the radius are considered by the person at the center as "affection ended" and are to be treated by him on the basis of the relationship of friends.

Thus according to traditional social theory every individual is the center of a social circle which is constituted of various social relationships. He is a person and is to be treated as a person. Whatever may be the merit or demerit of traditional Chinese society and its family system, it is quite wrong to say that there was no place for the personality of the individual.

I mention these arguments only to show that, although traditional Chinese society is radically different from a modern one, it is not so irrational as some of its critics may suppose. In saying this I have no intention of supporting it as a working social system in present-day China. In order to live in the modern world in a position worthy of her past China must be industrialized. When there is industrialization, there is no place for the traditional family system and the traditional social structure. But this does not mean that we should not try to have a sympathetic understanding of them and their underlying ideas.

I shall try to give a brief account of these ideas as expounded in the classics and accepted by most of the educated people in traditional China.

THE IDEA OF HSIAO OR FILIAL PIETY

The central philosophical idea at the basis of traditional Chinese society was that of filial piety. "Filial piety" is the common translation of the Chinese word hsiao, which in Chinese traditional literature has a very comprehensive meaning. In the book *Hsiao Ching,* or the *Classic of Filial Piety,* translated by Ivan Chen under the title, *The Book of Filial Piety,*[2] it is said that there is a "perfect virtue and essential principle, with which the ancient kings made the world peaceful, and the people in harmony with one another." This perfect virtue is hsiao, and this essential principle is also hsiao, which was considered as "the foundation of all virtues, and the fountain of human culture."

In the *Li Chi,* or *Book of Rites,* one passage reads:

The body is that which has been transmitted to us by our parents. Dare anyone allow himself to be irreverent in the employment of their legacy? If a man in his own house and privacy, be not grave, he is not filial. If in serving his sovereign, he be not loyal, he is not filial. If in discharging the duties of office, he be not serious, he is not filial. If with friends he be not sincere, he is not filial. If on the field of battle he be not brave, he is not filial. If he fail in these five things, the evil (of disgrace) will reflect on his parents. Dare he but be serious?

The fundamental lesson for all is filial piety. . . . True love is the love of this; true propriety is the doing of this; true righteousness is the rightness of this; true sincerity is the being sincere in this; true strength is being strong in this. Music springs from conformity to this; punishments come from violation of this. . . . Set up filial piety, and it will fill the space from heaven to earth. Spread it out, and it will extend over all the ground to the four seas. Hand it down to future ages, and it will be forever observed. Push it on to the eastern sea, the western sea, the southern sea, and the northern sea, and it will be everywhere the law of men, and their obedience to it will be uniform.[3]

This passage was attributed to Tseng Tzu, one of the great disciples of Confucius. The *Hsiao Ching* also consists of a dialogue between Tseng Tzu and Confucius, so it too was attributed to Tseng Tzu or some of his disciples. It is not our purpose to inquire into the authenticity of these works. It suffices here to say that during the third century B.C. the theory that filial piety is the foundation of all the virtues of man had already prevailed. In Book XIV of the *Lu-shih Ch'un-ch'iu,* which is a work of this century and a product of the eclectic school, it is said: "If there is one principle by holding

which one can possess all the virtues and avoid all the evils, and
have a following of the whole world, it is filial piety." All the social
and moral philosophers of later times agreed with this statement.
Even the emperors of the following dynasties in Chinese history
used to say proudly with the *Hsiao Ching:* "Our dynasty rules the
world with the principle of filial piety." [4]

Such is the very comprehensive implication of the word hsiao,
which the simple English phrase filial piety can hardly suggest. To
those who are not familiar with its Chinese equivalent, filial piety
may mean simply taking care of one's parents. But as the *Li Chi*
says: "To prepare fragrant flesh and grain which one has cooked,
tasting and then presenting before one's parents, is not filial piety;
it is only nourishing them." [5] This is no doubt an overstatement, but
from the above quotations we can see that taking care of one's
parents is certainly only a very small part of the comprehensive implication of the word hsiao.

One would not be surprised to find that the virtue of hsiao was
so much emphasized in the traditional Chinese social philosophy
if one realized that traditional Chinese society is founded on a
family system and that hsiao is the virtue that holds the family together.

THE BACKGROUND OF THE TRADITIONAL CHINESE SOCIAL SYSTEM

It must be remembered that China is a continental country. To
the ancient Chinese their land was the world. Since it happened that
the Chinese people found themselves in a continental country, they
had to make their living by agriculture before the industrialization
of their economy by science and technology. Even today that portion of the Chinese population which is engaged in farming is esti-
mated to be 75 to 80 per cent. In an agrarian country land is the
primary source of wealth. In the minds of the people in traditional
Chinese society land was the symbol of permanence and safety. One
could not be considered well established in society unless one had
possession of some land.

Farmers have to live on their land, which is immovable. Unless
one has special talent or is especially fortunate, one has to live where
one's father or grandfather lived and where one's children will continue to live. That is to say, the family in the wider sense must live
together for economic reasons. So people in traditional Chinese so-

ciety, when they possessed some land, meant to live there permanently. For them their land was not only their own home during their lifetime but also that of their children and grandchildren, in whom they saw the continuation of their lives and works.

In the *Li Chi* it is said that when Chao Wu, a minister of the state of Chin in the sixth century B.C., completed the construction of his residence, the officers of the state went to the housewarming. One of the officers said: "How elegant it is, how lofty! How elegant and splendid. Here will you have your songs! Here will you have your wailings! Here will you gather together your great family!" Then Chao Wu replied: "If I can have my songs here, and my wailings, and gather together my family (it will be quite enough). I will then only seek to live peacefully to follow my ancestors in their graves." Commenting on this story the *Li Chi* says: "A superior man will say (of the two gentlemen), that the one was skilful in the expression of his praise and the other in his prayer." [6]

Such praise and prayer expressed the aspiration of agrarian people who built their houses on their land and wished to live there permanently. The praise and prayer are both well said because they are very human. They did not pretend that there would be only happiness and no sorrow. They did not express belief in life after death. They only expressed the desire of the owner of the house and land that he might remain there whether happy or sad, whether alive or dead. The sentiment is that of attachment to the land, and the praise and prayer well expressed this sentiment.

Agrarian people are attached to the land both physically and sentimentally. Their family trees are really like the trees that have their roots deep in the earth and spread their branches in different directions. The family in the wider sense must live together because they cannot separate. Since they must live together, there must be some moral principle to serve as a sort of unwritten constitutional law of the group, and the principle is that of filial piety.

THE TRADITIONAL CHINESE FAMILY SYSTEM

Filial piety is the organizing principle of a society based on a family system. Such a society is the product of an agrarian economy, which is in turn conditioned by geography. There have been other continental countries and agrarian societies besides China. But it happened that traditional Chinese society, because of its long history, had become such a society in the most developed form. The traditional Chinese family system was no doubt one of the most complex and well organized in the world. The complexity of the system can be seen in the different terms for various family relationships. Thus, in the *Erh Ya,* the oldest dictionary of the Chinese language, dating from before the Christian era, there are more than one hundred terms for various family relations, most of which have no equivalent in the English language. When Mr. A says in English that Mr. B is his uncle, to the Chinese it is a very ambiguous statement. Is Mr. B the brother of Mr. A's mother, or the husband of his mother's sister? Or is Mr. B the brother of Mr. A's father? And, if that is the case, the elder or the younger brother? In the Chinese language there is a term for each of these relationships. When Mr. A says in Chinese that Mr. B is his so-and-so, one knows exactly what the relation is between them. There is no Chinese word for "uncle" as such.

The family system *was* the social system of preindustrial China. The family was the foundation of the social structure. The state was an organization which might be called "united families." In the United States of America there are different states each with its own constitution and tradition, and over and above these states there is the Federal Government taking care of matters concerning all the states. Traditional Chinese society might be called politically the "United Families of Asia." In that union there were different families, each with its own traditions, and among these families there was one taking care of matters that concerned all the families. This was the royal family of the reigning dynasty, the head of which was called the Son of Heaven. Was this family also over and above the other families? In one sense, yes; in another, no. This is a very interesting point which I will discuss later.

Traditional Chinese society was organized with what were known as the five social relationships. They were those between sovereign and subject, father and son, husband and wife, elder and younger brothers, and friend and friend. Each relationship was governed by a moral principle. As Mencius said: "Father and son should love each other. Sovereign and subject should be just to each other. Husband and wife should distinguish their respective spheres. Elder and younger brothers should have a sense of precedence. Between friends there should be good faith." [7] These relationships and the moral principles governing them were considered as the "common way of the world," [8] which should be followed by all men.

Later, Tung Chung-shu (c.179–c.104 B.C.), a great Confucianist philosopher of the Han dynasty, selected out of the five relationships those between sovereign and subject, father and son, and husband and wife as the more important and called them the three *kang*. The literal meaning of kang is a major cord in a net, to which all the other strings are attached. Thus the sovereign is the kang of his subjects, that is, he is their master. Likewise, the father is the master of the son and the husband is that of the wife.

Besides the three kang there were the five *ch'ang*, which were upheld by all the Confucianists. Ch'ang means a norm or constant, and the five ch'ang were the five virtues of Confucianism, namely, *jen* (human-heartedness), *yi* (righteousness), *li* (propriety, rituals, rules of proper conduct), *chih* (wisdom), and *hsin* (good faith). The five ch'ang were the virtues of an individual, and the three kang were the organizing principles of society. The compound word *kang-ch'ang* meant, in olden times, morality or moral law in general.

All the acts of an individual were regulated, in olden times, by these social relationships. Each term of the relationships, according to Confucianism, is a *ming* or name which represents a moral principle. Every individual must have some name in terms of the relationships, and it is his duty to behave according to the moral principle represented by that name. For instance, if an individual is a son in relation to his father, he must behave according to the moral principle represented by the name son; in other words, he must behave according to what a son ought to do. If he later becomes a father in relation to his son, he must behave according to the moral principle represented by the name father, which is what a father ought to do. This whole theory was known in olden times as the *ming-chiao*, or instruction based on names.

Of these five social relationships, three are family relationships. The remaining two, the relationships between sovereign and subjects and between friends, though not family relationships, can be conceived in terms of family. The relationship between sovereign and subject can be conceived in terms either of that between father and son or of that between husband and wife. The relationship between friends can be conceived in terms of that between brothers. Such, indeed, was the way in which they were usually conceived.

That is why hsiao or filial piety was considered the foundation of all virtues. The whole structure of social relationships can be conceived as a family matter, and hsiao is essentially loyalty to family.

THE IDEA OF CHUNG OR LOYALTY TO THE SOVEREIGN

The relationship between sovereign and subject can be conceived in terms either of that between father and son or of that between husband and wife. That is why I say that in ancient times the royal family of the ruling dynasty was considered in one respect as a family over and above the other ones but in another respect as theoretically only one of the many families.

It was quite common to consider the Son of Heaven as the Father of the people. It was a common saying that "the serving of the sovereign by the subject was analogous to the serving of the parents by the son." In the *Book of Filial Piety* it is said: "From the way in which one serves one's father, one learns how to serve one's mother. The love toward them is the same. From the way in which one serves one's father, one learns how to serve one's sovereign. The respect shown to them is the same. To one's mother, one shows love, to one's father both love and respect." [9] In these sayings the relationship between sovereign and subject is conceived in terms of that between father and son. If this relationship is considered in this way, then the royal family of the ruling dynasty must be considered as a superfamily over and above all other families.

But it was also very common for the relationship between sovereign and subject to be conceived in terms of that between husband and wife. One of the similarities between the two relationships is that the tie between sovereign and subject, like that between husband and wife, is, as the Chinese philosophers said, a "social or moral" one, not a "natural" one. That is to say, the tie is not one of blood. That is why, as it is said in the above quotation, one shows one's father both respect and love but to one's sovereign only respect, which is also, according to the Chinese philosophers, what husband and wife should show to each other.

One does not have a chance to choose one's father. That is something determined by fate. But one can choose one's sovereign, just as a girl, before her marriage, can have a choice as to who should be her husband. It was a common saying that "the wise bird chooses the right tree to build its nest; the wise minister chooses the right sovereign to offer his service." It is true that traditionally all the people of the Chinese Empire were theoretically the subjects of the emperor. But it is also true that traditionally the common people had not the same obligation of allegiance toward the emperor as those who entered the official ranks of the government. It was to the officials that the relationship between sovereign and subject was specially relevant. So even in the time of unification when there was only one sovereign, one still could choose whether to join the official ranks or not, just as a girl might choose to remain single, even though there were only one man whom she could marry. In Chinese history, if a scholar chose to remain outside the official ranks, he was a man, as a traditional saying puts it, "whom the Son of Heaven could not take as his minister, nor the princes take as their friend." He was a great free man, without any obligation to the emperor except the paying of taxes.

Traditionally the analogy between the relationship of sovereign and subject and that of husband and wife was carried further in the common saying that "a good minister will not serve two sovereigns, nor a good wife, two husbands." Before a man decided whether to join the official rank or not, he was quite free to make the choice, but once it was made the choice was final and irrevocable. In the same way, traditionally, a girl before getting married was free to choose her husband, but after marriage her choice was made once and for all.

Traditionally, a marriage was a transference of a girl from the family of her parents to that of her husband. Before marriage she was the daughter of her parents; after it she became the wife of her husband. With this transformation she had new duties and obligations, and above all she had to be absolutely faithful to her husband. This faithfulness is called *chen* or *chieh* and was considered the most important virtue for a wife.

Traditionally, when a man joined the official ranks, he was in a sense "married" to the sovereign. He transferred himself from his own family to the royal family, which in this sense was but one of the many families. Before this transference he was the son of his parents, but after it he became the minister of the sovereign. With this transformation he had new duties and new obligations, and above all he had to be absolutely loyal to the sovereign. This loyalty was called chung and was considered the most important virtue of a minister.

When a man "married" himself to the royal family, he should devote himself completely to his new duties and obligations, just as, after marriage, a woman should devote herself completely to the management of the household of her husband. Such a change in a man's status was called in olden times the "transformation of filial piety into loyalty to the sovereign."

In traditional Chinese society chung and hsiao were considered the two major moral values in social relations. A loyal minister and a filial son both commanded universal respect. But this does not mean that hsiao is not the basic moral principle underlying traditional Chinese society. In the transformation mentioned above a filial son does not cease to be a filial son. On the contrary, in his new circumstances, this is the only way in which he can continue to be a filial son. As shown in the above quotations, a son becomes truly filial by being loyal to the sovereign, if that is his duty. So in traditional Chinese society chung or loyalty to the sovereign was considered an extension of hsiao or filial piety, but hsiao could not be considered an extension of chung.

THE CONFLICT BETWEEN CHUNG AND HSIAO

This fact can be illustrated with certain historical moral situations. In history there were moral situations in which the conflict between chung and hsiao, that is, between one's duty as a son and that as a minister, became so great that it was a grave moral question which of them should receive the first consideration. The classic case in Chinese history is that of Chao Pao of the second century A.D. He was the governor of a frontier province in present Manchuria and was attacked by an invading force of a certain tribe. The invading army happened to get hold of his mother who was on her way to join him. They then told Chao Pao to surrender or they would slaughter his mother. For Chao Pao there was a real moral dilemma. He made the decision and said: "Before, I was my mother's son, but today I am a minister of my sovereign. I cannot do otherwise." He fought the enemy and defeated them with the sacrifice of the life of his mother. After the war was over Chao Pao said: "My mother died because of me, I cannot live after her death." He died of grief at his mother's grave.

There are many historic discussions of the moral implications of Chao Pao's conduct. The *History of the Later Han Dynasty* regarded him as an extremist who took only one aspect of the situation into account. But what Chao Pao should have done if he had considered all the aspects, the *History of the Later Han Dynasty* did not say.

Several hundred years later a great philosopher of the Neo-Confucianist school, Ch'eng Yi (1033–1108), made the suggestion that Chao Pao might have resigned his post as the governor of the province and transferred his military power to a deputy. In that case the enemy might not have killed his mother because there would not have been any point in it. Even if the enemy still had done it, Chao Pao would have been less responsible for her death. Anyway he should have made some attempt, even if unsuccessful, to save his mother.

Ch'eng Yi's reasoning had the support of the authority of Mencius. According to the book of *Mencius,* he was once asked: "When Shun (a traditional sage emperor) was the emperor, and Kao Yao (a traditional very just judge) was the chief justice, suppose Ku Sou (Shun's father) committed the crime of homicide, what would Shun have done?" To this question Mencius answered: "Shun would have stolen his father from the jail, and run away with him. He then would have hidden himself with his father in a corner at the seashore, and gladly lived with him through his whole life, and have entirely forgotten the empire." [10] This imaginary situation is similar to that in which Chao Pao actually found himself. In both cases there is a conflict of a very serious nature between one's duty as a functionary of the state and one's duty as a son. There is a moral dilemma for which Mencius and Ch'eng Yi suggested similar solutions.

I have mentioned this extreme case in order to show the moral temper of traditional Chinese society. The point is that, normally, if one chose to join the official rank, one had "to transform filial piety into loyalty to the sovereign"; but that when these two virtues seriously conflicted it was the duty of the son as a son that should receive first consideration. This is further evidence that the family system was the foundation of traditional Chinese society and filial piety the basis of all its moral principles.

THE CONTINUATION OF THE FAMILY

According to traditional Chinese social theory, of the five social relationships that between father and son is the first in importance but that between husband and wife is the first in origin. In the *Book of Changes* it is said: "Following the existence of Heaven and Earth there is the existence of all things. Following the existence of all things, there is the distinction of male and female. Following this distinction, there is the relationship between father and son. Following this, there is the relationship between sovereign and subjects." [11]

Before the establishment of the relationship between husband and wife, "people only knew that there were mothers, but not that there were fathers." In this situation men were the same as the beasts. The establishment of the relationship between husband and wife was the first step in the development of the distinction whereby men distinguish themselves from the beasts. Hsun Tzu, one of the great Confucianists in the third century B.C., said:

Man is not truly man in the fact that he, uniquely, has two feet and no hair (over his body), but rather in the fact that he makes social distinctions. Birds and beasts have parents and offspring, but not the affection between father and son. They are either male or female, but do not have the proper distinction between male and female. Hence in the way of humanity, there must be distinctions. No distinctions are greater than those of society.[12]

In other words, that there are males and females and their offspring in the animal world is a fact of nature, but that there are the relationships between husband and wife and between father and son is a fact of social organization. It is this that distinguishes men from other animals.

In traditional Chinese society the establishment of the relationship between husband and wife was considered the first step toward social organization. In the *Book of Odes,* one of the ancient classics, it happens that the first ode is a love song. According to the traditional moral interpretation, this is so because the relationship between husband and wife is the "first of the social relationships."

The marriage of man and woman becoming husband and wife is the beginning of the family. Once there is the family, the marriage of its younger members is needed to continue its existence. In the continuance of one's family one enjoys an immortality that is both biological and ideal. In this continuance one has both the remembrance of the past and the hope of the future.

An individual must die, but death is not necessarily the absolute end of his life. If he has descendants, they are actually portions of his body that are perpetuated. So he who has descendants does not actually die. He enjoys a biological immortality which is possible for all living creatures. This is a fact of nature, but it is only with the social organization of the family system that this fact is brought into bold relief.

With the social organization of the family system, one who has descendants enjoys not only a biological immortality through their bodies but also an ideal immortality through their works and their memories. In their works one's own work is continued, and in their memories one continues to be known in the world. Thus in the family system one is kept both from physical extinction and spiritual oblivion.

Traditionally, marriage was considered in this light. It is said in the *Li Chi* that the purpose of marriage is "to secure the service of the ancestral temple for the past, and to secure the continuance of the family for the future." [13] Marriage provides a means for the transference of the life of the ancestors in the past to the children in the future. Traditionally, it was a great duty of a son to become a father. If he failed to do this, not only would his own life face extinction, but what is more important, the life of his ancestors, carried on by him, would also be terminated. So Mencius said: "There are three things (meaning many things) that are unfilial, and to have no posterity is the greatest of them." [14]

In traditional Chinese society, to have a son or sons was the greatest blessing of human life and to have none the greatest curse. The proverb says: "If only one has a son, he should be satisfied with everything." "To play with the grandchildren" was considered the greatest happiness that an old man could have. In traditional Chinese society, when a man had sons and grandsons, he could look on them as extensions of his own life. Hence in his old age he could regard his existence and that of his ancestors as already having been entrusted to others and so could await death calmly, without further care as to whether his soul after death would continue to exist or not. Why should he be anxious about an immortality that was extremely doubtful when he already had one that was assured?

ANCESTOR WORSHIP

Here we see the essential meaning of the practice of ancestor worship. In traditional Chinese society, the function of this practice was both social and spiritual. Socially it served as a means for achieving the solidarity of the family. Since the traditional Chinese family was a very complex organization, its solidarity depended upon some symbol of unity, and the ancestors of the family were the natural symbol.

In traditional China, in places where the family system was carried out in strict accordance with the ideal pattern, the people of the same surname living in one place used to have a clan temple. The temple had its own land and income, which were considered the common property of the clan. The income of the temple was to be used for preparing sacrifices to the ancestors, for helping the widows, orphans, and needy of the clan to live, and also for offering scholarships to the promising youth of the clan to study or take state examinations in the capital. Thus the temple functioned actually as a social work center for the clan.

In the practice of ancestor worship, according to the theory of the Chinese philosophers, the dead are called back by the living descendants, not as ghosts coming from a supernatural world, but as forms cherished in the minds of the descendants. This is the spiritual or emotional, personal side of the practice, as it comforts the individual and strengthens his morale, in addition to fostering the solidarity of society. In the chapter entitled "The Meaning of Sacrifice," the *Li Chi* says:

During the days of vigil (in preparation of the sacrifice), the one who is going to offer the sacrifice thinks of his departed, how and where they sat, how they smiled and spoke, what were their aims and views, what they delighted in, and what things they desired and enjoyed. . . . On the day of sacrifice, when he enters the apartment (of the temple), he will seem to see (the deceased) in the place (where their spirit-tablets are). After he has moved about (and performed his ceremonies), and is leaving at the door, he will seem to be arrested by hearing the sound of their movements, and will sigh as he seems to hear the sound of their sighing.

Thus the filial piety taught by the ancient kings required that the eyes of the son should not forget the looks (of his parents), nor his ears their voices; and that he should retain the memory of their aims, likings, and wishes. As he gave full play to his love, they seemed to live again; and to his reverence, they seemed to stand out before him. So seeming to live and standing out, so unforgotten by him, how could sacrifices be without the accompaniment of reverence?[15]

Thus in the practice of ancestor worship the departed, no matter whether they are good or bad, great or insignificant, become familiar once more in the living world. They are not in the world of oblivion but in the living memory of those who are actually the perpetuation of their own flesh and blood. He who practices the worship has the feeling that he will be known to his descendants in the same way also. In such circumstances, he feels that his life is one of the links in a series of an indefinite number of lives, and this fact is at once the insignificance and the significance of his living.

So, in theory there is nothing superstitious in the practice of ancestor worship as conceived by the Chinese philosophers. The fundamental idea of this practice, as they conceived it, is quite scientific. Westerners used to call the practice "religion." I do not wish to argue about terms, especially about such an ambiguous term as religion. But I wish to point out that, if this practice can be called religion, it is one without dogma or supernaturalism. It takes life and death as biological facts. Yet the psychological effect is that a man is "saved" from the momentariness of his life and gains a genuine feeling of a life beyond. Through ancestor worship a man can have salvation without a God or divine savior.

ACKNOWLEDGMENT is due to my colleague Professor V. M. Ames and Mrs. Ames, who read the manuscript and made suggestions.

NOTES

1. *Sacred Books of the East,* F. Max Müller, ed. (Oxford, The Clarendon Press), XXVII, 209.
2. *Hsiao Ching,* trans. by Ivan Chên (London, J. Murray, 1908).
3. *Sacred Books of the East,* XXVIII, 226–227.
4. See reference 2 above, chap. viii.
5. *Ibid.,* reference 3 above.
6. See reference 1 above, p. 196.
7. *Mencius,* IIIa, 4.
8. *Chung Yung,* XX, 8.
9. See reference 2 above, chap. v.
10. *Mencius,* VIIa, 35.
11. *Book of Changes,* Appendix VI.
12. The *Hsun-tzu,* chap. v.
13. See reference 3 above, p. 428.
14. *Mencius,* IVa, 26.
15. See reference 3 above, p. 211.

III

THE PHILOSOPHICAL BASIS OF CHINESE PAINTING

CHIANG YEE

IN 1927 the English art critic, the late Laurence Binyon, wrote in his *Introduction to Chinese Paintings in English Collections:*

It cannot but seem strange that while porcelain, lacquer, textiles, and all kinds of Chinoiserie had been so long and so enthusiastically appreciated in Europe, no European during the eighteenth century and the greater part of the nineteenth had the curiosity to enquire whether behind all this exquisite decoration there might not be a creative art comparable to the painting of the great European schools. The Chinese regarded us as barbarians and we repaid the compliment. Or if we did not consider them quite as barbarians, we thought of them as outlandish people with fantastic customs—exquisite craftsmen indeed, but whose art was in a different and altogether inferior world from the classic art of Greece and Italy. We absorbed, half unconsciously, the Chinese love of floral design, besides imitating directly Chinese motives of decoration. Hand-painted wall-papers imported from China were among the earliest wall-papers used in England, and are still to be found in English country houses. But it was not, I imagine, till about the last quarter of the nineteenth century that any pictures by artists whom the Chinese would recognize as Masters arrived in England. Whether they came earlier to France or Holland, I do not know. In any case, whatever single works may have been imported by chance, there were no collectors, for the whole subject was entirely unexplored. The first English Collection was brought home in 1880, by Dr. William Anderson . . .

Laurence Binyon was one of the first enthusiasts of Far Eastern art to study it seriously. He wrote many beautiful essays on the art of the Far East in general and on Chinese painting in particular. His understanding eye and poetic mind brought a glowing light to bear on the subject, and he was soon followed by other Western scholars. His enthusiasm, expressed through the medium of his powerful yet delicately penetrating pen, aroused in many people as strong a feeling for Chinese painting as had long existed for the classic art of Greece and Italy. Numerous books on Chinese painting have since appeared in Western languages; and a number of Chinese master-pieces have found their way into the collections of public institu-tions and private homes in the West. Indeed, it is not too much to say that the writings of Laurence Binyon and other Western schol-ars have made many Chinese aware of their own pictorial art.

I believe that with regard to beauty and to artistic value there is no difference between the arts of any two nations or cultural regions in the world. But there are obvious differences in technique and medium. Art speaks to the human heart and appeals to the human soul; and Chinese masterpieces have come to be admired in the West just as much as Western masterpieces have appealed to Chi-nese minds. One point of difference still remains: the inward be-lief which the artist consciously or unconsciously expresses in his work and conveys to the beholder. No art can reach an established manner in a flash; it must undergo a good deal of change and de-velop gradually. The course Chinese painting has followed can only be ascribed to our traditional philosophy.

Every art represents the mind of the people that creates it. The mind of the people has been molded gradually within the frame of their conventional thoughts. These thoughts did not take their form all of a sudden but arose by deduction from collected observations of daily life as lived under the natural conditions, or rather the geo-graphical conditions, of the area concerned. China has her typical geographical phenomena which have influenced Chinese conven-tional thoughts and traditional philosophies. I will not attempt to analyze the trends of the different civilizations of the world, nor am I capable of dealing with the historical and esthetic aspects of world art; I propose only to select a few points for illustration by comparison.

Though the origin of the Chinese race and culture is still a sub-ject for speculation by scholars, it is generally accepted, at least by Chinese scholars, that Chinese civilization originated along the valley of the Huangho, the Yellow River, far inland, but gradually extended to its mouth and then turned southward. Why did it turn southward and not remain along the coast or push across the sea? If the southern part of China proper had presented obstacles to the pioneers instead of land much more fertile and habitable than the northern part, it might not have attracted them, and our ancient thinkers might then have followed a different trend of thought. Accepting that in prehistoric days all peoples were nomads, it seems clear that the early Chinese people did not find life as difficult as did some peoples in other parts of the world and that it was not necessary for them to battle against the wanton weather near the coast. Therefore they did not try to become familiar with the sea, which remained obscure and mysterious in the Chinese mind for centuries. In the whole history of China her people have never in wholesale fashion crossed any sea to make a stand for life. It can be said, I think, that the Chinese race is a land-people, a people living entirely on land and as far away from the sea as possible. If they could not get enough to live on from one piece of land, they went on in search of a better piece. This did not necessarily involve every member of the group moving on. Many were presumably quite contented with the fruits of their labors. But one pioneer, with his closest kinsfolk, would set out to look for another piece of land. This way of finding a means of existence cannot be described as a life-and-death struggle. Life in general must have been rather easy for our most remote forefathers. In the Temperate Zone, where China is situated, they did not have to cling to each other in order to ward off wild beasts and other such dangers. So long as they could find a way to exist, one or two persons could live in the heart of the mountains far from the sight of any other human being. Community life seems to have been an unknown conception in the beginning of the Chinese race. Today, despite the enormous population of China, the characteristics of "trying to find an easy way of existence," "detachment," and "indifference" still have deep roots in the Chinese mind. I personally think this is because they are the fundamentals on which Chinese conventional thoughts and traditional philosophies have been built.

I venture to use a simple term for Chinese culture—*land-civilization*. European civilization, I think, is a *sea-civilization*. The latter originated in Egypt and Greece. The areas along the seacoasts of Egypt and on the islands of Greece are limited, and those who lived on them must have had to struggle hard for their existence, in other words "to fight for existence." When one's existence is the result of a hard struggle or a decisive fight, naturally one treasures dearly one's life and possessions. "Lust of possession" and "self-importance" soon developed. As the number of people in a limited area increased, so did the struggle for existence become harder than ever, bringing bitter consequences. Things could not be allowed to go on like that, so some sort of system had to be worked out to prevent the recurrence of these bitter consequences. By degrees the system was subjected to the judgment of both the spiritual and material sides of human nature and steadily improved. The persons who originated the system became superior and divine in the eyes of ordinary human beings, and those who carried it out were hailed as great leaders. Eventually the people worshiped them. Again, the struggle for existence in a limited area near a seacoast or on an island could not be carried on successfully singlehanded. Much had to be undertaken collectively. For instance, one man would simply vanish in a strong gale or a high sea-flood, but several might be able to withstand the danger by a united effort. Nor could one cross the sea entirely alone. Thus one experience and another taught the people to cling together in emergencies and to render mutual help when necessary. I do not need to analyze further. To my mind, "the battle for existence," "lust of possession," "the importance of authority," "organizing ability," and "public spirit" are the fundamentals on which European civilization is based. The ancient thinkers of China also tried in their own way to stress these points, but they found no great support from the people who could still find an easy mode of independent existence, pursuing life peacefully.

Having once fought for existence, one unconsciously continues to fight for a better existence until "to go on fighting and struggling" becomes a habit. Consequently, the standard of living in European civilization has improved through the ages. When it will cease to do so is not for me to say. I want to show that the evolution of European civilization has mainly been concentrated in human affairs. No human being can lead his life without being involved in human affairs in one way or another, but European civilization seems to have stressed the importance of man. The progress of science and inventions is for man's benefit.

This immense interest in man and the culture centered around human affairs can be well illustrated by the development of European art. The history of European art is often divided into periods such as pre-Christian, medieval Christian, Renaissance, and modern. It is unnecessary for me to go through them in detail in this essay. Consider the Egyptian Sphinx and pyramids, the sculpture of an Assyrian cherub or of a Greek satyr. They are all man-beasts, supernatural beings with a beast's body and a man's head, the enormous strength of man being expressed by the body of a lion, an ox, a horse, or an eagle. The Assyrian cherub with its man's head and winged-bull body symbolizes the power of the king. So does the

Egyptian Sphinx. So does the Greek satyr, though it also symbolizes lustfulness. What interests me in these sculptures is that the man-head is always male, not female. From the very beginning of the history of mankind the male wins regard for his power and strength. But gradually the female contribution to living in a confined space near a seacoast or on islands became considerable and could not be ignored, any more than her task of childbearing; so woman also began to figure in pre-Christian art. With these precedents, it is easy for me to understand why the winged man and female angel and then the little naked winged child so often appeared in Christian art.

Medieval Christian art and Renaissance art are chiefly occupied with subjects arising out of the Christian religion. An artist's work is not a realistic representation of the object as seen by the ordinary eye but a representation of it as seen through his natural gift of insight. So the object is often molded with special emphasis on certain points and rearranged to suit the artist's insight, while still looking real and natural to the ordinary eye. Since, in the beginning, "power" or "strength" was the factor in man to be particularly admired and worshiped, nothing could better illustrate this than to emphasize his facial expression and exaggerate his muscles as in the early Greek sculptures. Gradually the figures of Apollo and Venus came to be established as ideal in the artist's vision.

Then the life story of Christ provided an enormous store of subjects for the artist's insight to penetrate. Each part of the story—the Nativity, the Crucifixion, the Resurrection—delighted great masters and continues to do so. Christ's life was glorified or dramatized in much the same way as the figures in Greek legends. I do not attempt to suggest that Western artists in the early days did not produce works of "art for art's sake," but it seems to me that most of them must have had a strong Christian faith within themselves in order to be able to reveal it to countless succeeding generations. The Christian leaders realized this powerful means of revealing and spreading the faith, and they began to decorate their churches and holy books. Soon artists found in the Christian Church a patron which freed them from the material worries of life. Without such patronage Western art might have developed along different lines.

Christian art did not reach its zenith until the Renaissance, for the Christian Church was divided into two—the Eastern and the Western Church. The former was more or less the slave of the Byzantine emperor, and the art which it established was also enslaved to the same master, who regarded it as an instrument to impress the people both with the might of the divine ruler and that of the Christian faith. Slavery is fatal to art. It was not until the Renaissance that Christian art offered a full revelation of the artist's faith. The glorification of the birth of Christ and of His resurrection through the medium of adoring angels, winged cherubs, and precious ornaments later led the artists to use rich designs and colors in drapery and decorations for the gorgeous pageants of history. Prominence was given to portraiture with rare jewelry and splendid costumes as well as to dramatic subjects in every walk of human life.

The interest in any Western work of art is concentrated on man and the doings of man, with landscape or other objects as subordinate background. Though pure landscape paintings were later produced by a number of great masters, they have not so far surpassed the prominence of portraiture or life subjects in Western art as a whole. The modern movement in European painting from the Postimpressionists up to the present day has shown many new developments of portraiture and landscape, but "human life" is still the main subject. Even in Surrealist, Cubist, or Abstract art most paintings have been given titles of life subjects. In the West anyone who is to be an artist must try life studies first, and nude subjects are the basic ones at the beginning of any artist's life. I do not insist that the early Greek sculptures of the nude figure have to do with the seaside life of the ancient Greeks, who wore scanty clothing or loose garments in their semitropical Mediterranean climate, but it is clear that the nude studies in Western art are directly connected with early Greek sculpture. In this sense I venture to say that in the whole history of Western art there is a consistent glorification or dramatization of human life. Indeed, the human form should be the most fascinating medium for the artist's insight. It is perfectly natural that being man himself, the artist should take a keen interest in man and in human forms with their infinite variety.

This simple statement of the general development of European art, however inadequate, may serve as a basis for comparison, while I am tracing the development of Chinese art. The Chinese race is as human as any other, and the Chinese artist should have the same insight into man and the human form as any European artist. But in the surviving archaic jades and ancient bronzes dating back to the eighteenth century B.C., there is nothing comparable to the Egyptian Sphinx, Assyrian cherub, or Greek satyr, in carving or molding. In other words, the symbolic representation of great strength by a winged beast with a man's head did not find root in the early Chinese mind of prehistoric days, though the early Chinese people were as primitive as any other human race in the world, full of fears and hopes. We had many early legends but in none of them was there any similarity with Egyptian and Greek myths or any hint of angelic beings. A number of ogre masks were designed as decorative patterns for bronzes, but every object is clearly shown, man as man, bird as bird, beast as beast. This may indicate that the ancient Chinese did not indulge in the worship of anthropomorphic images. Why not? I think the invention of the ancient Chinese script may have been one reason. According to traditions in the oldest books, a genius of the twenty-eighth century B.C., T'sang Chieh, after observing the footprints and shadows of birds and beasts, invented the script. Each character represented an image of the object seen in nature. Reality could not be perverted, since the image was used to convey the meaning of the object it represented. So the object is often much simplified, with unnecessary detail eliminated. As life became more complicated, more scripts were designed, imagination, reasoning power, and logical combination all playing their part in the process. This led the early Chinese mind to pursue metaphysical ideas rather than to construct anthropomorphic images. The Chinese ancient script for "man" gave no hint that he was considered superior to bird or beast. He was just another object in nature. And the lack of community life in the early days of the Chinese race also helped to prevent over-emphasis of the importance of man.

In the most ancient days the forefathers of the Chinese race, like any other race in the world, doubtless made acute observations of the many distinct natural phenomena—rain, snow, wind, how birds fly, and how plants grow—and could not help expressing their bewilderment, amazement, and awe at the power of nature. Thus sprang up in their minds some idea of worship of heaven, earth, and other features in nature. As they did not live in close groups, they could carry on their worship in the way which suited them locally. (Through lack of urgency there was never any systematically organized worship in the very early days in China.) This explains why some customs and superstitions differ from place to place, though they have a similar purpose. Even if some kind of system was later invented, it was and still is a very loose one. It seems never to have occurred to the early Chinese to inquire what sort of supernatural Being—man, beast, bird, or insect—created and regulated the great host of natural phenomena, though they probably believed in some such Being.

Indifference to any kind of worship was prevalent in ancient China. A ballad supposed to date from the days of Emperor Yao, more than four thousand years ago, ran as follows:

> Work with the sunrise,
> Rest with the sunset,
> Dig the well for my drink,
> Plough the land for my food;
> What do I care for the Power above?

In the peaceful pursuit of existence and in hard work for it, the early Chinese mind was completely free from any abstract attachment or entanglement. All were living on the same level of bare existence in those days and they could learn nothing from one another. Although in time the population increased and human affairs grew complex, the peaceful and easy way of pursuing life remained native to the Chinese, and still so remains. Imbued with the quality of detachment, the Chinese race has come to be known to the world as a people without desire for adventure or exploration. The bulk of the four hundred million Chinese of the present day still know very little about the sea. Most of them have never seen it. They have not acquired the habit of becoming inquisitive about things outside their own domain. (I have often smilingly reflected that there have been many more people living far away from China who are eager to know about Tibet and Mongolia than there have been Chinese. I can state with assurance that the Chinese Government will never raise an expedition to go and claim some part of Antarctica!)

"Pacifism" alone speaks to the mind of the Chinese. But pacifism can assume different forms. Among the many forms of thought current after the great turmoil of wars toward the end of the Chou period (1122–222 B.C.), three—Confucianism, Taoism, and Mohism —prevailed. The last-named suffered from having no great disciples or ardent followers and from being wantonly attacked by the great Confucian disciple, Mencius; so it exercised much less influence in the history of China than Confucianism and Taoism. Just as Christianity is largely responsible for the development of Western art, so Confucianism and Taoism are responsible for the development of Chinese art, but by no means so directly and coherently. The part played by Buddhism, when it was introduced from India, is more comparable, Buddhism being a form of religion as definite as Christianity, though with a negative principle of life. But Buddhism was an alien form of thought to the Chinese mind and so its influence, as we shall see, did not become widespread.

The workmanship and artistic quality of Chinese archaic jades and ancient bronzes of the Shang-yin and Western Chou periods, dating roughly from the eighteenth century B.C. down to the eighth century B.C., reveal that Chinese culture had already reached a highly developed stage and that the people had become prosperous and pursued their life peacefully under good rulers who apparently did not interfere with them. The population was not big then and there was plenty of land for all.

Gradually, however, things changed and developed and multiplied. Human nature has the same passions and desires—love, hate, joy, grief, anger—all the world over, and the Chinese people are no exception. When descendants became numerous and it was not easy to keep on moving to find a new and easy existence, quarrels took place incessantly, and wars were the consequence. From the eighth down to the second century B.C. China experienced ceaseless wars between her feudal states. The result was endless suffering. As these disturbances were contrary to the fundamental characteristics of the Chinese race in their peaceful pursuit for life, there naturally arose cries for peace and thoughts on how to regain it. These long years of war were curiously a period of outstanding intellectual activity. Hundreds of thinkers were born and hundreds of forms of thoughts fermented. Two thinkers, Confucius and Lao Tzu, stand out and have influenced the whole of the succeeding thought of their race.

Confucius, the originator of Confucianism, was born in 551 B.C. and died in 479 B.C. In the seventy-two years of his life there was hardly a single day of peace over China as a whole. He naturally wanted to do something to end the unnecessary sufferings of the people. Being a historian and engaged in historical research, he had probed the reasons of war, and knew that it first comes from disorders in society. To end war and regain peace for the people one must put the disordered society back into good order. Confucius thought there could be no better way of doing so than to restore the system which, under wise rulers such as the Emperors Yao, Shun, Yu, T'ang, Wen, and Wu, had obtained in China's early history. He had a passion for history and based his whole teaching upon the early history of China, which to him was not very remote.

He spoke of himself as a transmitter, not as an originator. To achieve order in society Confucius concentrated on the study of human values—the values of human relationships and of human behavior. Good order in society comes from the correct appreciation of human relationships between man and man. Confucius encouraged everyone to be a good son, a good brother within the family, a good friend, and a good citizen in the society, and a good official and a good ruler in the government. He took the innate goodness of human nature as a matter of course and stressed the cultivation of this goodness as the foundation of one's personal conduct. By cultivating this goodness in one's personal life one would establish the characteristics of a "standard" man or "superior" man, who differs from the inferior man in being benevolent, righteous, well mannered, wise, and honest. Confucius once said: "A single word may spoil an affair, and a single man can set the country in order." This single man must be a superior man. The ruler of a country should be a superior man.

Witnessing the great sufferings of the people around him, Confucius seems to have stood up and cried that there would be no war if the ruler were a superior man and that peace would reign again only when the ruler had educated himself to be a superior man. Confucius thought he could put the country in order if the feudal princes would listen to him, and he went from state to state trying to persuade the princes to follow his teachings. In years of wanderings his efforts met with no success, but with confidence unshaken he labored at the Five Great Classics, *The Book of Songs, The Book of History, The Book of Changes, Spring and Autumn,* and *The Book of Rites,* until his death. In addition to the *Analects,* the record of Confucius' sayings by his disciples, these five books represent the doctrine of Confucianism. Confucianism is pure humanism; it is ethics; it is the study of human relations in their moral sense. Its principles are deduced from the human nature of the Chinese race as a land-people with the habit of pursuing life peacefully. Yet Confucius' contemporaries could not accept it. They had not been brought up in it, and indeed many thought his efforts were futile and made fun of him.

Lao Tzu, the originator of Taoism, was probably born in 570 B.C. He had a different idea about the cause of the endless wars. He was Royal Librarian at one time, and he too must have studied the history of the early emperors and kings thoroughly. While in office he saw the feudal princes breaking away from their allegiance to the Royal House of Chou, paying the Imperial Head no respect and ignoring the imperial laws and canons which had been handed down from the early emperors and kings to guide, protect, and bind together the people. Each of the feudal princes simply craved power and wealth to overcome his fellows, and therefore war had started and continued. If, as Confucius claimed, the laws and canons of the early emperors and kings were good enough to keep the princes and people in order, there could never have been war. Thus in his retirement Lao Tzu probed a step deeper into the integrity of human nature. Confucius was convinced of the innate goodness of human nature and thought he or anyone could put the country in order if people would follow carefully the example of the early wise emperors and kings; his was a plain, straightforward principle for social reform. But Lao Tzu sneered at it, saying, "The virtuous man is for patching things up . . ." To him Confucius' plan was no preventive of future wars. He thought the trouble had sprung from a breakdown in the integrity of human nature. The integrity of human nature is centered in the free will and pure soul of the individual, which together regulate the rhythm of life. When the free will is upset by innumerable fallible laws and the pure soul spoiled by ever-increasing desires, the rhythm of life becomes confused, and wars ensue. Lao Tzu's remedy was to urge every individual to go back to the original natural state of being, free of fallible laws and superfluous desires. He also stressed the unity of all natural phenomena, urging people to see the "Secret of Life" in nature and to identify themselves with the procedure of the Secret of Life or the sense of the Eternal Law, which he called "Tao," "The Way," or "The Nameless," or just "Being of Not-being." He said: "All creatures under Heaven are the offsprings of Being, and Being is the offspring of Not-being." Again, he stressed the importance of keeping the original simplicity of human nature, saying: "The unnamed simplicity will extinguish people's desires. The people's desires being extinguished, there will be peace, and the world will be in order by itself." In other words, the ruler should not try to increase the people's desires by giving orders, creating rites and laws, or holding processions and ceremonies. He should "accomplish do-nothing" by the principle of Wu-Wei or "nonaction" (perhaps "noninterference"), for "Nature does nothing, yet everything is done." Over-government, interference with the carefree, simple life of the people, the folly of power, of pride, and of self-assertion, all lead to war. "Action without deeds," which implies "Exalt not the wise," is Lao Tzu's idea for maintaining the integrity of one's nature.

Lao Tzu condensed his thoughts into a book of only five thousand words called *Tao Teh Chin* or *The Book of Tao,* which is the doctrine of Taoism. Theoretically, as well as practically speaking, Taoism reveals the mind of the Chinese more truly than Confucianism; its advice on protecting the integrity of human nature matches the spirit of the ballad of the days of the Emperor Yao. What the Chinese people have always wanted is to pursue life peacefully without interference from anybody or from anywhere. Unfortunately it was not easy for people to grasp Lao Tzu's ideas while war was being waged and when the integrity of human nature had already been broken up and disturbed by ever-increasing desires and the folly of power, of pride, and of self-assertion. Besides, Taoism, with its focus on the mystical "Tao" or "The Nameless" or "Being of Not-being" or "the sense of the Eternal Law," is more than everyone can grasp. Consequently, Lao Tzu did not exercise much influence toward ending the war and re-establishing peace. Not that this was his immediate object; he meant rather to indicate that those who understand "Tao" can avoid war and find peace.

Taoism therefore represents a contrasting point of view from Confucianism, which urges the "exalting of the wise" to make full use of the innate goodness of human nature. Yet Confucianism and Taoism did not directly conflict, for one was endeavoring through the control of personal conduct to maintain order in society, while the other was urging the maintenance of the integrity of human nature in the rhythm of life under the Eternal Law. As a matter of fact, Confucius went to see Lao Tzu on a few occasions and acknowledged his wisdom. But in Confucius' mind the urge for social reform was too strong; he had to keep on teaching pure humanism and precise ethics, for he thought "The measure of man is man."

The third great Chinese thinker, Mo Tzu, the originator of Mohism, lived probably from 441 to 376 B.C. As he was born after the death of Confucius, whose influence must by then have spread widely, he studied Confucianism and was taught the Confucian method of keeping social order. But he was disillusioned, for in his time the war went from bad to worse and he saw no chance of securing social reform and peace by Confucius' method. He therefore rose in revolt against Confucianism. He was a realist and taught and practiced altruism, frugality, and the hard life in order to achieve his aim of world peace. He attacked Confucian belief in fate and Confucian extravagance in rituals and ceremonies. He also compared Confucianists to bells which would sound only when struck, and not sound when not struck. In other words, the Confucianists only taught principles, but did not try to put them into practice. Mo Tzu condemned aggressive wars. To check aggressive war he developed the technique of defensive warfare. Once he actually visited the prince of a neighboring state which was to wage war with his own state and brought hostilities to an end by announcing that he and his many disciples had made every preparation for defense. He evolved a principle of his own, with universal love as the basis of society and of peace. When nobody in the world loves any other, he said, naturally the strong overpower the weak, the many oppress the few, the wealthy mock the poor, the honored disdain the humble, the cunning deceive the simple. Therefore all the calamities, strife, complaints, and hatred in the world have arisen out of want of mutual love.

While war was being waged and the sufferings of the people were intense, Mohism gained a strong hold over the minds of many who wanted to see the war ended quickly and were prepared to act heroically toward that end. But this kind of extreme altruism and impulsive heroism did not make a strong appeal to the mild Chinese temperament, and Mohism collapsed eventually without playing any effective part in the later history of China. Mo Tzu had many followers in his time but no great disciple to uphold and throw new light on his teachings. In the meantime there arose Mencius, the greatest disciple of Confucius, who lived from 372 to 289 B.C. and who interpreted Confucianism with unmatched force, with the "expansive spirit."

Confucianism, Taoism, and Mohism all failed to halt the wars being waged among the feudal princes during those much troubled years of China's early history. Mere forms of thought can never do anything about war directly. War is a straightforward contest of physical strength. After perhaps years of great suffering and weariness, the weaker side is subdued by the stronger. Thus in 221 B.C. China was at last reunited under the powerful House of Ch'in, whose prince, having overcome all the other feudal princes, proclaimed himself "Shih Huang Ti" or "The First Emperor." So China regained peace by force. This "First Emperor" set no store by Confucian or any other principles. He did away with his enemies ruthlessly, burning all Confucian books and burying hundreds and thousands of Confucian scholars alive. He then became the greatest tyrant and absolute dictator ever known in the history of China. However, this did not help him to govern the country long, for the carefree, peace-loving mind of the Chinese race could not be subdued indefinitely. Either they moved out of the ruler's reach or they gathered together in revolt. The House of Ch'in was pulled down by the Chinese peasants after reigning only fourteen years.

The first ruler of the succeeding Han Dynasty (206 B.C.–219 A.D.) and his ministers were wiser. With the disastrous experiment of the Ch'in totalitarianism in mind, they tried to govern the country by letting the people alone. Far from suppressing Confucianism, they made great efforts to revive and spread it by all possible means. They sent people out in search of the hiding, surviving Confucian scholars and reproduced Confucian books. They created rites for court ceremonies and also for family ancestral worship according to Confucius' teachings. They also set up rules and regulations for behavior between the emperor and ministers, between governmental officials and the people, between man and woman, between elders and youngsters, and so on. They honored the memory of Confucius and his great disciples by giving them posthumous titles and providing their descendants with honors and wealth. They also built state temples for Confucius in the capital and big cities to hold nation-wide ceremonial offerings twice a year. Confucianism, though not a religion, became almost the state religion. Indeed, the Han Emperors and ministers made full use of Confucianism to foster their ambition, and nothing delighted Confucianists more than to be occupied with governmental tasks. After the great oppression and ruthless treatment under the short-lived Ch'in Dynasty, the Han Confucianists employed their triumph to work out Confucius' teaching in minute detail and often carried it to extremes. As long as their peaceful pursuit of life was not interfered with, the people did not mind. By and by they accepted these detailed rules, rites, and regulations as habitual customs. And generation after generation became so soaked in them that thenceforward every Chinese was a Confucianist by birth, no matter what he may have become afterward.

This account of how Confucianism finally became the dominant form of thought in the mind of the Chinese as a whole may suggest that it must have made a major contribution to the development of Chinese art, particularly Chinese pictorial art. This is not so in a positive sense. Let us see why not. I have just said that the first Han emperor and his descendants almost made Confucianism the state religion of China. But Confucianism was not a religion. It had no system of communal worship of Confucius as the religious leader, no Bible, Sutra, or Koran. The Confucian temples built in the Chinese capital and big cities are only a kind of monumental building for reverence and remembrance to show the high esteem in which the people of China hold Confucius. Until recently every young Chinese child, when he entered his school for the first time, and twice a month until he left to attend the local civil examination or to enter upon another career, was made to kneel down in front of a small Confucius shrine made of paper or wood to pay his respect to the great master. But this was not a religious service and the schoolmaster was not a Confucian priest. The child was not told to expect help or guidance from Confucius while kneeling before the shrine; he was to make his obeisance simply because Confucius was the wisest man China had ever possessed. This paying of respect and esteem to Confucius was not demanded from everybody in the country. Women were virtually excluded from it, though they all offered it in their minds.

The Confucian scholars of the Han Dynasty worked out a system of ancestral worship according to Confucius' teaching on filial piety; but when the family gathered to pay their respect and esteem to their ancestors for what they had done for them, Confucius was never mentioned as the one whose teaching had inspired the ancestors' character or work. All great Confucianists in China at all ages have taken the influence of Confucianism for granted without thinking of how to spread his principles and win converts among mankind at large. Scholars in large numbers have gone on studying Confucianism and writing commentaries on it, but these are all individual, separate enterprises, restricted in their effects to the learned.

Again, the Confucian scholars have only studied Confucius' *teachings;* very few of them, even in the early Han days, ever entered upon the study of Confucius' *life.* The Chinese have not the habit of working things out systematically or scientifically, and they have been trained not to probe into the private life of another. Without the authentic and exact details of Confucius' life it is therefore not easy to dramatize or glorify it. He performed no miracles. Once or twice he did run a specific risk of his life, but neither he nor any of his disciples suffered martyrdom for the cause of his teachings. Confucianism never encountered a dangerous rival philosophy

except the short-lived Mohism; Taoism just lets it alone or sometimes sneers at it. Our modern mind can but wonder how Confucianism, without being a religion, can have rooted itself so deeply
in the mind of the Chinese people, as deeply as Christianity has
rooted itself in the European mind.

There being no definite institution comparable to the Western
Church, devoted to the task of spreading Confucianism, the early
Chinese artists did not enjoy Confucian patronage at all. However,
in the first chapter of *Li Tai Ming Hua Chi* or *The History of
Famous Paintings* by the T'ang historian and Confucian scholar,
Chang Yen-yuan, painting is cited as a means of promoting culture
and strengthening the principles of right conduct. In many early
records we read that pictures of the ancient wise kings and emperors were painted to make one look at them with respect and venera-
tion, while evil beings were portrayed in such a manner as to make
one feel sad. It seems one would simply grind one's teeth on seeing
pictures of rebels and unfilial sons, but would forget one's meals
when facing pictures representing men of high principles and great
thinkers; one would feel exalted when looking at pictures of loyal
subjects who died at the call of duty, and sigh over pictures of exiled
citizens and expelled sons; one would be reluctant to contemplate
pictures of vicious men and jealous women, but would admire
deeply those of faithful, kindhearted empresses and court ladies.
Painting was employed to uphold morality and to be a mirror of
conduct. These were the words left by the famous young poet,
Prince Ts'ao Chih, who lived in 192–232 A.D., at the end of the Han
Dynasty and the beginning of the Wei Dynasty (220–264 A.D.).

During the Han period, when Confucianism was first established,
many artists must have been busy depicting subjects connected with
Confucius' teachings and must therefore have shown great interest
in human life as subject matter—not only in a certain group of men
but in all types of men and women. In what way these works of
the Han artists were employed is not known. Whether the Han
artists were themselves convinced Confucianists no one can tell. Unfortunately very few examples of Han pictorial art remain for our
examination. There are embossed engravings on Han bronze mirrors, and Han bas-reliefs on tombstones and in family temples, such
as those from Hsiao-tang-shan and Wu-liang-tzu of Shantung.
Most of them show a rather rough craftsmanship, and the figures
appear to be very much formalized, all having more or less similar
gestures. The only Han pictorial art which can be examined clearly

is the "Scene of an animal fight in the Shang-lin Park," which forms part of the Ross Collection in the Boston Museum of Fine Arts. Here each figure has a lively expression and gesture, yet all are more or less similarly arranged. Ku Kai-chih's "Admonitions of the Imperial Preceptress to the Ladies of the Palace" in the British Museum, London, must be similar to the type of painting prevailing in Han days, though Ku was a fourth-century artist. For artistic skill in connection with Confucian subject matter, Ku Kai-chih's work shows the highest development, reminding us by its flowing, graceful brush strokes that calligraphy and not sculpture is the foundation of Chinese graphic art. In this same century lived Wang Hsi-chih, the greatest calligrapher of all ages. It is possible that Han Confucian scholars made use of calligraphy to enlighten the minds of their fellows about Confucianism, and so felt no need to urge the claim of pictorial art.

However this may be, we cannot fail to feel that Confucianism, with its interest in man and conduct, *ought* to have played as great a part in the development of Chinese pictorial art as Christianity did in that of European art. Unfortunately, Confucianism lays too much emphasis on the humanistic, rational, and ethical sides of human nature. Its range does not extend beyond the span of a natural life. It stresses how to live and how life *should be,* and neither deals with the essence of life as it *is* nor investigates the origin and end of life. With such definite limits, the artistic rendering of its principles is restricted and cannot go far or deep. The plain, straightforward Confucian account of the example set by ancient wise kings and emperors offers very little inspiration to artistic and imaginative thought. Pictorial descriptions can only parallel the verbal ones. This might not weaken the value of the work if the artist were given entire freedom in rendering his subject matter, technically as well as artistically. But the strict rules and rigid regulations of ritual behavior which were created by the Han Confucian scholars to foster the principle of the right conduct of man set up further barriers for the artists when they tried to employ their talent and skill in working out compositions, etc. In a word, art was not free.

The chief and most important issue in Confucianism is the moral sense or moral virtue of man. To emphasize the importance of this moral sense man must cover his body with clothes. The Han Confucianists made an intensive study of the dresses worn in earlier times, particularly in early Chou, the period which Confucius praised and held up as a model. They made clothes a symbol of civilization. It did not matter whether the clothes fitted well as long as they complied with the moral requirements and maintained their symbolic importance. There are no relics in existence to provide adequate information about Chou and Han costumes. The figures appearing in the Han bas-relief of tombstones do not display much variety. A naked figure was strictly forbidden. Artists were not even given freedom in rendering bodily movements and facial expressions. Confucianism expects a man to maintain a dignified air and a serene complexion at all times. Confucius once remarked: "Clever talk and a pretentious manner are seldom found in the good." Again, he told one of his disciples concerning personal conduct: "Don't look at a thing if it is not in accordance with propriety; don't talk of it if it is not in accordance with propriety; don't listen to it if it is not in accordance with propriety; and don't go to it if it is not in accordance with propriety." These tenets may not originally have been very rigid, but the later Confucianists made use of them to insist that morality meant absolute suppression of one's emotions, feelings, and moods both at home and in public. Barriers were set up between man and woman so insurmountable that a young man could be approved by Confucianists for not extending a helping hand to his sister-in-law if she were drowning. This led further and further away from natural life. (No wonder the Chinese became known as people of inscrutable countenance!) A man living so rigidly is little better than a wooden figure. How could any artist want to work on such a figure for his composition? In "life" of this kind the artist could find no inspiration at all. This is probably why there was not any outstanding Confucian art produced in the Han period. Confucianism was the slave of the government and as such as little able to inspire great masterpieces as Christianity in the Eastern Church was under Byzantine tyranny.

By Ku Kai-chih's time (fourth century A.D.) it was already clear that not every human being could become a "standard" Confucian man however hard he tried. Han Confucianists did not give enough thought to Mencius' principle of benevolent government, nor to his statement that "the people are most important and the ruler least important." They made the emperor a supreme head, far above the people, open only to condemnation by Heaven; as they did not define what power "Heaven" might have, the Emperor felt safe to do as he liked. When he was a good ruler, China was prosperous and at peace; when he was not, calamity came upon the country. Many a

Confucian official joined in intrigues in order to remain in office; the temptation of authority and wealth is always hard to resist. Even in the smallest Chinese village the headman, with the scantiest ability to read or write (the lowest qualifications for many so-called Confucian scholars), has plumed himself on being more important than his fellow villagers. So Mencius' teachings were thrown to the winds. Personal influence, bribery, and corruption took a hand, and the unfortunate people who did not benefit thereby were filled with discontent and disgust.

Again the artist found no inspiration in the life around him. Sincere Confucian scholars took to heart the disillusionment, discontentment, and depression of the people, and when they could make their way into the government tried to make improvements but only became the more disillusioned, discontented, and depressed themselves when their efforts were frustrated. For consolation they turned to Lao Tzu's teachings and to Taoism. Without Taoism's activity at the back of people's minds, the Han Confucianists with all their rules and regulations for behavior would have had all Chinese living like automatons. But Taoism came to the rescue, bringing humor, romance, and even cynicism to keep the Chinese soul alive. Confucianism is the natural form of thought for Chinese conduct, and Taoism is the natural form of thought for Chinese sanity.

At the fall of the Han Dynasty many good Confucian scholars turned their minds to Taoism simply because they had come to see how futile was the Confucianist ideal of completely regulating the conduct of life, instead of letting the Rhythm exercise its sway. They became Confucian-Taoists, still guiding their personal conduct according to Confucian principles, but with the modification of a Taoist outlook. Some wandered deep into regions of high mountains far from the public gaze; some became hermits, even within a city; some, drinking more deeply of Taoism, ultimately discarded Confucianism and no longer behaved according to propriety. There have come down to us many stories and tales of this and that well-known scholar being drunk, behaving idiotically, even letting himself drift into madness. This was the period when Taoism first came out into the open and showed that Confucianism was not alone to dominate the Chinese mind.

If it had not been for this period, with its spreading and nourishing of Taoism, Chinese culture and civilization might never have reached important fruition. Painting and literature benefited directly. Poetry, particularly the poetry of nature and the countryside, was its chief product. After Confucius compiled the *Book of Songs,* there is little to be said about Chinese poetry till Chu Yuan of the later Han Dynasty wrote *Li Sao.* This is a long mystical poem already imbued with Taoistic thought. The Confucian emphasis on morality by absolute suppression of one's emotions, both at home and in public, stifled poetry as well as painting. It was natural for those who wanted to express their emotion and were prohibited from describing human life to turn to nature.

The leading poet in the development of Chinese nature poetry was T'ao Yuan-ming. A good Confucian scholar, he went into public life to become the district governor and magistrate of Peng-cheh, Kiangsi. When told to learn the rites for receiving an official slightly superior to himself, he found them so tedious and futile that he hung his official seal on the central beam of his office and ran away. Thereafter he led a life of constant poverty, but he enjoyed it to the utmost because he retained complete freedom and possessed the integrity of his soul. He became for all Chinese the perfect model of a true lover of life. His poetry shows his immense joy in nature and country scenes, and opened a path for later Chinese poets and scholars.

Chinese painting received a similar stimulus from the increased influence of Taoism. But it did not develop so quickly, owing to the simultaneous enthusiasm for Buddhism. Buddhism had made its appearance in China quite early in the first century but was not firmly settled until the fourth or fifth century. A huge golden image of Buddha appeared in a dream to the Han Emperor Ming-ti, in 64 A.D., suggesting a paradise far in the west of China. The country was at peace again after a few years of trouble and war just before the beginning of the first century. Nevertheless the people felt discontented with their life and longed for something else either to satisfy the body or to solace the soul. Dreams of immortality and long life were prevalent, roused by the corrupt mixture of alchemy, witchcraft, and native superstition which formed the so-called Taoist religion—a very different thing from Taoism or Lao Tzu's teachings. This superstitious worship brought no satisfaction, so the idea of a new paradise roused great interest. In 66 A.D. Ming-ti sent envoys to India to ask for the golden image of Buddha, and some Indian monks came to start the building of Buddhist monasteries in China in 68 A.D.

Little mention is made of Buddhism after that, until the latter part of the second century and the early part of the third, when China was once more immersed in a series of wars. Many Chinese people moved away from the capital and big cities and settled the border regions of the southwest. More stories about Buddha's life in India came through to them. More Indian monks came to China as missionaries and told of the Buddha's life with its many miraculous incidents. Born a prince and heir to a great throne of India, Gautama discarded everything to become a beggar in order to study the sufferings of mankind and how to cure them. This action alone won the Chinese heart, because of the traditional admiration in the Chinese mind, following Mencius' teachings, for those who lead a simple life of righteous conduct and who cannot be seduced by riches and honors, nor made to bow to force and power, nor disgusted by poverty and obscurity.

Again, the stories about Buddha's previous life and his enlightenment made the Chinese believe that their dream was true and that there was a paradise in the world, in India, west of China. Many early Buddhist converts went to live in India to experience the paradise. They came back intent upon making China into a paradise too. Indian monks accompanied them.

The Indian Buddhist monasteries, decorated as they were with monumental sculptures and frescoes and paintings of Buddha's life and enlightenment, must have made a great impression on the Chinese converts, who naturally wanted to found similar establishments in China. Continuing war conditions greatly hindered their work, yet they only felt the more eager to share their new experiences in order to alleviate grief and suffering. By the beginning of the seventh century China had thousands and thousands of Buddhist monasteries, big and little, scattered over the country. The stories of Buddha's life and activities now offered a huge store of subject matter for artists. Indian sculpture and painting were a revelation to them. The demand for artists to decorate the Buddhist monasteries in China was so great that for the time being they were diverted from Taoism and from the newly developed Chinese poetry of nature. Chinese Buddhist sculptures and paintings produced during this period, such as those found in Tun-huang, Lung-meng, Tien-lung-shan, and Yun-kang, far outnumber and outshine works of art of the preceding period, when Confucianism was the sole influence over the mind of the people.

However, the Buddhist sculptures and paintings produced in China are unlike those in India or Cambodia. Indian artists may have come to China with the monks, but it seems likely that some Chinese artists were sent to India to study Indian art in the Indian monasteries in order to be able to produce similar works for the Chinese Buddhist monasteries. Apparently these Chinese artists, whose minds were already imbued with the Confucian standard of moral virtues, could not entirely accept the sensuous and exuberantly rhythmical body-movement expressed in Indian sculpture and paintings; so they produced a rather restrained, austere, and aloof type of Buddhist art. Very few Chinese Buddhist figures were naked, nor did Chinese artists imitate the Indian sculptors and painters in representing dancing girls and temptresses with soft swelling curve of breast and hip. Chinese Buddhist artists made Buddha, Bodhisativa, his disciples, attendants, and worshipers wear graceful draperies in order to appease their own Confucian upbringing. A calm, half-smiling expression of otherworldliness and light-in-the-emptiness became the admired feature of the Chinese Buddhist sculptures and paintings. Then both sculpture and painting became formalized and there was little further development.

Chinese Buddhist art, particularly as far as painting is concerned, is only a branch development and cannot be said to be representative of Chinese painting as a whole. The Chinese artists who painted Buddhist subjects were not all Buddhists themselves, unlike the European artists who painted Christian subjects in medieval and Renaissance days and who were ardent Christians—or at least do not suggest that they were not. While Buddhism offered so much inspiration to Chinese artists, many of them did not confine themselves to its inspiration. This is again unlike those early European Christian artists who painted nothing but what was inspired by Christianity, which is of course connected with every walk of human life. There are many miraculous tales about the wonderful Buddhist wall paintings of Ku Kai-chih and Wu Tao-tzu, but of Ku Kai-chih's painting nothing survives except his Confucian work, "Admonitions of the Imperial Preceptress to the Ladies of the Palace." Ku Kai-chih was a Confucian scholar by upbringing. Wu Tao-tzu, as recorded in books, painted over three hundred frescoes in Buddhist monasteries in Ch'ang-an, Lo-yang, and the neighborhood. Ch'ang-an was the capital, Lo-yang the secondary capital, for the T'ang emperors (618–906 A.D.). Unfortunately all these frescoes have perished. But we can see something of Wu Tao-tzu's style, if not of his spirit, in the few Chinese frescoes of the Eumorfopoulos Collection now in the British Museum.

Yet although Wu Tao-tzu was largely responsible for the high standard of Chinese Buddhist paintings, his greatness in the Chinese mind lies in his inimitable achievement in landscape painting. Many interesting and inspiring tales about his work on landscape subjects have been handed down, and Chinese artists are proud to repeat them. Indeed, Wu Tao-tzu is a pioneer-master in the development of Chinese landscape painting. His second name, "Tao-tzu," indicates that he or his parents were soaked in Taoism.

No Chinese artist painting Buddhist subjects was *strictly* Buddhist. Far more Chinese Buddhist monk-painters preferred to express their artistic inclination and inspiration in landscape subjects than in Buddhist ones and have left big names in the annals of Chinese art, such as Ch'u-jan, Mu-chi, Shu-ku, Kun-tsan, Shih-tao, and others. The first of these established his own school of Chinese landscape painting, while the influence of Shih-tao has lasted through three hundred years up to the present day. This is no accident.

As Buddhism came to China from India, no Chinese Buddhist could ever be a born Buddhist. There have been tales about people who had led a former life in the bosom of Buddhism, refusing to take meat food, according to the Buddhist religious rules, when they were reborn, but such tales are apocryphal. I have said that Buddhism did not catch the Chinese mind at all, when it was first introduced. When its influence did at last begin to grow it spread rapidly and the authorities, all Confucianists by upbringing, were at a loss. Some became infatuated and followed the tide, others attacked the new ideas violently. While the miseries of war were being suffered, the people naturally sought relief either in Taoism or in Buddhism. Those who ran away into the mountains and became Taoist hermits simply disappeared and did not worry the authorities. But those who went over to Buddhism, which has a definite form of worship and is a religious system, as their numbers grew presented a menace. Thus Buddhism invited attack, but not from Taoism. This attack came from Confucianism.

The Confucianists attacked Buddhism on two scores: first, because Confucius had never mentioned God or an unseen Being, and secondly, because the Buddhist convert would lose his family name when he cast away his family connections and became a monk, which in Confucian eyes was an outrage to the Confucian principle of ancestral worship. The greatest Confucian scholar of the T'ang Dynasty, Han Yu, wrote many fine essays attacking Buddhism.

These attacks were focused more on the religious form of Buddhism than on its philosophy.

As a matter of fact, the *Dhammapada,* a book of Buddhist aphorisms—Buddha's advice on good friends, his distinction between the wise and foolish, and on moral strength—is closely akin to Confucianism. Again, his emphasis on self-examination, freedom from fear, and on inner repose do not conflict with Taoism. That is why Buddhism, when it came to China, found a ready reception in the Chinese heart and stayed, despite attacks on its religious form by some ardent Confucian scholars.

On the other hand Buddhism did not take the place of Confucianism, which was too firmly rooted, nor did it displace Taoism, for a similar reason. It would probably never have swept over China even for a time had not China been in turmoil and strife at the end of the Han Dynasty. But it could never have been made a state religion, as in Cambodia (Siam) or even in Japan. It stayed in China, as I have said, because Buddha's teaching has much in common with Chinese native thought and also because one of the two Buddhist schools, Mahayana, captivated the inner mind of many Chinese thinkers and scholars, both Confucian and Taoist.

Hinayana, called "Lesser Vehicle" in Chinese, is the other school of Buddhism, dealing with the saints and gods of all degrees presented in Buddha's sermons. It evokes the principle of prayer and devotion by continuous works, and therefore emphasizes religious ceremonies and the illumination of Buddha's life through imposing statues, pictorial records, and so forth. But Mahayana, called in Chinese the "Greater Vehicle" school, or more generally "Ch'an Buddhism," is centered on *Bodhisattvas,* the incarnation or rebirth of the Buddha, for the purpose of converting all mankind into Buddhas and thus saving the world. It stresses salvation by faith rather than by works. Having faith in Buddha, everyone can become a Buddha. Buddha is everywhere and Buddha is one's heart, or the heart is the Buddha, if it is full of faith. Many great books of the Mahayana school have been translated into Chinese since the sixth century and are the main sources of the interesting phrases and sayings which occur over and over again in the works of Chinese poets and writers, incorporated with either Confucian or Taoist thoughts.

This is not the place to go into more detail. But one sure thing is that to the Chinese scholars who became interested in Buddhism it was its philosophy, not its religious form, which appealed. Very few Chinese Buddhist scholars could name any Buddhist saint or god except Buddha and Kuan-yin. The different names of the saints and gods in Hinayana Buddhism proved much too difficult for the conservative Chinese to pronounce. I doubt if any Chinese monk of today can give the names of any of the Buddhist statues in Yun-kang Cave, for instance, or explain their importance for Buddhism. They must have signified something when they were sculptured, unless the sculptors just carved all the figures alike under the name of Buddha or Bodhisattva. Similarly, Chinese Buddhist paintings remain obscure to the onlooker because the life story of Buddha and his disciples was never popularized in China as the life of Jesus Christ has been in the West. Apart from one or two names such as Manjusri and Ananda which have some special significance in Chinese Buddhist paintings, the Chinese artists have very seldom painted other Buddhist subjects than Buddha and Kuan-yin. After the early part of the T'ang Dynasty few Chinese artists painted Buddhist subjects with a religious intent, but only in connection with the philosophy of Ch'an Buddhism.

When the philosophy of Ch'an Buddhism became incorporated with Confucianist and Taoist thought it stayed forever and became a native thought itself, known as Chinese Buddhism. In 527 A.D. the great Indian monk Bodidharma, or Darmo, came to China on a special mission and was later worshiped by all Chinese Buddhists as the first patriarch of Chinese Ch'an Buddhism. He taught by example, not by scripture, and meditated in faith, not through work. Thus arose the meditation practice in China. He was known to have meditated facing a huge rock, without food or sleep, for nine years, as deeply sunk in the faith as if his flesh were not exposed to physical sensation. Once someone in China brought the books of the Confucian Classics to him to ask what he thought of them. He put the books close to his nose and said, "They bear a sort of quarrelsome smell"! It can be imagined how this tale has delighted the hearts of Taoists, and also how it made real Confucianists see how often Confucianism had failed to solve human difficulties. This tale alone won Darmo great support from both Taoism and Confucianism, so he stayed and his teachings went further and deeper into the people's mind.

It will sound strange when I say that Confucianism supported Ch'an Buddhism. The reason is that China, with Confucianism dominant, has not often or for long enjoyed glory and prosperity. This is not due to errors in Confucius' own teachings but to Confucian scholars in authority who failed to follow Confucianism truly. Had the fault lain in Confucianism itself instead of in pseudo-Confucianists in authority China would have disintegrated when troubles arose about the beginning of the Christian Era after nearly two hundred years of Confucian rule. China did not fall chiefly because the essence of Confucian philosophy is the principle of the Middle Way, developed by Confucius' grandson Tzu Ssu. Troubles and wars came to China owing to Confucianists in authority going to extremes. Happily there were always others who strove to get China back into the Middle Way. In the Middle Way Confucianism can see things for itself; it can accept Darmo's joke about the quarrelsome smell of the Confucian Classics, as well as the Taoists' sneer at their futility. Good Confucian scholars, understanding the principle of the Middle Way, easily accepted either Taoism or Ch'an Buddhism when they were unsuccessful in life or when they encountered difficulties and injustice in public service. Consequently, besides being Confucianists they became either Taoist or Ch'an Buddhists. Many scholars have been Confucianist by birth, Taoist in spirit, and Ch'an Buddhist as regards the life beyond. Confucianism tends to regulate life; Taoism considers it unnecessary to regulate life which regulates itself through the work of Tao or the Nameless Being; and Ch'an Buddhism adds that life, whether it needs regulating or not, proceeds in a cycle of rebirths until, through faith, the state of a Buddha is attained. The contrast between the three is relative: their interfusion has every possibility.

After nine years of meditation, Darmo was said to have identified himself with Buddha; he became a Buddha completely free from bodily worries such as the need for food, drink, and sleep, and also from any human entanglements. Thus he was able to save mankind by setting an example of how to identify oneself with Buddha through the faith of Buddha. At one time he was seen meditating in front of a massive waterfall, at another on the top of a precipice, at another inside the hollow trunk of an aged, rugged tree, or inside a rock cave. Other tales tell how a good many years after his death and burial at a certain place in the north of China, Darmo was seen crossing a river in the south on a single plate of weeds. This kind of carefree and conscience-free life has delighted many a Chinese heart and suited its temper. Darmo's example was followed by many Ch'an Buddhists and monks. Chinese artists then used their insight, were inspired by these disciples of Ch'an Buddhism, and began to paint with the aim of identifying themselves with or revealing the faith of Buddha. This was a later development of Chinese figure painting. Buddhist religious subjects had limited the artist's ability through the stories, names, costumes, and gestures associated with them; Buddhist philosophical subjects gave the artist every freedom.

From the Chinese point of view, the artistic value in the Chinese Ch'an Buddhist paintings is higher than that in the painting of religious subjects because it expresses the insight and spirit of the artists and therefore is a work of art in the true sense. For example, most of the Chinese Ch'an Buddhist paintings depict a Ch'an monk or Lohan or even Darmo himself meditating among various phenomena of nature. The favorite theme is Darmo crossing the river on a single plate of weeds. This further step in the development of Chinese figure painting has brought direct, close contact between man and nature.

While those artists who had faith in Ch'an Buddhism continued their carefree expression in Ch'an philosophical subjects, there must have been many other artists who did not adopt the Ch'an faith, yet refrained from entangling themselves in the too rigid conventions of Confucianism and devoted their talent and insight to the expression of their feeling and mood in Taoism. The growth of Chinese nature and countryside poetry, with the great poet Tao Yuan-ming as pioneer, must have inspired many artists to turn their thoughts to the relation between man and nature. They began to paint poets, who were either Confucianist-Taoists or Taoists, in their doings among the various natural phenomena. We find among the titles of their paintings, "Tao Yuan-ming Picking Chrysanthemums at the Eastern Fence," "The Scene of the Gathering [of men of letters] at Lan-t'ing or Orchid Bower," "A Taoist Scholar Reclining inside a Bamboo Grove," and so on. These paintings aim at expressing the tranquil harmony between man and nature. They developed into paintings of all kinds of stories of the activities of men in natural surroundings as related in Chinese literature, but without any suggestion of intrigue between man and man. When this stage was reached, Chinese figure painting became conventionalized with one or a few human figures in a natural surrounding. Unlike Western figure paintings, with their intense feeling and love for life, it has gone no further.

No artist can be happy when working within a rigid conventional form, especially when even the free rendering of this conventional form is handicapped by a conventional conception. So again, as under the restrictions imposed by the Confucian code of moral behavior, Chinese artists became dissatisfied with any attempt at figure painting and found their release in pure landscape painting. But this development was not sudden. It is difficult to assert when a pure landscape was first painted. There was a small portion of landscape in Ku Kai-chih's "Admonition of the Imperial Preceptress to the Ladies of the Palace," but it was rather crude and primitive by comparison with his figure subjects and did not convey any special feeling. Tsung Ping (357–426 A.D.), though none of his works is left today, was perhaps one of the first pure landscape painters, according to his essay "Introduction to Landscape Painting":

I have lost my heart to the mountains of Lu and Heng, and am so constantly thinking of Chin and Wu, which I have not seen for such a long time, that I forget old age is approaching me. Regretting that I am unable to enjoy myself—body and soul—by lingering around the waterfall of Stone-Gate, I paint their form and color from imagination, and create these cloudy mountaintops . . .

As I have said before, the newly introduced influence of Indian Buddhism after the Han Dynasty proved too rich a source of inspiration for artists, so that they did not at first follow the growth of Chinese landscape poetry very closely. By Mid-T'ang, at the beginning of the eighth century, we find the greatness of landscape painting in Wu Tao-tzu's work. It is said that he and another landscape painter, Li Ssu-hsun, were commanded by the Emperor Husan Tsung (reign 713–755 A.D.) to paint for him some scenery of the Chia-ling River along the Upper Yangtse. Li Ssu-hsun began immediately and in three months' time finished the work, which showed careful touches in detailed form and rich color. But Wu Tao-Tzu awaited the moment of inspiration and revealed his vision of the landscape in one day's work with his brush and ink. Both paintings were equally admired and treasured. From this story we see that by Mid-T'ang Chinese landscape painting was not only firmly established but two distinct styles had been evolved.

It was Wang Wei (699–759 A.D.), a successful official and man of letters, who welded landscape painting and poetry into one. From that moment landscape painting became the chief flower of Chinese civilization. Wang Wei was a Confucianist by birth. He won distinction in the civil examination and was made a high official. Later the country was disturbed, and he experienced great difficulty in his career. Then his Taoistic instinct and inclination led him to study Taoism and even more Ch'an Buddhism. A good calligrapher, he painted pure landscape paintings as well as writing landscape poetry which is in a direct line from that of Tao Yuanming, incorporated with Ch'an philosophy. Many record him as a Confucian scholar converted to Ch'an Buddhism simply because he did not marry again after the death of his wife in his middle age. But I think from his poetry and landscape painting he was more a Confucian-Taoist than a Ch'an Buddhist, though it is recorded that he did more paintings on Ch'an Buddhist subjects than on Taoist ones. His poetry is his landscape painting in words; his landscape painting is his poetry in form. He is the first artist responsible for this happy combination, which has become an inexhaustible spring for the Chinese artist's insight and interpretative power ever since.

Chinese landscape painting did not reach its peak until the Sung Dynasty (960–1276). There were more great masters in the Sung period than at any other time in the annals of Chinese pictorial art. Great names such as Li Cheng, Fan Kuan, Tung Yuan, Kuo Chungshu, Chao Ch'ang, Hsu Tao-ling, Kuo Hsi, Tsui Pai, Li Kung-ling, Wen Tung, Su Tung-p'o, Mi Fei and his son, Mi Yujen, Chao Pai-chu, Ma Ho-chih, Li T'ang, Chiang Seng, Liu Sunglien, Ma Yuan, Hsia Kuei, Kung Kai, the monk Ch'u-jan, and, of course, the painter-emperor Hui Tsung (1101–25) are all now associated in our minds with masterpieces. Except for one Ch'an Buddhist monk, all were Confucian scholars with Taoist inclinations, and many held high official positions. Nearly all are great landscape masters, but two specialized in bamboo paintings, and a few painted other subjects as well.

The development of bird-and-flower painting and the painting of animal subjects, including fish and insects, were natural consequences of the establishment of landscape painting. Artists studied these before introducing them into their landscapes and soon painted them separately. This new development also reached its zenith in the Sung period. The artists were happy in revealing their insight and thought and in giving their minds free play. They could choose any subject that suited their talent or pleased their taste. After the Sung Dynasty figure painting or life study never reregained any prominence. Landscape remained the favorite subject. Innumerable treatises and essays on landscape painting have been written by great masters. It is on landscape painting that Chinese esthetics is based. Just as every Western artist must have served an apprenticeship to life study, so must every Chinese artist to land-scape study. But he is only able to identify his soul in his land-scape work through being steeped in Chinese philosophy—Con-fucianism, Taoism, and Ch'an Buddhism.

The Chinese term for "landscape" is *shan-shui,* "mountain-water." In English the term is perhaps better written "mountain water," for the first word does not qualify the second. It signifies a painting in which the chief elements are mountains or hills and water of some kind—river, stream, waterfall, lake, or pond. In the West a picture of a garden would qualify as "landscape"; in China it would not. In the West, too, a landscape painting almost invari-ably has some specific representational aim: Constable's "Flatford Mill" or "Dedham Lock" expresses the local quality of these places; and man, or man's works, are seldom absent. In China, a master-piece of landscape art is not a realistic study of a particular moun-tain and an actual river but an imaginative representation of nature in essence, of the rhythm of life of which the artist discerns the mountain and water and the space between to be the expression. For this purpose, a mass of realistic detail is not merely unnecessary; it is irrelevant, and destructive to the rhythm which the artist seeks to express. To define this rhythm is difficult. It is nothing disturbing or extraneous. It is the power which we feel keeps nature working in fullness, unity, and balance. Man, in such an environment, be-comes diminished to the proportions of one live creature among all the hosts of nature.

This feeling for the rhythm of life has more affinity with Taoism than with either Confucianism or Ch'an Buddhism. Confucius ex-pressed his belief about nature in the famous—and typically moral —saying: "The wise take pleasure in rivers and lakes, the virtuous in mountains." His disciple Mencius lamented the deforestation of the hills occurring in his time. Both displayed the characteristic Chinese feeling for nature. Nevertheless the prime concern of Con-fucianism is human life and human affairs. Ch'an Buddhism spec-ulates on the life before birth and after death, and thus brings man nearer to nature, in which it sees the means of emancipating him from his many restraints. Only Taoism is without preconception, and strives to see life as it is—not, like Confucianism, as it should be; nor, like Ch'an Buddhism, as it may be. Taoism imposes upon its believers the obligation to see life whole, and to understand the balance in the relations of living things with one another which constitutes the rhythm of life.

According to Lao Tzu, it is the Eternal Law which is responsible for the rhythm of life in nature. He said:

> He who knows the Eternal Law is tolerant;
> Being tolerant, he is impartial;
> Being impartial he is kingly;
> Being kingly, he is in accord with nature;
> Being in accord with nature, he is in accord with Tao;
> Being in accord with Tao, he is eternal,
> And his whole life is preserved from harm.*

He also said: "Tao models itself after nature." In other words, to identify oneself with Tao is to identify oneself with nature. Hence, to paint nature, as it is in essence and as a whole, not as it should be or could be, is to follow Tao, the Way. The Chinese love of nature thus differs from the Western love of nature in that its aim is identification with her, not imitation or "conquest" of her. And to identify oneself with nature is to find one's own place in the rhythm and thus preserve the integrity of one's being and the complete freedom of the soul.

But the human self is not a simple entity. Chuang Tzu, the great disciple of Lao Tzu, said:

> The crowd cares for gain,
> The honest man for fame,
> The good man values success,
> But the true man, his soul.†

Taoism teaches that a man has two selves: the Great Self or soul and the Small Self or body. When one is preoccupied with material things one is not "oneself," not free. A free soul is not constrained by logic or ethics or man-made laws. It lives in simplicity and harmony and sees life as a great whole. When this wholeness of outlook is attained, one is a true man with a free soul. Taoism is not escapism, as is so often suggested. It advises one to be a true man with a free soul in the interests of intense life. Tsung Ping said that he painted landscapes in order to *ch'ang sheng,* relax or free his soul. After him the belief arose that an artist could *incarnate* his Great Self in his work.

A legend of the death of the great painter Wu Tao-tzu illustrates this point. It is said that Wu painted a large landscape on a palace wall, and the Emperor, when he saw it, became lost in admiration.

---

* Translated by Lin Yutang.
† Translated by Arthur Waley.

Wu Tao-tzu then clapped his hands, a cave in the painting opened, and Wu stepped into it and was seen no more. The object of the story is to show that Wu had so freed his soul through his painting that the picture had *become* his Great Self, and it was therefore of no consequence that his body or Small Self should disappear.

Chuang Tzu wrote that he once dreamed he was a butterfly. Fluttering hither and thither, he was conscious only of his happiness as a butterfly and unaware that he was Chuang Tzu. When he awoke he found himself unsure whether he was a man dreaming he was a butterfly or a butterfly dreaming it was a man. This story embodies a guiding principle for the poets as well as the painters of China. When the soul is free it is possible to enjoy a butterfly's fluttering happiness exactly as the butterfly does. Leonardo da Vinci's affirmation that "art seeks to vie with nature" is incomprehensible to a Chinese artist.

Taoistic insight is the source of the intense delight which Chinese poets and artists take in the flight of one small bird, in a single flower blooming in the sun or waving in the wind, in a fish gliding through water, or an insect's acrobatic leap from blade to blade of grass. Nature is not "red in tooth and claw," though birth and death are inevitable and incomprehensible: creation and extinction take place rhythmically under the Eternal Law or Tao. By embracing Tao one can enjoy life as it is, without anxious seeking for the life before birth and after death.

Sympathetic insight is also practiced in dealing with inanimate objects—mountains, rocks, streams—for sticks and stones are felt to possess selves or souls. It is the soul which must emerge from the picture, and the technique which achieves this is permissible—the simpler the better, for the less obtrusive the medium the clearer the truth. This is why Chinese artists prefer monochrome to color, and slight color to rich color. They do not aim at naturalism. Su Tung-p'o painted the dark green leaves of the bamboo with red ink, and yet his work has a powerful feeling of bamboo life.

Taoism is also responsible for two marked and closely connected characteristics of Chinese landscape painting: asymmetry and the use of space. Only the important parts of a subject are included—often the top and not the foot of a mountain, one blossom-laden bough and not a whole neat bush—lest the less important parts obscure the really significant. The detailed composition and rich color of Li Ssu-shun gained many fewer admirers and imitators than the agility of Wu Tao-tzu or the brushwork of Wang Wei. The

Sung masters considered their greatest achievement to be their use of *space,* and space had become the most typical characteristic of Chinese landscape painting. A small mist-shrouded, snow-clad landscape sketched with a few strokes of the brush does not depict every material object in the scene, yet to the eye of the imagination everything necessary is there, vibrating with the rhythm of life. But man and man's works will be inconspicuous. If a whole city can be reduced to the proportions of a dot, how small must be a single man! In the Taoist view of life man has no superiority over nature's other creatures. In the depth and distance of Taoist thought man forgets himself; is freed of the follies of power and wealth, of pride and self-assertion. In the depth and distance of Chinese landscape painting the onlooker finds his soul relaxed and freed, not saved nor enlightened.

Appearances to the contrary, I think it is not an exaggeration to say that the temper of the Chinese race is more akin to Taoism than to Confucianism. But this was not realized until lyric poetry, drawing inspiration from Taoism, joined hands with the visual arts. In Mid-T'ang days thousands of lyric poems expressing delight in identification with nature were written by Li Po, Tu Fu, Po Chu-i, and many others. The Sung poets followed them. For this prolonged outburst of song, Taoism was almost exclusively responsible.

Then Confucianism underwent a modification in the direction of Taoism. This movement, which came to be known as Neo-Confucianism, was led by Chu Hsi (1130–1200 A.D.), a prominent official and voluminous writer. His best-known work is a metaphysical treatise on Yin-Yang, the dual principle of the universe first propounded by Taoism. His teachings for the young bear obvious signs of Taoism:

> Do not bother the gods with too many prayers.
> Do not make allowances for your own shortcomings.
> Do not seek to know what has not yet come to pass.*

His poems show great feeling for nature. His name, even during his lifetime, was a household word throughout literate China.

But Chu Hsi was not the first Confucian scholar to tread the path toward Taoism. The great philosopher Chou Tun-i (1017–73) and his two disciples, the brothers Cheng Hao (1032–85) and Cheng Yi (1033–1101), had made an intensive study of Yin-Yang

* Translated by H. A. Giles.

and written several important works on it, in Sung times. The painter-emperor Hui Tsung, also of Sung, revered Lao Tzu as his "first ancestor," because both bore the family name of Li. But for the releasing influence of Taoism many of the great Sung masters of landscape, most of whom held high government posts, would have been in real danger of succumbing to the thralldoms of power, wealth, pride, and self-assertion.

The achievement of the Sung period stands out in the history of Chinese pictorial art. After it, the flow continued unbroken for six centuries. Then the Small Self triumphed and the great days came to an end. Until the Great Self once more triumphs, Chinese pictorial art will remain chained by materialism. The philosophical basis of Chinese painting lies in Taoism, driven there by the rigidity of Confucianism and supported there by Ch'an Buddhism. The dominant motives in European art are love and life; the dominant motives in ancient American and other primitive art are fear and death; but Chinese art is concerned with neither love nor fear. It simply reveals the artist's true self.

IV

THE PHILOSOPHICAL ROOTS OF
WESTERN CULTURE

CHARLES M. BAKEWELL

IT is customary to speak of Greek philosophy as ancient philosophy. This is quite misleading. It is evidence of our inveterate
temporal provincialism. For there is a provincialism that comes
from isolation in time which can prove a more formidable obstacle
to understanding than that which comes from isolation in space.
Before the Greek came upon the scene, for hundreds of thousands
of years, men had been struggling up the long hard road that leads
from the brute and the savage to the civilized man. Civilizations had
arisen and perished long before the dawn of recorded history, leaving behind them monuments in stone that are eloquent testimony
to a skill in engineering that could only be matched in comparatively recent times and by the aid of machinery that harnesses the
forces of nature in the service of man. And how many civilizations
had preceded these and gone down in ruin without leaving a trace
behind?

The fact is that viewed in the true perspective of time Socrates
lived but yesterday. And who is there who can read Plato's *Dialogues* today without finding himself saying over and again, "How
like ourselves are these men he brings before us; how well he understood human nature; how clearly he saw, and how much he has
contributed to an understanding of the deepest and humanly most
interesting problems that still perplex us and still await a final solution." It would be far more accurate to regard the Greeks as having
written the first chapters in modern philosophy. Greek philosophy
is our own philosophy, and science, in its beginning.

Thales of Miletus started it. He appears to have been something
of a universal genius—engineer, courtier, politician, statesman, student of mathematics and astronomy. He predicted the eclipse
which occurred in 585 B.C., according to the calculations of our
astronomers, and put an end to the war between the Lydians and

the Medes. In all the lists of the fabled seven wise men of Greece his name leads all the rest. For us he is important because he is in very truth the father of science and philosophy when these terms are used in the stricter sense to denote a wholly and consciously reasoned view of the world, man included. He was the first to ask what are all things made of and then go to nature herself for the answer.

He and his followers wrote the first chapter. It is a philosophy of naturalism; nature is all there is, for man is a part of nature; if you can find what nature, this visible and tangible world about us, really and truly and changelessly is, you will at the same stroke have discovered what man is. It then only remains to explain *how* the variety and change of the world as it appears can be conceived as arising from the one changeless ground. For we must "save the appearances." Since these philosophers generally viewed this changeless ground as divine, it might be said that we have here also the beginning of natural theology.

The attitude of the Greek thinkers was, from first to last, singularly detached and objective. They attacked their problem in entire freedom from religious prepossessions, and there was no concern for mere utility. It was simply an eager desire to know, to understand the world in which we live, and to gain this understanding by observing, and reasoning from the facts observed. It is an interesting story, one that has no parallel in the history of any other people. We have not the time to follow it in detail, but a few general observations are in order.

The thinkers of this period, with one exception (Xenophanes), did not openly attack the religious beliefs and practices of the people. They simply ignored them and went their own way. But while they were free from religious prepossessions, there was one principle which they all took for granted, even before they had given it definite expression; namely, that out of nothing nothing comes, into nothing nothing that truly *is* can ever pass away. And they all sought to find behind the confusing variety of experience some unity, behind the changing appearances something that remained always the same. Being innately logical, it was not long before Parmenides of Elea, a Greek colony in southern Italy, drew the inevitable conclusion: the real is one and changeless. Therefore variety and change are illusory. He made clear and sharp the distinction between Being—one, definite and perfect, like a well-rounded sphere, at once the object and the source of the quest for truth—and the things that come and go, indefinite and imperfect, the world of appearances where men wander in doubt and perplexity and the opinions of men usurp the place of truth. But he found no way of bridging the gap between the changeless reality and the changing world of experience. At the opposite side of the Greek world, in Ephesus, in Asia Minor, Heraclitus grasped the other horn of the dilemma: all is change and nothing stays put. To be sure, Heraclitus did not entirely give up the idea of the permanent. He found it in the *logos,* the Word, the story that is being told, the wisdom that guides all things through all things, and that is the same for all men, though, he sorrowfully adds, "Most men live as if each had a private wisdom of his own." Here is a principle that might well have started philosophy off in a new direction, but it lay dormant until revived by Socrates and Plato. Heraclitus identified the Word with fire and fell back into the camp of the naturalists. For his followers, all things change; the very idea of sameness must be given up. Plato called them humorously the "flowing philosophers." From their philosophy comes the skepticism of the Sophist Protagoras with the doctrine that man is the measure of all things, as from the Eleatic philosophy, with equal inevitability, the skepticism of the Sophist Gorgias, who wrote on "Nature or the Non-Existent" in which he sought to show that the Being Parmenides talked about did not exist; if it did, it would be unknowable and incommunicable.

A way must be found to combine these polar opposites. This was done by assuming a plurality of elements, each indestructible, and interpreting the variety and change as due to the diverse combinations of the primal substances. And then it was not long before it was seen that each one of the many substances must have the characteristics of the Being of Parmenides, and that it was necessary to affirm the reality of empty space (of the void) for the many to move in; and this step the atomists took.

Leucippus, who started the atomic theory, said to have been a disciple of Parmenides, broke up the solid sphere of his master into an infinite number of minute particles, called atoms, so small as to be invisible, so solid as to be indivisible, differing only in size, shape, position, and arrangement, ceaselessly moving in the void. This atomic theory was further developed by Democritus. All things are made of atoms, including mind or soul. Mind is made of the smallest atoms so smooth and round and swift in their motion as to penetrate all other things. The action of atom upon atom is by impact, but the resulting combinations are not the result of chance but of necessity. And this is the first appearance of the conception of the universal reign of law in the physical world. Greek naturalism thus culminates in a complete and thoroughgoing materialism and mechanism. So thoroughly did these men do their work that their atomic theory, with but slight changes, held sway in the interpretation of the physical world almost throughout the Newtonian era.

Here ends the first chapter. Naturalism has in less than two hundred years run its course from its initial premises to its inevitable conclusion. But it is a conclusion which makes plain the necessity of a fresh start in philosophy. The unity of nature is lost in the infinite variety of the atoms and of their arrangements. Moreover, what about the objects of the senses, of sight, hearing, smell, taste, and feeling? "They are supposed to be real," says Democritus, "and it is customary to regard them as such, but in truth they are not. Only the atoms and the void are real." They are by *"convention,"* not by *"nature,"* by which statement he merely means that colors, sounds, etc., are not characteristics of the universal nature, that is, of the atoms. But if we throw out the objects of the senses as unreal, we throw out at the same time the whole world of our daily experience.

Moreover, it may well be asked if the mind is merely a congeries of the finer atoms, how does it know at all, how does it know that the atomic theory itself is true?

And how about conduct? Democritus has much to say on this subject. His ethics is a form of hedonism, not systematically developed but popularly expressed in maxims which are partly the deposit of the general experience of mankind and partly the result of his own reflections—maxims that give rules for the guidance of conduct which must be followed if one is to achieve a tranquil and happy life. But his ethics has no connection whatever with his atomic theory.

There is a strong undercurrent of skepticism in his writings. "Verily we know nothing," he says, "truth is buried deep." And again, "In truth we know nothing, but every man shares the prevailing opinion." The problem of knowledge becomes henceforth central in philosophy; how do we know anything for sure, either about nature or about right conduct? In seeking the answer to this question philosophy is led to a new conception of being—of what it means to be, or to be real. The story of naturalism ends. That of idealism begins.

The impulse to this new movement comes, however, not from

Democritus but from the thoroughgoing skepticism of his older fellow townsman, the Sophist Protagoras.

Before taking leave of the naturalist philosophers we must consider an aspect of their thinking which has indeed been hinted at above but which needs emphasis and further clarification because of the central part it played in the next phase in the development of philosophy, and that is the distinction of form from matter. This was implied in the work of the earliest of the naturalists when, in addition to discovering what they took to be the substance of things, they felt obliged to show *how* the things we experience might be conceived as arising—to discover "the go" of the process. But it was Pythagoras who first definitely made the distinction. He had discovered how to measure the intervals of the notes of the octave—that these could be represented by numerical ratios which always remained the same. He had also discovered strange things about numbers: add together in succession the numbers in the whole number series, and if you represent the units by points (or pebbles), you always get an equilateral triangle; add together in similar fashion the odd numbers and you always get a square; add the even and you always get an oblong figure. Put these shapes together to form a solid, and you get from the first series pyramids, from the second cubes, from the third no fixed pattern, for they are never the sides of a regular solid. Pythagoras also discovered the dodecahedron, each facet having the shape of the pentagram. This is the regular solid that most approximates a sphere. If made of material slightly elastic, you can stretch it into a ball. Here are all the elements necessary to build up a world out of figures. It is not unusual for one who makes a striking discovery to be carried away by it, and attempt to swing it full circle. Many examples might be adduced, drawn but from science and philosophy. So it is not surprising to find Pythagoras saying all things are made of numbers. But as he nevertheless seems to regard numbers (figures, shapes, forms) as a sort of stuff of which things are made, it is customary to include him with the naturalists.

And I think, though this is still matter of controversy, that Heraclitus with his logos doctrine was trying to separate reason, the form of reason, from the things of sense, though he never quite succeeded in doing so.

Finally, Anaxagoras tried hard to distinguish the animate from the inanimate, to separate mind from matter and give it the rulership over all things. However, he not only fails to make use of this principle, to show how it works, but also finds it necessary to make mind, since it is real or has being, itself a body, though it be, as he says, the finest of all things and the thinnest of all things.

These philosophers prepare the way, and at the same time point the direction which the next movement in philosophy must inevitably take.

And now, for the sake of brevity, I shall get ahead of my own story. The Pythagorean school continued to flourish throughout the fifth century B.C. and well into the fourth, devoting itself chiefly to the study of astronomy and mathematics, and this work was taken up and carried forward by Plato in the Academy. Many discoveries were made in astronomy which were lost to subsequent ages (partly through the reactionary views of Aristotle in this field), but these were finally revived by Copernicus. The work in mathematics was so completely carried out that Euclid, in the third century B.C., could write a treatise on the subject which provided the basis of the textbook still in use in our universities at the time I entered college. Mathematics was the one perfect gift of the Greeks to science. Now Plato was much impressed by the fact that the entities that mathematics deals with are intangible, invisible, and perfect, and yet real, more real than their sensible images which we encounter in experiences. They are stubborn too. You can get around a physical object but you cannot take liberties with numbers. The side and the diagonal of a square are incommensurable and resist your every effort to find a common measure. And you actually grasp certainty in your mathematical conclusions.

What if the whole world were governed by number and measure and mathematical patterns! Might we not then find in the "mathematicals" the unity and permanence which reason requires in order to make nature intelligible, and still "save the appearances"? This is not the whole of Plato's theory of ideas but an essential part of it. One cannot understand that theory unless one bears in mind the fact that Plato was a great mathematician.

But it is time to take up again the thread of our story.

The second chapter in our philosophy was begun by Socrates and finished by Aristotle—with an appendix added by the Stoics.

It would be hard to exaggerate the influence that Socrates exerted upon his contemporaries and, through them, upon the whole course of Western philosophy. That he was a favorite with the youth of Athens and that he liked nothing better than to be with them and draw them into an argument is well known. With his customary irony he at once put them at their ease. They met on the level and were soon engaged in the joint pursuit of truth. It was a great game, this game of question and answer. Ah, but it was far more than that. Socrates had led them to the discovery of themselves. It was their own selves, their own souls, they were exploring in the attempt to discover how to make the most of their own lives. Yes, he talked strangely about the self, the soul. They had never heard anything like this before. They did not know that there was such a thing. What they had heard called by that name was no concern of the living. It was a shadow or image that floated away from the body at death to join the gibbering shades of Homer's Hades or wander about aimlessly on the dreary asphodel moors, a witless, hapless, senseless, unreal thing. Or perhaps they had heard the more modern view that the soul was just the breath which at death left to join the upper air while the body returned to earth. They might have heard of the Orphic mysteries and the religious revival of the sixth century b.c., whose influence can be traced in many subsequent thinkers, including Socrates and Plato. These centered in the story of the battle of the Titans and Dionysus Zagreus and in the consequences of that struggle. It is one of the most savage of the Greek myths. But its details do not concern us here. Enough to say that this story, presented and visualized in a drama, was intended to emphasize and drive home the belief that there is a fragment of the divine imprisoned in the body, and this the Orphics called the soul. But they did not identify the soul with the normal conscious life. Its true nature was revealed in ecstasy, a foretaste of the final ecstatic union with the divine when the soul would be free from the body prison and from the cycle of births. Now the Eleusinian mysteries were relatively sober and dignified, restrained and moderate. It was a religion of good form. To be initiated was itself enough to secure a passport to at least a somewhat better life after death. Not so the Orphic. That was a violent religion, to borrow a term sometimes used in America to describe certain Christian sects. Initiation was only the beginning of a long struggle for purification and release from the body prison.

Now what goes over into subsequent thought is this conception of life as a struggle between soul and body, and of the need of salvation through purification, and of release not from the body, as with the Orphics, but from the *chains* of the body. For undoubtedly the body does get in our way in our pursuit of truth and beauty and goodness. But whereas the Orphic votary sought release in sacrifice and in mystic rites, Pythagoras sought it in mathematics and in the realization of harmony between the elements of which the body is composed; Socrates and Plato in the study of philosophy. Socrates had been early interested in the speculations of the nature philosophers, but was greatly dissatisfied with them and could find no way of reaching certainty there. So he turned from the world without to the world within and made the "examined life" the life most worthy of man, and in doing so introduced a new concept of the soul and with it a new conception of philosophy, and religion too.

The soul he identified with the normal waking conscious life of man. It is the soul that feels and thinks and that seeks after and can achieve wisdom and righteousness. Now Socrates was that rare combination of religious enthusiast and clear sober thinker. So if he could even dimly descry the chief end of man he would seek to reach it with single-minded devotion; and if he only knew the path that led in that direction he would take it as surely as would the man who desired to go to Thebes, and knew his geography, take the road to Thebes and not the road to Corinth. This is what he means when he identifies virtue with knowledge.

Socrates made a genuine discovery.[1] It was the discovery of the individual, the self, of the ego or person, as we might say. His name for it was soul. And this soul is real on its own account; it has its own *nature,* and it is the first business of philosophy to find out what that nature is. It is the same question the early philosophers asked about body that he asks about soul. What is the common or universal in the soul, what is it that gives unity and steadfastness to the soul? So Socrates' answer to the Sophist Protagoras, who said man is the measure of all things and seemed thus to bar the way to truth, is that it is precisely that doctrine which opens the door to truth. If I did not measure for myself I could never tell whether or not I was being deceived. But it is this universal in man, which is common to all, which is the real measure of truth.

But philosophy as thus viewed is nonetheless an individual adventure. Socrates can do nothing except with the fertile mind. The barren he can only send to Prodicus or some other Sophist to be pumped full of sham wisdom. With the fertile he can bring to birth an idea, and then scrutinize it to see, as he humorously says, whether it is a genuine birth or only a wind egg. Socrates did not lay down the law, or hand out a set of ready-made copybook maxims to those whom he wanted to help; he did not tell them, he asked them—and that was something novel too.

We must return to the Athenian youth. Too long have we kept them waiting in the gymnasium. We can now better appreciate the tremendous effect Socrates had upon them, why they were so fond of him, why, when he would "follow an argument all over Attica," they were eager to join in the chase. We can understand why they were so thrilled by his conversations, even by scraps repeated at second hand. They hung upon his words, and their souls were stirred within them as by no other speaker. It is Alcibiades who thus describes the effect he produced, and adds that more than once he was moved to tears, as were others also, and that he was angry at the thought of his own slavish life. Socrates had made him ashamed, and he was the only person who had ever done that. When the love of popularity got the better of him, Alcibiades would stop his ears and fly from him, but was ever drawn back by the irresistible charm of his words.

But the elders were equally and more profoundly impressed by Socrates. Men came from far and near just to be with him. Plato has given us a partial list of those who, during the month that elapsed between Socrates' condemnation and execution, came daily to the prison to pass the time with him in philosophical discussion, and who on the last day came earlier than usual in order that they might be admitted the moment the door was opened and not lose a word that fell from his lips. Included in this Socratic circle were the foremost philosophers of the time, and they all looked up to Socrates as their master. A number of them later founded schools of their own. One, Aristippus, seizing upon the cheerful side of Socrates' disposition, his serene happiness and contentment under all conditions, and exaggerating this, founded the school at Cyrene which developed into the school of Epicurus. But there was another and sterner side to Socrates, shown in his exceptional powers of endurance, whether of cold or hunger, in his independence of things, in his complete self-mastery, his life being always steadied and ordered by reason, and in the extreme simplicity of his mode of life. ("No one," says Xenophon, "could earn so little as not to have enough to satisfy the wants of a Socrates.") Seizing upon this side of his character, and exaggerating it, Antisthenes founded the Cynic school, which developed in a straight line to the Stoics. And there was Euclid, head of the Eleatic school at Megara, who was especially interested in the logical aspect of the Socratic method. His devotion to Socrates is illustrated by the story of how, when there was a feud between Athens and Megara, and the gates of each city were closed to the citizens of the other, he used to smuggle himself into Athens in disguise so as to be with Socrates. And he is represented by Plato as having been present at the discussion of the meaning of truth which is described in the *Theaetetus,* and as having written it down from memory after his return to Megara, then bringing his manuscript back to Socrates for correction. It is a long dialogue and the argument is intricate.—The Greeks had great memories.—Perhaps this story is not a fiction of Plato's but a record of what actually happened. If so, it is not impossible that Plato may have seen Euclid's copy when he went to Megara to sojourn with him after the death of Socrates and been allowed to use it in constructing his own dialogue. Who knows?

Other members of this group founded other but less important schools. And then there was Plato himself, not present at the last scene, having been "detained by illness." Socrates' most understanding and devoted disciple, who gathered together all the threads of his master's thinking, following them through to their logical conclusions—some of which Socrates himself would scarcely have recognized—and weaving them into the pattern of the most magnificent philosophic vision ever created by man.

In later times, for the Stoics, he was, barring Zeno, the one instance of the complete realization of their ideal of the wise man. "When in doubt what to do, ask yourself what would Socrates have done, for though you are not yet a Socrates you ought to live as one seeking to be a Socrates." For an Alexandrine Christian he was a Christian before Christ, because he lived in company with the logos; while the pagan Emperor Julian declares: "It is thanks to Socrates that all who find salvation in philosophy are being saved even now." [2]

That the philosophers were captivated by Socrates should occasion no surprise. He *had* introduced a new subject of inquiry—man, human nature—and, in doing so, he became the father of philosophy viewed as a discipline other than, and, in a manner, independent of, knowledge of the physical world, and at the same time he became the father of metaphysics. He *did* introduce a new method of attaining truth, and was exceedingly skillful in its use. His conclusions are generally not final, but just the starting points for further inquiry. And so, although he had no finished system of philosophy, he had an extraordinary genius for awakening the minds of men and stimulating them to creative activity.

He wrote nothing. Xenophon wrote a great deal about him, and no doubt honestly portrays him as he appeared to him. But Xenophon's was a commonplace mind and he was quite innocent of philosophy. The man he describes is a good man, a very good man, and a good moral influence. This is not enough. Such a man could never enthrall the youth, fascinate the philosophers, and arouse the anger of conservatives, politicians, and the unthinking mob to such an extent that they put him to death. We must turn to Plato. We run right into a controversy, started by Schleiermacher, and still continuing. Is the Platonic Socrates the historic Socrates, or is it Plato himself speaking through the mouth of Socrates? Futile, I think, is most of this discussion. Bear this fact in mind: Plato was not only a great philosopher, he was also a consummate artist and a man of letters, the first man of letters who wrote for the sheer love of writing. He describes scenes and discussions, the most absorbing experiences of his life. Now a modern essayist discussing a current problem would probably bring up the various points of view, critically analyze them, sifting, discarding, and combining them into a finished paper. Plato brings before you real men who hold the different views, each having a distinct personality, and you observe the drama of embattled minds. And each of the dramas might be described, to borrow and adapt a phrase of G. B. Shaw, as a leaf from the life of reason. Now Socrates, whom Plato seems to have regarded as philosophy itself walking about the streets of Athens, is the hero of them all. Was it not inevitable that as time went on Plato would put more and more of himself into the character of his hero, and quite legitimately, so long as he was developing and applying, perhaps in novel ways, the teaching of his master? Socrates would grow into Plato by imperceptible degrees, so that it might be difficult even for Plato himself to tell just where to draw the line between his own philosophy and that of Socrates. Where he was not presenting views that could be regarded as logically developed from his master's teaching, he would no longer give Socrates the title role. We should speak of the Socratic-Platonic philosophy as if it were all of a piece, one philosophy developing through two successive lives, and growing and expanding all the while.

I hold that our point of departure for the understanding of Socrates should be with the *Apology,* which we must take as the record of what he actually said. I doubt if even Plato's genius could have invented the speech reported in the *Apology.* Plato must have swelled with pride as he listened to that noble and triumphant defense—triumphant, for though his enemies had a temporary victory, Socrates won for the ages. And piety to his master's memory must have made Plato want to preserve Socrates' very words—that is the way his disciples felt about him—and Plato, we may be sure, had a good memory. The *Apology* is a defense of freedom of thought and of speech which justifies the encomium of Gomperz, that it is the lay breviary of all free souls. It is a defense of Socrates' way of life, and at the same time a defense of philosophy itself from the charges brought against it in all ages, that it creates doubt which undermines authority, civil, religious, or both. What Socrates says in the *Apology* is, on all points there raised, final. If they are not his very words, they have in any case the full authority of Plato.

The problem, you see, is to find in this new subject of inquiry— the soul or self—something that will give the unity and permanence which it must have if it is to be real, something that will be universal and common to all souls. This, as we have seen, is taken for granted in all thinking. It is an instinctive belief to which we are committed by the very structure of the language we use, and in the categories of speech—substance, quantity, quality, and so forth. We speak in terms of subject and predicate, substance and attribute, the thing and its qualities, and so on. Now Socrates thinks we can find this "nature" of the soul if we use the new method of inquiry which he has discovered, and this, be it noted, is a strictly scientific method. I say "new" though it may be regarded as a generalization of the dialectic method of Zeno. Perhaps the brilliant success of mathematical science suggested it. *That* science gives certainty, and it deals with reals that are intangible, ideal—the perfect forms or patterns, the perfect square, circle, etc. It reaches certainty by starting with the common or universal, the generally accepted hypotheses, or axioms, and the proof is deduced from these. In ethics, however, we have no such axioms to begin with, so we must start with the particular and discover the universals. "Inductive reasoning and universal definition" is the way Aristotle describes the contribution of Socrates, and he adds that these are the foundation of all knowledge.

In the "examined life" we are seeking to find the perfect form or pattern of the life that is supremely worth while. Socrates' attitude is still objective; virtue is just human worth or excellence. As the virtue of a pruning hook is to do its job well, so the virtue of man is to do well the job of being a man. We start with experience. There are certain kinds of human excellence that have come to be generally recognized—wisdom, courage, etc. We begin by examining one of these virtues, going to someone who would, by common consent, be regarded as its very embodiment, as for example, Charmides of temperance, and explore with him the meaning of the virtue he represents. Usually the first answer is to name some particular kind of action or behavior. Thereupon the Socratic method takes hold. Is not the opposite kind of action sometimes required by the very virtue under discussion? What then is the general idea which guides us in determining, in a given situation, which kind of action is called for? So we seek a more inclusive definition and examine it in the same way and with similar result, and so on and on, making progress toward that totalizing idea or universal which will be all-inclusive. In the case of each virtue we are led finally to the conclusion that the general idea that governs action is the conception of what is good for the soul as a whole. But this conclusion only starts a fresh inquiry. How are we to interpret it concretely? To make a long story short, Socrates—or is it Plato?—finds that there are three distinct activities of the soul: wisdom, the spirited element, which we might call effective will, and the appetitive; and that virtue or human excellence consists in the perfect functioning of all, but in such wise that no one preys upon another. It is the completely integrated life. Reason is here the judge and it in turn is guided by the inherent attractiveness of the ideals of perfection—the unconditioned, that is, complete knowledge, the essential form of the good, and beauty absolute. "The fiend that us harries is love of the best" (Emerson). Herein is the paradox; these ideals are infinitely far away. I can at best find them feebly adumbrated in the finite experience. True, but that finite experience gets its unique value in reference to these standards of perfection. These directive ideals are not merely possibilities but are now actually realized. In short, there is a God. And the individual person is or may be even now in touch with the Being in whom these ideals are realized. Now man, whatever he makes his chief good, is always asking for more. If his chief desire is centered in things, in power, and in the means of attaining them, the result is endless strife and dissension within and without, for there is a limited quantity of these things. But not so with the higher ideals which we have been considering. *All* can share to the fullest extent in all of them. For these values can be multiplied indefinitely without being divided once.

So the struggle for virtue is a struggle to escape from the "chains" of the body and to rise from the natural to the spiritual. As Socrates says in the *Apology,* "I spend all my time going about among you persuading you, old and young alike, not to be so solicitous about your bodies or your possessions, but first of all and most earnestly, to consider how to make your souls as perfect as possible; and telling you that wealth does not bring virtue but that rather virtue brings wealth and every other human good, private or public." The good life is simply the reasoned life, the integrated life, the life organized by reason in the light of the ideals of perfection. And this is the meaning of virtue and therefore at the same time the revelation of the true nature of man.

This view which thus exalts man, which makes him a being of infinite worth, at the same time brings with it a sense of deep humility with the realization of the short distance that one has traveled in the direction of the ideal which is at once his end and goal. This is the meaning of Socrates' saying that if the oracle at Delphi declared him to be the wisest of men it was only because he knew that in truth he knew nothing. He knew that all his knowledge was as nothing in comparison with the complete wisdom that was the goal of his aspiration.

We find in this philosophy not only the essential pattern of the good life for man but also the pattern for the social order, or the State. *Its* value also must be measured by the same ideals; and its purpose must be to secure an order in which every citizen shall be able to make the most of himself that he is capable of making, always with an eye to the welfare of the whole.

What we have been saying applies, I think, equally to Plato and to Socrates. But while Socrates confined himself to ethical problems and did not give his universals, or ideas, independent or separate existence, Plato parted company with him in both of these respects, and extended the doctrine of forms or ideas to the interpretation of nature. The same method is here employed, finding ever the larger or more comprehensive idea within which the less comprehensive gets defined—in other words, discovering the pattern or the idea which fixes meanings in the flux of things. Experience is, for him also, the starting point. One whose intellect is at the lowest level of activity sees merely the surface of things, sees them as passing shadows, and, as Plato says, gives the prize to the "best guesser of the shadow that is coming next." A higher stage, but still in the realm of opinion, is attained when man sees things as definite objects in definite relations empirically discovered. He only obtains a true knowledge of nature, however, when he can interpret it in the light of mathematical relations. But there is a higher knowledge still, one which aims at nothing less than vision in the light of the whole. That Plato regarded this last as the highest form of knowledge does not mean that he discredited the other type or that he looked down upon, as unworthy of man, the observation and classification and description of facts.

It is sometimes said that Plato condemned the observational or empirical study of facts and thus definitely blocked the path of science. Only one who is ignorant of what Plato actually said and did, or ignorant of the history of science, could make such an assertion. Precisely the opposite is the case. Professor G. C. Field has recently,[3] and as I think conclusively, shown that Plato did encourage exact observation of phenomena, and regarded this as part of the necessary training for the philosopher; that astronomy was one of the chief subjects of study in the Academy and other empirical studies were not neglected; that the most flourishing period of science in the ancient world was the century and a half following Plato's death. Some of the men who carried on this work were trained in the Academy. Others were Plato's enthusiastic admirers and received their inspiration from him. When we come to modern times Kepler and Galileo, the founders of modern physics and mechanics, regarded themselves as followers of Plato's philosophy rather than Aristotle's, which was then in vogue, and all because Plato had found the key to the understanding of the physical world in number and in measure. That the Greeks did not make greater progress than they did in the use of this discovery is explained in part by the fact that they could only see in nature what the naked eye could discern. They had no telescopes, no microscopes, no cameras to extend their vision, and they had no instruments of precision such as modern science possesses. Most important of all, they had not learned how to question nature rightly and, by carefully devised experiments, force nature to say definitely of their hypotheses "right" or "wrong." It remained for Galileo to start science squarely on that pathway which made possible the discovery of the specific laws of nature, and enabled man through obedience to these laws to conquer nature and make her serve his ends. The rapid progress of science once started on this path, which has been going forward at an ever accelerating rate, especially in the last fifty years, and the stupendous discoveries which have completely transformed man's environment and increased his power, make the scientific achievements of the Greeks seem meager indeed. If it is otherwise with philosophy it is because human nature has changed but little and because for keenness in observation of human nature these Greek idealists have had few equals. But it is especially because they *had* learned how to "question a *man* rightly." The fact that thinkers of all ages have kept returning to this philosophy for light, from Philo in the century before Christ down to Whitehead, Eddington, and many others in our own day, is an impressive tribute to the Greeks.

Aristotle who in all his major works borrows heavily from Plato, though generally without acknowledgment of his indebtedness, gave a dynamic interpretation to Platonic idealism and definitely introduced the time factor as necessary to give meaning to the universal or the idea. Wherever we step into the stream of events we find matter taking on form only to become in turn the matter for further form. Dynamically interpreted this means that we find potentiality becoming actualized only to become in turn the possibility of further actualization. This change makes it possible to put meaning into the conception of the individual, the living individual, as the unity of a single life process which is self-determined, and thus genuinely to unite the polar opposites which had troubled the Greeks, the one and the many, the permanent and the changing. Aristotle uses the word "entelechy" for the individual so conceived. It is a process whose meaning is not given either in its beginning or end or in the summation of its episodes, but one in which, we might say, every part is in functional relation to every other and also to the unity of the whole, as is the whole to every part. And it is in this unity or wholeness that we discover the essence of the individual and the source of its activity.

Aristotle also attacks the problem of the relation of body and soul. It is absurd, he thinks, to speak as if the soul could enter into and depart from the body in the same casual way in which a person might step into and out of a boat. The relation is far more intimate than that. The individual is matter ensouled or soul embodied. The soul is then viewed as the essential form of the body, and the body as the manifestation in nature of the kind of a soul the individual is. But in the case of man the soul is much more than this. For in knowing, willing, in constructive imagination, and in creative art, creative reason is the active principle. *This* reason is "separate from and uncompounded with material conditions" and is therefore separable from the body. It is reason thus conceived that Aristotle regards as either divine or that in man which comes nearest to the divine. It is the essential form of man, and inasmuch as Aristotle views the higher form always as giving the true meaning and significance to the lower, it is here that we find the explanation of all the lower forms. In this conception also he finds the measure of human excellence. We ought, he tells us, not to listen to those who advise us as men and mortals not to lift our thoughts above what is human and mortal, but ought rather as far as possible to put off our mortality and make every effort to live in the exercise of the highest of our faculties which in power and value far surpasses all the rest.

Like Plato and Socrates before him, Aristotle's philosophy leads him inevitably to the conception of God. Aristotle struggles hard to put positive meaning into the idea of God and in doing so follows the only path possible. Man has always made his gods in his own image, and the higher religions have been such because they have taken what is highest and most valuable in human experience to give them their inkling of the divine nature. As Aristotle says, "What life is for us in our brief best moments, that God's life is always." And since for Aristotle the highest for man is found in pure contemplation of truth, God's activity is conceived as that of pure theoretic vision. This is what makes his concept seem to us so empty of meaning. His God is all alone; he has no friends; he does not know the meaning of the word "alas!"

If, however, we wish to reach a more satisfactory concept of the divine being, this can only be done by showing that the highest for man is not found in the mere contemplation of truth. There is a still higher that finds expression in love and loyalty, in courage and justice, and in the vision of beauty as well as of truth. If in ascribing such activities to a supreme being one finds oneself involved in further difficulties, one simply evades the issue by finding the divine ideal embodied in the human, in a Buddha or a Christ.

In Aristotle the idealistic movement initiated by Socrates finds its final expression. He is an idealist because for him the lower is always explained in the higher, because what comes last in time is first in reality, because in the final analysis mind is the ground of reality as well as of truth; or, in a word, because he "begins with Zeus and not with chaos." He is indeed more of an idealist than Plato, just because he finds his ideal in the actual, and, we may add, because he has combined his idealism with common-sense realism.

For all three of these thinkers philosophy is a way of life, one that is suggested and justified by the theory of the true nature of the self or soul which Socrates had made an independent object of inquiry, and by the theory of the physical order to which they had been led, starting with self-knowledge. All of them make education central just because they conceive it as liberal, that is, as setting men free. For Aristotle, the highest life (the diagogic life) is that which finds pure joy in those things which are "fair and sweet" on their own account, and these are to be found in the fields of all the muses, in music, poetry—in all creative arts—and in history, science, and philosophy, the intangible values that mark the civilized life, the cultured life.

Now for Plato also philosophy is a way of life that finds human excellence in the pursuit and enjoyment of the intangible, the spiritual values. But there is a religious fervor in his writings which is lacking in Aristotle. When those who are being trained to rulership have completed the arduous course he prescribes, with frequent tests both of intellectual ability and strength of character, the few who survive the ordeal may, by the time they reach their thirty-fifth year, catch a glimpse of the vision of the essential form of the good, that is, of God, and be qualified to begin their *apprenticeship* as rulers. The essential form of the good, or God, is beyond knowledge, for He is the source at once of intelligibility in the object and intelligence in the knower. One can only know Him through His image in the visible world, and then darkly. As, when the sun rises in the visible world, all things are clear and distinct and in definite relations to one another, so the essential form of the good brings order and definiteness into the eternal realm of the ideas, and the eye of the soul can behold in the eternal light that lightens all things the pattern according to which men are to order their own lives and also establish order in the state. They are not to rest in enjoyment of the vision: first, because education is a life-long enterprise—that is the beauty of it!—and second, because the duty is laid upon them to descend from time to time to the cave to aid those imprisoned there and help set them free. Now this education is for a small group of chosen men, sound in body and mind, selected for their steadfastness in holding to the principle of justice, to the identity of their own interests and the interests of the community, and for their mental alertness. Plato has given us a description in the sixth book of the *Republic* of the ideal or true philosopher who can vanquish all the tests with approval. He must be a man of quick mind and retentive memory, devoted to truth and abhorring falsehood in every shape, temperate and thoroughly uncovetous, with no taint of meanness or little-mindedness or cowardice, gentle and just in his dealings with men; one whose spirit is full of lofty thoughts and privileged to contemplate all time and all existence, and who is, therefore, fearless in the face of death; one who is enamored of all learning that will reveal somewhat of that real and permanent existence which is exempt from the vicissitudes of degeneration and decay, and of the whole of that real existence, willingly resigning no part of it, great or small, honored or dishonored.—A counsel of perfection, like the state itself over which these philosopher kings are to rule. And, as they said in the Eleusinian mysteries, "Many are the thyrsus bearers, few the inspired."

There is, however, another plan of education described in the *Laws* which is for all citizens, and Plato would have it made compulsory.

Let us look a little more closely at this educational enterprise. The first step is, as Socrates saw, to purge the soul of ignorance, and especially of that most blinding form of ignorance—conceit of knowledge where no true knowledge exists—and thus bring about the conviction of ignorance which, like the conviction of sin in later times, is the necessary preparation for the higher life. The mind can then be trusted to bear the fruits of wisdom.

Now the goal of perfection that we seek is a flying goal; the further you go toward its realization the more do new avenues of inquiry open up offering fresh opportunities for abundant living. If you can only assure yourself that you can set aside once and for all the less complete for the more complete knowledge, you are on the path. And this is life—to keep going ahead. You must keep going forward or you will slip backward. There is no standing still. Things of beauty, to be sure, give the momentary resting places on the journey toward Truth and Goodness. They are examples of perfection found: this poem, that line, this painting. Momentary, we have said, lasting just long enough to enable one to catch one's second wind for the climb ahead; and there is a ladder of beauty as well as of dialectic. When one stops going forward one's race is run. One may linger on for a while, but it is not life but dying long drawn out. Education—going forward—is the breath of life for the soul. All education is liberal education. Professional training is like learning a trade—carpentry, shoemaking, etc.—it is a means to earning a livelihood, it is not education in the proper sense of the word. For education, rightly understood, has no end beyond itself; it simply is *living,* living the life ever more and more ordered by reason as one makes progress in knowledge. It begins with the kinder-garten, is continued in the secondary school, for Plato invented both of these institutions, and he has much to say about curriculum and methods, from which our own educators might profit.

When the religions of the East found their way to Alexandria, that melting pot of ideas, and sought to make their beliefs under-stood of all men, they naturally turned to Greece, for it was there that the very tools of reason had been forged; and, for the Christians, the task of interpreting was greatly simplified by the fact that they had found so much that was congenial to their own way of thinking in the systems the Greeks had fashioned with those tools. When St. Paul, educated in a Greek school at Tarsus, speaking Greek and familiar with Greek thought, the friend of Seneca the Stoic, went to Athens as apostle to the Gentiles and preached that famous ser-mon on Mars Hill, he took his text from the hymn of Cleanthes the Stoic: "For we are also His offspring," tying in his own message with what the Greeks had themselves discovered. (If all mission-aries would take St. Paul for their model how much more effective their work would be.) And many are the sayings of St. Paul that might be matched with passages from Plato. The first chapter of the Fourth Gospel might have been lifted bodily from Plato and the Stoics—the logos or Word that "was in the beginning," "was with God and was God," "All things were created by Him." He was "the Light that lighteth every man that cometh into the world." Yes, all of it, except for one little addition—seemingly little, but of infinite significance: "The Word was made flesh and dwelt among us." An addition which leads straight to the doctrine, or better, the mystery, of the Trinity, an emphatic affirmation that even in the Godhead there is a many in one, a one in many, and that through the Holy Spirit there is room for man, for the "Communion of Saints." For the Greek conception of God, because of its exclusive insistence upon the unity and changelessness of ultimate being, tended, in spite of the efforts of Plato and Aristotle, toward a pan-theism, which came to clear expression in the Stoics and in the Neoplatonists.

The *Timaeus* of Plato, his "hymn of creation," as it has been called, was known throughout the Christian era; and at sundry times this Greek philosophy has entered directly into the course of Western civilization—Aristotle with St. Thomas and Dante, Plato at the time of the Renaissance. In the Renaissance it was chiefly the esthetic side, with a return to nature, and to Plato's fine appreciation of the love of the beautiful as a power that draws men onward and upward to the higher vision. Michelangelo came under the spell. This shows not only in his sonnets but even more, I think, in his painting and sculpture. That wonderful painting on the ceiling of the Sistine Chapel is thoroughly Greek in its purity, its strength, its simplicity, its perfectness. It is as if Michelangelo had painted it under the inspiration of Plato's vision of "Creation and birth in beauty absolute." Much that is greatest in art and literature, from that day to this, may be traced to the influence of Plato. We have already spoken of the part he played both in the origin of modern science and in its latest developments. Whenever direct contact has been re-established with Greek thinking there has been a fresh awakening of creative activity. The great vision of their philosophers has a value independent of time, place, and circumstance. It is part of our eternal inheritance. We shall always be returning to it for light and inspiration.

"You Greeks are ever young."

NOTES

1. Professor Burnet, in a paper on the "Socratic Doctrine of the Soul" (first published in *The Proceedings of the British Academy,* Vol. VII, 1915–16), has traced the history of the concept in Greek thought, and after examining every instance of the word ψυχή in the extant Athenian literature of the fifth century, has shown that Socrates was the first to identify the soul or self with normal consciousness, to regard it as real, as that in us—by whatever name called—which strives after wisdom and goodness, and that it needs and deserves constant care and nurture. It is because of this original contribution that he is properly regarded as the founder of philosophy.
2. I have borrowed from Professor Burnet (*op. cit.*) this quotation from Emperor Julian.
3. Philosophy: *The Journal of the Royal Institute of Philosophy,* 1947.

V

THE PYTHAGOREAN AND PLATONIC SCIENTIFIC CRITERION OF THE BEAUTIFUL IN CLASSICAL WESTERN ART

MATILA GHYKA

THE title of this essay might easily be expanded to "The Influence of Pythagorean and Platonic Scientific Conceptions on the Development of Western Art and Thought"; but I shall try to confine myself as much as possible to the realm of esthetics, and especially to the study of the transmission and evolution of certain esthetic theories and techniques. We shall have to examine on our way certain questions bearing as much on philosophy proper as on the history of art and even on archaeology.

The Western cycle of art considered here embraces, besides European art proper, Egyptian art, which had such influence on the beginnings of Greek art, and also the offshoots of European art in post-Columbian America and the white Dominions of the British Empire.

All this forms a cycle distinct from what may be called Asiatic art, with its four main foci—Persia, India, China, Japan—and also distinct from American pre-Columbian art. The latter is linked to Chinese and Scytho-Siberian art in what Fenollosa and O. Sirén call the Pacific cycle. These two great domains, Western art and Asiatic art, have not been without influence on each other, to their mutual profit. Asiatic art through Persia and Byzantium has enriched Romanesque and Gothic decorative art and imagery. We have Dieulafoy's original theory, based on impressive arguments, according to which the Gothic pointed arch is of Persian and Arab origin, with a trajectory passing through Cairo and Spain; and we need only mention the Crusades, the eighteenth-century invasion of *Chinoiseries,* and the latest wave of Far Eastern influence due to contact with the higher levels of Chinese and Japanese art. In the same way, through the Hellenistic movement which, after Alexander's death, spread throughout Asia Minor and gave rise between

Transcaucasia and India to the Greco-Buddhist Gandhara cycle, a strong Western influence introduced the Greek sense of proportion into Hindu statuary and painting, was reflected in the Ajanta frescoes, and through the flowering of art under the Tang dynasty in China reached as far as Japan, in the great Nara period. Statues like the magnificent Prajnaparamita, the Goddess of Infinite Wisdom, from Borobbodur (Java), now in the Leyden Museum, bear witness to this temporary meeting of Western and Eastern ideals of beauty.

But what I intend to examine here, without attaching to them any label of superiority, are the characteristics which specifically distinguish Western art as defined above from all the other cycles; then I shall show the origin and the permanence of these characteristics through more than twenty centuries, and their correlation to a more general logical, or rather analogical, principle derived from the same origin.

These specific Western concepts and the corresponding methods of composition are, as I hope to show, entirely based on certain viewpoints and formulae of Plato, borrowed in their turn from the dominating ideas of Pythagorean philosophy and esthetics, those two disciplines being here closely welded, almost fused into the concept of cosmic harmony regulated by number. The key or foundation stone of this point of view is the Pythagorean statement that "Everything is arranged according to number," a formula which we find already in the *Hieros Logos* or Sacred Speech of Pythagoras, as written shortly after his death by his disciples, probably even by one of his sons.

Let us point out that in Greek the words and ideas of number and rhythm were more or less equivalent, *rhythmos* and *arithmos* having the same root, from *rhein,* to flow. This equivalence was still accepted in Elizabethan England. In the biography of Pythagoras composed by Heraclidus of Pont, as recorded in a fragment quoted by Clement of Alexandria, we read that the Master found the supreme happiness, literally "the eudaïmonia of the Soul," in the contemplation of "the perfectly ordered purpose" of the "numbers" of the universe. Plato, in the *Timaeus,* composed a musical superscale of 35 notes which he called the "Number of the World Soul." This scale was produced by inserting arithmetical and harmonic means between the elements of two geometrical progressions joined into one complex progression, 1, 2, 3, 4, 9, 8, 27. And according to him, the numbers or rhythms of the well-balanced human soul reflect by consonance the harmony of the universe. The term "cosmos" was invented by Pythagoras himself, like the word "philosophy," and even then meant a well-ordered universe.

Plato underlined the importance of number in two short sentences of his *Epinomis:* "Number is the highest degree of knowledge" and "Number is Knowledge itself." But he did not confine himself to these generalities. He examined, explored, and worked out the concrete idea which was to become the main tool of Western artistic composition, that is, the concept of proportion. He developed it especially in the *Timaeus,* and his point of view guided not only the Neo-Pythagoreans (he himself received the notion of proportion from the Pythagoreans of Magna Graecia, especially from his friend Archytas of Tarentum) but also Euclid and Vitruvius, and later, as we shall see, the Gothic master builders and the humanists and architects of the first Renaissance, in the forefront of whom were Luca Pacioli, Alberti, and Leonardo. Pacioli was the author of the beautiful treatise *Divina Proportione,* illustrated by his friend Leonardo (Venice, 1509). Like him, Piero della Francesca studied the five Platonic bodies (the regular polyhedra) and the proportions linking them together, and Dürer afterward published his work on proportions under the influence of Pacioli, whom he appears to have visited in Bologna. But this is anticipating.

Plato's introduction of proportion in the *Timaeus* is worth quoting because of its "logistical" generality: "But two things cannot be held together without a bond which most completely fuses into one the things bound. Proportion is best adapted to such a fusion."

It was the role of the "proportional mean," or "harmonizing" link between two magnitudes, which especially appealed to Plato, as shown in his above-mentioned treatment of the "Number of the World Soul."

From the concept of proportion, more precisely from the geometrical proportion (A is to B as C is to D, or A is to B as B is to C, if reduced to three terms), in Greek *analogia,* derive two more complex but concrete concepts and techniques through which proportion was used in Greek and Gothic architecture and in Western art as a whole, and a still more general principle of which they are the spatial and temporal reflections: the principle of analogy.

These concrete spatiotemporal concepts are openly associated for the first time in the following statement of Vitruvius, which is the visible link between Plato and Neo-Pythagoreanism on one side and Gothic and Renaissance architecture on the other:

Symmetry resides in the correlation by measurement between the various elements of the plan, and between each of those elements and the whole. . . . As in the human body . . . it proceeds from proportion—the proportion which the Greeks called analogia—which achieves consonance between every part and the whole. . . . This symmetry is regulated by the *modulus,* the standard of common measure for the work considered, which the Greeks called "The Number." . . . When every important part of the building is thus conveniently set in proportion by the right correlation between height and width, between width and depth, and when all these parts have also their place in the total symmetry of the building, we obtain *eurythmy.*

We shall notice first that the original meaning of the word "symmetry," as found before Vitruvius in Plato's *Theaetetus* and after Plato in Pliny, in Plotinus' *Enneads,* and in the terminology of Gothic architects, was quite different from the modern one. Symmetry means for a modern the repetition of identical elements or patterns on each side of an axis or "plane of symmetry." It meant for Greek, Roman, and Gothic architects and artists generally the "commodulation" or concord of proportions obtained between the elements of a design, and between the elements and the whole, by the correct use of the geometrical proportion or analogia. This produces modulated recurrences and reflections of the same theme throughout the design, leading thus to the desired eurythmy. That this is the Greek, Roman, and Gothic meaning is demonstrated by the Vitruvius published in 1521 and written by Caesare Caesariano, who was the Master of the Works for the Duomo of Milan.

Vitruvius has been wrongly interpreted, even by Hambidge, as advising the use of a static or arithmetical modulus or ratio. To be sure, Vitruvius, like all architects and master masons in antiquity and all through the Middle Ages, undertook under oath not to divulge the key secrets of his art. Nevertheless, in spite of the self-imposed vagueness in which he veils the essential technique of "symmetry," he says explicitly that ". . . the more subtle questions concerning symmetry are solved by irrational ratios and methods" (*difficilesque symmetriarum quaestiones geometricis rationibus et methodis inveniuntur*). Thus the use of geometrical, i.e., irrational, ratios and proportions which he advises and which is based on the "dynamic symmetry" of Plato, recently rediscovered and interpreted by J. Hambidge, is quite a different thing from that of the static, i.e., arithmetic, modulations tolerated for standardized elements like columns.

The mention of the human body as a model of perfect symmetry is interesting. We find the same hint in Plato, and after Vitruvius in Galen, Plotinus, and all through the Middle Ages, in the theory of the correspondence between the microcosmos (man) and the macrocosmos (universe) accepted by architects. Here the complete correspondence was the progression or proportion, or analogia, man-temple-universe. This proportion was also accepted by alchemists, cabalists, and "scientific" magicians like Agrippa and Paracelsus. Very important in the Vitruvian text is the statement that the perfect composition or plan, using proportion and symmetry, leads to eurythmy. This is what we may call the principle of "symphonic composition," which, with the conscious use of proportion, is the dominant characteristic of classical Western art.

Symmetry was then the science of linking together proportions, in order to get eurythmy or symphonic composition. The use here of a musical term is entirely justified by the musical starting point of the Platonic theory of proportions, taken from the Pythagoreans. That this science or technique of symmetry was the essence of the discipline for Greek and Roman architects is confirmed again by Vitruvius, quoting the most famous Greek treatises of architecture which he always calls treatises of symmetry or symmetries, among others: Silenus, Philo, and Argelius.

All these works without exception are lost, and it is only by correlating the above-quoted sentence of Vitruvius with the words *dynamei symmetroi* and by noting that dynamic symmetry is defined in terms of irrational numbers or ratios which are commensurable "only in the square," such as $\sqrt{3}$ or $\sqrt{5}$ referred to in Plato's *Theaetetus,* that Jay Hambidge found the key to this essential concept of *dynamei symmetroi* as a technique of composition. It is to be noted that two lines which, in their relation or ratio to one another, are by themselves arithmetically incommensurable, generate, when squared or when treated as the sides of their respective squares, numbers or geometrically equivalent squared areas which are commensurable. Hence the expression "commensurable only in the square." Furthermore, because such squared surfaces produced out of lines forming their respective sides with irrational ratios are linked by commensurable ratios or proportions, the use of dynamic symmetry, rooted in irrational ratios, generates a whole concatenation of similar surfaces of different sizes dominated by a specific proportion or "theme," and this in a subtle and prolific way which the use of the simple, static, arithmetic ratios like ⅔, ⅕, etc., could not emulate.

This might be the place to define more accurately the Greek scientific concepts of ratio and proportion on which the whole theory of symmetry is based, and which are generally confused. A ratio is the quantitative comparison between two measurable mag-nitudes A and B, expressed mathematically by the fraction $\frac{a}{b}$, where a and b are numbers measuring the two magnitudes with the same unit. It is the mathematical aspect of the most general operation of intelligence or judgment which combines (1) the perception of a fundamental relation or hierarchy of values between two or several objects of knowledge, and (2) the valuation of the relation, the comparison of the values, qualitative or quantitative. When this comparison results in a quantitative "weighing," the result is a *ratio*.

Proportion, as briefly defined by Euclid, is the equivalence or equality of two ratios, and its most important type, the geometrical proportion of analogia of Plato and Vitruvius, is A is to B as C is to D, written $\frac{a}{b} = \frac{c}{d}$, when the four magnitudes A, B, C, D, can be measured with the same unit, a, b, c, d, being the respective meas-urements in numbers. We have seen already that, as in Plato's defi-nition, this expression can be reduced to three terms, A is to B as B is to C, or $\frac{a}{b} = \frac{b}{c}$. This is the *continuous* geometrical proportion.

The geometrical proportion A is to B as C is to D is the mathe-matical aspect of a more complex logical operation than simple comparison. It is the perception of a similitude, an analogy. This word derives of course from the Greek *analogia,* from *ana logon,* meaning according to reason. It is in fact a special case of a still more general principle of analogy which, as we shall try to prove, played in Western thought in general a part as important as the principle of symphonic composition in art, the two principles being closely related.

A proportion need not be limited to the equality of two ratios but may have any number of terms, like

$$\frac{a}{b} = \frac{c}{d} = \frac{e}{f} = \frac{g}{h} = \ldots \text{ etc., or } \frac{a}{b} = \frac{b}{c} = \frac{c}{d} = \ldots \text{ etc.}$$

The latter is a *continuous* geometrical proportion. But in all cases the characteristic of a proportion is always the *permanency* of a specific ratio. This of course explains why the notions of ratio and proportion are generally confused, although the concept of proportion adds to the simple quantitative comparison the idea of this permanent quality, of a ratio-value transmitted from one term to the next, of an *analogical invariant* which, when those proportions are between lines, surfaces, or volumes, implies the recurrence of similar shapes. Incidentally, the Greeks wrote the equation of continuous proportion as a series; for example: the proportion 1, 2, 4, 8, 16 . . . , the permanent ratio here being 2.

It might be as well to note that the geometrical proportion, the *analogia* of Vitruvius, the mathematical projection of the general principle of analogy, is not, in spite of its dominant role in architecture, sculpture, and painting, the only type of proportion. We have first two other types also used by Plato: the arithmetical and the harmonic proportion. The three main types can be symbolized as follows for proportions with three terms a, b, c:

arithmetical proportion $b - a = c - b$ like 1, 2, 3

geometrical proportion $\dfrac{a}{b} = \dfrac{b}{c}$ " 1, 2, 4

harmonic proportion $\dfrac{1}{b} - \dfrac{1}{a} = \dfrac{1}{c} - \dfrac{1}{b}$ " 2, 3, 6

The proportional means are respectively $b = \dfrac{a + c}{2}$

$$b = \sqrt{ac}$$

$$b = \dfrac{2ac}{c + a}$$

These three main types of proportion were evolved by the Pythagoreans. Proclus (410–483 A.D.) writes (*On Euclid*): "Eudoxus of Cnidus, . . . an associate of Plato's School . . . to the three proportions added another . . . and increased the number of theorems about the *section* which had their origin in Plato." Incidentally, as pointed out by Bretscheider in 1870, this *section* "par excellence," was probably the "golden section" which we shall meet presently.

To the six proportions of Eudoxus the Neo-Pythagoreans added four more types, bringing the total number to ten. We shall not enumerate these ten types of proportions but only mention that the tenth, figured by the equation $\dfrac{c - a}{c - b} = \dfrac{b}{a}$ (e.g., 3, 5, 8), corresponds to the Fibonacci series (1, 1, 2, 3, 5, 8, 13, 21, 34, 55, . . .) in which each term is the sum of the two preceding ones, and the ratio of two successive terms approximates very quickly to the golden section ratio, 1.618. . . . This series plays a great role in botany. Ten or the decad, as we shall see, played a dominant role in the Pythagorean society of numbers. Besides these ten types of proportions, the Neo-Pythagoreans, to their great satisfaction, established ten types of ratios.

The golden section ratio or proportion, which has already been mentioned, is the simplest asymmetrical (in the modern sense) proportion obtained when reducing to two the three terms of a proportion a, b, c, by applying "Ockham's Razor," or the law of economy of logical entities (*Entia non sunt multiplicanda sine necessitate,* i.e., "Logical entities must not be multiplied without need").

In $\frac{a}{b} = \frac{b}{c}$, we suppose $c = a + b$; algebraic reduction leads to $\left(\frac{b}{a}\right)^2 = \left(\frac{b}{a}\right) + 1$ or (if we symbolize $\frac{b}{a}$, the desired ratio, by x), $x^2 - x - 1 = 0$. The roots of this quadratic equation are $x = \frac{1 \pm \sqrt{5}}{2}$; the positive one, $\frac{1 + \sqrt{5}}{2} = 1.618 \ldots$, is the golden section ratio or proportion.

This irrational number $\frac{1 + \sqrt{5}}{2}$, generally symbolized by ø, has the most remarkable properties. It is, in fact, the most important algebraical invariant. To mention a few of its properties, $ø = 1 + \frac{1}{ø} = 1.618 \ldots$; $\frac{1}{ø} = 0.618 \ldots$; $ø^2 = ø + 1 = 2.618. \ldots$

More generally, $ø^n = ø^{n-1} + ø^{n-2}$ and $\frac{1}{ø^n} = \frac{1}{ø^{n+1}} + \frac{1}{ø^{n+2}}$. The infinite series $1, ø, ø^2, ø^3, \ldots ø^n \ldots$ has the unique property of being at the same time a geometrical and a two-beat additive progression. This occurs because each term is the sum of the two preceding ones. This allows a very simple graphic manipulation of lines proportional to its terms, enabling one to construct any term or number of terms by simple additions and subtractions.

The general definition of the golden section deduced from the initial quality $\frac{a}{b} = \frac{b}{a + b}$, can be expressed logically as follows: Two lengths, or magnitudes, whether surfaces or volumes or weights, are in the golden section ratio or proportion when the ratio between the greater and the smaller one is equal to the ratio between the whole (the sum of both terms) and the greater one.

Here follow some of the more important geometrical properties of this proportion: In any regular pentagon, the ratio between a diagonal and the side is equal to the golden section, or number ϕ. Or, in other terms, in a pentagram (star-pentagon), obtained in tracing the five diagonals of the regular pentagon, the ratio between the sides of the pentagram and the sides of the pentagon is ϕ. In tracing indefinitely the internal pentagons and pentagrams, we obtain an infinite nest of ordered golden proportions, a *symmetria*.

The regular decagon is also directly ruled by this proportion: The ratio between the side of the star-decagon and the radius of the circumscribed circle is ϕ. So is the ratio between this radius and the side of the regular decagon inscribed in the circle. These properties, as we shall see, play a dominant role in the plans of Gothic cathedrals and churches (Moessel's theory).

It follows that the two more complex regular solids, the dodecahedron, which is a regular polyhedron having twelve pentagons as faces, and its reciprocal, the icosahedron, which is obtained by joining the twelve centers of these pentagonal faces, have also as leading proportion or theme the golden section. And as we can pass from these two polyhedra to the three simpler ones, the tetrahedron, cube, and octahedron, by simple constructions, we can say, like Campanus of Novara in the thirteenth century, that the golden section (*proportionem habentem medium duoque extrema*) binds the five regular bodies in a logical way (*rationabiliter*) into a symphony ruled by an irrational proportion (*irrationali symphonia*).

Another simple geometrical figure derived from the golden section is the golden rectangle or ϕ rectangle, called by Hambidge the "rectangle of the whirling squares." The ratio between its longer and shorter sides is ϕ. Together with the related $\sqrt{5}$ rectangle and the related $\sqrt{\phi}$ and ϕ^2 rectangles it plays a great role in Hambidge's theory of dynamic rectangles and in his treatment of "harmonically divided" surfaces, as well as in the analysis of Greek temples, Greek vases, and the human body.

As we have seen, Plato attached great importance to the theory of proportions. He is one of the few estheticians to have analyzed proportions between volumes. His theory of proportions, however, and the bulk of his esthetics, or theory of forms, based on proportion, symmetry, and harmony, were of direct Pythagorean inspiration. Hence, it will be useful now to examine the Pythagorean sources themselves, beginning with a brief exposition of the life and legend of Pythagoras.

Born in Samos at the beginning of that extraordinary sixth century B.C. which makes him a contemporary of the Buddha, of Confucius, Lao Tzu, and Zoroaster, Pythagoras spent many years traveling between the different schools of wisdom of the period. Incidentally, as a young man he had won the pugilistic crown at the 48th Olympiad. Like Plato, nearly two centuries later, he lived for some time among the priest-scientists of Egypt, and was initiated into their mysteries as well as into their mathematical knowledge. The legend woven around his life mentions other periods of initiation in Chaldea, Syria (Mount Carmel), Thrace (the Orphic mysteries), and even India. What is certain is that, having returned to Samos between 540 and 530 B.C., he started to teach his new philosophy, and soon provoked the suspicions and displeasure of the tyrant Polycrates. Forced to leave the island, he arrived a little after 530 B.C. in Magna Graecia.

There the success of his mathematical, ethical, and political teachings was such that it led to the foundation of the famous Brotherhood which in a few years succeeded in wielding political power over a loose confederation of cities, known as the Crotoniate League. Although it was not under the direct rule of the Order, many of its members, whether exoteric (the "nomothetes," second degree of initiation) or esoteric (the "mathematicians," third degree, in possession of all the doctrine), were executive agents of the governments of the various cities belonging to the League, so that Croton, headquarters of the Order, was the de facto capital of the confederation.

In the same way that the Pythagorean Brotherhood was to be the model for most later secret or semisecret societies, so the Crotoniate League, its political emanation, inspired Plato with his ideal state ruled by an elite of philosophers. The League stood for law, order, and tradition. It generally allied itself with the democrats against tyranny, but sometimes also with the conservative elite against demagogy. This regime lasted successfully for about eighty years, but around 450 B.C. a widespread anti-Pythagorean outbreak, culminating in the massacre at Metapontum of the most important leaders of the Order, led to the first emigration of its members to the Greek mainland. Those who remained in Italy transferred their headquarters to Rhegium. About 390 B.C., probably because of their conflict with the tyrant Dionysius of Syracuse, they were all forced to hide or leave southern Italy, with the exception of Archytas and his group at Tarentum. Tarentum was the last successful Pythagorean state, of which Archytas was regent and seven times generalissimo. About 387 B.C. Plato had occasion to visit Tarentum and its philosopher-regent, who was one of the great mathematicians of antiquity, and a strong friendship developed between them. The tradition mentioned by Diogenes Laertius, according to which Archytas, pupil of Philolaos, one of the Pythagorean leaders who escaped the massacre at Metapontum, initiated Plato into the core of the Pythagorean doctrine, seems to be confirmed by Plato's Seventh Letter. This is one of the most remarkable documents of Western culture, at once in part a confession and in part an autobiography of its most outstanding mind. In this letter Plato calls Archytas and his Tarentine entourage his "friends and brothers in philosophy." This philosophy is obviously the secret doctrine of the Brotherhood. He adds: "To the one who has once understood this teaching, there is no danger that he should ever forget it. It is summed up . . . in a few very short formulae. . . . Very few men alive have knowledge of the doctrine."

The fundamental axiom of Pythagoreanism was that "everything was arranged according to number." Plato's elaboration in the *Timaeus* reads: "And it was then that all these kinds of things thus established received their shapes from the Ordering One, through the action of Ideas and Numbers." Nicomachus of Gerasa states that the "numbers" and patterns of all permanent things, structures, relations, as distinct from illusory and transient things like corporeal entities (matter), pre-existed in the mind of "The God Ordering with Art." This of course corresponds very closely to the point of view of modern physics, which has also replaced substance by pure numbers, waves or "matrices" or probabilities, and structural "invariants." This made Bertrand Russell write: "The oddest thing about modern science is its return to Pythagoreanism." The same observation was made by Professor Whittaker of Edinburgh in his Riddle Memorial Lecture at Durham University.

The other main tenet of the doctrine, also bodily taken up by Plato, was that the cosmos is a harmoniously ordered whole. This harmony and its rhythms were reflected in the harmony of the well-balanced human soul and even in the proportions of the human body and of other living beings, and in the perfect work of art.

This was to lead to "symphonic composition," itself related to a general principle of analogy, the first formulation of which is also found in the *Hieros Logòs* of Pythagoras, quoted by Jamblichus and Stobaeus: "You will know, as far as it is allowed to a mortal, that Nature is from all points of view similar to itself."

Music plays a dominant part in Pythagorean teaching and doctrine, both as a reflection of the harmony and rhythms of the cosmos and as a mathematical theory leading to the theory of proportions in general. Music also played its part in creating the right atmosphere for the meditations of the adepts.

The invention of the diatonic scale, starting from a pulsation of fifths brought back within the octave, which was the foundation of all Western scales, is also attributed to Pythagoras himself. In the part of the *Timaeus* where Plato states the affinities between the five regular bodies and the elements of the universe, it is to the general principle of harmony in the cosmos that he correlates the dodecahedron. This body in space, like the pentagon and decagon in the plane, has in fact as its leading theme the famous "divine proportion" of the golden section, which was later to be extolled by Campanus, Pacioli, Leonardo, and Kepler. The construction of a pentagon with a given side and the inscription of the dodecahedron in a sphere, both based on the construction of the golden section, were precisely two of the mathematical secrets of the Brotherhood, the divulgation of which by Hippocrates of Chios and Hippasus of Metapontum brought about their excommunication.

The secret geometrical symbol and pass sign of the Brotherhood was the pentagram. As stated by Lucian in his *On Slips in Greeting:* "The Pentagram, which the Pythagoreans used as a symbol of recognition among the members of the School, was called by them Health."

It is evident, therefore, that the principle of symphonic composition, of "commodulation" between the parts and the whole leading through proportion (analogia) and symmetry (in the Vitruvian sense, not the modern one) to eurythmy, had its origin in the Pythagorean concept of cosmic harmony. This concept, as we shall show later on, was transmitted from Plato via Vitruvius, the Neo-Pythagoreans, St. Augustine, Plotinus, St. Thomas, and the Gothic master builders, to the leaders of the Neoplatonic revival in the first Renaissance.

This, of course, although of capital importance for the creative technique of Western art, especially architecture, is far from being

Plato's sole contribution to esthetics. We shall see that the correlated Platonic idea of the organic unity of the work of art, already hinted at in the *Gorgias,* has also been taken up recently by S. Alexander and others. But to Plato, too, is due the concept of absolute beauty, the archetype or Idea of Beauty, or rather two distinct concepts of absolute beauty. The first, which we might call the mystical or properly the idealistic one, is developed in the *Symposium,* where we see the transition from the love of a beautiful body to the love of corporeal beauty, as it were, in the abstract, then to the love of beautiful minds, of beautiful actions; finally, the earthly Eros is transformed into the divine Eros, creating the urge for inner perfection and the quest for the essence of beauty ("Beauty uncreated, imperishable, . . . which remains by itself eternally identical to itself") culminating after mental and moral ascension in a mystical union with absolute beauty merged with absolute love.

The other conception of absolute beauty in Plato, according to which beauty is considered from a purely morphological point of view, is presented in the following extraordinarily dry sentence in the *Philebus.* It could be adopted as a manifesto for cubist and abstractionist art: "What I mean here by beauty of form is not what is commonly understood by that name, such as for instance the beauty of living beings and of their representations, but something straight and circular, and surfaces and solids produced out of straight lines and curves, by lathes and rulers and squares." Here the archetypes, instead of projecting the organic symmetries of living forms, have contracted into abstract geometrical shapes.

Even the striking image of St. Thomas about beauty as splendor (*splendor entis* or *splendor secundum propriam formam,* "splendor as being," or "splendor according to its appropriate shape,") is already sketched in Plato's *Phaedrus:* "But of Beauty, I repeat again that we have her there shining in company with the celestial forms, and coming to earth we find her here too, shining clearly through the clearest apertures of sense."

To return now to the subject of Pythagorean number mystic, we shall mention the importance there of the decad, or archetype of ten. In this mixture of mathematics and metaphysics the Pythagoreans did not consider the "vulgar" numbers used in counting or in practical arithmetic, but what they called "divine" or "pure" numbers, which were supposed to be the archetypes of the former ones, pre-existing, like the other "ideas," in the mind of "The Great Ordering One." The definitions of these divine or pure numbers coincide strangely with the modern conception of number in Dedekind, Cantor, and Bertrand Russell, i.e., numbers as classes or classes of classes.

This remarkable convergence is illustrated in the *Introduction to Arithmetic* by Nicomachus of Gerasa of the first century A.D. It is the only complete treatise on Pythagorean numbers to escape destruction. Owing to its translation by Boethius and the careful preservation of manuscripts by the Benedictine monks, at Monte Cassino in particular, the Pythagorean concept of number was kept alive all through the Middle Ages, even in the *Quadrivium* or four major disciplines taught in the universities. This fact explains not only the familiarity of Gothic architects with the concepts of proportion and symmetry but also the apparition of Pythagorean number mysticism in the printed works of the great "magicians" and dabblers in occult sciences of the sixteenth century, such as Agrippa of Nettesheim, Paracelsus, John Dee, and Henry Kunrath. This underground channel of transmission of Pythagorean ideas embraces also alchemists, Rosicrucians, and cabalists.

Here is an extract from Nicomachus' treatise:

All things in the universe that nature has arranged systematically with an artistic method seem, both in their component parts and as wholes, to have been distinguished and ordered in accordance with number by the foresight and intelligence of the One who created all things—the model having been established, just like a preliminary sketch, due to the fact that number, purely ideal and completely immaterial, yet real and eternal essence, was dominant, being pre-existent in the thinking of the divine Creator of the world, in order that in reference to it, as if conforming to an artistic plan, all these things were created—time, motion, the heavens, the stars, and the cyclical movements (the rhythms) of all things.

One sees here the ideological contact with Plato's theory of ideas. After this majestic introduction of ideal or divine numbers as archetypes, Nicomachus presents the decad, and the relations between the theme or symmetry of the archetypal ten and the harmony of the cosmos:

But as the whole was illimited multitude . . . an Order was necessary . . . and it was in the decad that a natural balance between the whole and its elements was found to pre-exist. . . . That is why the All-Ordering God [literally "the God arranging with art"], acting in accordance with his reason, made use of the decad as a canon for the whole . . . and this is why the things from Earth to Heaven have for the wholes as well as for their parts their ratios of concord based upon the decad and are ordered accordingly.

This is a paraphrase, on a wider scale, of Vitruvius' hints on architectural eurythmy; Vitruvius himself insists on the perfection of the number ten and its role in the relationship between the parts of the human body and the whole. We see here the influence of the conscious analogia universe-temple-man on the Pythagorean aspect of Greek and Roman esthetics.

After the decad, the most important number was for the Pythagoreans the pentad, or archetype of the *five;* we have already seen that the pentagram, or five-pointed star, was the secret sign and passport of the Brotherhood, the letters YGEIA, composing the Greek word for health, being sometimes associated to the points of the star (or SALUS in Latin). But independently of its geometrical symbol, the pentad (as "divine number") was revered in itself; if ten was the number of the cosmos (of the whole, or macrocosmos) the pentad was not only correlated to health as harmony but also to love (as a combination of the first "male," or uneven number, three, and of the first "female," or even number, two) and to nature as a living force. We shall see a striking justification of this intuition in the part played by pentagonal symmetry, the associated golden section, the ø and Fibonacci series, in organic morphology and harmonious growth, the growth called "gnomonic" by the Greeks, producing homothetic, similar shapes, by simple addition of identical units or cells.

The pentad was therefore called by the diverse names of nature, Aphrodite Gamelia (Venus Genitrix), the Unconquered, and the Half-Goddess (being half the "divine" decad).

We shall now present still another channel of transmission of Pythagorean concepts and symbols deriving from the fact that, in the same way that Greek music was based on the diatonic scale of Pythagoras, the technique of symmetry in architectural composition, as summarily mentioned by Vitruvius, had been entirely evolved from the Platonico-Pythagorean theory of proportions. As already stated, the allusion to dynamic symmetry, or symmetry in the second power, "in the square," of surfaces with irrational linear dimensions, in Plato's *Theaetetus,* gave J. Hambidge the key to the jealously kept secret of Greek planning. Like the physicians through their Hippocratic Oath, the architects and master builders in Greece and Rome took an oath of secrecy, inspired perhaps by the oath of the Pythagorean Brotherhood, from which they had borrowed their theory of proportions. Their secret method for obtaining eurythmy through dynamic symmetry was transmitted from father to son or adopted son, and this esoterism of architectural science was kept in force all through the dark period from the fourth to the ninth century A.D. and through the Middle Ages proper, the secret planning diagrams themselves being mainly transmitted through the guilds of stonecutters and masons which were linked without interruption to the *collegia* of antiquity.

In Rome the *Collegia Opificum* of masons were the depositaries of the secret Greek techniques, having as social counterparts associated *sodalitates,* with which they shared ceremonies such as *agapes* and initiation rituals and elections of honorary patrons, borrowed partly from the "mysteries." The legendary foundation of these professional guilds was attributed to Numa. The Roman collegia are first mentioned historically in the third century B.C., and for the last time in a decree of the Emperor Majoranus in 461 A.D. The corresponding Greek guilds were still in full operation under Justinian in the sixth century A.D. The titles of their officials were borrowed from the Eleusinian and other mysteries, their ritual both from the mysteries and from the related Pythagorean ritual. To quote Eric T. Bell's *The Magic of Numbers:* "The influence of the Pythagorean Brotherhood has lasted to the present day . . . [it] fixed the pattern of secret societies for hundreds of years."

As we know from inscriptions found in France and Italy, the existence of these collegia in Western Europe was not interrupted by the barbaric invasions. Between the eighth and tenth centuries the monastic schools or workshops of master builders and masons grouped around the magnificent Benedictine abbeys of Cassino, Corvey, St. Gallen, and Cluny, learned from the collegia, which they Christianized, the still esoteric tradition of architectural planning. From this collaboration there resulted, after the Carlovingian period, the fully organized federation of guilds and lodges which appeared in France, Germany, and England, and which in the Holy Roman Empire formed the powerful body known as the "Bauhütte," with the Great Lodge of Strassburg as its headquarters.

The gods or tutelary genii of the old collegia had been replaced by the "Quatuor Coronati," four architects or master builders, St. Castor, St. Symphorian, St. Claudius, and St. Nicostratus, martyred under Diocletian. But the antique ritual was transmitted with few alterations, including the election of honorary patrons; also the core of professional secrets including the teaching of symmetry and the oath not to reveal them to any but a brother in the craft.

There is no room here to give more particulars about this continuous filiation, which also links these professional lodges to "speculative" free masonry, founded with the Great Lodge of London in 1717. Let us only mention that the Cooke Manuscript in the British Museum after underlining the importance of geometry as the principle of all other sciences, and the special importance of Masonry which is its direct application, narrates how Pythagoras and Hermes found the two columns on which were engraved the rules of these two sciences.

The mention of Hermes (Hermes Trismegistos) is interesting. We have already seen that another parallel line of transmission of Pythagorean symbols starting from Ptolemaic Hermetism and Hebrew Cabala leads through the school of European magic associated with alchemy and Rosicrucian speculations.

The famous John Dee, English Elizabethan magician and alchemist, in his preface to the first English translation of Euclid, writes in a thoroughly Pythagorean style: "All things . . . do appear to be formed by reason of number. For this was the principal example or pattern in the mind of the Creator."

Like Paracelsus, Agrippa of Nettesheim shows the pentagram, with a man inscribed in it, to be the symbol of the microcosmos, or man; the decad and decagon corresponding to the macrocosmos, the living universe, *natura naturans,* as distinct from the material universe, *natura naturata,* symbolized by the number six. Agrippa does not forget to mention that, as a result of the combination of the first even-female number and of the first uneven-male one, the pentad possesses a very special perfection and power. Moreover, it is the half of the "whole," or decad, and "it was for the Pythagoreans the number of marriage, of happiness, and beauty. . . . The pagan philosophers placed the pentad as high over the tetrad as the animated dominates the inanimated. . . . Of the power of this Number in living nature, we have an example in pentaphyllon . . . etc."

We will see later on that there was a curious intuition here, in the association of pentagonal symmetry with the geometry of life, of the hexagonal and quadratic symmetries with unorganized geometrical patterns (like crystal lattices).

This correspondence of macrocosm to microcosm (developed in antique architecture as the proportion universe is to temple as temple is to man) is of course the main axiom or proportion of cab-ala, alchemy, Hermetism, and magic, condensed in the

> *Id quod inferius*
> *Sicut quod superius*
> (As it is below
> So it is above)

All this is in direct filiation with the axiom of analogy (nature always similar to itself) in the *Hieros Logos* of Pythagoras. Curi-ously enough we find literally the same sentence in Alberti's *De Re Aedificatoria: "Certissimum est naturam in omnibus sui esse per-similem,"* i.e., "It is certain that nature is always similar to itself." And in St. Thomas: *"Pulchritudo enim creaturae nihil aliud quam similitudo divinae pulchritudinis in rebus participatis,"* i.e., "Be-cause the beauty of the created being is nothing but the reflection of the divine beauty in the things emanating from it."

Before we examine the role of Pythagorean diagrams in the special domain of Western architecture, it may be noted that the pentagram was transmitted, together with many rites, by antique and medieval "operative" masonry to modern speculative free-masonry, where the "flaming" five-pointed star is one of the master symbols. What perhaps few brothers know is that the letter "G" in the center of the masonic flaming star does not stand for "Geome-try" or "Gnosis" but is the Latin transcription of the Hebrew letter *Yod,* which numerically stands for ten, the Pythagorean decad, symbol of the macrocosmos.

To return to art, we shall now find that those graphic symbols associated to the concepts of proportion, symmetry, and organic and cosmic harmony, transmitted by several underground channels, were not only correlated to the secrets of architectural planning jealously kept by collegia and guilds of masons but were in certain cases *identical* in part or *in toto* to the "regulating diagrams" which condensed these secrets. All through the nineteenth century estheti-cians and architects tried to discover these principles of Greek and Gothic architectural planning, and the obvious part played therein by proportion. However, it is only during the last thirty years that the converging researches of three independent investigators have given us the solution to this archeological and esthetic problem. The key to this solution is the technique of symphonic composition or eurythmy, derived from a universal principle of analogy. The latter principle and its attendant technique permit the elucidation of many questions in what may be called esthetic biology. The morphological laws of living shapes and growth are forthwith demonstrated to be equally based on number and proportion, and the mathematics or geometry of art and the geometry of life are shown to be identical, a conclusion reached long ago by Plato and Vitruvius.

The three main explorers in this field were Jay Hambidge in the United States, F. Macody Lund in Norway, and Ernst Moessel in Germany. They quite independently discovered that the solution of the problem lay in the right interpretation of the expression "dynamic symmetry" found in Plato's *Theaetetus* and other dialogues, and in the appropriate use of the corresponding technique, once rediscovered, in order to produce the eurythmic compositions and subdivisions postulated by Vitruvius. Also, the process of "gnomonic" or homothetic growth, in geometry and living organisms, has been specially treated by Sir D'Arcy Thompson in *Growth and Form*.

The right interpretation of dynamic symmetry had been given, in addition, by other scholars indifferent to the esthetic approach. For example, John Burnet in his *Greek Philosophy* holds that in the *Epinomis* Plato presents the view that "Geometry can be an assimilation by reference to surfaces of numbers not similar to one another by nature." In other words, dynamic symmetry, which, as its etymology indicates, means commensurability "in the square" or second power, can be produced practically by combining surfaces which, although their linear dimensions are incommensurable ("irrational" ratios like $\sqrt{3}$, $\sqrt{5}$, etc.), are themselves correlated by commensurable proportions (like the squares or rectangles constructed on $\sqrt{3}$, $\sqrt{5}$, etc.).

In order to illustrate practically this logical interpretation of dynamic symmetry, Hambidge imagined the manipulation of dynamic rectangles having as proportions between their longer and shorter sides irrational ratios like $\sqrt{2}$, $\sqrt{3}$, $\sqrt{5}$, or the golden section ($\phi = 1.618 \ldots$), and its relatives $\sqrt{\phi}$, ϕ^2. These, when combined or subdivided by Hambidge's graphic method of tracing diagonals, then perpendiculars to these diagonals from opposite summits, and parallels to the sides through all possible points of intersection, produce a "harmonic" system of surfaces linked by an ordered chain of correlated proportions in accordance with the Vitruvian definitions of symmetry and eurythmy. It is to be noted that the "static" rectangles with rational proportions ⅔, ⅘, . . . , etc., *do not* produce this elastic interplay of themes.

Measurements or studies of the plans of Greek temples, vases, and ritual objects by Hambidge and Dr. Caskey, the curator of Greek vases in the Boston Museum, gave a striking confirmation of Hambidge's theory. Out of 192 Greek vases of the best period in the Boston Museum only 9 have a static rectangle as over-all frame; all the others have dynamic rectangles, the margin of error being smaller than 1 mm. Out of 120 vases "dynamically" analyzed, 18 are based on the $\sqrt{2}$ theme (6 having as over-all frame the $\sqrt{2}$ rectangle, 1.4142, itself), 6 on the $\sqrt{3}$ theme (3 having the rectangle $\sqrt{3}$ itself as frame); all the others on themes connected with ϕ or $\sqrt{5}$. The golden section theme ϕ and its "relatives" $\sqrt{\phi}$, ϕ^2, $\sqrt{5}$, etc., give of course a much greater number of harmonic combinations than $\sqrt{2}$ or $\sqrt{3}$, which explains their predominance in the plans of Greek temples, vases, etc., and the frequency of the occurrence of the ϕ and $\sqrt{5}$ over-all rectangles as frames. Hambidge also applied his method of analysis of proportions by dynamic rectangles and their harmonic subdivisions to the human body, and found that there, too, the ϕ and $\sqrt{5}$ (especially the $\frac{\sqrt{5}}{2}$) rectangles appear in the great majority of cases to the exclusion of static rectangles and even of the rectangles $\sqrt{2}$ and $\sqrt{3}$.

The role of the golden section in the proportions of the human body had already been rediscovered in modern times by Zeysing, about 1850. He found, in measuring the proportions of a great number of human bodies (not skeletons in his case), that the average ratio between the height of the whole body and the vertical distance between the navel and the floor level was ϕ or 1.618 . . . , the golden section. This ratio appears also between the total height and the distance from the top of the skull to the finger tips stretched vertically, as well as in many other dimensions of the human body.

Incidentally Vitruvius, in comparing the proportions of the beautiful temple with the ones of the ideal human body, states that the navel is the center of symmetry of the latter: *"Item corporis centrum medium naturaliter est umbilicus."*

Hambidge's intuition about the preponderant role of dynamic rectangles and irrational ratios is confirmed by the previously mentioned sentence of Vitruvius *("difficilesque symmetriarum quaestiones geometricis rationibus et methodis inveniuntur,"* the geometrical ratios being the irrational ones), and also by a key sentence in Pacioli's *Divina Proportione,* a treatise on the golden section published in Venice in 1509 and illustrated by Leonardo da Vinci. Pacioli's statement underlines explicitly the superiority of dynamic, irrational proportions. In Chapter V of his treatise he elaborates the statement of Vitruvius that the architect has to use irrational symmetries, "which like the ratio between the diagonal and the side of the square cannot be specified by integers and their aliquot parts," and in Chapter XX he specifies that "when one cannot make use of the simple symmetries like ½, ⅓, ¾, ⅔, etc., but has to use irrational proportions, the important points of the plan, instead of being obtained by numbers, can be found by lines or surfaces," because "proportion has a much wider use in the realm of 'continuous' quantities (the irrational, dynamic numbers) than in that of the integers."

Hambidge summarizes the origin of this conception as follows: "The materials for the study of Dynamic Symmetry are obtained from three sources: from the symmetry of the human body and of plants, from Egyptian and Greek Art, and from the five regular polyhedra." With reference to Egyptian art, we can only mention that the Great Pyramid has as half-meridian section a right-angled triangle in which the ratio between the hypotenuse and the shorter side is ∅, or the golden section, which makes the whole body of the pyramid a concatenation of remarkable geometrical properties.

The Chamber of the King, of dimensions proportional to 2, 1, $\frac{\sqrt{5}}{2}$ has remarkable relations to the icosahedron, the human body, and the pyramid itself.

Although Macody Lund and Moessel gave the same interpretation as Hambidge of Plato's dynamic symmetry, they used different graphic techniques or methods in analyzing Greek or Gothic plans. Lund, especially for the plans of Gothic cathedrals, produced beautiful stellated diagrams composed of double-square rectangles and pentagrams, where the center of the controlling pentagram coincided with that of the main altar. Moessel evolved circular regulating diagrams based on the subdivision of the circle of orientation of the temple or cathedral in a certain number of equal parts, 4, 8, 16, or 32, for Byzantine, Carlovingian, or Romanesque plans, but nearly always 5, 10, or 20 for antique temples and Gothic cathedrals. In view of the intimate connection between the golden section, the pentagon, and the decagon, it is not surprising that, like Hambidge, Lund and Moessel find the golden section and the associated $\sqrt{5}$ ratio dominant proportions in their regulating diagrams; in fact, although obtained through different systems of dynamic symmetry, the resulting diagrams produced by the three methods are often identical.

We are therefore entitled to say definitely that the interpretation of symmetry and dynamic symmetry produced and applied by these three explorers of the secrets of Western architecture is the correct one. It has given us the long-sought key to the whole problem. Furthermore, whereas Greek architects and artists seem to have used Hambidge's dynamic rectangles as over-all frames and his diagonal method of harmonic subdivision, the Gothic master builders probably used Moessel's method of the subdivision in 5, 10, or 20 parts of the circle of orientation.

Miss Irma Richter has applied Moessel's system with success in analyzing the composition of many early Renaissance paintings. There is an additional confirmation of his theory as applied to Gothic architecture in some of the mysterious slogans appearing in the few texts left by the Federation of Guilds of Stonecutters and Masons on the continent of Europe in the Middle Ages concerning their ritual and technical secrets, and also in the only regulating diagrams published by the Gothic master builder, Caesare Caesariano, Master of the Fabric of the Duomo of Milan, in his Como edition of Vitruvius of 1521. In this book Caesariano printed two of the original Gothic fourteenth-century plans on which he was working. The "symmetry" of the plans and the "center of the circle" are mentioned on his diagrams, and the regulating circle itself is traced on the elevation exactly as in Moessel's constructions.

We know that in antiquity the line from north to south in the circle of orientation was found by the shortest (noon) shadow of a pole; also that any right-angled direction could be traced on the ground with the help of a rope knotted in 12 equal parts and reproducing thus the right-angled triangle of Pythagoras, with sides proportional to 3, 4, 5. The subdivision of the circle of orientation in 5 or 10 parts was easily done by the construction shown in Ptolemy's *Almagestes*.

Moessel's two standard regulating diagrams in which can be found the plans and elevations of nearly all Gothic cathedrals and churches are very striking. The circle of orientation is divided into twenty segments, and the star-decagon and two or more pentagrams appear together with the correlated golden sections. Those two standard diagrams can be joined into a single one which may be called "the Gothic master diagram." It was probably the great technical secret communicated only to the third grade of operative masons, or masters of the works, whereas the other diagrams based on the square and the triangle were known to the second grade masters, as they had to be able to "place" and "prove" their geometrical signatures or marks within the specific lattice, on keystones, etc.

The uninterrupted transmission from Greek scientists of the notion of symmetry, as defined by Vitruvius, and as itself related to the conception of the work of art as an organic whole, reflecting the symmetry of living organisms and the parallel harmony of the cosmos itself, is demonstrated by the following quotations: St. Augustine (*De Ordine*): "Reason, turning to the domain of sight, that is, to the earth and sky, noticed that in the world it is beauty that pleases the sight; in beauty, figures; in figures, measures; in measures, numbers"; Plotinus (*Enneads*): "What is it that impresses you when you look at something, attracts you, captivates you, and fills you with joy? We are all agreed, I may say, that it is the interrelation of parts toward one another and toward the whole, with the added element of beauty in color as perceived by the eye; in other words, that beauty in visible things as in everything else consists of symmetry and proportion."

When speaking of beauty, St. Thomas also consistently uses the words *consonantia* (equivalent to *symmetria*), *proportio, ordo,* or *situs partium.* He also writes: "Sense delights in all things well proportioned, as in what is like itself."

I have already mentioned the important sentence of Campanus of Novara in the thirteenth century, observing how the golden section by an irrational proportion binds the five regular solids in a rational symphony. This sentence is quoted *in extenso* by Luca Pacioli in his *Divina Proportione.*

With the Reformation, which brought the end of the architectural monopoly of the Catholic Bauhütte, with the Neoplatonic revival beginning with the foundation of the Platonic Academy by Cosimo de Medici about 1450, with the translation of Plato's dialogues by Marsilio Ficinus, and with the publication of Alberti's and Pacioli's treatises, the well-guarded secrets about symmetry, proportion, and the golden section became public property. In his *Trattato della Pittura* Leonardo writes: "Every part of the whole [of the human body] must be in proportion to the whole . . . I would have the same thing understood as applying to all animals and plants."

But curiously enough, both these concepts and the correlated techniques were soon forgotten and replaced by mechanical copying and juxtapositions of standardized classical elements, as in the "orders" of Serlio, etc. The very meaning of the word "symmetry" was completely obscured in the seventeenth century and replaced by the modern one: repetition of identical elements on each side of an axis or plane of symmetry.

Palladio seems to have been one of the last architects to work consciously on eurythmic plans, and to have manipulated proportion, even the harmonic proportion, in the Platonic sense. After him Christopher Wren appears to have planned the Sheldonian Theater in Oxford on a rigorous vertical modulation of the golden section. It reappears nearly identically a century later in Gabriel's façades on the Place de la Concorde.

Kepler, who was led by Pythagorean reflections concerning the music of the spheres and the proportions of the five Platonic bodies to the discovery of his three laws, was the last author to mention the golden section, which, in his *Mysterium Cosmographicum de Admirabili Proportione Orbium Caelestium* (1596), he calls "a precious jewel, one of the two treasures of geometry."

The golden section was rediscovered by Zeysing about 1850. Forerunner of Hambidge and Moessel, he showed its all-ruling presence in the Parthenon, in the proportions of the human body, and in botany.

There is no space here to exhibit in detail the role of the golden section and of pentagonal symmetry in biological morphology. Three items are significant: 1) the correlation between gnomonic or homothetic growth, where the shapes, surfaces, or volumes, as in marine shells, remain similar; 2) the properties of logarithmic spirals each of them corresponding to a geometrical progression or proportion, or pulsation; and 3) the fact that the ∅ or golden section series and its asymptotic approximation, the Fibonacci two-beat additive series, are the only progressions which, by addition of identical elements, produce a geometrical, homothetical progression or pulsation. There is no space either to show the radical difference between the morphology of living growth and that of crystal lattices and shapes, where combined regular lattices and equipartitions of space ruled by the principle of least action can produce only quadratic or hexagonal systems of symmetry. This is the case because among the regular polygons only the square, the hexagon, and its subdivision, the equilateral triangle, can fill the plane by repetition. The pentagon, or its three-dimensional representative, the dodecahedron, or the star dodecahedron, which plays a predominant part in the system of proportions of the human body, is *never* found in crystalline, inorganic arrangements, whereas it dominates botany. Like the *genus rosa,* the lotus family, sunflowers, all fruit and trees or bushes that bear berries, as well as orchids have either five petals or a number multiple of five. The lily, the tulip, the hyacinth, the three-petalled trillium, on the contrary, are modulated on the "crystalline" hexagonal symmetry.

These correlations between the golden section, pentagon, and living growth and morphology were, after Zeysing, rediscovered and explained scientifically in Sir Theodore Cook's *The Curves of Life* and in D'Arcy Thompson's *Growth and Form.* As Professor Jaeger in his *Lectures on the Principles of Symmetry* has noted: "A certain preference for pentagonal symmetry in the case of superior animals as well as in that of plants seems to exist here, a symmetry clearly related to the important proportion of the *Sectio Aurea,* and unknown in the world of inanimate matter." In Germany the great botanist R. Francé also noticed this predominance, which is apparent too in marine organisms like starfishes and sea-urchins.

Hambidge's and Moessel's theories have a subsidiary aspect. When combined, they give us not only a satisfactory working hypothesis and solution for the problem of Greek and Gothic planning but also, irrespective of the validity of the hypothesis, a very interesting and easy method of enabling modern architects, draughtsmen, painters, and designers of all sorts to plan their compositions eurythmically. And in fact architects, painters, silversmiths, especially in France (Jean Puiforcat, sculptor and goldsmith, among others) and Switzerland, have been using both dynamic rectangles and harmonically divided circles to their great satisfaction.

At the beginning of this essay it was indicated that the conscious use of proportion and symmetry in space, and of rhythm, which is symmetry in time, is but the reflection of a more general principle of analogy which was and is also one of the most specific mental tools of Western thought. In the domain of the plastic arts, including architecture, this principle has been summed up by Thiersch in the conclusion of his book, *Die Proportion in der Architektur:* "We have found in examining the greatest works of art of all times that in each of them a fundamental shape is repeated, and that its elements produce similar shapes by their composition and disposition. Harmony results from the repetition of the principal figure (shape) of the work of art throughout its subdivisions."

This ordered recurrence of similar shapes of different sizes is precisely what is produced by Hambidge's and Moessel's methods of realizing dynamic symmetry. The same observation has been made in the musical domain. As W. R. Spalding writes in his *Handbook of Musical Analysis:* "It is not an exaggeration to say that systematic repetition in one form or another is the most important principle of musical structure."

It is interesting to follow the transmission of the general principle of analogy from Pythagoras, who said, "You will know, as far as it is allowed to a mortal, that nature is from all points of view similar to itself." It is echoed by Alberti: "It is absolutely certain that nature in everything is similar to itself." F. Bacon adds, in the *Novum Organum:* "Men's labor should be turned to the investigation and observation of the resemblances and analogies of things as well in wholes as in parts. For these it is that detect the unity of nature." Whether in the arts of space or in those of time, including poetry, in logic or in pure or applied science, the greatest minds in the cycle of Western culture have been the seers of analogies.

Plato's special influence on esthetics was, as already mentioned, not confined to the mathematical theory of proportions and shapes or to the pursuit of the abstract geometrical archetypes mentioned in the *Philebus.* The quest for absolute beauty, liberated of earthly shape, as defined in his *Symposium,* has not been forgotten in spite of all empirical, physiological, or behavioristic explanations of esthetic feeling.

The contemplation of beauty can indeed, by the action of the higher Eros, the urge to elevate one's self to the highest level of beautiful spiritual achievement, bring us a shining vision of essential, transcendent beauty. This idea has, after Plotinus and St. Thomas, found new expressions in modern times. As Stephen C. Tornay writes in his "Symbolistic Theory of Aesthetic Experience" (published in Vols. 19 and 20 of the *Proceedings of the Utah Academy of Sciences, Arts, and Letters*): "Aesthetic experience is not a draught from the waters of Lethe, the grand way to forget, as Schopenhauer thought, but a progressive adventure toward self-fulfillment on the wings of symbolic self-anticipation."

But in this adventure the study of the theory of forms, even of geometrical forms, plays its modest part, and this special exploration, if made at all, has to be made in the thorough manner of which Plato, too, showed us the methods and the purpose.

A great French poet, the late Paul Valéry, has perceived the essence of this mathematical criterion of the beautiful in classical Western art in a sentence placed in the mouth of a Greek architect: "Where passing men see only an elegant little building . . . I have inserted the memory of a shining day of my life. O sweet metamorphosis! This delicate temple . . . is the mathematical image of a daughter of Corinth. . . . It reproduces faithfully her particular proportions."

VI

FRANCISCAN PHILOSOPHY AND GOTHIC ART

ROBERT GRINNELL

IF there is any one characteristic of medieval art that distinguishes it most clearly from that of other periods and styles, it is the extraordinary consistency with which medieval artists expressed the coordination of visible signs to intellectual values. Esthetic forms embodied in themselves—in their subject matter as well as in their principles of composition, and even in certain types of materials out of which they were constructed—principles of a metaphysical sort that made of the work of art a universe in miniature. The very word "art" had connotations far broader than in our understanding of the term, linked as it was to the ancient Greek notion of God as a "maker," a creator that produced a universe or *cosmos,* an exquisite balance of form, structure, energy, and value. In its widest sense the word "art" signified the whole realm of man's creative effort, the sum of the principles by means of which predictable results could be achieved. It included the whole scope of man's attempt to impress upon a world of receptive possibilities the mark of his contributive purposes and the pattern of his moral values. And because he was considered to be incapable of acting without at the same time fulfilling the purposes of God, it seemed reasonable to find the principles of all art in theology, and to bring to art a final rationale rooted in ethical values and metaphysics.

So it was that each of man's activities reflected, in medieval eyes, the formalizing activity of God. Perfections stemming from God were immanent in the world of sensory experience. Man's own activity in this world was to actualize the moral values which it thus presented to his choice, and to achieve thereby his own moral maturation. And because of the profound conviction that this world of esthetic experience contained in a luminous and sacramental plenitude the intelligible power of God and the materials of their own redemption, men not only lavished great care on the subjects of their artistic production, which were largely drawn from God's revealed word, but they perceived in their own activities, in the psychology by which things were known and could be said to *mean,* and in the materials of which they were composed, vestiges of a divinity that subsumed and supported the entire process. Consequently, although an artist presented pictorial images of redemption or of man's moral history, and so might be regarded as dealing, in a limited sense, with symbols, in a more general sense his work was symbolic, in that his estimation of its very being and of the processes of its production and apprehension was based on an awareness of what might be called metaphysical symbolism—each moment of which was rooted in God's inner life, and of which its very existence spoke.

It has long been recognized that medieval art, and indeed much of medieval life generally, was profoundly symbolic in intent. Emile Mâle, in his classic works on the iconography of religious art in France, showed most clearly the directive ideas of the subjects carved and painted on medieval churches. But though major themes of decoration and the complex symbolism in which these themes were expressed formed the main subject matter of his investigation, the intimate interaction between ideas and major characteristics of organizations of space and form suggests that medieval art was symbolic in a more fundamental way than one might have at first supposed. The structures of space and form in medieval art seem to react most sensitively to the general character of the ideas and relations of ideas that they are designed to express. And even though one might not be inclined to assert a causal relation between a given philosophical theory and a specific style in art, they do seem to be related in a more fundamental way, as parallel expressions of an underlying set of structural beliefs that in part defines a culture. Thus, in the following discussion, only one system of philosophical speculation will be used to provide a contemporary theory of meaning for Gothic art of the later thirteenth century—the Franciscan philosophy of St. Bonaventure. But the questions he discussed and the interpretations he advanced are intimately related to general problems in medieval philosophy, so that in spite of the distinctive coloring which makes Bonaventure's philosophy his own, by implication the traditional speculation of Augustinian Platonism as well as the sharp modifications initiated by Aristotelian influences in the twelfth century are present in his thought; nor is our general thesis of the parallelism of esthetic and rational modes of expression contradicted by points at issue between two systems. Problems of knowledge, fact, value, and cosmology are ones which unite philosophers even in their disagreement. A philosopher's solutions to these problems are metaphors on a common set of beliefs—as metaphorical in their expression of his relation to the primary convictions of his intellectual environment as artistic forms are metaphorical in theirs, in uniting the individual artist's experience to the stylistic first principles in his esthetic world.

This metaphorical character of expression leads one to believe that there may be a double layer of significance in an understanding of medieval art and its symbolic value. The first layer, that of literary and pictorial symbolism, with which Emile Mâle dealt in so masterly a fashion, need not concern us here. But the second layer reveals several dimensions. In the first place, the way medieval artists used their materials, their notion of the characteristics of space, the relation of space and form, the relation between decoration and architectural structure, or the relation of voids and solids in structure are, if not the appearances of ideas, at least indications of a habit of thinking. Or a dominant technique, whether architecture, sculpture, or painting, which not only goes far toward defining a style but also exerts a profound influence on the way ideas are visualized, will give us insight into the meanings of plastic form. This dimension of meaning may properly be called the esthetic dimension.

A second dimension of meaning emerges when we examine the structure of ideas of which plastic forms are modes of expression. This may be called the semantic or ideal dimension of meaning. What did a person mean, in the thirteenth century, by matter, space, and form? Since an artist felt that he was dealing with real things, what were the general characteristics he ascribed to them?

A third dimension of meaning appears if we ask how the artist envisaged his own creative activity. What did he hope to say, not merely in terms of subject matter but also in the very method and materials of a work of art? What were, for him, the common and validating grounds of communication? For a spectator presumably participates more actively in a sculptor's thought than a statue does, even though a statue may represent an adequate vehicle for what an artist has to say. How was this participation conceived? This third dimension we may term the moral or operational dimension.

A final dimension of meaning emerges if one asks what an educated man in the Middle Ages thought ideas as such were. What were their relations to particular objects, what was their status, and how did they affect mind and each other? And if ideas were considered to reveal truth, what was truth and its relation to facts and to values? In short, what was the meaning of meaning, and in what sense was meaning real? This dimension of meaning we may term the intuitional dimension.

These dimensions of meaning have not been arbitrarily chosen. They are the modern terms for the fourfold method of interpretation by which, in the thirteenth century, men tried to organize all information. Thus, the esthetic dimension is equivalent to the literal or factual character of a thing. It refers to things as in some sense physical facts and as data in sensation. Our ideal or semantic dimension is comparable to the allegorical level of meaning—the words or ideas equivalent to things. The operational dimension the medieval philosopher termed the tropological level of meaning—a thing considered as a constituent in purposive action or as relevant to moral value. And the intuitional dimension suggests what was called the anagogic or mystical meaning of a thing—a thing as given simultaneously with the infinite coherent relations of its total context—in short, as an expression of Truth or God. Emile Mâle has shown that these dimensions of meaning, which were the basis for the organization of Vincent of Beauvais' great encyclopedia, the *Speculum Majus,* also govern the relationships of the details in medieval iconography, in which all the wisdom of mankind, sacred and profane, finds its appropriate place and pictorial representation.

Certain salient characteristics of space, form, and structure in medieval art will serve as an introduction to the esthetic dimension of meaning. For example, the Romanesque style is defined primarily by architecture as a technique. As architecture, it is a style based on an equation between masses of masonry and a continuous thrust along the springing of the vaults. Sculpture and painting are conceived of in architectural terms. Figures are distorted and contorted to fit the space that architecture makes available for them, and their contours underline the architectural tensions of the points where they are placed. The space in which sculpture appears seems to press relentlessly on the planes of the figures, flattening the modeling, attenuating proportions, weaving a figure sometimes only distantly reminiscent of its natural prototype into a restless geometry of line and plane surface. And the iconography of the

Romanesque style reflects this same sense of the omnipotent power of a divine environment that wrests a natural being into quite ideal abstractions. The apocalyptic power of God, as the dominant theme of the great Romanesque tympana, finds a counterpart in the transcendental idealism of Erigena, where things are simply images of ideas formed eternally in the divine mind, borne in the power that, like space, presses upon them from all sides.

Each of these aspects of the Romanesque style undergoes radical modification in Gothic art. Structurally, Gothic architecture can be defined as a coherent and finely balanced system of thrusts and forces concentrated in ribs and flying buttresses. It is a style conceived in terms of periodic moments of tension, achieving dramatic effects by elegant structural means in which each rib, each course of stone, is dynamically related to the whole structure and each course becomes a slender armature for lines of force.

These stylistic principles in Gothic architecture permit of a far more complicated relation of interior spatial volumes than was the case in the Romanesque style, so that when the differences in physical proportions of a Romanesque and Gothic building are left out of account, the architectural elements of a later thirteenth-century cathedral seem rather sutures in space than the limits of mass. For the first time in architecture the main element in the building is the enclosed space and the complications of its limits and volumes, rather than the supporting solids.

This sense of the integral and fluid character of space is also seen in the tendency toward increased fenestration. The logic of Gothic structure is such that the large areas of wall surface between the buttresses no longer perform a supporting function in the building, and are consequently promptly turned into windows. For the structural murality and limiting space of the Romanesque style the Gothic builders substituted the psychological or esthetic murality of the great stained glass tracery window and a plastic space and light that seem to ebb and flow through the harp-string supporting elements of the building like currents of water through the rigging of a sunken vessel.

This tendency of mass and form to evaporate into a receptive space in a complicated and sinuous interplay of lights and darks and voids and solids governs also the decorative canons of the Gothic style. For Gothic decoration is no longer defined by architecture. Rather, sculpture emerges as the dominant technique. In building it is a style of sculptural architecture in which space is modeled by structural forms and sharp lines are obliterated by crockets. The structure of the windows reflects this same sculptural tendency, resulting in a vibrant play of mullions and traceries and fractured light that elaborates decoratively the structural principles of the ribbed vaults and flying buttresses. Architectural elements are now conceived of in decorative terms, not only structurally in the elaboration of fan vaulting but also in other techniques, as, for example, in the painted pinnacles and buttresses framing figures in windows and illuminated manuscripts. Perhaps the most dramatic example of the evolution from architectural to sculptural dominance is seen in the development from the statue columns of the Royal Portal of Chartres to the smiling angels of Reims or the great Teaching Christ on the South Portal at Chartres. This evolution is the evolution of the free-standing statue, begun in slender figures hardly more than incised on the affixed columns of the portal, ending in full rounded figures whose pedestals and decorative architectural canopies alone attest the architectural method of thinking that gave them birth. Structure has become a frame for particular things and no longer defines, as previously, their particular characters.

It is clear that concepts of space, structure, and form have undergone profound change. Space is no longer a compressing limit but rather a vast area of receptive potentiality into which form proliferates freely, actualizing the esthetic possibilities of space in terms of patterns of lights and darks in a manner quite as calculated in purpose as was the treatment of solid surfaces. Likewise, in regard to decoration, the elegant structural equations of Gothic architecture framed naturalistically proportioned figures—figures that in the thirteenth century still retain something of the monumental generalization architecture imposed on their ancestors of the previous century, but which point, in their dramatic postures, smiling faces, and sinuous axes, to the variations of psychological types seen in Renaissance portraits. To a certain extent decoration has become descriptive of natural forms, even though these forms are happily related in mood to the monument on which they appear. They reflect a dual influence in thinking—an empirical and descriptive and nominalistic tendency still perfectly accommodated by a traditional habit of thinking that saw things in terms of ideas and universals and deductive relationships. Thus, the facility with which things conceived of naturally and in the integrity of their individual being came to be incorporated into medieval thought is matched by the felicity with which natural forms were organized but unmodified by the structural logic of thirteenth-century architecture.

The natural integrity of things and their organic relatedness is seen in the relation a church had to its physical environment. Here again space has a relational function, binding esthetic facts to moral significances. Not only are the flowers, vines, and birds of the *pays* reproduced in the sculptures and paintings of the cathedral, along with a meticulous attention to the *métiers* and seasonal pursuits of the inhabitants, but also the very spatial directions in which the portals face have their appropriate subjects and meanings. The church is usually oriented with its main axis toward the east, so that the rays of the morning sun illuminate the windows of the sanctuary. The north portal and northern windows are usually reserved for scenes from the Old Testament and lives of the Prophets, the south for the New Testament and the ministry of Christ, while the western façade, illuminated by the last rays of the setting sun, presents the gloomy climax of the Last Judgment, the Wheel of Fortune, the Crucifixion, and the works and days of mankind.

Here, as in other regards, space acquired meaning and was defined (as space generally was in medieval thought) by light, and what one might call the moral quality of the light that struck a given surface. Thus, the cold light of the north was the esthetic equivalent for a moral idea of life before the revelation of Christ, that of the east signified the emergence of a new life and a new hope, and that of the west the final reckoning of all activity.

The esthetic quality of these various types of light is apparent enough in the interiors of the great cathedrals and the sensitive responses that the windows make to the quality of illumination that transfigures them. It must have been equally apparent on the exteriors when the sculptures were painted and the building glittered with the high lights of gold leaf.

Painting, which was to become the dominant technique of later years as interest in description, narration, and the historical increased, clearly reflects this tendency. Painting may simply try to represent light or it may try to incorporate light. In Gothic painting it is the second type that predominates. The stained glass window is, of course, the most dramatic example of this attempt. But by the use of gold in backgrounds and as a base for translucent color the same sparkle of light *in* a painting is achieved as Byzantine mosaicists achieved by leafing the bottoms of their bits of glass with gold or silver. And in Giotto's "Death of St. Francis" in the Santa Croce of Florence the nimbus surrounding the saint's head is not only carved on the surface of an otherwise flat painting but is also gilded, so that a jewellike radiance and sparkle come from the surface of the wall. It thus represents an experiment in conceiving of space and light from the standpoint of painting, but also it represents a happy union of the sculptural and architectural techniques of his immediate tradition.

Such an attitude toward art, an attitude seeking to include light as a constituent within things rather than regarding it as an external and reflected phenomenon, suggests an attitude toward the world in general. In some sense, the world and the things of the world seemed luminous because of an internal principle that made each thing something real and meaningful. The naturalistic sculpture suggests a world of natural forms. The internal luminosity of medieval decoration suggests a picture of this world of natural forms as likewise luminous, radiating moral and ideal as well as esthetic meanings. Together they form elements in a point of view that could see and love nature without fear of prejudice to moral value— a world unreconstructed by an austere metaphysic but susceptible to organization—a world in which each thing *is* itself but even while thus honestly existing expressing in its existence values that link it to the moral goals of man.

The personality that seems to have typified and inspired this picture of the world suggested by the spacious naturalism and luminous character of Gothic art is St. Francis. For St. Francis the world seems to have been in a vital sense a reliquary directly illuminated by God, whose presence transfigured it into a prayer of desire and thanksgiving. In Francis, the rather stereotyped symbolism of the twelfth century was transmuted into a vehicle of poetic metaphor and lyrical creativity. The world became, for him, a vast collection of symbols for perfection, mirroring the moving power of God with Whom men lived in a more or less conscious and intimate communion. St. Francis' sermons to the birds and the sun, his love for a world that bore God, in one of his aspects, in its bosom, seemed to Francis' followers to have turned his life into an ecstatic prayer of peace and joy, a journey of the mind to a God who was never very distant. For St. Francis, prayer was in some sense expressed in every action and event in the world. It was the passionate voice of desire, the irresistible force of life and God himself, the cry for perfection that imperfect beings raised by the very fact of their existence to the giver of all things and all existence.

The character of Franciscan philosophy as it was defined by St. Bonaventure, a half century later, was fundamentally an attempt to work out the general principles which such a life seemed to express and the spiritual radiance with which it shone. Consequently, what started as an esthetic appreciation and pious admiration for the holy life of an *illuminatus* of God ended in a philosophy that seemed adequate to deal with all reality and all experience.

St. Bonaventure's interpretation of St. Francis' life and the character of St. Francis' world will serve to open to us the semantic dimension of Gothic art. Gothic art, as we have seen, presents an esthetic interpretation of what an artist considered the world and its structural relationships and values to be. But lying behind this esthetic interpretation were certain theoretical meanings for matter, form, space, and light which, though perhaps not explicitly avowed, were certainly as much presupposed by the artist as by the "illuminated" temperaments of St. Francis and his companions.

Perhaps as clear an indication as any of the intimate relationship between mystical, esthetic, and philosophical types of expression is found in St. Bonaventure's definition of matter. Matter he defines as a confusion of desires, rather than as a confusion of elements. As such, as a process rather than as some existent thing, as an inner conatus and drive toward self-realization and perfection that in part defines a being, matter becomes a continuous and pervasive element involved in the whole dynamics and structure of the created universe. Reflecting, as this definition does, the Franciscan attitude toward prayer as a cry wrung from the very imperfections of all beings apart from God, matter becomes like prayer in human experience, a mother and origin of all upward action. Matter, defined by Aristotle as a tendency toward motion and by Plotinus as a process rather than an essence, takes on for Franciscan philosophers an entirely new meaning as a constituent in the universe and in human experience. It becomes, as a capacity for change, as desire, and in some sense analogous to prayer, a binding relation between existence itself and the moral goal and completion of existence that was God. And because experience was esthetic in so far as the material principle was present in it, all knowledge was in some degree esthetic and colored by the moral character of matter's aspiration. From this standpoint each particular detail of the world, each sculptured detail on the façade of a church was, as far as its material element was concerned, a syllable in the recorded time of aspiration. And time, change, and process were measured by goals achieved and the fruition of desire in the formal reality of accomplishment. The reality of matter was measured by the character of the form it gained; the meaning of matter as a constituent in an esthetic fact was measured by the formal degree of the intelligence in which it found itself absorbed and its moral levels evaluated. In things, matter spoke as the raw material of sensation. In works of art, it mirrored explicitly the higher qualities of moral significance that were implicit in matter and reflected in it as a fact.

The relation between matter and form was an intimate one. Considered concretely, matter could exist only in conjunction with some form, and form could exist only in conjunction with matter. In this combination matter represented a condition of change in the sense that, possessing one form, it was still capable of a higher degree of organization that would enable it to possess another. Thus matter and form at one level of being became the constituent matter for a higher form. Matter, as "desiring" change, and form as the attractive cause "prompting" change, evinced a certain reciprocity of activity, a tendency to vaporize into each other. Forms, instead of limiting possibilities, as is the case in St. Thomas' view, on the contrary represented the goal and measure of matter's achievement as an element in a thing, and the higher goals to which it might aspire.

It is apparent that there was a radical imperfection and insufficiency in both matter and form, from the standpoint of Franciscan philosophy. Apart from matter, form had only an ideal existence. And matter, abstractly considered, was mere brute potentiality, devoid of any existence whatsoever. Consequently, at the moment of creation some principle was necessary as the polar coordinate of matter to act as a catalyst for its brooding potentialities. This principle philosophers in the Augustinian tradition identified as light. Light was the first application of divine power, and on the first day of creation produced space, on the one hand, and spiritual being, on the other. It was not physical in any other sense than that there was thought to be an element of contingency present in it as in all beings other than God. And because of its primitive position in the creative process, it permeated to the core of all spatially extended things, and in an analogous way to the core of spiritual essences in the realm of spiritual matter, from space through the whole complex of mineral, vegetable, and animal substances, to the intelligence itself. Light was an indwelling and constituting energy. The light of sensory vision was simply one wave length in the whole continuous spectrum of analogies relating the universe to God that light itself included as the primary imitation of God's unity and the immediate vehicle of his power.

This metaphysical light represented the first emanation and the first imitation of God. It was rooted in the nature of the Son of God, the *Logos* or Light of *John*. In its diffusive and generative character it reflected the productive aspect of substance. In its ability to define limits it reflected the intelligible attribute of substance. In its warmth and fructifying character it reflected the valuational character of substance. Radiated immediately from God into the silent potentialities of matter, it illuminated and mirrored God's infinity against the infinite passivity of matter, refracting and in a sense generating out of itself and matter the infinite number of finite things of creation—the infinite complexities and degrees of organization in things physical and spiritual that in one aspect are mirrors of God's being and in another aspect are vehicles of his expression. Light was regarded as centrifugal, in the diffusion of itself to the very limits of possible being. But its effects were centripetal in that, with the initial character of being which light conferred on matter, it communicated also to the inmost structure of things the images of the other two attributes of substance—intelligibility and value. In so doing, with its bestowal of being it awakened desire in the universe—desire of things to participate in truth and desire to participate in value.

If we were to try to imagine the relational character of this indwelling light in things, we might imagine a lamp surrounded by mirrors. The mirrors themselves would correspond to matter. The mirrors would exist in proportion as the light emitted from the lamp actualized their reflective capacity. And the images in the mirrors would represent precisely the degree to which the mirrors would have been realized, while the lamp would represent in a sense the archetype and goal of the mirrors' aspiration. In so far as an image was present in the mirror, the mirror could be said to express the lamp. And in turn, the lamp might be regarded as expressing itself through the mirrored images, through the irradiation of its own light, or the effective aspect of that essence which makes it what it is.

The problem now would be to specify the character of those reflected and expressive images. Each of the images is, from the standpoint of the light upon which it depends, a connotation of the lamp—an image generated against the plastic and reflective capacity of the mirror. Yet, in another sense, each of the infinity of images so radiated represents an individual and unique expression, and has a certain inner integrity of its own, which is contributed precisely by that radiant light. Each image is unique in the sense that each is different; each reflects the lamp from its own point of view. No one image could ever be an instance of another, nor an instance of the lamp, since no one of the images ever gives the lamp in its own completeness. At best, the images are interchangeable only in terms of the light that is equally present to them. An adequate reflection or expression of the lamp would require the simultaneous presence of the whole infinity of radiated images—although even so an impassable gulf separates them from *being* the lamp simply because they are dependent upon it for their own existence. Yet the very existence of the lamp entails the existence of the images, and they are necessarily involved in it.

Now, if we substitute God for the lamp, and the world of natural things for the images in our analogy, we can gain some insight into the nature of creation and its relation to the Creator as the Franciscans viewed it.

God, for St. Bonaventure, was a *Deus exprimens,* matching the reflecting universe or *Deus expressus* in which men find themselves. The character of this expression was considered to take place as follows. The essence of God is pure intelligence and pure intelligibility. But since his essence is to know, and the only object of his knowledge is himself, it follows that from this act of knowledge is generated an image that is a perfect and unique similitude of God's infinity. Since God's character is eternal, so likewise the resemblance is eternal, deriving its total content from God as pure intelligence and pure intelligibility. Being an adequate similitude of God, this image *is* God—an eternal attribute or expression of substance. This similitude is the Son, generically related to the Father, and named in Christian theology the Light or Logos of the divine substance. Within the generation of this similitude are contained all of the possible imitations of God—the totality of finite beings, as connotations of the divine Logos. The Word is, as Bonaventure calls it, the "art" of God, the metaphysical support for the infinity of finite expressions of substance in creation.

Now God's expression, viewed from his own standpoint, is an eternal event contained within himself and a sort of interior conversation. But this conversation is accompanied by external signs or images as vehicles of diffusion and communication, much as we express our thoughts by means of spoken words. These signs, like spoken words, are the connotations of an idea, radiated like light or magnetic lines of force from the introspective intensity of God. Thus, God's internal life is the life of *Creator creans;* his external expression or his "works of art" is the life of *natura naturata.* These creations are the infinite number of meanings radiated from God as Truth, being true meanings in so far as God expresses himself through them. Viewed as expressions, things are adequate vehicles of God's meaning to the extent that each is understood as a mode of substance implying the totality of expressions flowing from God.

The individual things of the universe are related to God as the images were to the lamp. Each is a unique reflection of God's being and mirrors God from its own point of view. Yet each thing in some sense expresses God because of the radiant energy that constitutes it. Each thing, as each image, has an internal structure that links it to a specific aspect of God and makes the object what it is. These links, which bind an expression to God, are universals. But they are not the abstract universals of the logician—rather they are concrete or *radical* universals, grounded in a certain reciprocity of capacities, or, in the case of our analogy, the reciprocal capacities of each mirror and the reflected lamp, and carrying to each image precisely the ability not only to reflect or imitate but to express.

Each of these images is a relational meaning, a proper name, joined to its exemplar by a radical universal. A meaning is a dynamic relation between a model and one of its radiated images—a radiation made possible physically through the instrumentality of physical light and its sensory analogue, and intellectually through the irradiation of that divine light to which sensory and physical light are related as images to archetype. The truth of an object, therefore, is the totality of its radiated meanings, and the trueness or validity of any one meaning depends upon and is derived from the coherence of the whole.

This relational theory of meaning and truth holds at every level of being. Sensory images are individual radiations from an individual object. Again, an individual object (as, for example, an individual man) is a connotative resemblance radiated from a divine idea in God. But the divine ideas themselves, the archetypes from which the infinite multiplicity of objects flow, are structural and internal relations, resemblances or connotations attending the eternal generation of the Son by the Father, the Logos who was at once Word and Light. The knowledge men have of things and the intelligible aspect of things was considered to be borne on the waves of an illumination stemming from the interior life of God. Down to the tiniest grain of sand, each individual thing finds its integral reality as one of the infinity of connotations of God's life, and in the resemblance which, after its manner, each thing bears to it. The coherence of created things and the fusion of their constituent matter and form into real beings lie in their analogical relationship to divine life and the interior light that constitutes it.

Consequently, it is clear that things *are,* to the extent that they imitate God. But this imitation has a certain active sense, active in the sense that an imitation is a dynamic mode through which substance expresses itself, and the total reality that a thing may claim is the infused reality that the divine act of expression may bring to it. This means that, from the standpoint of creation, or God's work of art, the fundamental constituent in its definition must be its operational dimension. Though in a partial sense the universe is a mirror of God, in another sense the universe entertains God, in one of his aspects, within itself. The degree to which the universe can be said to *mean,* therefore, must be measured by the degree to which it expresses and the level of expression conveyed.

Franciscan philosophers interpreted the levels of imitation of God in the following way. The universe in one sense is a "shadow" of God in that it does not specify any other form of existence than the mere brute fact of being. At a higher level, the universe may be termed a "vestige" of God if there is detected in it some predominant quality referring to God as formal, efficient, or final cause. Again, at a still higher level of adequacy, certain constituents in the universe may be called "images" of God to the extent that they confess God as their object as well as their cause. Where the shadow and vestige were silent witnesses of God's being, the image is an active and explicit level expressing God's goodness. And finally, to the extent that an image achieves a qualitative identity with its model it becomes a "similitude" of God, suffused with God's perfections.

We can suggest this more clearly if we return to our analogy of the lamp and mirrors. The mere undifferentiated luminosity of the mirror can be regarded as equivalent to a shadow of God, or mere brute existence. The form of the image that differentiates the surface of the mirror can be regarded as equivalent to a vestige of

God. But if we could imagine in some way certain of those reflections as endowed with a capacity to speak and to point toward the
lamp that makes them what they are, they could be regarded as
equivalents to images of God. And if from among those speaking
images certain ones were able to move, and to place themselves
face to face with the origin of their light, and to reflect that light
with an intensity equal in quality to the lamp's, they could be regarded as being equivalent to similitudes of God.

The explicit recognition of the operational or moral dimension of
meaning by Franciscan philosophers appears in this notion of man
as an expressive image of God. As we have seen, they regarded
created being as a continuous and pervasive esthetic element mirroring God, and as a receptive potentiality against which he expressed himself. This continuous and indeterminate element was
modified by forms reciprocally related to this material or esthetic
principle, so that in so far as an object was at all, it was in a fundamental sense both esthetic and formal. Each object was related to
God by a radical universal—by a relation without instances. And,
from the standpoint of creation as a whole, each of these relations
was real, each implied all others, and each entered into certain stable
collections of relations, from which facts, it was thought, were
constructed. These facts and relations were analogically related to
each other and to God. And the actualizing principle that matched
the continuity and passivity of matter was a continuous, dynamic,
and transcendent principle of light. But from God's standpoint no
created thing could be really related to him. Consequently, though
within the limits of creation, relations were real, and matter's continuity was a continuity of radical possibility, from God's standpoint all relations were ideal—ideal analogies contained within
himself. Matter assumed its esthetic character—its conative character of indeterminate desire—precisely because its being was rooted
in the mental life of God and the transcendent character of the light
that actualized it. The meaning of objects lay in the ideal origin of
their formal constituents and the luminous principle that supported
their factual existence as vestiges of God.

As far as man was concerned, relations and facts in his environment were viewed from without, as entities suggesting in some
sense autonomous reality. Yet as far as his own introspected experience was concerned, man was considered to discover one relation
that could be viewed from within, as it were—that is, himself as
a dynamic mode of being referring to a pole that was transcendent

and, as far as knowledge was concerned, ideal. For the reality of the soul was not known, directly, but rather, *felt*. Relatedness to God was experienced initially as pervasive desire, in which environmental facts were reconverted into their ideal constituents and re-expressed as the material components in the soul's own search for itself and its happiness. Thus, the esthetic dimension of things became active, in the soul, through their absorption into the conscious desires of its own esthetic life, and in its own distinctively expressive nature. In short, the soul imitated God in its moral life, by transfiguring the real essences and relations of its environment into ideal connotations elicited from its own esthetic possibilities.

This means that though relations were real, and the structure of the universe in relation to the soul could be expressed in terms of analogies, yet from the soul's own point of view, in its effort to find its own validity as a fact in creation, they became truncated and inadequate. The soul knew itself, according to this view, not directly but in terms of its activities. These activities might be presumed to be analogically related to an expressive substance, as the rest of the universe was, morally, to the soul. But this could not be known, directly, nor in terms of what could strictly be called knowledge. It could only be intimated, symbolically expressed, and all other knowledge became involved in and colored by the soul's symbolic perception of itself, because of the immanent yet transcendent character of its relation to God. Thus, the images of things entered the lower limits of consciousness as the stuff of desire; but in its higher reaches they became the symbols for the objects of prayer, shadowing forth the city of God wherein the soul would find its own habitation and name.

It followed that, from the standpoint of Franciscan philosophy, man's life was in a fundamental sense the creation of a work of art, and that, from the material possibilities thus presented by the esthetically given facts of the world, a man's soul expressed its own goals and its own desires. In the fact of their expression and re-interpretation of nature, men were images of God's own expressive life. In the quality of their expressions, and in the goals so intimated, they became similitudes of divine substance. Life represented a continuous process of discovery of God's meanings implicit in the world and actualized explicitly in the soul. It was, in its entirety, a search for the goals of prayer amid the elements of desire, and a journey of the mind to God.

The journey begins in the perception of material forms bathed in visible light. The conclusion of the first stage occurs in the composite image of the outer world mirrored in the light of mind. The second stage begins in the rational abstraction of ideas and forms from the images contained in memory, and is completed in the intellectual illumination revealing underlying transcendentals like Being and Truth. The third stage begins in the perception of valuational transcendentals like Good, revealed in moral illumination, and reaches its fruition in the *apex mentis* where the unity of God is presented in divine illumination. Each stage represents the explication of meanings implicit in creation as a whole. Each stage represents the absorption of lower forms of truth as the material element in a higher form of being. The first half of each stage represents the esthetic factor in the soul's expression, the material element in its self-creation and search for God. It ranges from desire, or God as mirrored in things, at its lowest level, to prayer, or God as mirrored in the soul, at its highest level. The second half of each stage represents the degree of reality that a soul achieves, ranging from the transfiguration of the universe by the perception of God as expressing himself through it, to the transfiguration of the soul itself, in its higher reaches, by the expression of God within it. Experience is rooted in these three levels of transformation, which the soul works in the world because of its expressive character— the re-expression of nature, the expression of itself, and the expression of itself in God.

Medieval art, in its use of space, in the relation of space and form, in the techniques by which space and form were related, in the natural proportions of figures and their relation to the structural logic of architecture, reflects those characteristics of thought which we have described. Space as the first actualization of matter's possibility and the first and muted reality of its desire represents the basis of both artistic expression and philosophical cosmology. Light represented, for both types of expression, the principle by which that initial reality was achieved and the means for the multiple modifications it assumed. Form's tendency to evaporate into luminous space, a characteristic of later thirteenth-century architecture, finds its counterpart in the philosophical concept of form as reciprocally related to matter, as fused in its pervasive continuity of desire.

In regard to the relational logic of structure: sculpture as a technique, as a mid-point between what one might call the a priori logic of architecture and the empirical technique of painting, finds its counterpart in philosophy. The respect for the natural individual form in art finds its philosophical justification in the radically empirical and esthetic character of experience as the Franciscans viewed it. This empirical tendency, nascent already in the Franciscan school of painters and lyricists, is likewise present in the philosophical position of the school—in the empiricism of Roger Bacon and the multiple-value logic of William of Ockham. On the other hand, the sense of intrinsic relatedness that the structural logic of architecture still expresses is matched in philosophy by the concept of the radical universal and by the relational logic of Bonaventure. Thus the implication of meaning-relations in a coherence theory of truth is reflected by the implication of esthetically given facts, in Gothic decoration, in the coherence logic of Gothic architecture.

In regard to light as the initial constituent in existence, as involved in the essences of things, we have the theoretical equivalent for the luminous character of Gothic art. Light, as the hypostasis upon which the modifications of artistic form were based, serves also as the hypostasis upon which the philosophical theory of creation and experience was based. Because light was a common substrate between material form and esthetic experience, and pervaded, along with matter, the whole continuity of creation, it represented the link between the existence of things and their presence in knowledge. Esthetic forms formed the beginning of knowledge in human experience. Light was the precipitating cause in this relation. Art forms represented the initial stage in moral knowledge in the sense that they were examples of the universe reconstructed by the expressive capacity of the soul and the soul's own moral goals. And the validity of artistic meanings, esthetic and moral, was grounded in the analogy they bore to the reality of things as radiated meanings stemming from God.

Finally, in regard to the process of artistic creation itself, we find the true roots for its validity in the notion of creation as the work of art of the divine substance, and man as an expressive image of God. The validity of his expression lay in the moral imperative of his nature and the analogical relation in which he stood to the Son or Art of God. As an artist, he expressed God from his own point of view, as did the mirrored images of the lamp, in our analogy. The materials he used were structurally related, by analogy, to principles involved in the very texture of the universe. But as reconstructed in terms of the artist's own inner knowledge and, one might say, by his own transformation growing out of that expressive activity, artistic forms occupied a fundamental position in the moral and creative life of other men. This was true simply because of the esthetic factor involved in all experience and knowledge. The quality of an artist's desire and the degree to which it achieved fruition in the transcendental esthetic of prayer were the proper gauge of the quality of his creation and his own quality as a man. But because his creations and his desire, and in an equal degree his prayers, were rooted in matter even while they referred to goals of a transcendent sort, it followed that they, like all strictly human experience, were defective. They were his prayers—"the source and origin of every upward progress that has God for goal," the first condition for the soul's activity, as Bonaventure says. But they were not the completion of those desires. They were testaments to their reality and symbolic references to a goal that escaped them at every point.

The inadequacy of all human expression, because of the pervasive influence of the esthetic component in nature and experience, and the transcendent nature of the goal to which it referred, brings us to the intuitional dimension of meaning. The existence of anything apart from substance, or of any truth apart from God, was considered logically inexplicable. The facts of existence and truth in some sense were clear enough. But the *why* of them completely eluded the soul's natural powers. Consequently, just as an esthetic and passive element was present at every level of the soul's expression, so belief was regarded as involved in every act of reason and faith in every act of moral judgment. They were evidences for God's existence, and of God's grace bridging the abyss separating him from his creation. They were the substance of the things prayer hoped for, which men perceived darkly as through a mirror. A mystical and miraculous factor, therefore, accompanied every conversion of spirit or inner transfiguration of essence into meaning by the soul. This miracle took place in a partial sense in every perception of truth that men expressed. But in the upper reaches of the soul's desire, as it sought most eagerly for God in his own nature, truth came as a miraculous infusion of grace, a vision of God that completely transfigured the soul and all that had entered it from below. It was thus that the soul became a similitude of God. Properly speaking, this final perception of truth was not an act of knowledge at all, because it was totally incommunicable. It could, like a revelation, only be symbolized and be experienced as a transforming miracle like Christ's transfiguration with Moses and Elias before the apostles.

It was at this point that symbolism became necessary, in art, as the transcendent completion of its moral meanings. A symbol, which refers to a reality beyond itself, and the meaning of which is in a sense an arbitrary fact, was an avowal of the miraculous and revelatory in all meanings. Symbolism was the recognition that while the factual existence of the universe was analogical in character, based on the radical universals uniting it to God, the why of the universe and the truth of its meanings were in the last analysis symbolic. God, Truth, and divine illumination were the conditions of knowledge, not the objects of knowledge.

In this final characteristic of experience as the Franciscan philosophers conceived it, we find what may properly be called the mystical and religious character of Gothic art—the fluid and elusive presence of light in a structure that is defined by it rather than contains it. Structure, in building, represents an analogy to the structure of the universe. But each floats, as it were, in the energy of divine power and the mystery of divine presence. A text to which St. Bonaventure often referred, and which seems to crystallize his philosophy, might also have served as the motto of the Gothic artist: "Every good gift and every perfect gift is from above, and cometh down from the Father of lights, with whom is no variableness, neither shadow of turning." (James 1:17.)

VII

PHILOSOPHIES AND ECONOMIC THEORIES IN MODERN OCCIDENTAL CULTURE

OVERTON H. TAYLOR

I. ANALYTICAL

1. *Introduction* Among human cultures, modern Western civilization has been distinguished chiefly by its achievements (1) in business enterprise and economic progress; (2) in natural science and technology—the development of the modern physical and biological sciences and the arts or techniques based upon them; and (3) among the social studies, in the science and art of economics. To other cultures, such as the ancient Western, the medieval Western, and native Oriental, must be credited outstanding achievements in a contrasting set of fields: the fine arts, religion, moral philosophy and codes, the ordering of life in stable and widely accepted patterns, refinement of manners in the upper classes, and the forms of philosophical and social thought associated more with art, ethics, and religion than with economics or any near approach to science in the modern sense. Now of course the esthetic, ethical, and religious interests generally predominant in those other cultures have been active also in the life and thought of the modern West; but here they have tended to be, too often, overshadowed by, and in confused conflict with, the stronger business, scientific-technical, and economic interests. It is with manifestations of this conflict, in the related histories of modern Western philosophical and economic thought, that I am concerned in the present essay.

In philosophy, this conflict has appeared in the clashes of philosophies of two general types, which I will call respectively visionary and prosaic. The visionary philosophies, either continuing the traditions of or akin to the great philosophies which originated in the ancient and medieval periods, have been such as Platonism, Thomism, the visionary side of the eighteenth century's natural order and human rights philosophy, German (Hegelian) Idealism, and, in one aspect, Marxism. These were bold elaborations of at once cosmic or historical and social-moral visions of a resplendent order in the universe and to be achieved in all human life, transcending man's empirical but, allegedly, not his rational knowledge.

In contrast with these, the prosaic philosophies have been those with such largely overlapping names as rational empiricism, naturalism, mechanism, utilitarianism, positivism, instrumentalism—the philosophies claiming special affinities with modern science and a careful, skeptical avoidance of exciting but nonscientific, transcendental, and moral-absolutist speculations. In our culture as a whole the predominance of devotion to business, science, technology, and the economic aspect of individual and social welfare has generally given the greater competitive advantage to the prosaic philosophies; for men tend to believe that the kind of knowledge they find relevant to their more avid pursuits exhausts reliable knowledge, and that what their keenest interests make them aware of alone makes up reality. But even in the modern West there have always been countless persons—chiefly among artists, devoutly religious people, and ethically sensitive and ardent social idealists—whose predominant interests have in the same way made visionary philosophies the more persuasive to them.

My subject, however, is not simply general philosophies of these two kinds considered in themselves, but their expressions and results in varieties of economic and social thought involving general presuppositions suggested by them. Hence, before going on to discuss the philosophies in this connection, I must speak of (1) the interconnection of the modern West's economic with its natural-scientific ardors and achievements; (2) the great prominence and development and the peculiar character this connection has given to the study of economics; and (3) how certain internal problems in the latter, and intrinsic connections of economic theories with social-moral philosophies, have brought not only prosaic but also visionary philosophic views into play in this field and into conflict within it.

2. *Business, Science, and Economic Science*   The vigorous pursuit of wealth in our culture not only has utilized but also has stimulated and supported the triumphant progress of the natural sciences. It is true that most leading scientists themselves have been chiefly motivated *not* by interest in the potentially profitable, technological applications of their discoveries but simply by love of work and discovery in "pure" science for its own sake; and I shall speak later of the philosophic significance of the experience of the scientist,

which I think may be described as an esthetic-intellectual enjoyment of the patterns of order in all parts of nature, which science progressively explores. But the immense development of science since the Renaissance has required also the widespread support arising from the prevalent desire and esteem for the kind of knowledge giving power to master nature and lift human life from poverty to ever-rising planes of wealth. Probably it has been this factor which has so largely channeled the pursuit of esthetic-intellectual enjoyment into exacting work in the natural sciences, where so much prosaic, logical, and factual investigation must be toiled through, in payment for the thrilling and potentially useful discoveries ultimately won. In any event, the prevalent enthusiasm in the pursuit of wealth has clearly stimulated the advance of science; and the latter in return, of course, through its effects in the sphere of technology, has made possible the phenomenal rise of economic productivity and living standards of all classes.

Now it is no wonder that a culture thus largely dominated by business and science has tended from the outset, in the sphere of the social studies, to isolate, emphasize, and develop most fully the study of economics. Just as naturally it has tended to make this study, as far as possible, a science emulating the methods and concepts of the triumphantly advancing natural sciences—and more especially, those of physics, the first-established and in many ways the most impressive science of them all. As the study of economics, then, has developed *in its main tradition,* it has been from the outset in the seventeenth century *a physics-emulating science of the pursuit of wealth* as one abstractly considered phase of social life. More precisely, the subject matter studied by this economic science has included (1) the conditions of the fullest success in the pursuit of wealth, in the situations and on the parts of the different individual actors in an economic society; (2) the quasi-mechanical "laws" of the social-economic processes *consequent and thus contingent upon* the regular, actual fulfillment of those conditions; and (3) the national, governmental policies required for the most effective furtherance and stabilization of *general* prosperity within each nation.

As thus delimited, the subject matter of this science has in fact proved amenable *in large measure* to successful investigation by a method and through concepts broadly similar to those of physics: the method of postulation, deduction, and empirical (in the case of economics mainly statistical) verification, and the use of "mechanistic" conceptual schemes or "models." In the case of economics the models are consciously much simplified envisagements of social-economic systems as quasi-mechanical systems, in which all the parts or individual actors are always gravitating to their best economic opportunities and interacting in predictable ways to the resultant situations and *attendant actions*. The economic science thus built up has advanced, not as triumphantly as the natural sciences but in the same accumulative way; and as the study of the conditions of maximal economic prosperity, it has naturally always attracted a wider public interest than any other social science.

My description of the character of this main-tradition economics has already suggested, however, one important respect in which it is unlike physics or any natural science: the peculiar fact that it combines inseparably a science and an art which mutually involve each other. Now this results from a dilemma which necessarily confronts any social science. In the case of a natural science and an art dependent on it (e.g., physics and engineering), the human practitioners and their practice of the art are *not* also included in the subject matter of the pure science itself; hence the latter is *not* obliged to take account of the potentialities of the art in framing its own descriptive propositions. But a social science inevitably is in the position of endeavoring simultaneously to develop knowledge which may be used to guide human actions and also to describe and explain the *actual* pattern of *the same* actions. In the main-tradition economics, the way of meeting this dilemma has been to include the theory of the art of economy among the fundamental assumptions of theory in the descriptive science; or in other words to assume—with the support of common knowledge of the character of business behavior—a natural tendency of all men in reacting to their economic situations and opportunities to act toward the wealth-maximizing goal of the economic art.

There has thus developed, through study of the requirements and consequences of effective practice of the economic art, a theory in the descriptive science of economic activities which gains increasing truth in so far as the progress and general use of this science and art reduces the gap between economically ideal and actual economic behavior. Too often dogmatic errors in economic theorizing have arisen from inadequate awareness of the implications of the peculiar, twofold nature of this type of theory; the gap just mentioned has been ignored or unduly minimized; empirical study of *actual human behavior* in business (as distinct from study of *the situations* of the actors and their economically best reactions thereto) has been neglected; and theory of a pattern of social-economic processes contingent upon universal fulfillment in fact of "ideal" assumptions, has been presented as literal description of a supposedly actual and strictly inevitable pattern. All this has involved not only neglect of an important type of empirical research which should accompany theoretical work but also a tendency to miscontrue economic theory as *just* like physical or mechanical theory. But these errors, however natural and common in the history of the main-tradition economics, have been not necessary consequences of its twofold nature as a mutually dependent science and art but failures to deal correctly with the problem.

Apart, however, from those errors and that underlying mutual dependence of the economic art and science, further problems arise from the abstractness of the purely economic subject matter and the fact that *it,* as one phase only of human life, is in concrete reality always involved with the whole. Neither as theory of an art nor as theory in a science—neither in its prescriptive nor in its descriptive aspect—can theory of the pursuit of wealth be as fully independent of other branches of social reflection and inquiry as many exponents of the main-tradition economics have imagined it to be. The economic art is neither in itself the whole art of life nor yet a special art which can be completely isolated; and the science which describes only those tendencies in individual and social life which have to do with adaptations of choices and activities to economic conditions and opportunities cannot by itself either fully or quite truly describe any actual or possible concrete activities. In each society economic life necessarily is framed within and affected by some noneconomic human and socio-cultural milieu, more or less specific to that society; and *in consequence* economic thought necessarily develops within and is affected by some wider context, or mental vision, pertaining to the rest of life and to the social order.

Despite those facts I think the main-tradition idea of a special science of the purely economic subject matter alone has fully vindicated itself long since, as most fruitful of real scientific achievements; though I shall speak later on of the contributions, and not only of the errors, of the anti-main-tradition "historical and institutional schools" of economists, who have drawn the seemingly obvious conclusion from the point I have just been emphasizing, and tried to broaden economics into forms of historical sociology. I am not yet ready, however, to discuss those efforts and the issues they have raised. Here I am concerned only with the fact that *all* economic theories have developed in wider intellectual contexts; and I think analysis of the nature of these contexts will also reveal the point of contact, so to speak, of all economic thought with conflicting views in general philosophy.

3. *Economic Theories, Ideologies, and Philosophies*   What, then, are the contexts of economic theories, and what are they about? I have so far only spoken vaguely of "the rest of life," and must now give meaning and precision to that phrase. The very assertion that all human life contains something which is noneconomic, or not included in the pursuit of wealth, may seem to come in question, if we think of wealth correctly, and in line with all recent main-tradition economic theory, as including not only material goods but all items satisfying any specific human wants or interests, and costing sacrifices of any alternative satisfactions obtainable only through alternative uses of the same "resources"—money, material goods, effort, time, or whatever. On this correct, inclusive view of the meaning of wealth it may seem that practice of economy includes all choosing, and thus everything in human life, and that nothing noneconomic is left to which the context of an economic theory can pertain. But the seeming is false. For besides all specific wants and goods, there also are in human life general desires, or ideals—desires expressed in, and producing efforts to realize, all-inclusive ideas of the good, imperative order, form, pattern, or structure of one's life as a whole and society as a whole.

The distinction I am making here, to put the matter in Aristotelian terms, is that between the "material" and the "formal" side of life. Not all wealth is material in the sense of consisting of solid, tangible things, but all is material in the different sense of consisting of *particular* items, making up in the widest sense the riches or richness of life. But life demands in addition to richness some attractive unifying pattern which will limit assertions of the otherwise indefinitely expansive and conflicting particular desires within each individual and within a society, thus assuring order in contrast with chaos and, beyond that, the type of order which is most desired. Thus economic life in any society goes on within some more or less restrictive form of order, having as its ideal expression the dominant ideology or philosophy of life in that society, and as its actual imperfect realization the institutions and generally observed mores of the society and its members. Moreover, whatever pattern of order in the scientific sense—a system of processes conforming, approximately, to predictive laws—emerges *in* the economic life, as such, of a society, is never the product of economic wants and conditions alone. It is always a joint product of those factors and the currently effective social-moral frame of order. Hence any *theory of* an economic order requires as its context a vision of the social-moral frame of order within which the adaptations of economic choices and activities to the specific wants and situations of the actors are envisaged as proceeding.

It is hardly surprising, then, that the contexts of economic theories —different systems of economic theory—generally have been ideologies—social-moral visions current in particular societies and epochs, and shared with other citizens by the economists concerned. Ideologies, to use another term, are the philosophies of life of societies through epochs, or of the dominant groups in them, or of insurgent social movements. Central in them are the general desires or ideals of their adherents; but they also include extensive bodies of beliefs supporting those desires. Among these are not only the beliefs commending realization of the envisioned "ways of life" as possible and imperative, but also overt or latent philosophical beliefs, representing either the order of nature or the past and destined future course of human history, as *necessitating* realization of the ideals in question. Now economists generally have been both citizens and students of the current economic life of the same societies. They have generally developed their economic theories in the contexts of the ideologies they have shared with other like-minded citizens, although often, in developing their personal variants of those ideologies, they have added important contributions. The results are compound systems of economic-scientific and social-philosophic thought.

Examples of two different types are (1) the nineteenth-century "classical" and the later "neoclassical" economic theories, in the context of the classical eighteenth- and nineteenth-century liberalism or liberal individualism and internationalism; and (2) Marxism in the nineteenth century—a special transformation and development of classical economic theory in the very different context of Marx's vision, as a socialist, of the history and destined salvation of mankind. In the former case, the ideology was already dominant, and its ideals were largely—though of course imperfectly—realized in the existing social order. Hence the economic theory consisted of analysis of those actualities and possibilities of the current economic life which were of interest to adherents of the ideology: analysis of the conditions of maximal satisfaction of all the economic interests sanctioned by the ideology, and of the pattern of processes in the *potential* economic order whose full realization was seen as contingent upon that of the ideal liberal social order. In the case of Marxism, on the other hand, the ideology was *not* anywhere dominant, nor were its ideals anywhere even partly realized in the existing social order; it stood everywhere in total opposition to the latter, and as purely a vision of a desired and predicted future "new order"; and the economic theory was chiefly analysis of the evils of current economic life under existing institutions, and a forecast of their intensification and resulting developments leading to attainment of the new order. But in *all* cases the "ideological contexts" of economic theories have affected, above all, *the fields of attention* or ranges of problems studied, and the angles of vision from which they were seen.

Is not the existence, however, of diverse economic theories tied up with rival, partisan ideologies serving as their contexts, a standing refutation of the scientific claims of economics? Not entirely by any means. The diverse biases infused into different economic theories by their ideological contexts have indeed made them all imperfectly scientific, at best; but these biases have generally *not* prevented them from attaining and including substantial scientific achievements. Facts—and economists do study facts—and logic enforce their own demands upon all conscientious, truth-seeking investigators; and few eminent economists, whatever their ideologies, have been seriously guilty of the *worst kind* of bias—distortion of evidence or reasoning in the scientific field and relating to the problems studied. What *has* infected the work of all—being inherent in the partial dependence of economic theories on their ideological contexts—is bias *in the different sense* of that direction of attention to some and not to other scientific problems, which arises from devotion to a set of social aims and pursuit of the knowledge relevant to the task of realizing them. But the effect of this has been only a production of economic theories which, while different, have all had much validity in their respective fields and been, in the main, not inconsistent with but complementary to one another.

There remains, however, a deeper, *philosophical* difficulty and source of conflict within and among varieties of economic and social thought, which reflects the general conflict in our culture between prosaic and visionary views in general philosophy. Economic-scientific thought as such shares with modern scientific thought in general a tendency to *seem* to involve exclusively prosaic, fundamental views of knowledge and reality and thus to seem irreconcilable with any visionary views whatever. But most ideologies, on the contrary, very clearly involve, or are at bottom, visionary philosophies—boldly imaginative, charged with faith and emotion, and, for their adherents, inspiring all life with a vision of the right, imperative order in all human affairs, and generally also of supporting features of the cosmic order or of the historical process. Hence the history of modern Western economic and social thought is full of instances of failures to achieve any full inner coherence in combinations of largely scientific economic theories with distinctly visionary ideologies; and also of attempts and failures in other quarters to establish satisfactory all-prosaic or all-visionary total systems.

Yet I do not believe that this dilemma is a final one or one that cannot be resolved. In philosophy and in all inquiries there are valid prosaic and other valid visionary insights; and despite the many failures of past efforts to achieve it, I think these *can* be combined in a both well-balanced and entirely coherent synthesis. In our culture the disbelief in this possibility is rooted chiefly in the conviction that modern natural science has exclusively prosaic foundations and lends no support to any, but discredits all, visionary views. Nevertheless I think despite the misleading special prominence of its prosaic side and the claims of prosaic philosophies to speak for it exclusively, natural science itself has a basic, visionary side.

At an early point in this essay I spoke of the scientists' esthetic-intellectual enjoyment of exploring patterns of order in nature; and I now make the further assertion that not only the enjoyment but also, in its primary stages, the process of discovery of those patterns of order has an esthetic-intellectual or visionary character. Before the clear-cut logical and empirical investigations which give science its prosaic aspect become possible, there must be hypotheses with implications to be elaborated and tested by those investigations; and hypotheses originate as imaginative and attractive visions, suggested by already existing knowledge *and* the scientist's *feeling for* the probable structural pattern of his subject matter. Moreover, while the vision is corrected in details in the later investigations, the *feeling* of its truth remains the indispensable basis of the knowledge that nature has an order or conforms to laws. Hume's discovery that this knowledge has no prosaic basis in definite sense perceptions or in logic should have made him skeptical not about the foundations of science but about the sufficiency of his own purely prosaic philosophy. Science involves the visionary reliance on feeling and imagination *as well as* the prosaic reliance on rigorous logic and exact observations. While in other fields we seem unable to achieve a coherent synthesis of our visionary and our prosaic insights, in its own field natural science embodies just such a coherent synthesis.

In social science, however, the task is more difficult, because here the patterns of order which must be first envisioned and later elaborated and confirmed in the realm of solid facts, are not, as in nature apart from human creations, simply existent in that realm; instead initially they are only subsistent as possibilities, realizable through human efforts. Their attractions must lead not only to the discovery of them, through feeling and imagination, as possibilities, but also to their approximate realization in actual social orders—man-made, though on a natural basis—before the study of them can be carried through in prosaic and thus fully scientific terms. And in fact, because all theories in a social science involve visions which *never* become *fully* realized and are always subjects of emotion-filled controversy, these theories never can become *fully* scientific by the natural science standard.

But it is time now to turn from purely general explanation of this situation as it affects economics to historic illustrations. I shall attempt a general sketch of much of the history of Western philosophical and economic thought, mainly in modern times but beginning with the ancient and medieval Plato-Aristotle-Aquinas tradition, mainly visionary throughout, which is both a seldom entirely discarded heritage and a contrasting background to the main varieties of modern Western thought.

II. HISTORICAL

1. *The Ancient-Medieval Background; Plato and Economics*
Both in the ancient and in the medieval European culture there was a degree of one-sidedness of the kind opposite to that which has been characteristic of modern culture. The dominant concerns were not economic and scientific-technical but esthetic, religious, and ethical. The primary stress was upon the formal, not the material side of life; not upon the pursuit of wealth to satisfy all specific wants more fully, but upon the pursuit of agreement in devotion to the right ideals, to assure well-ordered lives and societies. Hence development of science in the modern sense was neglected. As to

wealth, it was held to be unimportant; not even the effort to raise
living standards above poverty was thought important; the tendency was to accept and in the Middle Ages even to honor poverty,
not to regard it as an evil. And the pursuit of wealth, as practiced
by the capitalists or businessmen, who existed but as rather humble
minorities, not only was not highly thought of; it was even regarded
by the leading minds with some antipathy, as a danger to spiritual
and moral health in both souls and communities—an expression
and a stimulant of the always potentially overexpansive and conflicting particular desires in men, leading to disorder if not strictly
curbed.

Now the great tradition of philosophical and social thought, begun by Plato and developed further, with modifications, by Aristotle and in the Middle Ages by Aquinas, expressed and by its influence strengthened all those related tendencies in those two cultures. For my purpose here, all the essential ideas in that tradition
can be found in Plato's dialogues, and I need say little about their
later developments and modifications. In the original Platonic as
in the later forms, the total scheme of thought was both a general
philosophy and a philosophy of life for all men and societies, *and
included also* the rudiments of an economic theory. For the latter
had its lowly place in the scheme, though largely as a branch of
social pathology—a study of the evil tendencies arising in the pursuit of wealth, which the moralist statesman should understand
and thus be able to control.

Important in giving Plato's thought its direction were his three
connected antipathies: to democracy, to capitalism, and to the philosophical views of the Sophists, which strongly anticipated what
have been the dominant modern Western views. He grounded all
three antipathies on the same foundation: a theory of knowledge,
reality, and ethics according to which the condition of attainment
of knowledge of reality and the consequent right ordering of lives
and states is the supremacy of "reason" over the senses, appetites,
and passions. Sense perceptions are of many, diverse, and ever-
changing apparent objects; the task of reason is to study them with
skeptical detachment and penetrate beyond them to apprehension
of the stable and divinely harmonious pattern of purely general
"ideas" or universals, which the sense objects *imperfectly* exemplify
and which itself alone is pure "reality." Unless "reason" does this,
the sense perceptions generate not knowledge but a maze of variable, confused, and misleading opinions. Moreover the sense per-

ceptions, through the opinions they create, stimulate the appetites and passions which disrupt order and engender chaos in lives and societies. To control them reason must (1) truly apprehend the pattern of the real cosmos and thus (2) awaken the soul's potential love and emulation of that divine order; and so, finally, (3) with the help of that enthusiasm make the will or "spirited principle" in each soul and in the state its loyal, executive arm, to "rein back" all the particular desires within limits, making them mutually consistent and consistent with the proper order in each life and in the community. Now the conclusions from this whole theory which Plato applied as criticisms of democracy and of the Sophists I pass by here as familiar and not in the line of my special interest. The conclusions that I wish to emphasize are those he drew regarding the businessmen and their pursuit of wealth.

Like the Sophists and democracy, so also the businessmen in their respective ways tended to be enemies of order or producers of chaos. Seeking unlimited wealth and stimulating beyond all limits the particular desires of potential customers in order to profit the more by serving them, the businessmen embodied in themselves and aroused in others the disordering forces. And the spread in society of their "money madness" diverted all the vocational arts from their true functions in the well-ordered state to that of enriching their practitioners; reduced political life to a sordid conflict of economic group interests; and, growing into a desire of the populace for luxuries or excessive wealth, engendered greedy imperialism and wars and growth of the victorious states to unmanageable size and complexity. Thus Plato had, as one branch of the tree of his philosophy, an economic theory—a theory about "economic forces," the results of their "unfettered working," and the need to "fetter" them in order to build and preserve well-ordered states. How serious was his view of the disordering power of economic wants and ambitions is best shown by his decree of communal asceticism for the members of his governing *elite*—the "guardians" who must, in the state, embody reason, knowledge, and love of the real cosmic and moral order and the rational will to keep order. If the guardians were allowed to have private property, even private family lives, or any encouragements to pursue and cherish satisfaction of their own desires, the latter would expand, disorder their own souls, and unfit them for their task. But this was not all. Although the subjects, unlike the rulers, were to be allowed to own property and seek wealth within limits, the notion of a theory of the proper limits and regulations to enforce them is implicit in the whole argument of the *Republic*. Detailed development of this theory was left for Aristotle and the medieval Schoolmen, and to it belong all their ideas about usury, just prices, and the rest.

The entire scheme of thought—basic-philosophical, social-moral, and economic—thus developed by Plato and those successors was, I think, admirable in just the respects in which the bulk of modern Western thought has been defective, and vice versa. Its inspiring and largely true vision of the formal side of all existence and all proper human life—the order of the universe and the order to be sought for in human lives and societies—gave the medieval culture, which it permeated, an admirable set of ideal aims, though in the circumstances of the time those aims could not be at all fully realized. But the total scheme or outlook was one-sided, overstressing forms, order, and an ascetic moralism, and in consequence unduly curbing and retarding economic enterprise and progress, while also both neglecting and hampering development of science in the modern sense, and of technology. Under the influence of this outlook the many particular desires and curiosities which must be the sources of a culture's vitality, richness, and progressive dynamism were curbed *too much* for the sake of social order and stability, a static harmony, and undisturbed cultivation of the genteel virtues and graces by the upper classes; and the "masses" remained immured in a poverty which confined them to a scarcely civilized or human existence. But modern Western culture, born in reaction against the restrictive aspects of its heritage, has erred in the opposite way; and so, while achieving immense economic and scientific progress, has been deficient in the power to give men's lives and societies any harmonious order, or to avoid that chaos which Plato feared.

2. *Modernity, First Phase: Hobbes and the Mercantilists*   The early modern revolt against medievalism and the transition from it to modernity in the West had many phases; all of them together produced the setting in which there appeared, in seventeenth-century England and western Europe, the first fully modern, complete pattern of philosophical, political, and economic thought. By this time both the Renaissance and the Reformation had made their contributions to the bold individualism and other ingredients of the new, modern, spiritual climate. In the social-economic sphere the great expansion and development of commercial capitalism had been long under way and now was booming along at a great

rate; and in the political sphere there had been a great change—the rise of the modern centralized and fully independent national states. Individuals and nation-states were now the important units; the unity of Christendom under Pope and emperor was gone, small region localism was declining, and there had begun a progressive loosening of many social bonds. And along with the economic, social, and political transformations an intellectual revolution also had by this time reached its floodtide: the rise of modern science, following and using both advances in mathematics and the earlier growth of a new interest in faithful, empirical observation of nature.

The development of the new science, thus far mainly physics, had involved a revision of methods and fundamental concepts which entailed a break with—though there was also much unacknowledged indebtedness to—the Scholastic Aristotelian kind of science. And with the new physical science had come, too, with Descartes, Bacon, and others, a revolution in philosophy, having two main aspects: in theory of knowledge, empiricism, and in theory of reality, the belief that "all is mechanism." Meanwhile, advances in many practical arts—such as military engineering, accounting and business management, and the arts of technical statecraft including large-scale bureaucratic administration—had done perhaps even more than the advances in pure science to develop and spread the modern spirit of close study of causes and effects or of means to ends, and minute accuracy in the required joint logical and factual studies. And finally, with all these social and cultural changes went a change in both economic and political life and thought from general prevalence of belief in the need for a predominance of religious-moral over worldly aims in all activities to wide prevalence of a very worldly point of view. Both the pursuit of wealth by individuals and, even more, the pursuit of national wealth and power by ambitious rival nation-states had taken on new vigor and expansiveness, thrown off restraints, and become accepted, primary preoccupations.

With the background of all those developments in mind, then, let us notice the characters and coherence of, first, the philosophy and political theory of Hobbes and, second, the economic theory of the merchants, bureaucrats, and scholars of that epoch who supported the set of policies for promoting national wealth which in retrospect we call mercantilism. To speak first of Hobbes, his philosophy was at all points antithetical to Plato's. (1) His sensationalist empiricism and nominalism stood in exact opposition to the

Platonic rationalism and, in the medieval sense, "realism"—the doctrine of "real" or objective ideas or universals. (2) His mechanistic materialism, again, was antithetical to Plato's cosmic-ethical teleology, or view that "reality" is a cosmic harmony—a harmonious pattern of real universals—which "lures" all particular, actual, active entities toward participation in it through actualization of their own real-ideal or best possibilities and functions. And (3) in the ethics and politics founded on his sensationalist-mechanist epistemology and psychology, Hobbes' central doctrine was that not reason, as in Plato, but only a ruler or ruling group with overwhelming despotic arbitrary power can subdue the chaotic conflict of desires and men and produce social order.

Let me slightly elaborate those points in turn. (1) All knowledge originates in sense perceptions; universals or concepts are only signs invented to designate our groupings of sense objects; and reason is only a power of "calculating," with the help of these signs, what sense experience adds up to. Thus reason cannot apprehend (intuit) any primary, nonsensory, objective ideals or premises of ethics, and therefore cannot govern conduct independently of or in any opposition to the sense-linked desires—appetites and passions—which are the only desires men have. Being merely a power to draw inferences from sense *data,* reason can only serve active life instrumentally, by discovering the conditions of satisfaction of the nonrational, inevitable and actual, sense-linked desires. (2) The only "reality behind" the sense perceptions is matter in motion; *all* existents are in last analysis simply physical mechanisms; and what humans know as their mind-states are, as Hobbes put it, only "phantoms" of brain-states. External events, through the sense organs, produce in our nervous systems "internal motions" which occur in "trains," and of which the phantoms appear to introspection as trains of experiences, thoughts, desires and aversions, and resultant volitions—all leading to our actions, the end results of this mechanical process. There is reasoning which tends to make actions "logical" in relation to the desires and situations of the actors, but this reasoning, too, is a part of the mechanical process. Finally, (3) the sense-linked desires are—as Plato also taught—conflicting and expansive without limit; hence, if not curbed, they inevitably drive men into mutual conflict—in Hobbes' picture a frightful, intolerable "war among all." And reason, in Hobbes' view of it, cannot itself directly curb the desires or quell the conflict and produce social order; being in each man only—as Hume was later to express the same view—

"servant, not master" of his sense-linked desires, reason itself is a tool of the disordering forces. What alone makes order possible is the predominance among each man's desires of the desire for safety from the aggressions of his fellows, and the discovery that this can be had only by joining in submission to an almighty despot who restrains all and thus protects all. Thus the human "natural" mechanisms are impelled to organize political (nation-state) societies, despotically governed, which are "artificial" mechanisms— mechanical monsters, "Leviathans," omnipotent over their subjects, members, and creators. Finally, one last corollary has for us here a special interest: in international relations, the several independent Leviathans *remain in* the "state of nature," i.e., a state of war, and each must simply carry on its conflict with the others with all possible vigor and resourcefulness, and no hampering scruples.

Thus on the foundation of a purely prosaic philosophy Hobbes logically erected an utterly grim and hard-boiled view of the basic, practical necessities inexorably controlling all human life. Now, although as a rule in economic writings it was mainly implicit, not explicit, I think essentially the same tough view of the necessary aims of individual and national life and imposed despotic order in the state was the ideological context of all the mercantilist economic theory which flourished in that epoch; and with one exception all the elements of the philosophy which Hobbes spelled out as the basis of that outlook were presupposed in the mercantilist writings —in *both* their economic theory itself and its ideological context. Hobbes himself, in the twenty-fourth chapter of *Leviathan* on "Nutrition of the Commonwealth," produced a bit of perfectly good and typical mercantilist economic theory, obviously fitting perfectly into his system. Indeed, the best scholar among the seventeenth-century English mercantilist economists proper, Sir William Petty, professed admiration for and indebtedness to Hobbes. Most other writers in this group, however, were not philosophers and undoubtedly owed nothing to Hobbes; they were merchants or public officials or both, men with more practical than speculative minds and interests, and unlikely to draw ideas from such a book as *Leviathan* or to express their own ideas on the same—the philosophical—level. Nevertheless, being also entirely hardheaded realists in the modern sense, with logical and matter-of-fact minds and cause-effect curiosities like those of the physical scientists of the time, and a keen interest in the search for effective ways of increasing national wealth and power through governmental stimulation and control of trade, the mercantilist economists all went at this search with a way of thinking which presupposed fundamental notions nearly identical with those of Hobbes.

(1) While not apt to formulate in philosophical terms the empiricist theory of knowledge, the mercantilists were in method generally better *practicing* empiricists than Hobbes himself. He, philosopherlike, announced that empirical evidence must support significant reasoning but scarcely bothered to gather and present any facts to support his own. But they were pioneers of the statistical as well as of the theoretical branch of modern economic science, and avid seekers and users of economic-factual knowledge; they generally theorized in the light of their information and in a very matter-of-fact spirit; and unlike the later liberal economists have never been accused, to my knowledge, of neglecting facts and relying on unverifiable, a priori premises.

Nevertheless, as regards the other basic doctrine of Hobbes, mechanistic materialism, I think a division must be made. The Mercantilists in general theorized constantly in mechanistic terms, but I see no ground for ascribing to them as a presupposition the metaphysical doctrine of materialism. Though the two ideas, "all is mechanism" and "all is matter," seem inseparable in Hobbes and to most philosophers, I think they are not; some of the philosophers and physical scientists of that epoch who shared the former idea were Cartesian dualists, not materialists, and Leibniz, for example, called the "soul" a "spiritual mechanism"—*automaton spirituale.* In any case, this question of the ultimate substance(s) need never arise in economic theory, and as far as I know never did among the mercantilists; nor is any one answer to it necessarily involved in supposing that all events, including human thoughts and actions, occur in mechanical patterns or can be explained with the aid of mechanistic conceptual models. The latter were certainly in the minds of the mercantilists; they all reasoned constantly in mechanistic terms about interdependent changes of prices, supplies, demands, etc., in the markets, and expansions or contractions of "branches of trade" and effects of governmental measures on them—long before Sir Dudley North, near the end of the century, wrote that "since Descartes, natural science has become mechanical and the *chimeras* of the Schoolmen are done away with; and to become as clear and solid the science of Trade also must become mechanical."

Unlike their liberal successors, however, the mercantilists thought of the national business economy as a mechanism *to be manipulated* by the state through policy devices—taxes, tariffs, bounties, controlled interest rates and other prices, subventions to favored trades and penalties against obnoxious ones—to *make* it work for maximal enrichment of the national state as such. Theirs was *not* the later idea of an automatically, socially beneficent, self-adjusting, harmony-insuring economic mechanism. They implicitly shared with Hobbes the assumption that not harmony but conflict of the interests of men and of nations is the fundamental fact; and hence shared also the resulting views about the practical necessities of despotism at home and war abroad—and strong governmental control of the national economy, and direction of its processes to maximization of *the national wealth significant as the basis of military power*. Their stress on amassing a national treasure of the money metals through a favorable balance of foreign trade was not, as later liberal critics supposed, the result *merely* or mainly of a simple confusion of wealth with money; neither was it due mainly to the natural tendency of a business community in which merchants, not physical producers, were dominant, to stress the money gains from shrewd trading rather than efficiency in physical production. The *main* foundation of their special concept of national wealth was the fact that not the liberal, humanitarian aim of higher living standards for all men, but readiness for war, *had* to be the supreme aim of all economic policy in their Hobbeslike view of struggle for security as the essence of life. In those times national security required an ample treasure of the money metals, strong home industries, and subservient colonies to make the mother country independent of markets and supplies in potentially hostile countries —precisely the objectives of mercantilism as a set of actual policies. And the body of economic theory which culminated in ideas of the most effective means to the ends of those policies was in the main, sound though rudimentary economic-scientific theory, empirical and mechanistic—in an ideological context and involving philosophical presuppositions closely similar to the political theory and underlying philosophy of Hobbes.

This whole pattern of thought, then, of Hobbes and the mercantilists, was, in my terms, all-prosaic and, internally, admirably coherent—not, like later systems, full of inner conflict between the economic-scientific element and a visionary ideology. But its grim assumptions of the iron necessities of despotism and war—a merely forcibly imposed and arbitrary order within nations and none in the world of nations—denied men's hopes and insights concerning the possibility of a more complete and better kind of human order —international as well as domestic, and in both spheres more largely spontaneous, truly harmonious, compatible with freedom, and based on reason, justice, and fraternity, not arbitrary might. A new expression, however, of these hopes and insights—modern liberalism, involving as we shall see a revised and weakened revival of the Platonic-Stoic vision of a divine-natural, cosmic, and moral order—was growing up meanwhile in other quarters and became dominant through much of the West in the next long epoch. The economic science which began its growth in the context of the out-look best expressed by Hobbes was to reach its maturity in the very different context of liberal thought; and to this I now turn.

3. *Economic Theory and Three Forms of Liberalism* In its long career from early modern times to the present, liberalism as a quasi religion with varying creeds has had three successive, general phases. In the first phase, which culminated in the eighteenth century, liberal thought relied in part upon ideas with a Stoic and thus ultimately a Platonic origin, current also in the Middle Ages: ideas of ethical-juristic natural law and the natural rights of all men, and the harmonious natural order of the universe, realizable in the world of men through conformation of their institutions and conduct to natural law or morality. It was in the context of this form of liberal thought that the Physiocrats and Adam Smith developed the first formulations of the economic theory of the self-adjusting mechanism of the free, competitive economy. In the second phase, extending through the nineteenth century, the bulk of liberal thought discarded the natural right and related ideas as nonempirical and nonscientific, and tried to replace them with the supposedly scientific principles of utilitarianism. This change did not lead, however, to any great alteration of concrete objectives or the liberal program; and the theory of the free economy continued its development, through the nineteenth and into the twentieth century, in the context of utilitarian liberalism. The classical economic theory of the early nineteenth century, however, although its chief architects were friends and co-workers of the first utilitarian liberals, did not apply Bentham's idea of calculations of amounts of "utility" for "happiness" directly to the problems of economic theory itself. Only in the great new development of economic theory after 1870, led by Jevons, the famous Austrian School, Walras, Marshall, and others, was this done; and even then only Jevons acknowledged the connection of the new utility economics

with utilitarianism. Meanwhile, there began a change in not only the philosophies but the practical objectives of the liberals and a growing division of their movement into conflicting wings.

Both the eighteenth-century natural-rights and the early nineteenth-century utilitarian reformers had supported the classical, liberal program—liberal individualism and internationalism. That is, they stood for maximal freedom of all individuals from external dictation of their views or actions, limited government, and a voluntary comity among nations. And they relied mainly on general "enlightenment," spontaneous morality, the interdependence of all men and nations, basic harmony of their major interests, and the "natural" processes of a free, unregulated world economy, to insure order and a steady progress and general diffusion of prosperity and happiness. But in urging this program they had been strongly reformist in temper, being not defenders of a status quo, but crusaders for a new, free world order, in opposition to the traditions of oligarchy, despotism, and mercantilism—the *first* modern, predemocratic and preliberal regime. In a degree of contrast, the Victorian liberalism of the later nineteenth century and quite early twentieth, while it still supported the classical, liberal platform and especially the planks of free enterprise and limited government, took on a conservative tone and became largely a business class gospel; being oriented now not against the original alternatives but against the rising menace of socialism and the expanding activities of democratic governments. And this change produced another: the original, humanitarian idealism and reforming fervor in the movement began to pass, and has since passed mainly into development of a new, third phase or form of liberalism in general, which is still inchoate—the semisocialist, more democratic (for mass welfare) than individualistic, liberalism of our time.

The philosophy, as well as the program of this new liberalism is still inchoate, but tends generally in the direction of pure pragmatism, avoiding formulation of any system of abstract social-moral principles, even of the type of those of utilitarianism, and aiming to develop "experimentally" institutions and policies found to "work" in terms of satisfaction of majority demands. Hence the "new" liberalism may be called pragmatic democracy. And the latest developments of economic theory in the liberal (nontotalitarian) world of recent years have been and are at least loosely related to that outlook. The theory of monopolistic competition tends to undermine the old faith in free enterprise and the automatic social beneficence of "natural economic laws," by refining the analysis of the "competitive" economy in a way which finds it to be full of "monopoly elements" working generally, in results, against public welfare, and thus by implication requiring either destruction or public regulation if the latter is to be best served. And more trenchantly and positively in another direction, Keynesian economic theory directly implements the new liberalism with ideas of a technique for making the business economy serve democracy or mass welfare by using governmental fiscal operations to control and stabilize it.

Now the instability over time of the philosophic base of liberalism has been due I think to an inner conflict present from the start, between the visionary element, originally boldly expressed in the natural-law and harmonious natural-order ideas, and the prosaic element of empiricist and mechanist ideas associated with modern science. In the long development I have just outlined the prosaic element has become more prominent in each new form of liberal thought, while the visionary has come to be denied philosophical expression; but I think this increasingly submerged, visionary element necessarily remains, all the same, the source of whatever the liberal movement retains of vigorous idealism and clarity in its goals or direction. Clarity of aims, in particular, requires an accepted, philosophical expression of the vision—of the pattern of the potentialities—of nature and human nature, and the good society to be achieved. But although modern liberal thought began its career with a philosophy which in a fashion supplied all that, the included and essential metaphysical and moral ideas in that philosophy were marred and weakened from the outset by their conflict with the even more emphasized, but mistaken, purely empirical and mechanistic formulations of modern scientific ideas. As these latter ideas have increasingly prevailed, the clarity of the liberal ideals or vision has declined.

The loss of clarity has become conspicuous in the present-day confused pragmatic liberalism, in which the idealism is only an emotional, vague humanitarianism, and the intellectual content is only a *mélange* of variable and often mutually conflicting, purely empirical and mechanical ideas of ad hoc remedies for diverse, particular social ills. And this state of liberal thought has adverse effects on any economic theory of which it is the ideological context. Thus the Keynesian economic theory, though it has much merit, analyzes only an unduly restricted range of features of the working of the present-day business economy, because it is solely intent on developing the knowledge on which to base ad hoc remedies for one particular, urgent evil—mass unemployment. And the Keynesian economists tend to be "political" economists of the worst kind—active in politics on behalf of their favorite policy devices, and lacking in this role a political philosophy or unambiguous vision of the type of social order they regard as desirable, and a theory of all the conditions of its realization, to guard them from ignorance and unconcern about the broader, institutional changes which may ensue from general adoption of their policy program.

Nineteenth-century utilitarian-liberal thought and the classical and later neoclassical economic thought connected with it were not as bad in those respects, because in the former and thus for the latter there remained the fairly clear vision of the good society and economy embodied in the classical-liberal program. But already the logically required philosophical foundation of that vision and program had been disavowed, in the effort to achieve a purely scientific, logical-empirical, and mechanistic way of thinking. The utilitarian formulas did not really in themselves prescribe the liberal program. The conditions of the greatest general happiness—simultaneous satisfaction of the greatest number of desires—in a society depend on the character of the desires of its members. If desires of a certain type predominate in the great majority, a bellicose, totalitarian despotism may best satisfy them. The utilitarian liberals, despite their denials, really presupposed a general if not universal agreement of men's spontaneous desires with their real needs or "true interests," and of both with that vision of the natural society of free men respecting one another's natural rights which the eighteenth century and earlier liberals had dared to formulate in half-Platonic, metaphysical and moral terms. But even that original liberal vision was made defective by the inconsistent mixing with it of the ideas which were to cause it to fade out or be disavowed in later explicit liberal thought.

The pioneers of liberalism of the sixteenth to the end of the eighteenth century were thinkers who did not depart as far from the ancient-medieval tradition as did Hobbes and the mercantilists. They carried on but modified its ideas. One modification made was only the rejection of one that Christian dogma had imposed on medieval thought. The latter held that sinful, fallen man's uncertain grasp of natural law and his still more enfeebled love of the good order in life to be had by obeying it must be helped and supplemented by supernatural revelation and grace if his evil passions were to be controlled. The founders of the modern liberal revised version of the natural-law philosophy rejected the supernaturalist additions. They asserted the full capacity of the natural reason in all men to apprehend and bring them to agreement on the rules of natural law, as well as the predominant attractiveness of the ideal natural order to all human nature—when the latter should become enlightened with modern knowledge or properly educated and freed from the corrupting influences of bad environments. Then, too, in rejecting the Christian-supernaturalist additions, the liberal revision went farther and discarded also the austere and pessimistic element in the original views of Plato and the Stoics—the distrust of the desires connected with the senses and regarded as too "naturally" predominant in "the many," and the belief that chaos could be avoided and the natural order be realized only through a repressive control of society by a ruling, wise, and good elite enforcing an authoritative formulation of a body of natural law, rather highly restrictive in relation to the mundane, "natural" desires of ordinary mortals.

What was retained was only the optimistic side of the ancient vision—the belief in the reality of the ideal pattern, the capacity of mankind for direct apprehension of it, and its great attractions for all human nature. Thus eighteenth-century liberal thought had a tendency to slide into a superficial and egregious optimism, almost identifying the *spontaneous* natural with the morally ideal behavior of mankind. And this was supported by the influence of the empiricist and mechanistic element in that mixed way of thinking, which tended to cause confusion of the characters of the moral, the Newtonian physical, and the social-economic natural laws. Yet those confusions and that overoptimism were not always as pronounced as they are often said to have been. Thus in the total systems of thought of the Physiocrats and Adam Smith, the included ethical and economic theories were really tolerably distinct, and related in the sense of being complementary. Deliberate reforms, directed by moral insight, to make the actual social order and legal system and effective moral code conform more closely to the ideal, rational, natural order were seen as preconditions for that socially beneficent operation of the mechanism of the free economy—free only from nonmoral, arbitrary controls and internal obstacles due to machinations by selfish special interests—which was envisaged in the economic theories.

4. *Romantic and Positivistic Alternatives, and Marxism*   In most

of the intellectual life of the nineteenth century the visionary and prosaic halves of the eighteenth century's composite outlook came apart, so to speak—with some change in the process—and went on developing to new results in, respectively, the romantic movement, and the trend in most nonromantic circles to pure positivism. Romanticists and positivists, while thus holding mutually opposed positions, were often mainly conscious of their oppositions to the full tradition and to all even relatively full continuations of the eighteenth-century way of thinking, in which each group tended to see only what it rejected. Now while, as I indicated in the last section, the development of liberal, and of economic, thought itself increasingly conformed to the positivistic or prosaic trend, it nevertheless remained visibly enough indebted to the entire composite eighteenth-century way of thinking to encounter opposition not only from romanticists but also from a few (in precept) thorough positivists.

The romantic opposition developed mainly in Germany, and is best represented by the line of German scholars including—in temporal order from the early nineteenth century to a very recent time —Adam Mueller, Frederick List to some extent, the first economists of the "historical school," and such recent figures as Werner Sombart and—on a lower level of ability—Othmar Spann, who was active at Vienna in the years just before the rise of the Nazis and had, intellectually, very much in common with them. In differing degrees and ways all those scholars were romantic-conservative nationalists and statists; opposed to liberal individualism and internationalism and the theory of a free-world economy; inclined to cherish romantic visions of a state-led German national society and economy. And the latter, they insisted, must be conceived as a unique and unitary spiritual "organism," having as members not separate individuals pursuing their private ends within a framework of agreed-on rules but persons and groups bound together as organs of the whole, with natures and functions formed by and serving the unitary, traditional, self-evolving national spirit— *Volksgeist*. Hence, with their opposition to the liberal ideology of Adam Smith and his successors, they joined inseparably a radical opposition to the character, method, fundamental concepts, and alleged philosophical foundation of the "science" of the liberal economists. And their primary object of attack in the latter was the ideal of emulating physical science. All declared this ideal to be wholly out of place in a social science, and to involve the metaphysical ideas of atomism and materialism and, as their corollaries, "practical materialism" in the sense of the sordid, mercenary view of life as only the pursuit of material goods, and "social atomism" or individualism in contrast with the romantic idea of "social organisms."

Also, they attacked the effort to discover or believe in a universal, timeless pattern of economic laws, and the predominantly postulational and deductive method—with its attendant stress on, and conception of theory. They insisted that each local or national culture in each stage of historical development does and must evolve, under the joint influence of *Volksgeist* and *Zeitgeist,* its own unique and unitary concrete pattern of all, including economic, institutions and activities; and along with that its own body of both economic theory and policy, entirely and solely valid for itself. Thus on a larger scale the only true method of economic study must be historical, and must aim to understand each local, temporal culture and economy through study of its special history. Furthermore, this study must be of a new type, investigating the facts of record only in order to reach intuitive or sympathetic "understanding" (*Verstehen*) of the special "spirit" (*Geist*) or set of ideas and feelings which produced the objective phenomena as its manifestations. Finally, in their attacks on the thought of economic liberalism and of liberalism generally these writers always emphasized its origin in the "wretched" philosophy of the Franco-British eighteenth-century "enlightenment," in which they saw only the prosaic elements. That the liberal vision of societies of free men living on a basis of mutual respect for each other's rights embodied a moral idealism and involved a visionary metaphysics which modified its prosaic side, was never recognized.

In contrast with this romantic opposition to economic and philosophical liberalism, which exhibited itself for the most part in German Eastern Europe, the positivistic opposition appeared mainly in "the Western democracies," where the number and influence of its representatives have been limited by the increasing conformity of economic and philosophical liberal thought itself to the prosaic trend in this part of the world. However, in company with others of no great importance, two widely separated, and in many ways dissimilar, representatives of positivism were not satisfied with that conformity. These two were August Comte and Thorstein Veblen.

Comte, as is well known, attacked the classical political economy as a mere continuation in its field of the eighteenth-century kind of thought which he called metaphysical or prescientific. By meta-physical he very clearly meant precisely what I call visionary thought—taken in its rationalistic, not its romantic form; thought positing, and seeking to grasp and reason from, abstract but real universals, forming a pattern and serving both to explain all nature and to define the ideal pattern for all human life. Only this element could Comte see in economic and general liberal thought; the stronger positive scientific element in classical economics and even (in aim at least) in utilitarian liberalism he could not see at all. In his view the economists and utilitarians reasoned not from observation of men's actual circumstances and behavior but only from a priori postulates about a universal human nature. Moreover, the attempt to keep economics a separate, special science entailed, he thought, its nonempirical or metaphysical character. In empirical social life the economic and other elements are so interdependent that positive social science must be all one single, unitary science—the sociology Comte sought to found. This must truly emulate the methods and concepts of natural science, in essentials, but in details develop its own variants adapted to its subject matter; thus it must be in part historical, in part descriptive of each society in each stage of its development. Above all, like natural science, social science must develop into or support a scientific art—of government, or the proper ordering of life in each society by a body of experts. Here he missed or fumbled the distinction between a scientific art and a philosophy of ends; his social science would also prescribe the moral code to be enforced in his "positive polity," which, in contrast to liberal individualism, would emphasize not rights but duties. The "metaphysical stage" had only destroyed the outmoded moralities and political systems developed in the first or "theological stage" of human development; liberal thought logically culminated in pure anarchism—a doctrine that everyone must obey only the promptings of his "nature"—and could not create a new social order. Positive social science would in its way fill the place once filled by religion and create a new, scientifically controlled society. Comte's kind of positivism, although philosophically at the opposite pole from German romantic idealism, likewise led to anti-liberal authoritarianism, as the next chapter demonstrates.

Veblen's partial agreement with Comte is obscured by important differences, and by the wholly different, informal character of the former's writings. But although it has never, to my knowledge, been pointed out before, I think the degree of agreement about nineteenth-century liberal "orthodox" economics, and what, for Veblen, should replace it, is fairly striking. To Veblen, also, the classical and neoclassical economics seemed a continuation in its field of the eighteenth-century, prescientific mode of thought, elaborating the vision or mythology of a universe ruled for good ends by natural laws—including human societies thus ruled by economic laws—the philosophy of which was bound up with that of the natural rights of property and contract, dear to businessmen. Oddly, Veblen thought the up-to-date kind of science was half a product of the machine age and half a product of Darwinism. How the machine age got started is not wholly clear, for his account of the features of eighteenth-century thought which made it prescientific would seem, as an earlier critic of Veblen has noted, to condemn Newtonian physics along with classical economics. In any event, the new age was habituating everyone having intimate contact with machines—working men and engineers—but not businessmen, preoccupied with rigging markets to make money and not familiar with the new ways of making useful things—to thinking of *all* processes in impersonal, mechanistic terms, as having no inherent purposes but only causes and effects which become new causes. Darwinism was diffusing into all sciences the idea that there is no immutable, timeless pattern of "kinds" of entities with appropriate relations and ways of interacting; there is only the temporal process of ceaseless change of all the kinds, and hence of all relevant categories and concepts. The "evolutionary" idea, to Veblen, meant only this and not the particular theory of "natural selection," which was suggested to Darwin by the work of Malthus and was used by Spencer and others to bolster up the economic and general social theory of "free competition."

Economic science then, according to Veblen, should get over being a laggard, still prescientific theory of the fixed categories, values, wages, etc., and their appropriate relations, and the beneficent, "natural" processes of a static or unchanging business economy. It should become a modern mechanistic evolutionary science of the temporal process of unending, goal-less social change. Actually, his new economic science as represented in his own writings was a kind of sociology, or cultural anthropology, applied to "modern" as well as to "primitive" societies. As such it was often highly perceptive and suggestive, but wholly unlike economics as conceived in its main tradition. More important, as "science" it wholly lacked any "vertebrate" structure of either precise or systematic theory, and also any statistical or other "exact" studies of particular facts; Veblen's writing was all intuitive and impressionistic, not scientific. Nonetheless, his gospel was science only, and his complaint against traditional economics was that it merely carried on the eighteenth century's prescientific, visionary, metaphysical moralism.

Now in turning, finally, to Marxism I apologize for having saved only an insignificant fraction of my space for comment on that imposing, complex, and in every sense important intellectual system. In this crumb of space I can only faintly suggest how I see it in relation to the others I have just considered.

Like eighteenth-century liberal and economic thought it combines, but again not coherently, I think, prosaic and visionary elements. The former include not only Marx's special transformation and development of old classical economic theory but also the solid, factual part of his own historical investigations which—I am told by experts whom I trust—were in and for his time excellent and highly relevant to economic science. The visionary elements include both the socialist vision itself, of the future ideal society, and the "inverted Hegelian" *philosophy* of history.

In the latter philosophy, termed "historical materialism," the so-called "materialism," it is my impression, does not quite conform to any non-Marxian, familiar meaning of the word. It is of course not the classical, mechanistic materialism, for its dialectical theory of history is a different, nonmechanistic idea of process. Further, I would say it has little more in common with classical metaphysical materialism than the fact of being metaphysical, in contrast with positivism in the sense of antimetaphysical "phenomenalism." The latter opposition is made clear in Lenin's essay *Dialectical Materialism vs. Empirio-criticism*. Not subjective human sense impressions but an absolutely objective reality the Marxian philosophy does insist upon; but in precisely what sense the reality is "material" may be open to question. I suspect that it is so only in the sense literally got by simply "inverting" Hegel: all that is "objective" in a concrete society through a given time—in the people and their social and total environment—is *not* a product or manifestation of their spirits, feelings, ideas, *etc.*; on the contrary, the objective social world is the reality which generates the subjective, the states and contents of the people's minds. In any case, a more serious error is to be avoided: Marxian "materialism" is not and does not imply or produce the practical "materialism" of aiming only at a society rich in material goods, or supposing wealth in the latter sense to be the main end of life, *or* the main actual aim of most human beings. This calumny is no more fair or true when aimed at Marxism than it was when aimed by romanticists at the nineteenth-century liberal economists.

The economic determinism in the Marxian theory of history is the notion not that "economic motives" are all-controlling but that objective, economic (and with them all social) *circumstances* engender, by psychological conditioning, the feelings, views, etc., and thus the aims of the human beings who live in those circumstances. For example, rich men and poor men, generally speaking, are sure to have different outlooks, because they have different experiences.

But the dialectic, in the form of the class struggle and, more generally, the dynamic temporal ebb and flow of "contradictions" or conflicts within a society as the behavior patterns and ideologies of diversely conditioned groups clash with and change one another and produce "evolution"—this concept, derived from Hegel who put ideologies in the primary causal position, I think retains in Marxism its romantic-visionary character. For it remains the notion of a process which occurs *in order* to realize an ideal; the idea of an "inherent logic" in history whereby the world "must" (ought to, and will inevitably, fused into one idea) become rational at last, free of contradictions (human conflicts), a perfect harmony. There is the relation to eighteenth-century liberal and economic thought that here too is self-enforcing, ethical natural law, only now in the historical dimension; the existing order is *not* natural, rational, harmonious, hence self-maintaining, but full of evil or conflict, hence fated to destroy itself and in so doing generate the harmonious order—in the ultimate historical long run. But this visionary and the prosaic side of the system are unreconciled; the whole claims to be a science but, as was the case with economic liberalism, it is half a science and half a religion in some mutual conflict.

POSITIVISM AND PORFIRISM IN LATIN AMERICA

LEOPOLDO ZEA

THE rule of General Porfirio Díaz in Mexico and the simultaneous influence of positivism, the accepted doctrine of the theorists of so-called Porfirism, form part of a remarkable experiment which was executed in more or less the same manner throughout Latin America.

I

When political independence from the Spanish Government was achieved the Latin American countries were quick to realize that this was not enough. The order imposed by the leaders of the emancipation differed very little from that which Spain had established. What had happened was a mere change of power; Creoles had taken the place of the Spanish ruling classes. But the social status remained as it had been in colonial times. Army and clergy enjoyed their old privileges—among them the right to rule the minds and bodies of their countrymen.

Andrés Bello, the great Venezuelan thinker (1781–1865), described the situation as follows: "We have wrested the scepter from the Spanish monarch but not from the Spanish spirit: our congresses, themselves unconscious of it, succumb to Visigothic inspirations . . . even our military, in clinging to special prerogatives which stand in marked contrast to the principle of equality before the law, reveal their allegiance to the ideals of that very Spain whose banners they have trodden under foot." The democratic idea, one of the tenets of the liberators, had not yet assumed its full meaning in the minds of the people. According to the Argentinean writer and statesman Domingo F. Sarmiento (1811–78), the South American revolution was actuated by nothing but "a passing wish to benefit from an opportunity of replacing the Spanish administration by a local one." And Juan Bautista Alberdi (1810–84), comparing Spanish American independence to that of the United States, says:

"Among North Americans freedom is not loudly praised but silently *practiced;* to them it is not an *idol* but an ordinary *tool* like a lever or a hammer. . . . San Martín, Bolivar, Sucre, O'Higgins . . . understood American liberty the *Spanish* way; to them it meant independence of the new states from Spain. . . . Washington and his contemporaries held the opposite view. What was foremost in their minds was the freedom of the individual, not the independence of their country."

Spain was present in every action of the Spanish Americans. Her habits, customs, ideas, and creeds were implanted in their minds. Those habits and customs had plunged them, once they were politically emancipated, into several decades of wanton bloodshed. In vain had the democratic idea which was written on their banners struggled to adapt itself to so hostile an environment. The authoritarianism inherited from Spain quelled all democratic intentions. The ideas proclaimed in those fratricidal fights were nothing but pretexts to justify strong impulses of personal rule. The ideas ceased to be valid norms and became embodied in the persons of the leaders who proclaimed them.

All Spanish America was divided into bands fighting against one another. In Mexico it was Centralists against Federals; in Argentina Unitarians against Federalists; in Chile *Pelucones* (big wigs) against *Pipiolos* (upstarts); and so on everywhere. But whoever won, the result was invariably the establishment of personal government. Some made no bones of their intention to re-establish the colonial order, with the one difference that the center was no longer Spain but the person of the respective rulers. Others, the enlightened ones, were all for democratic government; but, for the time being, while the masses were yet unfit for it, an equally personal government would see to their being prepared. There were those also who opposed central government for the sake of democracy but defended another of the political forms inherited from the colonial period: the *cacicazgo* or rule of local political bosses.

In the name and for the benefit of the people, Dr. José Gaspar Rodriguez Francia (1766–1840) imposed upon Paraguay one of the cruelest dictatorships recorded in history. In Argentina the Federalist Juan Manuel Rosas (1793–1877) set up another dictatorship of ill fame which had the support of the former caciques of the provinces. In Mexico Antonio López de Santa Ana (1795–1877) alternately used the Federal and the Centralist platform to establish one of the most sinister dictatorial rules. Only two dictatorships, those of Gabriel García Moreno (1821–75) in Ecuador and Diego Portales (1793–1837) in Chile, made no attempt at camouflaging their aim to re-establish the colonial order independently of Spain. The first set up a personal government with religious leanings; the second devised an impersonal government making use of the same psychological incentives which had caused Spanish Americans for several centuries automatically to obey not King Carlos III or King Carlos IV but simply the king, i.e., the government.

In those diverse guises Spain never ceased to be present in the minds and habits of Spanish Americans. As the Chilean José Victorino Lastarria (1817–88) put it: "No sooner had the revolution of independence come to an end than inevitably, as an effect of the laws of society, a reaction set in of the *Colonial spirit* and of the interests brought low by that very revolution. Through education and instinct the very officers who had fought the revolutionary battles incorporated that spirit." And Sarmiento cried out: "Do not laugh, peoples of Latin America, at the sight of such a disgrace! Remember you are Spanish, and the Inquisition made Spain. This is the disease we carry in our blood." What was needed, urgently needed, was another emancipation, the intellectual emancipation of Spanish America. Those habits and customs inherited from the colonial period must be torn up, root and branch.

To quote Lastarria again: "Society ought to improve upon the ways of its forefathers to secure its future." "And does this our civilization, this legacy of Spain," he asked, "not need correction? It must be completely mended, for it is the very opposite of the democracy we have in mind." And the Argentinean Esteban Echeverría (1805–51) wrote: "We cannot accomplish the social emancipation of Latin America unless we repudiate our Spanish heritage." This was to be the task incumbent upon the statesmen and thinkers quoted above: Sarmiento, Alberdi, Echeverría, Bello, Lastarria, the Mexican José María Luis Mora, the Ecuadorian Juan Montalvo, and many others. The instrument for shaping such emancipation they held to be education. The means to educate, or rather re-educate, the Spanish Americans, would be many; professorships and the press were among the foremost. These people dreamed of creating a new type of man.

The model for the new man of Spanish America was found in the Anglo-Saxon nations, England and the United States, particularly the latter, where the Spanish American reformers saw their ideals realized to an admirable degree. "In North America," said Sarmiento, "the settlers developed the economic life of the land; in South America they exploited it for the benefit of the mother country. . . . There the conquerors brought with them the ideal of labor; here they were satisfied to loaf as bureaucrats and parasites." One America had been colonized by Anglo-Saxons, inspired by the spirit of democracy, the other by a Latin race used to absolutism; hence the greatness of the first, the disgrace of the latter. Or in Lastarria's words: "In the North the people were supreme, actually and legally; they made the law and administered all its interests through their representatives. In Spanish America the people did not exist, society was alive only as far as it lived for the glory and benefit of its sovereign, an absolute ruler." With his accustomed impetuosity Sarmiento pointed out the remedy for Spanish American grievances: "Let us not detain the march of the United States! Let us catch up with the United States! Let us be America as the sea is the ocean! Let us be United States!" [1]

II

In Mexico the admiration the United States enjoyed throughout Latin America was tempered by distrust, a consequence of the war of 1847. Mexico felt she was weak and inferior in comparison with the "Northern Colossus"; and this weakness and inferiority she blamed on the fact that she was a member of the Spanish or Latin race, an irrational, anarchic race incapable of such organization as had made North America a powerful nation.

To South Americans their own race appeared romantic, idealistic, given to utopias and to sacrificing reality to dreams. A race scorning material exertion and preferring to live suspended in a world of idealism without consequences. Nations founded by this race, the argument went on, could not but be inferior to those with a practical sense, such as England and the United States. History was on the side of the latter. England had defeated theocratic Spain, and in America the sons of England had defeated those of Spain. The United States had found itself pitted against a weak nation. And this weakness was due solely to racial defects. Since their independence Mexicans had done nothing but kill one another for ideas which were mere words and for leaders who claimed to represent those ideas. Hence the necessity of getting rid of so unfortunate a disposition.

To bring about the desired change no vehicle appeared more suitable than education. A doctrine had to be found, an ideology, a body of thought, and it presented itself in the Comtian system. Positivism was the philosophy of practical people like the Anglo-Saxons who had made great nations of their countries; it would make the Mexicans fit for true liberty and democracy. One of the champions of positive philosophy, Telesforo García, wrote:

"In a country where positivism is innate in the national character, where it moves on its own ground, where the experimental method is applied to all manifestations of life—in England, in short—liberty is at its safest, and law and order are best guaranteed—whereas countries which have developed metaphysical philosophies and absolute idealisms, as for instance Germany, the cradle of all absolute idealisms; France, mother of all absolute rights; Italy and all the other nations that have indulged in such fancies . . . fell prey to all sorts of tyrannies, despite the priests who, in the name of the absolute, burned and beheaded everywhere. Practical, positivist peoples like those in England and the United States knew how to take care of their liberties while metaphysically inclined nations such as Germany, France, and Spain interpreted liberty metaphysically and thus made liberty itself impossible."

Positivism would teach the Mexicans how to establish order, mental and social—order in their own minds being an indispensable presupposition of the direly needed social order. Philosophical doctrines or systems not grounded on positive principles were considered unsuitable for the Mexican mind. How can we expect to regenerate, asked Telesforo García, if we increase the defects of our race, yielding to them instead of checking them with the help of rationally erected dams? We Latin people are "given to dreams and mysticism"; under such circumstances is it not absurd that "instead of disciplining the mind with rigorous scientific methods, instead of directing our activity toward clearly defined, positive ends, we indulge in fantasies and dreams and take the zest out of labor through which man makes himself the master of nature?"

"We may say," García went on to explain, "that in history the Latin race appears as a synthetizing race, the Anglo-Saxon as an analyzing one. As for its complement, the second must look for syntheses, the first for analyses." Thus the Mexicans, members of the Latin family, ought to acquire the qualities particular to the Anglo-Saxon race: a practical sense of life and a willingness to work. To develop an "inquiring, experimenting, and practical mind" they must "adopt suitable methods and procedures of teaching" and not such methods and systems as foster racial defects instead of reducing them. Of the qualities developed by educational systems based on metaphysical principles they have enough and to spare, he affirmed.[2]

Justo Sierra (1848–1912), one of the greatest educators of Mexico, made it clearer still that only through a mental and social change could Mexico survive in the struggle for life. A transition from the *military era,* the era of revolutions and continuous intestine wars, to the *industrial era,* the era of labor and a maximum personal effort, had to be achieved. And it had to be accomplished quickly, "for the giant nation that grows by our side and moves closer and closer in on us as a consequence of the industrial and agricultural prosperity of her border states and the extension of her railroads, threatens to absorb and dissolve us if she finds us weak." [3] History had already spoken a few years before. Mexico had been defeated by the northern country—defeated, however, by a superior mental and social organization, not by a superiority of arms. In vain had the men of the liberal party endeavored to give the Mexican people a progressive education and organization; the old interests of the military and the clergy, a residue of colonial times, had proved stronger and had obstructed all progress. Those very interests had vanquished Mexico and not the arms of the North. Thus, when the war was over, the progressive party was firmly resolved to enforce a program that would put an end to such a situation. This program, said Sierra, proposed "to educate the people in absolute independence of the Church, to break down the barriers of religious intolerance, to release churchland from mortmain." Thus and thus only one might hope to build up what had been so badly missing in the war with the northern neighbor: national consciousness.

Such was the work to be accomplished by the generation that assumed political responsibility in Mexico from 1880 to 1910. Their aim was to establish order in Mexican minds and in Mexican society. They set up a new type of national education, and they endeavored to set up a new type of social order, claiming science as the foundation of both. Mental order was based on positivism, social order on Porfirism.

III

In 1878, shortly after General Porfirio Díaz had seized power in consequence of a rebellion against President Sebastian Lerdo de

Tejada, the Mexican capital witnessed the rise of a new political group whose organ was the newspaper *La Libertad*. For their device they used the motto of Comtist positivism, "Order and Progress." [4] Several of the editors had been the pupils of Gabino Barreda, the man who has introduced positivism into Mexico and who in 1867 had been charged by the government of Benito Juárez with the execution of an educational reform based on this same philosophy.

The people grouped around *La Libertad* began to stir up public opinion with the catchword "order," insisting, however, that their type of order was new and had nothing to do with the notion of order taken over from colonial administration and defended by the conservatives. They called themselves conservative, too, but liberal-conservative. Their goal, they said, was liberty. But their methods were conservative. They were opposed to achieving liberty by revolutionary methods. Liberty, they said, rises by way of evolution, not revolution.

The thing immediately to be achieved, as the prerequisite of the longed-for liberty, they said, was order. The liberals, failing to understand this, had wanted to give the masses liberties for which they were unprepared; the result was anarchy. People must first be educated, must be taught what liberty means and what duties it involves. As long as that knowledge was lacking all the laws and all the constitutions aspiring to create liberty by simple decree would prove futile. Such aspirations were utopian—a product of the unpractical mind of the Mexicans.

Now at long last a group of people had appeared who were blessed with common sense and versed in the methods of positive science. They would take it upon themselves at some future time to institute democratic government based on social liberty. For the present, however, and until such a thing proved feasible, social order must be established at any cost. An end must be made of those sanguinary revolutions, of anarchy become permanent. The liberal Constitution of 1857 was one of the obstacles to such an order: it had been made by utopian minds for a utopian people—utopian because nonexistent.

Francisco G. Cósmes, one of the editors of *La Libertad,* said it was most provoking that there still were people of so obsolete a mentality that they continued to believe in the ideas of the legislators of 1857 "after half a century of incessant warfare for an ideal which, when realized, produced nothing but grievous consequences for the country. . . . It makes one sad indeed to see that while the fearful wounds sustained by the Mexican Republic in her endless revolutions have not yet stopped bleeding, the revolutionary ideals are still hailed among us." And the chief editor of *La Libertad,* Justo Sierra, criticizing the very members of the constitutional assembly, wrote:

Our supreme law was made by men of the Latin race, who believed that a thing is practicable the moment it is found to be logical; who are bent upon realizing at once and by violence any ideal whatever; who pass in one day from absolutism to relativism without transitions or nuances, compelling people to act out in real life what only holds in the sphere of pure reason. Such men—and who knows, we too are of their kind—confusing heaven and earth, have supplied us with a noble and exalted code but one in which all elements conspire to promote the individuality and autonomy of the single person to such a degree that social duties cease to function, and nothing is left except individual rights.

This utopian and anarchic liberalism had to be replaced by a realistic one promoting order—a liberal conservatism. As Justo Sierra put it:

We want the formation of a great conservative party comprising all the country's elements of order which are fit to guide public life. . . . For leadership we look not to a person but to an idea. Around it we wish to rally all those who feel that the epoch is over when political aspirations could hope to be fulfilled by revolutionary violence, all those who believe that the time has come to organize a party seeking *practical* rather than rhetorical liberty, and who are deeply convinced that progress has its origin in normal social development, i.e., in order.

"For leadership we look not to a person but to an idea." These words express the ideal of the new order, an order independent of the will of a *caudillo,* an impersonal order deriving from the Mexicans' own minds. But this order proved, at least for the time being, another utopia. The people had to be educated for it; but to that end order must first be established. The problem looked insoluble. The goal was to get rid of an order dependent on the personal will of a leader; on the other hand, a man was needed who had sufficient personal prestige to prepare the ground for such an order. This man could be considered only as a sort of amanuensis, a transitory institution to function while the Mexicans were acquiring the mental habits indispensable for an autonomous order.

As for the immediate measures, it was necessary to repeal liberties the utopian character of which had become obvious; the trust put in the people had to be withdrawn; no other way was open to initiating their regeneration. "Rights!" exclaimed Francisco G. Cósmes:

People are fed up with them; what they want is bread. To constitutions teeming with sublime ideas which no one has ever seen functioning in practice . . . they prefer an opportunity to work in peace, security in their personal pursuits, and the assurance that the authorities, instead of launching forth on wild goose chases after ideals, will hang the cheats, the thieves, and the revolutionaries. . . . Fewer rights and fewer liberties in exchange for more order and more peace. . . . Enough of utopias. . . . I want order and peace, albeit for the price of all the rights which have cost me so dear. . . . I daresay the day is at hand when the nation will declare: We want order and peace even at the cost of our independence.

That order and peace, so ardently clamored for, how could they be contrived? Not indeed by arbitrary rule; not by personal government which had proved so harmful to the nation. In an editorial of *La Libertad* we read: "Nothing is more loathsome and more contrary to progress than the reign of one or several men whose powers are not carefully defined. That is our opinion about dictatorships." However, the peculiar character of Mexico had engendered dictatorships and tyrannies. Hence, to put an end to them this character must be changed. Yet before it could be changed it had to be coped with. "To get rid of recurrent dictatorships . . . it is necessary to find a practicable constitution." But as this proved impossible under the actual circumstances, "we content ourselves with asking in this extraordinary situation for extraordinary authorizations." In another of his articles Cósmes explained: "Since we have gone on granting rights over rights which have produced nothing but misery and malaise, we will now try a little *honest tyranny;* let us see what that can accomplish." This honest tyranny was exercised by General Porfirio Díaz.

IV

Which social agents were represented by the group that would use some honest tyranny to improve Mexico's social situation? They called themselves the "bourgeoisie," formed by the "middle class" of society. "The middle class," said Justo Sierra, "supplied our cause with officials, generals, journalists, representatives, ministers, martyrs, and victors." [5] From its beginnings this new social group dreamed of achieving in Hispanic America what the great middle classes had achieved in Europe and the United States. Those of England and the United States were considered the best models, because they had given strongest proof of their power. In Mexico and in most of the other Latin American countries the members of this middle-class group would, first of all, model their countrymen on the Anglo-Saxon pattern. To create a middle class was the aim of Sarmiento and Alberdi in Argentina, of Lastarria in Chile, of Barreda and Sierra in Mexico. They all broke away from the classical parties in their respective countries, parties which had been exclusively concerned with working out a definite constitution. Themselves neither Unitarians nor Federalists, neither *Pelucones* nor *Pipiolos,* neither Centralists nor Federalists, they wanted to achieve not merely a political change but a change of mind.

The first theorist of this middle-class group in Mexico was José María Luis Mora (1794–1850). His theoretical sources were the utilitarian philosophy of Bentham and James Mill and the doctrines of Pierre Jean George Cabanis and Destutt de Tracy. He also drew upon the traditionalist Benjamin Constant. But the strongest of these influences was that of English utilitarianism. Mora lived during one of the most important and most violent epochs of Mexican history, the Revolution of Independence and the intestine struggles following it. He saw a Mexico fighting for her political independence and a Mexico torn by factions which contested one another's right to the newly acquired power.

Behind those factions stood the vested interests of definite groups fighting for their privileges. To these groups political power and the state were mere instruments in the service of their particular interests. The Revolution of Independence had destroyed a rule benefiting only Spain and Spaniards, merely to give rise to another rule with equally limited designs. "The Revolution of Independence," said Mora, "worked as a universal solvent which did away not only with class distinctions but also with ancient pedigrees, aristocratic privileges, and race discrimination," but "independence proclaimed on religious grounds increased the power of the *clergy,* and independence conquered, fought over and obtained in its most visible results by the force of arms, brought about the predominance of the *army* and the habit of considering brute force and ecclesiastic aspirations as the only effective powers." What was really achieved was a change of privileged groups, Spanish interests being replaced by those of the clergy and army. The people which had fought for liberty "not to change its master but to shake off servitude" had gained very little; it had rid itself of a foreign overlord only "to fall prey to a native one."

But a government concerned only with furthering the group interests it represents, or a ruler with the sole intention of turning government into an instrument to serve his stakes, can but breed chaos. With such a government there must be incessant revolutions, in fact, as many as there are groups interested in usurping power for the purpose of obtaining or maintaining special privileges. In Mora's opinion those interests had to be directed into other channels and kept apart from public power. Public power ought to be an instrument used in the service of society. Personal or group interests must look for other ways and means, such as had already been tried out and proved conducive to progress and liberty by the increasingly powerful middle classes of England and the United States. What were these ways and means? Mora referred to them in the following words: "Work, industry, and wealth make a man really and reliably virtuous. In rendering him independent of all the rest, these three imbue him with the firmness and noble valor of character which resist oppression and baffle any attempt at bribery. He who has never had to toady to power and to beg from it his means of subsistence is certain not to support power in its devious ways, its schemes of disorganization, its tyranny." That is to say, the day the Mexicans ceased to regard public power as a means of subsistence they would have gained true independence instead of merely having exchanged one dictator for another. Authentic authority would then rest with each Mexican; he would exert exactly as much power as his work was worth, and the state would be merely the guardian of the fruits of his own labor. Clergy and army, instead of exploiting public power, would be what they ought to be: servants of society. In Mora's words: "Let us discard the error that a form of government is a magic formula conjuring up prosperity. Let us replace this false idea by the right one that welfare depends on the promotion of morality and *industry*."

How was such a change to be brought about in the minds of the Mexicans? Through education, Mora answered. A new revolution had to be executed, a mental revolution, not an armed one. If the new class that emerged in the first years after the declaration of independence wanted its reforms to endure, this was the course it must follow. "For a reform to be stable," says Mora, "it must arise gradually by way of *mental revolutions* which take hold of society and modify the opinions not merely of a few persons but of the mass of the people."

In 1837 José María Luis Mora anticipated the Mexican positivists in his effort to shape, in accordance with a new philosophical doctrine, the mentality of a new social class fit to take over power and to realize the ideals of that "bourgeoisie" or "middle class" of which Justo Sierra was to speak. We need an education, said Mora, able to produce "the elements of a middle class which will be forthcoming in the next generation and which is so badly needed in this." The new schools must dispense knowledge which, rather than being an adornment of the mind, leads to practical results. They must "arouse in the young the questioning and searching spirit which never tires of pursuing truth and sometimes comes near it." In 1833 he said that all men of good will were called upon to aid the reformation, particularly in education. For the old educational system falsified and destroyed "all the convictions which make a *Positive man.*" Mora himself belonged to the group of "Positive men" who strove to see those reforms through; but in vain. A long civil war thwarted their efforts. "Reactionary forces" stubbornly opposed "progress." [6] Those forces had to be vanquished; their allies, the French troops of Napoleon III, had to be expelled before Mora's educational ideals were accepted and a new middle class emerged. This was the work of the Mexican positivists and so-called Porfirism.

V

The group which, according to Sierra, had formed "a minority the day after the American invasion" and had become "the majority of the country at the eve of the French invasion," definitely triumphed in 1867. In Cerro de las Campanas the ill-advised Emperor Maximilian paid with his life for the treason of the clericals and the ambition of Napoleon the Little. In that same year in the city of Guanajuato the doctor and lawyer Gabino Barreda (1818–81) pronounced a "Civic Prayer" [7] in which he interpreted the history of Mexico, dividing it into three epochs: the theological, the metaphysical, and the positivist. The first was represented by the colonial period, the second by the war of independence and the struggle against the reactionary forces in Mexico, the last was being inaugurated by the victory of the reformers. In Mexico, said Barreda, the spirit of positivism, after having triumphed in Europe, won its last battle—a victory not only for Mexico but for humanity.

Between 1849 and 1851 Barreda had attended several of Comte's courses in Paris where he had gone to finish his medical studies. On his return to Mexico he joined the reform group. In the above-mentioned "Civic Prayer" he applied Comte's famous division to Mexican history, replacing the Comtist motto "Love, Order, Progress" by "Liberty, Order, Progress" in allusion to the peculiar Mexican situation, for the victorious party, the party of progress, had called itself *liberal*. How to reconcile two such contrary conceptions as *order* and *liberty* was to be the great problem of Barreda and his followers. Ere long liberals and positivists were to join battle over the meaning of liberty.

Shortly after the pronouncement of the "Civic Prayer" the same year, in fact—the President of the Republic and leader of the victorious party, Benito Juárez, entrusted Gabino Barreda with the educational reform of the nation—a reform through which Mora's old dream was to come true. The young generation which would determine the future destinies of the country had to be prepared. It was Barreda's task to change the minds of the Mexicans. The change had to be radical. All that had caused the endless internal disorder must be discarded. In Justo Sierra's words: "As Juárez knew that political and social leaders must of necessity, owing to the very structure of modern society, be taken from the middle class, he wanted the middle class to receive an education that would pave the way for the future." The revolution that had been victorious, thanks to the force of arms, now assumed, in order to secure its reforms, the shape of a *mental revolution*. The nation's independence advanced another step by what Gabino Barreda called "mental emancipation." This is the task to which Barreda, the educator of Mexico, devoted himself. From the schools he had improved and from his own lecture halls stepped forth the young men who were to mark out new roads for their country. An experiment was initiated, the results of which mattered not only to the history of Mexico but to the general history of culture.

The era of armed revolution ended; that of mental revolution began. The old political order which had served definite political bodies was destroyed; a new order began to take shape. The new order, as Mora had pointed out, ought to serve society as a whole. The old order had relied on bodily and mental coercion, represented by the army and the clergy respectively. The new order would rely on persuasion. Mora had said: "The effects of force are fast but fleeting; the effects of persuasion are slow but lasting." In freedom, without violence, through persuasion, the Mexicans were to establish a genuine order—a constructive and progressive order in accordance with liberty. Recognizing their social duties they would freely institute an order in agreement with these duties.

Barreda saw in the state "the guardian of material order," i.e., of that social order in which the rights of any one individual are limited by the rights of all the others. Respect for the rights of others is the best safeguard to insure respect for a man's own rights; and knowledge of this fact is the best guarantee of order and peace. Juárez had expressed this same idea: "Respect for other people's rights is tantamount to peace." Thus order would abide in people's minds, thanks to logical conviction. The state would take it upon itself to insure by means of law this order which, if respected, would leave the individual in absolute liberty. No force would be capable of acts of violence in such an atmosphere of individual liberty. To Barreda, this atmosphere was tantamount to freedom of conscience —that same freedom which permits the individual to recognize the limits of material freedom. In Barreda's own words: "May that full freedom of conscience, and of thought and speech, giving free scope to all ideas and all inspirations, spread light everywhere and forestall any commotion not purely spiritual and any revolution not merely intellectual." This liberty, he hoped, would be guaranteed by a material order accepted on the strength of persuasion and protected by the state. "May material order enforced by the government and respected by the citizens be a firm guarantee and a sure way of steady advance along the road of progress and civilization."

The idea of material order was associated with that of the sources of disorder, one of which Mora had pointed out: government as an instrument in the service of definite privileges. Government, it was thought, ought to be merely the keeper of social order; privileges belonged to another sphere, the private sphere. There a man was entirely free. His rights, as Barreda's pupils later demonstrated, reached as far as his capabilities. But he ought not to turn to the state to obtain his rights. The state has no other function than to see to it that they are respected. However, Barreda, nurtured in the ideology of Comtian positivism, could not help believing that some privileges, such as wealth, must have social limits. Like Comte, he considered wealth a social good; but he differed from Comte in that he did not approve of state intervention. All he admitted was that the rich must be convinced that, once their real needs are satisfied, "they ought, for reasons of *moral responsibility,* to use the surplus as a public means entrusted to them by society for the common good and progress." The object is not to control wealth but "to humanize the rich."

Gabino Barreda, like his pupils after him, promptly clashed with the old liberals over the definition of liberty. The liberals were quick to realize that behind the ideas on freedom and order expounded by the positivists there loomed a new dogmatism—a dogmatism as dangerous as that of the ecclesiastics because, like theirs, it sought *to impose,* by means of a definite education, certain definite ideas. Such procedure was contrary to the freedom of conscience the liberals had fought for.

The liberal idea of liberty Barreda contrasted with a positive one. "Liberty," he said, "is commonly believed to be the faculty of doing and wanting whatever one desires, heedless of any law or guiding power. If there were such a liberty it would be immoral as well as absurd because it would make impossible all discipline and, consequently, all order." True liberty is compatible with order; it consists in unreserved submission to the laws of order. A thing is *free* when it follows its normal and natural course and encounters no obstacles alienating it from its own law and peculiar order. Taking an example from physics, Barreda explained that when a body is said to fall *freely* it is not because it falls where it likes but because it falls according to the law of gravitation; whereas the body is said not to fall freely when it encounters an obstacle deviating its fall. Thus true freedom recognizes that a man is limited by his social environment, from which he receives his laws. His liberty consists in his acting in accordance with these laws.[8]

VI

The generation of men educated by Gabino Barreda, those men who were to guide the nation along the road of progress, felt restrained in the ambit of Comtian positivism. Try as Barreda might, positive philosophy did not justify the freedom that most interested the middle classes: the freedom of getting rich without other limitations than a man's own capability. In Comte's philosophy individuals were subordinate to society in all material respects. This was the meaning of his *sociocracy* and his Religion of Humanity. Comte's politics and religion were not accepted by Mexican positivists, in contrast to those in Brazil and a group in Chile, because his political and religious doctrines were contrary to the end for which that philosophy in general had been adopted. That end, as pointed out before, was the formation of a middle class similar to that in England and the United States.

The theorists of the Mexican bourgeoisie were not long in discovering a doctrine fit to guide and to justify their actions; it was provided by the English positivists John Stuart Mill and Herbert Spencer (particularly the latter), and by the theory of evolution of Charles Darwin. The theories of those men appeared to mark the safest way and, at the same time, to coincide to a considerable degree with the ideas set forth by the first of the Mexican middle-class theorists, José María Luis Mora. In a way, John Stuart Mill and Spencer had merely developed the ideas already contained in Adam Smith, Bentham, and James Mill. All these thinkers together were the exponents of common sense so much admired by the Mexicans, and their doctrines appeared most appropriate for the education of the Mexicans. Indeed, English positivism could not be reproached by the Mexican liberals with being contrary to the idea of liberty. There were the great examples of liberal rule in England and the United States. There was Spencer assailing state coercion, and Mill defending individual liberty. To each of them the state was more what Mora had wanted it to be, an engine for the protection of the individuals living in it, an engine which could be discarded as unnecessary once the individual mind had learned to respect other people's interests without being under state compulsion.

Here then we come upon the group of young positivists who, from the pages of *La Libertad,* called out for a new order and proposed an honest tyranny as an emergency measure. This group no longer followed Comte, as their master Barreda had done, but Mill and Spencer. What was there in the doctrines of those two thinkers to justify an idea which at first sight seemed so flagrantly to conflict with them? The main justification was furnished by Spencer's idea of evolution. "To me it is beyond doubt," wrote Justo Sierra in one of his articles in *La Libertad,* "that society is an organism; it may differ from other organisms—that is why Spencer calls it a *super-organism*—but it shows undeniable analogies with all living organisms. . . . Society, the same as any living being, is subject to the laws of evolution." These consist essentially "in a double movement of integration and differentiation, a march from homogeneity to heterogeneity, from incoherence to coherence, from indetermination to determination. That is to say, the component parts of each body or organism grow more differentiated and specialized in proportion as the organism grows more unified and integrated. This double movement marks the increasing perfection of the organism, a perfection which, in societies, is called progress."

Thus adherence to Spencer's *Principles of Sociology* entailed disagreement not with the idea of liberty held by Mexican liberals but with the belief that Mexican society was ripe for that kind of liberty. Unlike the followers of Comte, those of Spencer did not contend that this type of liberty belongs to a stage of metaphysical transition; they regarded it as an aim to be reached; not as something past but as something to come. To realize this liberty Mexican society must first reach the corresponding stage of evolution. The new conservatives were opposed to the liberal constitution of 1857 because they deemed it utopian, or rather, untimely. Constitutions of that kind might be suitable for advanced countries like England and the United States but not for Mexico whose progress was lagging. "Is it not foolish," they asked, "to erect a gigantic building on swampy ground before first laying a solid foundation?"

In their opinion, the first thing an acceptable Mexican constitution had to see to was the material advancement of the country. Liberties were useless in a materially underdeveloped country. Once a satisfactory material status had been reached liberty would follow by itself, through natural evolution. "The day we find that our charter has produced a million settlers, we may say we have found the right constitution, a constitution no longer amounting to merely a phrase on our lips, but to ploughs in our hands, locomotives on our rails, and money everywhere." Ideal liberty would come; surely, it would. "We prefer normal and slow progress to rash and violent proceedings." These men were partial to progress by *evolution* instead of *revolution*.

The immediate need was to strengthen society, to integrate and homogenize it. For in proportion as society becomes more integrated and more homogeneous, its elements, the individuals, become more differentiated and more distinct. With social order growing more stable, individual liberty becomes more secure. Up to their time, so the positivists argued, Mexico had been a country without order, hence a country that had not complied with Spencer's law of progress. There was no passing directly from anarchy to liberty; a stage of order had to be interposed.

Looked at in this way, it was natural and in keeping with English positivism that the reform group should ask for a strong state capable of establishing that order which was so indispensable to the progress of Mexico. As Justo Sierra put it: "A nation which, owing to the motley and disparate quality of its elements, suffers from exceedingly poor living conditions needs, above all, a strong center fit to lend support to the forces of cohesion. Else dispersion will become more and more marked; the organism will not integrate; and the society will prove abortive." Disorder, Sierra went on, "is to blame for our nation's ranking among the weakest and worst defended social organisms of the civilized world." While Mexico is ruining itself "a sturdy collective animal for whose enormous insides no amount of food suffices lives next to us ready to devour us." We are in danger "of supplying a good instance for Darwin's theory with our chances of survival being very small indeed." [9]

VII

Political evolution and evolution of political liberty had to be sacrificed for what Sierra called *social evolution,* that is, for that degree of social organization without which political evolution must remain a chimera. To wean the Mexicans from their habits of disorder proved a very difficult undertaking. "Those ingrained Mexican habits," says Sierra, "are a thousand times more difficult to get rid of than the old regime and the ruling classes it established. Nothing short of a total change in our working and living conditions can bring about a transformation of this order." Only a strong state could work such a miracle. Once a group or a party was able to maintain for some length of time a state of organization, political evolution would be set going. "And the mass of the people, which is more important in democracies than in aristocracies, will follow suit; for the function creates the organ." All political power and with it all political liberty were to be handed over to one strong man, General Porfirio Díaz. "To accomplish the great task enjoined on him," Sierra went on to say, "the President needed a maximum of authority, not only legal but *political, social* and *moral* as well." As to the first, he had to be in a position to take over the actual direction of political bodies: legislatures and governments of the states. As to the second, he must, with the consent of all, constitute himself the *supreme justice* of the peace of Mexican society. But all this renunciation and delegation of power to one man was to be compensated by the state's taking action in that matter on which Sierra, like all the champions of intellectual independence in Hispano-America, had set their high hopes: education. "To educate people," said Sierra, "means to make them strong. Liberty, collective and individual, is the patrimony of strong men only. The social evolution of Mexico will come to nothing unless it comes to this all-embracing end: liberty." [10]

On November 26, 1876, General Porfirio Díaz, who had led a victorious revolution against the government of Sebastián Lerdo de Tejada with the battle cry "no re-election," was nominated provisional president. On December 6 of the same year he ceded the power to General Méndez, but took it back provisionally on February 16, 1877. On September 25, 1880, Manuel González was elected with the consent of Díaz; but in 1884 Díaz took office again, this time to stay until May 25, 1911, the day of the Mexican Revolution. All political forces of the country rallied around his person. He became the symbol of that peace and order the men educated in positivist ideas had so much at heart. A strong feeling of material well-being, which became more and more dehumanized, prevailed among the generation that supported him: industry, money, railways, more money. Mora's ideal seemed to be fulfilled; a new class, the bourgeoisie, seemed to determine the destinies of the country. Progress seemed to triumph, social evolution to advance with gigantic steps. But with all this well-being the purpose for which order had been established—liberty—fell into oblivion. People were content with a very special form of liberty: the liberty to get rich—a liberty in which not all classes could participate. Sierra himself had a premonition that the lack of true freedom would, in the end, undo what had been accomplished in the sphere of social evolution.

The new type of Mexicans emphasized their difference from the previous generation. "We are taken to task," they said, "because of our lack of faith, our positivism, our ill-concealed contempt for the institutions of the past." This was true, of course; and the reason for it was the different education they had received. "In philosophical matters," they told the old liberals, "you relied on Voltaire and Rousseau, on the Encyclopedists and the *Choix de Rapports* of the French Revolution, and the most advanced of you studied high metaphysics from the works of the German School, while we have learned logic from Mill and Bain, philosophy from Comte and Spencer, science from Huxley, Tyndall, Virchow, and Helmholtz." So different an education could not but produce different people. "You stepped forth from college campuses," the positivists proceeded, drunk with enthusiasm for the great ideas of 1789. Quoting Danton and the Girondists you dashed to the mountains to fight the ecclesiastics, you set up reforms, you brought down reactionaries, you moulded our laws on the pattern of beautiful utopias which, at that time, were honored as good money in philosophical transactions. Whereas we, less enthusiastic, more skeptical and perhaps more egoistic, dedicate ourselves to Newton's theory of gravitation, to natural selection, to sociological studies, and are concerned with our terrestrial destinies rather than with celestial spaces. We do not care for questions that cannot be subjected to the control of observation and experience. We disregard the portion of the world that cannot be investigated by means of telescopes or other instruments of scientific research. We do not arrive at our truths forthright; to attain them we need constant ardent efforts and patient, elaborate investigation.

These young positivists regarded themselves as destined to guide their country. Their methods were sure and precise—the methods of science learned in the new schools Barreda had reformed. This scientific method they intended to apply to all the problems of Mexico, in particular the political ones. In 1881 they spoke of nothing less then the "Scientific Political School of Mexico." In 1880 a number of the members of the new generation entered the Chamber of Deputies, among them Justo Sierra, Pablo Macedo, Rosendo Pineda, Francisco Bulnes, and Jorge Hammeken Mexia. All of them except Mexia, who died prematurely, had a hand in setting up the new regime and initiating the epoch in Mexican history that has been given the name of Porfirism.[11]

VIII

In 1892 the political party called the Unión Liberal published a manifesto in which were set forth the principles on which the Porfirist regime reposed. The purpose of the manifesto was to support a fourth re-election of General Porfirio Díaz. To this end a program had to be presented that would satisfy the ever more powerful and numerous Mexican middle class. As the manifesto promised to analyze the social situation of Mexico "scientifically," the opposition party and the angry mass of the people which had been cheated out of their political rights soon dubbed the Unión Liberal "the Party of the Scientists."

Among other things the manifesto dealt with the necessity of increasing the rights of the Mexican people as they had obviously reached a higher stage of development. Formerly it had been necessary to endow the executive with greatest authority; now the time had come to extend the people's rights.

The manifesto continued: "Our party is now capable of enough rational self-discipline to be allowed fully to speak its mind within constitutional bounds and to participate more actively in the direction of public affairs, marking out the road toward our supreme ideal, the ideal of freedom in permanent coalition with order." The new party called itself the heir to the ideals of the old liberal party, but with one difference: it knew that liberty presupposes a definite degree of order. Thanks to Porfirio Díaz' government this order now seemed to exist. Order being established, liberty could advance another step.

The party around General Díaz considered the condition for liberty fulfilled.

We believe that the time is ripe for starting a new period in the history of our party; we believe that the transformation of its directive organs into organs of government is accomplished; now that peace and material progress are achieved we believe that political activity must consolidate order and provide that henceforward rebellion and civil war remain accidents, and peace based on the interest and the will of the people becomes the normal state; to this end political activity must be put to the crucial test of liberty.

An increase of liberties was to show whether or not Mexican society had reached the high degree of order required for making good use of freedom.

The new party proceeded to propose a number of liberties for which they considered the people sufficiently mature. But of these liberties, said the manifesto, the most important is not the freedom to vote. There are others of more consequence:

The nation would wish its government to prove that it considers the present peace a final state and, accordingly, reorganizes from an economical point of view some branches of the administration. . . . It would wish that, by suppression of internal custom duties, nation-wide liberty of commerce may become a fact instead of being a periodically renewed aspiration. . . . Thus and only thus peace will extend to future generations of Mexicans, whose resources have been taxed for the purpose of furthering our credit and our progress, and *allow them to support themselves,* nay to accumulate savings for greater well-being and strength. Under such circumstances peace will not have been paid for too dearly.

What is the meaning of these words? Their authors insisted on the necessity of granting more liberties, only to go on explaining that the least important of such liberties is *the freedom to vote,* i.e., political freedom. What they propose is freedom of commerce or, more generally, *economic freedom,* permitting savings and accumulation of capital. They ask for less state interference but only in the economic sphere, not in the political sphere. Political liberty may go by the board if only what we have called the *liberty of getting rich* is preserved—a liberty which, of course, benefits none but those who already possess means that can be increased. Clearly this is not a matter of granting the kind of liberty the old Mexican liberals had in mind.

The ideals of the Mexican bourgeoisie were political order and economic freedom. Political order maintained by General Díaz was expected to protect the economic liberty of the middle class. Political rights ranked second; they were of no interest unless they jeopardized economic liberty. There was no objection to curtailing political liberty or the right to elective government if this benefited an order agreeable to middle-class interests. This order was represented by General Díaz. Hence the necessity for his re-election.

Under Díaz the Mexican bourgeoisie felt it had reached its apex. The order it needed had become synonymous with national order. Now the people might be granted such liberty as suited middle-class interests. Díaz was the man to watch over this liberty and to see that it was not upset by the interference of any other class. In the words of the manifesto: "The Republic is aware of being the cause of her own progress and peacefulness. But she also knows that it is one man who has given practical form to the general tendencies; and this citizen the Convention has elected . . ." again to the presidency.

If Porfirio Díaz is re-elected for the fourth time, the manifesto continued, it is not because his services are deemed indispensable but because he has proved able to rule in accordance with the interests of the nation. He is not indispensable, he is useful. The middle classes renounced their own political rights and those of the Mexican people because it thus suited their interests, i.e., their economic rights. They had succeeded in making Porfirio Díaz their own "honest tyrant." As long as this situation prevailed they supported him and would go on supporting him. From the outset, the theorists of the Mexican bourgeoisie had distinguished between what they called personal dictatorships and social dictatorships. The first served what Mora had called group interests, as for instance the dictatorships of the military and the clergy. The second were dictatorships concerned simply with looking after the interests of society.

As it was feared that the autocratic rule of Díaz might turn into a personal dictatorship or the dictatorship of a group from the entourage of the President, that very manifesto advocated permanency of the judicial power in an effort to guarantee its independence. The manifesto also considered the formation of political parties which would exercise control over the political activities of the chambers and keep an eye on the chief executive. Thus the middle class sought to forestall the possibility of a personal dictatorship. What they were willing to put up with was a dictatorship of and for the bourgeoisie. And General Díaz was expected to act as their stooge.

But Díaz, a powerful personality of exactly the mentality the new group had declared war on, would not let himself be used as a mere instrument. He opposed the proposed reforms which would have curtailed his political control. He had no intention of maintaining an order agreeable to the Mexican bourgeoisie upon any basis other than the unconditional surrender of political power to him. He was prepared to concede to the middle class whatever economic benefits they wanted, viz., economic liberty or freedom to get rich; but he would not share political power. Economic control remained with the middle class; it was taken over by José Ives Limantour, one of the signers of the manifesto, as Minister of Finance.

When a nation surrenders all political liberty for the prize of economic control by one class, what is going to happen? Justo Sierra, with the keen intuition that distinguished him among the rest of the generation to which he belonged, foresaw grave dangers:

The nation has built up the power of this man through a series of delegations, nay abdications, which are extralegal since they lie in the sphere of social order; he has not requested this, but neither has he, for a moment, tried to elude so frightful a responsibility. And that is dangerous, exceedingly dangerous for the future. It *establishes habits* contrary to self-government, habits incompatible with the existence, perhaps not of great men, but certainly of great nations. But Mexico has confidence in her future even as the President has in his stars; she believes that once the supreme condition of peace is fulfilled beyond any fear of its crumbling and vanishing again, everything else will follow, will follow at its appointed time. May she not be mistaken![12]

IX

What was happening? The opposite of what the pioneers who had fought for the creation of a new type of Mexicans were expecting. Positivist education had not produced men similar to those who had made great nations of England and the United States. Positivism had become another instrument serving the desire of power and dominion that had distinguished Spanish Americans at all times. Scientific absolutism had superseded religious absolutism. And behind this phenomenon stood precisely those group interests Mora had battled against, except that the privileged classes were no longer the army and clergy but a new group that called itself the Mexican bourgeoisie—a group that had become narrower and narrower through the selection it practiced among its own ranks. A small but powerful oligarchy had formed around the President who had granted them the right of getting rich. This small group held all the wealth of the country; its members gave preference to their friends in the apportionment of prosperity. Cliques springing up in the shadow of local banks monopolized all profits and made of social progress but another legend. Blind to the problems of their country, those people were concerned with nothing but their own gains. And all this under the name of scientific and positivistic politics.

Social evolution, so dear to the disciples of Spencer, its impulses checked, was reduced to the evolution of middle-class wealth. The political and financial leaders of the country considered their own success the best index of progress. August science found itself harnessed to the interests of industrialists and financiers. Their methods lay beyond the reach of the great masses for which they felt an Olympian contempt. The people continued to be a minor that had to be ruled with an iron hand and could not be trusted with major liberties. Snobbism and luxury stood out against a background of general misery. The lower classes lived in utter poverty while the ruling classes arrogantly displayed their luxury. But had at least material progress been achieved, the indispensable requirement for the formation of a powerful bourgeoisie? Had the middle class been freed from its bonds to state and bureaucracy, as Mora had wished it to be?

No! The government continued to be the principal source of privileges; and the material progress that might have engendered a powerful bourgeoisie was not achieved. Despite all positive education middle-class mentality remained the same as in colonial times.

The principal source of wealth remained the same: the exploitation of the rural worker. The social structure set up by Spain remained the same: on the one hand the great landowner, on the other the peasant who had no claim to the soil he tilled. It all boiled down to a political change: the colonial lord of the manor had given place to the Porfirian landowner. If there was progress, it worked toward greater efficiency in the methods of exploitation. Under Díaz the official machinery permitted the landed gentry to accumulate more acres than they could ever have held under the viceroys.

Industrialization, which Mora had regarded as the rightful source of middle-class power, never materialized. The Mexican bourgeoisie contented themselves with such income as they derived either from exploiting the land which, as often as not, they had never seen, or from speculating with the economy of the country. Instead of exploiting industry, they exploited peasants or the Treasury. Such industries as sprang up were due to the great European bourgeoisies, French and English in particular, to whom the progress of the country was of no concern. The Mexican bourgeoisie never got beyond playing the handmaiden to foreign interests. The brightest members of the generation which had been taught positive science took service with foreign enterprises. Instead of themselves exploiting the riches of the country, they turned them over to foreigners for exploitation. With all their education they had remained as unpractical as ever. As to order, which the positivists had so much at heart, reality was to reveal that it had not struck root in the Mexican mind. And it had not done so because that would have involved a change of mind impossible to bring about by mere teaching or training. The thesis that the function creates the organ turned out to be completely wrong. Thirty long years of dictatorial rule had failed to build up the desired order. The best procedure, so Mora, Barreda, and Sierra had taught, was to use persuasion, to have order accepted because it served the interests of the entire nation. But there was the rub: the nation would not let itself be persuaded that the order in question suited any interests except those of a small group which regarded itself as representative of all national interests. Nor was the progress those reformers had in mind the progress of the nation.

Discontent, not order, made itself felt in Mexican minds throughout the country—discontent and disgust at a doctrine the practical results of which had been *nil;* at a regime concerned with the interests of a very small circle of people; at a social situation which differed in no way from that of the colonial period. The next generation of intellectuals rebelled against education based on positive philosophy; and the people rebelled against Porfirist government. The order that had claimed to be everlasting was followed by one of the longest and most sanguinary revolutions. The entire political apparatus that bore the name of Porfirism was abolished as useless, and its downfall sealed the doom of the philosophical doctrine supporting it. Thus ended the great experiment of Mexican Porfirism.[13] (Translated from the Spanish by Helene Weyl.)

NOTES

1. A more extensive study of these ideas is to be found in my forthcoming book, *Positivismo in Hispanoamérica*. For an acquaintance with the facts themselves I recommend *Antología del pensamiento de lengua española en la edad contemporanea*, selección, prólogo, y notas del Dr. José Gaos (Mexico, Editorial Séneca, 1945).

2. See my study, *Apogeo y decadencia del positivismo en México* (Edit. El Colegio de México, 1944).

3. Justo Sierra, *Evolución política del pueblo mexicano* (Mexico, 1902–3; republished by El Colegio de México, 1940).

4. *La Libertad*, periódico político (Mexico, 1878–84). A detailed analysis of the articles it contains may be found in my book, *Apogeo y decadencia*.

5. Sierra, *op. cit.*

6. José María Luis Mora, *Obras sueltas* (Paris, 1837). A selection from Mora's ideas, together with an interesting introduction, has been given by Arturo Arnáiz y Freg in his work *Ensayos, ideas, y retratos* (Mexico, Biblioteca del Estudiante Universitario Ediciones de la Universidad Nacional Autónoma, 1941). See my book *El Positivismo en México* (El Colegio de México, 1943).

7. Gabino Barreda, *Opúsculos, discusiones, y discursos* (Mexico, 1877). The work is contained in the *Antología* mentioned under 1 and in a new collection made in the Universidad Nacional de México with the title *Estudios* (Biblioteca del Estudiante Universitario, 1941).

8. A thorough analysis of Gabino Barreda's ideas is given in my book, quoted above, *El Positivismo en México*. See also Samuel Ramos, *Historia de la filosofía en México* (México, Imprenta Universitario, 1943).

9. Justo Sierra, "El programa de *La Libertad*," *La Libertad*, 1879. Sierra, we have seen, expounded the same ideas in 1903. See note 3.

10. Sierra, *Evolución política del pueblo mexicano*.

11. See *Apogeo y decadencia*.

12. Sierra, *op. cit.*

13. See *Apogeo y decadencia*. On the feeling of cultural discontent see Alfonso Reyes, *Pasado inmediato* (El Colegio de México, 1941). On social and political discontent, Manuel Calero, *Un decenio de política mexicana* (New York, 1920); Antonio Manero, *El antiguo régimen y la Revolución* (Mexico, 1911); José López-Portillo y Rojas, *Elevación y caída de Porfirio Díaz* (Mexico, 1921).

SOVIET LAW AND ITS ASSUMPTIONS

JOHN N. HAZARD

POPULAR opinion among common law lawyers of England and the United States holds that Soviet law has introduced conceptions which create an impediment to relations between the Anglo-American world and the USSR. Soviet jurists are equally sharp in their denunciation of the concepts of the common law. It is the purpose of this chapter to explore the charges and countercharges and to search for the basic assumptions on which they appear to rest.

The center of interest in the debate has been the relationship between the individual and the state. Common law lawyers have said that the individual loses under Soviet conceptions the freedom which was gained in the Magna Charta. Soviet jurists have said that the individual has found a new freedom, surpassing previous conceptions. The issue is joined. It is not a new issue, however. For both schools it has its origins rooted in the past. It is well to consider that heritage before advancing to current differences of opinion.

Evidence concerning the course of Russian legal theory before the eighteenth century is limited in extent. What evidence there is shows that the rulers associated law with their own power. No effort was made to incorporate into political life the theories developed by the Greek philosophers of a law above man. Russian scholars rarely traveled in the West. One of the few landmarks was the sixteenth-century treatise of Peretsvetov who urged a democratic monarchy under which the privileges of the boyar aristocracy would be abrogated in favor of a strengthened middle class. Ivan the Terrible incorporated some of these ideas in his struggle with the boyar aristocracy who sought to dethrone him, but he remained the supreme law giver.

The development of the "natural law" school in the West had little influence in Russia until the time of Peter the Great; but when "natural law" ideas finally reached Russia, they had to be coordinated with Peter's peculiarities. This coordination resulted in their distortion, for the absolutism of the Tsar was thoroughly established. It was explained that Russia had entrusted all authority to Peter, and he, therefore, was the spokesman for law. Later, in 1764, Zolotnitsky defended authority and the existing order in terms of the "natural."

Catherine the Great, on ascending the throne, was determined to introduce some of the liberal ideas of Voltaire and Montesquieu, but she was not entirely successful. Her ministers dissuaded her from going far, and their task of dissuasion was facilitated by the peasant uprisings of Pugachev in 1773 and 1774. Russia was to remain outside the influence of the Renaissance and Reformation until the nineteenth century. Even then the more liberal ideas which Alexander I espoused for a time and which were to influence his soldiers were not those of Voltaire but of Rousseau. Society was identified with the state in these ideas, for the French Revolution had not been a victory for political toleration or for the rights of the individual against the state.

It was the liberalism of France to which the liberals of Russia looked forward. It was the world of Rousseau and not of Locke to which they aspired; but even their limited aspiration was held in check by the tsars. Not until the twentieth century were the people able to force the tsar to grant a parliament. Even then the events of 1905 did not introduce a great change in political theory. The new fundamental law of the Empire, promulgated in 1906, stated the position of authority in Article 4 in these words: "To the Emperor of all the Russias belongs the supreme autocratic power. To obey his commands not merely from fear but according to the dictates of one's conscience is ordained by God himself."

Rebellion against constituted authority emerged with new vigor in Russia under the new ideas of the nineteenth century. The first attempts to introduce new political philosophies from the West failed with the "Decembrists" in 1825. The country was not yet ready. Agrarian unrest, emphasized by the conditions of serfdom, stirred the peasantry until liberation in 1861, but these peasant uprisings were ineffective in shaking the throne. Industrialization had not come to Russia until the latter quarter of the eighteenth century. Even the industrial revolution became effective slowly. Discontent with long hours, low wages, and disciplinary fines aroused the workmen, as they had aroused industrial workmen everywhere in the West, but the discontent was not channeled in political directions.

It was into these fertile fields of discontent that the ideas of Karl Marx and Frederick Engels finally filtered. Here, at last, was to be found a philosophy supporting rebellion on political grounds. It called for revolution to snatch power from the rulers of Russia so that power might be wielded for the benefit of greater numbers of citizens. It attacked the misuse of power by the tsars. It argued that there was no hope that the tsars might be persuaded to use power for the benefit of the masses. Power would have to be taken away from the rulers and transferred to others who were to come up to positions of leadership from the masses. Power would then be used for new purposes, but it would still be a strong authority. There was no concept such as the basic philosophy of the English revolution of rights of the individual against the state. No Russian Marxist argued that the rule of law meant the enforcement of the rights of the individual against the state. There was no feeling that democratic government meant weak government.

The pattern of organization of the political party formed by the Marxists to further their cause indicated the tenor of their thinking. There emerged with the twentieth century a Russian Social Democratic Labor party. Some of its members conceived of this party as one to be modeled along lines familiar in the West—with a broad membership organized in local units and bound together by a loose central organization. These members lost out in 1905.

The party was developed as a relatively small, closely knit group of professional revolutionaries, who were organized in local units bound closely to a strong central organization to which they owed complete allegiance. Policies were determined by debate, but when they were agreed upon they became binding upon all. Authority of the center was supreme. Adherents were not sought on the basis that here was a mild organization which required of its members a minimum of discipline in furthering a program designed for the general good; they were recruited with an argument in favor of speedy progress toward elimination of the tsar as a prerequisite for any development of programs for the masses. For this rapid progress it was explained that the strictest discipline would be required, and members were trained in techniques which Marxists believed proved by history. It was the objective of defeat of tsarism and development of a program designed to benefit the masses in the manner Marx had outlined as the result of his historical studies which was the vision of Social Democratic leaders. It was not a state in which authority would be lessened nor one in which the individual might enforce rights against the state.

With the victories of 1917 the Russian Marxists came to power. They immediately set about establishing the principles for which Marx had argued. First and foremost was the principle of Marx's *German Ideology,* expressed in these words: "Only in the collective can the individual find the means of giving him the opportunity to develop his inclinations in all directions; in consequence personal freedom is possible only in the collective." Secondly, the Russian Marxists called for the complete smashing of the old state apparatus and its replacement by a new mechanism manned by persons devoted to the goals set by Marx. The state was to be placed in the hands of men trained to lead in the direction which Marx believed beneficial to the masses and to society generally. The individual was to be benefited, but it was believed impossible to benefit him if he became the subject of attention apart from the society in which he lived. Russian Marxists looked to the state as the instrument by which the individual would be led to a better world.

Very few Americans would now call themselves anarchists. Almost all would declare their agreement with the principle that the individual must live in society to prosper, and that society requires an organized authority powerful enough to maintain order. To this extent Soviet Marxists and American non-Marxists would agree. Disagreement arises when the next step is taken. Dominant schools of American political thought would grant the essentiality of the authority of the state only to preserve orderly conditions. After order is assured, the individual is to be left free to work out his own salvation in accordance with his own concepts of truth.

Schools of such nature abhor any suggestion that the mechanism of the state should be utilized as an instrument of leadership. They doubt whether any single individual or group of individuals knows or can know the direction in which the state should lead in order to achieve the maximum benefit to the individual. They prefer to rely upon the interplay of the social and economic forces of the nation to produce measures which have proved their worth in the school of experience. They believe that the only way to be certain of progress is to let trial and error decide.

Such Anglo-Americans believe experience has already demonstrated that matters such as those related to public health, highway maintenance, and water supply can best be administered by the state. By degrees they have reached the conclusion that the aged and unemployed can best be cared for by social security. In the main, however, they prefer to see the state's activities held to a minimum, so that individuals may develop their future without the restrictions of an official program. They fear that official programs become too inelastic to permit changes in policy as experience indicates that changes are desirable.

Soviet political philosophers take sharp issue with such views as to the place of the state in social organization. They acknowledge that the test of experience is to be sought in proving the desirability of any policy, but they differ from the Anglo-American schools in maintaining that experience has already provided its lesson for the twentieth century, and perhaps beyond it. They argue that once the lesson has been learned every force of society should be concentrated upon the achievement of the objective. For the Soviet theorist, nurtured in the authoritarian tradition of old Russia and the political theories of Karl Marx, the most effective and speediest way of concentrating the forces of society upon achievement of the objectives is by utilizing the state.

By pressing forward with the state as the guide and the authoritarian leader, Soviet philosophers hope to achieve their goals faster and with less anguish and suffering than a society which chooses to progress by the slower methods of laissez faire. Soviet jurists expect that there will be occasions for review of policy as interim objectives are achieved. In these reviews they may find it desirable to adopt a new tactic because of the changed conditions which the pursuit of their policy has brought about.

Divergence of views between the Soviet jurists and dominant schools of thought in the United States emerges at the point where the state's functions are considered. There is no divergence of views on the ultimate objective, for both groups believe that it is the function of society to seek benefit for the individual.

Evidence of the Soviet aim is found in the well-known interview with Roy Howard in 1936, when Stalin said, "But we did not build this society in order to restrict personal liberty but in order that the human individual may be really free." Soviet political philosophy holds no doctrine of the total immolation of individuals in society; there is no difference of opinion between the Anglo-American and Soviet schools on this score. It is rather the question of the role of the state in its relation to society which is in issue.

The split of opinion between the legal philosophers of the USSR and of the Anglo-American world can be traced with some ease, when their differing assumptions as to the duties of the state have been clarified. The Soviet jurist looks upon law as an instrument of policy—a tool of social engineering. We have seen that his ultimate social objective is benefit to the individual, and that this is expressed even as freedom of the individual. We have seen also that this ultimate objective is believed achievable if the method chosen to seek it is the state, acting as a positive guide toward the objective. Law becomes for the Soviet jurist the principal tool in the workshop of the state.

Anglo-American thinkers have clashed with Soviet jurists over the conception of law as a tool of the state. Much diversity of opinion exists among American jurists as to the nature and functions of law, but the most popular conceptions spring from ideas which are old indeed. Perhaps the most familiar classic statement about the common law is that of St. Germain in 1518:

The law of England standeth upon general customs of old times, used through all the realm, which have been accepted and approved by our sovereign lord the king, and his progenitors, and all his subjects. And because the said customs be neither against the law of God, nor the law of reason and have already been taken to be good and necessary for the commonwealth of all the realm; therefore they have obtained the strength of law, insomuch that he that doth against them doth against justice: and these be the customs that properly be called the common law.

Anglo-Americans have learned to think of the law in their lands as the product of custom, sometimes crystallized in legislation but always essentially the product of the wisdom of society in the mass. Those among the Anglo-Americans who have believed that custom must develop in accordance with some pattern have accepted the principle enunciated by the ancient Greek philosophers that there has been a guide to this development in the form of a superior "Reason," beyond the complete comprehension and control of man. Those among the Anglo-Americans who have been moved by spiritual experiences have accepted the principle enunciated by St. Thomas Aquinas that divine wisdom is manifested in the course of the development of law as the embodiment of social custom. Both groups unite in support of a modern version of natural law.

To the natural-law proponent society develops and will continue to progress in accordance with a wisdom which is beyond the individual's control. The state itself must accede to the dictates of natural law. It cannot use law as its tool, because natural law is above the state itself. In a sense, the state is an instrument of natural law, through which its principles are enforced in society.

The natural-law school is, however, no longer entirely representative of American thought. Sharp criticism of its position has emerged relatively recently. The school of thought which has come to be known as pragmatism looks askance at proponents of natural law. Pragmatism's principal philosopher, John Dewey, has written, "But we also find that one of the chief offices of 'nature' in political and judicial practice has been to consecrate the existent state of affairs, whatever its distribution of advantages and disadvantages, of benefits and losses; and to idealize, rationalize, moralize the physically given—for customs from a philosophical point of view are part of the physical state of affairs."

Pragmatism has been popular in the United States. Metaphysics is not believed by pragmatists to be a means of determining how law emerged or why it remains necessary and continues to exist. Pragmatists insist that one must explore practical consequences to determine whether a principle of law is good. One must look for expediency to determine the desirability of continuing to apply a principle of law. As William James has said, " 'The true,' to put it very briefly, is only the expedient in the way of our thinking, just as 'the right' is only the expedient in the way of our behaving."

Soviet jurists are in agreement with Dewey that philosophers have erred when they concluded that God or Reason, and their variations as found in Rousseau and Kant, lie at the base of law. But Soviet jurists believe that Dewey cannot deny that the pragmatists have come to support as of practical value and expediency the same theses which they call erroneous when they are traced to a "natural law." Dewey is complimented by Soviet jurists because he does not claim to have found eternal verities and eternal sources of law. On the other hand he and his followers are criticized because in their search for what is practical and expedient they have come to look in a mirror and see only themselves. Soviet critics say that pragmatists have come to accept the values of the social organization in which they live as the expedient ones. In consequence, they are found to have resisted change as effectively as the proponents of the natural-law school, even though they do it in the name of the scientific method. To the Soviet jurists the pragmatists seem to be apologists for current bourgeois law.

Understanding of the Soviet view rests upon an analysis of how they have come to adopt it. Soviet jurists, like the pragmatists in America, base their conceptions upon what they believe to be a scientific analysis of the sources of law; but their conclusions are not the same as those of the pragmatists. The pragmatists have examined the history of society from early times, and have reached the conclusion that law emerged with the state at the time of the breakdown of tribal society.

To the Soviet jurist the state appeared only after division of labor became possible and man achieved a level of production which left a surplus over tribal needs, from which trade emerged. With this phenomenon, accelerated by the fact that it facilitated specialization in certain types of production with the expectation that the products could be exchanged for others necessary for continued existence, the concept of "property," or ownership of things, emerged. Once the concept of property had come into society and trade brought outsiders into the family community of the tribe, later to be swelled with slaves captured in warfare with neighbors, individuals emerged with varying amounts of property. Those who had led the tribe required more than tribal custom to assert authority and preserve the advantage of wealth. The apparatus of compulsion, to become known as the state, was created and exploited to the advantage of those owning property. Law was developed as an instrument of government—a means of class domination.

Having reached their conclusions that the origin of the state and law is related to the emergence of the concept of private property, Soviet jurists trace the expansion of this relationship through the course of history. They find a pattern, which often lacks clearly defined lines but which gains clarity as one approaches modern times. They find that the essential feature in the definition of the pattern is production. As mankind has developed new means of production which have exceeded in volume the quantities of wealth produced by previously existing means of production, the social structure has changed. Those who had profited by ownership of property which was capable of maximum production in one epoch either come to own the new form of property which has outstripped the production level of the property they used to own or are forced out of their position as the dominant class by those who have come to be the owners of the more productive source of wealth.

Slaveholders were superseded by those who owned land and became feudal lords. Feudal lords were superseded by those who owned the machines developed by the industrial revolution. In each epoch—slaveholding, feudal, or bourgeois—the Soviet legal scholars find that law has been utilized to preserve the power of a dominant class, the owners of whatever is the most productive type of property at the time. The conclusion is reached that law is not above the state; it is a tool of the state, and it is utilized to further the policy of the governing class. Marx and Engels summed up the conclusion in their Communist Manifesto in 1848: "Your jurisprudence is but the will of your class made into law for all, a will whose essential character and direction are determined by the economic conditions of existence of your class."

Having reached the conclusion that the function of society is to benefit the individual, that the state is the instrument of leadership, and that law is the tool of the state, the Soviet jurist turns to his statesmen for guidance as to what law should seek to achieve for the state. He is told that economic abundance is the first objective. The emphasis placed upon the economic aspects is easily understood by him. Two world wars, a revolution, and a destructive civil war have depleted stocks of goods and the means of replenishing them to a dangerous level. Life itself depends upon the immediate provision of a minimum of the essentials of food, clothing, and housing. Society is called upon to sacrifice almost everything to the end of providing material goods so that Soviet citizens may continue to live. Even if there were no political theory supporting emphasis upon production, it is hard to see how such an emphasis could have failed to emerge from the conditions of Eastern Europe. The urgency of achieving the objective is based upon more than self-preservation, however.

Soviet statesmen believe that the perfect society is one in which there are enough commodities to supply all that each citizen needs not only to survive but to enjoy life. Marx's goal of a society in which every member will receive in accordance with his needs is ever before Soviet citizens. It is more than a goal expressed in terms of food, clothing, and housing. It includes the education necessary to enjoy the pleasures of the mind, and the resources and inspiration from which the cultural commodities of the fine arts, music, and literature emerge. The dream of a society in which there shall be freedom from want is ever present. The general acceptance of such a goal, rather than one of an élite of privilege such as that fostered by the National Socialists in Germany, is presumed to be universal among Soviet citizens.

Marxist analysis of productive forces in the history of social development is relied upon to determine how such a goal of abundance may be achieved. Private enterprise and capitalism are recognized as vastly more productive than feudalism, and therefore potentially beneficial to all the citizenry of a state which has remained essentially feudal in character. There is found, however, a limitation upon the productive forces as capitalism advances to the stage which Lenin called "imperialism," when wealth becomes concentrated in the hands of groups that grow so powerful they can control markets, reduce production to maintain or raise prices, and influence the governments of states to make war to extend the markets available to the financial groups seeking markets, with resulting destruction of wealth and limitation of the general productive level in the conquered lands. In addition to these activities, the capitalists are believed to be ready to restrict the share of the laborers in the profits made from production, with the result that purchasing power is not expanded as rapidly as it might otherwise be. The absence of economic planning is believed to result in the squandering of wealth in private ventures for which there could be no hope of success, although the individual entrepreneur with his limited vision is unable to foresee his failure.

In the light of such an analysis, capitalism seems less productive than a planned economy in which the state assumes the role of the producer and entrepreneur. Planning is expected to minimize loss of wealth and to maximize production by facilitating evenness of development in related industrial and agricultural fields. Profits from production become available to the state for reinvestment or social services, rather than to the private factory owner or owners who may not utilize them for the public good.

Socialism, with its basic principles of state ownership of the means of production, and central planning, is believed by Soviet economists to be the form of social and economic organization that can achieve the goals which have been set. Everything which is found to be useful in achieving the objective of socialism is acceptable. Everything which retards its coming is bad. The achievement of the objective is not expected to be easy, the less so since a people which has not enjoyed even the necessities of life for thirty years can be expected to look longingly at the successes of private enterprise in the more advanced Western countries. It is assumed that citizens will have to be guided and some of them even coerced into patterns of conduct designed to achieve production of the most extensive sort.

Sacrifices can be expected to be required for a considerable period of time before results appear. Stalin has stated the matter clearly in his interviews with Roy Howard: "Of course, in order to build something new, one has to economize, accumulate means, temporarily limit one's requirements, borrow from others." Soviet law rests upon the assumption that sacrifices will be required—in many fields—but that they bring nearer the attainment of the ultimate objective.

Anglo-American scholars likewise accept the necessity of sacrifices when the nation is in danger. Experience in the United States, and even more dramatically in England, has indicated a willingness to sacrifice. This willingness went so far in England during the past war as to permit even the sacrifice of some of the safeguards long associated with individual freedom. Labor was mobilized and the privileges of the writ of habeas corpus were suspended. During the Civil War in the United States the privileges of the writ had also been suspended.

The Western quarrel with the basic Soviet assumption that sacrifice is required is not so much a quarrel with the principle itself, when used in moderation. It centers rather on the fear that the sacrifice will become nearly permanent, because it is believed that a socialist form of economy will not only fail to exceed a capitalist form in productivity but will not even equal it. Suspicion of socialism is further enhanced in the West by the feeling that by placing ownership of the means of production in the state the economic and political power of the leadership is increased to a point where it may become headstrong. No force sufficiently strong to check an abuse of power by the leadership is left outside of the leadership's control.

Criticism such as the above falls on deaf ears in the USSR. In view of the Marxist thesis that the bourgeois state is in the control of those who own the means of production, any formal control over state officials is thought to be ineffective in practice. With a basic assumption, supported by research in the origins of law, that law is but a tool of the state, the Soviet jurist cannot accept a thesis that there is a means of control over the state available in law. On the contrary, the Soviet jurist argues that the state, and law as its tool, must be turned to the achievement of maximum production as the first step, and as a prerequisite to development of the conditions in which the individual can say that he is free.

Emphasis upon production and the sacrifices required for it is not so great that the Soviet jurist is permitted to overlook the individual. Times have been numerous when Soviet administrators let their enthusiasm for speedy progress toward the economic objective overcome their sense of long-range perspective. Efforts to stem such tides have appeared, as evidenced by Stalin's restraining hand upon the use of methods of collectivization which had forced individuals very much against their will into forms of agricultural management thought necessary for maximum production. The same restraint was exerted again in 1935 after industrialization had been pushed at such a rate that the individuals who manned the factories were overlooked and became restive.

The fact that law is treated as a tool of the state does not mean that it shall be utilized without reference to the interests of the individual. The interests of the state have been declared to be the long-range interests of the individual. It is thought to be to the interest of the state in reaching out toward its objectives to restrain arbitrary action of its officials. Soviet jurists, therefore, insist that there be observance of laws designed to convict only those who violate the rules deemed essential to social progress, and to result in acquittal of the innocent. There is thought to be room for a system of law protecting the individual, while the state at the same time utilizes law to preserve the discipline deemed necessary to speed toward the achievement of economic abundance.

Soviet jurists hold before them Lenin's admonition, "I have discussed soberly and categorically which is better, to put in prison several tens or hundreds of instigators, guilty or not guilty, or to lose thousands of Red Army men and workers? The first is better. And let me be accused of any mortal sin whatever and of violating freedom. I admit myself guilty, but the interests of the workers will win out." It is a doctrine which calls for sacrifices, even of the innocent, when the preservation of the Soviet state and its promise of socialism are in peril. But it is a doctrine which also contains in it the assumption that when the peril has passed, those who are not guilty will not be put in prison.

During the interwar years there was a noticeable tendency to emphasize the importance of adhering to measures designed to assure the protection of the innocent. Defense attorneys who had been maligned during the early years of the revolution as instruments of reaction, standing in the way of progress, were restored to a position of importance. The accused was given a constitutional right of counsel at his trial.

Procedural law, which was looked upon during the early years as a necessary evil to keep a court case from being lost in irrelevancies, was restored to importance. Judges were advised by the Supreme Court that procedural law must be observed, since it had an important purpose: protection of the innocent, and aid in determining who is really guilty of a crime against society. Civil law with its many rules designed to preserve orderly relations in social intercourse was restored to a position of importance just before the war. Finally, the article of the criminal code permitting the punishment of acts which were deemed by a court to be socially dangerous even when there was no pertinent article of the code concerned was restricted in application. The Supreme Court ordered that the principle of analogy be applied sparingly and only in the exceptional case.

The war years reversed the trend. The Soviet state was endangered, and law was called upon to protect it. At the height of the German advance in October, 1941, the State Committee for Defense ordered the shooting on sight of spies, provocateurs, and other agents of the enemy enlisted to disrupt the public order. The principle of prosecution of dangerous acts by analogy to articles of the criminal code when there was no article specifically concerned was extended to several activities which had become dangerous under wartime conditions. The principle of Lenin's early admonition was illustrated in practice. Survival of the Soviet social system was at stake, and the individual was the sufferer when there was reason to believe that he was guilty of endangering that social system's fight for life.

With the end of the war the calm of the middle 1930's has been restored. The Supreme Court has instructed lower courts to apply the principle of analogy sparingly. Lower court decisions are being reversed when procedural requirements have not been observed. The death penalty for crime has been abolished, in a decree stating specifically that this has been found possible because the cause of peace can be considered secure for a long time.

There remain, however, the Special Boards in the Ministry for Internal Affairs. These boards have jurisdiction over actions which do not constitute crimes but which give rise to a suspicion of social danger. In such instances the Special Boards may take protective measures and banish suspected persons for periods up to five years to a specific place named by the board, exclude a suspected person for periods up to five years from the capitals, large cities, and industrial centers of the USSR, intern a suspected person in a corrective labor camp for periods up to five years, and expel foreigners from the USSR. Such boards are considered by Soviet jurists concessions to necessity and by no means indicative of their hopes for the future. On the contrary, they look forward to a society in which the entire apparatus of compulsion—army, police, and courts—shall have become unnecessary and shall disappear.

It is this assumption that law and its enforcement agencies will eventually be unnecessary which has received particular attention from the West. The Anglo-American jurists look for no such time to come in their own social organizations or in any other. Soviet thought on this subject is based largely upon the work of Engels. He reached the conclusion that a socialist society in which means of production were owned by the state would see the end of economic classes, defined in contrasting terms as those who owned the factories or the land and those who toiled as factory hands or tenant farmers upon the land.

In the light of the conclusion that a classless society was an eventuality and that the state as an apparatus of compulsion had developed to maintain the dominance or ruling position of a class over other classes, Engels decided that the state eventually would not be required. Law, as its tool of authority, would likewise become unnecessary. Members of society would enjoy physical and cultural abundance, meeting all their needs. They would have learned to live amicably together in accordance with social custom which had proved its worth. The state and law would "wither away" as unnecessary social instrumentalities.

No clear explanation was given by Engels as to the manner or speed with which the withering process might be expected to proceed. Some schools of Soviet thought have assumed that it would be a gradual observable process in which legal regulation of civil law relationships would become unnecessary, while criminal law could be applied on the basis of a few general principles without regard for specific sections of a code, defining crimes in detail and providing for penalties varying with the predetermined danger of each type of activity. Other schools argued that the process would not be gradual. The state and law would remain as powerful instrumentalities guiding society toward its ultimate goal of abundance and customary order, to be known as Communism, and when that was at last achieved the state and law would be unnecessary and would cease to have any being.

The latter school of thought has become dominant. Soviet leaders declare that the state and law are to survive and to be strong until they are no longer needed. This is declared to be a phenomenon dictated by Marxist dialectics, an example of the application of the principle of the negation of the negation. Soviet law will be a powerful tool in the hands of those guiding society toward Communism. It will eventually, however, wither away when Communism is achieved.

Soviet jurists do not lose hope because the period before society achieves Communism appears to be long; they are prepared to wait for the time necessary for such a development. But it is their primary assumption that such a pattern of social organization can ultimately be achieved if the goal is kept before them, if the state is utilized to guide society in this direction as fast as it will go, and if law is utilized as a tool of the state rather than as an instrument above the state restraining its progress at the fastest rate possible. The individual is expected to come into his inheritance and to be free from want and from restrictions which are now enforced by law.

English and American jurists of the non-Marxist schools refuse to accept the validity of such assumptions. They find nothing in the experience of history to prove that power is relinquished by those in authority, if no checks upon the exercise of that power exist. They are prepared to acknowledge that classes, in the Marxist sense, may be abolished when means of production are owned by the state, but they believe that there are sources of continuing power other than in the ownership of property. They anticipate the emergence of a new ruling stratum, deriving its power from the positions of authority within the apparatus of the state which it has achieved. The aristocracy of wealth is expected to be replaced by a self-perpetuating bureaucracy which will forget its high principles and utilize in its own interests the apparatus over which it has obtained control.

In comparing the divergence of views existing in the USSR and the Anglo-American world, the difference of opinion seems to lie deeper than the relationship of the state and the individual. Both schools feel that they are striving to benefit the individual. Both believe that it is the function of the state to participate in that effort. But at this point the Soviet jurists evidence more faith in the individual than the Anglo-Americans are prepared to manifest. The Soviet school believes that it has found a pattern in the historical development of society and that by progressing as swiftly as possible in accordance with that pattern the goal of maximum benefit to the individual can be achieved. The state and law as the most powerful instruments which society has developed are to be utilized in the speedy course toward the objective.

The Anglo-Americans doubt that any such pattern as the Marxists find in history is really there. They expect that society will continue to evidence changing relationships, and that to solidify social relations at the present or any later time hampers the development of other forms and procedures which might result in greater benefit to the individual. The maximum of freedom to develop new forms and procedures commensurate with the preservation of order is to be maintained by preserving a state of moderate strength and a system of law designed to permit restraint upon the state if those at its helm at any time seek to usurp its authority for their own benefit.

Each side seeks a last word after reviewing the arguments of the other. The Anglo-Americans question whether the Soviet goal is not utopian. The Soviet jurists question whether the preservation of an orderly society in which the individual can work out his salvation is not distorted into the preservation of the kind of social organization in which those who do not have power cannot introduce their new ideas without violent revolution.

X

THE NEW DEAL AS A CULTURAL PHENOMENON

T. V. SMITH

When Franklin Roosevelt and his administration began their work in Washington in March 1933, the New Deal was not a plan with form and content. It was a happy phrase he had coined during the campaign, and its value was psychological. It made people feel better, and in that terrible period of depression they needed to feel better.

As Roosevelt described it, the "new deal" meant that the forgotten man, the little man, the man nobody knew much about, was going to be dealt better cards to play with.

Frances Perkins, *The Roosevelt I Knew.*

THE resurgence of North American courage under the leadership of Franklin D. Roosevelt was both a "deal" and a diversion. It was a deal in that it was professedly and actually an effort to restore morale and to distribute, yea, to redistribute, the mass economic increment.

Action is proverbial as an American ideal, but equally indigenous to Americans is the cooperative mode. Americans are for whatever can be done together, thus achieving through common endeavor the functional semblance of a game. Where everybody puts something into an enterprise, everybody gets something out of it, if nothing more than the highly important unearned increment of being "in on the know" and "in at the kill." Sportsmanship is the key to contemporary American life, and indeed the background of America suggests hardly less than the foreground that cooperation is justified of its process whatever may or may not issue as a product thereof.

Both de Tocqueville, traveler-observer of the early nineteenth century, and George Santayana, the Spanish neighbor-observer of the twentieth century, were alike impressed by a certain carry-over in America from British background: "the spirit of free cooperation," as Santayana calls it. "Everywhere," he declares, "cooperation is taken for granted, as something no one would be so mean or shortsighted to refuse. . . . The general instinct is to run and help, to assume direction, to pull through somehow by mutual direction. . . ." The pragmatic movement in American philosophy has but sought to establish in theory what the "progressive education" movement in pedagogy has grounded in practice—the notion, as Shakespeare has it:

> That no man is the lord of anything,—
> Though in and of him there be much consisting,—
> Till he communicate his parts to others;
> Nor doth he of himself know them for aught
> Till he behold them form'd in the applause
> Where they're extended. . . .

Of all this Anglo-American living, the *game* is a fitting symbol. Long before baseball came to furnish the chief metaphor of American life there was (and there remains) another game—a game of cards: "poker" it is called—in which "to deal" was but to initiate a cooperative activity that could be its own exciting reward, even to those who "lost their shirts" in its honor. Politics is in common American parlance a game, and in expert parlance it is "the great American game." Moreover, the symbolism carried over into business: a deal is a trade, any transaction for gain from which both sides are presumed to profit. Thus the very name of the Rooseveltian movement in question raises connotative echoes in the culture organic to America, in its full multi-dimensionality.

Franklin Roosevelt's extended administration was, then, a deal, but with new "wrinkles," as the colorful word goes. It was indeed a game played by old rules, but with now a few new plays: a *diverting* game. The stakes were vague but high: heightened morale for peacetime, deepened unity for war. It is our chief business now to spell out what was new and distinctive about the New Deal. The novelty of it, however, can be appreciated, and particularly can be evaluated, only in terms of its relations to what was not novel: to what had gone before and what still persisted to furnish context to the new.

There had been before it, within the memory of older New Deal personnel, two movements (to both of which Roosevelt himself was indebted: indebted to one by ties of family name; to the other by political participation and party loyalty), as preludes to this third. There was what Theodore Roosevelt had called "the Square Deal" and then what Woodrow Wilson had called "the New Freedom." Though the one movement was Republican and the other Democratic (in terms of party politics), Franklin Roosevelt, the Democrat, drew as impartially as he drew generously from both streams, in order to give body and form to his own movement, the New Deal. His was indeed the Square Deal consciously revivified, and it was the New Freedom streamlined into numerous alphabetical agencies of reform and made eventually exportable through war propaganda for the Four Freedoms.

These movements had both originated in or received impetus from the West, though neither was led by men native to that vast American region. Each movement caught up a great demand where numerous votes were congregated, each coined that demand into a political purpose if not a program, each with a catch-title and appropriate symbols for times that were hard. In doing so they but connected with Populism (a popular movement headed by William Jennings Bryan who *was* a Westerner) and reached back to connect with our traditional deference to pioneerism. For before these modern reform leaders there was Thomas Jefferson and there was Andrew Jackson, only the latter, of all our major political leaders, being in the current sense himself a Westerner. All these leaders were alike, however, in articulating frontier aspiration, in thriving upon Western support, and in revivifying at various levels the sense of pioneering.

These democratic leaders were alike, too, in much more. They were all against concentrated industry, against monopolistic capital, against regional dominance from the East. "Wall Street" became the continuing symbol of what was to be curbed, if not destroyed, through governmental action. In a certain sense they were all against cities, Jefferson at the beginning fearing for America if it ever became fully urbanized, and Roosevelt at the end hoping from his ample acres at Hyde Park for a healthful restoration of agrarian life in a soundly restored rural economy. If they shared a fear, they throve also upon a common hope. Henry Wallace, at the time Secretary of Agriculture, touched the common positive spring in a succulent little essay, entitled "The Strength and Quietness of Grass." "I have always had," he avowed, "a great affection for grass." Symbolically, that affection for the "grass roots" as the word goes—has been a wellspring of American life.

The hope common to these political movements had to do with that ancient thing men ever call Justice. And this meant a better chance for the millions who possessed little. In early days it meant land, free land, or at least cheap land—and so it was spelled out as homestead acts. In later days it meant better wages and more attractive working conditions, including shared initiative for determining both. Always it meant a rising standard of living, one not so obviously discrepant between the economic floor and the cultural ceiling. And always it meant for children, growingly and insistently for the children of all, an education which would nurture those hopes often frustrated in pressing for their more direct fulfillment. Free religious worship, free public lands, free public and nonsectarian schools, free opportunities for economic advancement—these were the freedoms which successive "deals" in American politics sought to further.

Onto this hand of hope, up-thrust from the past, Franklin Roosevelt's idealism fitted like a glove made to order. In the beginning indeed the New Deal was the lengthened shadow of this one man. Roosevelt was less driven by frustrations than most reformers, less led to compensate for frustration by aggressiveness. What alone in his life might have frustrated him was so pitilessly a matter of chance and fate that it matured him intellectually and mellowed him emotionally, without daunting his drive or diverting his aim. He himself belonged to the wealthy class—though in America, where every man may hope to better himself wealth does not constitute a ready basis for "class-consciousness." Being wealthy, however, and Eastern-born, Roosevelt was bred in our older culture; Groton-Harvard educated; sensitized by early foreign travel; but romantic as touching the land, innocent of industry, and largely inexperienced in corporate finance. Destined to be accursed by his peers for having "deserted his class," Roosevelt was informed of hope by temperament and disciplined of brotherhood by personal pain. Humbled in the flesh by the onslaught of poliomyelitis, and chastened in pride by the sight of suffering to which he had been intimately introduced, he compensated for intrepidity of the physical with an innovative mind and a bold imagination. This thrust of the spirit is the easiest identified birthmark of the New Deal, representing as it does the incidence of temperament upon national morale.

"Nothing to fear but fear" was the cry in 1933 of a soul self-triumphant over the despair tutored of failing banks and crashing corporate structures. Not only did Roosevelt innovate; he was proud of inventiveness in the social field, as proud of it as most Americans have been of inventiveness in the physical field. His appreciation of the inventive process far outran his appreciation of its given products, as his patronage of painting as a public work indicates, when he knew little of or cared little for paintings as products. He was indeed his own variegated patent office, promising escape from fear and prepotent for hope. Many a blueprint from many a private sensorium was mailed to utopia via the White House. Speaking of the early days of the Roosevelt administration, Miss Perkins says: "Washington was so hectic that it was difficult to concentrate on concrete programs. There were on my desk over two thousand plans for federal action to cover unemployment and as many more on the President's."

To distract attention from his physical condition—which at the time was feared to be more politically serious than it proved to be— as well as to enjoy what was boldly different, the nominee flew out to Chicago in 1932 to accept his first party call to the presidency, composing his acceptance speech in the upper air, as one who ascended to get a mandate from a purer region. This was symbolic of an expectation which Roosevelt put into words in his acceptance speech. He assured his friends and warned his political enemies what to expect from him: "Let it be symbolic," he told the Convention that had made him leader, "that I broke the tradition. Let it be from now on the task of our Party to break foolish traditions," leaving "it to Republican leadership, far more skilled in that art, to break promises."

In his inaugural address, on March 4, 1933, he promised, for the trust reposed in him, to "return the courage and the devotion that befit the time," resorting, if necessary, as he went on, "to broad Executive power to wage a war against the emergency, as great as the power that would be given me if we were in fact invaded by a foreign foe."

Roosevelt began his innovations with governmental personnel. Though choosing for Secretary of the Treasury (after an early interregnum) his wealthy farm neighbor, Morgenthau, easy and soothing symbol to great finance, he hit as readily upon Harold Ickes, self-confessed "curmudgeon," to be Secretary of the Interior and hatrack for many a subsequent agency, though Ickes was at the time but a little man from a big town, the "cut of whose jibs" Roosevelt said he liked. The first woman Cabinet-member—Miss Perkins —was also his selection. The President surrounded himself personally, and gradually charged the whole governmental structure, with idea-men, facile of projects and fecund of experiment. It was a poor idealist indeed who could not land some sort of a job in Roosevelt's Washington. And few ideas were too bizarre to be listened to, if divertingly presented. Nor were many plans of reconstruction too flighty to leave at least some flavor in the potpourri called national policy. Roosevelt himself rode many horses in many directions, for he could not wholly resist the temptation to experiment.

The pattern of policy which resulted was mottled; it was the despair of the logical. "He wanted a balanced budget," as his intimate biographer, Miss Perkins, genially says, "but he also wanted to do the right thing by his unemployed fellow-citizens." The multidimensionality of his policies resulted partly from the variety of his advisers, to none of whom was he inclined to give a categorical nay. Among early intimates were both the methodical Moley and the idea-tugging Tugwell, the project-hatching and manhandling Corcoran and the statute-implementing Cohen. The wild-eyed radical and the costumed college professor became the cartoonists' standard caricature of Roosevelt's love of the different and his audacity in perpetrating novelty at the level of national policy.

Nor was his stomach for variety confined to personnel. It actually issued as public policy. The climate of opinion in the New Deal was continuously Jeffersonian and Jacksonian, not to say Wilsonian; but the weather was—well, was what American weather is—changeable. Roosevelt came to power with the promise to balance the budget, for instance; but he embraced the Keynes' philosophy, which led the other way; and he reconciled the two in a moving logic which held that the only way to balance the budget is to balance what the budget is really about, the people's welfare. He balanced his conscience by keeping two budgets, one of which, for a while, "balanced." The farm program became a symbol of the multidirectional nature of many national policies: an economy of abundance realized through an interregnum of scarcity. Nor was it merely a matter of tacking right and then left, as politics often requires; it was, at times, also a matter of tacking both right and left at the same time.

Little wonder that when President Hoover heard, during the campaign which replaced him by Mr. Roosevelt, that Candidate Roosevelt had promised "self-liquidating public works—to provide employment," as Roosevelt blithely put it, *"for all surplus labor at all times"* (italics mine)—little wonder that the engineering-minded Mr. Hoover blurted out: "It is a promise no government could fulfill." Little wonder, either, that Hoover later in impatience uttered over the radio a paralyzing aside: "Thank God, we have a government in Washington that knows how to deal with a mob." It is great wonder, however, that Roosevelt was able to sustain the pervasive feeling that he was fulfilling the promise, in the light of concrete exceptions all too visible.

It is an approximate characterization of the New Deal to say that it differed from what went immediately before it, even from Mr. Hoover, more in the spirit of the doing than in the amount or nature of what was done. Under the impact of the depression President Hoover initiated many movements that Roosevelt was merely to consummate. But Roosevelt as President proceeded to do gladly what Mr. Hoover had tried to do grudgingly. The difference in national morale was immense, for the Lord's people loveth a cheerful doer. Initially, then, it is enough for us to characterize the New Deal as a new spirit and a glad spirit walking on troubled waters, domestically troubled and internationally troubling.

"Looking back on those days," says Frances Perkins, "I wonder how we ever lived through them. I cannot, even now, evaluate the situation. One thing I do see—it was dynamic. It was as though the community rose from the dead; despair was replaced by hope."

Measured against our national background, the New Deal was a resurrection of America's ancient spirit of hope. If the summit of its resurgence seemed to rise higher than before, it was because the valleys were deeper. So deep indeed was the economic valley that other nations wallowed in its trough too, sank deeper than we, and rose even more ecstatically than we from the valley of dead bones. Americans know, or should know, from the New Deal—its inception, its influence, its elation—how Fascism felt to the war-weary Italians, how Nazism felt to the inflation-groggy Germans, how Communism felt, and feels, to the reawakened Russian people.

Turning now from its national background, let us project the New Deal upon the international foreground: how like was it to its foreign counterparts, how unlike them? That double question answered, we shall return to characterize it more fully as the cultural phenomenon it was in the American environment.

The New Deal was like these other "isms" of the depression epoch in precipitate action and in resorting to a dynamic philosophy by way of explanation and justification.

It was like them in opportunistic strategy.

It was like them in triggerlike response to a public opinion which it itself had cleverly helped to create.

One need go little further than President Roosevelt's first inaugural address to document these similarities:

It is to be hoped [he said] that the normal balance of executive and legislative authority may be wholly adequate to meet the unprecedented task before us. But it may be that an unprecedented demand and need for undelayed action may call for temporary departure from that normal balance of public procedure.

I am prepared [he continued] under my constitutional duty to recommend the measures that a stricken nation in the midst of a stricken world may require. These measures, or such other measures as the Congress may build out of its experience and wisdom, I shall seek within my constitutional authority, to bring to speedy adoption.

But [he warns] in the event that the Congress shall fail to take one of these two courses, and in the event that the national emergency is still critical, I shall not evade the clear course of duty that will then confront me. I shall ask the Congress for the one remaining instrument to meet the crisis—broad Executive power to wage a war against the emergency, as great as the power that would be given to me if we were in fact invaded by a foreign foe.

All this he promised in the faith, as he proceeded to declare, that

the people of the United States have not failed. In their need they have registered a mandate that they want direct, vigorous action. They have asked for discipline and direction under leadership. They have made me the present instrument of their wishes. In the spirit of the gift I take it. . . . I will return the courage and the devotion that befit the time. I can do no less.

There followed, and followed immediately, in the spirit of the foregoing promise, a sustained period of crisis government: executive orders, "must" legislation, creation of special agencies, direct approach to the people via radio, immediate response to waves of public opinion from the people, clever use of the press to inspirit the administration's following and divert the opposition, efforts to warp the Democratic party into a "liberal" mold and to rid it of functionaries who did not fit the form. And then at a longer remove there followed the heroic and ill-fated effort to bring the Supreme Court around to like-mindedness as to the call of the hour for action and as to the resiliency of the Constitution to that call as heard and interpreted by the executive.

Moreover, Roosevelt broke a tradition coeval with the North American Republic: that presidents would not continue in office longer than two terms, eight years. This tradition he broke once, this tradition he broke twice: broke it first under the impact of a European war which the opposition said he welcomed for his own ends, and then broke it under the darker aegis of a Japanese attack which his personal enemies said he provoked in order to perpetuate his power uninterruptedly.

All these items became familiar also to Italian, German, and Russian citizens of the same period. (Roosevelt and Hitler came to power at the same time, as indeed they died the same year.) There was similarity enough to European totalitarianism to beget and in a way to explain a constant cry in America from the political opposition that the New Deal was despotic, that Roosevelt was or wanted to become a dictator, that his family was feathering the nest for a dynasty, that Congress was decadent, a mere "rubber stamp" for the executive will, that the Court would be a martyr if it escaped becoming a satyr, that free enterprise was gone and freedom of speech, if not also of worship, was going.

And yet the ancient freedom survived in America: it survived fully and wholly in the right of conscience and the practice of worship. It survived, and weathered the severe stress of a World War, in freedom of speech and press, less interrupted under Roosevelt through the severer World War II than under Wilson in World War I. Not only did these old and stable freedoms survive; others were instigated and extended. In the Atlantic Charter the traditional freedoms of conscience and expression were augmented by two more, newly formulated: freedom from fear and freedom from want, "linking in a plausible formula," as Raoul de Roussy de Sales says, "the inheritance of the past and the hopes of the future." The roots of these later freedoms had been nourished in America under Roosevelt throughout the time that he was being charged with undermining all freedoms. The freedom-from-fear constellation had derived from the "firm belief" of his inaugural address "that the only thing we have to fear is fear itself"—and so why fear? It had fed itself through ever-expanding movements, beginning with the Civilian Conservation Corps, to restore access to confidence for "the forgotten man." The freedom-from-want constellation had derived from Roosevelt's insistence upon public works to save face and to keep alive the pride in skill, while forfending hunger, for unemployed millions, as the wheels of industry got to humming once more.

That Roosevelt had never intended, or even thought, to subvert American constitutionalism is as nearly certain as any public judgment is likely to be. He was intent only upon making capitalism work, work as humanely as possible. With all the surface similarities of the New Deal to the new despotisms of Italy, Germany, and Russia, there were crucial dissimilarities. The greatest of these, whence came the saving grace of the American phenomenon, was the fact that the New Deal was a "deal" rather than a doctrine. There was little of the doctrinaire about it, and even less about its personalized symbol, Roosevelt. It was dynamic but not philosophic; it was idealistic without being ideological.

There may have been on the periphery of Roosevelt's orbit those who had their blueprints of utopia and who sought to insinuate them under Roosevelt's vest. But he had no pocket to hold such insinuations. His mind was too innocent of ideologies to become host to philosophies of even the ideas he did put to use. The Keynesian economics is a dramatic case in point. That the New Deal profited from Keynes technologically, so to say, is well known. The founding of prosperity upon purchasing power extended to the masses became a New-Deal truism. The supplementation of employment by public works was soon taken for granted. The increase of taxes during prosperity and their decrease in adversity became orthodox.

These techniques, however, were one thing; the general theory was, to Roosevelt, quite another. The former he utilized as occasion seemed to warrant. The other he could hardly be said to have understood at all. Miss Perkins reports that on the first meeting of Roosevelt and Keynes the Englishman had "supposed that the President was more literate, economically speaking"; and the American President had said: "I saw your friend Keynes. He left a whole rigmarole of figures. He must be a mathematician rather than a political economist." This intimate biographer puts the right light on the whole matter by concluding her report upon the meeting she had arranged between the two: "I wish he [Keynes] had been," she said wistfully, "concrete when he talked to Roosevelt, instead of treating him as though he belonged to the higher echelons of economic knowledge."

Whether de Tocqueville was right a century ago in holding that "the Americans are much more addicted to the use of general ideas than the English" is a matter to be doubted, certainly to be doubted contemporaneously, and indeed to be disputed in the meeting of Roosevelt with Keynes. But another observation de Tocqueville makes in the same connection was, and remains, sober sense about American culture. "The Americans," said that percipient Frenchman, "have not been required to extract their philosophical method from books; they have found it in themselves." Roosevelt was a typical American in depending for his philosophy upon *pre*suppositions rather than upon any systematic "suppositions."

Miss Perkins is the source also of a story which puts this matter in national perspective.

A superficial young reporter once said to Roosevelt in my presence, "Mr. President, are you a Communist?"

"No."

"Are you a Capitalist?"

"No."

"Are you a Socialist?"

"No," he said, with a look of surprise as if he were wondering what he was being cross examined about.

The young man said, "Well, what is your philosophy then?"

"Philosophy?" asked the President, puzzled. "Philosophy? I am a Christian and a Democrat—that's all!"

Not only was that "all," that was also *enough,* for Roosevelt; and it would be enough for most Americans. That is the reason Americans are so economical in their use of general terms. "Communist" is a term adequate to cover nearly anything, for instance, that is neither "Democratic" nor "Republican." There are presuppositions that lie deep in America: John Locke's theory of government as contractual retains its place among the people, even though to the intellectual it is long since "an exploded theory"; Christianity, meaning whatever it means, is enough to cover a multitude of virtues—and a few vices of provincialism mixed in.

"Roosevelt," observes Miss Perkins in concluding the previous story, "took the status quo in our economic system as much for granted as his family. They were part of his life, and so was our system; he was content with it. . . . I am certain that he had no dream of great changes in the economic or political patterns of our life."

It may be that on the periphery of Roosevelt's official family from time to time there hovered doctrinaires, but they could never consolidate their position under his generalship; for, not understanding them, he was constantly cutting across their various conflicting formulations. There may have been those who were for "planning" wholesale; he was for planning, but only retail. It may be, to specify, that Gen. Hugh Johnson was under the influence of Raffaelo Viglione and wished in the National Recovery Administration to imitate that author's *Corporate State,* which he is said to have carried around with him. It mattered little, for nothing could come of it in the whirlpool of Roosevelt cross currents. It may be that Rexford Tugwell had systematic notions about the *Industrial Discipline*. It mattered little, for nothing could come of it in the New Deal welter. Roosevelt was not an ideologist. He operated as he thought, opportunistically. He shot, when firing became necessary, "shot from the hip," as the pioneers said. The advisers of Roosevelt who made the greatest impression on the country were men who—unlike Wallace, who has ideas but can hardly himself boast a consistent ideology—shared Roosevelt's neat approach to problems.

And yet there was a certain method, half understood, in all this unmethodological madness: what George Santayana would call this "normal madness" of America. Roosevelt really thought that the only way to solve collective problems was to solve them collectively. A man cannot go off to himself and settle issues that exist between him and other men; there are no personal solutions of interpersonal problems. Ideologies are centralized solutions of collective conflicts through the presumption of personal vantage. The ideologist represents only a given point of view, whereas the essence of collective conflicts is that there is—and, alas, there is operative!—more than one point of view. All points of view must be represented if a solution is to emerge. So of course all points of view must be confronted in the form of persons representing them, in order to see what can be made to come out of the conflicts themselves. Otherwise, there is no solution—only "resolution," if anything at all. It was Roosevelt's distrust of political solitaire that turned him away from ideologies. Only a god or a brute would settle a public issue in private. It was Roosevelt's confidence in the method of *social solution of social problems* that made him the great democratic leader he was. We shall see presently how his distinctive contribution arose from this confidence—his politicizing of the whole of American life; and we shall see, too, his disadvantage in dealing with ideologists: with the Kremlin, for instance, or the Vatican.

Meantime, let us make two observations: one on the British Labor party; the other on the type of man who, under Roosevelt, was most influential in the country.

For all the commotion about the National Recovery Act, and for all the heart searching which attended the birth and maturation of the National Labor Relations Board (including the change now from the Wagner to the Taft-Hartley Act), there has hardly been a trace of the more ideological controversy which has marked the rise to power of the Labor party in England: whether, that is, workers should have any more direct participation in management under the state than under private ownership of an industry. American workers know little or nothing of the theoretical issue between syndicalism and Fabianism. With us the labor issue has been a much more practical matter of hours, wages, conditions of work, all of which are to be determined through the representative process of bargaining. There has been the question, of course, as to whether the government should be merely the umpire of the game, as it has been, or whether it should weight the rules unequally in favor of the weaker party. That there would be skilled managers, however, is taken for granted, in spite of the question as to whether the managers themselves should be allowed to organize. American labor has assumed the solution which British labor has arrived at through vehement controversy. There is not nor has there been any dogma influential in America as to "surplus value" or as to "moral management." Management has, of course, always been with us more a matter of promotion than of prerogative. American labor has thought, largely opportunistically, that it is entitled to whatever it can get out of the bargaining process; and it has been largely satisfied, opportunistically still, to accept any management that accepts these premises. The game's the thing, again: the game and its rules. The whole matter would rightly strike the doctrinaire as perversely *un*principled.

For the same reason, the spokesmen who under Roosevelt commanded most confidence were in this regard most like him, i.e., least contaminated by ideas. Jesse Jones, whom both parties alike supported in Congress throughout the New Deal, came to the Cabinet from successful management of the government's great domestic lending program (outside of agriculture). In the Cabinet he is reported by his fellow member, Miss Perkins, to have made on one occasion this authentically American analysis of the then national predicament:

Mr. President, [he said], at the depths of the depression the national income was $42,000,000,000. In 1934 the national income was $49,000,-000,000. In 1937 the national income was $71,000,000,000. If we can get the national income up to $90,000,000,000 in the next year or two, and I see no reason why we shouldn't, we don't have to give another thought to the budget. It will balance without the slightest difficulty. Mr. President, what we have discovered is that the national income grows by economic movement. The taxing power of the government applied to those truly economic processes of buying and selling and hiring and manufacturing and paying wages and spending the wages will make for a taxable income sufficient to get us out of this hole without any damage to our program. If nothing unforeseen happens, Mr. President, we shall be out of the woods.

A leader whose only "philosophy" was that he was a "Christian" (undefined) and a "Democrat" (unanalyzed) would have understood that speech with its dynamism of "economic movement" (unspecified).

Empirically typical as that approach is in what was called the New Deal, the something "unforeseen" did happen: the war. But that too was approached in the same ad hoc spirit. The war was run empirically—and the peace as well (as Mr. Secretary of State Byrnes was sadly to learn months after Yalta). Roosevelt liked Stalin and saw no reason why any ideological matter should stand in the way of getting ahead with the war. Stalin did not forget ideological matters, however, in any accommodating splurge of fraternalism; nor did he disconnect such concerns from the meaning of current issues. Roosevelt liked Churchill, and approached their common tasks in a spirit that was linear: linear with the multidimensional Churchill, who had no thought of presiding at the funeral of his Tory ideology. Roosevelt liked the Pope; and in a gracious burst of Christian fellowship proceeded to facilitate from Rome an immense wave of sectarian proselyting in a Protestant land and to further, beyond what any man can yet foresee, the steady attrition here against that crucial separation between church and state on which American liberty has long been based. Roosevelt liked all sorts of men, and did not see why men who liked each other should not get together and settle disputes through mutual give and take. As a Democrat he thought himself committed to accept whatever came out of conference; and as a Christian he felt himself committed to accord as the end of life. Not being a doctrinaire himself, he did not steadily understand that the doctrinaire always takes more than he gives (otherwise refusing to confer), leaving the empiricist to take what is left. So Roosevelt's friendly opportunism did not long outlast the war in international relations, any more than the New Deal as a domestic phenomenon is likely to leave any notable ideological legacies.

Without dogmatic ideology, save the presuppositions of democracy and Christianity, and minus a philosophy in the systematic sense, the New Deal embodied permanently only what is most typical of American two-party practice, with what has long been theoretically foregone. The New Deal serves to remind us that the profoundest philosophy of American life is that no philosophy is adequate to the free man's vocation. As William James, America's most typical professional in philosophy, says: "There is no conclusion. What has concluded that we might conclude in regard to it?"

Justice Oliver Wendell Holmes, whom Roosevelt constituted by an early dramatic presidential call the Delphic Oracle of his administration, wracked his philosophical mind to demonstrate how an American may operate judicially without a doctrine. His official conviction was that in the noblesse oblige of a tripartite government Congress should be allowed to do whatever it pleased and that his judicial duty was to permit it, as much what he disliked as what he approved. He had early learned, and happily—so he says—that "he was not God." Truth was to him in his youth "the majority vote of that nation that could lick all others"; but in the sedateness of his maturity truth came to be what he *could not help believing,* though whether his "can't helps" were those of the universe he declared he did not know. Nor did he profess to know whether there is any "truth of truth." It was enough for him as a public functionary to see to it that the majority got what it wanted, even though, as he adds, "personally I bet the crowd if it knew more wouldn't want what it does—but that is immaterial." That logical immateriality is crucially "material" to American democracy. Absolute truth is always irrelevant to action in America; and every secular ideology and every sacerdotal orthodoxy renders itself suspect to the extent that it builds upon the contrary supposition.

Proudly modest as he was, Holmes, as our judicial sage, refused to claim public relevancy for his private convictions. Roosevelt came through the method of conference to the *determination* of his convictions on public matters. There was this further difference between Roosevelt and Holmes: Holmes was older and culturally tired. He thought, as he said, that the only hope for men is that they should grow more intelligent: an onerous prescription with no date named in its statute of limitation. Holmes thought that no social planning is disinterested; that all legislation is, in fact, but the shifting of burdens from tired backs to backs unwilling. Roosevelt, leaning to the side of optimism, felt that giving the farmers something, labor something, the unemployed something, more could be had for all (alas for the logical fallacy of "composition"!)

without taking anything away from anybody—unless a compensating little away from businessmen! Roosevelt's hope was organismic, while his thought was individualistic; Holmes' thought was organismic, while his concern was individualistic. But both were typically American in that both thought the culture the healthier the greater the social distance it maintains from the doctrinaire.

Mr. Justice Jackson, in a contemporary decision against the undertow of patriotism, has given immortal embodiment to what was common in this regard to Roosevelt and Holmes. "If there be any fixed star in our constitutional constellation," says he, "it is that no official, high or petty, can prescribe what shall be orthodox in politics, nationalism, religion, or other matters of opinion. . . ." And then, broadening his purview to the orbit which all orthodoxy tends to inscribe, the Justice hurls this broadside against the fateful notion that meaningful consent can ever be distilled from convictional impetuosity: "Those who begin coercive elimination of dissent soon find themselves exterminating dissenters. Compulsory unification of opinion achieves only the unanimity of the graveyard."

A New Deal columnist at once sympathetic and circumspect—it was Mr. Ernest K. Lindley—undertook during Roosevelt's first administration to rationalize the New Deal's lack of rationalization: "The contradictions of the New Deal," he averred,

have bewildered many people. From time to time long lists of them have been published. Contradictions should worry no friend of the capitalistic system. Its very justification is the supreme contradiction that when every individual pursues his own selfish interests, in contradiction to the selfish interest of everyone else, the result is a maximum of social good. When these individual selfish interests merge into group interests and are reflected in contradictory governmental policies, they might be expected to achieve the maximum of social good. . . . When contradictions become blatant and obstructive, they have to be resolved by the victory of one side or the other or by compromise. . . . Most of the contradictions of the New Deal have been merely the extension into the realm of government of well-known contradictions of our economic system.

The foregoing was addressed primarily of course to the business community. But another friendly critic—it was Thurman Arnold, later to be Assistant Attorney General of the United States, and later still to be Associate Justice of the United States Court of Appeals, under Roosevelt—slanted a similar defense toward the intelligentsia. "The only path," says Mr. Arnold, "of *orderly* change leads through a confusion of principles. Clearcut and logical systems suddenly imposed bring the violence of Russia, Germany, or the French Revolution."

These rationalizations of Roosevelt's lack of ideological center are interesting enough in their own right. But Roosevelt's approach to the matter was important positively, elemental as it was. If his sympathy discerned some action that would relieve the object of sympathy, the sympathy was reason enough for action—and the consequences were self-justifying; or, that failing, other actions could produce other and better consequences. "The nation or state," said he, "which is unwilling by governmental action to tackle new problems . . . is headed for a decline and ultimate death from inaction." In other lands such confidence in action, especially in collective action, would have taken another type of man where—well, where it took Mussolini, where it took Hitler, where it takes Stalin. But Roosevelt was not a Mussolini, nor a Hitler, nor yet a Stalin. He was Roosevelt, and the land where he had to act was America. The dominance upon him of his background prevented temperament from offering dictatorial temptation to him. So he was what he was—and that we have sought to describe. Since he was what he was, the movement called by him the "New Deal" was the ideological potpourri which it was.

But the matter can be put with full effectiveness only when it is clothed in the majesty of ebullient affirmation. Roosevelt's voice knew how to articulate only the everlasting Yea. The positive implication of this temperamental preference for action and yet tolerance for directions of action quite diverse can better be put by another than the prime actor. From the summit of maximum New Deal achievement the philosophy has been well articulated by Mr. David Lilienthal, long in charge of the huge Tennessee Valley Authority, and now promoted upon the strength of that success to direct the United States Atomic Energy Commission.

Diversity and flexibility, rather than a stereotyped hard-and-fast system, is an essential part of such a noble concept of society as is ours. We get our economic services in the way that at the time seems to work best, that will in a particular situation best advance our underlying purposes. We do not start with all the answers, the economic answers or political answers. We make the answers up as we go along. Thus, American industry is owned and operated, by and large, by competitive private enterprise; yet . . . the Senate of the United States voted unanimously to establish public ownership and management in one of our largest industries, and make it a government monopoly—I refer of course to the atomic materials industry. That appeared to be the thing to do at the time, for reasons related to the facts of atomic energy, not for ideological reasons taken out of some book of economic dogma. The most rock-ribbed mid-Western town I know has for many years owned and operated its own electric power and light plant. Is this then a "socialist" town? Hardly! Its water service has been privately owned for the same period. There is a privately owned university; a public junior college. No one considers that these things are inconsistent; and of course they are not, except to the dogmatist who thinks we have a fixed "system." In the same town there is a farmers' feed coöperative that is not quite private or quite public, operating side by side with a big privately owned feed company. There are private banks, there are non-profit insurance companies, there are state-owned liquor stores. We would never consider adopting government ownership or control of newspapers partly because of their educational character; but our school system, the cornerstone of American education, is almost entirely publicly owned and managed. This is all part of the familiar picture of American diversity, of American flexibility.

The fact is that we have hardly an ounce of economic dogmatism in us. . . .

That is an up-to-date assessment from an intellectual whose success has been in the New Deal field which is most assured of permanence, though itself shallowly grounded ideologically.

No doctrinaire, Mr. Roosevelt was enormously successful in *politicizing* the whole of American life. Given economic activity on the one side, which he least understood, and given religious feeling on the other side, with which he was most sympathetic, Roosevelt pursued the great game of politics so as to make economics more humane and religion less fanatical. The golden mean between economic dogma and theological orthodoxy—each of which would achieve its logical goal in "the uniformity of the graveyard"—is the resiliency of democratic politics. Roosevelt thought politics so much the final art and economics so little a science that he did not take seriously objections to action that were urged on theoretical grounds. The result was that he was much inclined to submit even the most technical economic matters—simplified in statement by him!—to a referendum—and that made up by replies to a "fireside chat."

This procedure clearly has the defect of its virtue. By its practice

Mr. Roosevelt set the nation on at least two tacks that may have far-reaching cultural results. With all his revivification of citizenly interest in government, it is a serious resultant that he made governmental policy so responsive to public reaction that it could no longer be responsible to *settled* opinion. To use the sound notion that democracy is government by public opinion to justify the unsound practice of veering policy every time the wind of popular reaction sets in is not only to go against all the wisdom of our American Fathers—who preferred the social distance of a "republic" to the immediacy of "democracy"—but to meet oneself coming out every governmental door. It is no service to reasonableness to make public actors trigger-happy to opinion which needs to be resisted in order that it may become stable enough to support a policy in its name.

A leader may be opportunistic who leads a people with an ideology, or a people may profit from an ideology in leadership if they themselves are largely opportunistic. But for both people and leaders to be either opportunistic or dogmatically ideological is an infirm foundation for cultural stability.

The other defect of Roosevelt's great virtue is seen in his dealing with religious dogma. With all his clairvoyance for man's spiritual aspiration, he dealt alike with the dogmatic and the undogmatic—a practice than which the dogmatic can ask nothing better in their effort to warp a culture in their direction. He fraternized as gaily with the Catholic hierarchy, which can and does consolidate its gains, as with individualistic Protestants, who dissipate their power in the friendly competition of virtue. His personal representative to the Vatican is proving not so easily dislodged as a friend to a friend should be. Roosevelt's successor finds harder than he thought the promise he made to Protestant America to discontinue this anomalous innovation. To recognize a church as a state is a radical departure in America and it is calculated to further the determined and incessant drive to abridge the final separation in the United States between church and state. If there be one dogma in American culture it is this separation of the will to power and the will to perfection—a separation from which we have rightly believed to be derived not only the reasonableness of the state but also the purity of the church.

The cultural vulnerability of a liberal society, in the competition between an opportunist and a dogmatist, is written large in Mr. Roosevelt's relation with Stalin, to the left; with the Vatican, to the right.

From defects as from virtues, one must nevertheless interpret the New Deal's course as America's penchant for the middle of the road. To settle everything by what our tradition presupposes is to politicize the whole of life; for our tradition in politics is to reach agreement by consultation and to agree to disagree, with mutual respect, where consultation fails us. This is what Mr. Roosevelt sought to do, and this is what his movement most stood for. "Whatever happened," says Miss Perkins, "he loved the game of politics, and he played it like a master." If the leeway with which he played the game leads to a doctrinaire debacle, to the right or the left, it is because the world has changed: Roosevelt's way of life is now for the first time in America flanked by authoritarianism: secular in Communism, sacerdotal in Catholicism.

Roosevelt's generous and uplifting spirit remains as a legacy to memory at least. He is himself entitled to summarize that spirit.

Apart from phrases and slogans, the important thing to remember is . . . that the change in our policy is based upon a change in the attitude and the thinking of the American people—in other words, that it is based upon the growing maturity of our democracy; that it proceeds in accordance with the underlying principles that guided the framers of our Constitution; that it is taking form with the general approval of a very large majority of the American people; and, finally, that it is made with the constant assurance to the people that if at any time they wish to revert to the old methods that we have discarded, they are wholly free to bring about such a reversion by the simple means of the ballot.

The "people" have reverted, and through the means which he not only allowed but recommended. When the dynamic proves tiresome, it is well for people peaceably to revert to the lethargic.

Whether the dynamic leaven implanted by Roosevelt will outweigh the sediment deposited as tradition is a question of prophecy. What does remain to buttress the memory of politically exciting years in America is the functional relegitimization, under the greatest stress ever felt, of the two-party system by which the reversion has occurred. Politics is confirmed as the great American game. Two-party hegemony succeeds still—succeeds through its success in difficult peace years, through its success in portentous war years. To have greatly cared for the nobodies of prestige, to have deeply trusted the efficacy of human effort for amelioration, and to have infused the whole body politic with uplifting surmise —this is the spiritual legacy of Franklin Delano Roosevelt's leadership. The American seems ever to be affirming with his folk poet:

> I do not like the way the cards are shuffled;
>   But still I like the game and want to play.
> And through the long, long night will I, unruffled,
>   Play what I get until the break of day.

XI

THE POTENTIAL INTELLIGENT SOCIETY OF THE FUTURE

P. W. BRIDGMAN

THIS article will attempt to suggest certain changes in the general atmosphere of human affairs which conceivably might occur if tendencies which are already discernible should be allowed in the future to carry through to their logical conclusions. These tendencies are most obviously associated with those activities which most people would classify as scientific. I believe, however, that we are here concerned with something much broader than the scientific in the conventional sense. My point of view is that intelligence, when it operates in certain fields and on certain types of material, uses methods which we call scientific; but when operating in other fields and on other subject matter must use methods which recognizably have much in common with the methods of science. The tendencies with which we are concerned properly pertain to intelligent activity in general rather than to scientific activity alone. The development of science during the last few centuries is, I believe, only the beginning of an evolution of our still primitive intelligence, which will be accelerated if we take to heart the lessons of science. Never in human history has intelligence been allowed full opportunity, nor have its potentialities for a revolutionary recasting of society and culture been adequately appreciated.

The present tendencies, if allowed to work themselves out to their logical conclusions, will affect human activity in at least two major respects, in addition to the improvement in all-round efficiency to be anticipated. In the first place there will be an effect on the general philosophical outlook. Professor Northrop has well emphasized the intimate connection between the fundamental philosophy of an epoch and contemporary cultural and political institutions. He has also emphasized the intimate connection between the prevalent scientific outlook and the accepted philosophy. If, therefore, scientific activity is merely a special case of the activity of intelligence, we may expect the more effective use of intelligence to react on both philosophy and social institutions in general. In the second place, and equally as important as the reaction on philosophy, will be the enhancement of *effective* intelligence by way of the reaction on the techniques of intelligence itself. A man's outlook is determined as much by the way in which he unconsciously or consciously handles himself intellectually as by his explicit philosophy. In fact, his philosophy is to a certain degree merely a reflection of his mental processes. At present there is very little general awareness of this matter of intellectual technique—one does not often think of his mind as a tool which it is in his power to handle well or poorly. In the natural sciences, particularly in physics during this century, the force of events has compelled a heightened self-consciousness of intellectual techniques which I believe has implications in all fields of intellectual activity.

Before attacking the main problem of this article, namely, an examination of some of the implications of an evolution of present-day society into an intelligent society, several preliminary matters demand our attention. For example, we must examine the implicit thesis that the evolution of an intelligent society is desirable. This thesis is by no means universally accepted, even in the West, where large segments of the population are convinced that intelligence is a futile tool for solving our problems, and that our only recourse is to return to the supernatural and the mystical. If to this element in the West we add the East, in which the predominant philosophies are now and always have been either mystical or formal and conventional, it must be conceded that the major part of the human race today is anti-intelligent in its instincts and aspirations. Obviously the world will not evolve into the temple of intelligence which we envisage unless there is a change of general attitude toward the desirability of intelligence in daily life. The present attitude results, I believe, in large part from misunderstanding of the nature of intelligence. A preliminary examination of this is obviously called for.

Intelligence is not a sharply defined concept, and may be used with various connotations. I shall interpret it loosely as what we use when we solve a problem by deliberate thought. The concept of "problem" I shall not attempt to define further. Consciousness of problems and continual concern with them is one of the distinguishing marks of the intellectual person. Now intelligence has minimum and maximum aspects. At the minimum, it must be recognized to be a neutral tool, useful and necessary for the attainment of certain ends but not in itself determining the ends or even concerned with what they are. I think that everyone will recognize that a minimum concern with intelligence is something unavoidable for the human animal, even for one "anti-intelligent" in his instincts. It is human to want things. When we want something the getting of it constitutes a problem, the solution of which involves at least a rudimentary use of intelligence. The more self-conscious and well considered our attempts to solve the problem, the greater the intelligence involved, by the very definition of intelligence.

In any practical situation the question soon arises as to how much intelligence we shall exercise: how self-conscious shall we be about what we are doing, and how fully shall we analyze the details and their implications? There is of course no absolute answer. We proceed by trial and successive approximation. If our first solution does not satisfy us, we think some more. We eventually arrive at a satisfactory solution or abandon the attempt and put up with an unsatisfactory one, either because we are not able to find the satisfactory solution or because the mental effort of searching for it is too irksome to be compensated by the anticipated good. For it is also a human characteristic to find mental effort beyond a certain degree difficult and to be avoided if possible. The average human being does not like to think too hard and will deliberately try so to direct his life that he will not find himself in situations where a distasteful amount of mental effort is necessary. Nearly everyone recognizes that there are many unsolved problems which he himself could solve if he would only think harder, or which could be solved by some neighbor with greater intellectual capacity than himself. The point at which we give up trying to solve our problems by the exercise of intelligence is therefore not well defined; one man will give up more easily than another. It is here that the maximum aspect of the use of intelligence appears. Some people enjoy the use of the mind for its own sake, up to certain limits of difficulty. If they are not occupied with the solution of some problem of practical importance, they will go out of their way to invent problems and occupy themselves with their solution merely for the pleasure of using their minds. Such a person will not easily give up the search for a solution, and is therefore, from the point of view of the community, a useful sort of person to have around.

If the problem to be solved is one of general public interest, the two types of person, the one who does not like to use his mind and is satisfied with the minimum use of intelligence, and the one who enjoys using his mind and strives for the maximum employment of intelligence, are likely to come into conflict. For the minimist will want to give up trying for an intelligent solution of a baffling problem and adopt some stopgap procedure sooner than the maximist. Since the minimists are always in the majority, or have been up until now, this conflict will always tend to result in the defeat of the maximists, unless their position can be made to appear to the minimists to involve advantages to compensate for the personal inconvenience of using their minds. It is, I think, becoming more and more evident that there are such compensating advantages. The eventual, sufficiently widespread recognition of these advantages offers the only rational ground for the expectation that society may eventually be intelligent. This recognition appears to be slowly operating to modify the position of the minimists and to secure from them a certain toleration for the maximists.

At present the most important single factor in this slow modification is doubtless the appreciation of the material benefits that result from the applications of science. There is, however, a conflict here with those who are convinced that the benefits are outweighed by the disadvantages, and who advocate a return to simple primitive times. The conflict will continue until the nature of science and of intelligence in general is better understood. In this conflict I think there is a certain bias in favor of the progressive faction. There is an element of irreversibility in the operation of intelligence in human affairs, for the world is never the same for us after we have acquired a new insight. If we have a new idea we cannot thereafter refuse to consider it or willfully put ourselves back where we were before we thought of it. For this reason our understanding of the world, other things being equal, continually progresses, and at an accelerated pace, as we accumulate an ever-increasing number of tools in our intellectual armory. Parenthetically, there is an interesting contrast here between the continually growing and differentiating effect of the irreversible impact of new ideas and the effects of the irreversible processes of energy dissipation which are the subject of the second law of thermodynamics of physics. The latter is usually considered to imply the eventual "heat death" of the universe.

We are perhaps now ready to consider some of the aspects of what is conventionally called the scientific method which are really characteristic of the use of intelligence in more general fields. I believe that many of the most important of the characteristics of the so-called scientific method are really tricks of intellectual technique, first discovered to be important in the field of scientific subject matter but actually of much wider application. These tricks, or at least their widespread use, are new in the history of the human race and are adding immeasurably to its intellectual power. With all due respect to the intellectual acumen of the ancient Greeks, they missed a lot of tricks, and in some of their points of view were woefully mistaken. One of the most important of these mistakes was with reference to the role of logic and human reason in the external world. The Greek thought of the external world as so intrinsically reasonable that its structure could be recovered by the sufficiently cogent use of the naked reason of an armchair theorist. The notion has persisted to the present day, perhaps in its most virulent form in Eddington, but is certainly completely opposed to the spirit of modern science.

I think it will be pretty generally accepted, both by those who rely on the dictates of common sense and by those who have critically discussed the nature of inductive and deductive reasoning, that there is only one reliable method of being sure we have the correct answer to any problem. This is the method of actual application to the situation in question; that is, we must test our solution by finding whether or not it works. Whether or not there are other methods of assuring ourselves of the correctness of our solution, the condition that it work in actual application is at least a necessary condition, as it is also sufficient, by very definition. No amount of a priori argument as to what "ought" to be the case, or consistency with preconceived notions, can safely be allowed to replace the check by actual trial. Furthermore, we must be prepared to find that the check may fail, and if it does, we must accept it as a brute fact, with the best grace we can, and hunt for our mistake. The conviction that this sort of procedure is necessary rests upon a background of centuries of experience.

The recognition that a solution has to be checked before it can be accepted has various ramifications. One of them is the controlled experiment; this in itself constitutes a new trick of intellectual technique without which the rise of modern science would have been impossible. The controlled experiment is a device which has its most useful application in the simpler situations of science, and is not so easy to apply in the more complicated situations of economics or society, where there are so many variables that their control is not usually practical. Even here, however, its use is recognized as an ideal. The more general demand that a solution be checked before it is accepted is one that must be made in all fields of intellectual activity, and the vision of the necessity of this is essentially modern. Whatever justification the Greeks may have had for their scorn of the direct check, it was based on an insufficiently extensive experience, which made possible a naïve view of the nature of human logic and reason.

What sort of checks shall be applied, and how thoroughly, and by whom? Here the question of authority comes in. Under what conditions shall we accept a solution on the say-so of another? The scientific method is usually supposed to involve, among other things, the requirement that under no circumstances is a solution to be accepted on the basis of authority only. Now this is an ideal which has to be modified in practice, because of such considerations as economy of time, but always with as many safeguards as possible. We accept the authority only of experts, who have proved their expertness by past checks, and we require that the statement of the expert be presented in such a form that we could subject it to our own independent check if we cared to take the time. No reputable scientific journal will accept a paper for publication unless it is written in this form. This attitude of science toward authority is obviously one which should be extended as far as possible to all other fields of intellectual activity. The reason for it is twofold: experience has shown it is the only safe practice, for experts have been mistaken or have even willfully exploited their fellows; and secondly it is inherent in the nature of checking or proof itself, for a proof is an affair for the individual which can be apprehended only by the individual and cannot be done for him by another.

One particularly important situation arises in checking a solution presented to us by our fellows. Most of us have found that often our fellow is brighter or quicker than we and can find the solutions of problems which would not yield to us in a lifetime of our own effort. Our fellow, being bright, realizes the situation, and is very likely to let us see that he realizes it. Often it is not within human nature for the bright man not to try to bully the stupid man into accepting his solution on his authority and without examination. The situation can be met only by resolution of character. Everyone, no matter how dull, can out of self-respect demand no less than the right to check for himself any ostensible solution. If he is not allowed to take the solution home with him, mull it over at his leisure, and apply to it any test which he is able to devise, he has ample historical precedent for the suspicion that he is being exploited. He may particularly suspect exploitation if he is told that he is too stupid to devise a check, and that he has no recourse but to accept the whole thing on faith and on the authority of his more gifted fellow. In practice, of course, compromises have to be made because of the necessity for action within a finite time. The greater part of the compromise usually has to be made by the stupider party. The brighter one, however, who seeks to impose a solution by authority is under obligation so to present his solution that it may be checked by anyone as easily as possible. If he shows no recognition of this obligation, he may expect to be justifiably suspected of exploitation. The only place for arbitrary authority in intellectual matters is as a timesaver in emergencies.

In many of the nonscientific situations of daily life the method of authority is in use today and is aggressively justified by those who use it. This is particularly true in politics and in religion. The prevalence of the method of authority is a symptom of an intellectually immature society. It would be easier to cope with the situation were it not that so many people enjoy submitting themselves to the direction of authority.

In carrying out the detailed checking of ostensible solutions it is not long before we discover that perhaps the archenemy to the success of the entire enterprise is ourselves. In the first place, we make mistakes. These may range from gross blunders of carelessness to errors due to inexperience and the novelty of the situation. We have found that one of the most effective methods of dealing with our own errors is repetition. If we are seized with doubt as to whether we have made a mistake or not, often our only satisfactory recourse is to repeat our performance, scrutinizing the while what we do with all the self-consciousness at our command to see if we can detect any blunder or any alternative procedure that we missed. In order to make this sort of check the phenomenon itself must obviously be repeatable. Furthermore, it is a fact of observation, I believe, that the material of any intellectual activity is always endowed with this quality of repeatability, quite apart from the process of checking. There are doubtless good reasons for this. It has often been suggested that rational thought becomes possible only when we can recognize in present experience the repetition of elementary situations of the past.

Whatever the reason, it appears that we do have to have this property of repeatability before we can have intelligent action. This applies not only to scientific activities primarily but also to economic or political or any other activity which is not purely receptive and sensational. I believe that it is here that a large part of the backwardness of economics or politics as compared with natural science is to be found. The matter of repetition is very closely connected with the matter of description. The one criterion for believing that we have adequately described a situation is that we be able to reconstruct or repeat the situation from the description. Adequate description is at the basis of all science, as it must be of any other precise intellectual activity. But it is seldom indeed that a practical economic or social or political situation is adequately described; and indeed seldom that we would know how to go about giving an adequate description if we were allowed free rein. Contrasted with the situations in science, particularly physical science, the still rudimentary development of economics or sociology is painfully apparent. It seems to me obvious, however, that the future of these disciplines is bound up with the development of analysis sufficiently powerful to isolate the repeatable situations and make significant description possible. Once this necessity is clearly and generally recognized, I think we need not despair of success in finding the elements demanded for our analysis.

In testing purported solutions the individual soon finds that there are other human weaknesses besides mistakes that he has to guard against. His personal tastes and desires have a way of intruding themselves; a solution pleasing for personal reasons is likely to be accepted with a less searching analysis than one less pleasant. A not very extensive experience is required to show the dangers here. This was a lesson soon learned in the conventional situations of physical science; in fact, disregard of the personal angle is popularly regarded as one of the characteristics of the scientific approach par excellence. It is obvious that it must no less be a characteristic of any intellectual approach dedicated to obtaining the correct answer, in the situations in politics or society or anywhere else.

We have been talking about checking the solutions of our problems. How do we obtain the solutions in the first place? This of course is the main question, to which we have been slowly finding an answer through all the past experience of the human race. At first everything had to be tried, since we did not find the solution growing inside our minds. Any conceivable correlation was fair game for examination to see whether there was anything in it. At first, and until it had been tried, it was only intelligent to try to foretell the future from the conjunction of the planets, or the configuration of the entrails of sacrificed sheep, or by consulting the medicine man. With the accumulation of millennia of experience certain regularities have been observed so universally that we have come to feel that it is not intelligent to expect certain methods for obtaining solutions to be valid. There are not many people, at least in this part of the world, who still regard the employment of the methods of astrology or of the scatology of ovian entrails as marks of intelligence. There is not so much agreement about consulting the medicine man. It is not always easy to know where superstition ends and intelligence begins. Thus there are not many people at present who, in view of the history of the subject, take "extrasensory perception" (ESP) seriously, in spite of the fact that no logical reason can be shown for its impossibility. Such questions have to be decided on a probability basis in the light of past experience and with due regard for the techniques which we have found are necessary to avoid self-deception and the erroneous reporting of factual material. It must be recognized, however, that there is danger here, particularly when it comes to new types of phenomena. The ordinary man, with limited time and other compelling interests, must usually take his chances of missing something new if it appears to him to be intrinsically improbable, and can only hope that if there is something genuine in such a phenomenon as ESP, for example, someone will happen by with a strong enough natural interest to take the trouble to put a sound foundation under it.

Since our minds do not present us with the solution of our problems without experience and trial and checking, it is obvious that our search for solutions must be subject to no restriction; we must have complete freedom to try anything or to ask any question that we are bright enough to ask. Freedom has been necessary to all the progress of the past. Without freedom we would not have been able to invent the methods of astrology or scatology or, having invented them, to prove that they were not valid. Without freedom we shall not in the future be able to penetrate into the unexplored domains of the mind or of the external world that encircle us.

The necessity for freedom is intrinsic in the nature of intelligence; let anyone imagine himself trying to understand some new situation without being allowed to ask certain kinds of questions. This necessity prevails not only in the field of science but in any intellectual activity. Furthermore, freedom is inherent in the individual and has meaning only for the individual, for the solution of any problem can be initiated only in the mind of some individual and the consummation by checking and proof can occur only there. For this reason I think that the emphasis on the "objective" or "public" nature of science is often overdone. At bottom each individual scientist demands that science be "public," in order that he be able to formulate his own programs and apply his own checks with greater economy of effort. It must be admitted that the economy afforded by a public science is so great as usually to obscure the private aspects, but they are there at bottom and they alone give meaning to the whole enterprise.

It seems to me that the fact that intellectual integrity demands complete freedom of thought and that the focus of this freedom is of necessity located in the individual has political implications that might well be more strongly stressed than is usual. I believe that here is the one cogent ideological justification for democracy and the refutation of totalitarianism and authoritarianism. If society is to be a society of intelligent beings, it has got to be a society with intellectual freedom, simply because of the nature of intelligence and quite apart from the personal preferences of the members. Intellectual freedom will carry with it freedom of political action, for an intelligent citizenry will not long be satisfied with the merely academic recognition that perhaps some other form of government would be preferable and not do something about it. One may perhaps expect appreciation of this situation to become more widespread and effective as an increasingly large part of the community learns to apply its intelligence to the affairs of daily life.

The matters that we have been considering so far—the checking of solutions, the controlled experiment, the necessity for intellectual freedom, the proper place of authority, the guarding against the intrusion of personal predilections in the coloring of observations and the warping of judgment—these are all questions of intellectual technique, applicable in all intellectual fields as well as in the scientific. The consciousness of these matters and of their importance is something that has been growing on us in the last few hundred years as a consequence of our scientific experience. This growing consciousness constitutes something new in human intellectual history; and it is now broadening from a consciousness of the importance of these particular items of technique into a consciousness of intellectual technique in general. This general awareness of technique has developed since the turn of the century as a result of the experience with relativity and quantum theory in physics. As an outcome we are, I believe, acquiring an essentially new understanding of our mental relation to nature. This new understanding is applicable to all fields of intellectual activity as well as to the natural sciences, and cannot but alter the entire intellectual outlook of the race and hasten the advent of that divine far-off event when we shall have become the intellectual masters of our fate.

One of the new factors is a quickened apprehension of the extent to which human construction, particularly verbal construction, permeates our intellectual world. Not only does the mystic live in a world of his own construction, but all of us—including the scientist—live in such a world, to an extent not often appreciated. This was essentially the new vision imparted by relativity theory, which came with such a shock to the physicist. The old Newtonian absolutes of space and time were discovered not to have the meaning that we had supposed. We had thought that these concepts described the external world; we discovered on analysis that they found their meaning only in what we said about what we did in the external world, and furthermore that what we said about what we did was not a truthful description. The physicist has tried to meet the situation and prevent its recurrence in the future by the use of a self-conscious technique for the analysis of meanings. In brief, the physicist has come to see that the only part of the meaning of a term which is of real interest to him is to be found in what he does when he applies the term to a concrete situation, and in particular in what he does when he checks to insure that he is applying the term in the way that he thought he was. For if the "operations" which determine the use of a term are known and adequately specified, it is insured that when the same situation is repeated the same term will be used by everyone, and furthermore that the situation can be reconstructed from the term. This is sufficient to secure unambiguous recording and communication. This method of analysis of meanings has wide applicability, far beyond the physical situations which gave rise to it. Application of the method to the common language of daily life discloses that the meanings of most of the great abstractions—such as reality, right, duty, necessity, certainty, free will, the good, or democracy—are to be found (to an extent much greater than we had realized), in our verbal response to situations which are themselves predominantly verbal, created either by us or by our fellows. We had implicitly assumed that the meaning referred to something not so closely tied to human construction. Realization that this assumption is not true leads to an appreciation of the extent to which we have constructed the world in which we live and the strongly verbal character of this world. Many of the traditional problems which have plagued human thinking since thinking began degenerate upon analysis of this kind into mere pseudo problems.

We may anticipate that there will be revolutions in such practical disciplines as sociology, politics, economics, and psychology when the predominantly verbal character of most of our thinking in these fields is realized and when new techniques shall have been forged to meet the realization. When these techniques have been forged and applied, we may anticipate that such of our present difficulties, among others, as arise from ambiguity or uncertainty of meaning will disappear. This will be particularly important in promoting understanding between individuals of different cultures and languages. It is well known that there is seldom precise correspondence between the abstract terms of different languages, so that precise translation is not possible. Consider, for example, the word "democracy," which is such a stumbling block between Americans and Russians. To analyze the meaning of this word in the two languages, both Americans and Russians would have to describe what they do in applying the word democracy to any specific society, and furthermore would have to describe what they do in terms so precise that the other could apply the same procedure and get the same answer. The difference of meaning in the two languages will then appear completely delineated in terms of what is done, and joint courses of action are susceptible of agreement, once the precise nature of the difference of language is brought out into the open. It will be especially difficult for willful attempts to confuse the issue to survive an analysis of this character. It need not be anticipated that willful attempts at obfuscation will be thereby eliminated from the human repertory, but at least their existence will be more plainly apparent, so that there will be a better chance of finding effective means of dealing with them.

The fact that the world in which we live is so largely a verbal world, and that we have not always been as successful as we had supposed in constructing this verbal world to agree with the "external" world, contains implications which, I believe, have been only very partially assessed by the philosophies of either West or East. Perhaps an example will make the point more concrete. Suppose that we are debating whether it can be inferred that there is a purpose back of the universe around us, and that we think an answer to this question is beyond human capability. We might conceivably express our feeling in one of two ways: we might say that the universe doubtless has a purpose but that it is not within human power to find what this purpose is; or we might take a more openly agnostic position by saying that it is not within human power to find whether there is a purpose or not. It is, I think, usually felt that these two forms of statement more or less exhaust the agnostic position. The new vision is that there is a third position, namely that the idea of purpose itself is not applicable to the whole universe, so that the question is only a pseudo question. The reason is that the operations which we perform in ordinary situations to justify the application of the term "purpose" and which constitute its definition are operations which are not applicable to the whole universe. We find ourselves stymied, not because our minds are not capable of dealing with the problem but because the problem itself does not exist. The appearance of it is a verbal artifact, due to our inveterate habit of verbal extrapolation by sheer verbal momentum. The realization of this begets a different attitude than does either of the conventional brands of agnosticism; we simply have to stop applying our minds to a situation which was a miscreation of our minds in the first place.

This sort of situation will be comparatively simple to deal with once its predominantly verbal character has been appreciated. But it is slowly becoming apparent that there are other situations in which the difficulty is more deeply rooted. These new situations form a sort of complement to the type we have just been considering. The latter were situations in which we were led astray by our verbalizing; we devised a method of verbalizing which was adapted to certain orders of experience, and then attempted to push it too far, into domains where it did not fit the construction of the world. The new situations which are just beginning to appear as so fundamental are those in which we are not able to establish mental contact with nature in the first place in order to start verbalizing. Of course we do the best we can in these situations, and we do verbalize, but the fundamental difficulty is not with the verbal process but with what is back of it. The realization that there are such situations has been growing on the physicist, particularly since his pondering on the significance of quantum theory. For example, the principle of Heisenberg teaches that we cannot ascribe position and momentum simultaneously to elementary particles. This situation was at first described by saying that the process of measurement was such that if we chose to measure the position accurately the process of measurement itself interfered, so that we could not measure the momentum precisely. That is, the implicit idea was that there is a conspiracy of nature which prevents us from finding what the momentum is. We see now that it is a much juster description of the situation to say that position and momentum are concepts which do not apply simultaneously to elementary particles, because the operations which by definition would be involved in measuring them are in contradiction with the structure of nature. If one replies to this by saying, "But the very concept of particle involves the possession of both position and momentum, whether or not we can devise a method for measuring them," then the answer must be that if this is the case we have indeed come to a place where our minds are estopped by the very character of their own construction from probing further.

The situation is even more hopeless when we consider that in the quantum world objects with identity disappear, for how can we think without our "objects" that persist? Not only do objects with identity fade out, but situations do not repeat themselves. For neither can we control situations sufficiently to make them repeat at pleasure, nor can the physical operations be performed which are necessary by definition to determine whether a situation is repeating or not. The concept of repeatability simply evaporates, and we have seen how fundamental this concept is to all thinking. The invention of some essentially new way of thinking seems called for. This appears, however, to be of doubtful possibility. The physicist is coming to see what would be involved here. Detailed analysis of what we do in thinking about the microscopic domain shows that all meanings in the quantum domain must eventually be expressible in terms of what we do on the scale of ordinary life. We cannot react to this situation with the faith that the external world nevertheless continues to exist beyond the reach of our minds, for the reason that such an assertion is meaningless. We cannot give meaning to even such an elemental concept as "existence"; all that is left to us is to shut up.

It requires a tough-mindedness which few possess to respond by simply shutting up; most of us will, I think, continue to kick against the pricks. The situation is made more difficult by the construction of language. It is one thing to say, "There are things which I do not understand," and something quite different to say, "I do not understand," although the grammar of everyday life would treat them as equivalent. Unless the reader intuitively feels the difference between the two statements he is not catching the point.

The vision that this is the structure of nature is given not only by what we are finding in the direction of the very small; it is slowly dawning on us that the new astronomical discoveries of the unsuspected wealth of structure of the universe in the direction of the very large indicate the same situation there. All our thinking about the world involves dividing the world into subsystems, each of them closed and isolated. Our concepts find their meanings only in terms of closed systems. For instance, the thermodynamic concepts of energy and of entropy, ostensibly the most general concepts we have, find their meaning only in closed systems. But the universe is open—how shall we think about it? What meaning other than purely verbal is there in such a question as "Where is the radiation now that left the sun a billion years ago?"

The vision that the human race is isolated in an oasis of phenomena which it cannot transcend in the direction of either the small or the large because of the nature of the processes of thought is the culmination of the vision vouchsafed to us by Copernicus, Galileo, and Darwin. When this vision becomes more general, I think we may anticipate a revolution in our whole intellectual outlook compared to which the revolutions we have already gone through will seem puny indeed. New intellectual techniques will have to be devised to make it possible for the mind to shut up at the proper place. The situation is not hopeless, nor is it without suggestive parallelism to other situations. The scientist has learned how to suspend judgment and action in the face of an unsolved problem, whereas his more impetuous fellow is impelled to seek relief in the action suggested by some nonintelligent process. The scientist's suspense in such situations is akin to the "shutting up" now demanded of him, although recognizably not the same.

There are difficulties and dangers here. The line of demarcation between a clear-eyed recognition of the existence of essential intellectual limitations and an intellectual defeatism will not always be evident. We must find how not to inhibit the impulse to intellectual experimenting or the resolution to drive as far as we can with our minds.

Not only will new intellectual techniques have to be devised but new social techniques as well. One can foresee that one of the embarrassing questions will be that of tolerance. It has always seemed to me that even in present-day society the problem of tolerance has not been satisfactorily solved, and we may anticipate increased difficulties in the future. When it is a matter of the emotions only, there can be no question of the desirability of tolerance. But in intellectual matters it is not so clear. We do not usually demand tolerance in teaching the propositions of Euclid. The question comes up most often perhaps in connection with religion. Here the conventional justification for tolerance of one creed by the holders of another is that no one can have absolute certainty in such matters and that even we may be mistaken. But this sort of thing does not cover the situation. We often know, and know without the possibility of being mistaken, that we are at least considering factors which our fellow does not even see, irrespective of whether we are correctly assessing the effect of these factors. What degree of respect ought we to accord to the opinion of our fellow under such conditions? The situation is not easy and will become more difficult in the future, when the vision of essential isolation, which a certain fraction of the human race, at least with its present education, is probably intellectually incapable of grasping, becomes more widespread.

The immediate impact of a realization of our essential intellectual isolation, or limited intellectual adaptability to the universe, will doubtless be greatest in philosophy and religion, but from there it will spread to all other phases of intellectual activity. The incorrigibly religious nature of man and the deep-seated involvement of his religious and philosophical views with all his other outlooks has been much stressed recently by Northrop and particularly by Toynbee. Not all aspects of what is ordinarily understood by religion are involved, for religion itself is a most complicated thing, as witnessed by the universal difficulty in finding a satisfactory definition of what religion is. But there is an attitude toward the universe as a whole which will, I think, be recognized to be at least a very common component of the religious complex, namely, the feeling that the universe is in some way friendly to the human mind. At the very least the universe is thought to be essentially understandable. Usually one goes further and thinks of the universe as in some way made of the same stuff as "mind" and creates God in his own image. This attitude pervades the philosophies and religions of both East and West, and appears to be a nearly universal characteristic of human thinking up to the present. Yet it is an attitude which is beginning to appear to stand the test of neither critical analysis nor comparison with the factual structure of the universe. The universe is not intrinsically friendly to our minds—it is neutral. Our minds are a phenomenon of the human nervous system, confined to operation in a range between the small and the large centering around ourselves. We cannot range beyond these limits, or even express what we would like to mean by "ranging beyond these limits," because of the nature of meaning and thought themselves. The general appreciation of this and the impact of the appreciation will be something new in the history of human thought. It will give a meaning other than he foresaw to the age-old cry of the psalmist, "The thought of God is too high for me."

It can be no final answer to say that human beings are so constituted that they have an irrepressible emotional necessity for the consciousness of a friendly universe. If the human race is ever going to integrate itself, the first and foremost consideration has got to be of truth, and the other emotional needs will have to adjust themselves to that. I believe that we have the techniques in hand for making this adjustment. An exceedingly important factor in making it will be the rearing of a generation of educators with the vision that the human race is now treading paths it has never trod before and that the destiny of the race lies all before it.

It seems to me that we can envisage for the future no more potent agent of improvement than the finding of the true place of religion and the clarification of the meaning of its concepts. That Toynbee and others are right about the importance of the role now played by religion must be evident to anyone who will take the trouble to ask Socratic questions of his neighbor as to why he approves or disapproves of this or that social institution. It will be difficult to find a social institution which does not vitally involve sentiments usually associated with religion. For instance, the projection of one's personality into the future after death, which receives legal status in the recognized right of the individual to tie the hand of society in the use it may make of property long after the original owner is dead, is connected with sentiments about the existence of a human soul and its survival after the death of the body. One will find, in attempting to carry out his Socratic program of discovering the meaning of such concepts as "soul" and "life after death," that a limit will soon be approached beyond which answers will not be freely given. It is a sinister feature of most conventional religions that the devotee regards his religion as a personal affair, into which it is an impertinence for the outsider to intrude too far. The result is that the program of clarifying meanings and finding a common ground for understanding, equally essential for any real meeting of East and West or for the mutual understanding of the different elements within the same culture, is frustrated at the very beginning. At present there does not seem to be even an effective desire that this clarification and mutual understanding should take place. The demand for clarification and mutual understanding is, I think, associated with the scientific or intelligent temperament, and we may expect it to become more effective in the future when intelligence comes into its own.

Right here is situated a program for the future in investigating the nature of the human animal, which as far as I know has never been formulated or the necessity for it appreciated. It appears to be a fact that all human beings of normal intelligence are capable of applying scientific method. They make the same factual reports in the same situation and, when instructed, are capable of reasoning about scientific theory in the same way. This fact is the basis for the "publicity" of science, which is such an important property of science and the "sciencing" of the human animal that it is often incorporated into the definition of science. The corresponding question with regard to religion is seldom asked, nor is the answer known. How much of the emotional experience of the individual which is at the bottom of his religion is sharable or communicable to his neighbor? It is not to be expected, as I think would be admitted, that all men would be capable of having the same religious emotion in the same situation any more than they have the same esthetic emotions. But to what extent can the religious emotion of one be made understandable by another, so that a man's neighbor will be able at least to anticipate what his fellow will feel in a given situation? Is the human race all one in this regard or is it divided into species which are emotionally isolated from each other? I think the answer is not known, and I do not see how it can be expected that religion has found its final place in our institutions until the answer is known.

Whether or not people of different emotional temperaments can communicate with each other or not, I think there can be no question that there is a fundamental conflict of temperaments here, and I think it has done no good to attempt, as has been so often done in the past, to gloss over the fact that there is such a conflict. Because religion itself is so complex, this difference of temperaments may manifest itself on different levels. There is in the first place the man who simply is not interested in clarification or understanding, but who finds the emotional experiences of religion good and is content to accept them without consideration. Then there is the man who simply says that the religious world is a different sort of thing from the physical world and the same sort of questions cannot be asked about it. Many people are satisfied to divide the world into watertight compartments, one containing religion and the other the "natural" world. Surprisingly, many good scientists are among them: for example, Faraday. Then there are those who do not want to analyze their religious concepts for fear of what they may find. They are afraid that if they should be forced to discover that such concepts as soul and life after death have an unsuspectedly large component of verbal construction, they would be compelled to stop using those concepts; and this they do not want to do. Finally, there are the really tough-minded religious people, who are capable of seeing and admitting that the religious world in which they live is a world of their own construction, perhaps largely verbal, and whose serene "so what?" is undisturbed by the vision or the admission. They like living in this sort of a world, and why should they not? People of this type are not common; perhaps the Oriental mystics are the most important. It is with this type that there occurs, I believe, in its purest form that irreconcilable difference of temperament which to some degree is always found between science and religion. What reason can the scientific man give for the mystic not to construct his own world and retire into it if he finds the external world unpleasant? I think he can show no reason why the mystic should not act in this way, provided he is willing to pay the price. The scientist can only point out that such a course is unsafe, for one can have no assurance that at some time the external world may not come crashing through to destroy the religious construction. But the risk of such a catastrophe may not be very great, particularly if the mystic lives in an old culture which has learned how to restrain the intellectual curiosity of its members within narrow limits. If the mystic is willing to run his risk, the scientific man can give no compelling reason for the mystic, as far as he personally is concerned, not to do it. The scientist, however, will find it very uncongenial to live in a culture which is committed to restraining intellectual curiosity in order to make the world safer for the mystic.

The opposition between the two temperaments cannot be reduced to a matter of logic, but there is at bottom an irreducible emotional residuum. I think most people of the scientific or intelligent temperament find something abhorrent and unclean in the idea that they should construct a world for themselves without regard for the external world. The motives that enter into this feeling are doubtless complex, and I shall not attempt to analyze them. An important constituent, however, is the realization that it is incomparably more difficult to construct an intellectual system which shall be consistent with the external world than it is to ignore the external world. The difficulty is felt as a challenge, and men who like to use their minds accept the challenge with joy. I think it would not be human nature if the man of intelligence did not feel a certain slight superiority over his fellow who is willing to adopt the easier course of constructing his own world. He will, nevertheless, be able to live with him more or less amicably, until the religious man, impelled by the necessity for maintaining his own construction at least during his own lifetime, seeks to impose limits on the inquiry or the publication of the scientific man. This gives rise to a situation which is intolerable, and the conflict breaks into the open. It seems to me that there is only one conceivable eventual outcome of this struggle, as long as the brain remains the most important human organ. There is no stopping short of asking every conceivable question and applying every conceivable test in every situation. We have not mastered our surroundings and reached equilibrium until we know the answer to every such question and the result of every such test.

All this does not mean that the eventual society will be one from which the life of the emotions or the religious man has disappeared. All human beings, mystic and scientist alike, have emotional needs which they will find how to satisfy. The emotional need of the temperamentally scientific man for truth is just as poignant as any of the emotional needs of the religious. It is merely that the religious man will have purged his emotions and have solved the problem of satisfying his emotional needs within a framework consistent with the structure of the external world and man's relation to it, instead of finding his solution in the realm of free construction. Perhaps we have an adumbration of the solution in the scientific humanism movement, although I think that the movement still leans too heavily on a feeling of the friendliness of the universe. The solution of the problem will not be gained without difficulty, but I believe the difficulties are incomparably less than the difficulties of the scientific man in finding the solutions of his other problems. This, I believe, is not the sort of future envisaged for religion by men like Toynbee. Although we may admit that Toynbee is right in his estimate of the place which religion has played in human affairs in the past, I can see no room for optimism in our forecast for the future if he is right in his belief that religion must continue to play the same role in the future that it has in the past.

XII

THE PHILOSOPHY OF THE BRITISH LABOUR GOVERNMENT

LORD LINDSAY OF BIRKER

THE British labour movement, like most things British, has always been empirical and very chary about formulating its assumptions. I think its most fundamental assumption is that it represents a policy which, though it may not be clearly formulated, is, all the same, quite clearly distinct from either capitalism on the one hand or Communism on the other. Most of us who have anything to do with the labour movement accept this assumption and would say that what has been wrong with Europe in the last generation is the prevalent assumption that there is no alternative between capitalism on the one hand and Communism or complete and absolute socialism on the other. The Labour party and the Labour Government maintain again and again that what they tend to call social democracy or British socialism is the movement which will satisfy the aspirations of their own working class and the working class of Europe without falling into the extremes of Communism. They will stress at one and the same time its socialist character and its democratic character. They will deny the very common assumption that democratic socialism is a contradiction in terms. They will assert that socialism, as understood in Britain, is the completion of democracy, and will repudiate the Russian claim that Bolshevism is democratic. The faith of the Labour party shows itself in certain quite simple ways: in its insistence on constitutional methods, its refutation of totalitarianism, its dislike of Communism and the Communist party just because of Communist disregard of constitutional and democratic procedure and of human good faith. The Labour party is indeed more democratically governed than any other of the British political parties. I do not think anybody could be inside the British labour movement without recognizing it to be one of the most democratic movements in the world. There are times when its leaders must think its elaborate democratic machinery and its continual insistence that nothing be done without consultation of the rank and file a great nuisance; yet it is a nuisance which must be borne because of its worth. The Labour Government very largely depends upon the support of the British organized labour movement. That means, in effect, the trade unions and the cooperative party. Its members have all been trained in trade-union branches or "chapels," in cooperative meetings, or in organizations like the Cooperative Women's Guild. They are ordinary men and women managing their own affairs, being accustomed to trust their leaders but to keep leaders in their place. The Labour Parliamentary party in its democratic convictions is only a reflection of the intensely democratic character of the working-class movement on which it depends.

This is my first point: the assumptions of the British Labour Government are the assumptions of the British working-class movement, and these are primarily democratic assumptions. No doubt the British labour movement sometimes wears a superficial coloring of more doctrinaire beliefs, supplied by its intellectuals, sometimes Marxian and sometimes syndicalist. But I do not think these theories supply more than superficial coloring. The labour movement is permeated with working-class theories and assumptions.

It is important to understand the British working-class movement and where it comes from. It is not quite like anything else I know of, and I do not think there is anything quite like it in America. The Webbs, in their book on *Industrial Democracy,* notice the importance of Nonconformity in the history of trade unionism in the early nineteenth century. Where Nonconformity was strong trade unionism was strong, and where it was weak trade unionism was weak. It was the Nonconformist chapels which supplied democratic experience and the leadership of industrial democracy, whether in trade unionism or in cooperation. The British labour movement inherited from this source its intense democracy, its belief in government by persuasion and consent rather than by force, or, more exactly, its preference for negotiation and discussion and argument rather than compulsion, its idealism and its inclination to pacifism. It inherited also from Nonconformity its experience of the power for leadership inherent in the most apparently ordinary people, its concern with and care of what it calls the "rank and file." Nothing is more astonishing to anyone accustomed to British trade unionism than the apparently dictatorial power of some American trade-union leaders.

What has produced the Labour Government is the gradual conversion of the working-class movement to the view that its ideals could not be attained without labour being in office, and without something which, without making very clear to itself what socialism meant, it called socialism. When it was told by clever Fabians or by students of Karl Marx exactly what socialism did mean, it was often content to accept their definition as long as there was no real prospect of the definition being effectively put into practice. But the movement knew what in fact it wanted, what it was accustomed to, and what it believed in. It had used democratic cooperation for over a century to improve the workingman's standard of life, to give him better conditions. It had found that this process was never completely satisfactory because of the power—in its view the completely undemocratic power—of the employing class, and it therefore worked in hope of a time when it should gain power in a labour government and be able to realize its ideals. The Webbs in their history of early trade unionism explained how powerful in that movement are certain quite simple and crude democratic notions not unfamiliar in America: the belief in an abstract equality, according to which everybody is as good as everybody else, a consequent distrust of skill or expert knowledge and a distrust of government by the clever and able. While there is still a good deal of that kind of egalitarianism in the labour movement, trade unionism, though a democracy, is a disciplined democracy. Long and bitter experience has brought home to the trade-union movement that the members have no power apart from their solidarity, and that therefore when all the democratic processes have been observed and there has been dispute and discussion and final voting for all, then all the members must concur in the result of the vote. If the strike is voted by the rank and file, everyone must come out, for divided they fall. Trade unionism in Britain has managed to hold on to both sides; to the right of every member to vote on the question of striking and the duty of every member to acquiesce in the decision of the majority; and the ordinary unionist has little sympathy with the middle-class complaints about trade-union tyranny. Democracy cannot get results without discipline; discipline there must therefore be, and break-away unions and nonunionists are people who will not play the game and who are looked on with disfavor. In so far as the necessity for collective action after democratic decision is concerned the working-class movement has moved some way from the complete liberty of minorities which its origins once suggested.

To say that the British Labour Government rests primarily on the working-class movement is as much as to say that it is not totalitarian. It would never dream for one moment that it was the business of the state to absorb either the trade unions or the co-operative societies. No one in the British labour movement has the smallest desire to worship the state, to think of it as something of value in itself, to set it over against the individual as a higher or more perfect end. Indeed, British labour looks with intense suspicion on such views, even in the mild form in which modern conservatives sometimes promulgate them. If socialism means a belief in the superiority of the state or the collectivity of the community as a whole over against the individual, the British labour movement is not in that sense socialist at all. It could well take for its motto that famous remark by Colonel Raynborough: "The poorest he that is in England has a life to live as the richest he."

There is no trace in the British working-class movement of the belief in the superiority of the state over the individual, or indeed in the superiority of the state over other forms of association. The state is an instrument to be used for the good life of the ordinary man or woman, and the extent to which it has to be used depends on circumstances. The greatly increasing extent to which the present British Labour Government proposes to use the state comes from the special circumstances of modern industrial society.

Now if we connect the Labour Government with working-class movements and trade unions can we find any positive assumption in the history of British trade unionism persisting from its first early days when it was merely a combination to raise wages? There is a famous chapter in the Webbs' *Industrial Democracy,* published nearly fifty years ago, which suggests a clue. The chapter is entitled "The National Minimum," and begins:

Within a trade, in the absence of any Common Rule, competition between firms leads, as we have seen, to the adoption of practices by which the whole industry is deteriorated. The enforcement of a common minimum standard throughout the trade not only stops the degradation, but in every way conduces to industrial efficiency. Within a community, too, in the absence of regulation, the competition between trades tends to the creation and persistence in certain occupations of conditions of employment injurious to the nation as a whole. The remedy is to extend the conception of the Common Rule from the trade to the whole community, and by prescribing a National Minimum, absolutely to prevent any industry being carried on under conditions detrimental to the public welfare.

The Webbs are summing up an old direction of trade-union action. They have showed how the unions, at first by collective bargaining and afterward by collective bargaining aided by state enforcement, carried out what they call "the policy of the common rule," which is perhaps better described as a rule of minimum conditions of employment. Trade unions in the nineteenth century had gradually more and more enforced, in their respective trades, minimum conditions of work, hours, and pay. They had been struggling all the time against what the Webbs called parasitism. The employer who pays less than the minimum rate or maintains worse than the minimum conditions undercuts the better employer. Hence the necessity of a uniform and enforced rule. The Webbs have shown through most of those illuminating two volumes how this notion of the common rule explains trade-union attitudes and even trade-union defects. They go on, in the chapter from which this passage is quoted to argue that, just as in any one trade, sweating conditions and low wages are parasitic, so the existence of low-paid sweating trade is parasitic in relation to the whole community. It gets more than its share of the market. The Webbs therefore argue that the logical conclusion of this trade-union action is that a standard minimum should be enforced for all trades in the country. This general idea has been adopted more and more since they wrote. Years ago the state established minimum wages in certain industries. It has interfered by the establishment of trade boards in the sweated industries. Above all, by taking over from the trade unions what people call "the great social services" it has done more and more to provide a minimum standard of economic life for the whole population.

I think there is more behind this policy than the Webbs themselves actually saw. They confined themselves to the economic aspects of the matter. But behind these is the more far-reaching and democratic assumption that society, if it is to have any meaning, must be a common life; that the common life is something which all members of the society must share, and that the conditions necessary to sharing in it must therefore be at the disposal of everybody. This is not in the least to say that you cannot have a real society unless all its members have equal incomes or live in exactly the same way. What is to be insured is the minimum conditions which are necessary for a man or woman to be an active member of a society which is a democratic society and therefore in some true sense a fellowship. No one who has the good fortune to belong to an academic

society, perhaps the most democratic kind of society which an industrial society affords, can think that it is essential to its fellowship
that everybody should have equal incomes. What is important is
that the differences between members' incomes are not great
enough to matter; or that those who receive the lowest salaries
should yet have enough to enjoy with the others the ordinary forms
of social life. One of the things most bitterly felt about the long-
continued unemployment from which we suffered in the 'thirties
was that the unemployed found themselves suddenly cut out of
society. They had no clothes in which they could decently go to
chapel. They had no odd shillings or sixpences to spare for football
matches or for drinks. Someone who understood their conditions
very well said they felt like ghosts—there, but not really there; in
society, but not of it—no doubt partly because of the low economic
level at which they were living but chiefly because they did not and
could not share the ordinary work and activities of their fellows. If
society is to be a reality it must be a common life. If it is to be a common life people must be able to share experiences and activities.
They do not need to have equal incomes to do that, but every one of
them needs a certain minimum. The early trade unions tried to
maintain that certain minimum inside their own trades. But in the
complex industrial society of the twentieth century it has been
found that that can no longer be done without the intervention of
the state.

Such state action is merely an application of fundamental democratic doctrine to the circumstances. If social conditions were such
that families enjoyed the necessary minimum of conditions for
fellowship, there would be no need for state action at all, as there
might be no need for trade unions. The simple agricultural society
of New England where Western democracy began had neither
trade unions nor that kind of state action, as it needed neither. But
in modern times to maintain, or even begin to approach, the essential conditions of a real democratic society enforcement of minimum conditions by the state is indispensable.

In all this there is nothing startlingly socialistic. It would not be
going too far to say that something like this doctrine is accepted
by all political parties in England. All political parties are behind
social insurance. All political parties are behind some national
health scheme. All political parties agree that the state has to do
something about unemployment. In these matters the differences
between political parties are differences of degree, of what each

party may be prepared to sacrifice to attain these social-security ends. The trade unions would say that it is they who for over one hundred years have fought for this principle, gradually established it by their own action when they could so establish it, and gradually converted all political parties to it.

Where then does the socialism of the Labour Government and its schemes of nationalization come into this picture, and did not something happen when the trade unions, long committed to the doctrine of the national minimum, became committed to socialism?

To answer this question we must turn to our social history. More than anything else, what helped to put the Labour Government into power was the country's experience of long-term and large-scale unemployment in the early 'thirties. People used to think that unemployment was the fault of the person who got unemployed. It was never easy to grasp the fact that whether there was unemployment or not did not depend only upon the individual, though it was true that the least capable workmen were dismissed first when there was only a little unemployment. But the large-scale unemployment of the early 'thirties was new. There were places I know of in Cumberland and South Wales where practically the whole village or the whole small town was unemployed. Anybody on the spot could see that these men were the victims of something over which they had no control whatever, something with which neither the individuals nor the trade unions could cope. These men and women were the victims of a mysterious thing called the trade cycle. Modern industry, it became clear, works normally with a reserve of labour with which it meets the fluctuations of demand. When demand is low that reserve of labour becomes a body of unemployed, who are to be taken back into work when the demand recovers. Modern industry, as it developed after the first World War, suffered great fluctuations of demand which had terrible results. More and more people came to feel that the results in human suffering were too high a price to pay for the boasted efficiency of this kind of industrial system. No doubt the system may produce great wealth. The men who are employed have a high standard of wages. Indeed, so much wealth did the system produce that the country could provide a standard of life even for the unemployed which was at least bearable. Nevertheless, the effects of long-term unemployment on those who suffer them proved to be so demoralizing that most of the people in the country were determined that such unemployment should not happen again. The economists turned round and expounded schemes by which full employment could be assured. All parties favored such schemes to some extent. But it was generally thought that the Conservative scheme was too cautious and tentative, too wedded to the conditions of the existing system to meet the desperate disease, and that we must combat more drastically the influences of the trade cycle.

The theory of full employment is simple. Instead of starting with existing demands for goods or services and considering how much labour these need, you start with the existing labour force and consider what standard of life can be produced by means of it, given the necessity for imports and raw materials, and so on and so on. But this operation requires a considerable control over investment in capital goods. After the first World War it was thought employers had increased unemployment by a restrictionist policy. If the state were to prevent the fluctuations of the trade cycle and the large-scale unemployment consequent upon them, it would have to control a considerable proportion of capital goods investment, and it could only do that by nationalizing a sufficient proportion of the industries which use most capital goods. Hence the necessity for at least a measure of nationalization.

But full employment clearly involves something more than that. It means using the available labour of the country on a considered plan: giving priority to this industry and withholding it from that. And thus the British working class, committed to a policy of full employment, are committed to planning, which for many people, though not of course for all, is only another name for socialism. They are also committed, though they do not all realize it, to a considerable amount of direction of labour. The problem they have to face, a problem as yet unsolved, is whether planning is compatible with democratic freedom. Anybody can plan and anybody can prevent unemployment if he can order men and women about from this industry to that and determine their relative scale of wages. That might mean a degree of compulsion entirely incompatible with the ideals and traditions of the British Labour party. The problem the party and the government are now facing is whether this problem, the solution of which entails planning, can be solved by persuasion and argument and exhortation and discussion; in short, on democratic principles.

The difficulties of democratic planning can be seen perhaps most interestingly not in the nationalization of industries but in town and country planning. What happens is this. With no conscious control towns spread in haphazard, unsatisfactory, ugly ways. There is a mass of what is called "ribbon development," or building along the roads because that is cheap, and so on; and it is easy to see how the growth of industry and population and the absence of planning make the countryside hideous. It is a simple matter to say: "Let us do this wisely and properly and with order. Let us have architects and men of vision to plan where new towns ought to be and plan them in the most advisable ways." The country then sets up a Minister of Town and Country Planning and he goes ahead to plan new towns. But although everyone knows that if the minister does not plan, there will be a hideous mess, nobody knows exactly where the mess is going to be and everybody hopes it will be somewhere else than near him. And when people are confronted with the conscious choice and decision of a minister that there shall be a new town here or there, all those whose interests are then adversely affected rise in angry protest. They are far less ready to accept even the fairly sensible decision of a responsible minister than the unplanned result which nobody has willed and for which nobody can be made responsible. Things that work out at random, even when results are hateful, seem to many people easier to bear than are the deliberate decisions which do not please everyone. That is why planning needs a great deal of conscious and strong government if it is to make way against a policy of doing nothing and hoping for the best.

The Liberal party was converted by Lord Beveridge to a policy of full employment and was prepared to go some way toward nationalization to secure that end. But while the Liberals perhaps had a prejudice against nationalization, the Labour party had a prejudice for it. The necessities of full employment are not therefore a complete explanation of why the Labour party was converted to socialism, though they had a great deal to do with it.

Let us consider again the experience of trade unionism. Trade unionism has been called by the Webbs "industrial democracy," but that industrial democracy has not produced democratic industrialism. The nature of capitalism has indeed changed, but it has not changed in the direction of democracy. It was originally and still is, in part, a system where the government of industry is in the hands of the owners of capital. By the development of the limited liability company the owners of capital became largely shareholders, who, as shareholders, nominally have the final word in the government of a business. But in practice that final word has come to mean very little. The shareholders ordinarily have only nominal control, and businesses are governed by directors, or what is impersonally called "the management." But if the shareholders have little control, the workers organized in their trade unions have no responsibility at all in the management of the business. Professor Whitehead in his *Leadership in a Free Society* has pointed out that the great defect of modern capitalism is that the employers have never regarded their businesses as social groups or societies, and therefore never thought of them as businesses which required government, the members of which had to be persuaded or led to do things. They have thought of their problems as technical problems, questions of the right arrangement and distribution and factors of production, and they have got their workmen to accept these technical solutions by compelling them through the fear of dismissal. The small, old-fashioned family business in England, where the employer knew all his men and their families, was, in spirit, though not in form, far more democratic than the large-scale industries we described.

Industry has therefore been governed oligarchically, or monarchically, and this arbitrary, irresponsible government by employers has stood over against the democratic organization of the employed—the trade unions. The trade unions have been able to insist on certain conditions of employment. They have enforced collective rules of wages, of hours, of conditions, but they have taken and been allowed no responsibility for management. Trade unions have therefore increasingly felt that a modern industrial society is a house divided against itself, a society politically democratic, industrially oligarchic, and they have come to think more and more that this house divided against itself cannot stand. The oligarchy of employers will make political democracy a sham unless the principles of political democracy are transferred to industry. Till that is done the dualism which marks an industrial society will persist.

It has to be remembered that dualism of some kind is a very old feature of English society. The trade unions are the descendants of the Nonconformist congregations, and the Nonconformists were the democratic half of an English society which was aristocratic and Anglican on the top. In political and social matters that dualism has greatly disappeared, or at any rate its contrasts have been greatly softened, but in industry dualism in the nineteenth century took on a new and more intense form.

Industrialism grew up in America in a society which was already largely democratic, where there was an upward movement in society far greater than there ever was in England, and it was therefore natural for American society to think that what mattered in democracy was that any person, whatever his upbringing and whatever the means of his parents, could rise to the top of society. Democratic equality in America was therefore thought of as the right of anyone to become unequal. It is an equal right to inequality.

But in England the democratic ideal formulated itself not as the right for individuals themselves to become employers but as the demand that this dualism of employers and employed, of managers and managed, of governors and governed, should disappear. As the trade unions in England grew and developed and became accepted and respectable, as they have been doing increasingly for the last three quarters of a century, they gradually ceased to be regarded as an irresponsible opposition. Employers came more and more to regard them as an indispensable element in the whole setup of industry. The government in both World Wars negotiated with trade union leaders. More and more things were done through joint committees of employers and employed until finally in the recent war considerable responsibilities of management were placed upon what were called works committees. Some responsibility for production was placed upon the trade unions themselves.

So the old dualism described above began to lose its sharp edges. It was natural therefore for the trade-union movement to think that the ideal to which it was moving was the position in which this contrast was entirely overcome; when the workers would include management in their work and run industry, and industrial democracy would at last produce democratic industrialism and show itself as full-blown socialism. The simplest, though not to my mind the most logical, way of conceiving this result was thought of as nationalization.

If recent bills for nationalization of such fundamental industries as coal mining or transport are examined, it will be seen that what fundamentally has happened is that the state has taken the place of the shareholders. There is a supreme board of directors which has much the same powers and position as a board of directors in any modern big business. The board will represent the interests of the trade unions as well as the interests of the executives, but the new board will be ultimately responsible to the nation as a whole, and will be represented by the minister in Parliament.

This move toward nationalization shows the theoretical development of British socialism. It starts with an intensely democratic society, the working-class movement, the democratic side of British society. It applies its principle to the establishment of common rules and standards in industrial life. Its members retain their strong and fervent democratic spirit, but as businesses grow bigger and trade unions become national bodies, it becomes more and more difficult to retain the democratic spirit in the vastness of our organizations. Nationalization meets some of the difficulties, and it is easy to see how it seems to be the climax of a long democratic development; but closer examination reveals ambiguities which are not yet resolved.

Nationalization as such is the answer to the objection that in capitalism power is in the hands of directors or managers who are responsible to no one. There is much to be said for the view that the existence of such irresponsible power is fundamentally undemocratic. No doubt in very many cases that power is not used without responsibility. Though they cannot be made so to do, the employers may pay attention to the national needs. Nationalizing the Bank of England, for example, has not fundamentally changed its behavior. Nevertheless, regarded institutionally, the government of industry is undemocratic because of its irresponsibility. Nationalization makes management responsible to the community as a whole. The transport system will have to give account to a democratically elected Parliament. Such schemes, however, do not necessarily alter the internal government of an industry or a business. A sharp distinction between those who manage and those who are managed might perfectly well remain under nationalization, and will remain unless something is done about it. And if the labour movement, or the Labour Government, had begun by asking how the internal government of industry could be made democratic, most likely it would not have started with nationalization. It might have ended with it but not have begun with it. Administration would have begun with asking the far more complex question of how the principle of democracy, the combining of efficiency and popular consent, could be applied to a technical business like industry. One of the most persistent ideals of early trade unionism was that of the "self-governing workshop," in which the distinction between the management and the managed had entirely disappeared. Unfortunately experiments made of setting up such workshops have always, or nearly always, been inefficient. It is interesting to notice that the Russians started with the same idea—that the worker, the ordinary simple worker at the bottom, should run the business—and they have had, in the interests of efficiency, progressively to give up any such notion. This need not mean that the management of business cannot be made in some sense democratic. On the contrary, there have been in recent years in Britain and in the United States many promising attempts to make businesses in some sense democratic societies. But it does mean that the democratization of industry is not a simple but an infinitely complex problem. Experience has shown that there is no single democratic pattern for the management of business, no one way how best to make a business or a plant into a society of men who cooperate, who are driven not by fear of dismissal but by incentives which work because there are trust and understanding and a sense of common purpose.

What I am concerned to point out is that making a business in itself democratic is not the same problem as making the management of an industry responsible to the community as a whole. Either of these problems could be solved without solving the other. Now that nationalization is beginning to be tried out in England the distinction between these two problems is becoming apparent, but it has never yet been clearly in the minds of the British labour movement before.

There is one sphere at least where the democratic character of the British labour movement and the present Labour Government must be clear to all, and that sphere is its foreign policy and its attitude to imperialism. There have been no differences in the Labour party in regard to the government's attitude to India or Burma. Indian independence has been one of the greatest achievements of the present Labour Government, and that achievement has been possible because of the Labour party's record in the past and because of the confidence which that record has inspired in all parties in India and Burma. Indeed, the difficulty with the Labour Government has been to reconcile its uncompromising idealism with the exigencies of international politics. The party acquiesced in conscription with difficulty and with bad grace. It dislikes the compromises with the ideal solution which practical politics have forced upon it. The World War and Hitler's obvious aggression did much to weaken the persistent pacifism of quite strong elements in the Labour party. The party has in regard to foreign politics the virtues and the weaknesses of democratic idealism, the same virtues and weaknesses which are obvious in American democracy. No one can study the record of the British Labour party in foreign politics without seeing its persistent determination to believe the best of other people, its sometimes pathetic belief that democratic principles, if applied unflinchingly to any people, will solve all problems. Such attitudes have their virtues, as the achievement of Indian independence shows, but they are apt also to produce a woolliness of thought and a failure to recognize obvious hard facts. Indeed, no party whose philosophy was founded on worship of "the state" and belief in the supreme value of the state and its power could possibly behave in foreign politics as the British Labour party does. The contrast between British Labour democracy and Russian Communism is perhaps nowhere better illustrated than in the Russians' determination to think ill of all foreigners and all foreign nations.

Is there then nothing at all in the view that socialism and democracy are incompatible? Does an indefinite increase in using the powers of the state really raise no difficulties for democracy? Is there nothing in the old connection between democracy and laissez-faire individualism?

I can imagine anyone who has followed the argument of this article saying something like this: This is all very well, but it does not somehow work out like that in practice. Whatever may be the underlying motive, in order to carry out these vast schemes of nationalization there has to be set up a great bureaucratic organization whose powers have to be put in the hands not of the people but of officials, and the ordinary man and woman is as powerless in the face of officialdom as he was in the past in the face of his employers.

Socialism may be in theory the final outcome of democratic principles but in practice it is something very different. This objection may be enforced by pointing out that few Western observers would think Russian Communism democratic. Russian Communism claims to be even more democratic than any Western democracy. We should regard this as a complete delusion. Is it possible that British democratic socialism is not also deluded in supposing that it can achieve its ends and yet remain democratic? Plato long ago said of democracy that its insistence on equality had the paradoxical effect of producing tyranny. Does democratic socialism by insisting on industrial democracy produce its opposite in the same paradoxical way?

Why are we forced into this paradox? By reason of the fallacy which explains many puzzles of democracy—the fallacy that size does not make any difference in principle to the working out of democratic ideals. The original ideal experience behind democracy is the working experience of the small democratic community. Once it is accepted that all are to count, that all equally are to have a voice, that no one has a right to command others, then in the small community all manner of blessed results follow: the community—that is, all the members of it—rule; the distinction between "they" and "we" disappears, as does the distinction between rulers and ruled. "We" are the community; "we" obviously govern in the communal meeting; "we" make decisions about "our" common property. There are some things which "we" the community have in common; other things "we," the single separate selves who make up the community, own separately. In the tiny community, once the distinction between the ruler and the ruled is denied in theory, it can be negated in practice. Democrats have tended to think that this blessed state of affairs, which they have known and enjoyed in the small community, will follow, if the same recipes are used, in any community whatever its size and therefore in the state. But of course this does not happen. Contrivance, thought, constitutional designs, well-planned democratic machinery can do a great deal to reproduce on a large scale the essential features of small-scale democracy. But to think that the practices of a tiny democracy can be realized quite simply in a large-scale democracy is to court disaster. The democratic experience of the tiny community depends on discussion between people who know each other personally and in which all can take a real part. As the community grows in size this ideal experience quickly becomes impossible. A public meeting of all is impossible and a discussion by all even more impossible. Authority has to be delegated. Individuals have to be allowed to do things "in the name of the community." Persons have to be elected to "represent" the community; their decisions have to be "deemed" to be the decisions of the community, and so on and so on.

The modern democratic state, with a population of many millions, has only the remotest resemblance to its original prototype. If it tries to retain some features of the original experience of the small community, it does so only by leaving others out. It is roughly true that American and English democracy thought that discussion was the essential experience and that their democracy is like primitive democracy in that it is government by discussion; but it is not like it in much else. Discussion *for* us is not the same as discussion *by* us.

Rousseau condemned representative government as a departure from the fundamental simplicity of the public meeting. He approved of the plebiscite or the referendum because it retained the right of each and every member of the community to vote. But that meant dropping the discussion; and a plebiscite has to be arranged by an authoritative person, its questions drawn up, its timing settled by authority; so that it too can easily become an instrument of tyranny. Yet the belief in the referendum as an essentially democratic procedure outlived Napoleon III's demonstration that it need be nothing of the kind and, for all I know, may have outlived Hitler's more convincing demonstrations to the same effect.

Democrats still often speak of successful modern democracy in the language of its simple prototype. They speak of "the voice of the people" as though that could be as simply discovered in their large states as "the sense of the meeting"; of "government by consent" as though the distinction between "we" and "they" could be abolished as completely in a wide-flung nation as it can be in a tiny society; of the people choosing their government as though they selected with a discerning eye the men most fitted to govern them instead of choosing, usually, between candidates selected by the party organizations.

But though the language of modern democrats is often mythical, its use reminds them that the object of their complex modern constitutional machinery is to enable them to capture at least something of the spirit of democracy's original prototype. Myths are useful so long as we remember that they are myths. We are coming to realize that if we are to make large-scale democracy even a tolerable, let alone a good form of government, the ordinary citizen must not act only on those democratic myths but must be realistic about democratic machinery, and think seriously and continually to prevent perversions.

Democratic socialism is still largely in the utopian or myth stage of democracy. It starts, as did early political democracy, in reaction against the denial of democratic equality. Early political democracy was up against the claim of some to rule others as of right, and tended to think that a vigorous repudiation of such antidemocratic claims would be enough to bring real democracy into being. Social democracy starts with the claim of traditional capitalism that the owners of capital may organize and command men in the processes of production. Now that production has got to the stage of complexity in which the organization and discipline, in fact the government of men, has become an essential element in production, the social democrat demands that the government of industry ought to be, like any other government, democratic. So long as it is realized that there is no single pattern of democracy, and that making what government there is in industry democratic is not a charm but a problem, this demand for general social democratic principle seems to me as irresistible as the original claim of political democracy. Only those who are willfully blind can deny the facts of economic power. When there exists power of men over other men, there are political problems, and the thoroughgoing democrat will insist that the solution of these problems of power must be in principle democratic. The early British socialists found that their solution in what they called "the self-governing workshop" was as democratic and as inadequate to modern conditions as a modern New England town meeting. Orthodox socialism was as much occupied with the wrongness of the rule of the owner of the means of production as early American political democracy was with the wrongness of the rule of kings.

The belief that once the democratic principle is proclaimed and the autocratic repudiated industrial democracy will follow by itself is of course seen in its crudest form in Russia. Men who have learned from Marx that economic power counts for far more than political power, and have themselves known nothing about political democracy and had no experience of it, find it easy to believe that once the great and decisive step is taken, once the undemocratic authority of private ownership has gone and public ownership has taken its place, the result is a democracy more perfect than ever existed before. The facts of the NKVD, the dictatorship of Stalin, the autocratic organization of the Communist party—all these are nothing compared with the fact that private economic power has given place to public economic power. To the outsider the social divisions of modern Russia are glaringly evident. But Russia claims to be a classless society because its social divisions are not based on private property in the means of production. Since that old and fatal principle of social division has been abolished, other evils do not matter.

Though it seems fantastic to us in the West to call modern Russia democratic, Russia is now a society in which one great source of undemocratic power has been abolished. That other much worse undemocratic forces are still operating there does not obliterate that fact. If that illuminating and convincing book by Mr. M. C. Crankshaw, *Russia and the Russians,* is to be trusted, the ordinary Russian feels that Russia belongs to him, that the achievements of the Five-year Plan and elaborate organization are somehow *his* achievements. The myth, for it is a myth, works to some extent because it has some reality in it. There is bound to be an awakening some day as to how much unreality there is also, as there was an awakening in America to the fallacies of the simple political democratic faith; but in the meantime the myth works, to some extent at least. Meanwhile the British labour movement can learn the danger as well as the achievement of too simple solutions.

The best British statement of what I call the social democratic myth of the simplicity of the problem can be read in the writings of Sir Richard Acland, the founder of the ephemeral but significant Commonwealth party. The democratic idealism of his writings will be apparent to all who read them. They are inspired by it in every sentence. He is determined to overcome the fatal undemocratic distinction between "we" and "they." Sir Richard believes that public ownership will do the trick. He seems to believe that public ownership and such measures as nationalization will enable "us" to own and manage as "we" think best for "our" mutual advantage as truly as the inhabitants of a small Swiss commune may own their forest or pastures.

The leaders of the British Labour party are far too old hands in democratic practice both in trade unions and in national politics to hold a simple faith of this kind. They know what democracy is in practice; they are thoroughly familiar with and devoted to democratic procedure. They have far too much democratic common sense to be taken in by the simple mechanical Russian myth. They know there is no single pattern of democratic procedure. Their trade unions have taught them that. The rank and file of the party may perhaps dream the myth that nationalization will of itself make industry democratic, but the Labour Government knows that at best it is only a beginning. The partnership in the Labour party of the cooperative movement is a symbol of their belief that there are other ways than nationalization of making industry democratic. The Labour Government is no doubt continually reproached by its opponents for being doctrinaire. Perhaps some of them are doctrinaires, and yet their program is the program of men who believe in a principle—the application of democracy to industrial production—but who are empiricists in practice and who know that much has to be done, many experiments made, to achieve what they mean by democratic socialism. All successful democratic government is a compromise between public control and efficiency; democratic socialism will be a compromise between public control, efficiency, and private initiative. It will take effort and thought to work it out, and of that the Labour Government must by now be well aware.

XIII

LITERATURE AND PHILOSOPHY IN CONTEMPORARY FRANCE

HENRI PEYRE

I

BENEATH every literature there is a philosophy," Taine asserted in the chapter of his celebrated *History of English Literature* devoted to Chaucer.

Beneath every work of art is an idea of nature and of life; this idea leads the artist. Whether the author knows it or not, he writes in order to exhibit it. Put a new great idea of nature and of life into all the minds of an age, so that they feel and produce it with their whole heart and strength, and you will see them, seized with the craving to express it, invent forms of art and images. Take away from all the minds of an age every great new idea of nature and of life, and, deprived of the craving to express all-important thoughts, they will sink to imitation, to silence, or to dotage.

In no country perhaps, not even in Germany, have the bonds between literature or the arts and philosophy been closer than in France. French education, which traditionally devotes the last year of secondary school to the sole study of philosophy, may account in part for it; its emphasis, throughout school and college, is on general ideas. There are few French artists and writers who have not felt impelled to extract a philosophy from their novels, poems, and paintings. Science and philosophy have often been practiced by the same men, not only in the century of Descartes and Pascal but by D'Alembert and Condorcet, Comte, Cournot, Claude Bernard, Henri Poincaré. Stendhal's novels cannot be fully understood without some account of the psychology of Condillac, Balzac's without Swedenborg and other mystics, Zola and the naturalists without some knowledge of Taine's ideas, Anatole France without Renan, much of Symbolism without Bergsonism.

Indeed, it is hardly possible to attempt a history of French literature without granting many a chapter to thinkers who were men of letters rather than professional philosophers but whose influence has been paramount on the ideas of their compatriots: Montaigne, Pascal, Rousseau, Renan, to a lesser extent Maurras, Péguy, Georges Sorel, Sartre in our own century. The glaring omission of Pascal (while Byron received a whole chapter) in the *History of Western Philosophy* published in 1945 by Bertrand Russell, and the scornful silence in which Kierkegaard was shrouded, appear at once to French eyes as depriving the volume of any claim to comprehensiveness. The fertility of a philosophy like that of Bergson, which stimulated political thought (Georges Sorel), literary criticism (Thibaudet), fiction (Proust), poetry (Péguy), and deeply impressed musicians and painters, constitutes a more lasting tribute to Bergson than his influence on philosophers who tried to think along Bergsonian lines. Through such writers and artists, Bergsonism has powerfully shaped not only the thought but the sensibility of a whole generation of Frenchmen. French literature, on the contrary, has regularly sunk to its lowest ebb whenever it has severed itself from philosophy, that is, from the meditation of great problems translated into the language of the novelist or of the poet.

The same is even truer of French politics. Historians, whether from the left or from the right, agree today that the French Revolution, which occurred at a time of actual economic prosperity for France and when the country was far better off than any other continental nation of Europe, was due primarily to ideological causes. The forces opposing that great upheaval lost, chiefly because they had not found a rallying point around a body of ideas. "Ce sont les idées qui mènent le monde" is a common saying of the French which is taught in their schools and repeated by their politicians and journalists. The French defeat of 1940 was due to complex demographic, industrial, military, and political causes; but it constituted in essence a defeat of the spirit. It was, then, to be expected that the men and women who had lived through such an upheaval would proceed to a radical re-examination of their Weltanschauung and search for a new philosophy by which to live. France, indeed, is now a prey to an epidemic of metaphysical "isms."

One may even predict with some assurance that the ultimate victory of democracy in France, and probably in western continental Europe, will hinge upon the success of the French people in evolving a new philosophical basis for the political and social system which they will adopt. The most ominous flaw in the Third Republic, in other respects an admirable regime, was its failure to gain intellectual prestige with the middle and ruling classes because it lacked a dynamic political philosophy. It happened in the nineteenth century, as in fourth-century Greece, that not one of the important thinkers wholeheartedly supported democracy: from De Maistre, De Bonald, Comte, even Tocqueville, to Gobineau, Taine, Sorel, Maurras, they all favored order, hierarchy, and conservatism at the expense of social progress. The middle parties which held the allegiance of the majority of Frenchmen suffered gravely from the lack of a forceful body of thought with which to face either Marxism or reactionary philosophy. Their prestige was thereby gradually tarnished. The French soon lose respect for a political party which lacks a doctrine. The following warning uttered by Jaurès, himself a former professor of philosophy, to his Socialist associates in 1907 is still valid today; for the forces of democracy may not withstand the onslaught of more aggressive doctrines unless they rethink and reformulate their creed with boldness: "The time is drawing near when the Socialist proletariat will have to possess an organized doctrine on life and the universe. The role once played by the Encyclopedia for the revolutionary middle class will have to be assumed tomorrow for the working classes by a new Encyclopedia infinitely bolder and more comprehensive."

Philosophers in France have never allowed barriers to divorce them from literature. They seldom—and they should be honored for it—indulged in perpetrating treatises of esthetics; but they respect in art the most universal language of civilized man and regard literature as the most powerful dynamite, laden with ideas or myths. With few exceptions, they have bowed before the insight of the artist. Typical of them is Bergson who, in his little book on *Laughter,* looked up to the artist as the one who can best tear the veil which screens us from our own consciousness and from the essential reality outside. What ordinary mortals do not normally perceive is accessible to the artist; he alone reaches what Keats called "the top of sovereignty." Elsewhere, commenting on the philosopher Ravaisson who deserted speculation for the study of Greek sculpture, he added: "From the contemplation of an ancient marble may spring forth more concentrated truth than is found in a whole treatise of philosophy." Maritain, likewise, has perhaps won a more lasting fame by the sympathy and the stimulus he bestowed upon painters, musicians, and poets than by his own reformulation of Thomistic epistemology. The talent displayed today by Existentialist dramatists and novelists has drawn to that much discussed movement more prestige than its metaphysical speculations.

Indeed the one common assumption of almost all French philosophers (Comte and Renouvier excepted) is that thinkers do not have to be obscure in order to be profound, and gain little by wrapping their meditations in abstruse jargon. Pascal is one of the supreme writers of France; Descartes, Malebranche, Diderot, Bergson are great masters of prose now lucid and incisive, now fluid and teeming with images. Pettifogging pedants have derided such philosophy which did not warn off the common reader by barriers of logomachy. Their concern for literary values should on the contrary stand to the credit of those men who follow not unworthily in the footsteps of Plato. Philosophical speculation does not have to be wrapped in clouds of awe-inspiring words!

II

A few warnings must be unambiguously stated before one attempts to define the ideological postulates implicit in contemporary French arts and letters.

a. Literature and art obviously do not *proceed* from any preconceived system of ideas. When a correspondence can be traced between the writers of an age and its theoretical thinkers, this correspondence is often but a felicitous encounter. The doctrine which ingenious scholars will some day extract from their works was put there unbeknown to them. Not infrequently the artist was the first to perceive intuitively some new truths which philosophers subsequently defined. Thus the Symbolist poets and musicians expressed what may be termed a Bergsonian conception of duration, of memory, of the flow of consciousness, several years before Bergson had so much as crystallized his own thoughts on these subjects. Proust probably knew very little of Bergson when he wrote his early volumes, and he never read much of him; in 1913, in an interview granted to Elie J. Bois, he disclaimed the phrase "Bergsonian novels" for his work. As early as 1896, in a curious attack against obscurity, he had chided the novelists and poets who crammed their books with philosophy, and maintained that writers must follow their own path, parallel to that of the speculative thinker but leading straight into the life of things. Similarly, the poet Apollinaire foreshadowed as early as 1905–9 the liberation which the new physics and the new psychology, with Planck or Freud, were going to establish. Other modern poets, Claudel, Eluard, have played their time-honored role of prophets. Malraux formulated in 1926 some of the feelings of anguish and of fascination before the absurdity of life and of death on which the Existentialists were to build their doctrine. Philosophers and artists travel along parallel roads.

b. Nor can it be contended that there exists but one philosophy at any given period, or even that there exists such a thing as French thought, distinguishable from Western thought as a whole. Everything coexists within every country: idealism and realism, mysticism and empiricism, rationalism and irrationalism. In a welter of conflicting currents of ideas, the national temper, as we like to call it, or the powerful prestige of one man, be he Bergson, Husserl, Bradley, Dewey, may insure the success of one tendency over others. But exceptions will always remain many; posterity may not ratify our ephemeral judgment on the representative value of American pragmatism or behaviorism, of German phenomenology, of French Neo-Scholasticism, of Croce's doctrine of esthetics. As to French thought, we shall define it as thought elaborated by philosophers who lived in France and expressed themselves in French but liberally absorbed the most contradictory influences from several other lands.

c. It is a truism to call every country a land of antinomies: Great Britain, for instance, with her poetry of dreamy, imaginative flight and her matter-of-fact empiricism; or Germany, whose worship of the State and of the Army parallels her fascination with the vertiginous abysses and spiritual heights of music and metaphysics. But, in spite of her geographic and social unity, France has always displayed in her culture the most contradictory features. Not one great man has ever faithfully and completely expressed her diverse traits. Every man of talent seems in France to have called forth at once his direct opposite. The spirituality of the medieval cathedrals coexists with the ironical realism of the *Roman de la rose* and of the Gallic *Fabliaux*. Rabelais and Montaigne, Descartes and Pascal, Corneille and Racine, Bossuet and Fénelon, Voltaire and Rousseau, Ingres and Delacroix, Lamartine and Hugo, Stendhal and Balzac, Taine and Renan, Valéry and Claudel seem to have been regularly created in antithetic pairs. Pascal long ago wrote that "one can only draw an accurate physiognomy by harmonizing all our contrary features."

d. It follows obviously that French philosophy and French letters cannot at any one period be adequately defined by one system. In only one century, the seventeenth, did French thought attempt to stop the fluid mobility which had succeeded the disintegration of the medieval synthesis: comprehensive systems like those of Descartes and Malebranche were then established. The new synthesis, which the French called their classical order, broke up in its turn with the decline of the age of Louis XIV. Except for three thinkers, who aspired to replace Descartes and may be called in their ambition and method, if not in the substance of their philosophy, Cartesian (namely Comte, Maritain, and Sartre), French speculation on man and the universe has since then most often eschewed systematization. Montaigne and Renan have been the most determined adversaries of any system *in se,* and their attitude is as representative of their countrymen as that of Descartes. They wrote on the assumption that disbelief is at least as beneficial for man, and more difficult for him, than hasty or dogmatic belief; that a system is only "a fine epic on things," true in what it asserts with fervor and beauty, false in what it denies. Bergson pointed to this reluctance to build systems as the leading feature of French philosophy.

Yet neither Bergson nor, in truth, Montaigne and Renan can be dismissed summarily as skeptics. Rather did they voice the latent conviction of their countrymen that any system entails some self-deception in driving one or several ideas to their furthest conclusions, while perfect honesty demands that we hold deduction in check and confront it at every stage with reality. Any system into which we force the totality of things to find, willy-nilly, a shelter or a prison can be disproved by an opposite system. It implicitly claims to leave no problem unsolved, or insoluble. But insoluble enigmas are the only ones that are worth our while and the most precious incentive for speculative thought. "Human thought," Bergson wrote in 1915, "instead of constraining reality to shrink to the size of one of its ideas, will have to expand so as to coincide with an ever wider portion of reality."

III

The assumption is commonly held abroad that French thought to this day is essentially Cartesian. And Cartesianism is equated with logic, order, and clarity. Such an assumption is not fully warranted, and such a reduction of the complex and difficult philosophy of Descartes to a few banal rules of common sense and clear reasoning is a murderous mutilation. Repeatedly but vainly have Frenchmen protested against such a cheap simplification. A shrewd German analyst of France, Ernst Robert Curtius, has similarly denounced the presentation of the French mind as purely rationalistic. Modern historians of philosophy have spared no effort to show Descartes in his true light, that is to say as a thinker who started from an intuition, who frequently challenged common sense, who made room in his system for experimentation and for passions, and ranked himself, in one of those letters where he is best revealed as a human philosopher, "among those who love life most."

In fact, no history, no political and economic life is less "Cartesian" than the French, if Cartesian means orderly logic, systematic application of long-range schemes, and consistency. Turbulence and unpredictability have for ten centuries characterized French life; and if the words "reasonable," "logical," "clear-sighted" are insistently proposed to French schoolboys, indeed hammered into their heads by their teachers from the elementary grade up, is it not because they were not born with those virtues and need them to offset their innate individualism, their distaste for discipline and order, and the mercurial fickleness which they seem to share with another gifted and unreasonable nation, the ancient Greeks? Even in his own day, Descartes exercised very little, if any, influence on literature and the arts, as the literary historian Lanson demonstrated in a masterly study. Racine, La Fontaine, Pascal, Poussin, Couperin either ignored Cartesianism altogether or battled against it. Any esthetics derived from Cartesianism would, then, have devitalized the novel and the drama which are founded on the delineation of passion and illogic; it would have withdrawn from poetry its fecund obscurity, its evocative vagueness, and from painting and music the sensuous or dreamy play of colors, shapes, and sounds on which they feed. Some elements of modern French letters and arts, as we shall see below, may be called Cartesian in the sense that they stress analysis, discrimination among the confused elements which go into the making of any given whole, and lucidity; but only if we temper such use of the word with careful nuances. Intellectuality, lucidity, and analytical discrimination, which were practiced by Descartes and by many a Frenchman before and after him, are indeed essential features of the French mind. To that extent alone, and in reference to method but not to content, may it be called Cartesian.

The dominant tendency in French letters and art for the thirty years or so which followed 1885, through Symbolism, even Bergsonism, to Surrealism was anti-Cartesian and probably antirationalist. Then, more vehemently than ever before, French poets took up the cudgels against the much vaunted French clarity and endeavored, in Rimbaud's phrase, "to regard as sacred the disorder of their minds." The *cognitio ex principiis,* the faith in reason as the provider of first principles superior to the data of experience, was battered. Impressionist painters proclaimed their allegiance to the changing appearance of objects; dramatists sang a paean to Life, the rights of passion, the validity of instinctive reactions, even of hereditary forces in men; Romain Rolland celebrated music, lashed out against Parisian intellectuality, then listened to the appeal of the East; Loti and Proust felt nostalgia for a past which intellect alone was powerless to recapture. Even positive science was assaulted by philosophers and scientists alike. The leading influence then, and perhaps now, was not Descartes but Pascal.

Pascal is indeed far more widely read than Descartes in French schools and by adults. His appeal is most potent to laymen and even to unbelievers: his thought, interpreted in many diverse directions, permeates a great mass of French writing. Even those who attack him, often because they fear his bold challenge to orthodoxy, like the abbé Bremond and Maritain, are secretly obsessed by him. "Any philosophy which has not refuted Pascal is vain," exclaimed an interesting French philosopher, Brice Parain, in 1946, echoing a view commonly held in France. Writers like Mauriac and Bernanos, painters like Rouault, poets like Reverdy and occasionally Supervielle, are spiritually akin to Pascal. Claudel aptly called him "the apostle *ad exteros* for us Frenchmen" when he hoped to convert Rivière, a doubter seeking to believe. Indeed, it is no exaggeration to say that more cultured Frenchmen are familiar with Pascal's thoughts on Christ, on charity, on the heart, than with the Gospels or the Epistles of St. Paul. Most modern doctrines which rank immediate cognition, intuition, and inner life above all else go back to Pascal; and those doctrines naturally offer readier inspiration to artists and writers than philosophies of pure reason.

Next to Pascal, Montaigne is probably the chief influence on French thought as expressed in literature. T. S. Eliot, commenting on Pascal who himself owes much to the author of the *Essays* whom he castigated, wrote in 1931: "It is hardly too much to say that Montaigne is the most essential author to know, if we would understand the course of French thought during the last three hundred years." Like Socrates for the Greeks, Montaigne led the French away from the exploration of the world outside toward the simpler question: "What am I?" He is in this respect the progenitor of Descartes and of his systematic doubt. But while Descartes erected an ambitious scaffolding over his clean sweep of prejudices and errors, Montaigne preferred to accept himself, and his fellow beings, as fluid, irrational, contradictory. He has been called, by one of Bergson's most acute commentators, Thibaudet, "the most Bergsonian of French writers." He reveled in change, delineated becoming and ignored being, and translated his observations and intuitions into a genial flow of spontaneous images. Proust, the son, like Montaigne and Bergson, of a Jewish mother, has by many been compared to Montaigne. Gide hailed the moralist of the *Essays* as his predecessor in a small volume devoted to him in 1929; in the following year he condemned, in an entry of his *Journal,* the Cartesian spirit as destructive of the main purposes of literature: the unprejudiced observation of reality, the pursuit of what in man is most elusive, the preference given to intuition over deduction and to complex synthetic wholes over analytical, lifeless dissections.

Two of the most gifted French essayists of the last thirty years, Elie Faure and André Suarès, were descendants of Montaigne, as Sainte-Beuve and Renan were in the nineteenth century. Bergson reshaped for our age, on a much firmer philosophical and scientific basis, the philosophy of change held by the old essayist. "For a conscious being, to exist means to change, to change means to mature, to mature is to recreate oneself unceasingly": thus wrote Bergson in the opening pages of his *Creative Evolution.* Montaigne illustrates and reinforces, if he does not cause them or directly explain them, two constant features of French thought and life: the readiness of many Frenchmen to accept without reconciling the old antinomies between the real and the ideal, the flesh and the spirit, man's deep-rooted moral instinct and the immorality taught him by nature, paganism, and Christianity; and the eagerness of many a French writer and artist to be rather, in Keats's words, "an imprudent moveable than a prudent fixture," to remain pliable and capable of continued self-development long after middle age and its temptation to stagnate. Gide and Claudel, Matisse, Rouault, and Picasso, like the elder statesmen and generals whom France calls upon to rejuvenate her in time of crisis, have, after their sixties or seventies, been admirable examples of creative old age, impervious to the erosion of time, because capable of serenely accepting it.

The motto of Montaigne, and of Bergson, which might be put as

"I think, therefore I change," and that of Rousseau which is akin to it, "I feel, therefore I am," thus hold greater sway with French artists and writers than the Cartesian "I think, therefore I am." But another name must be added to those whose ideas seem to underlie most of our recent and present writings: that of Nietzsche. His action upon creative artists and even upon political thinkers has been wide and deep; in part because Nietzsche is easier to grasp than Hegel or even Marx, and far more contradictory than either: hence the variety of interpretations which have been placed upon his message. To some, he has been dear because of the stark sincerity of his thoughts, torn from his flesh and written with his blood. Malraux, for example, has been obsessed by him from his earliest ideological essays to his *Noyers de l'Altenburg* (1941) where the most moving passage is an evocation of Nietzsche in his madness. Giono repeatedly echoes Zarathustra's teaching in its most pagan aspects. Even Mauriac, a Catholic novelist, confessed in 1945 that "no philosopher had remained so dear to him as Nietzsche, the poor anti-Christ."

To others, Nietzsche has been a liberator. Literary artists like Gide and Montherlant, repelled by philosophical jargon, have been drawn to a thinker easily accessible to laymen. To them and many other Frenchmen, the author of *The Will to Power* has been a master of revolt against orthodoxy and conventionality, a rebel against the very elements of Christianity which had not been attacked by Voltaire or Renan: humility, pity, tenderness, charity. Others still have drawn from Nietzscheism a fresh vision of Greece as the land of Dionysian passion sublimated by Apollonian harmony. The encyclopedic Elie Faure, physician, art critic, and philosopher, learned from him the ruthless lesson of history: that the creations of man's imagination must be nurtured not in secluded quietude but in violence, strife, tragedy, and in death, perpetually giving zest and significance to life.

Strangely enough, Nietzsche, who is not an important political thinker, has acted upon much of recent French political thinking as a strong ferment. George Sorel's doctrine of violence owed as much to him as to Bergson. The Royalists and other antidemocrats drew some of their contempt for gregarious masses from Nietzscheism; they also borrowed from the German thinker a sense of renunciation of happiness which was to prove an intoxicating draught to the youth of several countries. Drieu La Rochelle, soon after the first World War, and the gifted essayist and thinker Thierry-Maulnier just before the second, did much to present modern European history as a symbolic duel between Marx and Nietzsche. In this duel the former only held his ground by adopting several of the elements of Nietzscheism: necessity of heroism, of ideological myths, of strong leaders, force of nationalism greater than any internationalism. Nietzsche, wrote Thierry-Maulnier in 1936, "gave to some souls tendencies, exigencies, and a temperature such that Marxism could no longer satisfy them and no longer did."

IV

These influences of thinkers from the past are blended, in French thought and letters, with those of more recent or contemporary thinkers, among whom Bergson, Maritain, and Sartre are paramount. There is not one of the important writers or artists of the last forty years who may be summed up by the epithet "Bergsonian" or "Neo-Thomist": for those who matter at all are also men of independent talent, who conceive and create in and through their medium—fiction, poetry, painting—and do not translate the cogitations of an abstract philosopher into their own mode of expression. But the spiritual climate in which they grew was Bergsonian, or Nietzschean, or Neo-Cartesian (if M. Maritain, who has harshly condemned Descartes, may be thus called), or Existentialist. Some examples will illustrate the working of philosophy through literary artists.

There are varied aspects of Bergsonism: it is a vindication of quality against quantity, of freedom against determinism, of intuition against abstract and deductive intelligence, of *élan vital* against mechanism. Above all, it has centered around our intimate experience of duration, identified with the deeper reality in man and in the world. It thus encouraged French literature to break away from naturalist fiction, which rested upon determinist and materialist assumptions, and to undertake the exploration of the inner man. It enabled poetry, which the rigid positivism of the years 1850–80 had tended to desiccate, to justify itself through theories as well as through beauty. It also brought many Frenchmen to a plane of intelligence all the higher for being on guard against the excesses of intelligence. Thanks to Bergson, literature was deflected away from the abstraction which solidifies the fluidity of consciousness toward a sympathetic espousal of the flow of life.

In the first rank of the important writers who would not have been what they were without Bergson stands Péguy. Bergson himself, to the dismay of the professional philosophers who had paid him homage, once declared that Péguy had "discerned the inmost secret of his thought as he himself had not expressed it and would have wished to express it." With the same fighting mettle as he had displayed against the accusers of Dreyfus, Péguy jumped to the defense of Bergson, maligned by conservative professors of philosophy and placed by the Catholic Church on the Index of unorthodox and perilous books. He saw in Bergsonism a doctrine which did not refuse to fight, while many other philosophies took cowardly refuge in security. He lucidly asserted that it was not an antirationalist doctrine because it denounced the sclerosis to which reason easily falls a victim. "In its principle, Bergsonism has been an attempt to lead reason to the grasp of reality." He assailed the stubborn prejudice which insists that reason is worthier of the name if it is rigid, while, to him, rigidity in reason is a pose or a willful cheating but suppleness in reason is fidelity itself. Finally, the Bergsonian thesis of duration became to Péguy, who had long hesitated on the threshold of Catholicism, the only means of reconciling what is temporal (the moment which is measurable by the clock) and what is eternal (the fragment of "lived duration"). It explained to him the mystery of Incarnation on which he rebuilt his original doctrine of Bergsonian Christianity. "Jesus is here among us as on the day of his death . . . eternally every day."

Proust may have disclaimed the direct influence of Bergson and may have contradicted him flatly when asserting the existence of two kinds of memory: voluntary and involuntary. His long novel is nevertheless Bergsonian in several ways. Like Bergson, Proust pictures human consciousness as covered by a hard crust of habit and automatism, beneath which our deeper and fluid self lives. A few privileged moments enable us to plunge into that "living reality," as Proust calls it: a cake dipped into a cup of tea, a perfume, a musical motive which reawaken the past dormant in us. Those rare moments of intense spiritual bliss, which mark the summits of the Proustian quest for essences, correspond accurately to the artistic ecstasy described by Bergson in his celebrated pages on the purpose of art, in *Laughter*.

In the same way, the Proustian characters change and grow old according to a process of inner duration which is unmistakably Bergsonian. Intelligence is sacrificed to a more intimate and more immediate communion with the flow of things in Proust as in

Bergson. Art alone triumphs over death and justifies life, as, in Bergson, it works the miracle of freeing us from matter and opening up for us a disembodied and loftier world. The very style of Proust is Bergsonian in its avoidance of the conventional phrases which cut up reality and in its rendering of the most elusive and the most valuable elements in our stream of consciousness or subconsciousness through an original syntax and a flow of images. Some very typically Proustian declarations of faith like the following, in *Cities of the Plain,* might have been signed by Bergson: "Since true reality is only extracted by the mind, through a spiritual operation, we know truly that alone which we have been obliged to re-create through thought, what is screened from us by daily life." Conversely, Bergson, in his remarkable *Introduction to Metaphysics* (1903), and elsewhere in the volume translated into English in 1940 as *The Creative Mind,* defined literature, art, and psychology in terms which one is tempted to call Proustian. "One knows, one understands only what one can in some measure reinvent."

The chief French critic of the twentieth century is probably Albert Thibaudet; for the rigidly dogmatic and rationalist criticism of his predecessors from Taine to Faguet he substituted a Bergsonian method of re-creating and evaluating works of the past. His purpose was to enter into a sympathetic communion with the author or with the movement that he was studying; to re-create within himself the original *élan* of the creator, and thus to avoid the pitfalls of dogmatism, of judgment according to exterior rules, and of artificial classifications, in which too many critics have been submerged. The other great critics of the same age, Jacques Rivière and Charles du Bos, were also driven to an organic recreation of the works of art which they interpreted by the indirect action of Bergsonism on their thought.

Even poets, who as a species are generally averse to metaphysics, may be said to have been encouraged by Bergsonism, if not actually inspired by it, in the bold evolution which has brought French poetry to the forefront of original creation in the present century. The clear-cut distinction established by Bergson in his *Introduction to Metaphysics* between the analytical cognition of science and common sense, and the *Einfühlung* or inner sympathy of the artist, strengthened poets in the claims first put forward by Baudelaire and Rimbaud. They disregarded many points of difference between Bergson's use of the word "symbol" and their own Symbolist predecessors. But they undertook to develop the suggestive powers of poetry, to reproduce man's innermost life, with their imagery and their music, and to act upon the readers willing to grant the required "suspension of disbelief" so as to plunge them into a trance. Modern French poetry is characterized by a metaphysical ambition: it has asserted its own validity as explorer of mysteries and as revealer of a new and higher reality, lying beyond rational thought and clear consciousness. It has, for many minds or souls, taken the place of religious mysticism. It has, moreover, revolted with more desperate energy than ever before against language, and attempted to break up the hard core of words, the solidified syntax, the network of familiar associations, with which inheritors of an ancient literary tradition are overweighed. In this heroic, probably superhuman fight, poets, and critics of poetry who traced new paths, have been assisted by Bergsonism.

Bergson's own rebellion against language and its prison of conventional signs came at a time, between 1900 and 1920, when Rimbaud's message was being deciphered by a new generation of poets. The beautiful ecstatic poem in which Rimbaud sings his joy at having forced time to have a stop and at recapturing eternity

> Elle est retrouvée,   Ame sentinelle,
> Quoi? L'éternité.   Murmurons l'aveu
> C'est la mer allée   De la nuit si nulle
> Avec le soleil.   Et du jour en feu.
>
> *(Illuminations.)*

had passed unnoticed for decades when it suddenly became attuned to ears and spirits fashioned by Bergson and Proust. Valéry, who in many respects stands at the opposite pole from Bergson and may be called one of the few truly Cartesian minds of modern France, nevertheless composed his *Jeune Parque* in a Bergsonian climate. Claudel's poetry is profoundly Catholic; its author is an impetuously imaginative genius, steeped in the Bible and in Dante more than in modern philosophy. Yet his own attempts at speculative thought spontaneously borrowed Bergsonian terminology; and the bouncing freedom of his *Five Great Odes,* his rending of the veil which normally divides the ego from the world, his jet of splendid images are better appreciated and understood if one connects them with the philosophy which impressed French art most powerfully in the early years of the twentieth century. Surrealism itself, in spite of numerous divergences (for Bergson showed little interest in dreams, which appeared to him as a relaxed, superficial activity, while subsequent poets were to dig joyfully into them as into a mine of concealed treasures), could hardly have come without the libera-tion previously effected by Bergsonism. "Boire à la source," to drink from the fountain of life: this title used by an eminent poet, Jules Supervielle, might be chosen as the fitting epigraph to Bergsonism as well as to a great deal of the most original French poetry since 1910.

V

No single name can be worthily opposed to that of Bergson in the years 1900–30 among the thinkers who advocated a restoration of rationalism: Benda, who campaigned most vehemently against the philosophy of intuition, was too purely a critical and dry intellect, combating all that was vital and spontaneous in the literature of his time, therefore unfit to inspire any novelists or poets. The professors of philosophy like Brunschvicg who distrusted Bergsonism re-mained read only by a narrow academic group. The two main ad-versaries of the current of thought and sensibility represented by Bergson were Charles Maurras and Jacques Maritain.

The former endeavored to reverse the tide which, since Rousseau, had made romanticism triumphant in the modern world. Accord-ing to him, sensibility must be held in check, for it leads to anarchy; man is fundamentally bad, and strict laws imposing order are nec-essary to repress individualism. All mysticism is foolish; most fool-ish of all is the democratic "mystique" which has turned words like Liberty and Fraternity into fallacious shibboleths. "There is no such thing as a generous idea; an idea is either true or false," Maurras repeated. Order and reason can only reign through the restoration of monarchy, which makes for stability, continuity, hierarchy in a state, and alone can curb the growing power of money which turns any democracy into a plutocracy. In endless articles and several books, Maurras hammered his traditionalist and pseudo-rationalist creed into the heads of his disciples. Even Cathol-icism became an orderly discipline for Maurras and his partisans, valuable because it represses irrationalism and rests upon a sound conception of man as a prey to original Evil unless he obeys strict rules and dogmas. Curiously enough, Maurras never entertained any phrase applicable to many other French doctrinaires of conserv-atism. He could declare, with one of his much admired pred-ecessors, Barbey d'Aurevilly: "I have established myself firmly in Catholicism, because it provides such a convenient balcony from which to spit upon democracy."

The doctrine of Integral Nationalism, preached with obstinate logic by Maurras and his disciples, exercised some fascination over an important group of French intellectuals. Its ruthless consistency, and the easy victory won by its scathing criticism of the political regime, led many logical minds to adopt also its positive creed: faith in monarchy and in a reactionary social policy which would restore to France the hegemony she had enjoyed under the Sun King. Several French poets, neoclassical at heart, and some novelists and essayists adopted the philosophy of Maurras. Their gifts were chiefly those of the intellect, and their work has struck no roots. Maurras' doctrine, after having served as a purveyor of coherent ideas for authoritarian regimes in Italy and Germany, and for the caricature sketched by the Vichy regime, has now fallen into utter discredit. Its rationalism, which mistook consistency for truth and repression of normal sensibility for reasonableness, became an absurd and sentimental fanaticism, a vain longing for a past irretrievably gone, and a doctrine of hatred separating Frenchman from Frenchman.

Maritain was once temporarily attracted by some features of the Maurrasian doctrine, as were T. S. Eliot in England and Irving Babbitt in America. But he soon rejected a philosophy which, while theoretically supporting Catholicism, lacked all humility and charity, distrusted the masses as fit only to bow to an established hierarchy, and advocated violence. He was more deeply impressed in his youth by Bergson's teaching, but turned against his "irrationalism," his "atheistic pantheism," and his "pragmatism" after adopting St. Thomas as his sole master. He also attacked Rousseau, Descartes, and, more surprisingly, Pascal.

Neo-Thomism, as expounded by Maritain in many volumes, is primarily a philosophy of intelligence, attempting to restore the human mind to order and advocating reason vivified by faith. Its appeal has been wide and its action deep in France and outside of France. Politically, Maritain's ideas may be said to form the basis of the socially minded Christian groups, such as the French Republican Popular Movement and the corresponding parties in Italy and South America. A generous and forward-looking democracy is presented as the regime most faithful to the Christian faith, rooted in its respect for the dignity of the individual person, affording proportional equality for men, that is, enabling them to achieve their human fullness, in whatever social condition they may be placed. Maritain's "Integral Humanism," as the title of one of his finest books goes, has been profoundly impressed by the strong and religious or pseudo-religious aspects of Communism; it agrees with Marx that the capitalist system has tended to alienate labor from the national community, and calls for a new humanism in which the proletariat would participate more fully.

Maritain has also attempted to extract a body of esthetic thought from the Schoolmen, notably in his *Art and Scholasticism*. While he attributed to the Scholastic doctors views which do not appear clearly in their works, and interpreted them along modernistic lines (presenting them as upholding Cocteau and Picasso, and asserting that Aristotle would have applauded the music of Eric Satie), he proclaimed some principles which have left an imprint upon the poetry and art of the years 1920–30. Maritain provided a haven for the artists who feel tragically their isolation in a world addicted to confusion: he listened to them with humility, encouraged them to develop their own views independently, and merely pointed to the mutual gain which artists and philosophers can find in association with each other. Reverdy, one of the leading French poets of today, Max Jacob, a Jewish poet converted to Catholicism, Pierre Emmanuel, Cocteau, Bernanos, Julien Green; Picasso and Rouault among the painters, Erik Satie and Stravinski among the musicians, have been influenced occasionally, if not inspired, by Maritain's views. At the same time, the lamentable mediocrity of much of so-called Christian art in our time was deplored by the philosopher of *Art and Scholasticism,* who discovered higher spiritual values in lay writing and lay painting done by men of unorthodox but authentic talent.

The main effort of Maritain's esthetics tended to defend intellectuality and reason. The pride of the Renaissance and of the Romantic artist, who has lost humility as well as religious faith, is to him the chief sin of modern culture. "Art is before all intellectual, and its activity consists in impressing an idea upon matter." Its first principle is reason; in every art there is a vivid experience of Logic, the liberal art par excellence. But this logic is the structural logic of the living thing, and not a deceptive search for clarity; its order is an internal as well as a sensuous order. From the Schoolmen to Baudelaire,[1] to the Cubists and Picasso, Maritain traces a repudiation of art that is imitative. True art is composition and construction of the object according to its own laws; its effect is one of joy through the possession of knowledge. Opposing the timid critics baffled by Picasso, Maritain, like Cocteau, praised the spiritual likeness of

Picasso's paintings, superior to any subservience to the mere appearance of reality.

Cubism, which had preceded Maritain's neorationalism by a dozen years, is indeed an offensive of classical reason against the descriptive technique of the Impressionists and their occasional superficiality. Matisse, following Cézanne, had emphasized the necessity of organizing one's sensations, the value of discipline and of simplicity, the preference granted to the lasting substance over the changing accidents. The Cubists sensed that Matisse had concealed a methodical, intellectual quest beneath the exquisite charm of his canvases. They submitted their artistic work to reason, rejected, as Maritain was going to reject, Bergsonian mobility and abandonment of the intelligence to the flux of reality or of consciousness; they opposed the *Fauves* and the Expressionists as well as the Impressionists, proclaimed the primacy of intellectual cognition over sense-perceptions and the superiority of cerebral composition over the prestige of color. "Les sens déforment, mais l'esprit forme," proclaimed one of them, Braque. "There is no certitude except in what is conceived by the mind." And again: "I love the rule which redresses the emotion." Juan Gris similarly called his technique classical and his method deductive, "because the pictorial relationships between the colored forms suggest to me certain private relationships between the elements of an imaginary reality." The weakness of Picasso's phoenix-like genius, unceasingly reborn from its apparent autodestruction, is probably the excessive role which his paintings grant to the abstract and voluntary powers of the artist, recreating a new reality at will. Apollinaire, the poet who was the prophetic conscience of many Cubists, aptly defined those seekers after an implacably rational absolute when he wrote in 1913: "Artists are, above all else, men who want to become inhuman."

If no rationalist trend may be traced in the years which preceded and followed the first World War, there remained nevertheless a profound thirst for order in the French mind and a fundamental disquietude because no orderly system, whether Neo-Thomistic or Neo-Cartesian, appeared to them as taking fully into account the complex and often irrational elements in life. The literature and the art of the years 1919–30 are characterized by a predominance of analysis. In a sense, this has been through the centuries a constant feature of the French temper. French philosophers have always insisted upon the need to discriminate among the confused data of reality, and to mark boundaries within realms of being or of thinking. Descartes and Pascal meet there on common ground, as do Fontenelle and Rousseau, Montesquieu and Comte, Bergson and Valéry. But the analytical and introspective tendency invaded the novel (Proust, Gide, Martin du Gard, Mauriac, Julien Green) in the first ten years after the Treaty of Versailles: it even spread to British fiction which, in the past, had been more attracted by creation of character and description of events and places than by ideas or by probing into the passions.

The peril of such intensely analytical literature has been repeatedly indicated. The novel disintegrated into kaleidoscopic scenes loosely linked by some frail thread, while the characters were themselves dissected into scattered fragments or into superposed layers of subconsciousness and unconsciousness populated by prenatal complexes and erotic urges. Writers of fiction juggled with time as they did with the once intangible ego and with the once sacrosanct rules of composition. Material objects were no longer described, and landscapes were no longer elaborately depicted as a background to human actions but dissolved into a halo of dimly perceived sensations fleetingly emerging into and disappearing from the consciousness of the characters. Traditional critics traditionally nodding their heads in melancholy reprobation of the literature of their time deplored the lack of any philosophical and moral message in their contemporaries.

As we see it with the perspective of one or two decades, the era of the 'twenties appears on the contrary as a period of rich and original literary creation. The philosophy of change and of superficial disintegration which inspired it proved in effect to be the inevitable critical phase preceding a new synthesis. In poetry, Surrealism cleared the path toward a liberation from conventional standards in morality, psychology, and literature. It opened up the oneiric domain to the artist, recaptured the magic purity of childhood in its imagery, and asserted the power of human imagination to change man, where reason and scientific knowledge had utterly failed. It boldly disclaimed the principle of contradiction and asserted its metaphysical ambition to step beyond the timidly self-imposed limits of philosophers and scientists. To unite in ourselves "contradictory and seemingly exclusive sentiments," as Alfred Colling puts it, became a more authentic mark of progress than submitting to a sterile logic.

In fiction, which was then the other leading literary genre, one phrase may be taken to sum up the age whose acknowledged masters were Proust, Gide, and Mauriac: intense and lucid analysis. Henry James once declared that "no good novel ever proceeded from a superficial mind." The intellectual and introspective novel of the years 1919–30 may indeed rank with that of Stendhal and Benjamin Constant, which has outlived many a ponderously naturalistic work of fiction in which the author conceals whatever ideas he might have nurtured, or refrains altogether from having any. Gide may not be a master of the art of fiction because he failed to conjure up life after analyzing it, or to give flesh and concreteness to his view of the world and of men. But Proust is, like Thomas Mann and Kafka, all the greater as a novelist for being also a philosopher. Joseph Conrad, on the morrow of Proust's death, aptly defined the chief originality of his French contemporary when he declared, in the *English Tribute* to Proust: "He has pushed analysis to the point where it becomes creative." Mauriac defined himself even more strikingly in his *Journal* as "a metaphysician working on the concrete." One of his most striking stories is entitled "Le Démon de la connaissance." Although ideological developments or philosophical ambitions never intrude into the works of this impeccable artist, a preoccupation with the metaphysical and religious implications of his novels is everywhere present, but concealed behind, or rather translated into, anguish of the soul and torments of the flesh. Even Paul Valéry, the fiercest negator among modern French writers, who reveled in exploding the claims of philosophy, proved by his very obsession the truth of Pascal's saying that "to deride philosophy is still to philosophize." He drove analysis to its farthest limits in his prose essays, because, like Descartes and Montaigne, he wanted to re-examine the basis for a few unconquerable truths. He confessed, however, that his aim was ultimately to rebuild: "To start from analysis in order to reconstruct" was his ultimate purpose, as he said to his friend Pauphilet.

The vexatious problem of the Cartesian traits in French thought and letters thus appears in its true light. Descartes is less admired by the French than foreign estimates hold him to be; clarity and logic are not innate gifts of French writers, and order hardly characterizes their political, social, and esthetic life. They are aware of the basic irrationality of the universe around them and of their own selves, as they are aware that art would have no place in a logical world. "If the world were clear, art would not exist," says one of the youngest writer-philosophers, Albert Camus. Yet they prize clarity in style as a triumph over the obscurity which comes from laziness and refusal to understand oneself. They distrust the pseudo-abysses, dear to some German and Russian writers, which appear profound because men have not courageously plumbed their depths. To them, true profundity is that which invites lucid exploration while it also resists it. But clarity, order, and knowledge of oneself are not hereditary virtues; they can only be reached through painful and ever renewed ordeals, and after plunging boldly into darkness and confusion. Pascal and Descartes, Bergson and Maritain are at one on this point, as are the modern French writers who have not been daunted by the most vertiginous depths in and outside themselves: Baudelaire, Rimbaud, Claudel, Picasso, Rouault. Proust stated the same creed when, toward the close of his long saga-novel, he declared: "What we have not had to decipher and bring to light through our own endeavor, what was clear before us, is not ours. Ours alone is what we draw from the darkness in ourselves, unknown to others." Péguy, Reverdy, the Surrealists themselves, who are far from being meek inheritors of traditional French values, have repeatedly voiced their conviction that clarity and profundity are not mutually exclusive. Mauriac conceives fiction as the art of bringing to light, while respecting their mystery, the darkest regions of man's passionate, sensuous, and mystical life. Montherlant, who expressed in flamboyant and sonorous sentences some of the deepest aspirations of the French youth of 1925 and rejoiced in contradictions, held to one deep-seated belief: that man must at no cost agree to dupe himself. To look things in the face and to refuse to bury one's head like an ostrich is to him the only law of morality. Stendhal, Pascal, La Rochefoucauld and Montaigne, and their admirer Nietzsche would not have disagreed with him there.

VI

Around 1930 a new trend became conspicuous in French literature which revealed a new philosophical attitude: it was to culminate in the Existentialist vogue of the years 1943–47 which is one of the most striking cases of an invasion of literature by philosophy. The literary works once more did not proceed from any doctrinal views; once again novelists and poets, through the nervous sensitiveness and the prophetic insight which are their privilege or their burden, first sensed truths which deductive minds were later to co-ordinate into a systematic whole.

Kierkegaard, irritated by the static concepts with which many professional philosophers are content, once said: "We live forward, but we understand backward." Not philosophers alone but many men of letters have divorced their thinking from action and from life: Proust, Gide, and their contemporaries had tended to concentrate on memory and to ignore will power, to dissolve the personality into subtle and evanescent hues, to isolate man from his fellow beings, and to cultivate his introspective knowledge of himself when at rest in a sheltered room, alone with his remembrance of the past. They endowed psychology with a new dimension which now makes most novels before Proust, Joyce, and Kafka appear thin or insipid. But by 1930 and even more by 1940 the world seemed no longer attuned to such elaborate and serene laboratory analysis. It was living through events which resembled rather the epics of violence and the crude colors of Dostoevski's and Balzac's fiction. It became obsessed by tragedy. "What have we to do with a life which would not be tragic?" asked Mauriac in his *Journal.* The same question echoes through the literature of the last fifteen years.

Saint-Exupéry, Giono, Céline, Chamson, Malraux, and the Existentialists, all born around the dawn of the twentieth century, are the representative novelists of this new generation; Eluard, Aragon, Michaux are its poets. All these men are obsessed by the desire not to remain unmoved by the anguish of other men suffering from the threat of war, by social inequality, or by economic injustice. Several of them have taken sides, usually with the extreme left, in political issues: but they have raised such issues to the height of metaphysical speculation and envisaged evil as a cosmic phenomenon, though one which it lies within the power of man to redress in part. If their art has occasionally lost in polished and serene beauty, it has gained in sincerity and in generosity. Malraux, Giono, Camus, Sartre, while not faultless in artistry, embody in their works the profound spiritual upheaval of our age and have listened to the symbolic warning of the Prophetess whom Keats, on the threshold of death, evoked in the revised version of *Hyperion:*

> "None can usurp this height," return'd that shade,
> "But those to whom the miseries of the world
> Are misery, and will not let them rest."

These men look forward, and not backward to their past or the past of their country. They no longer believe that the most authentic elements in us are also the lowest and are reached by laborious delving into our semiconscious states. Some of them have been aviators in the Spanish Civil War and in the second World War, others resistance leaders in their invaded land. They have lived their ideas, and have admired the achievements and potentialities of man all the more warmly as the world appeared to them more absurd and meaningless. In the very midst of action their minds reflected most intensely; on the brink of peril they perceived more clearly the value of art, friendship, love. Their characters are as remote as they conceivably could be from Leopold Bloom and Mrs. Dalloway, from Proust's hero and from his barons and marquis imprisoned in their abnormal loves. They live with and for other men. Two ideas recur in their message; communion with their fellow beings and need for grandeur or, to use a less literal but truer translation for the French word, for nobleness. Malraux, who is typical of them all, remarked in an interview given in 1945 to the review *Horizon* that he and his most widely read contemporaries should be linked with the Pascalian tradition or tendency. Each of them could indeed be, and has been, called a Pascal without faith or without Christ.

Malraux's philosophy owes much to Nietzsche, to Stendhal, to Pascal, and to Eastern thinkers: but it is definitely the philosophy of an artistic creator, in which intensity counts more than logic. Its starting point is a negation, or rather a refusal of the comforting belief in God. "We have killed God," as the Nietzschean mouthpiece, Zarathustra, joyfully exclaims; but man has also discovered an essential absurdity in life. The inevitability of death at first blights human joy; but man soon learns to find an exaltation in the challenging presence of death. Life is absurd, but it is possible to endow it with significance through adventure. Revolution is the great gamble which tempts Malraux's characters. They plunge into it in order to forge new reasons for living and perhaps to find the opportunity for an heroic death rather than to improve the fate of their fellow beings. "To gamble one's life on a stake higher than oneself" is one of the author's favorite formulas.

Malraux's novels are steeped in a metaphysical anguish which torments all the actors of his stories of revolutionary conspiracy. Their ultimate purpose is not to gain power, wealth, or fame: it is to acquire a clearer and fuller consciousness of the universe and of themselves; and such a consciousness cannot be reached in quietude. Men are hungry for myths, in Malraux's psychology; they passionately seek to justify their existence through them, and to rise above mediocrity, to become the equals of gods. Some of the peremptory assertions of his characters who engage in metaphysical discussion in the midst of battle give the key to their creator's deepest obsessions. "Every man dreams of being a god." "Men only die for what does not exist." In *Man's Hope* two airmen suddenly engage in conversation and voice Malraux's definition of the purpose of our frail and yet heroic life: "How can man best make use of his life?—By transforming as wide an experience as possible into consciousness."

Such novels (and those of Saint-Exupéry, Bernanos, Giono were not remote from Malraux's preoccupations) paved the way, in the 'thirties, for the Existentialist invasion of French literature in the 'forties. Philosophy and literature, indeed philosophy and action were then to be linked as never before in France. Action did not become the criterion of truth, as with the pragmatists whom the French, with their insistence on theory, have always distrusted. But action alone provides man's freedom with a significance and humanizes the free speculations of philosophers. Goethe had already said in his *Wilhelm Meister* that to act is more difficult than to think, and to act according to one's thought is the truest of all challenges. Along with a few eccentricities and a sonorous publicity which has disfigured their true message, the Existentialist movement has crystallized some of the deepest and sincerest aspirations of the French mind, seeking to examine all its assumptions anew and to build a philosophy in harmony with the tragic temper of the age. Never perhaps since the medieval debate over the Universals or since the time when fashionable seventeenth-century belles swooned with rapture over Descartes' vortices, has French social, esthetic, and political life been thus permeated with discussions over abstract ideas. Every issue, be it the attitude to be adopted toward Communism or Germany or the economic policy to be followed for French reconstruction—even, they say, what hat should be worn by one's philosophical lady friend, or what drink should be absorbed by anguished metaphysicians so as to forget, before dinner, the nauseating absurdity of man's fate—becomes a pretext for abstruse ontological and epistemological disquisitions.

In spite of some ridiculousness which was quickly seized upon by critics and in spite of the inevitable herd of imitators which success always brings in its train, Existentialism is to be taken seriously, at least as a literary phenomenon. It has attracted several of the most powerful talents in present-day French fiction, drama, and criticism, and influenced even those who disagreed with its tenets or opposed it on ethical or philosophical grounds.

Existentialism is by definition a repudiation of the essentialist attitude, which asserts the ontological precedence of essence over existence. Man was not created by God according to any preconceived pattern of human nature. Indeed, everything happens as if God did not exist; man, in Sartre's phrase, proclaims himself "a widower of God." The human creature is given: it is only what it makes itself. It uses certain actual conditions surrounding it to become what it chooses to be. For man is free.

Freedom is a burden and a source of anguish, expressed by metaphysical, occasionally physical, nausea; but it is also the sole justification of man's life. Man embarks upon a choice, freely and lucidly accepted. Through action, and especially through solidarity with other fellow beings, he endows his freedom with a content which gives it a meaning. "Man is responsible for everything before everybody" is a motto that the Existentialists are fond of quoting from *The Brothers Karamazov*. His task is to justify a universe which is otherwise absurd, and to act in order to fulfill himself and to alleviate the miseries of his companions in this world of anguish. Literature must desert the sterile ivory towers of the tenants of art for art's sake and become determinedly "engaged." Writers and thinkers can no longer enjoy the comforts of civilized society while scorning the workmen, the engineers, and the politicians who made them possible, or while playing their flute as Rome is burning. They must be prepared to fight for, and to improve, the political and social order in which they happen to live. Existentialism, which has been hastily branded as debasing pessimism, leads in truth to an ethics of stoicism and grave optimism. Its danger lies in the excessive burden it lays upon man, who, rejecting the comforting but, according to those philosophers, cowardly belief in God as a redresser of wrongs and in another life as justifying the injustice of the present one, must assume the immense responsibility of changing this world into a more logical and more moral one.

Such philosophical assumptions underlie the novels of Simone de Beauvoir, *L'Invitée* and *Le Sang des autres,* and are expressed in abstract language in her treatise vindicating the necessity to act in order to bring one's potential liberty to actuality: *Pyrrhus et Cinéas.* They have been labored at great length by Sartre in his bulky philosophical works, applied by him in many a penetrating article of criticism in his magazine, *Les Temps modernes,* and embodied in his novels, short stories, and plays. Sartre, in spite of occasional paradoxes and of a dialectic subtlety which borders on sophistry, is a philosophical and literary figure of very great stature.

He is probably the most powerful novelist since Proust and Mauriac, the most gifted dramatist since Giraudoux, and his prestige as a philosopher has not been matched in France since the vogue of Bergson at the dawn of the present century.

His big novel in several tomes, *Les Chemins de la liberté,* has turned resolutely against the literature of analysis and of disintegration: it has rejected the easy solutions of escape or of isolation on the part of the writer, and brought the heroes, through many varied experiences and some mud and vice, to the realization that their freedom has to be fought for through action and solidarity. Man must transcend himself, not toward God, but toward other men. Several other novelists and essayists follow and will follow in the footsteps of Sartre, and, without subscribing to the tenets of a philosophical system which might be too narrow a cell for them, will compose works inspired by the same fundamental metaphysics. The professional philosopher who stands, with Sartre, in the forefront of Existentialism is Merleau-Ponty. Meanwhile it may be said that the literature of France, and of a good many other countries, in the middle years of our century, is tinged with this doctrine.

An illustration is Albert Camus, who does not accept the dogmatic assertions of Sartre and his disciples but shares the emotional reactions which lie at the root of that philosophy, and steeps his writings, clad in a remarkable style, sensitive and restrained at the same time, in metaphysical anxiety. "A work is great through its ever-renewed power to call the world into question," says one of the heroes of *Caligula;* and again, in the same play: "Insecurity is what makes man think." Camus is a great artist who distrusts the fiction and the play with a purpose, the pitfall of Existentialist writing. His two novels, *L'Etranger* and *La Peste* (the latter a masterpiece of condensed and living embodiment of ethical and philosophical views), never preach or teach. His two plays have shown less mastery of the difficult technique of the stage, but the promise they contain for mature work in the years to come is very great. In a philosophical essay on the myth of Sisyphus, Camus voiced, with more sincerity and emotion than logic, the anguish from which his meditations sprang. Born with a passionate hunger for life and beauty, then stricken with a grave disease with which he is still constantly threatened, faced with the monstrous disorder of the second World War and of the concentration camps, Camus found only one basis for the re-examination of all his thought: the world is absurd. He then debated the "only serious philosophical problem, that of suicide." But suicide can only be tantamount to the disappearance of the one conscious force opposing the irrational absurdity of the universe. Man, Camus concludes, must not silence "this passionate desire for clarity whose call surges up from his very depths." His role is to revolt, to create, which is in truth to live twice, to triumph over the absurd through clear thinking and courageous acting. Thus Sisyphus, the King of Corinth, doomed to roll his stone eternally uphill, proudly walks down the slope again to pursue the vain task assigned to him by jealous gods or by a senseless universe. "He is superior to his fate, stronger than his rock. . . . No fate cannot be surmounted by contempt. The very struggle toward the heights is enough to fill a man's heart." Elsewhere, in an eloquent declaration, Camus had summed up the noble creed of his Existentialist contemporaries: "I insist upon believing that there is no transcendent significance to this world. But I know that one part of it has significance: man, because he alone demands that he have some. . . . Why not agree that a mind which judges man's fate without illusions may feel in itself a deep solidarity with the companions of its prison, and find therein reasons for action?"

The future will tell if the baffling problems of French economy, of French political life, of French turbulence undoing periodically the work of French logic, of French ideological intransigence contradicting French skeptical realism, will reach a practical solution in the years to come. It is meanwhile clear that the decade which preceded the catastrophe of 1940 and the years which followed it have brought the French to a radical re-examination of all their ideas about the world. This has entailed confusion, temporary severance of the links with the past, but also courageous acceptance of the new vision of the world proposed by tragic events and by the revelation of instincts and forces in man, working for good or for evil, incomprehensible through the more serene psychology and the superficial faith of the nineteenth century. Through Cartesian lucidity and the Pascalian sense of tragedy, through an original fusing of Bergsonian grasp upon the concrete, of Nietzsche's anguish, even of Heidegger's metaphysics, the younger French generation has evolved a philosophical approach of its own. Others will one day tell how valid or how lasting such doctrines may be in the periodic shipwreck of man's systematic attempts to embrace the world in his intelligence.

But the appeal offered by this new cosmic anguish to artists and writers has proved irresistible. Philosophy has gained by spreading outside of doctrinal seminars into the realms of beauty, of emotion, and of action. It is being lived, and not merely thought in repose. Literature has gained by becoming much more than a pastime and by envisaging the implications of any description of life, of any delineation of passion. Far from abdicating its autonomy by drawing more closely to philosophical issues, it has grown in originality and in significance. For its purpose is to treat, and to solve in the concrete, some of our eternal dilemmas. An American poet who was also a prophet, Whitman, proclaimed this many years ago in a book too little meditated even in his own country, *Democratic Vistas:* "Viewed today, from a point of view sufficiently overarching, the problem of humanity all over the civilized world is social and religious, and is to be finally met and treated by literature."

NOTES

1. "All genuine craftsmen draw according to the picture inscribed in their brains, and not according to nature." Baudelaire. The views of Matisse alluded to in the text have been strikingly expressed by him in an article in *La Grande Revue,* December, 1908.

XIV

THE IMPACT OF POLITICS ON SCIENCE

MANUEL SANDOVAL VALLARTA

THE second World War brought to all of us, scientist and layman alike, untold miseries and problems. It also had the virtue of throwing into sharp focus fundamental questions bearing on the relation between politics and science. Whether it be called planned versus free scientific research, or secrecy surrounding scientific results, or government sponsorship of scientific work, the actual problem involves the question of the impact of politics on science. For a long time scientists thought they could get around it by living in ivory towers and remaining aloof while engaged in their patient researches from which anything might spring—from a brand new industrial giant to a cure for pneumonia or to the atomic bomb. Such isolation, however, belongs to the past, and today they are forcibly reminded that they are part and parcel of this world and that what they do plays a vital role in the realm of politics.

Let us stop briefly and examine how this change came about. About the time of the first World War politicians and military men discovered that certain scientists played an essential part in the handling of matter and energy and that therefore they were needed to carry out victorious war—for what else is warfare if not the directed use of matter and energy against the enemy? So chemists—the scientists who know how to control matter—were put to work to find out how to make better explosives and better synthetic substitute materials, and physicists—the men who know how to govern energy—were asked to see how their knowledge of sound waves under water could stop the deadly submarine. Long before that they had been asked to use their knowledge of the laws of mechanics to determine how a projectile could be made to hit its target. These modest aims were expanded with a vengeance during the second World War, when it was not only a question of stopping the deadly submarine but also of detecting the bomber and downing it with antiaircraft fire, of building faster and more maneuverable bombers and fighters, of directing rockets and increasing their range, of making bigger and better air bombs—an endeavor which culminated in the atomic bomb. It soon became evident to all that without scientists, mainly physicists, chemists, and engineers, no nation could ever hope to wage successful war. Since the political importance of war is equally obvious, politicians were forced to become interested in the fortunes of science and scientists. The ivory tower went down with a resounding crash.

This crash has had consequences in two directions. Not only does the government today take an interest in the doings of scientists but scientists as a body are paying close attention to the activities of government. Politicians have come to realize that what scientists discover may not be devoid of practical importance in the realm of political affairs, while scientists have found out that it is impossible, indeed highly dangerous, for them to hide behind the attitude that scientific discoveries are essentially morally neutral and that the use they are put to by politicians, military men, industrialists, and the public at large is of no concern to them.

All this development has brought along a host of new, unsolved, and, I fear, perhaps insoluble, problems. To begin with, let us try to be clear about the primary aims of science. I do not believe there can be any reasonable challenge of the statement that the primary function of science is the discovery of objective truth and that all other aims are, or should be made, secondary to this. Public welfare, better industrial developments, a higher standard of living, or even the winning of a war, are all secondary aims of scientific research. Be it noted that all the subsidiary objectives of scientific work involve not its primary function but the wholly different question of deciding to what use scientific results are to be put. Clearly they cannot be used in any way whatsoever, good, bad, or indifferent, before they are obtained. Once a scientific result is available, someone must decide to what use it shall be put, and it is there that those in politics have found that the decision involves questions of political power. Hence the interest shown by politicians in the doings of science. The classical point of view that scientific results are essentially neutral from the moral point of view and that consequently the scientist cannot be held answerable for the use of his discoveries is obviously of no help at all at this juncture. I seriously doubt, for instance, whether a scientist could make a fundamental advance in nuclear physics anywhere in the world today without becoming an object of great political interest to all and sundry governments and having his work carefully watched by whatever means at their command.

Thus we come now to the question of secrecy surrounding scientific research. The procedure is for scientists to join a sort of glorified fraternity pledged to confine to members of their chosen circle the revelation of their results. In the past scientists have always made up a large, loosely knit fraternity, but its purpose was to make their results known, not to keep them secret. Free interchange of information has been a keynote of scientific work and indeed a vital link in the chain of its progress. If scientific papers have not always been accessible to the general public, this has not been due to a conscious desire to keep them secret but rather to the necessity of couching them in such technical language that they have been a closed book to the uninitiated. Even the development of atomic bombs, considered solely as a scientific problem and aside from its political and military implications, was greatly helped before the war through the free exchange of scientific information. I do not believe any responsible physicist would question the statement that if Hahn, Strassmann, Meitner, Frisch, and Bohr, the discoverers and early workers on uranium fission before the second World War, had been prevented from making their information known to physicists on this side of the Atlantic, atomic bombs might not have been ready for many years.

Once the political and military implications of scientific research were clearly recognized, a plan to keep the political advantage derived from it was carefully worked out by politicians and military men and a cloak of secrecy was thrown over many aspects of scientific work. The idea of secrecy has always presented a particular appeal to military men, and as applied to ordinary military operations it certainly appears thoroughly justified. There is an essential difference, however, not always clearly appreciated, between military plans and operations which depend on the will of one man, or a small group of men, and the solution of a scientific problem which depends on the application of natural laws, known or accessible to a great many men. Secrecy surrounding the former can be kept indefinitely—at least so far as there are no leaks; secrecy about the latter cannot be maintained indefinitely at all, for the solution of a scientific problem depends only on the discovery of the proper natural laws, that is, of an objective truth, and on the skill of the scientist in applying these laws to the solution of the problem in hand. Secrecy in scientific work can at most retard, but hardly ever stop, the general spread of the information involved.

There are still two more aspects of the problem of secrecy. In line with the desire to use scientific work in order to increase the political power of a nation or a group of nations, secrecy is maintained around the work of a number of scientists in that territory. If any nation could be certain of a monopoly of all the scientific talent in the world, this might lead to the desired result. But the history of science proves that this is a futile notion. Some of the most astounding and important discoveries of the past have been made by men far away from all scientific centers and working under conditions which amount to complete isolation. Consider, for example, the case of Lobachevsky, the discoverer of non-Euclidean geometry, who worked in seclusion in Kazan, far away from the important scientific centers of his time; the case of Ramanujan, who obtained marvelous new results in the theory of numbers while secluded in a remote spot in India; and in our own day the case of Eliezer who has greatly advanced our understanding of the laws of force between elementary particles while working in Colombo, Ceylon. Genius and talent are unpredictable and may arise unexpectedly in the remotest corners of the earth. But a genius cannot play his part unless free flow of information keeps him abreast of developments elsewhere and he in turn makes his own progress known. If either half of the exchange is lacking, science is the loser and probably mankind as well.

The second point I wish to discuss here is the distinction between pure science and the applications of science. It has been argued that secrecy should apply to the latter but that unimpeded exchange of information should proceed where the former is concerned, just as in the past. The difficulty with this solution is that frequently pure science and applied results are so inextricably bound together that revelation of information bearing on the former amounts to fairly complete disclosure of the latter. Moreover, since the decision as to what constitutes pure science must frequently be left to men who are not scientists, and who may or may not, as they see fit, listen to the advice of scientists, this type of distinction, rather than helping toward the solution of the difficulty, is likely to prove no solution at all.

We come now to another aspect of the impact of politics on science: the case of so-called planned research. This aspect of the general question has a great many different angles, of which we can discuss only a few. A group of scientists in close touch with the political powers of a nation decides in advance which scientific questions are important and should be tackled forthwith, and obtains the necessary funds for the purpose, usually from the proceeds of the nation's budget. Within this system a scientist may be left free to pursue his own work in any way that he sees fit, provided— and this is important—that his research finds a place in the general plan which has been drawn up. Much has been written regarding the merits of free versus planned research, and I do not intend to repeat the arguments which have been developed elsewhere by other writers. Here again I fear that if the history of science is any guide the verdict must be against those who defend the theory of planned research. The most fundamental, the really unexpected, big scientific advances spring up when a man with the gift of genius sets out along a totally new path of which no one had any inkling before. Would Michael Faraday, the discoverer of electromagnetic induction and the real founder of the huge electric industry of our day, have been able to carry out his work if there had been a board of scientists charged with planning the general line of scientific development in Britain during the first half of the last century? Or would he have been asked to concentrate his attention on the carbon arc or the electric cell? Would Josiah Willard Gibbs' work on statistical mechanics have found a place in the plans of the scientific board of his day, had there been one? I willingly grant that these and similar questions are largely hypothetical, but I fear that the weight of the evidence bears toward a negative answer.

If a certain pattern of philosophical theory is set up as a guide to decide questions bearing on the planning of science, then the case for it unquestionably becomes much weaker. For this amounts to forgetting that the essential task of science is the discovery of objective truth, and that objective truth cannot be made to conform with ideas set up a priori. Thus I suspect that one strong reason for the apparent backwardness of the economic and social sciences as compared with the mathematical and physical sciences is that economists and sociologists have been concerned not so much with the discovery of objective truth as with defending preassigned points of view. Where would physics be today if physicists had for centuries only tried to defend Aristotelian ideas or the tenets of materialistic philosophy? The answer is that our civilization would undoubtedly be quite different from what it is today, and there is scarcely any ground for the assumption that as a result our lot would have been made easier.

There is still another and more insidious aspect of planned research which raises a host of difficult moral questions. I refer to the case of scientists who are requested to do a certain type of work specifically intended to secure superiority of weapons and armament. In the first place, it is clear that such scientists are not primarily concerned with advancing knowledge as such, and they can hardly take refuge behind the statement that all scientific advances are in essence morally neutral and that what use is made of them is not for the scientist to decide. A superficial answer might be found in the attitude that even scientific discoveries specifically meant for war can be applied to peaceful purposes calculated to promote the welfare of mankind. Does this answer relieve the scientist of all responsibility? I fear it does not. There is clearly a very great difference between the cases of the scientist who in the course of his research accidentally discovers something vital for war and that of his colleague who, as a result of his conscious effort, devises a superweapon for mass destruction. Another type of solution for this problem involves the argument that there are instances where the end justifies the means. This kind of argument in turn depends on the problem of when a war is a just war, a question involving deep moral issues which I am not prepared to discuss here.

Still another problem, and a vital one, arises when planned research is directed to the applications of science and neglects research in pure science. First let us note that it is of the essence of the case that fundamental new discoveries cannot be planned. In the second place let us be clear that if no attention is paid to pure science there comes a time sooner or later when there is nothing left to apply. I mean by this that eventually all the possible applications of known fundamental facts will have been worked out and the source whence they spring will have run dry. Politicians, military men, and industrialists, unless they are exceptionally far sighted or listen carefully to the advice of scientists, are likely to be interested only in results leading to the development of power vested in their own hands, and hence are not interested in pure science. Last, but not least, let us carefully note that this question involves the essential function of science and therefore strikes deep at the very roots of knowledge.

I must confess that I do not share the apprehensions of many who see in any program involving government sponsorship of scientific work a disguised form of planned research. Whether such a program is used in this way or not depends exclusively, so far as I can see, on the type of men who are entrusted with its administration. If they are true scientists and keep always in mind the primary function of science they will see to it that research is completely free. The danger is not inherent in the plan; it enters only if science is used to press political aims. It becomes acute if the administering board is composed chiefly of persons without a thorough scientific background and whose interest is directed mainly toward furthering political aims. The modest experience of Mexico might be adduced as proof of the truth of this statement. In 1943 a Commission for the Promotion and Coordination of Scientific Research (Comisión Impulsora y Coordinadora de la Investigación Científica) was created as an agency of the Federal Government. Its cardinal policy since its foundation has been to avoid formulating a rigid program which would bar all work not conforming to it. Each of the great diversity of projects which it has sponsored has been judged on its own scientific merits, and subsidies have been unhesitatingly granted even to some that were very far from the beaten track. For it is precisely from research in new and unexplored fields that the outstanding developments of the future are most likely to come.

We now come to the task of drawing a general conclusion from these somewhat random observations. I fear that it must be rather pessimistic as regards the future of science. In the first place I believe it will be a long time before scientists, no matter what political influence they may be able to wield in the future, are in a position to decide in what direction their discoveries may be used. As a corollary, they may have to work toward results which will not always have as their chief aim the discovery of the objective truth. Further, as long as science is used as the chief support of political power, and as long as nationalistic rivalries determine national policies, there is no way in sight to avoid the impact of politics on science, with all that it entails. Thus we must look forward with apprehension to a period of political interference with the fundamental aims of science. At best this interference will only slow down the rate of growth of knowledge, at worst it may wreck both science and civilization. Bearing in mind that scientific advances can always be used for the good of mankind, it is clear that if political interference retards their rate of development, it will also react on the chances for the improvement of human welfare. The most deplorable situation conceivable would arise if science were used to wreck our civilization. As a humble scientist I must therefore hope for the day when it will no longer be necessary to think of science in terms of political power, for the day when nationalistic rivalries will vanish and with them the host of largely insoluble problems brought about by the impact of politics on science.

XV

UNESCO: ITS PURPOSE AND ITS PHILOSOPHY

JULIAN HUXLEY

AS Executive Secretary of the Preparatory Commission of Unesco, in 1946, I was asked to prepare a statement as to Unesco's purpose and aims. This gradually developed into a lengthy pamphlet which the Executive Committee of the Preparatory Commission very properly considered should be published as a personal statement of my own views rather than as an official document of the Preparatory Commission. Accordingly, it was published in the autumn of 1946, under my name, with the title "Unesco, Its Purpose and Its Philosophy." The present article is a considerably abbreviated and slightly amended version of that pamphlet.

I should like to preface the article by reiterating that the views therein expressed are purely my own; they do not commit Unesco and are not to be taken as in any way an official policy for Unesco.

Further, since I wrote the pamphlet my views have somewhat changed. In the first place, I do not now feel that Unesco, in the present stage of its career, should even aim at formulating an explicit philosophy. This would at best lead to interminable and on the whole pointless debate, and might promote serious ideological conflict. What the first conference of Unesco and our subsequent years' work have taught us is that Unesco can best achieve its aims by undertaking a program of concrete and limited projects, and that on such a program a remarkable degree of agreement can be reached among delegates with astonishingly different philosophical, racial, and cultural backgrounds.

In the second place, although I still believe strongly in the need for the world to reach an eventual agreement on some basic creed or philosophy, I would now lay less stress on the urgency of this task and more on the immediate necessity of securing mutual comprehension between different and apparently alien or even hostile cultures, as the inevitable first step toward the later, unified "world philosophy."

With this brief preamble I can pass to my main subject: whether it is possible to build a unifying and unified body of ideas to underlie the modern world.

Unesco—the United Nations Educational, Scientific, and Cultural Organization—is by its title committed to two sets of aims. In the first place, it is international and must serve the ends and objects of the United Nations, which in the long perspective are world ends, ends for humanity as a whole. And secondly, it must foster and promote all aspects of education, science, and culture, in the widest sense of those words.

Its Constitution defines these aims more fully. The preamble begins with Mr. Attlee's noble words: "Since wars begin in the minds of men, it is in the minds of men that the defences of peace must be constructed." It continues by stressing the dangers of ignorance: "Ignorance of each other's ways and lives has been a common cause, throughout the history of mankind, of that suspicion and mistrust between the peoples of the world through which their differences have all too often broken into war." And it then proceeds to point out that the late war was made possible by the denial of certain basic principles, "the democratic principles of the dignity, equality, and mutual respect of men," and by the substitution for them of "the doctrine of the inequality of men and races."

From these premises it goes on to point out that "the wide diffusion of culture, and the education of humanity for justice and liberty and peace, are indispensable to the dignity of man and constitute a sacred duty which all the nations must fulfill in a spirit of mutual assistance and concern"; and draws the notable conclusion, never before embodied in an official document, that a peace "based exclusively upon the political and economic arrangements of governments" would be inadequate, since it could not "secure the unanimous, lasting, and sincere support of the peoples of the world," and that "the peace must therefore be founded, if it is not to fail, upon the intellectual and moral solidarity of mankind." And finally, the states which are parties to the Constitution assert their belief "in full and equal opportunities of education for all, in the unrestricted pursuit of objective truth, and in the free exchange of ideas and knowledge"; they agree "to develop and increase the means of communication between their peoples and to employ these means for the purposes of mutual understanding and a truer and more perfect knowledge of their lives"; and they "hereby create the United Nations Educational, Scientific, and Cultural Organization," whose purpose is then specifically laid down as that of "advancing, through the educational and scientific and cultural relations of the peoples of the world, the objectives of international peace and of the common welfare of mankind, for which the United Nations Organization was established and which its charter proclaims."

In Article I of the Constitution the methods for realizing these aims are broadly defined under three heads.

In the forefront is set Unesco's collaboration in "the work of advancing the mutual knowledge and understanding of peoples, through all means of mass communication," and in the obtaining of international agreements "necessary to promote the free flow of ideas by word and image."

Next is listed the giving of "fresh impulse to popular education and to the spread of culture." Here there is asserted "the ideal of equality of educational opportunity without regard to race, sex, or any distinctions, economic or social," and the specific aim is included of suggesting "educational methods best suited to prepare the children of the world for the responsibilities of freedom."

And finally we have the enormous scope of the third head, to "maintain, increase, and diffuse knowledge." The methods here listed are, first, "the conservation and protection of the world's inheritance of books, works of art, and monuments of history and science"; second, "cooperation among the nations in all branches of intellectual activity," which is to include "the international exchange of persons active in the fields of education, science, and culture," and also "the exchange of publications, objects of artistic and scientific interest, and other materials of information"; and third, the initiation of "methods of international cooperation calculated to give the peoples of all countries access to the printed and published materials produced by any of them."

But in order to carry out its work an organization such as Unesco needs not only a set of general aims and objects for itself but also a working philosophy, a working hypothesis concerning human existence and its aims and objects, which will dictate, or at least indicate, a definite line of approach to its problems. Without such a general outlook and line of approach, Unesco will be in danger of undertaking piecemeal and even self-contradictory actions, and will in any case lack the guidance and inspiration which spring from a belief in a body of general principles.

From acceptance of certain principles or philosophies Unesco is obviously debarred. Thus, while fully recognizing the contribution made to thought by many of their thinkers, it cannot base its outlook on one of the competing theologies of the world as against the others, whether Islam, Roman Catholicism, Protestant Christianity, Buddhism, Unitarianism, Judaism, or Hinduism. Neither can it espouse one of the politico-economic doctrines competing in the world today to the exclusion of the others—the present versions of capitalistic free enterprise, Marxist Communism, semisocialist planning, and so on. It cannot do so, partly because it is contrary to its charter and essence to be sectarian, partly for the very practical reason that any such attempt would immediately incur the active hostility of large and influential groups and the noncooperation or even withdrawal of a number of nations.

For somewhat similar reasons it cannot base itself exclusively on any special or particular philosophy or outlook, whether existentialism or *élan vital,* rationalism or spiritualism, an economic-determinist or a rigid cyclical theory of human history. Nor, with its stress on democracy and the principles of human dignity, equality, and mutual respect, can it adopt the view that the State is a higher or more important end than the individual; or any rigid class theory of society. And in the preamble to its Constitution it expressly repudiates racialism and any belief in superior or inferior "races," nations, or ethnic groups.

And finally, with its stress on the concrete tasks of education, science, and culture, on the need for mutual understanding by the peoples of the world, and on the objectives of peace and human welfare on this planet, it would seem debarred from an exclusively or primarily other-worldly outlook.

So much for what Unesco cannot or should not adopt in the way of philosophies or guiding principle. Now for the positive side. Its main concern is with peace and security and with human welfare, in so far as they can be subserved by the educational and scientific and cultural relations of the peoples of the world. Accordingly its outlook must, it seems, be based on some form of humanism. Further, that humanism must clearly be a world humanism, both in the sense of seeking to bring in all the peoples of the world and of treating all peoples and all individuals within each people as equals in terms of human dignity, mutual respect, and educational opportunity. It must also be a scientific humanism, in the sense that the application of science provides most of the material basis for human culture, and also that the practice and the understanding of science need to be integrated with that of other human activities. It cannot, however, be materialistic, but must embrace the spiritual and mental as well as the material aspects of existence, and must attempt to do so on a truly monistic, unitary philosophic basis.

Finally it must be an evolutionary as opposed to a static or ideal humanism. An evolutionary approach provides the link between natural science and human history; it teaches us the need to think in the dynamic terms of speed and direction rather than in the static ones of momentary position or quantitative achievement; it not only shows us the origin and biological roots of our human values but gives us some basis and external standards for them among the apparently neutral mass of natural phenomena; and it is indispensable in enabling us to pick out, among the chaotic welter of conflicting tendencies today, those trends and activities and methods which Unesco should emphasize and facilitate.

Thus the general philosophy of Unesco should, it seems, be a scientific world humanism, global in extent and evolutionary in background. Our first task then becomes that of clarifying the notion of desirable and undesirable directions of evolution, for on this will depend our attitude to human progress—to the possibility of progress in the first place, and then to its definition.

It is of major importance that biology has enabled us to detect a direction in evolution as a whole, and not merely within the small domain of human life, to which the term progress can properly be applied. This evolutionary progress, we find, is directed toward an increase of the following characteristics. Throughout evolution, an increase in complexity of organization; on this, in the biological and human sectors, is superposed a more important trend toward greater control over and greater independence of the environment, and, in later phases, one toward an increase of mental capacities; and finally, in the human sector alone, an increase in the understanding and attainment of intrinsic values, which now in its turn becomes the most important characteristic of progress. Throughout, progress has the further characteristic of always permitting further progress, never shutting the door on later advance.

In general, Unesco must constantly be testing its policies against the touchstone of evolutionary progress. A central conflict of our times is that between nationalism and internationalism, between the concept of many national sovereignties and one world sovereignty. Here the evolutionary touchstone gives an unequivocal answer. The key to man's advance, the distinctive method which has made evolutionary progress in the human sector so much more rapid than in the biological and has given it higher and more satisfying goals, is *the fact of cumulative tradition,* the existence of a common pool of ideas which is self-perpetuating and itself capable of evolving. And this fact has had the immediate consequence of making the type of social organization the main factor in human progress, or at least its limiting framework.

Two obvious corollaries follow. First, that the more united man's tradition becomes the more rapid will be the possibility of progress: several separate or competing or even mutually hostile pools of tradition cannot possibly be so efficient as a single pool common to all mankind. And secondly, that the best and only certain way of securing this will be through political unification. As history shows, unifying ideas *can* exert an effect across national boundaries. But, as history makes equally evident, that effect is a partial one and never wholly offsets the opportunities for conflict provided by the existence of separate, sovereign political units.

With all this Unesco must face the fact that nationalism is still the basis of the political structure of the world, and must be prepared for the possibility that the forces of disruption and conflict may score a temporary victory. But even if this should occur, Unesco must strain every nerve to give a demonstration of the benefits, spiritual as well as material, to be obtained through a common pool of tradition, and specifically by international cooperation in education, science, and culture, so that even should another war break out, Unesco may survive it, and in any case so that the world will not forget.

Against this background our scientific humanism can pick out certain general principles which will be useful as general encouragements or detailed guides to Unesco in pursuing the broad aims laid down for it.

In the first place, our evolutionary analysis shows clearly enough that a well-developed human individual is the highest product of evolution to date. This provides external and scientific support for the democratic principle of the dignity of men, to which by its Constitution Unesco is committed. It also constitutes a complete disproof of all theses, like those of Hegelian philosophy, of fascism, or of Nazism, which maintain that the State is in some way higher than the individual and that the individual exists only or primarily for the State.

On the other hand, we have been brought to realize that the evolution of man, though a natural continuation of that of the rest of life, is quite a different process, operating by the essentially social method of cumulative tradition and manifesting itself primarily in the development of societies, instead of in the genetic nature of the individuals composing them. And this at once makes it equally obvious that the opposed thesis of unrestricted individualism is equally erroneous. The human individual is, quite strictly, meaningless in isolation; he only acquires significance in relation to some form of society. His development is conditioned by the society into which he is born and the social traditions which he inherits; and the value of the work he does in life depends on the social framework which benefits by it or transmits it to later time.

Special attention should consequently be given by Unesco to the problem of constructing a unified pool of tradition for the human species as a whole. This, as indicated elsewhere, must include the unity-in-variety of the world's art and culture as well as the promotion of one single pool of scientific knowledge. But it must also eventually include a unified common outlook and a common set of purposes. This will be the latest part of the task of unifying the world mind; but Unesco must not neglect it while engaged on the easier jobs, like that of promoting a single pool of scientific knowledge and effort.

From this global aim another principle immediately follows. It is that Unesco should devote special attention to the leveling up of education, scientific, and cultural facilities in all backward sectors where these are below the average, whether these be geographical regions or underprivileged sections of a population. To use another metaphor, it must attempt to let in light on the world's dark areas.

It will be impossible for humanity to acquire a common outlook if large sections of it are the illiterate inhabitants of a mental world entirely different from that in which a fully educated man can have his being, a world of superstition and petty tribalism in place of one of scientific advance and possible unity. Thus mass campaigns against illiteracy and for a common fundamental education must form part of Unesco's program. Further, a satisfactory common scale of values can obviously not be attained so long as large sections of mankind are preoccupied with the bare material and physiological needs of food, shelter, and health.

Again, science will not achieve its optimum rate of advance, either in research or in its application, until its light is more evenly shed over the dark surface of the world's ignorance, so as to provide a more equable distribution of scientists, of apparatus, and (equally important in the long run) of popular understanding of science.

Finally we come to a difficult problem—that of discovering how we can reconcile our principle of human equality with the biological fact of human inequality. Perhaps the problem is not so difficult as it appears when stated in this paradoxical form; for the contradiction largely disappears as soon as it is realized that equality is used in two very different senses. The democratic principle of equality, which is also Unesco's, is a principle of equality of opportunity: that human beings should be equal before the law, should have equal opportunities for education, for making a living, for freedom of expression and movement and thought. The biological absence of equality, on the other hand, concerns the natural endowments of man and the fact of genetic difference in regard to them.

Concretely, genetic human inequality is of two types. First, there is the inequality of mere difference. Some people are fair, others dark; some are tall and thin, others short and stocky; some have a natural gift for music, others for athletics; some are introspective, others practical and extrovert. Indeed, we can now definitely state that no two human beings, with the single exception of the members of pairs of identical twins, are biologically equal in the sense of possessing the same genetic constitution, so that biological difference is, for all practical purposes, universal. Furthermore, the range and degree of genetic variety in man is greater than that to be found in any other animal species. This is largely due to one of man's biological peculiarities, namely that his local differentiation into races is not continued to the stage of separate and intersterile species, as in almost all other organisms, but has always been followed by migration and interbreeding.

Secondly, there is difference in quality or level. Human beings are not equal in respect of various desirable qualities. Some are strong, others weak; some healthy, others chronic invalids; some long-lived, others short-lived; some bright, others dull; some of high, others of low intelligence; some mathematically gifted, others very much the reverse; some kind and good, others cruel and selfish.

It is of the greatest importance to preserve human variety; all attempts at reducing it, whether by attempting to obtain greater "purity" and therefore uniformity within a so-called race or a national group, or by attempting to exterminate any of the broad racial groups which give our species its major variety, are scientifically incorrect and opposed to long-run human progress. On the contrary, Unesco should aim at securing the fullest contribution to the common pool from racial groups which, owing to their remoteness or their backwardness, have so far had little share in it. While the social difficulties caused by wide racial crossing may be too great to permit the deliberate large-scale use of it as a means of still further increasing the extent of human genetic variability, we must assuredly make the best use of the variability which already exists.

There remains the second type of inequality. This has quite other implications; for, whereas variety is in itself desirable, the existence of weaklings, fools, and moral deficients cannot but be bad. It is also much harder to reconcile politically with the current democratic doctrine of equality. In face of it, indeed, the principle of equality of opportunity must be amended to read "equality of opportunity within the limits of aptitude."

Biological inequality is, of course, the bedrock fact on which all of eugenics is predicated. But it is not usually realized that the two types of inequality have quite different and indeed contrary eugenic implications. The inequality of mere difference is desirable, and the preservation of human variety should be one of the two primary aims of eugenics. But the inequality of level or standard is undesirable, and the other primary aim of eugenics should be the raising of the mean level of all desirable qualities. While there may be dispute over certain qualities, there can be none over a number of the most important, such as a healthy constitution, a high innate general intelligence, or a special aptitude such as that for mathematics or music.

Somewhat similar considerations apply to cultural inequality. Here, too, the inequality of difference is desirable: cultural diversity is in general a positive good. On the other hand, too great a degree of difference may be an evil, notably with philosophies and ideologies. There are ideologies, like that of Nazism, which must be rejected; and the divergence between philosophies should not be so great as to preclude the hope of reconciliation and eventual synthesis. Even in the realm of the arts, differences may go so far as to render mutual comprehension impossible; and this, too, is obviously an evil. There are many examples to remind us that failure to understand an alien art or culture may be our own fault—witness the seventeenth-century contempt for Gothic art or the nineteenth-century rejection of Negro sculpture. In such cases the essential error was precisely in attempting to set up a single canon of art or beauty; once cultural and artistic variety is recognized, both as a fact and as a positive good, much incomprehension melts away.

It needs no emphasizing that cultural inequality of level and standard is as undesirable as is biological. Bad taste, cheap art, shallow philosophy are evils. It may be that you cannot have good art without having bad art, but you can reduce the quantity of the bad.

These considerations indicate that science, in Unesco's program, must be taken to include all aspects of the pursuit and application of organized knowledge of phenomena. In the last few centuries this set of human activities has become increasingly dominated by what is generally called the scientific method. Negatively this implies the rejection of purely dogmatic authority, whether of tradition or revelation, and the cessation of reliance primarily on erudition or pure reason, let alone hearsay or anecdote. Positively it implies first the development of the age-old practical method of trial and error and of empirical practice into that of scientific research, whereby new discoveries (as well as old ideas) are regularly checked against the broad facts of nature, by experiment wherever experiment is possible, by observation or by mathematical analysis where it is not. And second, it implies the development of the equally immemorial intellectual methods of myth, rationalization, and logic into that of scientific explanation, whereby increasingly comprehensive theories are built up (again with constant reference back to the touchstones of fact and confirmatory experiment) to account for the body of established phenomena.

The scientific method has firmly established itself as the only reliable means by which we can increase both our knowledge of and our control over objective natural phenomena. It is now being increasingly applied, though with modifications made necessary by the different nature of the raw material, to the study of man and his ways and works; and in the hands of the social sciences is likely to produce an increase in our knowledge of and control over the phenomena of human and social life almost as remarkable as that which, in the hands of the natural sciences, it has brought about and is still bringing about in regard to the rest of nature. Consequently, Unesco must see that its activities and ideas are not opposed to this body of established scientific doctrine, just as it must encourage the use of the scientific method wherever it is applicable. Thus it cannot and must not tolerate the blocking of research or the hampering of its application by superstition or theological prejudice. It must disregard or, if necessary, oppose unscientific or antiscientific movements, such as antivivisection, fundamentalism, belief in miracles, crude spiritualism, etc. In order to do this effectively, widespread popular education is required in the facts of science, the significance of the scientific method, and the possibilities of scientific application for increasing human welfare.

The nations represented in Unesco are guided by men's thoughts and principles as well as by their material surroundings. Witness their failures to agree practically because of differing political, economic, or religious ideologies. Anthropology and history support the same conclusion. The history of art gives us, explicitly or implicitly, a history of the changes and developments of esthetic judgments and values, and comparative religion and the history of morals do the same for moral judgments and values; while esthetics, politics, and ethics, as branches of philosophy, go further still, since they aim at finding criteria for correct judgments in esthetic, political, and ethical matters.

This necessary bridge between the realm of fact and the realm of value, between the business of practical control and the creation of what is good or right, between means and ends, can be strengthened by the use of those social sciences which utilize the scientific method but endeavor to apply it to values, or at least to fields where values are involved. They can for one thing discuss the physical and biological correlates of values, as well as their historical origins and possible evolutionary basis. And for another, they can make a comparative and analytical study of the effects of different dominant values on society.

Philosophy, therefore, must be fostered by Unesco, since it cannot be neutral in the face of competing values. Even if it were to refuse to make a conscious choice between them, it would find that the necessity for action involved such a choice, so that it would be driven eventually to the unconscious assumption of a system of values. And any such system which is unconsciously assumed is less likely to be true than one which is consciously sought after and studied. The same is true of the scientist who says he does not believe in philosophy but in point of fact unconsciously or uncritically makes certain far-reaching philosophical assumptions in approaching his work; it is true of the man in the street who, when he says, "I don't understand art, but I know what I like," has in point of fact set up for himself a whole scale of esthetic values; it is true of all those who refuse to examine their beliefs on morality but yet, in every action they undertake or opinion they utter, are operating according to a scale of ethical values which is all the more insidious because not consciously recognized as such.

Unesco must accordingly promote the study of philosophy as an aid in the clarification of values for the benefit of mankind in general. It must also do so in order to have its own clearly thought-out scale of values to guide it in its own operations, both positively in what it should undertake or assist and negatively in what it should avoid or discourage.

Because the value-judgments of Unesco must apply to and be valid for all nations, its philosophy can hardly be based solely on the traditional value-judgments and ideology of any one of them; instead, it must be scientific, first in studying objectively the ideological assumptions of all nations, thereby fitting itself to understand them sympathetically and as far as possible to reconcile them; and, second, in constantly referring back to the facts of existence common to all peoples, and in particular to the facts of biological and social evolution.

Also, its philosophy must consider social as well as individual values. The social aspect imposes itself because social mechanisms provide the chief basis for rapid human evolution and it is only through improvement in social organization that progress can be secured. And the personal aspect arises from the fact that the individual human being is the highest product of evolution and that it must be through his further development that progress can be made manifest. Looking at ethics from this point of view, we can see that some systems of ethics have laid too little emphasis on the claims of the individual, others too little on those of society; or again, we perceive that some have laid too much emphasis on the present and attempted to bind a dynamic process in static ethical bonds, while others have gone to the opposite extreme and have so much disregarded the present that they have sought to relate their ethics not to this world but to the next.

Further, even if there are broad ethical principles which are general and lasting, yet their detailed formulation will and must change from age to age. The ethics of tribal life differ inevitably from those of feudalism or of industrial civilization. Our ethical systems today are still largely predicated on a prescientific and nationally fragmented world. We have to relate them to our new knowledge and our new closeness to each other. Thus, for instance, the rise of modern bacteriology at once gave new ethical responsibilities to man in such fields as water supply, pasteurization of milk, quarantine regulations, and public health in general; while the shrinkage of the world has for the first time made a famine in China or an epidemic in India a matter of ethical concern to the peoples of Europe and America. Similarly the new techniques of mass murder carried out by Hitler's exaggerated nationalism have led at Nuremberg to the formulation of a new crime against international law—the crime of genocide. In general, we may say, it is becoming necessary to extend our personal ethical judgments and responsibilities to many collective and apparently impersonal actions—in other words, to undertake a considerable socialization of ethics.

It will be one of the major tasks of the Philosophy division of Unesco to stimulate, in conjunction with the natural and the social scientists, the quest for a restatement of morality that shall be in harmony with modern knowledge and adapted to the fresh functions imposed on ethics by the world of today.

While realistically facing and encouraging the variety and richness resulting from the diverse philosophical ideologies of its member nations, Unesco will have to stimulate the quest, so urgent in this time of over-rapid transition, for a world philosophy, a unified and unifying background of thought for the modern world. Otherwise the basic minimum of ideological agreement necessary for the United Nations to function will not be present. In this matter Unesco must clearly proceed by means of conferences and discussions between leaders of thought from every region of the world and from every domain of thought and learning. The only assumptions that Unesco can make are that success in this task is possible, that certain ways of thinking are inadmissible—the dogmatic, for instance, or the exclusively logical, or the uncompromisingly absolutist—that scientific method can play its part, and that constant reference back is needed to scientific data and principles, including those of human consciousness as well as of physical nature.

In addition, the Philosophy section of Unesco will certainly have to undertake a number of special tasks which are philosophical in the narrower sense—such as a clarification of the philosophy of science and scientific method; a new formulation of esthetics which will take account of the arts of primitive peoples, the various modern movements in art, the relation of depth psychology to esthetic expression, and the function and value of art in the life of the individual and in the community; and in particular the different philosophies of the different nations and cultures of the world and their social relations.

For this task the help of art critics and artists will be needed as well as of art historians; of anthropologists, psychologists, sociologists, and students of comparative philosophy and religion as well as of divines and theologians; of archaeologists as well as of classical scholars; of poets and creative men of letters as well as of professors of literature; as well as the whole-hearted support of the historians. Throughout, of course, the development of culture in the various regions of the Orient must receive equal attention to that paid to its Western growth. Once more Unesco can help by being true to its many-sidedness, and by bringing men together from all these various fields to help in one or another facet of this huge work.

One of the most important things which Unesco can do in the field of the social sciences is to see that they pay attention to their own methodology. In them, as already set forth, traditional scientific method is no longer sufficient, since values are involved as well as ethically or esthetically neutral facts, and special methods must accordingly be devised for taking values into account.

In the arts, the individual work is pre-eminent, and no amount of quantity can offset low quality. And since each work of art, be it poem or play, painting or sculpture, symphony or ballet, is by its nature an individual creation, it can never simply be pooled with others; and accordingly variety and multiplicity must always be encouraged. Thus what Unesco must here aim at is not the promotion of a single movement but the orchestration of diversity. The only unity which can be contemplated is a world unity comprising regional and local diversities, in the same sort of way that diverse elements are fused into the single expressive unity of a symphony or a drama—in L. K. Frank's words, "the orchestration of diversity."

In treating of this important group of human activities (which has never previously been adequately dealt with by any intergovernmental organization) Unesco will insist on keeping their creative aspect sharply distinct from their aspect as objects of learned study. It seems for some reason much simpler for an organization to concern itself with the history of art than with the encouragement of contemporary painting, with the study of classical authors than with helping living writers, so that Unesco must be careful that the creative side of the arts shall not elude it.

Art is also social. It can serve to express, as no other medium can do, the spirit of a society, its ideas and purposes, its traditions and its hopes. In this respect the so-called primitive peoples and those of nonindustrialized countries are frequently superior. Their arts are often of extraordinary beauty or force, and show us new modes in which the spirit of man can express itself and its reactions to life. But these arts and their accompanying crafts are in danger of disappearing entirely or of being debased or distorted by contact with industrial civilization.

A number of attempts have been made, with varying success, to remedy this state of affairs. Like all results of culture-contact between cultures at very different social or technical levels, this problem is a difficult one. But it appears to be capable of solution. In regard to it, Unesco should attempt two things. It should help to secure understanding, both by the world at large and by the people of the regions concerned, of the value and interest—which is always a unique value and interest—of the art of nonindustrialized peoples the world over. And it should undertake a survey of the various methods so far employed to prevent the extinction or debasement of such arts, with a view to making recommendations for action.

It must also concern itself with the industrially advanced countries. For, paradoxically enough, it is precisely in these that the possibilities of art as a means of community expression are often least realized. There are exceptions such as France; but in both Britain and the U.S.A., for example, it is fair to say that the creative artist, even if he has not retreated into an ivory tower, too often caters only for a highbrow or an intellectually escapist minority or for a group so unrepresentative of the community as to deserve the name of clique. This is not to imply that the creative artist is ever likely to reflect the ideas of the majority. He may, however, truly express something essential in the life of the community, regarded as a social organism, and will often be the spearhead of its perception, the pioneer of new modes of vision and expression.

Above and beyond all other interests and needs at the moment is the need for peace and the interest of large groups in every country in achieving peace. Merely by preaching peace we shall not achieve much. We can achieve much by indirect methods—by demonstrating the fact that interests and needs transcend national boundaries, and by building a world in which international co-operation is actually operative, and operates to promote better health, and full employment, and the provision of adequate food for all, and safety and ease of travel, and the spread of knowledge. Finally, however, we can achieve a good deal more if we can give people the world over some simple philosophy of existence of a positive nature which will spur them to act, in place of the apathy, pessimism, or cynicism which is so prevalent today, and to act in common instead of in separate groups.

Not much remains to be said in conclusion, but what remains is important. It is that the task before Unesco is necessary, is opportune, and, in spite of all multiplicity of detail, is single.

That task is to help the emergence of a single world culture with its own philosophy and background of ideas and with its own broad purpose. This is opportune, since this is the first time in history that the scaffolding and the mechanisms for world unification have become available, and also the first time that man has had the means, in the shape of scientific discovery and its applications, of laying a world-wide foundation for the minimum physical welfare of the entire human species. And it is necessary, for at the moment two opposing philosophies of life confront each other from the West and from the East and not only impede the achievement of unity but threaten to become the foci of actual conflict.

You may categorize the two philosophies as two supernationalisms, or as individualism versus collectivism, or as the American versus the Russian way of life, or as capitalism versus Communism, or as Christianity versus Marxism—or in half a dozen other ways. The fact of their opposition remains, and the further fact that around each of them are crystallizing the lives and thoughts and political aspirations of hundreds of millions of human beings. Can this conflict be avoided, these opposites be reconciled, this antithesis be resolved in a higher synthesis? I believe not only that this can happen, but that, through the inexorable dialectic of evolution, it *must* happen—only I do not know whether it will happen before or after another war. Since another war would be so appalling as to set back the march of human progress by centuries, I am convinced that the task of achieving this synthesis in time to forestall open conflict must be the overriding aim of Unesco.

In pursuing this aim we must eschew dogma, whether it be theological dogma or Marxist dogma or philosophical or any other form of dogma: East and West will not agree on a basis for the future if they merely hurl at each other the fixed ideas of the past. For that is what dogmas are—the crystallizations of some dominant system of thought of a particular epoch. A dogma may, of course, crystallize tried and valid experience; but if it be dogma, it does so in a way which is rigid, uncompromising, and intolerant. What, for wanting a better term, I have called doctrine may also embody valid experience; but it may be flexible, may be capable of growth and development and adjustment. Some dogmas may represent a more recent past than others; but that does not render them any the less rigid and accordingly any less dangerously out of date, any less incapable of reconciliation with opposing systems. If we are to achieve progress we must learn to uncrystallize our dogmas.

The two opposing philosophies of today differ essentially on one point: the relation between the individual and the community. But this one central difference provides differences in every field with which Unesco has to deal, as well as in many others. It engenders different moralities and systems of ethics, different methods of education, different conceptions of the role of art in society, different ways of integrating science with national life, different interpretations of the fundamental human freedoms, different conceptions of the possibilities and limits of international cooperation.

I believe that these differences, though they will undoubtedly become irreconcilable without armed conflict if they are permitted to express themselves as dogmas, to embody themselves in rigid social systems, and to become translated into terms of politics and power, can in principle be reconciled. Unesco might well undertake an objective philosophical inquiry into the basic assumptions of these competing philosophies, with a view to reaching a positive philosophical solution, acceptable to all parties, of the problems which they generate.

This constructive solution may take the lines of some such evolutionary humanism as I have sketched in my opening sections, in which, though the full development of the individual is recognized as the central aim and criterion of further evolutionary progress, the proper organization of society is recognized as the indispensable mechanism of that progress. Put in another way, society as such embodies no values comparable to those embodied in individuals; but individuals are meaningless except in relation to the community (though that community transcends the nation both in space and in time) and can only achieve fullest self-development by self-transcendence, by interpenetration of the self with other reality, including other selves. The problem is thus not merely one of metaphysics or social principles; it is also essentially practical: how best to adjust or, still better, to reconcile the claims of two concrete sets of realities: individual human beings and human social organizations.

Accordingly, I believe that this reconciliation can be approached from two directions. It can be approached from above and from outside, as an intellectual problem, a question of agreement in principle; and it can also be approached from below and from within, as a practical problem, a question of agreement through action. The world is potentially one, and human needs are the same in every part of it: to understand it, to control it, and to enjoy it. Anything that Unesco can do to satisfy these needs through promoting education, science, and culture, will be a step toward a unified way of life and of looking at life, a contribution to a foundation for the unified philosophy we require.

And finally, I believe that a body such as Unesco, which is charged with promoting both the higher activities of man and their practical application, and of doing so on an international scale, is the most likely agency to make this dual approach and so to speed up this necessary process of reconciliation.

XVI

THE CONCEPT OF META-ANTHROPOLOGY AND ITS SIGNIFICANCE FOR CONTEMPORARY ANTHROPOLOGICAL SCIENCE [1]

DAVID BIDNEY

MODERN scientific thought has not been favorably disposed toward metaphysics. Owing largely to the empiricism of Francis Bacon, John Locke, and David Hume, the critical idealism of Immanuel Kant, and the positivism of Auguste Comte, metaphysical theory has come to be regarded generally as the antithesis of the scientific approach. Even philosophers themselves, the custodians of the metaphysical tradition, are not in agreement as to the role and validity of metaphysical concepts, the general tendency since Kant, and outside of Catholic circles, being to relegate metaphysical postulates to the realm of religion and faith, while denying their significance for empirical or verifiable knowledge.

SOME THEORIES OF THE RELATION OF SCIENCE TO METAPHYSICS AND THEIR BEARING ON ETHNOLOGICAL THOUGHT

On the whole, it would appear, one may distinguish three main positions as regards the relation of metaphysics to science.

First, one may mention the positivistic, evolutionary position of Comte according to which metaphysics is said to be prescientific. Metaphysical thought is held to be a stage intermediate between primitive, animistic, theological thought on the one hand, and positive, empirical, scientific thought on the other. The metaphysical mentality shares with animistic thought the acceptance of nonobservable entities and forces but differs from the latter in being critical and in formulating distinct logical categories. On this basis, cultural progress is measured by the extent to which the last vestiges of metaphysics have been successfully eradicated from contemporary thought and by the effort which has been made in promoting a positivistic, scientific mentality, especially in dealing with human, societal affairs. Sociology, according to Comte, is the last frontier of natural science and was envisaged by him as a study of society whereby the laws of sociocultural development may be investigated and human life regulated in a scientific way.

Émile Durkheim and Lucien Lévy-Bruhl applied Comte's positivistic approach to the comparative study of "social facts" in modern as well as native cultures. Lévy-Bruhl in particular made a thorough survey of the extant ethnographical literature and, as a result of his wide research, set up the distinction between the "prelogical" character of the "collective representations" of natives on the one hand, and the logical, scientific character of the civilized, collective mentality.[2] In characterizing the native mentality as "prelogical" he was careful to note that he did not mean that it was illogical or contrary to logic but only that it was indifferent to our accepted logical categories. The native mentality in its collective representations accepted a pattern or mode of thought which permitted natives to think in terms which apparently violated our Western principles of logic. Thus instead of the principle of contradiction and identity which is fundamental to our accepted mode of thought, they implicitly utilized the notion of "participation" which contradicted our notion of discrete entities and permitted them to think of one and the same thing as participating in the very essence of things other than itself.

Lévy-Bruhl's choice of the term "prelogical" was not a happy one and has given rise to much misunderstanding and criticism of his position. By identifying the logical with the scientific mentality, he led his critics to believe that native thought was irrational or illogical, notwithstanding his constant reiteration that such was not his meaning at all. Even so great a scholar as Ernst Cassirer [3] took Lévy-Bruhl to task for his conception of the prelogical and once more pointed out that native thought and custom were logical and rational provided one understood their basic premises or presuppositions. Cassirer failed to recognize that Lévy-Bruhl's own published works provided a wealth of material to demonstrate this very thesis; namely, that native mentality as manifested in its social or collective representations operated, on the whole, from premises radically different from those accepted in modern European cultures, although it was quite logical in terms of its own assumptions.

What Lévy-Bruhl really meant by his unfortunate use of the

term prelogical was, as may be gathered from the context of his works, that native thought was *prescientific* in the sense that it did not clearly distinguish the sphere of empirical, verified knowledge and practice from myth and magic. He agreed that native culture did comprise much data that were based on empirical observation but pointed out that the natives themselves failed to differentiate clearly and consistently between the sphere of the empirical and the nonempirical, between verifiable and nonverifiable notions, and hence were indifferent in their mental culture to the scientific or logical categories which characterize our own predominantly scientific mode of thinking. In this respect, native mentality may be compared with the folklore of so-called civilized peoples, which may be said to be prescientific in the sense that folklore is a mixture of empirical observation and uncritical imagination. The distinction between the prescientific and scientific mentality is not a psychological but rather a cultural one and does not reflect upon the inherent ability of a group of people to think logically and rationally.

Furthermore, Lévy-Bruhl, owing to a positivistic, antimetaphysical bias, failed to appreciate the point that the disparity between native and modern mentality was owing to ontological factors rather than to purely logical procedures. In other words, what appear at first sight as differences in psychology or logic were in fact differences in metaphysical or ontological perspective, the native mind manifesting an uncritical acceptance of a "natural metaphysic" which presupposed the unity of all life and the inherent interrelatedness or merging of things, while the scientific mind tended to assume a uniform order of nature and causal interrelations between physical phenomena which precluded physical or mystical influence on physical events. Lévy-Bruhl himself exhibited an ethnocentric prejudice in assuming that only the positivistic, antimetaphysical position current in his time was logical as well as scientific and that metaphysical postulates were a priori prelogical as well as prescientific. Had he not made this assumption, he would have been able to grant that native mentality was logical without being scientific, thereby obviating a great deal of unnecessary criticism.

A second approach to the problem of the relation between metaphysics and science may be described as *postscientific* and is that position which regards metaphysics as supplementing science, as stepping in, so to speak, where the scientific angels fear to tread.

The classical expression of this view is undoubtedly that of Immanuel Kant who in his *Critique of Practical Reason* acknowledges the validity of such nonempirical entities as God and the human soul as regulative notions or postulates essential for morality and faith, while denying any scientific knowledge of a metaphysical or noumenal reality.

Among anthropologists, the position of Bronislaw Malinowski comes closest to the above view. In opposition to Lévy-Bruhl's evolutionary conception of the prelogical, cultural mentality of the native, Malinowski maintains that natives clearly distinguish between the sphere of the natural and secular on the one hand and the supernatural and holy on the other. The native is said to resort to myth and magic not because he fails to differentiate the objects of scientific knowledge from the magical and mythological but precisely because he does in fact make this distinction. In his lectures on *The Foundations of Faith and Morals* [4] Malinowski states explicitly:

Primitive man has his science as well as his religion; a myth does not serve to explain phenomena but rather to regulate human actions. . . . It is rather the recognition of his practical and intellectual limitations and not the illusion of the "omnipotence of thought," which leads man into ritualism; which makes him re-enact miracles, the feasibility of which he has accepted from his mythology. . . . In short, *myth is not a pseudo-science of Nature* [italics mine]; it is a history of the Supernatural. It invariably refers to a unique break in the history of the world and mankind.

According to Malinowski, therefore, there is no need to assume a mythical mentality which gradually evolved into the logical, scientific mentality of civilized man. Myths are expressions of acts of faith in the existence of supernatural forces and as such are characteristic of man at all stages of human culture. Myths as beliefs in the supernatural thus supplement or complement scientific knowledge and practice; they neither substitute for science nor are antithetical to scientific thought.

Mythology [he writes] is definitely the complement of what might be called the ordinary knowledge or science of primitive man, but not its substitute. . . . Since they have their own science, mythology cannot be their system of explanation in the scientific sense of the word. Myth serves as a foundation for belief and establishes a precedent for the miracles of ritual and magic.

Thus metaphysical myth may be said to begin where scientific knowledge ends and yet myth is pragmatically significant in providing assurance of, and faith in, the harmony of man and his cosmic environment. Although the pragmatist William James would not have used the word "myth," his religious "will to believe" is an instance of this position in a sophisticated modern Western culture.

It is of interest to note in this connection that Malinowski in his earlier, comprehensive essay on "Magic, Science, and Religion" accepts (in contradiction to his later view quoted above) the view of Sir James Frazer that "we can appropriately call magic a pseudo-science." Thus he writes:

And the spurious character of this pseudo-science is not hard to detect. Science even as represented by the primitive knowledge of savage man, is based on the normal, universal experience of everyday life, experience won in man's struggle with nature for his subsistence and safety, founded on observation, fixed by reason. Magic is based on specific experience of emotional states in which man observes not nature but himself, in which the truth is revealed not by reason but by the play of emotions upon the human organism. Science is founded on the conviction that experience, effort, and reason are valid; magic on the belief that hope cannot fail nor desire deceive. The theories of knowledge are dictated by logic, those of magic by the association of ideas under the influence of desire. As a matter of empirical fact the body of rational knowledge and the body of magical lore are incorporated each in a different tradition, in a different social setting and in a different type of activity, and all these differences are clearly recognized by the savages. The one constitutes the domain of the profane; the other, hedged round by observances, mysteries and taboos, makes up half of the domain of the sacred.[5]

This statement comes close to affirming that the native has a theory of double truth and double reality, one for his intellect, which is empirical and logical, and the other for his heart, which is nonempirical, emotional, and illogical. The native is said to recognize clearly the differences between his rational, secular, scientific knowledge and his sacred, irrational beliefs involved in his myth, ritual, and magic. Thus native science and pseudoscience or magic may exist side by side since they are incorporated in different traditions and applied to different spheres of activity.

I find it difficult to reconcile this conception of native thought as involving a scientific and a pseudoscientific or magical epistemology at one and the same time. It is one thing to maintain that

myth complements scientific knowledge in the sense that it transcends but does not contradict scientific knowledge. It is another and
conflicting proposition to maintain that the native differentiates
clearly between scientific and nonscientific knowledge and yet retains his belief in a spurious pseudoscience called magic. The belief
in, and practice of, magic is contrary to science, whereas the belief
in metaphysical powers is, as Kant realized, quite compatible with
scientific theory and practice. The former position involves an
epistemology of double truth which is essentially self-contradictory;
the latter position implies a dualistic epistemology which is logically coherent.

In his paper on the "Historical Relations of Religion and Science"
published in the same volume, Charles Singer also raises the problem as to whether the savage has any science, but his answer differs
fundamentally from that of Malinowski, notwithstanding the
former's attempt to minimize the difference as "almost entirely
verbal." According to Singer,

Science involves, and must involve, something far more than the mere
power to observe and record. It is true that much of scientific practice is
little else than the systematic collection and record of observations, and
our savage has perhaps in certain matters attained to the systematic
stage. But behind the vast systematic collection of observations that occupies the main scientific effort throughout the ages there is a motive, an
aspiration, that is absent from the savage mind. It is just that motive
which makes science. The scientific motive is provided by a conscious
faith in the existence of general laws underlying the multiplicity of
phenomena. Science is the purposeful search for such general laws that
can then be used to link together the observed phenomena. The savage
has none of this faith, this aspiration. If he had, he would cast off his
magic and cease to be a savage. This faith, we have said, is a thing consciously held. It is something moreover which is by no means necessarily
implied when the savage resorts, as he often does, to reason. *While many
modern anthropologists are disposed to deny the existence of a pre-logical
stage of human development, they must, we believe, admit a pre-scientific
stage.* [Italics mine.] Where there is no science or where science is not yet
differentiated, we cannot hope to trace anything which concerns us here.[6]

This passage is of the utmost importance as providing a clear
and sharp formulation of the problem of science in primitive culture. Science, according to Singer, is more than the record of empirical observations systematically arranged; empirical data per se are
but scientific elements and provide material for "science in the

making." But science properly so called involves "the self-conscious investigation of nature with the direct and avowed object of educing general laws," and this is lacking in the native cultural mentality. Singer, therefore, posits a "pre-scientific stage" of human cultural development while denying the existence of a "pre-logical" stage. In other words, he differentiates between logic and science, holding that native mentality contains empirical and rational elements but denying that it is on that account to be regarded as strictly scientific. If, he argues, the native really had faith in the rational, lawful order of nature he could not possibly retain his belief in magic but "would cast off his magic and cease to be a savage."

Malinowski, by contrast, maintains that native science and magic are quite compatible since they apply to different spheres of interest and motivation. Seeking to avoid merely verbal issues, he remarks,

The question, however, whether we should call it *science* or only *empirical and rational knowledge* is not of primary importance in this context. We have tried to gain a clear idea as to whether the savage has only one domain of reality or two, and we found that he has his profane world of practical activities and rational outlook besides the sacred region of cult and belief.[7]

The issue, then, is not whether native culture comprises empirical and rational elements of knowledge but whether the native clearly differentiates between this type of evidence and nonempirical, irrational thought. According to Singer, and we may add Lévy-Bruhl, the native does not yet clearly distinguish empirical from nonempirical knowledge and faith, even though he undoubtedly does utilize empirical observations and logical thought in his theoretical and practical constructions. If the native were conscious of the radical difference between these two modes of thought he could not possibly retain his belief in magic, just as modern civilized man gave up his belief in magic once he became aware of the scientific method and the uniform causal interrelations obtaining among natural phenomena. The scientifically trained ethnologist, for example, may make a scientific study of the folklore and magical practices of his preliterate contemporaries but he can hardly share their beliefs or follow their practices, since to do so he would have to cease being a scientist. According to Malinowski, it would appear, science and pseudoscience may be quite compatible for the native but apparently not for the scientific anthropologist. The issue, then, far from being "merely verbal" is of fundamental importance, since the answer one gives has a bearing on one's interpretation of native culture as well as one's interpretation of cultural history.

Since Malinowski makes mention of Sir James Frazer in his interpretation of primitive magic as pseudoscience, it is well to recall in this connection that Frazer, like his contemporary E. B. Tylor, maintained that native magic and myth were to be explained in rational, intellectualistic terms. The native mind is said to be essentially rational or logical, and myths are interpreted as rational constructions motivated by intellectual wonder but based on erroneous major premises. Thus animism, according to Tylor,[8] is a logical theory which offers a plausible explanation of death on the analogy of sleep and as such represents a rational, primitive philosophy. Malinowski, it would appear, seeks to combine the rationalistic theory of Frazer and Tylor with the mystical, prelogical interpretation of Lévy-Bruhl, and therefore holds that the native mind is both rational and irrational in different contexts of experience. The native is said to be empirical and rational in his secular, everyday experience and practice, but irrational, emotional, and prone to wishful thinking in times of individual and social crises when his rational knowledge proves to be inadequate. As against Frazer and Tylor, he holds that native myth, magic, and religion are not the product of intellectual wonder and do not originate as an etiological explanation of natural phenomena. He agrees rather with Lévy-Bruhl and Durkheim that the function of native myth, ritual, and magic is primarily sociological and that the latter are to be understood as rationalizations of emotional needs which promote social solidarity and a feeling of cosmic harmony. But then Malinowski reverts to the rationalistic approach of Tylor and Frazer in maintaining that the native is conscious of the difference between rational-empirical knowledge applicable to the sphere of nature only and mystical, sacred tradition applicable to the sphere of the supernatural. Hence, he holds, the native mentality, far from being prelogical as Lévy-Bruhl claims, is essentially logical even when it has recourse to magic and myth. On this basis, therefore, the distinction between rational and irrational thought tends to disappear, since even apparently irrational thought serves a rational, social function.

A third approach to the problem of the relation of metaphysics to science may be described as the *superscientific view*. According to the classic formulation of Henri Bergson,[9] intuition provides genuine insight into the fundamental reality of nature and life, whereas the scientific intellect, while providing useful, pragmatic tools, tends to falsify the notion of reality. Metaphysical intuition provides insight into the "vital impetus" which underlies the evolutionary processes of nature. The scientific intellect, by abstracting the static forms and structures from the cosmic flux or process, enables man to contemplate and measure natural phenomena in their spatial relations but fails to grasp the fundamental flux and duration of things. In setting up the dichotomy of metaphysical intuition and scientific intellect, Bergson thus rendered support to the mystics and romanticists who posited superrational faculties which transcended the evidence of reason and science. From the supposition of the superrational sphere of experience, it was a short, though tremendously important, step to the realm of the irrational, since in either instance the validity of reason and science is questioned. Thus in seeking to combat the excessive mechanism and materialism of his day which he identified with the scientific approach, Bergson went to the opposite extreme in divorcing metaphysics and science and in accusing science of falsification. As subsequent developments in relativity theory and the philosophy of science have demonstrated, the concept of process and the historical view of nature may be adequately comprehended in scientific terms without recourse to a superior faculty of intuition. Bergson, it appears, mistook the limitations of the science of his day for an inherent defect of the human intellect and of science in general, and while he himself was much too close to the scientific tradition and to Hebrew-Christian culture to realize the full significance of the divorce between metaphysics and science, he unwittingly gave support to the ethnocentrism and "closed society" [10] which he personally abhorred so sincerely.

METAPHYSICS AS AN ASPECT OF SCIENTIFIC THOUGHT: THE CONCEPT OF META-ANTHROPOLOGY

As against the view that metaphysics is either prescientific or superscientific, the thesis is here advanced that metaphysics is, or may be, in part the theoretically postulated aspect or element of science as well as postscientific ontological speculation, such as theology, compatible with science though not an integral part thereof. In so far as metaphysics is scientific it may be subjected to indirect verification and validation, and hence the concept of a scientific metaphysics, far from being a contradiction in terms, is a genuinely valid notion. Each science may be thought of as having its own metaphysical aspect, and thus one may speak of meta-physics, meta biology, meta psychology, meta-anthropology, meta-ethnology,[11] or meta linguistics. It is merely an accident of the history of philosophical thought that the term metaphysics, originally employed by the editors of Aristotle's works to indicate the book which came after the physics, has come to comprise the whole of ontological thought, thereby obscuring the fact that ontological postulates constitute an indispensable element in every one of the sciences.

It should be noted, however, that metaphysics as an aspect of a given science is not simply to be identified with theory in general but only with ontological theory. Thus meta-anthropology or meta-ethnology, for example, is not merely another name for anthropological theory but refers to a special kind of theory, namely, the theory concerned with the problems of cultural reality and the nature of man. One may also advance anthropological theories which are not ontological, such as whether a given type of artifact was invented independently in a given society or whether its presence there is to be attributed to the process of cultural diffusion. In general, it may be said that purely descriptive theories, namely, those which are postulated in answer to the question *how* two or more phenomena are correlated, may be regarded as scientific theories which are not essentially ontological or metascientific theories. In the last analysis, an ontological or metascientific theory is an attempt to answer *why* phenomena are related in a given manner by referring to some aspect of reality which provides an intelligible ground or condition for their occurrence and interrelation.

It should be obvious from the above, that *the category of the logical and that of the scientific are not identical.* In the first place, as noted, metaphysical thought may be postscientific in the sense of going beyond the data of science and yet being compatible with scientific thought. The concept of God, for example, is not subject to scientific verification though it may be a postulate of thought quite compatible with all available scientific evidence. Furthermore, any system of metaphysical thought may be logical in the sense that it is a deductive system which may be inferred or deduced from given premises, and hence it may be argued that there is no "pre-logical" metaphysics, no matter how primitive the stage of cultural development. But only those metaphysical postulates are genuinely scientific which have been subjected to indirect, empirical verification and are in accord with the facts or data of the sciences. Metascientific thought in this sense is an achievement of our Western scientific culture which began with the ancient Greeks but has really taken on its modern forms since the time of the Renaissance. Prescientific or nonscientific metaphysical theories are therefore characteristic of most human cultural thought whether it be literate or preliterate.

With reference to the problem of native thought in particular, it would seem more in accord with the facts of ethnology to accept the thesis of Charles Singer that native culture is prescientific. Notwithstanding the empirical and rational elements to be found in native culture, especially as regards the manufacture and utilization of artifacts, native thought, like the folklore of the peasants of modern states, does not yet differentiate clearly between scientific and nonscientific evidence. The folklore and folk practices of all peoples, whether literate or preliterate, provide ample demonstration of the uncritical mentality which permits them to follow rational and irrational procedures indiscriminately. Thus natives will avail themselves of modern medical and hospital services only *in extremis* and *after* having exhausted their own traditional expedients, thereby demonstrating that they have little faith in, and attach a minimum of importance to, strictly scientific procedures. This, of course, is not to say that the mentality of natives or of peasant folk is prelogical in the sense of being indifferent to the principle of contradiction, but only that such folk, in their uncritical, pragmatic frame of mind, are indifferent to scientific methodology and do not yet realize the logical incompatibility of their empirical-rational procedures on the one hand and their magical rituals on the other.

Put in ontological terms, it would seem more in accord with ethnographic evidence to say that natives do differentiate between secular, everyday experience and sacred, superhuman tales and traditions about gods and spirits, since they have special terms to designate the different categories of narrative.[12] This, however, does not mean that they distinguish between the sphere of the natural and that of the supernatural, since gods and spirits are just as much a part of the order of nature as men and animals. The dichotomy of the natural and the supernatural implies a scientific epistemology and critical, metaphysical sophistication which must not be assumed without indubitable evidence. And modern ethnography does abound in evidence that sacred as well as secular traditions are *equally* credible to the native mind and differ only as regards the motivations for belief.

Strictly speaking, natives, like other peoples at a prescientific stage of thought, do not regard themselves as believing in myths, since the distinction between scientific knowledge and myth is one which the scientific ethnologist has constructed in his analysis of native cultures but which is unknown to the natives themselves. This point may be demonstrated in everyday experience even with reference to our own culture, for it may easily be shown that the concept of "myth" is relative to one's accepted beliefs and convictions, so that what is gospel truth for the believer is sheer "myth" and "fiction" for the nonbeliever or skeptic; e.g., compare the typical Freudian or Marxian position on religion with that of the firm believer in any one of the major religious faiths. Once we bear in mind the relativity of the category of myth to scientific conviction and faith in general it becomes apparent that there is no fixed category of myth and that the very notion of myth itself presupposes a critical scientific consciousness which may not be attributed to the prescientific mentality. Myths and magical tales and practices are accepted precisely because the native or prescientific folk do not consider them merely as "myths" or as "magic," since once the distinction between myth and science is consciously accepted, the acquired critical insight precludes the belief in, and acceptance of, magic and myth.

One may make a scientific study of folklore and of prescientific cultures in general precisely because the dividing line between science and folklore is real and significant. The fact that what is sometimes presumed to be scientifically established turns out, upon later evidence or more critical analysis, to be fictitious or mythical merely shows how narrow is the margin between our scientific and prescientific mentality, and how much of the latter still lingers on even in critical minds. But in all such instances, the very fact that one is able to re-examine critically "the folklore of science" and to record the "history of human error" is ground for optimism and trust in man's faltering rationality, and in his ability to transcend gradually the limitations of past perspectives and cultural traditions. It is, as James B. Conant has pointed out so freshly in his study of the methodology of science,[13] this self-corrective function of scientific method which has enabled the scientist to transcend the self-perpetuating myths of primitive or uncritical, prescientific thought and has put the modern scientist in touch with immense resources of power which the native magician and uncritical metaphysician could scarcely imagine.

There is, indeed, a logic or "method" to native ideology, as there is in all forms of irrationality—a method which the rational mind may come to understand and utilize—but this does not obviate the radical and irreducible distinction between the category of the rational and the scientific on the one hand and that of the irrational and mythical on the other. There may be "a reason" for everything in a cultural ideology, but not everything therein is in accordance with reason and much of it may be contrary to reason and scientific evidence. The genuinely rational mind may understand the "logic" of the irrational mind, but the converse does not hold. Ernst Cassirer's study of *The Myth of the State* has demonstrated this thesis by pointing up the conflict between the quest for rationality on the one hand and the modern resurgence of irrationalism consciously brought about by those who have made a "science" of mythical propaganda.

It is worth noting in this connection that there is a strong tendency among contemporary cultural anthropologists, sociologists, and social psychologists to assume that native ideology as well as modern ideologies in general are to be understood primarily from a sociological-functional-emotional perspective. Native thought is said to be a function of a given social organization and therefore provides a rationalization for social needs and requirements. Furthermore, owing to the impact of contemporary psychoanalysis, a concerted effort is being made to explain genetically the pattern of social institutions and the ideology which sustains them by reference to the child-training programs and the family relations which prevail in any given society. Thus the sociological as well as the psychoanalytical approach tends to stress the relativity of native ideology either to a specific societal context or to a given pattern of child conditioning. The adherents of both these positions tend to assume a unitary motivation for native ideology and agree implicitly in precluding objective, intellectual wonder or the free play of imagination as significant factors in the formation of native ideology.

It would seem, however, that the sociological and psychoanalytical approaches to native and modern culture tend to go to extremes in their reaction against the intellectualistic approach. If some of the nineteenth-century ethnologists and sociologists tended to go to one extreme in attempting to explain native thought in purely logical or intellectualistic terms, the modern tendency is to go to the opposite extreme in failing to reckon with intellectual wonder and theoretical speculation as significant factors in the development of native thought. Both the nineteenth-century rationalists and the twentieth-century irrationalists make the mistake of assuming a single source or motivation for native ideology, thereby setting up erroneous antitheses and promoting futile controversies. But, as Franz Boas [14] pointed out long ago, there is no single source or motivation for native myth and thought in general. Furthermore, on the assumption that native thought is prescientific rather than scientific or prelogical, it follows that one must admit more than one source for native ideology, and one may, therefore, acknowledge that there may be an objective ground in the phenomena of nature for some part, at least, of native culture.

META-ETHNOLOGY AND THE METACULTURAL BASES OF CULTURAL IDEOLOGIES

One of the important tasks of the student of meta-anthropology or meta-ethnology is the investigation of the basic or logically primitive assumptions as to the nature of the world and of man involved in any one given cultural system. The task of rendering explicit these fundamental ontological postulates and assumptions is said to be meta-ethnological, since the reality with which the investigator is here concerned is metacultural, that is, it is presupposed as given and ultimate by the adherents of any given culture, as something which their empirical cultural institutions and behavior must conform to and reckon with, rather than as something which is the product of their own creation and invention. *Nature as a whole may be said to be metacultural because it provides an indispensable condition for the cultural process and may not therefore be regarded as derived from culture alone.* There is nothing mystical about this concept of metacultural reality; it connotes simply that ontological element or factor within experience which provides the precultural conditions for any cultural processes whatsoever. The analysis of the metacultural postulates of a given culture, whether deductively inferred or intuitively conceived, is essentially a philosophical or meta-anthropological undertaking and as necessary a part of anthropological and social science as is the collecting of empirical data. To appreciate properly the philosophy of life and Weltanschauung which serve as leitmotifs for a given culture requires a measure of philosophical discipline and insight which necessitates that there be professionally trained philosophers working in the social sciences as well as philosophically minded social scientists.

The notion that the philosophy of a culture determines the general pattern of its empirical traits and institutions and provides it with a unity of meaning is one that modern, historically minded philosophers in particular, such as Hegel and Dilthey, and historians such as Burckhardt and Spengler have explicitly acknowledged. The concept of philosophy as a *way of life* has been an integral part of the Occidental as well as Oriental philosophical tradition, although, to be sure, this view has often been stated in individualistic rather than social terms. The point is one, however, which requires restatement for our times because social scientists, in their ill-considered attempts to imitate the radical positivism and empiricism of the natural sciences, have largely tended to neglect or disregard this philosophical approach.

It is highly significant, therefore, that a sociologist of the stature of Pitirim A. Sorokin has endeavored to introduce this metacultural perspective into contemporary sociology. His study of *Social and Cultural Dynamics* is based upon the major premise that the "presuppositions of a culture determine its empirical manifestations and institutions." His analysis of all cultures into the supertypes of sensate, ideational, and idealistic is an attempt to provide a "logico-meaningful" basis for the integration of any given culture (in so far as it is integrated) in terms of its ultimate epistemological-metaphysical presuppositions. Sorokin, however, would tend to exclude the philosopher from undertaking this logical analysis of cultures, claiming that this is primarily the task of the sociologist.[15] While it is most encouraging to find an eminent sociologist so zealous in the cause of fundamental, theoretical analysis, his tendency to exclude the philosopher from the study of the major premises of cultures is hardly acceptable either as a historical fact or as an ideal of systematic research. The great social thinkers of all times have been those whose critical evaluation of their culture and whose ideal visions have contributed most to the cultural development of mankind. The point I am concerned to make here, however, is that there is a real functional difference between the self-allotted task of the meta-anthropologist or meta sociologist and that of the anthropologist or sociologist which serves to differentiate meta-anthropology and meta sociology from empirical anthropology and sociology. The fact that so few sociologists tend to follow the path indicated to them by Sorokin demonstrates how exceptional is his philosophical interpretation of the role of the sociologist.

F. S. C. Northrop's study of world cultures entitled *The Meeting of East and West* provides ample demonstration that the professional philosopher has something significant to say on questions of cultural presuppositions. In common with other contemporary philosophers, such as A. N. Whitehead, Ernst Cassirer, and John Dewey, he maintains that the major cultures of the Western and Eastern worlds "involve basic theoretical assumptions from which the social institutions and practices that they value proceed." What is especially novel and thought-provoking in Northrop's approach is his particular thesis as to the nature of these basic theoretical assumptions which are said to underlie all historical cultures and which serve in each instance as a focus of integration for a given culture. This thesis, as expounded in *The Meeting of East and West,* as well as in his collected essays on *The Logic of the Sciences and the Humanities,* is that the philosophy of natural science which is presupposed by the adherents of a given culture determines largely, though not entirely, the particular character of their cultural ideology, together with its practical and empirical manifestations. The philosophy of science underlying any given historical culture is a composite of the data of empirical observation and intuition supplemented by logical inferences or constructs suggested by these data. All cultures alike are said to have their philosophy of science, the differences between cultural ideologies being ascribed either to the diversity of the empirical data of which cognizance is taken in a given society or to the disparate logical inferences which are drawn to supplement these data.

In the last analysis, Northrop's thesis would appear to blur the distinction between the scientific and nonscientific stages of the evolution of human culture. In this respect, it is the antithesis of the evolutionary approach of modern anthropology and sociology according to which science marks a late stage in the development of human thought. Since all cultures equally are thought to presuppose a given philosophy of science, cultural progress may be said to lie in the extension of empirical observation and intuition and in the refinement of logical theory so as to include and explain the totality of phenomena—a process which does not require any significant change in methodology but only in content. As Northrop puts it:

The difference between a modern Western society and a society of natives in the South Sea islands is not that the ideology of the former is scientifically grounded, whereas that of the latter is nonsensical hocus pocus and illogical. The ideologies of both express logical thinking, once one discovers the conceptual standpoint of each. Furthermore, both conceptual standpoints are empirically and hence scientifically verified. The difference is that the native South Sea islanders pass to their generalization with a particular group of observable factors in nature and the natural man attracting their attention, whereas modern Westerners have come upon different empirical natural facts and have achieved empirically verified generalizations which perhaps include a larger number of observable facts. Even so, as *The Meeting of East and West* has demonstrated, our traditional modern Western scientific and philosophical theories overlook or neglect certain facts of nature, especialy those in the realm of aesthetic immediacy, which the empirically supported philosophies of the Orient and the native South Sea islanders, such as the Balinese, take into account.[16]

In other words, Northrop's point is that it must not be assumed uncritically, as Westerners tend to do, that Western scientific culture is superior in all respects to that of the East and to native culture. The Western mentality, in neglecting the element of esthetic intuition and the ontological esthetic continuum which it presupposes, presents a one-sided perspective of nature, just as the Oriental and native mentality is impoverished through its neglect of the theoretically postulated and verified constructs of modern technological science. Both types of culture are equally scientific in the sense of being empirically verified and differ only as regards the phenomena which are recognized.

Northrop's concept of the philosophy of science implies an all-inclusive epistemology which comprehends the whole of human knowledge. Whereas critics like Sorokin regard science as but one epistemological approach which requires to be supplemented by those of religion and philosophy, Northrop, on the other hand, does not admit any special "truths of reason" or "truths of extrasensory and metalogical intuition" in addition to those of natural science. Thus he concludes:

We must, by means of nothing but the directly apprehendable data, together with inferences grounded in traditional, formal, logical methods applied to those data, construct a new set of integrated assumptions defining a new idea of the good for our time and the entire world which will surpass the modern assumptions in taking care of our increased knowledge in precisely the same sense in which the modern assumptions replaced those of St. Thomas and Aristotle and the latter in turn replaced those of Plato and Democritus. It is by moving forward to a new and more adequate theory, not by going back to assumptions which even the incomplete knowledge of the sixteenth century was sufficient to prove inadequate, that the problems of our time are to be met.[17]

Thus, on this basis, once the philosophy of science of a given culture undergoes radical change, its social and political philosophy together with its theory of religion must change likewise, since the latter are but a function of the former. Northrop's philosophy of culture is monistic in the sense that he postulates one predominant factor, namely, the philosophy of natural science of a given culture, as the focus of integration and in this respect his position may be compared with other monistic cultural theories, such as those of the Freudian psychoanalysts or the Marxian materialists. Unlike the latter theories, however, Northrop's philosophy of culture tends to fall into the ideational tradition, since the major emphasis is upon the role of ideas rather than upon social movements or institutions, although parenthetically, he does acknowledge that other factors are involved.

Northrop's thesis has met with vigorous resistance as well as with sincere praise from the most diverse sources precisely because it is so challenging and stimulating.[18] To the theologians, whether Protestant, Catholic, or Jewish, it presents a challenge, since it makes a universally valid religion dependent upon natural philosophy and denies the need for the autonomy of faith or any extra-scientific knowledge. Among the humanists, and especially among the philosophers, it has raised anew the problem of whether philosophy, notwithstanding the important role ascribed to it in his philosophy of culture, is destined to function primarily in relation to the data provided by the natural sciences when one considers universal values, or whether the philosopher in common with other humanists has something of universal value to contribute to human culture which does not depend for its validity upon the conclusions of the natural sciences. Finally, the social scientists, and especially the anthropologists and sociologists, are inclined to question whether philosophical presuppositions, even if present in every culture, do exercise so predominant a role in cultural dynamics as this theory prescribes and whether nonideational, social and technological factors may not be equally, or more, significant. The social scientists are also disturbed by the central, predominant position ascribed to the philosopher and the natural scientist, especially since this theory would exclude the former from participating on an equal footing in the task of formulating normative social theories and objectives. In sum, Northrop's challenging theory of cultural integration has raised a host of significant problems which go to the very foundations of all spheres of contemporary culture. Not the least importance of his thought lies in the fact that it may provoke theologians, philosophers, and humanists as well as natural and social scientists to re-examine the basic presuppositions of their respective disciplines with a view to bringing them into closer harmony.

Furthermore, Northrop's contention that the philosophy of natural science of a given culture defines its ethics and its concept of the good for man and the state leads him to reduce the category of the good to that of the true. Thus he writes:

The heart of the matter is that the method identifies the good for a given people with its philosophical theory of the nature of man and the universe and makes the basis for this theory for a given people the factual knowledge and logical inferences from those facts discovered by that people. *Thus the good for a given people is its scientifically grounded theory of the truth.* [Italics mine.][19]

In thus identifying the theory of the good with the theory of the true, Northrop has broken with the classical tradition, which has maintained that the categories of the true, the good, and the beautiful are distinct and irreducible. To my mind, Northrop's categorical position appears as the opposite of that of the Neo-Kantians who would reduce the category of the true to that of the good. That is to say, whereas Neo-Kantians, such as W. M. Urban, argue that "what ought to be" is the criterion of "what is" taken as factually true, Northrop holds that "what is" ontologically, as defined by a given philosophy of natural science, is the criterion of "what ought to be" in cultural life or ideology. This problem as to the relation of the basic value categories is, undoubtedly, the most significant issue in contemporary axiology or value theory and is one which the philosophers themselves must resolve. It is a metacultural problem which few professional anthropologists have faced or envisaged as yet, but one with which they are bound to be confronted when they turn their attention next to problems of value.

With reference to ethnological theory in particular, Northrop's interpretation of the role of a philosophy of science in native cultures is reminiscent of the intellectualistic approach of E. B. Tylor and Sir James Frazer. But whereas Frazer,[20] for example, adopts an evolutionary approach and traces the stages of cultural development from magic through religion to science, Northrop, it would appear, in attributing a philosophy of science to any given native culture, allows for no such logical, evolutionary development. There is, according to Northrop, quantitative progress as regards the accumulation of the data of experience and qualitative progress as regards the logical constructs or theoretical concepts by which they are supplemented. But with respect to method, Northrop has evolution only within scientific procedure from one stage of scientific inquiry to another, whereas Frazer has evolution from prescientific to scientific methods.

The full significance of Northrop's position for ethnology will become more apparent if we examine briefly the main theories of native culture which have appeared in modern ethnological thought.

First, according to the rationalistic or intellectualistic position of Tylor and Frazer, one may indeed speak of a primitive philosophy and of "the primitive philosopher" who makes logical inferences upon the basis of unverified, pragmatic data. For the nineteenth-century anthropologists, however, primitive thought as revealed in magic, religion, ritual, and myth, while fully logical, is at best but "pseudoscience." Second, by contrast, we have the theory of Lévy-Bruhl discussed earlier, that native thought is prescientific as well as prelogical in the sense of being indifferent to the principle of contradiction. Native thought is said to be motivated primarily by emotional and social needs rather than by intellectual inferences. Third, there is Malinowski's theory that natives do distinguish clearly between the sphere of the natural and the scientific on the one hand and that of the supernatural and the mythological on the other. Accordingly, native ideology is held to be composed of empirical, scientific concepts and metaphysical, mythical assumptions. Fourth, there is the position of Charles Singer, mentioned earlier, which, on the whole, is also the position taken by modern anthropologists, such as Boas, Kroeber, Lowie, Sapir, Radin, Linton, Osgood, and Benedict; namely, that native thought is prescientific and has its rational as well as nonrational aspects, its empirical traits along with its nonempirical folklore and myth. On the whole, it would appear, most contemporary anthropologists are cautious about assuming that native cultures represent well-integrated ideological wholes and so far have presented few such examples. Ruth Benedict's well-known *Patterns of Culture* has pointed up an esthetic leitmotif in Pueblo and Plains Indian cultures, but so far she has found it difficult to extend her thesis to modern cultures.

In relation to the aforementioned theories, Northrop's position may be regarded as the opposite extreme to that of Lévy-Bruhl, since the former affirms that native thought is both logical and scientific while the latter denies that it is either logical or scientific.

It is important at this stage to distinguish between the general thesis that native cultures reveal basic, philosophical or metacultural presuppositions which serve to integrate their cultural perspectives and the special contention that any given native ideology is based upon a specific philosophy of natural science. The general proposition is acceptable to most anthropologists and many sociologists, whereas the special theory is not. Northrop's analytical study of contemporary cultures has rendered a significant service to contemporary culture theory in making explicit the philosophical, metacultural presuppositions of contemporary cultural ideologies and in counteracting the growing influence of the sociological and psychoanalytical approaches which tend to ignore the objective, intellectual element in the cultural process. It would appear that in reacting against the excessive intellectualism of the nineteenth-century anthropologists and sociologists, modern anthropologists have gone to the opposite extreme in neglecting the "logico-meaningful" postulates and assumptions which serve as a focus of integration for a given culture. Northrop has undoubtedly made a strong case for the recognition of the ideational element in the study of human cultures, and there are signs that his point of view is winning a measure of serious consideration among social scientists. The question remains, however, whether, in claiming that native cultures together with all other historical cultures are based upon specific philosophies of science, he has not claimed too much and has not gone beyond the available ethnological evidence.

A major source of difficulty for readers of Northrop's work concerns the relation of the factual and the normative conceptions of science. On the one hand he employs science in a purely historical, relativistic sense as pertaining to all types of culture. On the other hand he conceives of science in a normative sense as a theory of truth about nature which alone is capable of winning universal assent and transcending the limitations of contemporary cultural traditions. In so far as he employs the historical, relativistic concept of science, the question of "historical fact" as to whether science does play the role he assigns to it in the history of culture is relevant. On the other hand, in so far as he employs the normative concept of science, the question of whether historical cultures have been scientifically grounded is irrelevant.[21] As may be seen from the context of this essay, I find myself in agreement, in part at least, with the normative function of natural science. I should, however, include social science together with the humanities and religion as well. But I differ as regards his historical, relativistic conception of science and its role in the formation of cultural ideologies in the past.

THE PROBLEM OF CULTURAL REALITY

The outstanding meta-anthropological or meta-ethnological problem of contemporary cultural anthropology is undoubtedly that of the nature of cultural reality.[22]

The most significant contribution of modern ethnology to contemporary thought has been the objective insight it has provided into the diversity of human cultures and the role of cultural conditioning in the development of the potentialities of human nature and in the structure of personality. Tendencies of behavior and thought once regarded as grounded in the instinctive nature of man or in the "soul" or "spirit" of a "race" are now seen to be due largely to historical, cultural factors. There is, in short, general acceptance among social scientists of the predominant role of cultural conditioning and of the sociocultural environment in shaping the life of man both individually and collectively.

There is serious disagreement, however, as to the connotation of cultural reality and the nature and number of the primary agencies involved in the cultural process. The problem arises, in what sense may culture be said to be real? Is it essentially an autonomous form or level of reality or is it an abstract pattern or configuration other than human behavior? In general, it appears, cultural anthropologists have tended to adopt one of five types of approach.

First, there is the realistic position according to which culture is defined as the aggregate of acquired customs, of folkways and thoughtways, together with the manufacture and utilization of artifacts. This implies that culture is a quality or attribute of actual overt or covert social behavior.

A second group, impressed with the role of linguistic symbols in the communication and acquisition of knowledge and experience, has been inclined to adopt an idealistic or ideational position. Culture is thus conceived as the aggregate or historical continuity of communicated ideas or meanings exemplified in artifacts, social institutions, and the behavior of persons. Others, regarding society as the *locus* of culture, maintain that social forces are the primary source of cultural ideology and cultural dynamics and that ideological systems are reflections of these primary social changes. Contemporary Marxism may be regarded as a variant of this general sociological approach inasmuch as it is based on the assumption that the economic-technological institutions constitute the primary, dynamic factor in determining the emergence of, and changes in, cultural ideology.

A fourth group regard culture as a kind of *ens rationis*, as a logical construct derived by abstraction from social behavior and thought. According to the latter position a culture is a configuration of patterns or forms abstracted by the mind and is to be differentiated from the actual behavior or instrumental products of human behavior from which it is abstracted.

Finally, there is the instrumental view of culture which derives from the functionalism of Bronislaw Malinowski and A. L. Radcliffe-Brown. The functionalists make the point that the unit of culture is not the trait or configuration but rather the institution, and tend to look upon culture as an apparatus designed to serve the collective needs of a society in relation to a given environment.

The issue between the cultural realists and instrumentalists on the one hand and the impersonal, transcendental idealists and materialists on the other takes on practical import when we turn to the conflicting philosophies of cultural history to which they lead. Here we find that the transcendental idealists (exemplified by A. L. Kroeber and P. A. Sorokin) together with the historical materialists (as, for example, Leslie A. White, among American anthropologists) view culture as an impersonal, "superorganic" entity or force which in the evolutionary process of history makes or develops itself. The cultural realists and humanists, on the other hand, in so far as they take an individualistic position, tend to take into account the voluntary directives and creativity of the human agents themselves in determining the goals they would pursue.

The contrast between the impersonal, superorganic, idealistic-materialistic position on the one hand and the humanistic, individualistic, realistic position on the other may be illustrated by the following passage from Sorokin's *The Crisis of Our Age:*

It was not the Hitlers, Stalins, and Mussolinis who created the present crisis: the already existing crisis made them what they are—its instrumentalities and puppets. They may be removed but this removal will not eliminate the crisis nor even appreciably diminish it. It will merely create new super-Hitlers and Stalins, Churchills, and Roosevelts as long as the crisis lasts.[23]

According to Sorokin's Neo-Hegelian organic theory, there is an organic logic to the life of culture which predetermines its own forms of development in accordance with the cyclic, triadic pattern as manifested by sensate, ideational, and idealistic cultural mentalities or thought systems. Individual leaders as well as social groups are thus said to be merely the instruments or vehicles of the culture forms by which they are possessed. Hence, on this basis, the term "crisis" refers to the mental or spiritual disintegration of a given culture type, the social ordeal or conflict being regarded as an empirical consequence and manifestation of this inner, conceptual or spiritual crisis. The materialistic superorganicists, however, while accepting the theory of the puppet role of the individual or group in sociocultural history, maintain that the cultural crisis proper consists of the socio-economic anarchy and strife, the ideological conflict being regarded by them as a consequence of these materio-technical and social conditions. Thus both idealistic and materialistic superorganicists tend to adopt a fatalistic philosophy of cultural history and to regard man taken individually and collectively in the role of cultural puppet or instrument.

Cultural fatalism as a philosophy of cultural evolution owes its plausibility to the divorce or abstraction of human achievements from the psychodynamic human agents and activities by which they are produced. Once human ideals, social institutions, and technical inventions are regarded as impersonal, superorganic entities and endowed with a force of persistence and development of their own, *as if* they were their own causal agents, then it seems logical to disregard their human creators or agents as the primary self-determining factor—a tendency which I have elsewhere[24] designated as "the culturalistic fallacy." In this manner it has come about that what began as a scientific quest for empirical factors or conditions involved in the cultural process has ended by becoming a transcendental metaphysics of cultural development in which impersonal, cultural forces are presumed to shape human destiny in accordance with their own special laws of development.

In practice, however, as recent history has demonstrated, cultural fatalism and humanism tend to fuse, since human effort and initiative are bound to assert themselves, notwithstanding the subtleties and learned, logical fictions of the "as if" theoreticians which are designed to exclude them in the name of "culturology." [25] In this connection it is interesting to note that Sorokin in his more recent *Society, Culture, and Personality* is emphasizing the role of persons as human agents of cultural change. Similarly Kroeber in the newly revised edition of his *Anthropology* has come to recognize the psychological motivations of the cultural process as manifested in personality structure.

The culture of contemporary Soviet Russia is of especial interest in this connection, since it involves an impressive attempt to combine a doctrine of humanism with Marxian historical materialism. As George Reavey has recorded in his study of *Soviet Literature Today*,[26] the new Soviet humanism is a social and historical humanism which, unlike the individualistic and antisocial humanism of the Renaissance and of the French rationalists and romanticists of the eighteenth century, refers "to the positive, social man, to *the maker of history*, to the man who transforms social conditions and who has the lever of history in his grasp, to the man building a new world society." It is this faith in man, and particularly in Russian man, as the agent of history in the transformation of the world which gives Soviet humanism its particular religious intensity and dynamic character. It is a humanism which takes time very seriously, because nature itself is held to be subject to perpetual change in accordance with the theory of dialectical materialism, and because social life also is subject to laws of development in time in agreement with the principles of historical materialism.

CULTURAL ANTHROPOLOGY: NATURAL SCIENCE OR HUMANITY?

In the development of modern cultural anthropology one may discern two major "themes." On the one hand there is the theme derived from the naturalistic, positivistic, evolutionary tradition of the nineteenth century that cultural reality represents an autonomous, superorganic, superpsychic level of reality subject to its own laws and stages of development or evolution. On the other hand there is the recurring theme, which dates back to the humanistic tradition of the Renaissance and the rationalism of the eighteenth-century philosophers of the Enlightenment, that human culture is the product of human discovery and creativity and is subject to human regulation.

The superorganic approach views culture as a level of reality which is, as it were, a *causa sui,* a process which is conceived through itself alone and which molds the experience of man as a member of society. The humanistic, personalistic approach, with which I should here identify myself, stresses human freedom and intelligence and the role of persons taken individually and collectively in determining their cultural destiny and in achieving a certain measure of rational progress. Thus while both schools of thought affirm a belief in human progress, the naturalistic, superorganic evolutionists tend to assume that progress comes about by natural selection and by the inherent logic of the cultural process itself, whereas the humanistic school maintains that progress is a function of human effort and thought as guided by normative ideals. The naturalists proclaim that the study of human society and culture is a natural science and is capable of revealing natural laws of cultural development similar to those found in the sphere of biological and physical phenomena. The humanists reply that in an adequate social science there is a radical dichotomy between natural facts and normative ideals and that this disparity of facts and ideals renders a so-called natural science of human culture impossible of realization. This claim, the humanists grant, is not to deny that human society and culture are subject to evolutionary stages of development and that there are necessary, empirical conditions for the processes of cultural development which it is the business of the cultural anthropologist and sociologist to investigate. But it should not be forgotten, the humanists would add, that the thesis of cultural evolution is quite compatible with the admission of human freedom in the sense of self-determination and creativity, since human freedom is not something absolute but is limited by human power in relation to a given natural and social environment. Thus, the humanists would argue, the scientific study of human culture is in large part an historical, critical study which, while it may reveal significant regularities and parallels, is nevertheless by its very nature precluded from attaining the status of a precise, predictive natural science.

The above analysis should make it clear that the problem of the status of cultural anthropology is itself one of the major meta-anthropological issues of our times. It is a metacultural problem precisely because it cannot be resolved by empirical data of ethnology alone, since the problem we are investigating concerns the very conditions of the cultural process itself. It is, in short, a problem in the philosophy of culture which must be resolved in logical terms and by appeal to the history of human experience.

THE METAPSYCHOLOGICAL PROBLEM: IDEOLOGICAL DETERMINISM AND FREEDOM OF THOUGHT

As the foregoing analysis implies, the problem of the nature and dynamics of the cultural process is closely bound up with the metapsychological problem as to the nature of human thought. The basic issue here is whether human thought is essentially culturally determined or whether, notwithstanding the influence of the cultural environment, one may still acknowledge the mind's inherent capacity for freedom or self-determination and creative invention.

If, on the one hand, one assumes, as Friedrich Nietzsche and Karl Marx for example do, that moral values and ideals always serve the special interests or will to power of some dominant group or of some subservient group in quest of power, then it follows that thought is necessarily determined by sociopolitical or economic conditions. On this basis, there is no logical way of overcoming cultural relativity and class perspective. The "logic of power" takes the place of the power of logic and reason. Instead of power in the service of ideals, we have the doctrine of ideals in the service of power.

On the other hand, if one agrees with Aristotle and Albert Einstein in postulating the fundamental creativity of the human intellect and imagination, then it follows that man is inherently capable of transcending the limitations of his sociocultural environment, notwithstanding the very considerable influence which the latter exerts upon him.

The attraction of the theory of thought-determinism for many historians, sociologists, and anthropologists lies in the fact that it purports to explain scientifically the natural laws of cultural development and to predict human social behavior. They seem to think that social science, unlike natural science, requires a radical determinism of human mentality and that to admit any significant indeterminism or creative spontaneity in human thought would preclude the possibility of a science of society and culture. Thus the social scientist tends to outdo the natural scientist in so far as the latter is content to postulate determinism for physical phenomena but is prepared to acknowledge the mind's freedom in constructing postulates and theories for the understanding of nature.

But this antithesis of absolute determinism versus freedom of thought is not at all necessary. The paradox of science lies in the fact that there could be no science unless the mind were free to reflect upon the evidence of nature and formulate its own concepts. *To deny freedom of thought in the alleged interests of science is to undermine the very condition of the scientific process.* The scientific intellect is capable of reflecting upon the phenomena of nature precisely because it transcends or stands outside of, or apart from, the phenomena it comprehends, since otherwise the process of observation and verification would have no meaning. Thus freedom of scientific thought is a prerequisite of science considered as the investigation of phenomena subject to natural law. The scientific mind which denies its own freedom is denying itself.

It is significant to point out in this connection that ideological determinists inconsistently assume their own ability to transcend the ideological relativism they discern in the historical process, and envisage some cultural state which somehow has an absolute, timeless validity obviating the necessity of further historical development. Hegel's idealization of the Prussian state of his day and Marx's ideal of a classless society are cases in point. In brief, historical relativism, whether it take the form of historical idealism or historical materialism, tends to be accepted as a scientific theory of cultural development precisely because its adherents claim to present a timeless or absolute perspective which overcomes or transcends its own limitations. In practice, this means that cultural relativists tend to deny the objective validity or ideal universality of any system of thought other than their own, and hence treat their opponents as deluded victims of their own respective sociocultural institutions according to the Marxists, or of their historical, intellectual traditions according to the idealists. Thus what appears to be a scientific, relativistic doctrine of the stages of mental and cultural development becomes in practice the justification for rigid intellectual dogmatism and authoritarian intolerance of dissent which precludes any genuine synthesis of, or respect for, opposing views.

THE METACULTURAL PRESUPPOSITIONS OF ONE WORLD

We of the twentieth century, living in this age of science and technology, are especially conscious of the unity of the world from a functional and geographic point of view. Modern means of communication and travel have made geographical isolation a thing of the past. Economically, too, the development of specialized industries and of world trade has made all nations dependent upon one another for their very subsistence and for the maintenance of their civilized standards of living. This lesson is brought home to us very vividly when normal trade relations are suspended and it becomes impossible to carry on the highly mechanized industrial life to which we are accustomed.

Culturally, however, we are still living in ethnocentric worlds of our own imagination, worlds which are the products of our diverse historical experiences and traditions. Because of the prevalence of mythological, prescientific views of human nature and the cosmos, the nations of the world tend to live in private cultural worlds of their own, somewhat like a dreamer who dwells in a world of his own imagination and does not participate in the common-sense world of wide-awake men. The question then arises, is it possible for men to emerge from their ethnocentric, imaginary worlds and to participate in a common cultural world, and if so, how is this to be achieved?

The answer to this problem would seem to be, as Plato originally discerned and as Northrop's *The Meeting of East and West* has lately reminded us, that it is possible for mankind to emerge from its cultural caves and behold a common, rational world in the light of human intelligence, provided men learn how to distinguish scientific knowledge based on reason and experience of nature from the subjective opinions and wishful notions derived from their limited, traditional cultural environments. Through critical, scientific knowledge alone can men conceive of one world subject to universal natural laws. This world of science is one and the same for all precisely because it is *the* world of *common* reason and *common* sense. Similarly, the world of culture *may become* one and the same for all, in essentials at least, provided it is based upon a scientific knowledge of the nature of man and of the sociocultural conditions which determine the modes of his existence.

Since the common cultural world of man is primarily an ideal world of common objectives, of moral values and principles, it must necessarily depend upon the common will and efforts of mankind for its realization. Hence we must not assume, as the positivists and functionalists among us tend to do, that because of the interdependence of modern societies the human world is in fact one. Mere functional or geographic interdependence of cultures is a mechani-

cal kind of unity which would apply to any kind of world organization or lack of organization. A genuine and significant world unity
is one characterized by the mutual acknowledgement of common
values or objectives; it is a *teleological unity* manifested in harmonious social and political relations among the peoples of the world.
Only in such a common universe of cultural participation can there
be real or enduring peace, a peace which is more than a temporary armistice between potentially conflicting factions. As Wendell
Willkie so clearly realized in his *One World,* unless the United
Nations dedicate themselves sincerely to the actualization of this
wartime ideal, the second World War, like the first World War,
will have been nothing more than a "costly fight for power" ending
"with an armistice, not a real peace." The ideal of one world requires that we substitute a genuine strategy of peace for the strategy
of war, since peace is not merely the absence of overt strife but is
essentially a positive social and mental state or attitude which must
be deliberately cultivated and promoted. In brief, the common
cultural world of man implies a common axiological world, a common world of values whose very subsistence must first be acknowledged in theory before it may be realized in practice.

Furthermore, the indispensable presupposition of a common scientific world is the assumption of an objective, ontological order
of nature which is independent of man but which man may discover
and utilize for his own ends. If one adheres to the subjective, idealistic, Kantian approach that " 'the world' exists only with reference
to the knowing mind, and the mental activity of the subject determines the form in which the world appears," [27] then indeed one is
logically compelled to oppose as "ontological dogmatism" the position which regards the world as existing independently of us in a
fixed and definitive form. From the position of Kantian idealism it
is but a short, though disastrous, step to the relativistic, historical
idealism of the Neo-Kantians and the historical materialism of the
Marxists. For, as Karl Mannheim argues in his *Ideology and Utopia,*
ideological relativity leads logically to a "sociology of knowledge"
which postulates a total "relationism" of all ideological perspectives
and denies any one ideology a privileged position as regards truth-
value.

The basic assumption of sociological "relationism" is "that there
are spheres of thought in which it is impossible to conceive of
absolute truth existing independently of the values and position of
the subject and unrelated to the social context." [28] On this premise,

there is no meaning to the concept of One World since there are as many worlds as there are disparate sociocultural contexts. If the only reality we know is a historically determined cultural reality, then the quest for world unity is vain and futile since no two major ideological perspectives are alike. One cannot arrive at the notion of One World through a summation of ideological perspectives, since there is no basis for evaluating the various perspectives in relation to one another. It is only on the assumption that man is able to transcend his limited, historical ideological perspectives and to achieve a scientifically verified knowledge of a metacultural, ontological reality that the concept of One World becomes intelligible as an epistemological as well as axiological ideal. In the final analysis, the theory of sociological relationism is self-refuting, since it is assumed implicitly that the theory of total, ideological relationism is itself "absolute" in the sense that it is not itself a function of a particular sociocultural context but provides objective insight which transcends the limited, socially conditioned ideologies to which it refers.

Upon the anthropological scientists and humanists especially, though not exclusively, falls the tremendous task of providing a common ideological frame of reference for the relative perspectives of the diverse sociocultural configurations of the contemporary world. Such a "general theory of relativity" for the human world is a formidable undertaking and will require the united efforts of the world's best minds in the years to come. For in the world of culture as in the political world the crucial practical problem of our time is not so much whether unity is desirable, as *what kind* of unity shall we have. A cultural unity which impoverishes human life and thought by excluding whole areas of cultural experience as meaningless may have the virtue of simplicity but will fail, nevertheless, of general acceptance, regardless of the learned and "scientific" support it may receive. We must remind ourselves constantly that cultural integration, like political unification, is not an unqualified good and that everything depends upon the nature of the final composition. To my mind, the problem of cultural integration is essentially one of harmonizing diverse polar interests and disciplines, each of which must enjoy a measure of autonomy to ensure its own creative advance. There is always the danger that the adherents of some one discipline or class will arrogate to themselves a role or "mission" which may upset the sociocultural equilibrium. There is danger in assuming that any one discipline or type of institution alone provides the key to normative or to factual cultural integration. A genuinely scientific and realistic view of cultural dynamics will be one which is based on a healthy respect for the complexity of cultural life and for the reciprocal influence of subjective and objective factors. Only by keeping in mind the Platonic vision that integration, whether of culture or society, is essentially a matter of harmonizing the one and the many can this objective be attained.

NOTES

1. A briefer version of this paper was originally presented before a meeting of the American Anthropological Association held in Chicago, December, 1946. The research involved in the writing of this paper is part of a larger project on meta-anthropology which is being conducted by the writer under the liberal auspices of the Viking Fund.
2. Lucien Lévy-Bruhl, *How Natives Think* (London and New York, 1926).
3. Ernst Cassirer, *Essay on Man* (New Haven, 1944); also by the same author, *The Myth of the State* (New Haven, 1946). For a more detailed analysis of the problem of myth in Cassirer and Lévy-Bruhl, cf. D. Bidney's forthcoming essay on "The Philosophical Anthropology of Ernst Cassirer and Its Significance in Relation to the History of Anthropological Thought," in *The Philosophy of Ernst Cassirer*, ed. by P. A. Schilpp (The Library of Living Philosophers, Vol. VI), scheduled for publication during 1948.
4. Bronislaw Malinowski, *The Foundations of Faith and Morals* (London, Oxford University Press, 1936), pp. 3, 5–6, 19.
5. Bronislaw Malinowski, "Magic, Science and Religion," *Science, Religion and Reality*, Joseph Needham, ed. (New York, The Macmillan Company, 1925), p. 80.
6. *Ibid.*, p. 89.
7. *Ibid.*, p. 36. In a footnote to the passage quoted earlier (see note 6) Singer remarks: "Dr. Malinowski regards science as a very early development. The difference between us is, however, almost entirely verbal. It is due to the fact that I have interpreted *science* as the self-conscious investigation of nature with the direct and avowed object of educing general laws. Such is science as we know it today and as the Greeks knew it. Dr. Malinowski, however, rightly considers that there are certain scientific elements even in the most primitive culture and it is these *elements* that he calls *science*. I should describe this early stage as *science in the making*. If the reader will bear these terminological differences in mind, he will perceive that there is little or no difference between Dr. Malinowski and myself." Notwithstanding the fact that Singer here tends to agree with Malinowski that the difference between them is "almost entirely verbal" I still think that the issue involved goes much deeper, since it is a question of an entire cultural mentality and not merely one of terminology. For a similar criticism see E. H. Ackerknecht's "Natural Diseases and Rational Treatment in Primitive Medicine" in *Bulletin of the History of Medicine*, XIX (1946) 467–497.
8. Edward B. Tylor, *Primitive Culture* (London, 1871).
9. Henri Bergson, *Creative Evolution* (New York, 1911).
10. Henri Bergson, *The Two Sources of Morality and Religion* (New York, 1935).
11. The term "meta-ethnography" has appeared previously in R. H. Lowie's *History of Ethnological Theory* (New York, 1937). Lowie, however, employs the term in a descriptive sense as referring to the study of cultural leitmotifs exemplified by Ruth Benedict's *Patterns of Culture*.
12. Cf. Paul Radin, *The Road of Life and Death: A Ritual Drama of the American Indians*

(New York, 1945), p. 54; also review by D. Bidney in *Journal of the History of Medicine* (Summer, 1947), pp. 406–407. The point is one also found earlier in Franz Boas' "Mythology and Folk-Tales of the North American Indians" in *Anthropology in North America* (New York, 1915).

13. James B. Conant, *On Understanding Science*, New Haven, 1947.

14. Franz Boas, "The Origin of Totemism," *American Anthropologist*, Vol. XVIII, 1916.

15. Cf. the comment of Pitirim A. Sorokin on Northrop's essay "Philosophy and World Peace" in *Approaches to World Peace*, Fourth Symposium, Conference on Science, Philosophy and Religion, L. Bryson, ed. (New York, Harper & Bros., 1944), pp. 678–680.

16. Chap. xxi, on "The Scientific Method for Determining the Normative Social Theory of the Ends of Human Action," in *The Logic of the Sciences and the Humanities* (New York, The Macmillan Company, 1947), p. 337.

17. Cf. Northrop's reply to Sorokin in *Approaches to World Peace*, p. 683.

18. Cf. the discussion of Northrop's essay on "Philosophy and World Peace" in *Approaches to World Peace* referred to earlier; also the critical review of Northrop's *The Meeting of East and West* by R. Demos in *Philosophy and Phenomenological Research*, December, 1947. For an evaluation by an anthropologist, cf. A. L. Kroeber's review of same in the *American Anthropologist*, April–June, 1947.

19. In *Approaches to World Peace*, p. 690. Cf. also "The Criterion of the Good State," in *The Logic of the Sciences and the Humanities;* also the essay on normative social theory referred to in note 16.

20. Cf. Sir James George Frazer, *The Golden Bough* (one volume ed. New York, 1942), chap. iv, on "Magic and Religion" and chap. lxix, on "Farewell to Nemi." Frazer even envisages a stage beyond science, "a totally different way of looking at the phenomena" which may supersede science (p. 712).

21. Cf. Northrop's statement in *The Logic of the Sciences and the Humanities*, p. 346.

22. Cf. D. Bidney, "On the Concept of Culture and Some Cultural Fallacies" in *American Anthropologist*, 1944; "Culture Theory and the Problem of Cultural Crises" in *Approaches to Group Understanding*, Sixth Symposium, Conference on Science, Philosophy and Religion (New York, 1947); and "Human Nature and the Cultural Process," *American Anthropologist*, July–September, 1947.

23. P. A. Sorokin, *The Crisis of Our Age* (New York, E. P. Dutton & Co., 1941) p. 23.

24. Cf. "On the Concept of Culture and Some Cultural Fallacies" referred to in note 22.

25. Cf. Leslie A. White, "Culturological *vs.* Psychological Interpretations of Human Behavior," *American Sociological Review*, December, 1947.

26. George Reavey, *Soviet Literature Today* (New Haven, Yale University Press, 1947), chap. x, on "The New Demiurge and the Window of Europe."

27. Cf. Karl Mannheim, *Ideology and Utopia* (New York, Harcourt, Brace & Co., 1936), pp. 58–59.

28. *Ibid.*, pp. 70–71.

XVII

THE PHILOSOPHY OF THE NAVAHO INDIANS [1]

CLYDE KLUCKHOHN

THE publication of Paul Radin's *Primitive Man as a Philosopher* did much toward destroying the myth that a cognitive orientation toward experience was a peculiarity of literate societies. Speculation and reflection upon the nature of the universe and of man's place in the total scheme of things have been carried out in every known culture. Every people has its characteristic set of "primitive postulates." As Bateson has said: "The human individual is endlessly simplifying and generalizing his own view of his environment; he constantly imposes on this environment his own constructions and meanings; these constructions and meanings are characteristic of one culture as opposed to another."

It remains true that critical examination of basic premises and fully explicit systematization of philosophical concepts are seldom found at the nonliterate level. The printed word is an almost essential condition for free and extended discussion of fundamental issues. Where dependence on memory exists, there seems to be an inevitable tendency to emphasize the correct perpetuation of the precious oral tradition. Similarly, while it is all too easy to underestimate the extent to which ideas spread without books, it is in general true that tribal or folk societies do not possess competing philosophical systems. The major exception to this statement is, of course, the case where part of the tribe becomes converted to one of the great proselytizing religions such as Christianity or Mohammedanism. But, before contact with rich and powerful civilizations, "primitive" peoples seem to have absorbed new ideas piecemeal, slowly integrating them with the previously existent ideology.

Although there are no organized groups of human beings without their own philosophy, there are, then, some tendencies toward differentiation between literate and nonliterate societies. The abstract thought of the latter is ordinarily less self-critical, less systematic, less elaborated in purely logical dimensions; more concrete, more implicit—perhaps more completely coherent than the philosophy of most individuals in larger societies which have been influenced over long periods by disparate intellectual currents. It must be remembered, however, that these statements are made at a relatively high level of abstraction. There are such wide variations in the philosophies of "primitive" folk that, in empirical detail, any black-and-white contrast between "primitive" and "civilized" philosophy would be altogether fictitious.

This consideration of a single nonliterate philosophy is, therefore, not offered as a representation of "primitive man's thought." It affords merely a single illustration of orientations which are typical of the members of one large (60,000) nonliterate group with a fairly homogeneous culture. In the earlier part of this chapter the presentation will be restricted to "native" (i.e., pre-European) ideas. Later, the effects of ideas from white American culture will be touched upon. By no means every adult, minimally acculturated Navaho would set forth all of the notions that will be described. There are Navaho intellectuals (mainly the singers of their ceremonials), and the more explicit systematic statements have been derived in part from talks with them. Yet it is maintained that "average" Navahos think and act in accord with these premises and concepts, even though they would be hard put to explain them in the fashion carried out here.

IMPLICIT PHILOSOPHY

There is a unifying philosophy behind the way of life of every individual at any given point in his history. Although each personality gives to this philosophy an idiosyncratic coloring, this is primarily in its affective or felt dimensions. The main outlines of the fundamental assumptions and basic abstractions have only exceptionally been created out of the stuff of unique biological heredity and peculiar life experience. They are usually cultural products. From the life-ways that constitute the designs for living of his community or tribe or region or socioeconomic class or nation or civilization the ordinary individual derives most of his "mental outlook."

Cultures or group life-ways do not manifest themselves solely in observable customs and artifacts. There is much more to social and cultural phenomena than immediately meets the ear and eye. If the behavioral facts are to be correctly understood, certain presuppositions constituting what might be termed a philosophy or ideology must also be known. The "strain toward consistency" which Sumner noted in the folkways and mores of all groups cannot be accounted for unless one postulates a more or less systematic pattern of reaction to experience as a characteristic property of all integrated cultures. In a certain deep sense the logic (that is, the *manner* of interpreting relationships between phenomena) of all members of the human species is the same. It is the premises that are different. Moreover, the premises are learned as part of a cultural tradition.

Synthesis within a culture is achieved partly through the overt statement of the dominant conceptions, assumptions, and aspirations of the group in its religious lore, secular thought, and ethical code; partly through unconscious apperceptive habits, ways of looking at the stream of events that are so taken for granted as seldom or never to be verbalized explicitly. These habitual ways of begging certain questions that are distinctive of different cultures may be clearly crystallized in the morphology of the language. For example, the tense system of European languages points to the enormous emphasis upon time in Western culture. To the outsider who is a student of the culture these linguistic forms may constitute invaluable clues to the structure of the implicit culture. But to the naïve participants in the culture these modes of categorizing, of dissecting experience along these planes and not others, are as much "given" as the regular sequence of natural phenomena or the necessity of air, water, and food for life.

Every group's way of life, then, is a structure—not a haphazard collection of all the different physically possible and functionally effective patterns of belief and action but an interdependent system based upon linked premises and categories whose influence is greater rather than less because they are seldom brought out into explicit discussion. Some degree of internal coherence which is apperceived rather than rationally constructed seems to be demanded by most of the participants in any culture. As Whitehead has remarked, "Human life is driven forward by its dim apprehension of notions too general for its existing language."

In sum, the way of life that is handed down as the social heritage of every people does more than supply a set of skills for making a living and a set of blueprints for human relations. Each different way of life makes its own assumptions about the ends and purposes of human existence, about ways by which knowledge may be obtained, about the organization of the pigeonholes in which each sense datum is filed, about what human beings have a right to expect from each other and the gods, about what constitutes fulfillment or frustration. Some of these assumptions are made explicit in the lore of the folk; others are tacit premises which the observer must infer by finding consistent trends in word and deed.

In highly self-conscious Western civilization that has recently made a business of studying itself, the number of assumptions that are literally implicit in the sense of never having been stated or discussed by anyone may be negligible. Yet only a trifling number of Americans could state even those implicit premises of our culture that have been dissected out by social scientists.[2] I remember an astute remark by Lloyd Warner: "If you could bring to the American Scene an Australian aborigine who had been socialized in his own culture and then trained in social science, he would perceive all sorts of patterned regularities of which our sociologists are completely unaware."

In the case of the less sophisticated and less self-conscious societies, the unconscious assumptions characteristically made by individuals brought up under approximately the same social controls will bulk large. The Navaho do talk about their ethical principles and their values. Navaho intellectuals discuss the purposes of life and the principles that govern the universe. But many distinctively Navaho doings and sayings make sense only if they are related to certain implicit convictions about the nature of human life and experience, convictions so deep-going that no Navaho thinks of talking about them in so many words. These unstated assumptions are so completely taken for granted that the Navaho (like all peoples) take these views of life as an ineradicable part of human nature and find it hard to understand that normal persons could possibly conceive life in other terms. Much of what will be said in the two following sections is at this level. This implicit philosophy is an inferential construct based on consistencies in observed thought and action patterns.

UNDERLYING PREMISES

The keystones on which the Navaho view of the world appears to rest may be stated schematically as follows:

1. The universe is orderly: all events are caused and interrelated.
   a. Knowledge is power.
   b. The basic quest is for harmony.
   c. Harmony can be restored by orderly procedures.
   d. One price of disorder, in human terms, is illness.
2. The universe tends to be personalized.
   a. Causation is identifiable in personalized terms.
3. The universe is full of dangers.
4. Evil and good are complementary, and both are ever present.
5. Experience is conceived as a continuum differentiated only by sense data.
6. Morality is conceived in traditionalistic and situational terms rather than in terms of abstract absolutes.
7. Human relations are premised upon familistic individualism.
8. Events, not actors or qualities, are primary.

Each of these presuppositions now needs to be elaborated and, in some instances, qualified. Up to a point the Navaho may be legitimately described as a "primitive mechanist." On the other hand, one does encounter some teleological notions. It is generally agreed that Changing Woman created livestock and other goods for the benefit of the Navaho. Some accounts state that death was created so that "everything would be coming new," that the earth would not get too crowded with people and with livestock. The myth with respect to livestock is obviously post-European, and there are other grounds for suspecting the influence of Christian theology in all versions that attribute an all-embracing purposeful design to the divinities. Recently created myths of flood and of the impending end of the world probably also have an indirect Christian source.

In general, Navaho philosophy makes small provision for teleology and for mysticism. History is not oriented in accord with the master design of all-wise and all-powerful beings; events are the inevitable results of previous events. Visionaries do occasionally appear in Navaho lore and legends. But they did not themselves seek mystical experience; the visions were caused, not willed. The ideas of fasting, self-torture, and pity that were so popular among Plains Indians seem ridiculous to earthy, hedonistic Navahos. Rites of purification occur in the curing ceremonials, but this is not a case of the individual's seeking mystical enlightenment. He is only following a cultural pattern that has nothing to do with his private motives.

It should be noted, however, that the Navaho, although they

usually think in terms of mechanical causation, are not thorough-going positivists. They do lay great stress on immediately apprehended sense data. This life is what counts, and experience is not defined mystically but in terms of one's sensations of pain and pleasure and of the existence of persons and objects outside oneself. On the other hand, mountains and other natural phenomena have their "inner forms" as well as the properties obtained from introspection of a succession of sense data. Words, as well as things and processes, are important. Mastery of an esoteric terminology gives one power over supernatural forces, objects, and events to which the terms refer.

The universe is orderly. Everything in the universe is interrelated. It is a lawful universe. The notion of causation is essentially mechanical. Although at the beginning of things certain happenings occurred at the will of the divinities, they themselves were henceforth bound by the consequences of their own acts. Once the machine had been started, it ran according to irreversible laws. There is no place in Navaho thought for a god who can capriciously (from the Navaho point of view) grant the petition of humans. The divinities, too, follow the rules. Every event has one or more specifiable causes. If rain does not fall at the expected season it is because "people are too mean" or because "whites are selling liquor to the Navahos." As Dr. Reichard has written: "The balance of all things may break down because of man's own behavior in breaking taboos, because of ghosts and witchcraft, or because of foreign influences, all matters which are considered as being 'out of order.' " However, it should be noted at once that possible causes are multitudinous. Hence, one must not be too disappointed if a ceremonial cure is not successful. There are causes, but identification is not easy. The universe is determinate, but human thought is not determinate. "Perhaps" is one of the words most frequently uttered in Navaho.

There is even in Navaho behavior a touch of the experimental, of the utterly pragmatic. Before committing himself to an expensive nine-day ceremonial the sick individual will try out a brief excerpt. Only if it works will he go on to the full version. Some (though not all) singers will freely admit what certainly goes on in practice: a new herbal medicine or song or bit of equipment will be tried out in a ceremonial; if the results are satisfactory, the new business will be incorporated as a standard procedure and taught to learners of the rite. Whole new ceremonials have been borrowed from neighboring tribes, slightly adapted, kept or discarded on the basis of experience. In secular life the Navaho is prone to try anything once. New foods, clothing, and gadgets are taken over with a freedom that contrasts sharply with the resistance of the Pueblo Indians to innovation.

Knowledge is power. The conception of "good luck" is hard to translate into the Navaho language. In their scheme of things one is not "lucky" or "unlucky." One has the requisite knowledge (sacred or profane) or one hasn't. Even in what European languages call "games of chance" the Navaho depends upon medicines, rites, and verbal formulas. The same is true with hunting. Getting a deer is never a matter of good fortune; it is a matter of ritual knowledge and of one's relations with supernaturals which, again, are controllable.

Complete knowledge, however, is unattainable: "Not even the white people who have been everywhere, go across the ocean, fly in the sky, can see all things and places—even up in the sky—not even they know where the sunrise is nor where the sunset is. Nor will they ever find out." While man can never hope completely to understand and control his destiny, he can, once he learns the right formulas, coerce even supernatural beings, for they too are subject to the lawful processes that control events. If the right mechanical procedures are followed, the divinities *must* restore the patient to health and harmonious living.

The basic quest is for harmony. In so far as Navaho philosophy is goal-oriented, it is directed toward the elimination of friction in human relations and toward the restoration of harmony in that total economy of things in which human affairs constitute only one facet. In the Navaho conception of the relationship between their divinities there is the mechanical notion of a balance of opposing forces. No one divine being has unfettered control over the others. Each is limited by the powers of others as well as by the remorseless working out of processes beyond the control of the whole pantheon. In this equilibrium of forces human effort in the form of observance of taboos and in the performance of compulsive rituals can play its part. Individually acquired knowledge can assist in the restoration of harmony in one person's life, in that of the community, in that of the whole universe.

This dominant conception of balance is reflected in the scrupulous symmetry of ceremonials, formal narratives, and art. Poetry is constructed in the fugue and coda style. In dry paintings, rugs, and silverwork an element rarely appears singly. There is a pair, or more often a group of four. In songs and prayers there are numberless balanced repetitions, four again being the favorite pattern:

That before us there being beauty as we shall walk about, we have told our stories to each other. That behind us there being beauty as we shall walk about, we have told our stories to each other. That below us there being beauty as we shall walk about, we have told our stories to each other. That all about us there being beauty as we shall walk about, we have told our stories to each other.

That our speech will become beautiful, we have told our stories to each other. That out of our mouths there will come beauty, we have told our stories to each other. That we shall walk about in beauty, we have told our stories to each other. That we shall walk about being "that which goes about at the rim of old age," we have told our stories to each other.

That today we are the children of the Earth, we have told our stories to each other. That we are the child of the Black Sky, we have told our stories to each other. That we are the children of the Sun, we have told our stories to each other. That we are the children of the White Shell Woman, we have told our stories to each other. That we are the children of the Changing Woman, we have told our stories to each other. That we are the children of the Talking God, we have told our stories to each other. That we are the grandchildren of the Hogan God, we have told our stories to each other.

Let there be beauty indeed. Let there be beauty indeed. Let there be beauty indeed. Let there be beauty indeed.[3]

Divinities in all forms of symbolism tend to turn up in pairs or fours (Changing Woman, White Shell Woman, Salt Woman, Turquoise Woman; Monster Slayer and Child of the Water). The final example is a pairing of older and younger—a repeated theme in Navaho culture. Another common form of balance is that between the sexes. Each male divinity has a female counterpart in a dry painting. There are male rains and female rains; male rivers and female rivers; male turquoise and female turquoise; male chants and female chants; male plants and female plants. In part, this is not so much a duality of the sexes as such but rather the complementary nature of stronger and weaker, dominant and submissive, etc.

One price of disorder is illness. In every ceremonial there is a patient ("one sung over"), although all rites, and some in particular, have purposes that go beyond the individual to the group and indeed to the whole world. Illness is not traced to what Europeans would consider "natural" causes. Even a broken limb from an accident may have a deeper etiology. Illness is one possible result of disharmony. The outward and visible form of the disharmony may be a disturbance in human relations, but this, in turn, is the manifestation of malequilibrium in the patient's relations to supernatural forces. The social group, the rest of the animate and inanimate world, and the supernaturals are all part of one scheme. Anything that disturbs the balance of this system as a whole can produce malfunctioning in any part of the system. The symptom may be a physiological disturbance, social friction, lack of rainfall, or a flood.

The universe tends to be personalized. This, if you like, is the familiar "animism." As a matter of fact, it is a broadly human tendency, found among peoples not considered "animistic." In contemporary American culture, for example, most persons find it psychologically more satisfying to blame "Wall Street operators" than "the laws of supply and demand," "Stalin's clique" than "Communist ideology." Navaho parallels are: "witches" as opposed to "bad weather," "the spirit of Old Age" as opposed to "physiological process." The Navahos, however, do carry the tendency further. Every feature of nature is animated and has some specific supernatural power. "The spirit of hunger kills me" is preferred to the intransitive "I am hungry." The English language describes the impersonal operation of natural forces, "I am drowning"; Navaho uses the active, personalized "water is killing me." Causes are not only identifiable; they are, up to a point, controllable in the way that people are controllable.

The universe is full of dangers. Every realist is aware that the world is a dangerous place. But the Navaho is distinguished by the variety of threats from the unseen world that he fears and names. Navaho philosophy seems a little like that of the Eskimo who said, "We do not believe; we fear." To be sure, he has also learned from experience in his difficult physical environment that living is hard and dangerous. It should also be understood that this view is interpreted in terms of the first premise. It is part of the nature of things that life is difficult and hazardous. No Navaho ever curses a divinity or a "malign fate." He accepts, though he accepts cheered by the realization that *some* misfortunes can be averted by applying obtainable knowledge and thus influencing the course of events. From old age and death there is no escape, but most mischances result from "error which is either incomplete knowledge or carelessness in the observation of rules which constitute the lubricant to minimize friction in the operation of the universal machine" (Gladys Reichard).

Evil and good are complementary, and both are ever present.

Some divinities can be influenced directly by human rituals, some only indirectly, others not at all. Some of the Holy People continually have human interests at heart, but the Sun and Moon each continue to demand a life a day, and First Woman and First Man persist in malevolent activity. But all are necessary to the scheme of things. According to some informants, even the most respected singers must know a little witchcraft—"or they'll go dry." The conception of perfection of personality is not a Navaho abstraction. Some frailties are recorded even of Changing Woman, who, of the divine beings, most nearly approaches the idea of benevolence. The most cherished and respected of family members are thought to have some evil in them, so that when they die their ghosts are feared, though majority Navaho opinion says that the good person who died in a ripe old age is harmless.

Experience is conceived as a continuum differentiated only by sense data. The Navaho find no difficulty in distinguishing one horse from another. The language delights in categorizing the concrete in precise and neat fashion. However, where the senses fail to provide evidence of sharp gradations, the continuum, with one important exception, is undifferentiated. A Navaho cannot conceive of absolute good or of absolute evil, though perhaps it is misleading even to use these two words. The Navaho conceive of what is to be desired and what is to be feared more than of the morally approved and disapproved. That is, to say that a person has evil in him really means in Navaho terms that he has properties that are to be dreaded. At any rate, the two qualities of the sought and of the avoided shade into each other and blend. Categories like "the social," "the economic," "the political" baffle the schooled Navaho. Life is a whole. There is likewise no mind-body problem for the Navaho. Although there is a Navaho word which may be translated "mind" and another which may be tendered "body," the two are conceived as interdependent, with the "mind" (the "in-lying one") as dominant. If a person has bodily aches and pains, his "mind" must be treated. If his mental reactions are aberrant, his body must be put through the same procedures as the man who has a fever. Psychosomatic medicine is no startling discovery to the Navaho! The behavior of the warrior's wife at home is as relevant to his safety and success as are his own actions, for all are part of a continuum of interrelated events. Navaho thought abhors the clear-cut time distinctions that are so necessary to Western thinking. Things have only the isolability evidenced by immediate sense perception. Events seem to be thought of as points in a continuous pattern. When they are separated out from the pattern, all their aspects in vivid specificity are isolated as a whole. The type of abstraction that is the central feature of what Northrop has called the theoretic component is almost entirely lacking in Navaho thinking.

Morality is conceived in traditionalistic and situational terms rather than in terms of abstract absolutes. Conduct that is not defined by custom or by rules involving the supernatural is ordinarily judged in terms of its practicality. But a pattern of conduct that has become invested with symbolic significance has its warrant in tradition rather than in rationality. "That is the old Navaho way." "Women must sit that way because the female Holy People used to sit that way." Any violation of the rules is a disruption of the harmony of things and a sure cause of trouble. There is no rain this year because the young men stamped their feet in the Girl's Dance, and that is not the old way. A woman is sick because she fired pottery in full sight of everyone. Since custom is king, public opinion and not "conscience" is the arbiter. Punishment is predominantly external, not internal. Navahos do not lie awake at night worrying about their secret sins. But the threat of being "shamed" by being publicly observed in a transgression of custom or the fear of setting in motion a set of supernatural sanctions is sufficient to induce proper behavior. The difference between Navaho morality and Christian morality is not at all that of the presence versus the absence of moral standards. It is rather a difference in the mechanisms for enforcing those standards.

Navaho morality is also contextual rather than absolute. This is characteristic of "shame" as opposed to "guilt" culture. Lying is not always and everywhere wrong. The rules vary with the situation. To deceive when trading with foreign tribes is a morally accepted practice. Acts are not in themselves bad or good. Incest is perhaps the only conduct that is condemned without qualification. It is quite correct to use witchcraft techniques in trading with members of foreign tribes. Behavior that is disapproved for a Navaho is acceptable for an outsider. There is an almost complete absence of abstract ideals. Under the circumstances of aboriginal life Navahos did not need to orient themselves in terms of abstract morality. They got their orientations from face-to-face contacts with the same small group of people with whom they have the overwhelming majority of their dealings from birth to death. In a large, complex society like modern America, where people come and go and business and other dealings must be carried on by people who never see each other, it is functionally necessary to have abstract standards that transcend an immediate concrete situation in which two or more persons are interacting.

Human relations are premised upon familistic individualism. The Navaho, particularly as contrasted with the Pueblo and some other communally oriented groups, is surely an individualist. Ceremonial knowledge is acquired—and paid for—by the individual. Certain animals in the family herd belong to definite persons. Some rites give considerable scope to individual self-expression. Yet this is equally certainly not the romantic individualism of American culture. No unacculturated Navaho feels his independence sufficiently to break from his relatives. There is a great deal of ordinarily submerged hostility among family members, but in his cognitive picture of his world the Navaho insists that family life is the hub of interpersonal relations. He does not consider himself primarily as a member of a local community, nor of his tribe—let alone of the United States or of an international brotherhood. His conception of the ideal society is that of a stable equilibrium between various groups of related persons. One's first loyalty is neither to oneself nor to society in the abstract but rather, in attenuating degrees as one moves outward in the circle of kin, to one's biological and clan relatives.

Events, not actors or qualities, are primary. Navaho is overwhelmingly a verbal language. Most nouns may be thematic, and adjectives are slightly altered verbs. The most fundamental categories distinguish types of activity. Similarly, Navaho thinking is relentlessly concerned with doing, with happenings. This fits with the view of the universe as process, with the belief that effective action influences the process, with the emphasis on the interconnections between events, with the stress on situation as opposed to qualitative absolutes, with the animation attributed even to natural phenomena. It is very difficult in Navaho to make fine precisions as to attributes; it is all too easy to indicate a hundred variations as to how an act of going occurred. Doing—neither being nor becoming—is the keynote of Navaho thought.

NAVAHO LAWS OF THOUGHT

Navaho reasoning proceeds consciously or unconsciously from the above premises. It remains to specify the forms of logical processes recognized as valid. First, negatively, it should be observed that the Aristotelian laws of "identity" and "excluded middle" are only weakly and not consistently observed in Navaho thinking. One never hears a Navaho say "a thing either is or it isn't." "Both-and" is a more familiar form than "either-or"—to the extent that one can point to many examples of the thought process that Lévy-Bruhl designated as *participation mystique*.

The following positive logical canons are by no means distinctly Navaho, but they are so emphasized as to be of indispensable significance for the comprehension of their mental horizon. They need only be listed here, since they have been discussed so frequently in approximately the same form that they are encountered among the Navaho:

(*a*) Like produces like (e.g., the eagle flies swiftly so that the runner can well carry a bit of eagle down).

(*b*) A part can stand for a whole (e.g., witches can work upon hair or nail parings as effectively as upon the victim himself).

(*c*) *Post hoc ergo propter hoc* (e.g., the grass no longer grows as high as in the old days when taboos were strictly kept; therefore, the decrease in vegetation is caused by carelessness in observing the rules).

(*d*) Every subjective experience must have its demonstrable correlate in the sense world. (It is not enough for a Navaho to say "I *know* a witch is after me." Witch tracks must be found or dirt must fall mysteriously from the roof of the hut at night. All interpretations must be documented in terms of actual sensory events. The unacculturated Navaho has difficulty in adjusting to clock time. This is arbitrary and unconvincing because it is not based upon natural phenomena.)

SOME BASIC NAVAHO CATEGORIES

In general the Navaho language is tremendously concrete. Referents of words are unusually delimited and precise. Verbalizations are taken with great literalness. Though some ordinary words have figurative connotations, loose denotations are uncommon, and, since most Navahos have had highly similar experiences associated with the same words, connotations do not spread over nearly as much territory as they do in English.

There are, however, some abstract words, extremely difficult to render adequately in English, which are of the greatest importance for the understanding of Navaho philosophy. Perhaps the most significant of these is conveyed by the Navaho root hóʒǫ́-. This is probably the central idea in Navaho religious thinking. It occurs in the names of two important ceremonials (Blessing Way and Beauty Way) and is frequently repeated in almost all prayers and songs. In various contexts it is best translated as "beautiful," "harmonious," "good," "blessed," "pleasant," and "satisfying." As a matter of fact, the difficulty with translation primarily reflects the poverty of English in terms that simultaneously have moral and esthetic meaning. A number of words in classical Greek come rather close.

Earlier it was remarked that the universe was not only lawful but also an interrelated whole. It is integration with the harmony of all forces, personal and impersonal—a harmony that includes both good and evil—that is sought in Blessing Way. It is sought not only for the individual patient but also for his family and for all present at the rite and indeed for all living beings (animal, human, and divine; Navaho and non-Navaho) and all natural phenomena (rivers, mountains, winds, lightning, and the like). The harmony exists, but no person, human or divine, can hope for complete and permanent participation in it:

> When my spiritual power was strong, I came up with it
> When I was holy, I came up with it
> > "Second Song of the Flood"

For a limited period a personality can become identified with this harmony, and the integration of all forces in it can be improved by performances of the ceremonial.

It is to be noted that this term is applied to a human being only while he is in a sacred situation (i.e., singer or patient in a ceremonial). This in itself implies that the state is not permanently attainable. It also implies that the word means something different from the actually realizable condition of relative moral goodness. "Holiness" is sharply distinct from "goodness." The descriptive adjectives that designate individuals who are "good" (in the simply moral, nonesthetic sense) have reference to a number of different qualities. The most general concept seems to include the notions of industry, responsibility (especially to one's relatives), frugality-generosity, strength-hardihood, pleasant disposition, avoidance of excess of any kind, tending to one's own affairs.

The conception of evil also has separate profane and sacred dimensions. The root, hóčǫ́-, however, is not a precise antithesis of hóžǫ́-. It does not refer explicitly to disorder as hóžǫ́- refers to harmony. Rather, its primary reference is to the malevolent activities of ghosts and witches who are the living embodiments of evil of the sacred variety. Ceremonials of Evil Way type (intended to free the patients from ghost or witch attack) are hóčǫ́ʾží which is sometimes translated "Ghost Way." Various words applied to persons who are disapproved of in the profane sense refer to qualities the opposite of those listed for the good person. Individuals who commit incest are abhorred and suspect of witchcraft. To be sure, some connection betwᵗeen the categories is evidenced. Those who are violent, lazy, irresponsible, meddlesome are more often accused of witchcraft than is the average Navaho. On the other hand, singers and the rich and powerful (who are at least industrious and strong) are still more frequently mentioned as witches.

Another basic concept of the sacred world is that of "immunity." The patient in a Holy Way ceremonial becomes identified with the Holy People of that rite, hence holy himself, hence immune to further attack from these divinities. This conception is, of course, congruent with the premise that many dangers can be averted through employment of the proper mechanical means. The word, *diʏin*, which is rendered above as "immune" may also in certain contexts be translated as "holy" or "sacred." "Charged with positive spiritual electricity" suggests in not too far-fetched a manner the core of the Navaho concept. One whole group of Navaho ceremonials is called the Holy (*diʏin*) Way group. One class of divinities is referred to as the Holy People (*diʏin diné*).

The category "property" is very prominent and has some special Navaho subdivisions: "hard goods," "soft goods," "flexible goods," etc. The Navaho concept of "place" is unusual and impossible to convey briefly and directly. Every thing and every act has spatial position which must be specified with great precision. Myths are replete with long lists of place names that are as tiresome to the foreigner as the "Catalogue of Ships" in the *Iliad*. Each verb has a special third person form that grammarians call "place person." Other secular categories tend to follow the lines set rather obviously by the visible world. Except for certain plant groups, there is little lumping in accord with use or function as contrasted with divisions derivable from descriptive physical features.

The absence of various abstract categories that are familiar to whites should be mentioned. It is not surprising in a "shame" culture that there is no notion of "sin." Nor can the Navaho easily conceive of "laying up treasures in Heaven." Indeed there is no heaven in our sense. The afterworld is a colorless, unattractive place according to Navaho thought. In the native ideology there is no concept analogous to our "personal success." Parents urge their children to be industrious, but this is in order that they may gain "security" or "relative harmony." The attainment of some goal through the correct employment of ritual means is also stressed, of course. Personal ambition—as abstracted from family welfare—is a foreign notion. Prestige for some activities, yes. But the Navaho characteristically shrinks from formal leadership, from being marked out as above his fellows. A hierarchical rating of human beings is avoided as much as is a hierarchy of divinities.

The European concept of personality has little if any counterpart in Navaho thought. There are words that may be translated "in-standing" or "in-lying" beings which express an idea that—in certain respects only—is similar to that of a soul. In Navaho conception a wind is blown into the conceived or born body of a human which is an entirely separate unit from the body. The body is animated and activated by the "in-standing one." This "in-standing one" is responsible for the actions of the individual, though not in a sense that Christians would define as "morally responsible." For instance, a child may become ill as the result of actions of the parents during pregnancy. However, an individual is thought to be mean, gentle, one-eyed, left- or right-handed because of the qualities of the "in-standing one."

There is no notion that a *persona* is a composite of "body and soul" in the sense that the union of the wind with the babe's body creates a person (*"homo hic et nunc"* or *"sic et sic"*). The in-lying one of Blanca Peak does not mean that this being and the respective physical mountain result in a specific personality. In the human case, at death the in-lying being is separated forever from that body. In life, if the in-lying one is sick (i.e., out of harmony) this can affect the body which the in-lying one activates. However, no ceremonial expiates a crime or makes provision for *expiation* of unethical actions. Since there is no total personality that is *morally* responsible, transgressions of taboos, clan code, and the like are not reacted to by the offender in terms of a "guilty conscience."

The concept *bahadzid* ("for it there is fear") is congruent with assumptions of causality, lack of personal *moral* responsibility, and the like. The word may be varyingly translated as "dangerous," "tabooed," "restricted." It is, if you like, "negative *mana.*" That is, certain objects, events, and persons are charged with negative power. If they are not approached circumspectly, they backfire with enormous destructive force.

Limitations of space make it impossible to discuss all basic Navaho concepts. The ones considered above seem to be especially important in Navaho thought and also very representative.

NAVAHO ETHICAL CODE AND VALUES

We now come to that portion of Navaho philosophy which even the average Navaho can present explicitly. The very fact that the Navaho find it necessary to talk about their ethical principles suggests that not everybody lives up to them (any more than is the case in white society). But this code is largely the working out in concrete terms of the principles inherent in the absolute logic that have been discussed.

In no human group is indiscriminate lying, cheating, or stealing approved. Cooperation is of course impossible unless individuals can depend upon each other in defined circumstances. Societies differ in how they define the conditions under which lying or stealing is forgivable or tolerable or perhaps even demanded. In their general discussions the Navaho make virtues of telling the truth and of fair dealing much as white people do. In the advice fathers give their children, in the harangues of headmen at large gatherings, these types of action never fail to be extolled.

The difference in presentation by whites and Navahos lies in the reasons advanced. The Navaho never appeals to abstract morality or to adherence to divine principles. He stresses mainly the practical considerations: "If you don't tell the truth, your fellows won't trust you and you'll shame your relatives. You'll never get along in the world that way." Truth is never praised merely on the ground that it is "good" in a purely abstract sense, nor do exhortations ever take the form that the Holy People have forbidden cheating or stealing. Certain other acts are commanded or prohibited on the basis that one or more of the Holy People did or did not behave in a similar fashion, but never in the modes which would seem "natural" to Christians: "Do this to please the Holy People because they love you," or "Don't do this because the Holy People punish wrongdoing." The Navahos do most definitely believe that acts have consequences, but the nature of the consequence is not wrapped up in any intrinsic "rightness" or "wrongness" of the act itself. In the matters of truth and honesty the only appeal to the sentiments (other than those of practicality and getting along with relatives and neighbors) which Navaho "moralists" permit themselves is that of loyalty to tradition. The old Navaho way was not to lie, to cheat, or to steal. The prevalence of such vices today, they say, is due to white corruption. So much for the theory.

When it comes to practice, it is harder to put the finger on the differences between Navaho and white patterns. One gets the impression that Navahos lie to strangers or indeed to their relatives with fewer qualms than the average well-socialized white adult would feel. (However, the white adult's easy acceptance of "white lies" must not be overlooked.) There are also occasions on which stealing is mostly condoned "if you can get away with it." Again, though, a qualification must be entered; in many parts of the Navaho country one can leave an automobile containing valuable articles unlocked for days and return to find not a single item missing. Thefts occur chiefly in the areas under strongest white influence, especially now at "squaw dances" frequented by ne'er-do-well young men who are souls lost between the two cultures. There is undoubted evidence that white contact brings about—at least in the transitional generations—some breakdown in the moralities. This much, however, seems to be a distinctive part of the native attitude: a Navaho does not spend much time worrying over a lie or a theft when he is not found out; he seems to have almost no "guilt" feelings; but if he is caught he does experience a good deal of shame. Ridicule is used to reinforce this sense of shame. The person who gets caught is the butt of many Navaho jokes.

Offenses more strongly condemned are those which threaten peaceful working together. The boaster and the troublemaker are strongly disapproved of. Incest and witchcraft are the worst of crimes. Murder, rape, physical injury, and any sort of violence are disapproved and punished, but some of the penalties seem relatively light to white people. By Navaho custom, murder, for instance, could be compounded for by a payment of slaves or livestock to the kin of the victim. To this day the Navaho way of dealing with violent crimes against the person is not ordinarily retaliation or even punishment of the offender but levying a fine which is turned over not to "the state" but to the sufferer and his family to compensate for the economic loss by injury or death.

The positive behaviors which are advocated center, as has been pointed out, on affectionate duty to relatives, pleasant manners to all, generosity, self-control, minding one's own business. The Navahos say: "Act to everybody as if they were your own relatives." A courteous, nonaggressive approach to others is the essence of decency. Polite phrases to visitors and strangers are highly valued. If an English-speaking Navaho wishes to speak approvingly of another Navaho with whom he has had a chance encounter, he is likely to say, "He talks pretty nice." Quiet strength is highly valued. "Make your mind into something that is hard." Generosity is uniformly praised and stinginess despised. One of the most disparaging things which can be said of anyone is, "He gets mad like a dog." Women will be blamed for "talking rough" to their children. The Navaho word which is most often translated into English as "mean" is sometimes rendered "he gets mad pretty easy." In short, one must keep one's temper; one must warmly and cheerfully do one's part in the system of reciprocal rights and obligations, notably those which prevail between kinfolk.

Health and strength are perhaps the best of the good things of life for the Navaho. If you aren't healthy, you can't work; if you don't work, you'll starve. Industry is enormously valued. A family must arise and be about their tasks early, for if someone goes by and sees no smoke drifting out of the smokehole it will be thought that "there is something wrong there; somebody must be sick." In enumerating the virtues of a respected man or woman the faithful performance of duties is always given a prominent place. "If you are poor or a beggar, people will make fun of you. If you are lazy people will make fun of you."

By Navaho standards one is industrious in order to accumulate possessions—within certain limits—and to care for the possessions he obtains. Uncontrolled gambling or drinking are disapproved primarily because they are wasteful. The "good" man is one who has "hard goods" (turquoise and jewelry mainly), "soft goods" (clothing, etc.), "flexible goods" (textiles, etc.), and songs, stories, and other intangible property, of which ceremonial knowledge is the most important. An old Navaho said to W. W. Hill, "I have always been a poor man. I do not know a single song." The final disrespect is to say of a man, "Why, he hasn't even a dog."

A good appearance is valued; while this is partly a matter of physique, figure, and facial appearance, it means even more the ability to dress well and to appear with a handsome horse and substantial trappings.

Thus possessions are valued both as providing security and as affording opportunities for mild ostentation. But to take the attainment of riches as the chief aim of life is universally condemned. This is a typical pronouncement by a Navaho leader:

The Navaho way is just to want enough to have enough to eat for your family and nice things to wear sometimes. We don't like it when nowadays some of these young men marry rich girls for their money and waste it all right away. The old people say this is wrong. You can't get rich if you look after your relatives right. You can't get rich without cheating some people. Cheating people is the wrong way. That way gets you into trouble. Men should be honest to get along.

Many skills carry prestige: the ability to dance, to sing, to tell stories. Skill at speaking is important and is expected of all leaders. "He talks easy" is high praise. Conversely, "He doesn't talk easy. He just sits there," is a belittling remark. Training in certain occupations is emphasized: a man will spend all the time he can spare from subsistence activities in order to learn a ceremonial; grandmothers and mothers are expected to teach young girls to weave. Knowledge is power to Navahos as to other peoples, but the kinds of knowledge which are significant to the Navaho are naturally limited by his technology and his social organization. The skillful farmer or stockman is admired. So also is he who excels at cowboy sports, but the runner comes in for his meed of praise too, even though this skill is today of minimum social utility.

Personal excellence is thus a value, but personal "success" in the white American sense is not. The Navaho lack of stress upon the success goal has its basis in childhood training but is reinforced by various patterns of adult life. A white man may start out to make a fortune and continue piling it up until he is a millionaire, where a Navaho, though also interested in accumulating possessions, will stop when he is comfortably off, or even sooner, partly for fear of being called a witch if he is too successful. This statement represents tendency rather than literal fact, for a few Navahos have in this century built up fortunes that are sizable even by white standards. The attitudes of the Navaho population generally toward these "ricos" are very mixed. Envy, fear, and distrust of them are undoubtedly mingled with some admiration. But there is almost no disposition for parents to hold these individuals up as models to their children. No elder says, "If you work hard and intelligently you might get to be as rich as Chee Dodge."

Navaho ideas of accumulation are different from those of whites.

Riches are not ordinarily identified so much with a single individual as with the whole extended family and "outfit." Indeed the social pressure to support and share with relatives has a strong leveling effect. The members of a well-off family must also spend freely, as in the white pattern of "conspicuous consumption." But all wealth is desired for this purpose and for security rather than as a means of enhancing the power and glory of specific individuals.

That individual success is not a Navaho value is reflected also in the avoidance of the types of leadership which are familiar in white society. To the Navaho it is fundamentally indecent for a single individual to presume to make decisions for a group. Leadership, to them, does not mean "outstandingness." Each individual is controlled not by sanctions from the top of a hierarchy of persons but by lateral sanctions. Decisions at meetings must be unanimous.

Some personal values which bulk large among whites have a place among the Navaho that is measured largely by the degree of white influence. Cleanliness, for instance, is an easy virtue where there is running water, but where every drop must be hauled five miles washing is an expensive luxury. Navaho social and economic life is not geared to fine points of time scheduling. If a Singer says he will arrive "about noon," no one takes it amiss that he appears at sundown, though an arrival a day or more late would call for explanation. Work is not, as it is in our Puritan tradition, a good thing in itself. The Navaho believes in working only as much as he needs to. Industry is praised only as a means to providing decently for one's family and oneself.

In sum, the Navaho concept of "goodness" stresses productiveness, ability to get along with people, dependability and helpfulness, generosity in giving and spending. "Badness" means stinginess, laziness, being "mean" to others, being destructive. The concept of value stresses possessions and their care, health, skills which are practically useful. Concerning all of these topics the Navaho are fully articulate. Such sentiments are enunciated again and again in the oral literature, in formal addresses, and in ordinary conversations. As John Dewey has remarked, "Ideals are goals which, though never completely attained, set the direction of intelligent effort."

THE IMPACT OF AN ALIEN IDEOLOGY

Personal and social disorganization is rampant among the Navaho people today. In part this is the consequence of objective facts,

Navaho country is overpopulated, and the range is overgrazed. Few Navahos have the occupational skills to compete with whites in the near-by towns and cities. But that Navaho culture is becoming an ugly patchwork of meaningless and unrelated pieces instead of a patterned mosaic is due at least as much to the power of foreign ideas. The Navaho recognize and respect the strength of white American culture. Many Navahos are saying frankly that their tribe's salvation rests in mastering the language and the way of life of the dominant group. The lack of selective blending and constructive fusion is not due to low intelligence. Navahos are perfectly capable of learning white skills and white customs. But when the traits of another culture are learned externally and one by one without the underlying concepts and premises of that culture, the learners feel uncomfortable. They sense the absence of the fitness of things, of a support which is nonetheless real because difficult to verbalize.

The adoption of our ideas is not, of course, due solely to choice on the part of Navahos. Missionaries, government officials, and traders are consciously and systematically trying to redeem the Navaho from "savagery." Some programs have conscientiously endeavored to take account of individual Navaho customs and even of the more external patterns of Navaho life. But because they have taken no account of underlying Navaho philosophy they have often produced results regarded as unfortunate by Navahos and whites alike. The rationally desirable innovations have failed to configurate correctly with the unconscious system of meanings characteristic of Navaho implicit culture.

This is no new experience in planned culture change. Many attempts at acculturating on the part of missionary groups have had the (to the planners) unexpected consequences of contributing to the reinvigoration of basically aboriginal religions. Education in white values in government schools has promoted "rugged individualism" without the limiting and integrating controls which the white American absorbs in the home as part of his largely unverbalized philosophy. Such phrases as "compatibility with the pre-existing culture of the borrowers" are frequent in discussions of acculturation, and they are necessitated by the universal experience of students of culture that, over and above the cases of externally observable pattern conflict, there are less tangible forms of compatibility "that you can't quite put your finger on." These relate to lack of congruence between the implicit ideological systems. It is as if there were forces "behind" the explicit culture which made for acceptance of one foreign idea but for rejection of the associated ideas that contribute to discipline and control of behavior. Certainly ideas are retailored with subtle distortion of borrowed patterns of thought and behavior to swing them into line with remarkably tenacious underlying ideas.

There is not space to follow out in detail the ways in which Western conceptions have disturbed or destroyed the relatively smooth fabric of Navaho social life. Let us look merely at some aspects of the effects of white premises and categories with respect to individualism, government, economic institutions, sex, and property. It will be easier to follow out the course of events in these rather concrete realms than to trace, at this time, the effects of ideas from Western culture upon Navaho ideas. The less tangible, more implicit aspects of Navaho philosophy have undoubtedly been altered by the impact of Christianity, for example, but the underlying premises and concepts change more slowly than does behavior. Nevertheless, it is clear that many contemporary deviations make sense only if understood in terms of the influence of Christian notions of individualism, personal responsibility, sex code, and the like.

The category "government," something fixed and powerful to white people, is foreign to Navaho thinking. Authority, to their minds, extends only indefinitely and transitorily beyond the established rules of behavior between sex groups, age groups, and, especially, classes of relatives. There are headmen, but the sphere of their influence widens and narrows with the passage of time, the emergence of a new leader, the rise of a new faction. The prestige of some headmen often spreads beyond their own local region. Through channels excessively informal they can sometimes "swing" most of the population of a number of local groups to a given course of action. By and large, however, control of individual action rests in the group and not in any authoritative individual or body.

The whole mechanism of Navaho social control is too fluid, too informal, too vague to be readily understood by white people who think of authority in terms of courts, police, and legislative assemblies. But Navaho social controls are extremely effective for those who remain within their own group. Never to be lost sight of is the fact that the basis of the system was and still is the family. To live at all in this barren region the individual must have the economic cooperation of others, and such cooperation is hardly likely to come to those who deviate from the "right way of doing things" as the Navaho see it. Thus the major threat which restrains the potential offender is the withdrawal of the support and the good will of his neighbors, most of whom are "family" to the Navaho. Gossip and criticism were and are major means of social control throughout Navaho society. These diffuse sanctions are less effective today than in former times because, by taking up wage work for whites, the offender can escape both the need for economic cooperation by the group and the criticism which the group aims at deviators.

The introduction of the white idea of individualism without the checks and balances that accompany it leads to the failure of collective or cooperative action of every sort. The substitution of paid labor for reciprocal services is not in and of itself a bad thing. But there is not a commensurate growth of the white idea of individual responsibility. There tends to be a distortion of the whole cultural structure which makes it difficult to preserve harmonious personal relationships and satisfying emotional adjustments. Widespread exercise of escape mechanisms, especially alcohol, is the principal symptom of the resultant friction and decay. Human groups that have different cultures and social structures have moral systems that differ in important respects. The linkage is so great that when a social organization goes to pieces morality also disintegrates.

A typical cause for confusion, distrust, and hostility arising out of a difference in the system of categories is the fact that Navahos are today dependent upon a distant and mysterious white institution called "the market." In the days of bartering raw materials, a sheep or a sack of wool maintained a rather constant value. At present, when both are sold to the trader, the Navaho never know in advance whether the lamb will bring ten cents a pound or only five cents, and they see no sense in these variations. They share the common distrust of farmer folk for those who buy and resell the products of their hard labors, but they are at a greater disadvantage than the white farmer because they are unfamiliar with white marketing customs and have no means of understanding the reasons for the apparently senseless fluctuations in price and demand. Moreover, since they feel that they usually are underpaid for their sheep and wool and that the price they will get varies with no rhyme or reason, they feel uncertain about improving their products. Why should they invest money, labor, and time simply to benefit the trader or the more remote livestock dealers? Similar confusion and irritation resulted from the government's program of killing "excess" livestock. From the Navaho point of view only production is ethical. Destruction—except to satisfy immediate hunger—is unethical.

The Navaho have only "object taboos" as regards sex, none of the "aim taboos" which are so marked a development of Western culture. That is, Navahos do feel that sexual activity is improper or dangerous under particular circumstances or with certain persons. But they never regard sexual desires in themselves as "nasty" or evil. In school and elsewhere whites have tended to operate upon the premise that "any decent Navaho" will feel guilty about the sexual act which takes place outside of marriage. This attitude simply bewilders Navahos and predisposes them to withdrawal of cooperation in all spheres. To them sex is natural, necessary, and no more or no less concerned with morals than is eating.

The Navaho and the white administrator may see the same objective facts, and communication may be sufficiently well established so that each is sure the other sees them. Naturally, then there is mutual irritation when the same conclusions are not reached. What neither realizes is that all discourse proceeds from premises and that premises (unfortunately taken for granted by both) are likely, in fact, to be very divergent.

Let us put this in the concrete. A wealthy man dies and leaves considerable property. He has a widow but no children by her. There are, however, two sons by another woman to whom the deceased was never married in either white or Navaho fashion. He left, of course, no written will, and it is agreed that he gave no oral instructions on his deathbed. These are the facts, and there is no dispute about them between the Navaho and the white administrator.

Nevertheless the prediction may safely be made that before the estate is settled the white man will be irritated more than once and some Navahos will be confused and indignant at what seems to them ignorance, indifference, or downright immorality. Each will unconsciously make his judgments and decisions in terms of his own presuppositions. Neither set of premises will be brought out into the open and discussed as such, but the following unstated assumptions will be in the background of thinking:

WHITE	NAVAHO
1. Marriage is an arrangement, economic and otherwise, between two individuals. The two spouses and the children, if any, are the ones primarily involved in any question of inheritance.	1. Marriage is an arrangement between two families much more than it is between two individuals.
2. A man's recognized children, legitimate or illegitimate, have a claim upon his property.	2. Sexual rights are property rights; therefore if a man has children from a woman without undertaking during his lifetime the economic responsibilities which are normally a part of Navaho marriage, the children—however much he admitted to biological fatherhood—were not really his: "He just stole them."
3. Inheritance is normally from the father or from both sides of the family.	3. Inheritance is normally from the mother, the mother's brother, or other relatives of the mother; from the father's side of the family little or nothing has traditionally been expected. Most of the father's property goes back to his relatives.
4. As long as a wife or children survive, no other relatives are concerned in the inheritance unless there was a will to that effect.	4. While children today, in most areas, expect to inherit something from their father, they do not expect to receive his whole estate or to divide it with their mother only; sons and daughters have different expectations.
5. All types of property are inherited in roughly the same way.	5. Different rules apply to different types of property: range land is hardly heritable property at all; farm land normally stays with the family which has been cultivating it; livestock usually goes back (for the most part) to the father's sisters and sororal nephews; jewelry and other personal property tend to be divided among the children and other relatives; ceremonial equipment may go to a son who is a practitioner or to a clansman of the desceased.

The white administrator would be likely to say that the only heirs to any of the property were the wife, children, and perhaps the illegitimate children. Such a decision would be perplexing or infuriating to the Navaho. To say in the abstract what disposal would be proper at the present complicated point in Navaho history is hardly possible. But it is clear that a verdict which seemed so "right" and "natural" to a white person as to require no explanation or justification would probably appear equally "unjust" and "unreasonable" to the Navaho involved.

The pressure of such double standards is highly disruptive. Just as rats that have been trained to associate a circle with food and a rectangle with an electric shock become neurotic when the circle is changed by almost imperceptible gradations into an ellipse, so human beings faced with a conflicting set of rewards and punishments tend to cut loose from all moorings, to float adrift, and become irresponsible. The younger generation of the Navaho are more and more coming to laugh at the old or pay them only lip service. The young escape the control of their elders, not to accept white controls but to revel in newly found patterns of unrestraint.

The Navaho are torn between their own ancient standards and those which are urged upon them by teachers, missionaries, and other whites. An appreciable number of Navahos are so confused by the conflicting precepts of their elders and their white models that they tend, in effect, to reject the whole problem of morality (in the widest sense) as meaningless or insoluble. For longer or shorter periods in their lives their only guide is the expediency of the immediate situation. One cannot play a game according to rule if there are sharp disagreements as to what the rules are. The incipient breakdown of any culture brings a loss of predictability and hence of dependability in personal relations. The absence of generally accepted standards of behavior among individuals constitutes, in fact, a definition of social disorganization.

A stable social structure prevails only so long as the majority of individuals in the society find enough satisfaction both in the goals socially approved and in the institutionalized means of attainment to compensate them for the constraints which ordered social life inevitably imposes upon uninhibited response to impulse. In any way of life there is much that to an outside observer appears haphazard, disorderly, more or less chaotic. But unless most participants feel that the ends and means of their culture make sense, in terms of a unifying philosophy, disorientation and amorality become rampant. Some major Navaho premises are incompatible with some major premises of our culture. A resolution must be sought in terms of wider assumptions.

In this chapter an attempt has been made to describe not only Navaho ethics and values but also some of those highest common factors that are implicit in a variety of the doings and sayings of the Navaho. In the not distant past these recurrent themes, these unstated premises, gave a felt coherence to life in spite of social change, in spite of the diversity of institutions, in spite of differences in the needs and experiences of individuals. These distinctly Navaho values and premises still do much to regulate group life and to reconcile conflicts and discrepancies. But these basic assumptions are now under attack from a competing set of assumptions. The majority of Navahos no longer feel completely at home and at ease in their world of values and significances, and an appreciable minority are thoroughly disoriented. This will continue and increase until new coherent philosophical bases for life are created and widely accepted. As Merton has written, "It is the dominating system of ideas which determines the choice between alternative modes of action which are equally compatible with the underlying sentiments."

NOTES

1. Certain statements in this paper are repeated (usually in somewhat altered form) from *The Navaho* (Harvard University Press, 1946). Thanks are due to the Press and to my co-author, Dr. Dorothea Leighton, for permission to re-use these materials. This paper has benefited from criticisms and suggestions by Father Berard Haile, O.F.M., Dorothea Leighton, M.D., Rev. Robert McNair, Dr. Gladys Reichard, Mr. Evon Vogt, and Dr. Leland C. Wyman.

2. Cf. Clyde and Florence Kluckhohn, "American Culture: Generalized Orientations," in *Conflicts of Power in Modern Culture* (Harper & Bros., 1947), pp. 106–129.

3. Edward Sapir and Harry Hoijer, *Navaho Texts* (Iowa City, Iowa, Linguistic Society of America, 1942), pp. 400–401. The word translated by Sapir and Hoijer as "beauty" could as well or better be translated "harmony." It is based on the root hóžǫ́-, discussed below (see pp. 20 ff.).

BIBLIOGRAPHICAL NOTE

It has not seemed appropriate to document this paper in detail. The best original sources are the Navaho texts that have been published by Father Berard Haile, Gladys Reichard, P. E. Goddard, E. Sapir, and H. Hoijer. These, however, are highly technical. Next best are the published autobiographies. These and the secondary accounts most useful for these purposes follow:

Walter Dyk, recorder, *Son of Old Man Hat; a Navaho Autobiography* (New York, Harcourt, Brace & Co., 1938).

Walter Dyk, *A Navaho Autobiography,* The Viking Fund Publications in Anthropology, No. 8 (New York, 1947).

Clyde Kluckhohn, "A Navaho Personal Document," *Southwestern Journal of Anthropology,* I (1945), 260–283.

Clyde Kluckhohn and Dorothea C. Leighton, *The Navaho* (Cambridge, Harvard University Press, 1946).

Alexander H. and Dorothea C. Leighton, *The Navaho Door* (Cambridge, Harvard University Press, 1944).

Dorothea Leighton and Clyde Kluckhohn, *Children of the People* (Cambridge, Harvard University Press, 1947).

Gladys Reichard, "Human Nature as Conceived by the Navaho Indians," *Review of Religion,* VII (1943), 353–360.

Gladys Reichard, "Distinctive Features of Navaho Religion," *Southwestern Journal of Anthropology,* I (1945), 199–220.

XVIII

MAN AND CULTURE

FRANCISCO ROMERO

MAN, culture, and spirit are three themes between which no absolute separation can be established. They are three distinct subjects, each with its own contents and its peculiar problems. They must, indeed, occasionally be examined separately in order to be disclosed in all of their multiple aspects and to be plumbed according to the vocation or competence of the author. But a thorough study of each of them presupposes a conception, even if only vague and, as it were, provisional, of the other two.

The study of man gives rise to anthropology; that of culture to the general theory, or philosophy, of culture; that of the spirit to the doctrine of spiritual being. Special investigations in these three fields abound. But even in the books and essays which treat the three separately it is easy to recognize their interdependence from the incessant references, explicit or implicit, linking one to the other two; and where such references are lacking the subject is arbitrarily cut short and remains incomplete.

Man is inconceivable without culture; the correlation between the two terms has become increasingly clear, although it may not yet have been stated in a sufficiently distinct and definite form. Culture is not only an expression and production of man and—in the form of objective culture—the medium or environment he creates around himself and inside which alone he can lead a human life; it is also the condition sine qua non of things human, the external and, as it were, objectified aspect of man's being and, for that reason, an essential part of man. Just as a satisfactory anthropology is inconceivable without at least a rudiment of a theory of culture, so it is not possible to set up a theory of objective culture without briefly expounding, or at least presupposing, a concept of man as the subject of culture, the agent who creates it, understands it, and benefits from it in most diverse ways. As regards the spirit, it is obvious that it cannot be separated either from man on the one hand or from culture on the other. Spirit as a living agency abides in subjects. Spirit in a solidified and coagulated form is inherent in cultural realizations; and any investigation into it must be careful not to lose sight of these entities in which it necessarily appears: men and cultural objectifications. To understand what spirit is, there is no other way but to seek it, and define its appearance, in subjects present and past, and in the works in which it is embodied: works of religion, art, philosophy, science, etc. Thus the three themes man, culture, spirit are actually inseparable, and their close connection cannot but be revealed from the studies devoted to them, however specialized these may claim to be.

This inseparability is not a question of mere chance. Nor does it spring from the simple fact that man is the maker of culture, and spirit is an attribute of man. Between the three a profound unity obtains in terms of an identity of origin and a continuous correlation. As the purpose of the following pages is to point out that unity and that continuity, references to the intrinsic being of man, culture, and spirit must be reduced to what is indispensable for the matter in hand.

Let us begin with the problem of the being of man and ask what it is in man that makes him particularly and specifically human. As a starting point and a plane of comparison it will be convenient to use the formulation Max Scheler gives to the problem in his book, *Man's Position in the Cosmos*. Although I fail to agree with Scheler, as will appear later, his exposition ranks, in my opinion, among the clearest and most apposite. Some authors, Scheler points out, admit a difference between man and animals and recognize it in that man possesses intelligence and is able to choose—two faculties lacking in animals. Others maintain that no essential difference exists, since animals also possess intelligence and man is only distinguished by possessing it to a very much higher degree. Scheler is at variance with both these opinions. According to him, animals do possess intelligence, but they are not, despite that fact, like man. For man is, in addition, endowed with another attribute, an exclusively human attribute: spirit—the characteristics of which are objectivity, liberty understood as man's autonomy with regard to his own impulses, and consciousness of himself.

To clarify the difference between Scheler's and my standpoint and to justify my own position, let me, instead of taking the concept of intelligence *en bloc,* as does Scheler, go back to the roots of intelligence, that is, to its component elements and processes.

Behavior of the instinct type or behavior based on associative memory (retention of whole situations, be they natural or arranged, as those used by man in training animals) requires no analysis and recomposition of reality. So-called intelligent operations, on the other hand, are known to ascertain solutions of new problems, to choose means in view of ends, to fabricate tools as a normal and habitual performance (and not as the result of a chance discovery or an accidental achievement both of which can be attributed to mere associative memory). All these activities presuppose an analysis or decomposition of reality and a conceptual recomposition of the elements resulting from such analysis. An intelligent being possesses two versions of reality: a primary one of things as they are perceived, and a conceptual one in which the natural entities and their elements appear reduced to classes, genera, and concepts according to a certain systematic order. If, for instance, an intelligent being has to ford a river, he will not mechanically repeat such procedures as he has, by chance or blind groping, found to be helpful on a previous occasion, but he will combine and suitably use the concepts of danger (getting drowned), of velocity (the current), of capacity to float (a board or a bundle of branches), of solidity (a tree trunk that may serve as an improvised bridge), etc. Even if he had never seen a river before he would, provided he possessed these concepts or others appropriate to the situation, be in a condition to solve the problem of crossing a stream.

Intelligence relies on *objectification*. The first step in objectification consists in turning sensations into perceptions and states into entities. A mere sensation occupies, as such, the entire consciousness. In passing from sensations to perceptions, the dawning consciousness of a merely sensorial being is transformed, clarified, and split up into the polarity of subject and object, although at the outset the subject is likely to be only functional and not conscious of itself. Something (at first not conscious of itself, but already set up as a focus inside consciousness) becomes conscious of something (an object). The something subjective, the active pole of consciousness, fulfills as its primary task an objectifying or intentional function. (The word "intentional," is used here in the sense that Franz Brentano and Edmund Husserl use it.) This something subjective is characterized by having objects. In my opinion intentionality, which philosophers have so far considered almost exclusively from the standpoint of the theory of knowledge, ought to form the foundation of anthropology. But to be able to fulfill this purpose, intentionality must primarily be understood not as a mere apprehension of objects but as an objectifying function, the function that constitutes something as an object and effects the transition from states to perceptions. The subject of states is not yet a subject proper; the true subject is born when his states have been objectified. Man is what he is only after objectification has confronted him, as a subject with a sphere of objects. If there is objectification in animals, it is rudimentary and arrested after its first steps, as is shown by the clumsiness and limitation of the intelligence even of higher animals and their lacking an objective language, the indispensable means of a permanent and normal objectification. The distinguishing characteristic of man is the intentional and objectifying mind; that he has a "world"; that he is a subject. Later, spirit combines with intentionality to consummate humanization.

The states which become objectified belong to different classes. Some are objectified in the perception as things. Others, kinesthetic states, for instance, become objective without losing their condition of states. That is to say, we may blindly live them without objectifying them, or we may live them and, at the same time, have cognizing awareness of them, elevating them to the rank of objects. Another class of objectification is that of our own selves when we behold ourselves as beings who exist among others. In this primary form of objectification, entities are given in the natural shape proper to them and in their original order in time and space. But the objectifying activity does not stop here. It proceeds to objectify the parts, qualities, modes, and relations of those primary objectifications, attributing existence and consistency to whatever may be given in an intentional act of seeing. This operation is a veritable analysis of reality, an incessant dissection of things. Let it be noted, this analyzing and abstracting operation is not a mere act of distinguishing and setting down separately all that is separable; rather it is a full-fledged objectification inasmuch as it attributes being to each instance thus isolated. Owing to this objectification, we can speak of color, of weight, of number, and relation as of autonomous and consistent entities, *enduring identical* with themselves. Objectification is possible of the content of apprehensions and intuitions as well as of conceptual syntheses, i.e., of groups or classes that ensue when similar or homogeneous things are assembled.

Objectification carries with it a free and most diverse manipulation of contents *qua* autonomous entities; it permits us to order and classify contents in different ways and to use them at each opportunity according to the demands of the respective interests or conveniences. Objectification thus forms the foundation of intelligence and turns the mind into a laboratory in perpetual activity. In fomenting the growth and continuous accumulation of contents on a scale a nonintentional mind would never be capable of, objectification initiates historicity, a specifically human phenomenon which later, amplified through the working of intentional community, prepares the ground for the spiritual attitude, that supreme form of objectification.

Spirit, as will appear later, presupposes, and is supported by, the capacity of executing intellectual acts. But man as such exists before he has spirit; he is human as soon as his objectifying faculty functions steadily. Plenary objectification includes conceptualization and entails conceptual and objective language. An objectification that stopped at natural objects and did not objectify their parts, qualities, modes, and relations could not construct concepts, not even generic concepts of those natural objects since, to that end, in a plurality of kindred objects the traits common to them all must be recognized. Nor is objective language conceivable without concepts; for a nonconceptual objective language would be a language in which each individual object had a linguistic sign of its own, which is practically impossible. Hence language is of necessity conceptual. Its words—nouns as well as verbs and even the signs indicating relations—must express general notions, with the one exception of proper names, strictly speaking. In such general terms singular objects and situations are expressed, thanks to a particularizing and determining procedure which resorts to diverse and effective means.[1] Language is at once the result and the condition of intentionality as a normal function. For objectifications naturally tend to express themselves; and what has been intellectually objectified subsists only by being laid down in perceivable signs. Previous to its communicating function—which is of cardinal importance for the constitution of intentional community—language thus serves as an indispensable instrument for the evolution of individual intentionality, although the actual structure of languages doubtless depends on their use as instruments for intercommunication.

In short, the first and decisive step toward the constitution of what is called humanity is, in my opinion, the intentional and objectifying consciousness. This consciousness of objects is, at the same time, the consciousness in which a subjective center is shaping and acting. There is no man who is not a subject, and there is no subject without objects.

I cannot afford to venture in these brief notes on any conjectures regarding the animal mind; let me only say that higher animals, as appears from their intelligent behavior, execute some objectifications, if only precariously and fleetingly, but that they do not succeed in splitting up consciousness into a firm subjective center and a stable, well-defined, objective world, neatly standing out against the ever-changing, continuous flow of sensations and states. In fact, how could the process of objectification progress in the animal mind without an adequate stock of objective signs? With the help of the linguistic tool, intentional consciousness effects the analysis of reality and puts reality together again in concepts. Intentional consciousness may be very advanced and yet not be accompanied by the spiritual component. However, increasing objectification, a maze of objects accumulating around the subject, and habitual intercourse with these eventually bring about the spiritual attitude. This attitude consists in dealing with objects for their own sake and in recognizing the right of each object according to its peculiar nature. In a merely intentional attitude consciousness gives objects to a subject; in the spiritual attitude the subject gives itself to objects, conforms to them. But the spiritual attitude I shall treat later.

The objectifying or intentional character of consciousness suffices to account for the peculiar and specific quality of human coexistence. What characterizes this coexistence and radically distinguishes it from animal life in common is its being an intentional community. The primary distinction between these two ways of living-together does not consist in a different quality of the affective ties; indeed, in some animal families we find a keener and more tender affection and more loving care of the parents for their offspring than in certain human families. Nor is the distinction due to the spiritual factor which, in fact, is missing in certain human associations. That human coexistence is an intentional community is enough for it to represent a type infinitely removed from any type of animal congregation. Animals consort with others of their kind in groups of different descriptions, characterized by biological and also by psychic intercourse, the psychic elements, however, being of a type immediately connected with life. But no matter how intensely this stream of vital and psychic relations may flow between the members, their aggregate will be far from resembling a human community, even one of the lowest rank, provided the latter is a truly human community, that is, an association of intentional beings. In an animal group, beings are joined that have no objectified inner world and are not endowed with an instrument of expression suited for communicating this world and thus making it a common property of the group. But it is exactly this which occurs in a human association and imparts to it the essential quality for which it may be called an intentional community.

Any reality which has been objectified and fixed in signs of an objective meaning by a member of the group is being shared, wholly or to a considerable part, with the companions and becomes the property of all. In exchange for his particular contribution each individual receives that of all the others, present and past. Something like a totalization or generalization of objectifying consciousness takes place. It is of cardinal importance that different generations live together; for thanks to this fact the common intentional consciousness becomes the sum total of present and past and accumulates all objectifications accomplished by the group in the course of time. Here we have an actual integration and a sort of inheritance that has little to do with biological inheritance or with the transmission of individual experiences. Even the latter doubtless occurs in certain domains of the animal kingdom in the form of a transmission restricted to what an animal may observe in its dealings with its parents and fellow creatures. The inner world of an animal is dim, and the larger part of it remains hermetically sealed. The human world, on the other hand, grows ever clearer, opens up more and more, and develops into a world of explicit contents which are largely communicable. This then is the second instance or second stage of the peculiar historicity of man. It is brought about through accumulation of experiences objectified in the course of time within the intentional community which is a community in time. The uninterrupted actual interchange of objectified experiences is strengthened and amplified by the powerful succor of objective culture, which imparts material fixation to many of the most valuable human objectifications and thereby not only preserves them in their original meaning but also sets up frames and grooves, models and patterns, procedures and goals for future developments of the intentional function.

Objective culture consists of the unending succession of man's creations which, surrounding him on all sides, constitute his environment; an environment which is something like his own inner being materialized and externalized: art, religion, law, and the State, with all the regular forms of coexistence: science and philosophy, technology, etc.—all these taken as "objects," i.e., as fixed and, so to speak, materialized creations. In the case of art we have the works of art; in that of religion: dogmas, current and traditional beliefs, religious books, buildings, and rites of the cult; in the case of law and all that refers to social and state life: institutions, constitutions, and, in general, the regulations of law and usage; in that of science and philosophy: the whole of expressed doctrinal content.

It cannot, of course, lie in the intention of this article to give even a rough characterization of objective culture; nor is this indispensable for the present purpose. Let us just recall the complex function of objective culture as the specific "medium" of man. To begin with, it gives material and concrete existence to objectifications which possess a meaning of their own and fulfill their purpose by merely acting through their presence: paintings, statues, religious doctrines, scientific theories. Secondly, objective culture stimulates, instructs, and guides the subjective activity, individual and collective. The esthetic sense is educated and prepared for creative work through contemplation of realized art. Generally speaking, a man keeps up and improves his faculties by frequent contact with outstanding or merely adequate works in his field. Thirdly, some cultural objectivities, such as the juridical ones, serve to establish a certain order in human communities, be it for the sake of mere convenience or with a view to higher values, such as justice.

Other cultural realizations, the technological for instance, increase the effective power of man, his rule over nature, and thereby not only his command of the material world but also his freedom and the triumph of the spiritual principle over any kind of natural coercion. Furthermore, we must not forget that culture is a veritable medium and atmosphere for man, which surrounds and enwraps him on all sides. No effects of nature reach him directly; all have to filter through the cultural medium; all are perceived, interpreted, and even felt in terms of culture. It would be interesting to examine what still exists in our body—down to its inmost biological recesses—that has not been touched, modified, and influenced by culture. It is part of the fate of man that he cannot jump across his culture, any more than he can jump across his own shadow.

But as I have said before, the general problem of objective culture

cannot be treated here. We are only concerned with the partial problem of the origin or generating principle of culture as a succession
of objectifications. We maintain that identity or strict correlation
obtains between the constitutive principle of man and that of culture.

The expressing activity in its first stage, before it has turned into
a vehicle of communication, is nothing but a spontaneous prolonga-
tion of the objectifying attitude, as can easily be observed in children. The act of naming or graphically representing things immediately follows upon perceiving them; it is, as it were, an explicit acknowledgment that things are, that they are there. The
initial sources of language and of art are one and the same, and
they ought to be related not to special values but to a spontaneous
exteriorization of something inward. Only later does language become a useful instrument of communication and for this purpose
work out a uniform system of signs, while representation assumes
an esthetic character. Hence the common root of the expressing and
the representing activities is the same as that of the human quality
as such: objectification.

It is easy to show that this also holds for any of the products which
jointly form the world of objective culture. A presumption or a
conviction assumes concrete form in a myth or dogma. The vision
of a certain social order, desirable for its practical convenience or
because it satisfies other needs or aspirations, engenders the objectification of this order in what we may call its pure geometric
form or linear pattern, that is, in the norms of usage or the decrees
of law. Such vision exists first in the minds of people as an aspiration and then in the sphere of outer objectifications as a cultural
entity. The same happens in the field of technology. To give an
example: Cognizing objectification, in which the natural world
is given as a world of objects, does not stop, as noted before, at whole
objects but proceeds to objectify their parts, modes, qualities, and
relations. In this continued analysis of reality the objectifying acts
ascribe identity and being to each aspect they consider, a process
which later evolves the conceptual syntheses. An interest, a need,
or a convenience initiates some definite synthesis of these concepts
for the purpose of creating, imaginarily first and materially thereafter, an instrument capable of satisfying that interest, need, or convenience. The random use as a hammer of any hard and heavy
natural object presupposes an examination of the object in the
light of pre-existent concepts pertinent to hammering. That is to

say, the object is found suitable for hammering, since it possesses the distinctive features of weight, hardness, resistance, handiness, etc., whereas the rest of its qualities, all that is irrelevant to hammering, is disregarded. When the tool is being made, this forgetting about what is not pertinent to the pursued end assumes reality, and only the constellation of concepts that fits the purpose is materialized. Cognizing objectifications are actuated by a motive or interest: existence. Something vaguely present in the form of a state or a merely lived sensation becomes an object when its presence is perceived, when it passes from being lived to being known, when it is ascribed existence.

The agency ascribing existence to states and sensations is the "I," the subjective pole of consciousness which is born simultaneously with the object because it is nothing but the faculty of objectifying, of being conscious of something. Of all contents of perception the one that is hardest to objectify is one's own subject as a totality, as identical with itself throughout its different situations in space and time; for the subject cannot see itself as it sees other objects, and the royal road to knowledge lies through vision. That is why the "you" precedes the "I," and why on the lowest stages of human life collectivity prevails over individuality.

It would be erroneous to ascribe to this fact any spiritual meaning, by interpreting it as unselfishness; it merely discloses a deficient objectification by the individual of his own individuality. While all objectification of a cognizing character is based on the fact that something is given or present, cultural objectifications spring from the impression that something ought to be, that an inner synthesis, a subjective objectification which has formed around a desire, an interest, a need, etc., must be materialized in order to serve the inner purposes of the "I."

The external objectification comes about in many different ways. If the thing that is to be made is a poem, if someone believes he must give concrete form in poetry, said with words, to certain visions and emotions, the work is in principle done by one individual intentional consciousness and its faculty of expression. But certainly not exclusively so; for the objective existence of a poem does not depend solely on the fact that someone makes it but also requires an opportunity of being heard, that is, of arousing in other minds identical or similar or kindred objectifications to those in the mind of the author. This is a common trait of all cultural objects, that they are expressions and something beyond that. Mere expression may disregard the community of intentional beings; but cultural expressions *live* within a community. If an author's work remains unintelligible to the community, contemporary or future, to which he belongs, it is simply the expression of a single intentional consciousness. Such a work may be perceived and interpreted as a sign or signal of something going on within this consciousness, but it lacks the full external objectivity peculiar to objects of culture. These must speak by themselves without the necessity of referring to their creator or to the processes and circumstances of their creation.

More actively still the community interferes in other cultural orders. There are those cultural products which are literally collective creations, as conceptual and communicating language, for instance—that fruit of intentional community. There also is a kind of appropriation by the community through adoption: when a felicitous phrase or a very fortunate metaphor, a song or a saying—products of an individual imagination—rouse so strong an echo in the great masses that these feel they themselves have invented them. Without entering upon any detailed discussion of the relation between morality and the positive law, we may state that a moral need that is strongly felt by many members of the community produces in them the impression that it ought to be established as an objective norm. Such a moral need is apt to become embodied in regulations or in laws; for whenever it is expressed by someone it meets with the consent of all. In short, we objectify what is present or existing, by recognizing it to have presence or existence; and thus we set up the natural world. And we objectify internally certain complexes around motives, interests, or values, and then realize these complexes (objectifying them again, now externally); and thus we create the sphere of culture. These are interdepending pursuits responding to the same principle, the objectifying principle—that mainspring of the peculiar character of man and of culture alike.

The three instances we have so far examined are intentional consciousness, intentional community, and culture. Their common root, we have seen, is objectification. These three instances function in close solidarity. Each benefits from the other two; each exerts, in a constant interaction, a powerful influence upon the others; and they form, in a way, one complex in which, as a rule, it is impossible to distinguish the contributions of each of them, although intentional consciousness forms the cardinal and primary element. Only

in an intentional community do the phenomena of expression develop into conceptual and communicating language. Even the intentional consciousness of each individual is indebted for most of
its contents to the intentional community, the storehouse of the objectifications achieved by the species; and it is indebted not only for
the accomplished objectifications but also for the instigation to
contrive others of its own accord. Culture, as we have seen above,
originates from the endeavors—different as to scope and manner—
of the individuals as such, and from the action of the community.
The ensuing cultural objectifications correspond to the several
functional modes or directions of the objectifying faculty. Each of
these subjective functional modes or directions is educated and forti-
fied through intercourse with the respective cultural objects (the
artistic faculty through frequent contemplation of works of art,
etc.). Moreover, from the several branches of objective culture
evolve certain canons or rules, apt to guide the subjective activity in
the corresponding field, rules which are unwittingly or deliberately
absorbed during a man's apprenticeship.

Even as it lies in the essence of intentional consciousness to sally
forth from itself, to express itself, and to engender intentional community, so intentional consciousness and intentional community
together fulfill the spontaneous and permanent function of creating
objective culture. For acquisition of what is given in objective terms
is tantamount to cultural objectification, i.e., to the effective and
materialized creation of subjective syntheses which have arisen in
view of certain ends or purposes. One side or aspect of intentional
consciousness consists in its perceiving reality and its own "I" as
objects and, furthermore, possessing the capacity of objectifying
parts, qualities, and modes within whole objects. This side or aspect is paralleled by another in which intentional consciousness is
occupied with projecting certain of its syntheses outside itself.

Perceptive objectification, as noted above, recognizes the existence
of the objectified entity. To objectify in an act of perception means
to recognize that something is, to lift it out of the blind flow of
experience, and to ascribe being to it as an external cultural objectification. The creation of objects of culture is based on an impression
or notion, be it vague or distinct, that something ought to be, this
something having shaped within the mind around some end or
purpose.

Consider a painting or a poem, or the plan of an institution or of
a machine. The individual's conception of such works is accom-

panied by a desire or a decision to realize them in the outer world because they appear convenient, useful, or valuable. Sometimes the conception emerges in the mind more or less perfect and entire with an intrinsic tendency to exteriorization, as, for example, when a poem is conceived and written at the same time.

In other cases, what is there first is a mere intention of supplying something that serves such and such an end. Then the resolution of producing in the outer world something suitable for a definite purpose precedes the conception or pattern of the object—for instance, when we decide to make a tool for a certain special operation and then, through trial and error and calculations, arrive at the conception of such a tool.

But this difference is accidental and of little importance. What matters is that we have in all these cases formed a subjective synthesis around a purpose, a synthesis accompanied by a tendency to exteriorization or by an impression or conviction that it ought to be realized. Of course, the creation of the external object of culture as such—the written and understandable poem, the constructed tool ready to be used—requires a series of technical operations which effect the transition from the conception to the materialization.

Intentional community enriches and supports the intentional consciousness of each individual to such a degree that today a solitary intentional consciousness is hardly conceivable. And similarly, objective culture serves as a frame and a multiform vessel for individual and collective life, which we should be at a loss to picture without the assistance of cultural objectifications. Objective culture is the proper environment of intentional life—a medium or environment composed of as many special media or environments as there are cultural capacities in the subject. The diffuse artistic faculty of the common man, as well as the special vocation or capability of the creative artist, the critic, or the connoisseur find their proper and adequate medium in existing art and are to a certain degree determined by its level. The same holds for the other cultural capacities. They benefit in most varied ways from previous achievements, using them as springboards toward new, similar realizations which otherwise would be impossible or would require exceptional efforts, if not the power of genius.

Intentional community is also essentially historical. But this historicity becomes more intense and profound through the presence and action of cultural objectifications. The historicity of intentional community by itself consists in accumulation through direct tradition, which is alive and operative in the reality of each moment. The accumulation and tradition of objective culture with its firm stratified structure and the round and neat outline of its forms impart to intentional community stability and protection against possible deviations and losses or lapses which otherwise would be inevitable.

In yet another way, objective culture makes itself felt. It imparts to intentional community the character of society by superimposing upon the spontaneous, mutable reality of such a community objectifications of a specifically social order, i.e., all those institutions and regulations which bring order into human coexistence. Collective human life needs these two elements, intentional community and society. The first is a mere aggregation of intentional unities, based on the spontaneous tendency of intentionality to sally forth from itself and communicate with others. The second is based on the capacity of external objectification. A rudimentary society begins to emerge as soon as the individuals have gained objective perception of their community. But socialization consists, above all, in an imposition of a whole system of cultural objectifications—the social institutions and regulations—upon the shapeless mass of intentional community which comprises all the biological and emotional ties and relations.

If the community component dwindles, collective life disintegrates or degenerates into a dry and abstract formalism. If the society component breaks down, collective life relapses into crude primitive ways. Although this point cannot be discussed here, we may at least mention that any primacy of the community over its individual members goes hand in hand with a deficient objectification of the subject by himself, with a hitch in the objectifying process. In a fully humanized state, community is community of individuals, a community with preponderance of the individual factor. Absorption of the individual by the community (the ideal and device of all totalitarianism) spells obliteration of the objectification of each individual by himself—an act which doubtless holds first rank among cognizing objectifications and marks one of the decisive steps in the making of man.

Here we have reached the point where we can no longer postpone asking what spirit is and which role it plays. To identify intentional consciousness, individual or collective, with spirit is in my opinion erroneous. If it is done, another word must be found to denote an attitude or function which does not coincide with mere intentional life and which we are wont to call spiritual. Intentional life, even on a very high level and when performed by a being of complex and agile intellectual capacity, may yet take place in a sphere of interests closely connected with individual man; it may serve his immediate egoistic purposes and remain oblivious of those sublime ends and interests which are called spiritual. Nor is it impossible for certain forms of objective culture to develop in this lower sphere. Generally speaking, cultural objectifications do not necessarily involve the spiritual factor. External or material objectification is possible without spiritual acts.

Intentionality in itself suffices to open a gulf between man and animals. "How does an animal see its environment?" a contemporary psychologist, Aloys Müller, asks himself. His answer is this:

It certainly sees neither persons nor trees nor houses nor stones nor any such entities. For these perceptions imply, as we know, a deposit of knowledge which animals do not possess. Animals only see complexes of color qualities. But curiously enough, such complexes an animal does not see as independent objects existing in its environment in a spatial order side by side with other things. The best description of the way an animal sees may be as follows. There are modern paintings which to a spectator standing very close show nothing but color blotches. Objects and a spatial order become distinguishable from some distance only. Perhaps an animal sees his environment in the way we see these paintings at close hand: as a totality of color qualities which, to be sure, possess extension. For an animal something stands out from this complex with the qualification of distance only when it moves.

This is one way of conceiving of animal perception. It is however, open to discussion whether the infra-human cognizing mind can be reduced to a single type, as though perception were the same in infusoria, in an insect, a fish, a chicken, a dog, and a chimpanzee. There probably exists in the animal kingdom an ascending line along which mere stimuli are more and more approaching perceptions yet without ever developing into full perception of objects as a permanent normal function and a steadily accumulating activity. The animals nearest to man seem to execute some objectifications, but precariously and sporadically, without developing a stable intentional consciousness. The objectifying faculty produces—and at the same time requires for its consolidation and progress—objective language and intentional community as well as objective culture, all of which are exclusive with man. With this we have already fixed a neat borderline between man and animal and need not resort to spirit, as does Scheler.

According to Scheler, man has a "world" in contrast to animals which possess only an environment of resistances; but this "world" is, in the first instance, a mere collection of objectifications, that is to say, simply a result of the intentional activity. With the transition from the blurred consciousness of states, characteristic of animals, to consciousness split up into subject and object, there indeed appears in reality a thing without precedent, comparable to nothing else. A part of reality reflects and embraces all the rest; an eye is born which looks intelligently at the world; a principle of universality arises in a particular being, although this universality is still limited and restricted to the cognizing sphere.

The length of this chapter does not allow me to describe and discuss what I think is the secret spring at the root of the intentional or objectifying faculty. Let me make only one point. The function which renders objectification possible and sets it going is the same as the one which later gives rise to explicit judgments. That is to say, it is owing to certain implicit and primary judgments that states and sensations, the shapeless and blindly lived psychic matter, are elevated to the category of objects. To be given, or to perceive, objects is to recognize something as present and existing, i.e., to attribute being and consistency to something. Objectification and judgment go hand in hand; to know objects is always to recognize, and to recognize is to judge. Already in the vague and undifferentiated preintentional consciousness, the individual focus begins to shape as a capacity for judging. But I must leave this point as it now stands, without proof or development; or I should be led too far away from the present purpose.

Intentional consciousness gives objects; it presents them to the subject as alien instances confronting him. Once the subject is well rooted in this world of objects and accustomed to objectivity, he apprehends objects as existing *by themselves*. But at first he manipulates them exclusively for the benefit of his individual and concrete subjectivity in an attitude of wholesale, ingenuous egoism. This egoism does not cease to be egoism when it extends its scope and becomes the egoism of a family, a clan, or a caste, or of any definite group the solidarity of whose members entails or presupposes an actual profit for each of them. But frequent intercourse with objective instances which confront the subject and make their autonomous existence constantly felt eventually produces the impression that each of those objects is something in and for itself; that, because they exist, there abides in them a certain right of their own;

that they are not merely minor figures in a drama in which the perceiving object plays the lead but that, from its own point of view, each is the center and protagonist. This new objective turn toward objects constitutes the spirit. Intentional consciousness *gives* objects to the subject; in the spiritual attitude the subject *gives himself* to the objects, turning entirely toward them.

To perceive intentionally is to have cognizing perception, to be aware that objects have being. To perceive spiritually means to add to cognizing perception—which is unconcerned with our ulterior behavior toward objects—the conviction that each object possesses a right of its own.

Herewith, objectification is consummated and carried to its furthest limit, the instance of right being added to that of fact. The merely intentional attitude apprehends objects but leaves them in a state of subordination to the apprehending subject, who uses them throughout as instruments in his service. The spirit executes a "Copernican revolution" by turning toward objects disinterestedly.

Acts of intelligence as well as the creation of cultural objects are possible without the intervention of spiritual instances. Mere communication of intentional contents, the contrivances of primitive technology, knowledge gained with a view to application, social regulations serving the sole purpose of rendering coexistence possible—all these are, in principle, achievements alien to the spirit. Spiritual activities and spiritual creations are realized by the subject when he operates not as a concrete and individual empirical center but as a universal subject, i.e., as a representative or agent of the ideal community of all persons created equal. In the spiritual attitude the subject may act against his spontaneous inclination and individual convenience and stand up for universal interests or values because he feels he is part of a collective spiritual subjectivity infinitely superior to his particular individuality.

Any act thus qualified must be called spiritual, no matter to which sphere of life it belongs. The merchant who might easily and safely cheat his customer but uses just weight and measure only because he feels it *ought to be thus* executes a spiritual act just as does the artist who creates beauty or the scholar who seeks truth. Spirit recognizes in everything existing a right of its own: not one and the same right in all things but a right determined by the hierarchy of entities and even of situations. Absolute right inheres only in entities of absolute dignity, i.e., in human persons. This principle is recognized by all great ethical doctrines and in the juridical and political order, where the superior forms of democratic rule aspire to realize it in practical institutions—without being opposed, however, to increased socialization, provided this leaves intact the absolute right of the human person. Thus intentionality and spirituality respectively recognize the existence and being of objects and the right of objects. From these two principles in conjunction man in his fullness is born as the one universal being, a part, no doubt, of reality but a part in which the whole is reflected and gathered together: observer, thinker, and conscience of the universe.

In short, I hold that the essence of humanity lies in the objectifying faculty. Objectification is among the greatest enigmas and the most important and surprising facts to be found in reality. Before this faculty appears, each entity or cell of reality is what it is without reduplicating itself or getting entangled with others except through natural ties, physical, biological, or instinctive; it reposes in itself without clear awareness of itself or the rest of creation. Owing to objectification, there arises an entity, called man, who possesses, in a cognizing way, that which he is not, and who also takes possession of himself. This is enough to upset the natural order and to initiate an unheard-of new order.

This objectifying entity, man, apprehends other entities. He apprehends himself. He amplifies, by means of objective communication, his individual consciousness to make of it a collective, accumulating, historical consciousness. He creates from his own substance a new reality side by side with natural reality: objective culture. He endows the cultural objects with intentions and meanings and maintains a continuous and most diversified intercourse with them. He performs spiritual acts in which he projects himself unreservedly toward objects and voluntarily recognizes the singular right residing in each object as well as in his own objectified self (the latter being a man's sense of his own dignity). Through the workings of the spirit he rises above himself, above his "here" and "now," above his concrete individuality and particularity, eventually to establish himself as consciousness of the whole, able to live with a view to universality.

Not all objective culture is of spiritual origin. A good many cultural realizations spring from mere intentionality guided by subjective interests, from the objectifying faculty which is yet alien to the disinterested turn toward objects. But the spiritual attitude holds sway in vast sectors of culture and tends to prevail upon the originally alien and rebellious parts. That is to say, the nonspiritual aspects of culture are being "colonized" by the spirit.

At the bottom of all this, as we have repeatedly stated, lies objectification, a function that involves—as its components and simultaneous facts—illumination of the hazy preintentional consciousness, splitting up of consciousness into a subjective and an objective pole, and the emergence of the faculty of judging, although at this stage only dim and inarticulate judgments occur. All this may be regarded as a single complex phenomenon or as the several sides of one whole. For to have objects means to judge implicitly that something is and is present, and presupposes the existence of one who has those objects, i.e., of someone who cannot be what he is unless he is able to be aware of those presences or existences. To be a man is the same as to be capable of judging. Any progress in humanization is founded on an increase of the objectifying and judging capacities, the sources of objective culture as well as of the spiritual attitude.[2]

Within the limits of this article I cannot discuss the bearing on the historical cultures of what has been expounded here; but I will say this. The fact that, out of the many cultures which have appeared in history, only three survive—the Indian, the Chinese, and the Occidental—seems to suggest that these three possess some particular advantage over the others. In my judgment, this superiority consists in the fact that the three, in contrast to all others, contain an answer (each a radically different one, of course) to the most profound and permanent questions and needs of man. Man is not only the one being that objectifies, he is also a being that objectifies endlessly and untiringly, and he needs the goal and lodestar of a supreme and absolute object to set his mind at rest. Every culture is likely to have aspired to satisfying this need. But while others were unable to supply more than myths, which in the course of time wear out and lose their charm, or halfway goals that proved unsatisfactory, the three mentioned above have each found a great clue or goal which has determined their organization. The clue of Indian culture is the *whole,* the cosmic infinity into which the individual yearns to dissolve, divesting his separate personal existence of all value. In traditional Chinese culture, the clue is the *social reality,* that vast community in which the ancestors live together with their descendants and rule over them, an immense family, held in religious reverence, of which the State is only a political continuation, and which interlaces, through the ties of magic, with the supernatural powers. Occidental tradition has always regarded as the last goal and supreme reality the "I" *qua* soul or person, that is, *qua* absolute entity, deviser of perfect order, and carrier of supreme dignity.

In Indian culture, and likewise in Chinese, the individual achieves reality by giving himself up and merging in a reality he regards as infinitely superior and as the one valid goal or end. This premature resignation and abandonment of the principle of individuality cannot but slow down and weaken the process of the objectification of the "I," whereas the realization of the ultimate goal of the Occident—the "I" as person or absolute subject, as soul or spiritual "I" —requires constant progress in self-objectification and persistence in that objectifying exertion which, as we have seen, constitutes man as such.

From the standpoint here taken, it becomes clear that the success of Occidental man is not an ephemeral historical accident but a consequence of the fact that the course of his culture coincides sufficiently well—at any rate, much better than that of any other culture, dead or living—with the general trend assigned to man by his inmost essence. Despite its limitations and its frequent aberrations, the Occident holds the keys of the future. To those who reproach it with lacking the cosmic sense of India or the social sense of China, one might reply that Occidental culture is not unlikely to accept in due time the holiness of cosmic mystery and to realize the ideal of the solidarity of humanity. For the person taken in his plenitude is a complex of disinterested and reverent intentions toward all that exists. Recognition of the equality of persons and realization of the ideal community of persons is by no means alien to him. Such a cosmic and social union, however, Occidental man will try to accomplish not through annihilation and surrender of his own "I" but, on the contrary, through an ascent from his intentional individual "I" to the spiritual "I." In the course of this ascent, the "I," growing in strength and depth, evolves within himself the person in the image of the personal God who is exclusively characteristic of Occidental culture.

These hypotheses—more they could not be—are borne out by many conspiring signs. Only the Occident is concerned with the concept of time; only the Occident really has history. The individual's flinging himself into the cosmic or social whole—characteristic of the other two great living cultures—is instantaneous; moreover, it is already implied in the central attitude of those cultures, whereas the empirical "I"—the imperfect subject, chained to nature in many ways—is aware, and conceives, of the person as an object to be realized, a duty or task. The process of history has been defined by the greatest Occidental thinkers as a march toward "humanity" (I should prefer to say "humanization") or toward freedom, or again as a progressive realization of the most exalted values. All this signifies nothing if not the gradual triumph of the personal or spiritual principle over concrete individual man who lives immersed in his particular aims and interests. Occidental man believes in time, in history, in progress because his being is given to him as something latent and potential. He endeavors to realize it in time and in history, valiantly taking upon himself the long task of giving existence to what ought to be, of implanting the ideal in the real.

India has worked out a grandiose metaphysics, while the other disciplines into which we are wont to divide philosophy are sporadically developed. The reason is that logic, ethics, and esthetics are meditations on the faculties that shape and consolidate the person in his intercourse with reality. But Indian culture holds such intercourse to be nothing but dream and vanity, for the one thing needed is the integration of the subject into the whole. Metaphysics is concerned with this integration. Metaphysics is conceived, however, not only as knowledge but also, and above all, as practice, as a way to salvation, the gate through which one enters infinite totality. In China formalism and ritual are predominant and all-pervading; they assume a thousand shapes, all very surprising to Europeans. The innumerable threads of an intricate social web knotted in the course of many centuries imprison the individual on all sides and reduce him to a coordinated link within a community which only as an interknit totality possesses value, nay sanctity.

The objectifying will of the Occident, its zest to obtain distinct and exact visions of things, its resolve to maintain intact, in the face of all such visions, the power of the subject have no equal in the Orient. Only Occidental man defines, that is, only he arrives—or believes he arrives, or is in need of arriving—at clear-cut concepts, identical with themselves and hierarchically distributed into rigorous systems of thought. Indian metaphysical systems are mainly interpretations, that is, versions, of traditional wisdom; they give expression to a truth which may be set forth in various and always fragmentary manners. China's greatest metaphysical work, the *Tao*, eludes any exact determination and any attempt at definition or clear characterization, whereas Western philosophy has, since its beginnings, advanced theses each of which claims to be the only truthful one. The being of things, we have been told, consists of water, air, the *apeiron,* Ideas, matter with its forms . . . Occidentals are uncompromising and intolerant because they do not for a moment doubt that there exists one true doctrine and many wrong ones. The Orient, save for transitory exceptions, has been tolerant. The faithful of Oriental creeds, for example, are partial to "religious congresses," an idea impossible to occur to Europeans, although they may consent to attend such congresses.

Good or bad, right or wrong, Occidental man goes on objectifying indefatigably. He never tires of coining concepts, of making things. His objectifying urge tends to lead him astray. At times he thinks he was born to fabricate countless things. But he continues, often inadvertently, in his self-objectification. He continues to forge in the dark smithy of his soul "the one thing needed."

(Translated from the Spanish by Helene Weyl.)

NOTES

1. About some aspects of linguistic determination through the situation cf. the author's essay "Comunicacion y situacion" in *Revista de Filologia Hispanica* (Instituto de la Filologia de la Universidad de Buenos Aires) 1943, 244–250.
2. This anthropological doctrine is closely connected with the metaphysical standpoint expounded in my articles "Programa de una filosofía" and "Transcendencia y valor" in *Papeles para una filosofía* (Buenos Aires, Losada, 1945). Cf. also the article "Intuición y discurso" in the same book and the note "Personas y trascendencia" in my book *Filosofía de la persona* (Buenos Aires, Losada, 1944).

XIX

IDEOLOGICAL MAN IN HIS RELATION TO SCIENTIFICALLY KNOWN NATURAL MAN

F. S. C. NORTHROP

IN the traditional Orient throughout its entire history and in the traditional West through Hegel, the importance of ideas held in common by men in ordering their social institutions was taken for granted as evident. Following Marx, however, and because of early mechanistic physics, neurological behavioristic psychology, and positivistic social science many competent students of historical and social phenomena were led to believe that particular economic or other environmental stimuli determining a particular behavioristic response are alone significant in the human behavior of either the individual or the social group. Consequently, the prevalent conclusion has arisen that ideological factors are at best mere verbal pseudo-rationalizations after the fact and at worst insignificant if not completely irrelevant. It becomes important, therefore, that an examination be made of the relation between ideological factors and biological factors in human behavior and its attendant cultural institutions, in the light of intuitive, introspective, radical scientific empiricism and of contemporary neurological and behavioristic psychological science.

Although the present inquiry is concerned primarily with the latter of these two scientific and philosophical approaches to human nature, it is not assumed that the "theoretic component" of human nature which is designated by experimentally verified neurological and behavioristic psychological theory exhausts the nature of man. There is also the "aesthetic" component of his nature, known intuitively or directly by immediate apprehension. Both approaches to and components of human nature are equally ultimate, important, and scientific. An adequate and complete conception of man must correlate and combine the intuitive, direct, purely empirical, and hence scientific, way of knowing man with the more theoretical, indirect, and experimental way of knowing him. Francisco Romero, in the previous chapter, examines the relation between ideas and human nature by the first of these two essential scientific and philosophical methods; the present inquiry does it by means of the second. At its end the results of the two methods of inquiry will be related.

Cultural institutions are, in part at least, the result of human behavior. Human behavior is conditioned by neurological processes. Comparative neurology shows that the nervous systems of men in so-called primitive cultures are practically identical with those of men in so-called more sophisticated cultures. It follows, therefore, that any conclusions which we reach concerning the relation of ideas to nervous systems will hold for any people in any culture.

The behaving human being is a member of society. If our problem is to be precisely formulated, it is important therefore that we begin with the problems which confront men in society.

THE ANALYSIS OF SOCIAL PROBLEMS

Social problems, unlike those of natural science, raise two fundamentally different kinds of questions. Of social phenomena we ask not merely "What are they, in fact?" but also "What ought they to be?" For example, the factual state of affairs in Western Europe at the present moment is reasonably well known by all the major peoples concerned—Western Europeans, Russians, and Americans alike. The deadlocks in the conferences of foreign ministers arise not over what is the case but over whether Marxist communism, free-enterprise capitalism, or parliamentary socialism is to define the form of what ought to be the case.

Theories of social science of the latter type, which designate the form of society at which one is aiming, are termed appropriately normative social theories. Theories, on the other hand, which designate the order of society in fact, may be called factual social theories. Since normative social theories present the real difficulty in any attempt to clarify the relation between ideological and biological factors in any culture, it is to normative social theory that this inquiry will direct attention.

That there are normative social theories has been amply demonstrated by the other chapters of this volume. The existence of normative social theories is a fact which even factual social theories must include in their subject matter.

The fashionable notion of the moment is, to be sure, to the contrary. Again and again one hears it said that normative social theories are pseudo-rationalizations after the fact, merely giving later verbal expression to particular social events brought about in a causal manner by previous particular events of a nonideological character. Among these nonideological causes economic factors are frequently given a primary place.

Several considerations must give one pause before embracing this popular thesis. First, even for directly observable contemporary social changes, none of the social sciences has laws of a causal type, like those of physics, enabling one to deduce the state of a social system tomorrow from its state today. Nevertheless, this is what one must have before there are scientific grounds for asserting that social events are caused by any previous specified events.

Second, the science of economics in neither its Anglo-American-Austrian nor its Marxist formulation is able to infer causally a future state of even the economic factors in the social system from a present state of the economic factors.[1] This means that there is as yet no scientific justification for saying that even the present economic factors in society are due solely to economic causes. How much more unscientific then and unjustified must be the claim of the economic determinists who assert that all the manifestations of culture and history are due to economic causes.

Third, were it true that normative social theories are mere verbal pseudo-rationalizations after the social facts, then it would follow that there should never be cases of the normative social theory arising first and of the facts conforming to the theory coming afterward. Yet history abounds in such instances, as the many chapters of this book have indicated.

For example, Lenin had a great deal to do with the specific form which Russian society took on during and following the Bolshevik Revolution. Both by his words and by his deeds in accordance with and following upon his words, he made it clear that he was guided by the normative social theory of Karl Marx. The Bolshevik Revolution took place in Russia in 1918. The Marxist normative social theory, as Lenin himself tells us, was completed in its main outlines in 1848. A theory created in 1848 and used by Lenin to make the Revolution of 1918 take the actual form it took can hardly be called a merely verbal pseudo-rationalization after the fact.

The cultural history of Mexico during the past four hundred years is also in point. It shows [2] that when any one ideology or normative social theory captures either a majority of the people or the political and social leadership of a community, then the de facto behavior of the people and cultural and social institutions are transformed toward the form of social organization defined by the normative theory in question. Furthermore, when, for any reason whatever, the traditionally accepted normative theory becomes replaced by another normative theory—a change usually marked by a revolution—then cultural and social institutions regarded as good under the old ideology often become regarded as bad under the new. Witness the tearing down of the old cultural and social institutions that occurred in Mexico when the Aztec and Toltec temples were broken into fragments which were used to build the baroque Roman Catholic cathedral of the Spanish Colonial period, which still faces the Zocaló in Mexico City. Similarly, when, in the Mexican Revolution of 1810, the democratic laissez faire normative social theory, like that of the traditional United States, derived by the Mexicans from John Locke by way of Voltaire and the French Encyclopedists, replaced the Spanish hierarchical, monarchical, and theocentric normative social theory, democratic political institutions replaced aristocratic, monarchical ones, and the church property was nationalized and turned to secular rather than the traditional religious usages. To be specific, the very large building on Avenida Tacuba which originally was a nunnery became in the nineteenth century, and still remains, a school of mines. The building which housed the Dominican Order that subjected the leaders of the democratic Revolution of 1810 to the inquisition, became, and still remains, a school of medicine. Similar examples can be multiplied in Mexico without number.

But Mexico is not unique with respect to the institution-transforming role of embodied normative social theory. Such a transformation occurred in the New England colonies when the Divine Right of Kings normative social theory was rejected for the more Lockean democratic normative political theory in our Revolution of 1776. The Civil War in the United States, which was fought to determine in a test case whether the federal principle with its transfer of specified political sovereignty from the state governments to the Federal Government was to stand, is another instance. The triumph of the present British Labor Government with its parliamentary socialistic ideology, is another example. The manner, as Gray Dorsey indicates in a later chapter, in which the classical Chinese conception of law differs from the Western concept and finds the root of this difference in a normative social theory defined by Confucian philosophy demonstrates the role of normative theory in the traditional East as well as the West. It is not an accident that up to the Chinese revolution in the first part of the present century every Chinese who took the examinations necessary to become a Chinese lawyer or judge found the first and most important of the three examinations confronting him to be on the great Chinese philosophical classics.

Whatever may be the evils and the depressing consequences of the contemporary world situation, it nonetheless has one very important merit so far as contemporary social science is concerned. It makes it inescapably evident that passionately believed and behavioristically embodied normative social theories have to be reckoned with as decisively significant. It was not because of economic facts but because of basic ideological differences that the recent conferences of foreign ministers have ended in failure. The inescapable fact is that the crucial difficulties and problems in the social field turn not merely around problems of fact but also around ideological or normative issues.

Recent developments in the social sciences are pointing toward the same conclusion. As other chapters of this book indicate, many are finding that one cannot understand the objectively observed behavior and social rituals, even of such so-called primitive people as the Navaho Indians, unless one stays with these institutions and practices long enough to discover the philosophy and its attendant specific normative social theory from the standpoint of which the practices and social rituals of the people and their culture in question take on meaning. *The Meeting of East and West* has shown that this is true also of other peoples and cultures, both Oriental and Occidental, in the contemporary world. The role of embodied normative principles in making de facto social institutions and behavior in part at least what they are must be reckoned with.

All these considerations indicate that philosophical ideologies have a much more significant connection with human nervous systems and human behavior than many modern scientists, historians, and philosophers assigned to them. Contemporary neurological and behavioristic psychological science supports this conclusion.

THE NEUROLOGICAL AND BEHAVIORISTIC PSYCHOLOGICAL BASIS OF THE ORDERING OF SOCIETY BY MEANS OF IDEAS

What, specifically, does it mean to assert that human behavior and its attendant social institutions are significantly determined as to their form by ideas? For one thing, it means that human beings in society are reacting not merely to particular natural events occurring just once at a given time and place, but also to symbols, to socially conditioned symbols, which keep their meanings constant during the period of decades or centuries, as the case may be, in which a given normative social theory captures their faith and thereby serves as a norm for their social behavior and cultural institutions. But to say that human beings in society are reacting to natural events is to say that their behavior is determined by what is called a particular. And to say that human beings are reacting to symbols which keep their meanings constant through many events is to say that they are reacting to particulars which are the embodiments of universals.

This permits the basic problem of the present inquiry as a whole to be put more specifically. This problem has to do with the relation between ideological and biological factors in social institutions. It has been noted that social institutions embody normative social theories and that these normative social theories are a significant cultural factor in the ordering of social phenomena. But we have just noted, also, that normative social theories, unlike specific events in nature, exemplify universals rather than mere particulars. Thus our problem of determining the relation between cultural factors and biological factors in social science becomes that, in part at least, of determining the relation between the processes of biological systems and the responses of people to particulars which embody universals.

But there is a second, more specific, portion of our over-all problem. When a given people are captured in the realm of their normative beliefs by a specific normative social theory, this theory serves in their behavior as an end. In other words, it defines a purpose. This means that if we are to clarify the relation between cultural factors and biological factors in social phenomena, we must determine the relation of normatively defined purposes to biological systems.

Previous attempts to solve this problem have produced two conflicting conclusions. Nevertheless, these conflicting conclusions rest upon a common assumption.

The one conclusion was that since human behavior exhibits responses controlled by purposes defined in terms of remembered norms which are universals rather than merely responses determined by physical events which are particulars, therefore human behavior must have its basis in extra-empirically verifiable extrabiological factors, the assumption being that in the realm of the biological there are only mechanical causes and no purposes, and only particular events and no remembered events with their persistent meanings and hence no universals. This has been the answer of the Cartesian and Lockean dualists on the one hand and of the idealistic philosophers and the German social scientists, with their distinction between the *Naturwissenschaften* and the *Geisteswissenschaften,* on the other hand. Purpose, memory, and the existence of universals, they maintain, unequivocally establish the existence and reality of nonbiological minds or mental substances or of a priori autonomous moral principles in human nature and social phenomena.

The other conclusion, represented by the early mechanistic biologists, the behavioristic psychologists, and the positivistic British and French social scientists and philosophers, was that since biological systems and all natural systems as known by the methods of natural and biological science are mechanical systems responding to stimuli which are particulars rather than universals, therefore purpose is a mere appearance or epiphenomenon and all ideas are particulars. Hence, universals do not exist, being, like the normative theories defined in terms of them, mere semantically misunderstood symbols which, when correctly analyzed, turn out to be mere pseudo-rationalizations after the nonpurposefully caused particular social facts, or else expressions of purely hortatory and noncognitive significance.

No two schools of thought would seem to be more unqualifiedly opposed than these. Nevertheless, the important thing to note about these two traditional conflicting answers to our problem is the basic premise upon which they agree. This premise is that scientifically verified knowledge of biological and other natural systems provides no meaning for purposes, for universals, or for human behavior which is a response to and specified as to its form by a temporally persistent normative social theory.

What is the present scientific status of this basic premise?

Recent investigations by Warren S. McCulloch and Walter Pitts show that certain biological organisms, because of the character of the neuron nets in their nervous systems, must know universals, responding to symbols as their exemplars, rather than as mere particulars. Other investigations by Arturo Rosenblueth, Norbert Wiener, and Julian Bigelow show that not merely a human being but also robots with inverse or negative feedback mechanisms have purposes that define their behavior. When this purpose can be determined by information, such robots are called servomechanisms. In other words, the basic premise of both the traditional philosophical dualists and idealists and the traditional, supposedly scientific naturalists and mechanists to the effect that natural and biological systems can have neither knowledge of universals nor normatively defined and behavior-controlling purposes must be rejected.

The scientific demonstration of these exceedingly important conclusions of revolutionary significance for natural science, moral as well as natural philosophy, and for one's theory of the normative factor in law, politics, religion, and the social sciences must now concern us.

The traditional theories rest upon an oversimplified notion of activity in the nervous system. They assume that neurons are always put together in the nervous system to form a path in or through the nervous system which is noncircular.

Consider the simplest possible case of a noncircular ordering of the nerve cells called neurons; the case, namely, of one afferent neuron a joined by a synapse to one efferent or motor neuron b. Assume also that the signal which is the firing of neuron a entails the behavioristic response which is the firing of motor neuron b. Then, assuming no further action upon a, the signal which is the firing of a perishes as soon as a has fired. Hence the response of neuron b is a response to a signal which is a mere particular. The number of noncircularly ordered neurons does not alter this conclusion. It follows therefore that if there were no circular paths within or through the nervous system a signal (i.e., the firing of a neuron) at any point within it could signify only what happened at a particular instant, and there could be neither purpose nor memory, and every action would be a response to a mere particular.

Suppose, however, that, for example, there are five neurons $a, b, c,$ $d,$ and $e,$ ordered in a circle in such a way that the signal which is the firing of a fires $b,$ which signal in turn fires $c,$ which by way of the firing of d and e in turn fires $a.$ Then assuming the time it takes the impulses to succeed one another around the circuit is sufficient to permit any neuron to restore its energy from the metabolic processes of the body, the signal which is the firing of a or of any one of the five neurons in the circular net will not perish. It will thereby persist through time. In other words, it will signify a universal rather than a mere particular. Also, memory will be achieved.

More than a century ago Majendie and Bell had defined reflexive activity and indicated its circular path from a part of the body through the nervous system back to the same part of the body. Cannon and his collaborator Arturo Rosenblueth were the first to call attention to this homeostatic property and to attempt to extend the concept to relations between the body and the world about it. But it was R. Lorente de Nó [3] who postulated and demonstrated the action of what he called reverberating chains of neurons so arranged in closed paths that each excited the next one around the loop, so that the last excited the first. Thereby the activity continued to regenerate itself around the loop.

Suppose also that an afferent neuron from a sense organ such as the eye excites one of the neurons in the regenerative loop. And in order not to mix in the same sentence words from different worlds of discourse, let us assume in addition that the epistemic correlate [4] of the postulated momentary signal or impulse which is the firing of this efferent neuron is in the consciousness of the person in question, the sense datum or "idea" denoted by the word "blue." Assume also that an impulse from the eyes fires a neuron which is a member of a regenerative loop and that its impulse is the epistemic correlate of the introspected "idea" or datum "blue." It follows from the character of a regenerative loop that this impulse will be transmitted continuously without ceasing around the loop, so long as the energy necessary to restore the neurons to a capacity to fire is maintained by metabolic activity. In other words, as McCulloch has put the matter, "a train of impulses in a regenerative loop preserves the form of the fact without reference to the one particular moment when it was experienced." This insures that one has the form of the fact remaining constant over time through different particular events. Hence, as McCulloch and Pitts [5] have noted, one has (the epistemic correlate of introspected) universals.

In their first paper on the subject, entitled "A Logical Calculus of the Ideas Imminent in Nervous Activity," McCulloch and Pitts have demonstrated also that very simply related neural nets made up of such regenerative loops have all the formal properties of the primitive ideas and postulates of mathematics and deductive reasoning of Russell's and Whitehead's *Principia Mathematica*. In other words, human nervous systems can reason deductively and, insofar as they possess and use nervous nets with this formal character, they must reason deductively in precisely the manner specified by an analysis of deductive reasoning and calculation in modern mathematics and symbolic logic. No manifestation of the use of universals and of rationalistic reasoning with universals could be more pure or unequivocal than occurs in the deductively formulated theories of mathematical physics and mathematics. This means that deductively formulated theories, whether they be the normative theories of social science or the factual deductively formulated theories of natural science of a Newton, Willard Gibbs, or an Einstein, are not epiphenomena of no causal significance; they are not mere rationalizations after the facts. They are, instead, because of the formal properties of the neural nets with their impulses in the central nervous systems of human beings, scientifically verifiable factors and scientifically verifiable factors of causal significance.

McCulloch and Pitts, in their paper of 1943, proved one other exceedingly important theorem. This theorem is that any robot or organism constructed with regenerative loops possessing the afore-mentioned formal properties, and thereby being a Turing machine, "can compute any computable number or, what is the same thing mathematically, can deduce any legitimate conclusion from a finite set of premises." It is not an accident that John Von Neumann and Norbert Wiener, in their designing of two of the most powerful contemporary machines for carrying through mathematical deductions and calculations, and McCulloch and Pitts, in their theoretical and experimental studies of the human nervous system, have influenced one another.

A neuron in a regenerative loop of neurons may be so related to a motor neuron that it not merely fires the neurons in the circle of its own loop but also fires a motor neuron, thereby producing a specific overt response of the system. When this happens the constant universal becomes manifest in a particular again, as a specific event here and now, but conforming to its universal.

Furthermore, with many regenerative loops in a single nervous system there can be many universals, and by joining these loops universals can be related. Thereby the postulates of any deductively formulated theory in natural science or any normative theory in social science can be constructed. As long as this related system of impulses in reverberating circuits never fires a motor neuron, it remains a covert universal, a mode of possible action, rather than a particular, or an overt, act. But when it fires a neuron leading out of the circuit, it generates a particular objective event. Thus we are able to understand how an abstract normative social theory, itself a mere universal and a possible, can, if it gets into a nervous system so as to define the form of its activity, determine the pattern of firing of motor neurons; and so, literally, causally, and neurologically determine an overt, objective, social and institutional fact.

Furthermore, if such a deductively formulated set of postulates is a theory in natural science, it can generate behavioristic responses upon the part of a physicist which put the theory to an empirical test with respect to particular events or facts in nature. Thereby the universals of the deductively formulated theory considered as a possible become related to particulars in a manner which introduces the quantifiers "all" and "some" of Russell and Whitehead's logic of propositional functions into the formal properties of neurological human behavior. This occurs when, as McCulloch has put it, "the universals are referred to the semels (the onces)."

But there is nothing to prevent man from constructing several different deductively formulated theories in natural science or in normative social science out of the universals which regenerative loops provide for him. It may and does happen that the firing of a motor neuron prescribed by one normative social theory is proscribed by another. Witness the capitalistic and the communistic theories known to all representatives at contemporary international conferences. Two such theories in one brain make choice obligatory for action. McCulloch, in his James Arthur Lecture [6] delivered on May 2, 1946, put the matter as follows:

How can the structure of the nervous system embody the possibility of choice? Clearly, if each circuit had a path separate from any other path each would go its own way to its own end. But many paths share nervous parts and others would result in contrary acts of some effectors. A few, like swallowing and drawing breath, working at once would destroy us. Conflicts and mental collisions are barred by inhibitory links from one circuit to another so that when both are excited only one works. Thus the net embodies the possibility of these decisions.

In their 1947 paper McCulloch and Pitts have carried their neurological theory of our knowledge of universals even further. Newton, among others, pointed out that the structure of sensed space and time is relative to the particular observer and quite different from the structure of public, mathematical space and time to which the theories of experimentally verified physics refer. Einstein continues this Newtonian distinction. An adequate, neurologically grounded theory of knowledge must account, therefore, for the manner in which the knower distinguishes the public, indirectly verified, postulationally designated structures and entities of natural science from the immediately sensed ones. This entails an account of how the nervous system, which receives impulses epistemically correlated with images varying from moment to moment and standpoint to standpoint, arrives at invariant entities and relations holding constant through the changing, immediately apprehended particulars. McCulloch and Pitts have shown that such invariants can be achieved by complicated neural nets which scan and average over a group of transformations. In their 1947 paper they not merely draw complicated neural nets which have this capacity, but they also give empirical neurological evidence that certain neural nets of actual nervous systems are of this character. Clearly, human nervous systems have the formal properties necessary to know universals and to construct deductive theories in natural science and in factual and normative social science which can causally determine particular human behavior and, through that human behavior, the character of cultural institutions.

It remains to see how neurological systems can be purposeful systems.

In any scientific inquiry the question being asked is crucial. With respect to the study of any behaving system, be it man, beast, or machine, Rosenblueth, Wiener, and Bigelow [7] note that there are two different but complementary types of scientific inquiry which one may pursue. The first type of inquiry they term behavioristic; the second type functional.

In a behavioristic inquiry one ignores the inner constituents of, and their relations within, the system. One concentrates attention, instead, upon what happens with respect to the response of the system when, everything else being kept constant, some specific stimulus or input is brought to bear upon the system.

In a functional study, on the other hand, the central subject matter under investigation is the intrinsic structure and internal properties of the system itself. In such a study the input and output are used merely to throw light on the character of the system which connects the one to the other.

In the investigations of both (a) McCulloch and Pitts and (b) Rosenblueth, Wiener, and Bigelow the subject under investigation is a behaving, biological system. The former approach is functional, the latter behavioristic. Yet each throws light upon the other.

Behavior is defined by Rosenblueth, Wiener, and Bigelow as "any change of an entity with respect to its surroundings." The usefulness of such a broad definition appears only when behavior is classified.

Their first dichotomy is between that which is active and that which is passive. In passive behavior, "the object is not a source of energy; all the energy in the output can be traced to the immediate input . . ." Active behavior, on the other hand, is that "in which the object is the source of the output energy involved in a given specific reaction." The response of a motor neuron not recently fired and fully stored with energy from continuous metabolic processes in the body is an example. The amount of energy necessary to fire such a neuron is a very small fraction of the total energy put out by the neuron. Thus the motor neuron itself is the immediate source of the energy released in its firing. So also is the total action of the nervous system or of the whole man.

Active behavior in turn falls into two classes, termed nonpurposeful, or random, active behavior and purposeful active behavior. The latter they define as active behavior "directed to the attainment of a goal—i.e., to a final condition in which the behaving object reaches a definite correlation in time or in space with respect to another object or event." They emphasize that "the purpose of voluntary acts is not a matter of arbitrary interpretation but of physiological fact. When we perform a voluntary action what we select voluntarily is a specific purpose, not a specific movement. Thus, if we decide to take a glass containing water and carry it to our mouth we do not command a certain set of muscles to contract . . . ; we merely trip the purpose and the reaction follows automatically."

Rosenblueth, Wiener, and Bigelow do not tell us in their important paper what they mean by "trip[ping] the purpose." They would be the first to admit, I believe, that without McCulloch's and Pitts' theory of universals to define the goal which is tripped, a given system such as a robot would have to have its purpose assigned to it by certain instructions fed into the mechanism by some purposeful being outside the system or mechanism. But if the system has the property of being an active system in Rosenblueth's, Wiener's, and Bigelow's sense and if this active system has reverberating circuits which permit the existence of universals and the construction of postulates or proposals out of these universals which can define ends, then the system itself has the capacity to project possible goals or purposes and the capacity to trip one of these purposes rather than another.

Purposeful behavior is again divided by Rosenblueth, Wiener, and Bigelow into two types called teleological and nonteleological. The important point to note with respect to this dichotomy is that mechanisms can be constructed exhibiting either type. The key to the difference between teleological and nonteleological purposeful activity is that in the case of nonteleological purposeful activity "no signals from the goal . . . modify the activity of the object in the course of the behavior." They give as an example a snake which may strike at its prey with no stimulus coming from the goal after the strike has started. Teleological purposeful activity, on the other hand, occurs in any mechanism in which signals from the goal alter the behavior after it has been initiated, so that it reaches its goal. The requirement of any mechanism in order to be thus not merely goal-directed but teleologically goal-directed is that it possess a "negative feedback" over the goal.

Feedback may be of two kinds, positive and negative. Both kinds involve activity in a closed path. Both kinds have this in common, that "some of the output . . . is returned as input." When this output which returns as input has the same direction and effect upon the system as the nonreturning input, the feedback is positive. Thus positive feedback reinforces the input. Negative feedback, on the other hand, counteracts the input "to restrict outputs that would otherwise go beyond the goal." In other words, negative feedback means that "the behavior of an object is controlled by the margin of error at which the object stands at a given time with reference to a relatively specific goal." Thus the modern gun is automatically controlled to hit its target. Electromagnetic waves returning to the mechanism from both the target and the projectile during the flight of the projectile give the error or deviation of the projectile from its intended course. This alters the input of the mechanism in such a way that the gun puts its next shell nearer the target.

It appears, therefore, that purpose, teleology, and mechanism, as Rosenblueth, Wiener, and Bigelow emphasize, are compatible rather than mutually exclusive concepts. Teleology is opposed not to mechanism but to nonteleological mechanistic systems—that is, to mechanical systems not governed in their behavior by negative feedback over the goal. Similarly, purposes are not antithetical to mechanism, but only to those whose behavior is random. Put positively, this means that a teleological system can be, and in human nervous systems it is, a mechanical system. It is a mechanical system in which the behavior of the system is controlled by a negative feedback over the goal. In fact, Rosenblueth, Wiener, and Bigelow suggest that "the main function of the cerebellum is the control of the feedback nervous mechanisms involved in purposeful motor activity."

It appears, therefore, that the traditional argument of the dualists and idealists that purposeful teleological behavior cannot be accounted for by means of scientifically verified psychology and neurology because the latter sciences give no basis for memory, universals, and purposes and the argument of the early modern naturalists, mechanists, and their sociological followers to the effect that purposeful teleological activities and the theoretical ideas defining human goals are mere epiphenomena of no causal significance, representing mere pseudo-rationalizations after the fact, because again such factors are incompatible with mechanism and a scientifically verified theory of human nature, rest upon a common confusion and a false premise. This false premise is that teleology and mechanism are incompatible.

Rosenblueth, Wiener, and Bigelow have made it abundantly clear that this incompatibility is justified neither by logic nor by fact. When purpose and teleology are carefully defined, one finds that each represents a particular kind of mechanism and that the real dichotomies are (a) between purposeful mechanisms and mechanisms giving rise to random behavior, and (b) between teleological purposeful mechanisms which possess a negative feedback controlling their behavior and nonteleological purposeful mechanisms which do proceed toward a goal and hence have a purpose but which do not have a negative feedback redirecting the behavior of the system on its way to its goal.

It remains to connect McCulloch's and Pitts' demonstration that scientifically verified neurological man can know universals and Rosenblueth's, Wiener's, and Bigelow's demonstration that scientifically investigated, behaving neurological man can have causally significant goals and teleologically controlled behavior toward those goals with the problem of our basic inquiry. This problem, it will be recalled, is that of the relation between ideological factors and biological factors in any culture.

Goals can be of two kinds. They may be some immediately apprehended particular enjoyed esthetically or used empirically to check a scientific theory of nature. But goals may also be the attempt to make the world conform to the theory of natural science as in engineering or to the normative theory of social science as in education, religious conversion, new legislation, and other social reforms. The former orders the things of nature to serve man's ends. The latter attempts to alter the behavior and cultural institutions of men to fit man's normative theory. The present inquiry indicates that if the latter type of goal-seeking is to be effective, attention must be directed less upon external factors and overt behavior and more upon the preservation or removal of the traditional universals embodied in the brains of men.

In both types of goals postulated theories constructed out of McCulloch's and Pitts' universals are necessary. The manner, however, in which the negative feedback controls behavior is different in the two instances.

In the case of the deductively formulated theory of natural science data from outside the organism coming through the sense organs of the scientist either correspond to what his deductively formulated theory, stated in terms of universals, specifies or they do not. If they do, the natural scientist, for the particular investigation in question, has reached his goal. His theory is verified. If they do not, the information fed back through the sense organs to the scientist forces him to reconstruct the postulates of his scientific theory. He may have to draw upon new reverberating circuits with their quite different universals or basic scientific concepts.

In the case, however, of a normative social theory—assuming it to be accepted—it rather than the empirical social facts given through the senses defines the goal. Thus the negative feedback comes from the normative theory itself to the motor neurons prescribing that the man's behavior conform to the prescriptions of the norm. It is in this manner that the censorship of personal and social norms arises and the prescriptions of an ideology for a given society operate through familial, educational, religious, commercial, and legal institutions and processes to mold *what is* in social institutions and behavior toward *what ought to be*.

Since the many reverberating circuits through the human cortex provide men with many different universals out of which to construct both their factual theories of nature and their normative theories of culture, one would expect rival hypotheses in natural science and the rival normative theories in the social sciences. That this is the case is well known. It is the presence of the latter which generates the ideological conflicts of the contemporary world.

It appears, therefore, that scientifically verified neurological theory of man makes deductively formulated theory in the natural sciences as well as normative theory in the social sciences both possible and significant. One aspect of the significance of normative social theory remains to be noted. Studies of the social behavior of ants by Theodore Schneirla and others show that they have a remarkable social organization but a very rigid one. Norbert Wiener has emphasized that this rigidity is due to the fact that the ants have a very poor system of communications. They follow their leader by scent. In other words, they respond only to particulars and to particulars of but one sense organ. Human societies in the West, as was noted earlier in this paper, radically reconstruct their social organization with the rejection of an old normative social theory and the acceptance of a new one. This is possible quickly only when a society or its leaders have reached majority agreement upon a systematic normative social theory and possess an excellent system of communications to acquaint and habituate the leaders of that society and, if possible, a majority of the people with that normative social theory.

The answer to the basic question of our inquiry may now be summarized: Cultural factors are related to biological factors in social institutions (a) by the biologically defined purposeful behavior of human neurological systems containing negative feedback mechanisms and (b) by the normative social theory defined in terms of the universals which are the epistemic correlates of trains of impulses in neural nets that are reverberating circuits in such negative feedback mechanisms. Because overt behavior can be tripped by impulses from reverberating circuits whose activity conforms to universals, as well as by impulses coming immediately from an external particular event, the behavior of men can be and is causally determined by embodiments of ideas as well as by particular environmental facts. And since the brains of men in early so-called primitive societies are provided with reverberating circuits just as are the brains of men in so-called modern societies, it follows, though the specific universals may be different, that normative social philosophies will be significant in any culture. In short, in any culture embodied ideas defining purposes or ideals really matter.

THE RELATION OF MORAL MAN TO SCIENTIFICALLY KNOWN NATURAL MAN

Two types of theory, each constructed out of universals, have been noted. One is the deductively formulated, indirectly and experimentally verified theory of natural science. The other is the normative theory of cultural science.

Each type of theory specifies a philosophy. Experimentally verified theory in natural science, when its method is analyzed to designate its epistemology and when its primitive assumptions are determined to specify its ontology, defines a complete verified natural philosophy. A normative social theory, when its assumptions are made explicit, defines an ideology or in other words a possible moral and social philosophy.

Consider what must happen in a single human nervous system when these two philosophies are different or incompatible. Then one has a dual, a split, or in other words a schizophrenic personality. The conflicts multiply when more than one normative ideology is impinging upon the individual. Contradictory universals are giving contradictory orders to the same motor neurons.

Need one wonder that such people must either live out their moral philosophy in an isolated institution or in an insulated retreat where they will be untouched as far as possible by the facts of nature which continuously impinge upon their nervous systems to enforce the acceptance of a natural philosophy or else, if they stay in the world, waver between moral indecision verging upon a nervous breakdown at the one extreme and dogmatic, hyperintense, ego-sustaining normative convictions at the other extreme. Need one wonder, also, why Socrates and Plato said in the *Republic* and at the end of the *Timaeus* that only the person who identifies the normative philosophy which he uses to define his personal and social purposes with the natural philosophy checked scientifically against the data of the senses from nature can be absolutely good and supremely happy. The reason is clear. With only one philosophy giving instructions to his motor neurons, and that one empirically verified so that he can have confidence in it, such an individual can be a single, a composed, and a whole man.

One other previously mentioned fact supports this conclusion. It was noted that one's normative social theory, i.e., one's humanistic philosophy, is not tested against social facts. Instead, it defines one's personal and social purpose and serves as a measure and censor or inhibiter of motor responses to stimuli from particular social facts. Hence, by itself, it has no way of being verified, since it tends to make personal and social behavior and humanistic cultural institutions conform to its form; it does not conform to them. Consequently, only by making the universals which define one's humanistic philosophy identical with the universals verified indirectly against the particular facts of nature and the natural man which define one's natural philosophy can one obtain moral philosophy which may be said to be verified and hence true. Thus escape from moral relativity and from personal schizophrenia both require that the universals which define one's moral and social philosophy be identical with the empirically verified universals which define one's natural philosophy.

The universals which enter into empirically verified natural philosophy are of two kinds.[8] They may refer to the immediately apprehended particular factor in things. This factor is appropriately called the aesthetic component of nature and the natural man. Or they may refer to a theoretically designated factor in things which is inferred from their immediately apprehended aesthetic component. This inferred, theoretically designated factor is appropriately called the theoretic component of things.[9]

Since the aesthetic component is immediately apprehended, knowledge of it is absolutely certain. Hence natural philosophy based upon it and its attendant humanistic philosophy will not change with time. So-called primitive societies and Far Eastern Oriental cultures, apart from Western influences, exhibit this temporal constancy.

Since, on the other hand, the theoretic component in nature and the natural man is inferred rather than immediately apprehended, the empirical verification of its specific character must be indirect rather than direct. This entails that although the knowledge that the theoretic component exists is absolutely certain, the knowledge of specifically what it is is subject to change with new empirical information. Hence societies such as those in the West whose humanistic philosophy is constructed out of universals referring to the theoretic component in man and nature are subject, as the history of Western civilization illustrates, to the reconstruction of their specific moral and social ideology with the advent of new experimentally and indirectly verified philosophies of nature and the natural man.[10]

The theoretic component of natural philosophy defines an absolute good, specific in content, holding for all people at any given epoch of empirical knowledge. It does not, however, for finite human minds, define an absolute good, specific in content, holding for all time. *That* there is the theoretic component in human personality and in the rest of nature is nevertheless true for all time. In fact, this theoretic component in human personality and nature generally is the permanent object of worship in all theistic religions as it is also the final aim of all experimentally verified, deductively formulated science and philosophy.

These considerations indicate that the traditional reasons for separating moral philosophy from natural philosophy no longer exist. This separation is of purely modern Western origin. It dates from Kant.

The Greeks identified moral philosophy with natural philosophy. It was only the fallacious reading of Kantian moral philosophy back into Socrates, Plato, and Aristotle by modern students of Greek philosophy that has made the modern Kantian exception to the classical Greek rule look like the classical Greek rule itself. There was no need of making moral philosophy different from natural philosophy in the case of Socrates, Plato, and Aristotle, since the science of their time was teleological and provided meaning for universals and for human purposes. Thus thoughtful, purposeful moral man, fulfilling his natural potentialities, could be kept within nature.

What led to Kant's separation of moral philosophy from natural philosophy was the seeming incapacity of modern mechanistic natural science, treating man as a natural animal, to account for memory, universals, human choices, human freedom, and human purposes. Now, however, when the analysis of McCulloch and Pitts gives a neurological theory of memory, universals, choices, and deductive reasoning, when the theory of Rosenblueth, Wiener, and Bigelow accounts for human purposes, and when this paper has shown how normative as well as natural scientific theory falls within naturalistic conceptions, the need for separating moral man from scientifically conceived and verified natural man no longer exists.

Literally, moral, thoughtful, choosing, purposeful individual and social man is the scientifically verified and conceived natural neurological man. Moral man should therefore not merely be identified with scientifically conceived natural man in theory in order to obtain verified moral philosophy and a happy whole personality; he is so identical in fact. Consequently, the identification of moral philosophy with scientifically verified natural philosophy is not merely a correct program for the future to work out; it is something which so far as human nature is concerned, is actually achieved now.

If this present achievement is to be grasped in all its intellectual fullness, one final point must be noted. It will be recalled that in the exposition of McCulloch and Pitts' neurological theory of universals, recourse was made to relations called epistemic correlations. The introduction of these epistemic correlations was necessary in order to avoid the mixing of two worlds of discourse—in this instance the world of discourse of emotionally felt, aesthetically immediate, introspected man and the world of discourse of formally and theoretically conceived, indirectly and experimentally verified neurological man. An inspected "blue" in the immediately apprehended aesthetic continuum is one thing. The impulse which is the firing of a neuron in a formally defined neural net is another thing. These two different things are epistemically correlated.

But these epistemic correlations are important also for another reason. They relate the immediately felt esthetic component of the self to the experimentally verified theoretic component of the self. These epistemic correlations are two-termed relations. This fact has tremendous significance. It means, as Chapter XII in *The Meeting of East and West* has demonstrated, that the emotional, immediately felt self is not a mere epiphenomenon or appearance of the inferred, indirectly and experimentally verified, theoretically conceived self. Instead, the one component of the self is as scientifically ultimate as the other. Accordingly, a scientifically complete natural philosophy must, in its conception of man, unite both components of man's nature.

NOTES

1. F. S. C. Northrop, *The Logic of the Sciences and the Humanities* (New York, The Macmillan Company, 1947), chaps. vi, vii, and viii.

2. ——— *The Meeting of East and West* (New York, The Macmillan Company, 1946), chap. ii.

3. R. Lorente de Nó, "La Corteza Cerebral del Raton," *Trab. Lab. Invest. Biol. Univ. Madr., 20,* 41–78, 1922; "The Vestibulo-Ocular Reflex Arc," *Arch. Neurol. and Psychiat., 30,* 245–291, 1933; "A Study of Nerve Physiology," *Studies from the Rockefeller Institute for Medical Research* (New York, 1947), Vols. *131* and *132.*

4. Cf. reference 1 above, chaps. vi and vii; also reference 2 above, chap. xii.

5. Warren S. McCulloch and Walter Pitts, "How We Know Universals," *Bull. of Math. Biophysics, 5,* 115–133, 1943; "The Perception of Auditory and Visual Forms," *Bull. of Math. Biophysics, 9,* 127–147, 1947.

6. Warren S. McCulloch, "A Hierarchy of Values Determined by the Topology of Nervous Nets," *Bull. of Math. Biophysics, 7,* 89–93, 1945. "Finality and Form in Nervous Activity," James Arthur Lecture delivered May 2, 1946, at Am. Mus. of Natural Hist., New York City. Mimeographed.

7. Arturo Rosenblueth, Norbert Wiener, and Julian Bigelow, "Behavior, Purpose, and Teleology," *Philosophy of Science, 10,* 18–24, 1943; Norbert Wiener, *Cybernetics* (New York, John Wiley and Sons, 1948).

8. Cf. reference 1 above, chaps. iv and v.
9. Cf. reference 2 above, pp. 296–306, 394–404, 439–454.
10. Cf. reference 2 above, chap. viii.

The middle section of this paper, on "The Neurological and Behavioristic Psychological Basis of the Ordering of Society by Means of Ideas," is substantially the vice-presidential address of Section L on the History and Philosophy of Science of the American Association for the Advancement of Science, delivered at its Chicago meeting on December 28, 1947.

XX

LASTING AND DYING FACTORS IN THE WORLD'S CULTURES

PITIRIM A. SOROKIN

I

NO less than sixteen out of twenty-six [civilizations] are by now dead and buried." These sixteen dead civilizations include the Egyptian, the Andean, the Sinic, the Minoan, the Sumeric, the Mayan, the Indic, the Hittite, the Syriac, the Hellenic, the Babylonic, the Mexican, the Arabic, the Yucatec, the Spartan, and the Ottoman. Of the remaining ten surviving civilizations—the Western, the Christian Near East, the Islamic, the Christian Russian, the Hindu, the Far Eastern Chinese, the Japanese, the Polynesian, the Eskimo, and the Nomadic—all, except the Western, are "in their last agonies," under the threat of either annihilation or assimilation by our own civilization of the West. Even this Western civilization is in a state of acute crisis.

Such are the conclusions of A. J. Toynbee respecting the death of civilizations.[1]

These conclusions are but a variation of similar theories about the death of civilization (or culture) proffered by many thinkers of the past. In 1869 Danilevsky, in his *Rossia i Evropa,* distinguished ten great cultures or civilizations: Egyptian, Chinese, Assyro-Babylonian, Hindu, Iranian, Jewish, Greek, Roman, Arabic, and European. In 1929 Spengler, in *The Decline of the West,*[2] with or without knowledge of Danilevsky's work, presented a theory essentially similar.

Statements of this sort appear at first clear and convincing. When, however, they are closely examined and tested, they raise a host of questions as to their exact meaning and their validity. Let us consider the foremost of these questions.

1. If the foregoing writers mean that the *total culture of each of these "dead" civilizations*—its language and its political, economic, social, scientific, philosophical, religious, ethical, legal, and other

cultural values—no longer exists, is no longer practiced, is not incorporated in living cultural and social institutions, is devoid of influence, or is actually forgotten, no longer constituting a topic of thought or discussion, then their thesis is obviously untenable with respect to virtually all these "civilizations," as well as to the culture or civilization of many preliterate groups of the past. The greater part of the supposedly "extinct" Greco-Roman civilization, for instance, is still very much alive: Homer, Hesiod, Sophocles, Aristophanes, and the bulk of its literature; Socrates, Plato, Aristotle, and most of its philosophies; Zeno, Epicurus, and the majority of its ethical systems; its fine arts, especially architecture, in its Doric, Ionic, Corinthian, and other "classical" forms; the mathematical and scientific discoveries of Greek and Roman thinkers; the Roman law, with its Corpus Juris Civilis; Greco-Roman forms of political and economic organization, including Athenian democracy, Spartan totalitarianism, and Roman imperial organization (in its republican and monarchical forms); its forms of the family, marriage, and divorce including such specific laws as lex Julia et Papia Poppaea; a host of its manners and mores. These and a multitude of other cultural values of Greco-Roman "civilization" are still the subject of thought and discussion, are still imitated, practiced, and incorporated in our civilization, culture, and institutions, in our mentality, conduct, and relationships. They live, function, and influence us, being much more alive than last year's "best seller" or yesterday's fads and fashions. With a proper modification the same may be said, in varying degrees, of the other fifteen "dead" civilizations, from the Egyptian to the Ottoman (witness Mohammedanism, certain forms of Ottoman art, and such practices—which we have borrowed—as polo playing, the wearing of pajamas, and coffee drinking). Nay, more: one may safely contend that many cultural values of preliterate, nomadic, pastoral, and agricultural tribes are still alive and function in our culture on a large scale, embracing such factors as modes of transportation, technology, economics, patterns of taste, art, magical and religious beliefs, and manners and mores. *None of the "great civilizations" is dead in toto.*

2. If the term "death of civilization" means the disappearance of *a part of its total culture*—say, its language or religion or an art pattern—the contention is valid in so far as we admit the validity of the definition. As a matter of fact, the phenomenon is incessantly going on in any culture or civilization, constituting a regular sociocultural process. But the disappearance of a *part* of a total culture

or civilization does not mean its *total* death. Our fashions and fads vary each season; our best sellers live on an average only about six months; types of machinery, tastes, beliefs, political sympathies, popular philosophies, and so forth change incessantly, emerging, gaining acceptance, and swiftly being consigned to oblivion. But this does not mean that American or European "civilization" is dead and buried. To be sure, only a few Egyptologists continue to use the Egyptian language; for the rest of mankind it is extinct. But it does not follow that Egyptian forms of art, political and social organization, or religious and ethical beliefs are necessarily likewise extinct. As a matter of fact these aspects of Egyptian "civilization" are still vital in two forms: in their original patterns, imitated and reproduced in our contemporary culture, and as the patterns that entered, as an essential ingredient, into the Greco-Roman, Western, and other civilizations and have thus been preserved to the present day. For example, many a religious and ethical belief of Egypt decisively fashioned the Hebrew religion and ethics, and through Judaism—and even directly, through the cult of Isis, Osiris, etc.—passed into Christianity and thus into contemporary religious and ethical systems. The political organization of Egypt (the "divine right" and unlimited autocracy of the Pharaohs) decisively influenced the Roman monarchical regime and, through it, subsequent Western autocracies and monarchies. With a reasonable degree of certainty one may claim that a substantial percentage of any of the foregoing "dead" civilizations—in some cases a very large percentage—is still very much alive. Hence Danilevsky's, Spengler's, and Toynbee's formulas of the death of civilizations are unduly broad and sweeping and should be replaced by a narrower and more accurate statement—namely, that *a part of every past civilization or culture* has become extinct.[3] Similarly, as we have seen, many features of our own contemporary culture are incessantly becoming obsolete, so that certain cultural traits of today are doomed to go into the discard tomorrow.

3. If by the "death of civilization" Danilevsky, Spengler, and Toynbee mean *the disintegration of its unity and individuality*— and that is probably the essential meaning of the term—then they might easily brush aside the above criticism. They might say that bricks, stones, boards, and other materials of a dilapidated house may remain, and yet the house is gone because its unity is destroyed. A divorced husband and wife continue to live; yet the family as such has ceased to exist. Likewise, aspects of a notable culture may

survive; yet, when its unity and integrity are lost, the civilization or culture disappears.

The validity of this sort of counterargument depends upon what is meant by the integration or unity of a civilization or culture, and whether the major civilizations or cultures of Danilevsky, Spengler, and Toynbee are such integrated unities. The terms "unity," "integration," and "individuality," applied to cultures or civilizations, are widely used nowadays in the social sciences. However, in most cases no definite meaning, no clear-cut criteria of social or cultural integration or unity, is given by those who employ the terms in question. The same author frequently applies them to very diverse cultural or civilizational conglomerations.[4]

Two or more cultural or civilizational phenomena may present a *mere congeries of spatial contiguity,* being connected only by their spatial adjacency. A copy of the Bible, an orange, a wornout shoe, an automobile tire, and a broken whisky bottle lying side by side on the pavement may serve as an example of such a congeries.

In other cases two or more sociocultural phenomena may be united by an *indirect causal tie,* each being causally unrelated to the others but all being so related to a given agency, external to them, that they are connected with one another. In our pockets we may carry a watch, a pen, a handkerchief, cigarettes, money, a registration card, a comb, and some papers. Each of these "civilizational objects" is causally unrelated to the others. But each *is* causally connected with the respective person and his needs—and through this common factor they are connected, by an indirect causal tie, with one another.

Again, there are cultural phenomena possessing *direct causal unity* in the above sense, namely, that when cultural A is given, B is given; when A changes, B changes. For instance, when, in a given group, there appears a serious emergency, such as war, famine, or pestilence (A), the extent and rigidity of governmental control and regimentation tend to increase in this or that form (B).[5] The emergency is thus causally connected with the extent and severity of governmental control.

Furthermore, two or more cultural or civilizational phenomena may be linked by the bond of meaningful—logical or esthetic—consistency and causal dependence in the sense of articulation of the same general principle or value. Such a relationship presents the highest form of sociocultural integration, that of *meaningful-causal unity.* In Western medieval culture the dominant architecture (the cathedrals) articulated the Christian Credo, constituting "the Bible in stone"; its major sculpture was an articulation of the same Credo and the Bible; its literature was an embodiment of the Christian religion; its greatest music was, again, an articulation of the same Credo and the Bible; so also was its painting. The Christian religion and theology were "the queen of the sciences," and all the rest were mere "handmaids." The highest political, social, and moral authority was vested in the Pope, as the supreme spiritual power. The various parts of the totality of medieval culture represented a meaningful-causal articulation of the same Credo and the same system of Christian principles; they all functioned and changed together, in meaningful-causal unity.[6] F. S. C. Northrop has convincingly shown that a large number of economic and political phenomena and a large percentage of the social, ethical, philosophical, and other phenomena of the total culture of the United States have been merely a meaningful-causal articulation of the principles of Locke, Hume, Bentham, Adam Smith, and a few others. However they may have differed from a perceptional standpoint, these phenomena have been welded into a single unity by meaningful-causal ties. He has demonstrated similar unities in the cultures of Mexico, England, Germany, Soviet Russia, and other countries.[7]

Thus in the *total* culture or civilization of any area we find all four kinds of "unities" or "integrations." We find them even in the *total culture of an individual,* as the smallest possible cultural area. If we analyze the total cultural endowment (ideological, behavioral, and material) of each of us, we find that it is made up partly of purely spatial congeries, partly of traits bound together by indirect and direct causal ties, and partly of meaningful-causal cultural systems, or unities.[8]

Having in mind these four forms of unity, we may now ask what kind of unity is claimed by Danilevsky, Spengler, and Toynbee for their great cultures or civilizations. Are they, in their opinion, a multitude of mere cultural-civilizational congeries, a kind of dumping-place for a phenomena bound together only by spatial adjacency? Or are they indirect and direct causal unities? Or are they meaningful-causal unities bound together by meaningful-causal ties?

As soon as we put the question, we find that none of the three authors has given us any definite idea of what he means by the unity or integration of the civilizations under discussion. We find hardly any clear-cut definition of "unity" or "integration," any criterion of such a unity, or any evidence of its embodiment in their civilizations.[9] They merely urge us dogmatically to accept their civilizations as genuine unities, without any specification of what kind of unity is meant. This point is very important. If the unity happens to have been a mere spatial adjacency of multitudes of diverse phenomena, their civilizations were never integrated into real causal or meaningful-causal unities and never existed as individualities. In that case they represented simply congeries of unintegrated and disunited phenomena. Since they were not integrated or united, they evidently could not disintegrate. Since they were not born as unified individualities, they could not die.

A careful analysis of each of these "civilizations" shows clearly that the total culture of Egypt or Sumeria, of India, of Greece and Rome, of the West, or of any of Danilevsky's, Spengler's, and Toynbee's civilizations has consisted of many related and unrelated meaningful-causal systems, of hundreds of causal unities, and of still larger numbers of purely spatial congeries. Not only has its total culture never constituted a single causal or meaningful-causal unity, but scarcely even a large part of it has been thus integrated. As mentioned above, the total culture of such vast areas and of such a multitude of populations, and even the total culture of the smallest possible area—that of an individual—is rarely fused into a single causal or meaningful-causal unity.[10] Being conglomerations of a host of meaningful-causal, causal, and spatially adjacent phenomena, these civilizations could not completely disintegrate. For this reason, as we have seen, certain features of these civilizations perished, whereas others survived. If they had been genuine unities, their disintegration would have been complete instead of partial and "spotty." Thus Danilevsky's, Spengler's, and Toynbee's conception of the death of civilization is untenable also in the sense of the disintegration of a previously integrated civilization. They took for a real unity what was not united, ascribed to their "civilizational dumps" a unity which these did not have, and pronounced their death without ascertaining which parts were extinct and which were not and what were the symptoms of actual extinction.

4. This conclusion is excellently corroborated by a closer analysis of the nature and structure of their "civilizations." If they were not causal or causal-meaningful unities, what were they? The answer is that *they were an odd assortment not so much of unified cultures as of social groups of very different character*. The scholars in ques-

tion made two fundamental errors in their theories: first, they confused organized social groups or inhabited areas with unified cultures or civilizations; [11] second, they chose for their "civilizations" social groups of different kinds, thus committing the error of uniting in one logical class groups of different character and giving them the same name. Indeed, their very classification of civilizations (given above for Toynbee and Danilevsky), whether Egyptian, Sumeric, Jewish, Arabic, Iranian, Hindu, Chinese, or Greek, is actually a classification of social groups or even of certain vast inhabited areas—not of systems of culture or civilization. This error is aggravated by an additional mistake: even as a classification of social groups or inhabited areas it is inconsistent in that it puts into a single class "civilization" groups and areas of very diverse character. Some of their "civilizations" are really *language* groups (the totality of persons having the same native language and many similar cultural traits). Others are *state* groups; *religious* groups; *locality,* or *territorial* groups; or more *complex* groups, such as the totality of individuals sharing the same state, territory, language, and religion. Such a "civilization" as that of Greece is primarily a *language* group; for Greece as a whole has hardly ever been united into a single state. Such "civilizations" as those of Sparta, the Ottoman Empire, and Rome are essentially *state* groups. The Spartans differed from other Greeks not in respect to language but through belonging to an independent state. The Ottoman "civilization" is the Ottoman empire group, made of a multitude of different language groups never amalgamated into one nation or one language or religious group. "Civilizations" like those of the Buddhistic Chinese, the Mohammedans, the Hindus, or the Near Eastern Christians are mainly *religious* or *territorial* groups. The Chinese, Iranian, and Russian "civilizations" represent essentially complex groups—the totality of individuals belonging to the same state and territory and having the same language. Finally, a "civilization" like the Hellenistic (in so far as it was a phase of Greco Roman "civilization") does not represent even an organized group: the term is merely a name covering a multitude of different groups not united by a common state, a common language, a common religion, or any other common cultural or civilizational trait.

Such is the curious assortment of heterogeneous social groups and areas covered by the same name, assigned to the same class of "civilization," and fused into an "organic unity." Logically this procedure is as sound as that of a biologist who puts into the same class—that of "mammals"—a lion, a bird, a fish, an ant, and an area of New England! The procedure explains, however, how and why Danilevsky, Spengler, and Toynbee reached their conclusion respecting the death of civilizations. The *longevity, or life span, of almost all organized groups is finite.* According to the nature of the group, it varies from a few moments to a few years, decades, or centuries—in rare cases, a few thousands of years. Thus the average life span of contemporary small economic organizations is about three years; that of bigger business firms about six years; and that of the large business concerns about twenty-eight years. Small local cultural groups survive, on an average, about two or three years. The longevity of the family ranges from a few days or years to some three hundred years, rarely exceeding this duration, a longevity of from one to three generations being modal. Seventy-seven per cent of the existing universities and colleges were founded after 1800, very few, if any, antedating the twelfth century. Of existing cities with a population of 100,000 or over, approximately 40 per cent emerged after 1600, 21 per cent were founded between the eleventh and the fifteenth centuries, and only 18 per cent antedate the fifth century A.D. The life span of contemporary small cities is considerably shorter. The duration of states varies from a few years up to two thousand years or over, most of the existing states (36) having an age of approximately one hundred years or less. Small religious groups disappear within a few years or decades. The life span of major religions, such as Hinduism, Taoism, Confucianism, Buddhism, Jainism, Judaism, Christianity, and Mohammedanism, has ranged from approximately 1,300 years up to 3,500 years or over. Similarly, many small language groups have had a life span of only a few decades. Larger ones have existed for several centuries; a few, for one or two thousand years.

All in all, most social groups rarely survive for more than a few centuries.[12] Virtually all organized groups—the state, the family, the language group, the political party, even the religious group—are mortal: after a time they disintegrate and dissolve as social individualities, though this dissolution does not mean either the death of their members or the disappearance of their total culture or civilization. While the group may dissolve, all or a considerable part of its total culture or civilization may be—and usually is—taken over by other groups, and often expanded and enriched by them. Although the Greek states were dissolved, yet Greek culture or civilization has been appropriated, in its greater part, by many other groups and has spread far beyond the confines of Greece and the Hellenic world. The same is true of practically any other great culture that has possessed vital values.

Danilevsky, Spengler, and Toynbee, having mistaken a motley assortment of social groups for civilization, and having observed that social groups are mortal, rashly concluded that both ordinary and major cultures and civilizations die *in toto*. The states of ancient Egypt, Sumeria, Babylonia, and Rome are extinct; so also are many past language, religious, and territorial groups. Nevertheless, a great deal of the total culture or civilization of these groups is still functioning in the contemporary sociocultural world either in its original form or in a disguised and modified form as a part and parcel of our living "civilization." The scientific discoveries of earlier civilizations; their philosophical systems; their religious systems; their law, ethics, language, literature, architecture, music, painting, sculpture, and drama; their forms of political, economic, and social organization; their manners and mores—these elements make up the lion's share of today's living civilization. If, indeed, we were to subtract from our Western civilization all the values inherited from the "dead civilizations," particularly those of the Greco-Roman and the Jewish world (including Christianity), the remainder would be unbelievably meager and paltry, as well as incoherent.

To sum up: Whichever of the foregoing meanings of the term "death of civilization" we take, the formulas of the "undertakers of civilization" appear to be essentially untenable.

The basic fallacy of the main premises of Danilevsky, Spengler, and Toynbee vitiates also many other conclusions of these authors, such as the inference that all great civilizations pass through a similar life cycle of childhood, maturity, and old age, or of spring, summer, autumn (including the "Indian summer"), and winter; that each is based, throughout its whole life process, upon one specific idea or value, the Hindu civilization being regarded as religious; the Greek, as artistic; the Western, as scientific; and so on.[13] Nevertheless, their works contain many sound, valuable, and even profound ideas, the analysis of which is beyond the scope of this paper.

II

Having cleared the ground from the encumbrance of fallacious theories, we may now ask, What is the real situation respecting the longevity, life span, and mortality of cultural or civilizational systems? The notions of life and death can be applied only to the meaningful-causal unities. These notions are meaningless with reference to congeries, to phenomena that exhibit merely spatial contiguity; for since these phenomena have never been united or integrated, and have never existed as individualities, they cannot die or be dissolved and disintegrated.

The life span of empirical sociocultural unities (or systems) seems to fluctuate even more widely than that of organized social groups. It ranges from almost the zero point to several thousands of years—for generic systems to virtually an indefinitely long period. Petty sociocultural systems—daily utterances of the type *A* is *B* embodied in our conversations, in radio talks, in newspaper and magazine articles, and the like; trivial songs, drawings, sculpturing, building, playing, and even praying—these lilliputian cultural unities are forgotten almost as soon as they are uttered or created.

When, however, we turn to vast sociocultural systems containing some real and important value—such as a great language, a major religion, a notable philosophical, ethical, juridical, scientific, political, economic, familistic, or kinship system, a significant artistic creation, an important technological invention—we find that they may endure for decades, centuries, or even thousands of years. The foremost of them tend to become virtually immortal, surviving, with ups and downs, for an indefinite period.

Such languages as the Chinese, Greek, and Latin have existed for more than two thousand years; other tongues, such as German, French, English, and Russian, for more than a millennium. The same is true of outstanding religious systems, such as Taoism, Confucianism, Hinduism, Buddhism, Judaism, Jainism, and Christianity; of notable philosophical systems, such as those of the Upanishads, of Plato, Aristotle, and Sankara; of scientific and technological systems where the basic discoveries and inventions go far into the past. The overwhelming majority of these discoveries and inventions (with the exception of a few that have been lost and then rediscovered or reinvented) have continued to live up to the present time—that is, for millennia.

The same generalization applies to basic ethical and juridical principles or systems, such as the Golden Rule, the Ten Commandments, the ethical systems of love, utilitarianism, hedonism, eudaemonism, cynicism, stoicism, and asceticism—all formulated long ago, certainly before our era. Even specific legal codes, such as the

Corpus Juris Civilis, the laws of Manu and Brichaspati, or the law system of the first books of the Bible, survive not only in books and the writings of scholars but in our contemporary social life, being embodied in law norms actually practiced and enforced. After the adoption of the Roman law in Italy in the twelfth century, it became the foundation of the law of almost all the countries of continental Europe.

Similar longevity is exhibited by noteworthy esthetic creations— the Mahabharata and Ramayana; the works of Homer and Hesiod, Sophocles and Aristophanes; the Gregorian chants; the compositions of Palestrina and Bach; and the architectural systems represented by the Egyptian pyramids and temples, the Hindu temples, the Doric, Ionic, and Corinthian orders, and Gothic architecture.

Finally, such prehistoric technological inventions and practices as the use of fire, the lever, and the wheel; the domestication of animals; many nomadic, pastoral, and agricultural technologies; and many technologies of the Stone, Copper, Bronze, and early Iron Ages are still very much alive, either as original systems functioning now as auxiliaries or as elements incorporated in more advanced and comprehensive modern systems.

These examples demonstrate that specific major sociocultural systems survive for thousands of years or even longer. Some of them, to be sure, have perished; others have been mutilated; but the rank and file tend to be immortal. They display now an exuberant vitality and wide diffusion; now undergo an anemic phase marked by a diminution of their influence; but, like an organism passing through alternate periods of low and high vitality, they persist. Now and then some of them, such as many of the Greco-Roman cultural systems, experience a state of sociocultural "coma" which lasts for years, decades, and even centuries, and then suddenly reawaken. The revival or resurrection of certain Greco-Roman systems during the Italian Renaissance affords a pertinent example.

Finally, if we take not a *specific* individual form of a major cultural system but its *typical* and *generic forms,* we find these to be virtually immortal. This or that particular language may disappear; but language per se, even its principal types, is perennial. This or that specific materialistic or idealistic, rationalistic or empirical philosophical system may perish; but materialistic and idealistic, rationalistic and empirical types of philosophies seem to be immortal. The same is true of theistic, pantheistic, and mystical types of religion; of classical and romantic, ideational and sensate forms of art. This or that scientific theory may decline and be forgotten; but science itself, as a system, even in its basic principles, appears to be perennial. The same generalization applies to generic and typical systems of law and ethics and to the fundamental forms of political, economic, and family organization. Plato's aristocracy, timocracy, oligarchy, democracy, and tyranny are perennial political systems which, despite their fluctuations and vicissitudes, never perish.

Finally, even the vastest sociocultural supersystems, such as the ideational, idealistic, and sensate supersystems, embracing in a single consistent unity several major systems—science and philosophy, the fine arts, religion, law and ethics, politics and economics—these too are virtually immortal. Each of their individual forms emerges, flourishes for centuries or even millennia, and then declines, becoming a mere minor element in a given total culture or population and being superseded, as a dominant system, by one of the other supersystems or by a temporary eclectic congeries. After centuries of latent existence (in the same or in another population) it re-emerges, becomes again dominant for a certain period, then once more declines and eventually reappears.[14]

Instead of the ideational, idealistic, and sensate supersystems, we may take Northrop's "theoretic" and "aesthetic" cultural supersystems.[15] While their concrete forms in different populations and periods vary, these forms as well as their synthesis seem to have been perennial.

In fact, when the overemphasis upon the death of cultures is eliminated, there is a remarkable agreement among investigators. Northrop's (Oriental and primitive type of) culture based essentially on the complete intuitive "aesthetic component" is fairly similar to my ideational culture; his culture of the modern Western positivistic type founded upon an aesthetic component of nothing but sense data is comparable with my sensate culture; finally his complete culture based on a synthesis of the aesthetic and theoretic components is similar to my idealistic culture. Furthermore, Toynbee's civilization, during its period of growth, is marked by traits similar to those of my ideational and Northrop's "intuitive aesthetic" culture; Toynbee's civilization at the phase of its disintegration is again comparable with my sensate culture and, in part, with Northrop's "theoretic culture" after one of its mature stages, when one determinate formulation of it is breaking down. This similarity of the main types of culture—or, more exactly, of the cultural supersystems—arrived at by scholars starting with very different premises and disagreeing with each other in several other respects is significant. It suggests that such cultural supersystems really exist and function in the sociocultural universe, and hence can be used to articulate and build a world order with lasting ideological and cultural roots.

NOTES

1. A. J. Toynbee, *A Study of History* (New York, Oxford University Press, 1939), IV, 1–2.
2. O. Spengler, *The Decline of the West* (New York, A. Knopf, 1929).
3. Compare A. L. Kroeber, *Configurations of Culture Growth* (Berkeley, University of California Press, 1944), pp. 818–834.
4. For the fantastic variety of meanings ascribed by different authors to "unity," "integration," and "individuality" with reference to sociocultural phenomena, cf. my *Society, Culture, and Personality* (New York, Harper & Bros., 1947), pp. 337–341.
5. For this causal law cf. my *Social and Cultural Dynamics* (New York, American Book Company, 1937), Vol. III, chap. vii, and my *Society, Culture, and Personality*, chap. xxx.
6. For the detailed evidence cf. my *Dynamics*, Vols. I, II, III.
7. Cf. F. S. C. Northrop, *The Meeting of East and West* (New York, The Macmillan Company, 1946), chap. iii *et passim*.
8. For the evidence cf. my *Society, Culture, and Personality*, chaps. xvii, xviii, xix, *et passim*.
9. Cf., for instance, the definition and analysis of "a species of society," "intelligible field of historical study," and "civilization" in Toynbee's work, I, 1–181. Still vaguer are the dogmatic statements of Danilevsky and Spengler.
10. For the evidence cf. my *Dynamics* and *Society, Culture, and Personality*.
11. For the distinction between the two cf. my *Society, Culture, and Personality*, chap. xvii *et passim*.
12. For other data and for details cf. *Ibid.*, chap. xxxiv.
13. For a criticism of these theories cf. my *Dynamics,* my *Society, Culture, and Personality*, and my article "A. J. Toynbee's Philosophy of History," *Journal of Modern History*, XII (1940), 374–387.
14. Cf. the factual study of the fluctuation of these supersystems in my *Dynamics* and my *Society, Culture, and Personality*.
15. Cf. Northrop, *op. cit.*, chaps. xii and xiii *et passim*.

XXI

TWO OBJECTIVE BASES FOR A
WORLD-WIDE LEGAL ORDER

GRAY L. DORSEY

PERSONS who propose a world-scale peaceable ordering of human conduct almost unanimously consider that some sort of world-wide legal order is necessary. They differ on how it can be established.

Some think such a legal order must come from a gradual development and extension of law-by-compact-of-nations for the conduct of nations into law-by-compact-of-nations for the conduct of individuals. Some think that nations will never contract away their control of the conduct of the individual, and that the people of the world will have to create at an instant a complete world government which will include and sanction a world-wide legal order. Some think that a scientific study of the de facto structure of society throughout the world will reveal what institutions for the ordering of human conduct the people will accept and put into practice. Dean Pound, earlier in this volume, has indicated his conviction that a "background of universality" must be formed by education before a "universal social and moral and legal order" can be shaped.

Faced with these various suggestions and with the obvious fact that there is no effective world-wide legal order today, it might be well to examine the basis and derivation of law in the two systems for ordering society which have most nearly approached universality—classical Chinese and Roman. It happens that these represent the two broad categories of culture that Sir Henry Maine called "stationary societies" and "progressive societies." [1] This will permit a comparison of the basis and derivation of law in the two types of society which Maine considered significantly different. Roman law will be treated as representative of the type of law in Western civilization which leads to universality. For the present it is assumed that in any Western ordering of society law is either derived by the same method from the same ultimate basis as Roman law, or if it is not, the law and the whole system of which it is a part lead not to universality but to national or individual plurality.

GENERAL APPROACH OF CHINA AND OF THE WEST TO THE PROBLEM OF ORDERING SOCIETY

S. Francis Liu, in a lecture at the Yale Law School, December 18, 1947, said that Confucian ethics, which was the dominant social force in traditional Chinese society, taught the people how to behave toward anyone whom they could classify within any of the five relationships of life—ruler-subject, father-son, husband-wife, older brother-younger brother, between friends—but that its great weakness and consequently the great weakness of traditional Chinese society was that Confucian ethics *did not teach the people how to behave toward strangers.* Social integration was therefore limited to the form that could be erected from the five relationships, since the people simply did not know how to behave toward any person outside such a form. Liu said that the great problem for the Chinese was to devise a set of rules that would tell the people how to behave toward strangers.

Subsequent inquiry will show that the whole difference between Chinese law and Western law rests in the fact that the Greeks, almost contemporaneously with Confucius, laid down the method for the solution of this problem. They solved it not by discovering how people should behave toward strangers but by discovering a way in which there are no strangers.

Though it seems entirely paradoxical, the Greeks arrived at their solution, the results of which in the fabric of Western civilization have caused the different and changing social patterns so sharply in contrast with the unchanging traditional Chinese civilization, by doing exactly the same thing Confucius and all the other Chinese scholars did—looking to nature as a guide for human conduct. Particularly pertinent to a discussion of the basis and derivation of law is a comparison of Confucius' prescription for the proper ordering of the world with the words of Cicero on the derivation of law. Confucius in his *Li Ki,* or *Higher Learning,* says:

In order to make the virtues evident in themselves to shine brightly in the entire world, the ancients began by governing well their state; in order to govern well their state, they began by establishing good order in their family; in order to establish good order in their family, they began by perfecting themselves; in order to perfect themselves, they began by obtaining rectitude of heart; in order to obtain rectitude of heart, they began by obtaining sincerity in their intentions; in order to obtain sincerity in their intentions, they began by perfecting their knowledge.

The perfecting of knowledge consists of pursuing the study of things. After having studied well the things, knowledge attains then its perfection. Knowledge having attained its perfection, the intention becomes sincere. The intention having become sincere, the heart becomes rectified. The heart having become rectified, the person becomes perfect. The person having become perfect, the family is well organized. The family being well organized, the country is well governed. The country being well governed, the entire world enjoys peace.[2]

What is this "study of things" that is the root of all ordering of society for Confucius? It is a study of nature! Siao King-fang writes:

The Chinese believe profoundly in the existence, in the universe, of an order of nature. When this order is in conformity with that of society, the government will be able to attain perfection. [Siao's note: For the Chinese, there exists, in fact, a universal order of which the two elements, natural order and social order, react constantly the one on the other. When an equilibrium is maintained between the two, the universe is in good order and enjoys great peace.] This sort of idea has very ancient roots. One finds it already expressed many times in the books of great antiquity, such as the first classic books: the *Book of Annals* (*Chou-king*) and the *Book of Verses* (*Che-king*), in which this natural order is the synonym of "Heaven" (*T'ien*).[3]

Marcel Granet in his study of the festivals and songs of ancient China shows that these festivals and songs, which became the revered *Classics,* the basis of classical Chinese society, arose from sounds and gestures expressing what was immediately observed by early Chinese man in his environment of nature. Even the names of things, as of birds, sometimes appearing as onomatopoeia, when uttered together with the appropriate movements of the body which were a part of the name, by the opposing choirs representing "Yin" and "Yang," the male and female elements, contained this link between the actions of men and the events of nature. Granet writes: "For example the expression Kouan kouan, for gulls, suffices to portray a certain manner of fluttering and crying out and to evoke the whole range of sexual customs common to men and to these birds." He says further:

One knows early that the verses of the *Che-king* appeared full of a profound sense, which, as one penetrated it, rendered one virtuous. They spoke with a strange authority. . . . How is it that what appears to us a simple image has the value of a binding prescription? It is not an image, at least in the sense that we take the word: *in the themes of the impro-vised songs were inscribed the correspondences which existed in fact be-tween the events of nature and the observances of men.* [Granet's italics.]⁴

The things observed were mountains, waters, the changing seasons, birds, animals, etc., and man in this setting. Thus, order in society is achieved by action which is in accord with the order of things in nature. Cicero testifies that in Western civilization (tak-ing Rome as representative) the basis for ordering society is also to be found in nature.

For there is no principle enunciated by the philosophers—at least none that is just and honourable—that has not been discovered and established by those who have drawn up codes of law for States. For whence comes our sense of duty? From whom do we obtain the principles of religion? Whence comes the law of nations [Ius gentium. Translator's note.] or even that law of ours which is called "civil"? Whence justice, honour, fair-dealing? Whence decency, self-restraint, fear of disgrace, eagerness for praise and honour? Whence comes endurance amid toils and dangers? I say, *from those men who, when these things had been incul-cated by a system of training, either confirmed them by custom or else enforced them by statutes.* [Italics added.] Indeed Xenocrates, one of the most eminent of philosophers, when asked what his disciples learned, is said to have replied: "To do of their own accord what they are compelled to do by the law." ⁵

What this system of training consists of Cicero tells us in his *De legibus*:

. . . it is certainly true that, since Law [Cicero distinguishes between Law which is the universal order of Nature and law which is a specific enactment of men] ought to be a reformer of vice and an incentive to virtue, the guiding principles of life may be derived from it. It is there-fore true that wisdom is the mother of all good things; and from the Greek expression meaning "the love of wisdom" philosophy has taken its name. And philosophy is the richest, the most bounteous, the most exalted gift of the immortal gods to humanity. For she alone has taught us, in addition to all other wisdom, that most difficult of all things—to know ourselves. This precept is so important and significant that the credit for it is given not to any human being, but to the god of Delphi. For he who knows himself will realize, in the first place, that he has a divine element within him, and will think of his own inner nature as a kind of consecrated image of God; and so he will always act and think in a way worthy of so great a gift of the gods, and, when he has examined and thoroughly tested himself, he will understand how nobly equipped by Nature he entered life, and what manifold means he possesses for the attainment and acquisition of wisdom. For from the very first he began to form in his mind and spirit shadowy concepts, as it were, of all sorts, and when these have been illuminated under the guidance of wisdom, he perceives that he will be a good man, and, for that very reason, happy.

For when the mind, having attained to a knowledge and perception of the virtues, has abandoned its subservience to the body and its indulgence of it, has put down pleasure as if it were a taint of dishonour, has escaped from all fear of death or pain, has entered into a partnership of love with its own, recognizing as its own all who are joined to it by Nature; when it has taken up the worship of the gods and pure religion, has sharpened the vision both of the eye and of the mind so that they can choose the good and reject the opposite—a virtue which is called prudence because it foresees—then what greater degree of happiness can be described or imagined? And further, when it has examined the heavens, the earth, the seas, the nature of the universe, and understands whence all these things came and whither they must return, when and how they are destined to perish, what part of them is mortal and transient and what is divine and eternal; and when it almost lays hold of the ruler and governor of the universe and when it realizes that it is not shut in by (narrow) walls as a resident of some fixed spot, but is a citizen of the whole universe, as it were of a single city—then in the midst of this universal grandeur, and with such a view and comprehension of nature, ye immortal gods, how well it will know itself, according to the precept of the Pythian Apollo! How it will scorn and despise as naught those things which the crowd calls splendid!

And in defense of all this, it will erect battlements of dialectic, of the science of distinguishing the true from the false, and of the art, so to speak, of understanding the consequences and opposites of every statement. And when it realizes that it is born to take part in the life of a State, it will think that it must employ not merely the customary subtle method of debate, but also the more copious continuous style, considering, for example, how to rule nations, establish laws, punish the wicked, protect the good, honour those who excel, publish to fellow citizens precepts conducive to their well-being and credit, so designed as to win their acceptance; how to arouse them to honourable actions, recall them from wrong-doing, console the afflicted, and hand down to everlasting memory the deeds and counsels of brave and wise men, and the infamy of the wicked. So many and so great are the powers which are perceived to exist in man by those who desire to know themselves; and their parent and their nurse is wisdom. [I.e. philosophy. Translator's note.]

Therefore Law is the distinction between things just and unjust, made in agreement with that primal and most ancient of all things, Nature; and *in conformity to Nature's standard are framed those human laws which inflict punishment upon the wicked but defend and protect the good.* [Italics added.] [6]

The above passages indicate that both in China and in the West the rules which tell the people how to behave are based on nature. Both China and the West assume that action in accord with nature will lead to peace and tranquillity. Most people will judge the system of rules, which may be called ethics in the broadest sense of that word, by its practical results, accepting the system if it proves satisfactory, looking for something else if it leads instead to conflict and insecurity. But anyone who so desires can go beyond the system of ethics to see for himself whether the basis on which it rests is sound, i.e., whether he finds to be true in nature the facts which the system of ethics assumes to be true. In China this verification was more simple than in the West. This greater simplicity has consequences that will be discussed later.

What the relation is between law and this system of ethics depends upon what definition is given to law. Under a philosophical or sociological definition law would coincide entirely or to a large extent with ethics. But since the popular notion of law more nearly approaches the Austinian definition, perhaps it would be best to use the term law in that sense. Thus law, or positive law, will mean a system of rules promulgated by some agency of the society and "enforced" by some agency of the society; that is, action in accord with the rules will be induced if necessary by the organized and authorized force of the society.

In this sense of the term law is derived from the system of ethics. Whether law is said to be derived from, to be a part of, or identical with the system of ethics, it must be in accord with that system as both are derived mediately or immediately from nature.

DERIVATION OF LAW IN CHINA

In China the Taoists looking at nature found, as William S. A. Pott puts it, that nature's operations "are accomplished without effort or seeming purpose. 'Heaven does not strive and yet it overcomes.' " [7]

E. D. Thomas interprets the same doctrine when he says:

According to Lao Tzu all maintain their position before society properly by nonassertion. . . . The basis of Lao Tzu's ethics is found in this expression, "Wei Wu Wei," which may be translated, "act non act," or "act without ado," or, "act without deceit," do not show or parade yourself, be not egotistic. This is the basis of the non-action or nonresistance idea.[8]

Thomas quotes from Chapter 37 of Lao Tzu's *Canon of Reason and Virtue,* that "If Princes and Kings could keep reason, the ten thousand creatures would of themselves be reformed. *While being reformed they might yet be anxious to stir, but I would restrain them by the simplicity of the ineffable!"* (Italics added.)

There can be no doubt that the Taoists advocate less action on the part of the people because they continually admonish a return to simplicity. In addition, it appears from the quotation above to be necessary to eliminate all action in order to know Tao. As E. R. Hughes quotes Chapter 48 of *Tao te Ching:*

> The business of learning is one of day by day acquiring more,
> The business of Tao one of day by day dealing with less.
> Yes, dealing with less and less,
> Until you arrive at inaction.[9]

Since Tao can only be known by inaction, it is difficult to see why it would not be lost entirely upon the first action subsequent to its realization, in which case Taoism could not guide behavior at all, except to counsel less of it—which is the essence of a large part of Taoist teaching. At any rate, being "ineffable," and therefore uncommunicable, Tao is essentially incapable of furnishing the people a concrete set of rules for behavior.

Motze taught that the love which Confucius said should exist between the people in the various relationships should be extended to all the people of the world impartially. He taught that even the discrimination between "self" and "other" was a source of evil. As Liang Chi-chao quotes Motze's *On Impartial Love:*

> "Impartiality must displace partiality." . . . When the ideal of impartial love is realized, the state of society is described as follows: "When the other man's house is looked upon as one's own house, who will steal? When the other man's interest is looked upon as one's own interest, who will offend? When the other man's home is looked upon as one's own home, who will violate it? When the other man's country is looked upon as one's own country, who will attack it?" [10]

While Motze's ultimate goal of world peace was the same as that of Confucius, Motze sought to attain it not by an extension of the fellow feeling or love for persons in the five relationships of life but by wiping out all categories of relation, all discrimination.

Motze was able to give the people a system of rules telling them how to act, but he could not meet the requirement that the system be based on verified facts. This was because the people could directly experience that they did not feel the same love for some person they had never seen in a distant country as they felt for the members of their own family, and that feeling was a true fact of nature, which contradicted the impartial love that Motze's ethics taught.

The Legalists began with the order of nature, which as Siao King-fang has noted was common to all schools. They accepted completely the Taoist explanation that when the rules of nature governed the world, before man made any rules, complete peace reigned because the object of men's covetousness and hence the cause of conflicts and disputes is not the material thing itself but the value which the name, assigned to the thing by men, represents in their minds. As Hu Yan Mung puts it:

In other words, in the Taoist conception, things, in themselves, have no bond with men; knowledge, as well as men's appreciation of things, is uniquely based on the significance of their names. That is why the object of men's covetousness is not such a material thing but the value that its name represents in their minds.[11]

For the Taoists, peace is to be found by a return to the order of nature, or Tao, which would involve the abolition of all names for things, and thereby all desires and all resulting disputes and conflicts. This would result in a very simple existence, since it would necessarily mean abolition of almost all means of communication. But the Legalists, while accepting the Taoists' analysis of the problem, did not accept their solution. They felt that since rules of nature did not suffice to govern men in a complex society, men should make their own rules, rules of law. And since names did not refer to reality but were mere conventions among men, the way to achieve peace was by defining the meanings of names precisely and then maintaining each meaning without change.[12]

The consequences of this position are much more far-reaching than they appear at first. This is because the Chinese character *Ming,* which is usually translated "name," has a broader meaning, more nearly that of "word" or "term." [13] Furthermore, for the Chinese, keeping the meaning of the word unchanged often involves making actions conform to the term. Thus, punishments must be administered according to the exact meaning of the word which designates the crime; otherwise the meaning of the word will become changed and there will be no exact standard which the people can know and by which they can determine their actions. If a word designates that the act of hiding a fugitive from justice is a crime, any person caught hiding a fugitive must be given the punishment provided for that crime, regardless of circumstances.

The rights and duties, and the sphere of freedom of action of the individual are defined by the conventions of men, by the law. Therefore in order to achieve peace in the world these rules of law must be made available to the people so they can know them, and must be kept invariant so that the people will always know how to behave. It is immaterial whether these rules are "just"; the important thing is that they are impersonal and invariant, so that they can always be the standard for judging the actions of men, thereby eliminating all dispute as to what conduct should be rewarded and what punished.[14] Thus peace will be established.

The laws which the Legalists proposed to promulgate were apparently naïvely intended to be self-executing, but there is a more fundamental difficulty in their position. While the Legalists could and did offer the people rules of behavior, they cut themselves off, by their original assumption, from any verification in nature.

The Confucian school likewise began with the order of nature, or Tao, but they believed that the names, words, or terms referred to real material things.[15] Consequently peace could not be obtained by simply doing away with names or by laying down an exact convention of names. They observed that men had pretty much the same desires, dislikes, and needs. Therefore, if all men were treated alike the supply of things would not be sufficient, and distasteful or laborious tasks would not be performed. Furthermore, who should be respected and who should pay respect, who should command obedience and who should obey, who should be cared for and who should render the care?

But if men were observed to be much alike in needs, desires, and dislikes, they were also observed to be different in their physical and mental capacities. As Hu Yan Mung, beginning with a quotation from the materialistic Confucianist Siun Tseu, says:

"All men living together have the same needs; they differ only in the means which they have at their disposal to satisfy them. Their desires are the same but their intelligence differs. This difference of means and of intelligence between men is entirely natural." One ought naturally to organize society following this natural differentiation.[16]

Hu Yan Mung quotes further from Siun Tseu:

"The highest dignity, as that of the emperor, and the greatest fortune, as the possession of the whole empire, are natural objects of covetousness. If all had the liberty to covet their comfort, it would be impossible to satisfy them. That is why the ancient sovereigns instituted the rules of 'li' and of justice in order to delimit the liberty of individual action and to establish the social classes in order that there would be a difference between nobles and commoners, between the ages, the intelligences and the capacities. These rules had for their unique goal to maintain each in the occupation which is proper for him and to satisfy in the measure which suits him. When these rules had been instituted, the ancient sovereigns followed the established measure for the distribution of goods to the people. Those are the only rules to follow in order to live harmoniously united. . . . It is in this way that some men create a revenue as important as that of a prince and yet it does not appear too much for them; and others receive a salary as moderate as that of guardian, of a coachman . . . but that does not seem to be too little for him. This rule is called 'equality conformable to "natural" differentiation' or 'union without injury to "human" diversity.' " [17]

Li in its broadest sense is the whole body of rules which govern the events of the natural world and the actions of men. Siao Kingfang and also Jean Escarra [18] have pointed out that the Chinese believed in a reciprocal action between the natural order and the social order, so that improper behavior of the emperor had its reaction in unfavorable weather conditions, proper behavior bringing good weather. But the sense of Li which was basic to the Confucianists was as the set of rules which would tell the people what behavior would be in accord with observed nature, taking into account in the observation the faculties, qualities, and relations of the people behaving. These rules were found in the *Classics*. Hu Yan Mung tells us that the Chinese *King,* usually translated "Classic," would be better translated "immutable rules." These rules were set down after their observations of nature by the "civilizing saints." The emperors, who were always considered "temporary saints," therefore had no power to change them.[19] As noted above, Granet has shown that these "immutable rules" were "the correspondences which existed in fact between the events of nature and the observances of men."

Since Li takes account of all things natural, and the differences between men are natural, it was necessary in order to follow Li that society be differentiated according to the various differences. Thus the various social classes of relationships were formed. The classification of the individual within the social framework defined for him his *Fen,* the whole of the rights and duties which are identified with that social class. Fen also determines the social class of the individual and thus designates what his rights and duties are toward all other persons, who likewise are classified in their respective social classes. There were five classes of social relationships: ruler-subject, parents-children, older brother-younger brother, husband-wife, between friends. There were also five general principles which governed the conduct of persons within these categories: one should treat his fellow men according to the degree of intimacy, better treatment being accorded to the more intimate; one should accord better treatment to the more aged; one should accord better treatment to those in a higher social or political class; one should treat his fellow men according to quality, as noble or commoner, legitimate wife or concubine; one should accord better treatment to those who have more personal capacity.[20]

All of society is thus arranged in categories of relationships, and the rights and duties of each individual toward any and all others can be determined accordingly. Therefore, all that is necessary in order to have peace in the world is that each individual should act toward every other individual in accordance with the rules prescribed by their respective social status. These rules come from the basic Li and are also called Li. The rules were Li; the result of the operation of the rules was Fen.

The rectification of names, *Tcheng Ming,* enabled the people to obtain true knowledge of nature and of what action would be in accord with nature, true knowledge of Li. But Tcheng Ming, as Hu Yan Mung points out, did not give sincerity.[21] E. R. Hughes tells us that sincerity (which he translates as "realness"[22]) in a person is a matter of the individual completing himself, and "The completing of the individual self involves 'Jen.' "[23] Liang Chi-chao indicates something of the nature of Jen.

. . . in order to know what "Jen" is, it is necessary first to know what man is. What is the origin of the conception "Man"? By inference from the existence of ourselves we know of the existence of others like us. As we have round heads, flat feet, horizontal eyes, and intelligence, therefore any being of similar appearance and possessing similar qualities we recognize as our own species "Man." The conception "Man" is therefore derived from a recognition of others and self. This recognition is "Jen." Therefore is the Chinese character "Jen" formed from the combination of the characters two and man. . . . Without the association of one man with another the conception "Man" cannot be formed. In other words, if there were only one man living on earth, that which we call personality would have no way of exhibiting itself.

Mencius says, " 'Jen' is what constitutes man. The harmony of Jen and Man is Tao." Hsuntze defines Tao as "the fullest development of Jen."

Confucius says, "When one who is 'Jen' desires to establish himself, he must establish others; wishing to elevate himself he must elevate others. To understand another's desires by inference from one's own desires is the way to 'Jen.' " *(The Analects)* . . . The real meaning of "establishing others," and "elevating others" comprehends not individuals but the whole of mankind. Since the whole of mankind consists of others and self, to elevate the whole of mankind is to elevate oneself. To try to understand this principle by inferring the wants of others from our own desires, is the way to "Jen." To be lacking in "Jen" is to be like a benumbed hand or foot which is insensitive to pains in other bodily members. So the wholeness of personality which comes from the association of two or more persons lacks "Jen" when it is insensitive to the pains of another; it attains "Jen" when sensitiveness is keen. In short, the lack of "Jen" is insensitiveness to fellow-feeling; the fulfillment of "Jen" is the state of keen sensitiveness.[24]

Jen is the link which enables the ineffable Tao, common to all men and all things, to guide the Li of Confucian ethics. Chiang Yee, earlier in this volume, has noted the importance of this guidance. Sincerity of intentions, through Jen, arises at the same time that the facts of nature are being immediately apprehended in order to perfect knowledge, since the fellow feeling, or love, is also a fact of immediate experience.

Government for Confucius, then, was essentially a process of education. Human nature being in essence good, through the fellow feeling of Jen, people would behave correctly if only they knew what behavior was correct. Thus, having true knowledge of Li through Tcheng Ming and sincerity of intentions through Jen, the people would rectify their hearts. The true meaning of this step toward world order is shown by Escarra's rendering of this phrase: "they rendered their will conformable to the rules. . . ." That is, in conformity with Li. Having made their wills conform to Li and possessing exact knowledge of names, they were able to communicate precisely their intentions to others and to perfect themselves by translating their will into action in accord with Li. When every

individual perfected himself it followed from the structure of society that the family would be well ordered, the country well governed, and the world peaceful.

It can readily be seen that writing down laws and publishing
them to the people was for Confucius a bad thing. Since correct
behavior, behavior in accord with Li, always depended upon the
circumstances, such as the status of the acting parties in the social
relationships, to publish a law which took no account of these circumstances was giving the people false information in direct opposition to Tcheng Ming. The way to guide the people was to set
them a perfect example.

Thus Confucius in writing to a prince of Tsin to rebuke him for
publishing a penal code said:

The ancient sovereigns deliberated on the circumstances in order to decide the punishment of crimes; they did not make criminal codes, in
the fear that it would give rise to a litigious spirit in the people. . . .

The people acquire thus a litigious spirit and make appeal to the letter
of the texts, hoping that, by chance, they will succeed in their argument.
One is not able to continue to govern them. . . .[25]

The consequence of this consideration of the circumstances is
illustrated in a provision of *Ta Tsing Leu Lee*,[26] the code of the
Manchu dynasty, which relates to the crime, mentioned above,
of concealing fugitives. Section XXXII provides that all members
of the immediate family, including servants and slaves, and relatives to the first and second degrees, when found guilty of assisting each other to conceal offenses or of sheltering and aiding the
escape of one of their number who is a fugitive, will nevertheless
be held innocent. Relatives in the third and fourth degree in the
same situation are to receive three degrees less punishment than the
crime calls for, and more remote relatives one degree less.

S. Francis Liu has recently noted[27] two effects in the practical
administration of law in China of the sensitiveness and love of
peace inculcated in the Chinese people by Jen. The Chinese judge
is so sensitive to the opinion of others that if, in a case before him,
the decision which he knows on the facts and the law to be the
right one could in any way appear to be advantageous to him personally, he may decide the other way in order to avoid any question of his probity. The peace-loving temperament and the sensitiveness of the people make it very difficult to obtain reliable oral
testimony. The witness, particularly if he is a friend of both parties,
is apt to turn his attention actively to an attempt to compose the

dispute, or to give testimony so vague that it will be worthless. Consequently in China oral testimony has been relegated to the lowest rank in probative value.

While the Legalists' point that a good example was not always sufficient, and that the people needed to be told the rules by which their behavior would be judged, had telling effect, yet when these rules were published they came to embody the Confucian teaching that correct action is that which is in conformity with Li. The laws almost always carried a penal sanction, being directed primarily to maintaining public order, not to establishing or protecting individual rights. Escarra notes the absence of Western concepts (as ownership, etc.) in Chinese law, and the "indifference to the principles of causality and of contradiction, the rarity of syllogistic deduction . . ." in the judicial technique, although presumptions and fictions were used and a sort of sorites and particularly analogy were employed in reasoning.[28] Furthermore, recourse to law was considered a last resort. The better thing to do was to go along with the fellow feeling of Jen, to compromise, give in a little, and settle the dispute peacefully. It was a bad thing to insist upon the strict recognition of a "right." [29]

Confucianism was accepted and followed and became the dominant force for the ordering of society in China because it told the people how to behave toward one another and because its rules of conduct had a verified basis in nature. Furthermore, action in accordance with these rules did not lead to conflict and uncertainty but to peace and tranquillity. If the above analysis of the systems which influenced law in China is correct, Confucianism was the only system which met these requirements. Therefore whatever law existed was essentially based upon Confucian ethics.

DERIVATION OF LAW IN THE WEST

The relation between nature, ethics, and law is abundantly clear in China. In the West there is a vague feeling that law does not stand entirely alone. As Sir Frederick Pollock puts it in his *Essays in the Law:* "The fact remains that law, on the whole, expresses the common conscience of those who are subject to it. If it did not, it would not be obeyed, at least in a free country." [30] But the existence of a relation between ethics and law, and particularly between these two and nature, is generally denied in European and American countries. This denial is itself the direct result of Kant's use of the very procedure outlined above. It simply happened that when Kant looked at nature the same facts which he found to be true in nature told him that there was no meaning for ethics because they did not give man any freedom of choice in his actions. Unwilling to affirm that man's actions are wholly predetermined, and accepting his previous account of nature as true, Kant set up his moral and religious philosophy as subjects having no connection with natural science. Thus the "social sciences" became divorced from natural science, and ethics and law came to be considered as separate disciplines and as having no connection with nature.[31]

The examination of this development in its significance for law is beyond the scope of the present inquiry. Of immediate concern is the fact that the relation between nature, ethics, and law did exist with respect to Roman law. Cicero indicates it in the passages quoted above. It is a source of wonder why this relation, particularly with regard to Roman law, has not been recognized. Perhaps Kant's influence has been too strong. Eugen Ehrlich devoted a considerable amount of study to an effort to discover the source of Roman law. In his *Fundamental Principles of the Sociology of Law,* he says:

In spite of the great amount of labor that has been bestowed upon the study of the history of Roman law, no satisfactory answer has been found to the question whence the Romans got their legal material. In time past the belief was universal that they had obtained it by a process of interpretation from the statutes and from the edict. But this answer would merely shift the question somewhat, for we should then be constrained to ask whence the statutes and the edict got their legal materials. But we may now regard this doctrine as generally abandoned. At the present time, we have sufficient knowledge of the Twelve Tables, of the later private law statutes, and of the edict to know that this great wealth could not possibly have been obtained there. At most, they have made contributions of consequence only to the law of unlawful acts and of intestate succession. Perhaps I may claim for myself the credit of having shown in my *Beiträge zur Theorie der Rechtsquellen* that Roman juristic science has created its material independently of any other source of law. The main root of the Roman law is the *proprium ius civile,* i.e., the juristic law which the jurists themselves have created. . . . Although in form an interpretation of the Twelve Tables, this *ius civile* was an absolutely independent creation of the Roman jurists. For a further discussion I must refer the reader to the book mentioned above, the conclusions of which have quite generally been accepted.

Even though it has been established that juristic science in Rome has itself furnished its material, the question where the jurists got it remains unanswered. On this point, the writings of the Roman jurists contain a great amount of information which has not yet been made accessible, and which I may possibly turn to account at some future time in a second volume of *Beiträge zur Theorie der Rechtsquellen*.[32]

Ehrlich died in 1922, ten years after the above appeared in his *Fundamental Principles,* but he did not publish a second volume of *Beiträge zur Theorie der Rechtsquellen.* Though stating that the question of the source of Roman law was unanswered, Ehrlich went on to give what appears to be an answer to that very question, for he says that the jurists got their law by universalizing the "inner order of the relations." These may be described as the ways of behaving which were accepted and followed in various relations of life, such as ways of behaving toward each other with respect to a certain piece of land, accepted and followed by all persons who had any connection with that land. But this explanation, if such it was meant to be, merely shifts the question somewhat as Ehrlich pointed out the previously accepted answer did, because the question then becomes: Whence came the rules as to how persons should behave in the inner order of relations?

One other fact may have served to obscure the relation between nature, ethics, and law in the West. This is the fact that with the Romans, instead of being a last-resort method of getting the people to conform to the ways of behaving prescribed by the ethics, law became the principal method. This was possible because the ethics which it supported made the application of a uniform law a good thing (in contrast with Confucianism), and it was no doubt desirable and perhaps even necessary because, instead of attempting to lead the people back into conformity with age-old precepts which had long been recognized in the society, the ethics which formed the basis of Roman law was asserting an entirely new system of ways of behaving, and was seeking to revise society.

The importance of law is illustrated in the immediate continuation of the passage from Cicero's *De re publica* quoted above. He says:

Therefore the citizen who compels all men, by the authority of magistrates and the penalties imposed by law, to follow rules of whose validity philosophers find it hard to convince even a few by their admonitions, must be considered superior even to the teachers who enunciate these principles. For what speech of theirs is excellent enough to be preferred to a State well provided with law and custom?[33]

In Rome in the last century of the Republic there were two sects offering to teach the people how to behave toward each other whose systems had previously appealed to nature for their verification. The Epicureans, on the basis of Democritus' atomism, asserted that the world was governed not by design and universal order but by accident, and affirmed a personal hedonism.

The Stoics, likewise on scientific evidence, which was based originally on Heraclitus but which borrowed where necessary from later investigators including Plato and Aristotle, asserted a universal order presided over by reason, or law, and affirmed that all persons were in one respect alike, each possessing within himself this reason (which he could only know by attaining wisdom), and that the true nature of man was to live "consistently with nature" in accord with this universal law. Their teachings became the dominant force in the ordering of Roman society, beginning in the last century of the Republic and flowering under the Empire.

Zeno of Citium, the founder of Stoicism, first studied under Crates of Thebes, the head of the Cynic school, from whom he absorbed the forcefulness of the Socratic character and learned that virtue, which is knowledge, is the supreme good. But, realizing the importance of dialectics and physics, Zeno turned to another Socratic school, the Megarians, of which Stilpo was then the head. As E. Vernon Arnold puts it:

From this time he no longer restricted his outlook to force of character, but sought also for argumentative power and well ascertained knowledge. The foundations of his state must be surely laid, not upon the changing tide of opinion, but on the rock of knowledge. That a wise man should hesitate, change his views, withdraw his advice, he felt would be a bitter reproach. If indeed virtue, the supreme good, is knowledge, must it not follow that knowledge is within the reach of man? [34]

Cicero records Zeno's subsequent study under Polemo of the Old Academy and his departure from the teachings of that school also. Speaking, through Varro, first of philosophy's debt to Socrates, he then says:

But originating with Plato, a thinker of manifold variety and fertility, there was established a philosophy that, though it had two appellations, was really a single uniform system, that of the Academic and the Peripatetic schools, which while agreeing in doctrine differed in name. . . . But both schools drew plentiful supplies from Plato's abundance, and both framed a definitely formulated rule of doctrine, and this fully and copiously set forth, whereas they abandoned the famous Socratic custom of discussing everything in a doubting manner and without the admission of any positive statement. Thus was produced something that Socrates had been in the habit of reprobating entirely, a definite science of philosophy, with a regular arrangement of subjects and a formulated system of doctrine. At the outset it is true this was a single system with two names, as I said, for there was no difference between the Peripatetics and the Old Academy of those days.[35]

Varro states the original doctrine of the two schools which was arranged under three heads, logic, physics (which for the Greeks meant all natural science), and ethics, and then notes departures from it by Aristotle, Theophrastus, and Strato. Varro says:

On the other hand Speusippus and Xenocrates, the first inheritors of the system and authority of Plato, and after them Polemo and Crates, and also Crantor, gathered in the one fold of the Academy, were assiduous defenders of the doctrines that they had received from their predecessors. Finally, Polemo had had diligent pupils in Zeno and Arcesilas, but Zeno, who was Arcesilas' senior in age and an extremely subtle dialectician and very acute thinker, instituted a reform of the system.[36]

Following Varro's exposition of Zeno's system, which retained the same form as the old doctrine, being arranged under the same three heads, Cicero replies:

You have certainly given a short and very lucid exposition of the theory both of the Old Academy and of the Stoics; though I think it to be true, as our friend Antiochus used to hold, that the Stoic theory should be deemed a correction of the Old Academy rather than actually a new system.[37]

Zeno's connection with the science of both Plato and Aristotle was undoubtedly very close. H. A. Wolfson notes that "the Stoic 'substance' and 'quality' correspond to the Aristotelian 'matter' and 'form.' . . ."[38] But for the essence of the content of his system Zeno turned to Heraclitus, from whom he took the logos, or divine law of the universe, and the eternal fire with its mutations into the other three elements, which is in the last analysis identical with the logos. As Arnold says: "The Logos brings into harmony the parts of philosophy; for it is also on the one hand the guide to right reasoning; on the other hand the law which prescribes what is right for the State and for the individual."[39]

The Skeptics denied the possibility of knowledge, and as Cyril Bailey points out, ". . . a pure scepticism can not satisfy any type

of mind, least of all the Roman." [40] This denial was a step further
into negativism than the Taoists of China, who asserted that a true
knowledge existed but said that it was an ineffable, uncommunicable knowledge that could only be experienced by complete still-
ness. (I speak of Taoism being negative only in the sense of its
ability to furnish the people a concrete system of rules of behavior.)
The Peripatetics and the Academics furnished strong opposition
to the Stoics in discussions of theory, and indeed forced the latter
to "suspend judgment" and sometimes to accept their own teachings on certain points.

But the attention of the Stoics was mainly directed at ascertaining
a system of rules for behavior as a guide to daily life, a work which
for the Academics and the Peripatetics awaited St. Augustine and
St. Thomas Aquinas and their successors. E. Zeller reports that
the Stoics "even expressly stated that the study of nature is only
necessary as a help to the study of virtue." [41]

Further stating this attitude, he says:

. . . the most important and most distinctive points established by the
Stoic School belong to the sphere of ethics. In logic and natural science
the School displays far less independence, for the most part following
older teachers; and it is expressly noted, as a deviation from the ordinary
teaching of the school, that Herillus, the pupil of Zeno, declared knowledge to be the highest good, thus making it the chief end in philosophy.

This view of the problem of philosophy is more precisely defined by
the Stoic doctrine of virtue. Philosophy should lead to right action and
to virtue. But right action is, according to the Stoics, only rational action,
and rational action is action which is in harmony with human and inanimate nature. Virtue consists therefore in bringing man's actions into
harmony with the laws of the universe, and with the general order of the
world. This is only possible when man knows that order and those laws;
and thus the Stoics are brought back to the principles of Socrates, that
virtue may be learnt; that knowledge is indispensable for virtue, or
rather that virtue is identical with right knowledge. They define virtue
in so many words as knowledge, vice as ignorance. If sometimes they
seem to identify virtue with strength of will, it is only because they consider strength of will to be inseparable from knowledge, so that the one
cannot be conceived without the other. Hence the practical study of philosophy conducts with them to the intellectual; philosophy is not only
virtue, but without philosophy no virtue is possible. Granting that the
attainment of virtue, and the happiness of a moral life, are the chief ends
which the Stoics propose to themselves, still the possession of a comprehensive scientific knowledge is indispensable, as the only means thereto. [42]

Stoicism and Confucianism are thus seen to be strikingly, but deceptively, similar: man should live in accord with nature, the true nature of man is good, therefore the essential process for ordering society is education. With the Romans, law became a part of the process of education, but how large or how small a part it played in this role is not known. Arnold points out [43] the great extent to which Stoicism entered into the Roman home as instruction for the children, foreshadowing a "theory of education," and to regulate the daily life of the adults. This explains why Ehrlich was led to believe that the law came from the "inner order of relations." There was indeed accord between them, but because they were informed by the same rules of behavior based on nature, not because one gave rise to the other. It is probable, however, that some principles were not incorporated into law until after they had become the "inner order of relations," so that in a limited sense Ehrlich was partially correct. It might be well to give a brief account of the influence which Stoicism had on Roman law, both directly and indirectly by way of ethically conditioned customs.

The first impact of Stoicism was of course among the intellectuals, probably in the Scipionic circle in whose mouths Cicero places the dialogue of his *De re publica*. About thirty years later, around 100 B.C., Q. Mucius Scaevola, "the pontifex," a Stoic, wrote the eighteen volumes on civil law which earned him recognition as the founder of Roman law. Sohm calls him "the most distinguished of all . . . 'veteres,' " and says of his work:

In this treatise the positive law was, for the first time, set forth in systematic order, i.e., arranged and classified according to the nature of the subjects dealt with. Scaevola's system remained the foundation for the subsequent labours of his successors. He abandoned the traditional legal arrangement, and with it the method of merely interpreting the words of statutes or of formulae relating to procedure or juristic acts. Nor did he confine himself to the discussion of isolated cases or questions of law. He arranged his work according to the subject-matter with which the several rules of law are concerned, and in which they are, so to speak, focused. He was the first to determine, in clear outline, the nature of the legal institutions (will, legacy, guardianship, partnership, sale, hiring, etc.), and the various kinds (genera) thereof. He made the first attempt to set out general legal conceptions, i.e., those elements which go to make up the checkered and, to all appearances, boundless mass of concrete facts. This is the secret of the great significance and enormous success of his work. His achievements rendered it possible, for the first time, to survey private law rising as a whole beyond all the complexities of detail.[44]

Of fourteen lawyers whom Jolowicz lists [45] as laying the foundation for and developing the Roman science of jurisprudence under the Republic, Arnold names eleven as men who were Stoics or were strongly influenced by Stoicism. Of the remaining three, one was the father of a Stoic, and of another Jolowicz says nothing is known. After Scaevola, the most prominent of these was the Stoic S. Sulpicius Rufus, a contemporary and intimate friend of Cicero, who was acknowledged as the head of his profession and who compiled 180 books on law.

The Stoic teaching that all men were equal under the law made itself felt in the reforms of the Gracchi and the revolt of the peoples of Italy—not to throw off the yoke of Rome but to receive its mantle of citizenship—but was not fully realized until the principate, although Sulla retained some of the reform measures in his constitution.[46]

Many men who were strongly influenced by Stoicism held high office during the last century of the Republic. Probably the most eminent, due principally to his exemplary personal life, was M. Porcius Cato, who, having sided with Pompeius, took his own life after Thapsus. Of him Mommsen says,

Just because the shrewdest lie feels itself inwardly annihilated before the simple truth, and because all the dignity and glory of human nature ultimately depend not on shrewdness, but on honesty, Cato has played a greater part in history than many men far superior to him in intellect. . . . But the greatest of those marks of respect was the involuntary homage which Caesar rendered to him when he made an exception to the contemptuous clemency with which he was wont to treat his opponents, and pursued him even beyond the grave with that energetic hatred which practical statesmen are wont to feel towards antagonists who oppose them in a domain of ideas, which is as dangerous in their view as it lies beyond their reach.[47]

During the first century of the principate, with the exception of Seneca, Stoicism was almost unrepresented by men in high public office. But the jurists who were further developing Roman law used the same methods that had been introduced by the Stoics, the result of Greek science, which will be discussed later. Of M. Antistius Labeo, the greatest of this period, Sohm says:

As in the domain of scholarship—for he was an accomplished scholar and thoroughly imbued with the Greek and Roman culture of his age—so also in that of jurisprudence, he was an "analogist," i.e., his method was to trace all that was natural, all that was united by a common underlying conception, in order that, by so doing, he might bring positive law under the control of the art of dialectics.[48]

During this period, while Virgil, Persius, and Lucan were weaving Stoicism into the fabric of Roman society, Stoics were chiefly found in the opposition to the government and were even persecuted under Domitian. But Arnold tells us [49] that

from the time of the death of Domitian in A.D. 96, the imperial government became finally reconciled with Stoicism, which was now the recognized creed of the great majority of the educated classes at Rome, of all ages and ranks . . . and in the times of the emperors Antoninus Pius (138–161 A.D.) and Marcus Aurelius (161–180 A.D.) it became the starting-point for a new development of Roman law, which is one of the great achievements of Roman history.[50]

The period of the reigns of the Antonines marked the era of the highest point of Roman jurisprudence. This era was introduced by Celsus, embraced the works of Julian, Gaius, and Q. Cervidius Scaevola, and was climaxed by Papinian.

SIMILARITY AND DIFFERENCE IN EASTERN AND WESTERN LAW

Thus the striking similarity between Stoicism and Confucianism had a counterpart in Chinese and Roman law—equally striking and equally deceptive, and this for the same reason, as will be seen. To be more precise, the similarity was in the method of derivation of Chinese and Roman law from nature. And yet it was by pursuing the same general method in the derivation of law that the difference between Chinese law and Roman law arose, a piece of the whole difference between Eastern and Western civilization. It all stemmed from one small bit of method: THE GREEKS LEARNED TO KNOW NATURE IN A DIFFERENT WAY!

The great contribution of F. S. C. Northrop is that by studying Greek natural science in connection with the Greek classic literature, he has shown that this central fact—a new way of knowing nature—was discovered by the Greeks, and has indicated its significance for science, philosophy, religion, politics, economics, and art.

The new way of knowing nature was by postulation, rather than by direct inspection, or in addition to direct inspection. As Northrop puts it, "Confronted with himself and nature, Western man arrives by observation and scientific hypothesis at a conception of the character of these two factors"; i.e., the factor given by immediate apprehension of nature and the factor designated by verified postulated theory.[51] The new type of knowing arises in this manner:

It may be necessary . . . to regard the observable data as entirely too gross, complex, and crude to provide the entities or relations necessary to resolve the problem with which inquiry begins. When this happens, unobservable scientific objects, such as electrons or electromagnetic propagations with incredibly high velocities, must be introduced. . . .

Since entities and relations of this type are not directly observable, they must be proposed by the method of hypothesis. This does not mean that their status is merely subjective. What is proposed is proposed as objective, as belonging to the character of the subject matter of scientific knowledge, not to the character of the scientist as positor. But the mere positing does not guarantee the existence of what is posited. How is this guarantee to be provided?

The methods are well known. They involve the construction of a deductively formulated system. The basic assumptions or postulates of this system designate unambiguously what is proposed to exist. To this proposal or hypothesis, formal logic is then applied to deduce theorems or consequences. Among these consequences one seeks for certain theorems which define experiments that can be performed, such as Galilei's famous inclined plane experiment. The experiment designated by the theorem or theorems of the theory is then performed. If in all instances the experiment gives the result called for by the theorems, then the hypothesis is said to be confirmed and the entities and relations designated by it are said to exist. If the experimental result is negative, the hypothesis or postulate set is known to be false and some alternative hypothesis . . . is put in its place and subjected to the same procedure.[52]

For us, the most important things to note are (1) that the objects and relations are posited to be real; they are determinate and are not relative to any observer, and therefore are the same for everyone; (2) they are posited to be timeless; to exist not when looked at, or for ten years, but just to exist; (3) the very fact that they are posited; the object is what it is stated to be or it is nothing, depending on the result of the indirect verification. Democritus posited an object, the atom. Heraclitus posited a relation, the logos, or law which determined the flux of his fire.

Now it is possible to understand the difference between Chinese law and Roman law. The Chinese law was based on a philosophy of science and an ethics built out of concepts by intuition, the complete meaning of which is given by direct inspection. This means that Chinese law and ethics rested on knowledge which was entirely given through immediate apprehension, and immediate apprehension when it gave knowledge through the senses of anything determinate also gave the knowledge that the thing would change, would be different for different observers in different positions and under different circumstances. Consequently Confucius very correctly asserted that the right thing to do was to take account of the change, the relation of the persons in the situation, and the circumstances, in determining how to behave. The only timeless, unchanging, nonrelative thing of which immediate apprehension gave knowledge was indeterminate; it could not be defined, described, or observed by any specific sense impression. It was simply what was left when all specific sense impressions had been eliminated. It was "ineffable." It was Tao. Therefore the only thing that was the same for all was a thing that was *not* as far as its capacity to furnish determinate rules of behavior was concerned—since if behavior was present it was not. It is no wonder that the Legalists began with Tao and were closely connected with Taoism, for Tao was the only universal verified by Chinese science. It is also no wonder that the Legalists were unsuccessful in translating this universal into an unvarying determinate standard for the measurement of behavior.

The Greeks found a way in which there are no strangers, by finding a way of knowing a thing which is universal and yet which is determinate. It would be more accurate to say that they found a way in which there are no strangers-in-action, for the East knew of a way in which there were no strangers in nonaction, since all have Tao in common.

Greek natural scientists posited a primary object or a primary relation (as universal law, logos), or both. Most important for us here is the concept of a universal relation or law in nature which was the heart of Stoic philosophy and became the basis of Roman law. Man, being of all the animals the only one possessed of reason, has been endowed with a small piece of that universal law, reason, or logos which orders the universe. Therefore, all men are the same in this: that they are *rational*.

Cicero, probably following the Greek Stoic Panaetius, emphasizes the importance of this fact in the passage from *De legibus* quoted above: "This precept [to know ourselves] is so important and significant that the credit for it is given, not to any human being, but to the god of Delphi." And why is its significance so great? Because: "For he who knows himself will realize, in the first place, that *he has a divine element within him,* and will think of his own inner nature as a kind of consecrated image of God." This element is in the mind, for in the next paragraph Cicero ceases to speak of the man and speaks of the mind. Of this he says that when it has attained knowledge it will enter "into a partnership of love with its own, *recognizing as its own all who are joined to it by Nature . . . ,*" i.e., all other rational animals, all other men.

This is why law is applicable to all and is the same for all, in whatever relationship, under whatever circumstances, at whatever time —because men are in their rationality the same, and this rationality stems from the universal law which is determinate, eternal, changeless, known only by the intellect, but the same for all men whether they know of it or not. Cicero says,

. . . but out of all the material of the philosopher's discussions, surely there comes nothing more valuable than the full realization that we are born for Justice, and that right is based, not upon men's opinions, but upon Nature. This fact will immediately be plain if you once get a clear conception of man's fellowship and union with his fellow-men. *For no single thing is so like another, so exactly its counterpart, as all of us are to one another.* [Italics added.] [53]

Furthermore, since the primary relation, or law, is posited as timeless, the specific laws derived from it are conceived as unchanging. Thus Cicero can say that "True law is right reason in agreement with nature; *it is of universal application, unchanging and everlasting;* it summons to duty by its commands, and averts from wrongdoing by its prohibitions." (Italics added.) [54]

The very fact of positing also gives rise to a significant difference between China and the West. Since the truths of nature which form the basis of Confucian ethics are those which can be immediately apprehended, anyone can directly verify in his own immediate experience the basis of the rules of behavior he is asked to follow. The method of verification of the posited objects or relations in the West, quoted above (not to be confused with the method of proving a concept within the deductively formulated system), is indirect, complicated, technical, and cannot be performed by the average person who is asked to adhere to the rules of behavior derived from the theory. More important, the direct verification of China has the result of affirming absolutely that the facts are as they are asserted to be. The indirect verification of the West merely affirms that no facts have been observed which are in contradiction with what the theory says they should be. [55] This means that in the West, while one fact found not to be in accord with the theory will dis-prove it—i.e., prove that the posited object or relation is not what it is asserted to be—yet the theory can never be absolutely proved to be true, since a previously unobserved fact may turn up at any time to disprove the theory.

In China, assuming that action in accord with nature will lead to peace and tranquillity, acceptance of and adherence to rules of behavior correctly derived from observed truths of nature could never lead to conflict and uncertainty. But in the West, making the same assumption (as both China and the West do), nevertheless acceptance of and adherence to rules of behavior correctly derived from a deductively formulated theory based upon posited objects or relations so far found to be verified may lead to conflict and un-certainty, since there may be some unobserved fact which would show the theory to be unverified. Thus, while Epicureanism and Stoicism might both be based on "valid" evidence in nature, since the theory on which each was based had not yet been found to be unverified, yet one or both could lead to conflict and uncertainty among the people when accepted and followed. Since the average person accepts or rejects rules of behavior on the basis of practical consequences, if the rules derived from one theory appeared to lead to peace and tranquillity, they, and therefore the theory, would be-come the dominant force in that society.

The difference in method of verification also explains the change-less society of traditional China and the differing and periodically changing societies in the West. In China the rules of behavior rested upon immediately apprehended and hence certain knowledge of the truths of nature. In the West rules of behavior rest upon a *common belief* in respect to the truths of nature, and therefore society in the West is based on a common belief in the concepts of a deductively formulated theory based on posited objects or rela-tions thus far found to be verified. Cicero expresses this fact with respect to the state:

Well, then a commonwealth is the property of a people. But a people is not any collection of human beings brought together in any sort of way, but an assemblage of people in large numbers associated in an *agreement with respect to justice* and a partnership for the common good. . . . For what is a State except an association or partnership in justice? [Italics added.] [56]

Consequently when the common belief is found to be wrong, when the basic postulates are found to be unverified, the whole deductively formulated theory, and the whole pattern of society, has to be changed. It would also seem, if it is a basic assumption that rules of behavior derived from the theory will, when followed, lead to peace and tranquillity, that if instead conflict and uncertainty result this fact is itself a proof that the basic postulates of the theory are unverified, since this is, in a sense, an experiment on a grand scale.

This way of knowing also means that the individual himself is known not merely by a personal sense of awareness but intellectually, as a term in a relation, as a part of a system which embraces the universe and is governed by fixed law which man is capable of knowing, if he attains wisdom. But to do this it is not enough to feel, touch, taste, smell, see, hear, and be aware, as it is to be wise in a Confucian sense, nor is it enough to be completely still, which will give the wisdom of Tao. In order to be wise in the Western sense, in order to know himself and to realize in what way all men are the same as he, a man must know the deductively formulated theory which specifies his character and the relation between him and other men in nature.

Louis Gernet has made a semantic study of the moral and juridical thought of Greece which shows the effect of this way of knowing. Although he gives an unsatisfactory answer for the emergence of the notions, placing their cause in the conflict between city and family (when in truth it was the new way of knowing, telling men they had something in common even though they had no family ties, that made the city possible and also gave rise to the new notions), he nevertheless very interestingly reports the simultaneity of their emergence and the birth of Greek science. He says:

Through the words which have interested us, we have seen worked out some of the fundamental notions under which humanity still lives, the *abstract notions of delict, of the person as subject to laws, of individual responsibility;* and it is from the same movement that we have seen emerge the *rational thought* and have seen asserted the *idea of the individual.*—For the conditions which here dominate the development of moral thought and the reflection of men and of society on themselves are also those, for one part, which command the birth of scientific thought and reflection on the external world . . . the *notion of 'injustice' tends to become positive at the same time that the first natural philosophers propose a true object of knowledge;* the moment of transition marks itself in the first cosmologies of the philosophers. . . ." [Italics added.] [57]

These abstract notions arose because they designate concepts by postulation, they indicate terms in a relation, parts of a system that can only be known intellectually, and which are entirely independent of the circumstances. "A concept by postulation is one the meaning of which in whole or part is designated by the postulates of some specific deductively formulated theory in which it occurs. . . . Such a concept has no meaning apart from a specific deductively formulated theory." [58]

Thus we see the importance of Scaevola's work, and why Roman law really began with him. What we know as Roman law is the working out of a deductively formulated theory of law. Knowledge by postulation was necessary before anyone could determine "the nature of the legal institutions (will, legacy, guardianship, partnership, sale, hiring, etc.), and the various kinds (genera) thereof." Scaevola, as a Stoic, had knowledge by postulation. Furthermore, being derived logically from the postulates in the deductively formulated theory of law, it was necessary that Roman law should be "set forth in systematic order, i.e., arranged and classified according to the nature of the subjects dealt with." This explains why Chinese law, not being derived from a deductively formulated theory, though promulgated in "codes," remained what Sohm calls "a series of legal rules" and never became a hierarchical system of abstract concepts until the Chinese brought in Western law. This does not mean that Chinese law had no system at all, but that it had only the limited type of system that analogy and sorites dealing solely with concepts by intuition could give it.

Since every concept in a deductively formulated theory has no meaning except that designated for it by the theory itself, we see the significance of Socrates' constant emphasis on definition, and why Cicero says: "And in defense of all this [meaning the knowledge of one's self, and of all of nature, known by postulation], it [the mind] will erect battlements of dialectic, of the science of distinguishing the true from the false, and of the art, so to speak, of understanding the consequences and opposites of every statement." We also see the significance of the three divisions of Stoic philosophy: nature (or physics), logic, and ethics. A study of natural science revealed the universal law; the concrete rules of behavior told the people how to regulate their lives in accordance with these rules; the art of deducing, arranging, and proving propositions effected the transition from the former to the latter. With this type of theory, proving a proposition became a matter of logic, the correct manipulation of concepts in relations according to strict rules in order to prove that the proposition correctly followed deductively from the postulates, a "classroom" operation. This is in sharp contrast with the method of proving a proposition in the Chinese type of theory, where it is a matter of merely being aware of one's self and environment, a "soaking in" process, which could never be accomplished simply by argument in a closed room.

One other characteristic of a concept in a deductively formulated theory is significant. Since its meaning depends entirely upon the theory, instead of denoting a factor in immediately apprehended experience, the word which indicates the concept, such as "person," when used in a different deductively formulated theory, will have a different meaning—the meaning designated for it by the new theory. In China the word, because it denotes a factor in immediately apprehended experience, would retain exactly the same meaning when transposed from one system of law or ethics to another.

Thus we see that traditional Chinese law and Roman law had the same ultimate basis—nature. Both the Romans and the Chinese derived the paticular *normative form* of their laws, designating which behavior was good and which was bad, from what the scientists or sages found to be either directly or indirectly verified in nature; or to put the matter more explicitly, in methodological and epistemological terms, they derived the universal normative component of their laws from the concepts or symbols and the attendant propositions involved in the experts' knowledge of nature. Yet the normative character of Chinese law was radically different from that of Roman law because of the different ways of knowing nature in the two cases.

IMPLICATIONS FOR A WORLD-WIDE LEGAL ORDER

Examination of the basis and derivation of law in the two representations of "stationary societies" and "progressive societies" that have most nearly approached universality has revealed two empirically verifiable, and hence objective, bases for obtaining the universally valid normative principles necessary for a world-wide peaceable ordering of society: nature known postulationally and nature known by immediate apprehension. Since these bases are both empirically verified factors in nature and all men, an adequate world-wide legal order must contain specific laws derived from both of them.

The objective basis of law upon which the Chinese concentrated their attention gives very little specific law; perhaps only that *men should never deny Jen.* (Confucius says the superior man "will lay down his life to preserve his 'Jen.'" [59]) But that little is extremely important. It commands men to recognize and appreciate the indeterminate factor, called Tao by the Chinese, which all men have in common with each other and with all nature. Tao fosters Jen, the fellow feeling that instills a sensitiveness to the needs of others, a spirit of compromise and a love of peace which lead to an elimination of disputes, violence and bloodshed, since maintenance of Jen is more important than a temporary gain or the momentary justification of a "right." Because this factor is directly verified, and hence certain, any precepts based upon it would be unchangingly valid and would give a world ordering of society stability.

The objective basis of law upon which the Greek and Roman West concentrated generates a detailed legal system of specific logically ordered, sanctioned precepts which are asserted to be valid standards for judging the behavior of all persons at all times under all circumstances. The fact that a present-day nation normally does not try to require persons beyond the reach of its coercive force to behave in accordance with its laws does not affect the basic nature of those laws. Rather, this fact demonstrates that these laws are asserted to be universally valid since the reason given for not attempting enforcement is not that the laws do not apply but that the courts of the country do not have "jurisdiction," i.e., the coercive force of the nation cannot be brought to bear upon the persons to compel compliance.

Detailed specific laws can be asserted to be universally valid in the West because they are derived from the determinate factor in nature which links together all men, strangers as well as the intimates of the family. But this factor can only be known by the method of postulation and indirect verification, with its attendant uncertainty. Such uncertainty does not mean that it is useless or wrong to assert detailed universal precepts, but it does have two important consequences.

First, it entails that while the method of determining the Western component of a truly world law can be that of the classical Greeks and Romans, its *content* must be contemporary. This is the case because scientific study of the natural man and nature has revealed new facts since the days of Zeno, Plato, Aristotle, Cicero and the great Roman jurists and some of these new facts require a scientific and philosophical conception of man and nature expressed in indirectly verified universal propositions different from those of the ancients. It is in terms of these contemporary, more adequate, empirically and indirectly verified universal propositions that the Western contribution to a universal law for our contemporary world must be formulated. Thus the way is indicated for obtaining what Dean Pound in the opening chapter of this volume says is needed—not merely a jus gentium but a *new* jus gentium.

Second, it entails that while law based upon the determinate universal factor in nature is verified and hence is a scientifically validated rather than merely a speculatively possible universal law, nevertheless law derived from this postulationally known basis is not absolutely certain. Precepts and laws derived from this basis have the probable certainty sufficient for moral and legal action, as the tremendous impact and lasting effect of the Roman law witnesses, and as Western scientific method generally demonstrates. But they do not justify disregard of the needs and feelings of others, stubborn dogmatism, blindness to alternative possibilities, religious or legal inquisition, or the use of force beyond that which is absolutely necessary for self-preservation.

Recognition of its more probable kind of certainty will permit the Western type of precepts and laws, asserting *determinate* universal propositions, and the Chinese, Oriental type of precepts and laws, based on the *indeterminate* intuitive or immediately apprehended universal to combine harmoniously in a truly world-wide peaceable ordering of society. Such an ordering will include a world-wide legal order, but it will also include, as we have seen with classical Chinese and Roman society, a whole body of precepts or an ethics, derived from the same bases as the specific laws which make up the legal order. This ethics builds into the behavior and relationships of men the patterns of actions and convictions that result in the overwhelming acceptance and support of the legal order, without which it would be ineffective.

This fact is the true basis of Ehrlich's "living law." The legal order must be supported in the hearts, minds, and actions of men to be vital. Hence, it is very important that the two aforementioned foundations for a universal legal order are found in the traditional cultures of what Maine considered the two significant types of societies. This means that the fundamental bases for a universal law are present in deep-lying, lasting cultural traditions of the world.

These can be the beginning of the "living law" necessary to build and sustain an effective world-wide legal order.

NOTES

1. Sir Henry Maine, *Ancient Law* (Charles Scribner & Co., 1871), p. 22.
2. Hu Yan Mung, *Étude philosophique et juridique de la conception de "Ming" et de "Fen" dans le droit chinois* (Paris, 1932), pp. 43–44.
3. Siao King-fang, *Les Conceptions fondamentales du droit public dans la Chine Antique* (Paris, 1940), p. 20.
4. Marcel Granet, *Fetes et chansons anciennes de la Chine* (Paris, 1919), pp. 229–231, 93–94.
5. Cicero, *De re publica*, I, ii, Loeb Classical Library (Cambridge, Harvard University Press).
6. Cicero, *De legibus*, I, xxii, 58 ff., & II, v, Loeb Classical Library (Cambridge, Harvard University Press).
7. William S. A. Pott, *Chinese Political Philosophy* (New York, Alfred A. Knopf, 1925), p. 87.
8. E. D. Thomas, *Chinese Political Thought* (New York, Prentice-Hall, 1927), p. 23.
9. E. R. Hughes, *Chinese Philosophy in Classical Times* (New York, E. P. Dutton & Co., 1942), p. 158, Everyman's Library.
10. Liang Chi-chao, *History of Chinese Political Thought* (London, Kegan Paul, Trench, Trubner & Co.; New York, Harcourt Brace & Co., 1930), pp. 94–95.
11. *Conception de "Ming" et de "Fen,"* p. 60.
12. *Ibid.*, pp. 60–61 ff.
13. *Ibid.*, p. 28.
14. Liang Chi-chao, *op. cit.*, pp. 122–123.
15. Hu Yan Mung, *op. cit.*, p. 61.
16. *Ibid.*, p. 88.
17. *Ibid.*, pp. 88–89.
18. Jean Escarra, *Le Droit chinois* (Paris, 1396), pp. 8–9.
19. Hu Yan Mung, *op. cit.*, p. 13.
20. *Ibid.*, pp. 123–129.
21. *Ibid.*, p. 41.
22. E. R. Hughes, *op. cit.*, p. 32.
23. *Ibid.*, p. 41.
24. Liang Chi-chao, *op. cit.*, pp. 38–43.
25. Siao King-fang, *op. cit.*, p. 57.
26. *Ta Tsing Leu Lee*, Sir George T. Staunton, tr. (London, 1810).
27. S. Francis Liu, "Some Observations on Judges, Lawyers, and Court Administration in China," *National Reconstruction Journal*, published by China Institute in America, April, 1947, pp. 3, 11.
28. Jean Escarra, *op. cit.*, pp. 63–64, 67.
29. *Ibid.*, p. 17.
30. Sir Frederick Pollock, *Essays in the Law* (London, The Macmillan Company, 1922), p. 274.
31. Cf. F. S. C. Northrop in *The Meeting of East and West* (New York, The Macmillan Company, 1946), particularly pp. 200–201. The whole approach to the subject considered in this paper was suggested and is conditioned by the views of Professor Northrop.
32. Eugen Ehrlich, *Fundamental Principles of the Sociology of Law* (1912), Walter L. Moll, tr. (Cambridge, Harvard University Press, 1936), pp. 260–261.

33. *De re publica, op. cit.,* I, ii.

34. E. Vernon Arnold, *Roman Stoicism* (Cambridge, Cambridge University Press, 1911), p. 67.

35. Cicero, *Academica,* I, iv, Loeb Classical Library. (Cambridge, Harvard University Press).

36. *Ibid.,* I, ix.

37. *Ibid.,* I, x, xi, xii.

38. H. A. Wolfson, *Philo: Foundations of Religious Philosophy in Judaism, Christianity, and Islam* (Cambridge, Harvard University Press, 1947), II, 107.

39. Arnold, *op. cit.,* p. 71.

40. *Lucretius on the Nature of Things,* Cyril Bailey, tr. (Oxford, Clarendon Press, 1929), p. 7.

41. E. Zeller, *The Stoics, Epicureans, and Sceptics,* Oswald J. Reichel, tr. (revised ed. London, Longmans, Green & Co. 1892), p. 20.

42. *Ibid.,* pp. 58, 59.

43. Arnold, *op. cit.,* chaps. xii–xv.

44. Rudolph Sohm, *Institutes of Roman Law,* tr. (from 4th German ed.) by J. C. Ledlie (Oxford, Clarendon Press, 1892), p. 61.

45. Herbert Jolowicz, *Historical Introduction to the Study of Roman Law* (Cambridge, Cambridge University Press, 1939), pp. 90–91.

46. Theodor Mommsen, *Rome, from Earliest Times to 44 B.C.,* Arthur C. Howland ed., Vol. III of The History of Nations Series, H. C. Lodge, ed. in chief.

47. *Ibid.,* p. 360.

48. Sohm, *op. cit.,* p. 65.

49. Arnold, *op. cit.,* pp. 401–402.

50. Fritz Berolzheimer in *The World's Legal Philosophies* (The Macmillan Company, 1929), p. 85, indicates some appreciation of the influence of ethics on Roman law; Ernest Renan in *Marc-Aurèle* (4th ed. Paris, 1882), at pp. 22–23, has a brief statement of the influence of Stoicism on Roman law; and see Maine, *op. cit., pp.* 53 ff.

51. Northrop, *op. cit.,* p. 294. Cf. Northrop, "The Mathematical Background and Content of Greek Philosophy," in *Philosophical Essays for Alfred North Whitehead* (New York and London, Longmans, Green & Co., 1936), p. 1.

52. F. S. C. Northrop, *The Logic of the Sciences and the Humanities* (The Macmillan Company, 1947), pp. 59–61.

53. *De legibus,* I, x.

54. *De re publica,* III, xxiii.

55. Northrop, *The Meeting of East and West,* pp. 294–300.

56. *De re publica,* I, xxv.

57. Louis Gernet, *Recherches sur le développement de la pensée juridique et morale en Grèce* (Paris, 1917), pp. 432–433.

58. Northrop, *The Logic of the Sciences and the Humanities,* pp. 62–63.

59. E. R. Hughes, *op. cit.,* p. 20.

INDEX

Index

Index